AF476929

Cheltenham & Gloucester

Cricket Year

Cheltenham & Gloucester

Cricket Year

Twenty-Fourth Edition

September 2004 to September 2005

Edited by **Jonathan Agnew**

with additional contributions by
Qamar Ahmed
Charlie Austin
Mark Baldwin
Tony Cozier
Gulu Ezekiel
Jim Maxwell
Derek Pringle
Telford Vice
Bryan Waddle
Shane Warne

A & C Black • London

Edited by Jonathan Agnew
Assistant editing by Mark Baldwin
with additional contributions by
Qamar Ahmed
Charlie Austin
Tony Cozier
Gulu Ezekiel
Jim Maxwell
Derek Pringle
Telford Vice
Bryan Waddle
Shane Warne
With special thanks to Richard Hobson, Bruce Talbot,
Kate Laven and Andrew Hignell

The publishers would also like to thank *The Times* for their kind permission to
reproduce the photograph of Mark Baldwin on page 54.

First published in 2005 by
A & C Black Ltd
38 Soho Square
London W1D 3HB

www.acblack.com

A copy of the CIP entry for this book is available from the British Library.

ISBN-10 0-7136-7505-5
ISBN-13 9-780-7136-7505-4

10 9 8 7 6 5 4 3 2 1

A & C Black uses paper produced with elemental chlorine-free pulp, harvested
from managed sustainable forests.

Project editor: Julian Flanders at Butler and Tanner
Design: Kathie Wilson at Butler and Tanner
Statistics and County information: Press Association
Pictures researched and supplied by David Munden at Sportsline Photographic –
www.sportsline.org.uk – except those on the following pages which are copyright
© Empics: 9, 12 (top right), 16 (bottom), 19 (bottom), 61, 72, 74, 75, 87, 89, 92, 93,
106, 109, 113, 122, 134, 136, 162-66, 173, 175, 179, 184, 186, 209-12, 218, 220,
228, 230, 247, 249, 250, 258, 266, 274, 275

Printed and bound in Great Britain
by Butler and Tanner, Frome and London

CONTENTS

A MESSAGE FROM
CHELTENHAM & GLOUCESTER

What a year it has been for England, and English cricket. We are all even now still trying to get our breath back after what was perhaps the greatest Ashes series of all time ... and getting used to the wonderful fact that it is England who now hold the urn.

As one of English cricket's main sponsors, Cheltenham & Gloucester is hugely proud of the achievement of Michael Vaughan and his England team. We are absolutely delighted, too, that it is Michael Vaughan, our very fine England captain, who was the unanimous choice to win C&G's third Man of the Year award.

When we took over the sponsorship of *Cricket Year,* in 2003, we initiated a new award designed to recognise the outstanding contribution to cricket of a player, or personality, who had been prominent to the public during the previous year. Alec Stewart

Michael Vaughan, the Ashes-winning England captain and the C&G Man of the Year.

won that inaugural award, and Andrew Flintoff was the 2004 winner. Perhaps no one, however, deserves to be Man of the Year more than the man who, after 16 years, brought home the Ashes!

Vaughan and Duncan Fletcher, the England head coach, have reacted to England's magnificent victory against Australia by re-emphasising their drive to make the team undisputedly the world's number one by 2007. That means, in turn, that the next cricket year – as we build up towards the 'return' Ashes clash of 2006–07 in Australia, and then the World Cup in the West Indies early in 2007 – will be a vital and exciting one of continued growth for Vaughan's predominantly young team.

This winter's tours of Pakistan and India will be a test of England's mettle, and next summer's series against Sri Lanka and Pakistan again will also ensure excellent further preparation for those massive challenges of the 2006–07 winter.

The current England side, however, have been making a habit of winning Test matches for a couple of years now. Indeed, since the beginning of 2004, Vaughan's team have won 16 out of 23 Tests. These are heady days for English cricket, with the promise of so much more to come, but everyone involved in the game in this country now has a duty to keep cricket's momentum going forward.

We at C&G, for instance, were very glad to be able to show our complete commitment to Team England during the Ashes series itself. Duncan Fletcher and his management team decided not to make available those England players who were due to take part in the C&G Trophy quarter-finals. England had just played two back-to-back Tests at Edgbaston and Old Trafford – both of them thrilling and draining encounters, of course – and it was felt that the whole of Vaughan's team should get maximum rest in the week before the build-up to the following Test match at Trent Bridge.

We were very happy for that to happen, and we felt that our public support at that time for England's incredible Ashes effort was crucially important. When England then went on to go 2-1 up at Trent Bridge, in yet another nerve-tingling Test match, everyone could see what a good decision England's management had made.

Kevin Pietersen cannot contain his joy as Hampshire's players kick off their champagne celebrations at Lord's.

When we reached the C&G Trophy final on 3 September, however, five days before the start of the Ashes decider at The Oval, we at C&G were thrilled that England had no qualms about releasing Ashley Giles, Ian Bell and Kevin Pietersen to play in the Warwickshire v. Hampshire showpiece at Lord's.

'England's Big Summer' was how the England and Wales Cricket Board marketed the 2005 summer, but I don't think anybody could have foreseen just how big the Ashes series – and because of that, English cricket in general – became.

This book, published within weeks of the end of the English season, now serves as the perfect reminder of a summer that none of us will forget. I hope, indeed, that this 24th edition of *Cricket Year* will become a true collector's item!

Jonathan Agnew has written fully on the Ashes drama in these pages, and has also provided a commentary on all England's cricket both home and abroad during the past 12 months. In addition, his Introduction always makes required reading.

There is also comprehensive coverage of every other international game played around the world since September 2004, and an in-depth review of the English domestic summer. Our congratulations go to Nottinghamshire for winning the Frizzell County Championship, to Hampshire for their C&G Trophy triumph, to Essex for taking the totesport League title and to Somerset for their success in the Twenty20 Cup.

Special features have been a part of *Cricket Year* since we became involved, and this edition carries the views of Shane Warne and Peter Moores and also includes a tribute piece on Graham Thorpe by Derek Pringle of the *Daily Telegraph*. Michael Vaughan, our Man of the Year, is profiled by Jonathan Agnew, who once again heads up a small army of regular *Cricket Year* contributors from around the globe.

We would like to express our thanks to A & C Black for producing this traditional autumn delight and to every contributor for their words and pictures, which will always bring back the memories of one of the truly great cricket years.

Nick Hale
Sales Director
Cheltenham & Gloucester

AGGERS' VIEW

The summer of 2005 was the most exciting, entertaining and dramatic that English cricket has ever experienced, and I defy anyone seriously to argue against that statement. It was a season in which the scriptwriter, who is undoubtedly a member of one of England's two great cricketing institutions, MCC or the Barmy Army, got everything absolutely right. For not merely was the nation gripped by the most compelling Ashes series, complete with its three consecutive heart-stopping climaxes, but Bangladesh rose from the wreckage of their dismal tour to beat Australia for the first time in their history. England's women buried 42 years of Australian domination, and the NatWest Series final at Lord's, between England and Australia, finished in a pulsating tie.

Millions of people were converted to cricket, either watching or listening, and were enthralled by the heroics of Andrew Flintoff, Kevin Pietersen and, indeed, each and every member of an England team which came from 1-0 down to secure the Ashes for the first time in 16 years. Even Gary Pratt – a substitute fielder unknown to the vast majority at the start of the summer – attracted cult status following his dramatic run out of Ricky Ponting at Trent Bridge. It was a key moment in the campaign – possibly even the turning point because Ponting's angry reaction to it gave the first glimpse of the intense pressure the Australian captain was suffering. As the media circus that avidly accompanied the tour expanded to bursting point, even Al Jazeera sent a crew to film England in the nets before the final Test at The Oval.

As a (relatively!) young cricket correspondent, one cannot help but wonder if this summer was it: the defining moment in one's career. That reflection is offered entirely in an upbeat manner because my colleagues and I have been outstandingly fortunate to have reported or commentated on the cricket this summer. It would, however, also be greedy – and, in the light of my opening sentence, unrealistic – for my generation to expect to see its like again. One wonders if the players feel the same way.

I was lucky enough to be with the England team on their open-top bus as they were paraded through the streets of London the day after they won the Ashes. It was a morning I will never forget. An illustration of the humility of these cricketers was that none of them really expected anybody to turn up! And yet, as we drove away from the Mansion House and turned left down Queen Victoria Street, as far as the eye could see there were thousands of people, waving their flags and clamouring for a sight of their new heroes.

The players – one or two of whom had not been to bed the previous night – were genuinely moved by the warmth of the reception, and when the bus turned into Trafalgar Square, the sight of tens of thousands celebrating in the sunshine took their breath away. It took me a few days to come back down to earth after that experience, let alone them, and it is a memory that I am sure will keep many going during the tough months that lie ahead this winter on the subcontinent.

Given the new fascination with cricket, it was hardly surprising that the issue of the television rights should develop into one of the major talking points of the summer. It is worth remembering that the deal, which gave all live cricket television coverage to the satellite channel British Sky Broadcasting (BSkyB) until the end of 2009, was struck a year ago.

Some cautionary voices were raised then, but by the time Channel 4 was broadcasting the final Test from The Oval, this had developed into a raging public debate. Serious questions were asked of Tessa Jowell, the Secretary of State for Culture, Media & Sport whose department, under her predecessor Chris Smith, had previously negotiated with the ECB to have cricket removed from the list of protected sporting events.

Lord MacLaurin, the former chairman of the board and the man instrumental in putting its case, revealed that there had been an understanding between the two parties at the time that Test cricket would remain on terrestrial television. This agreement, he claimed, had now been breached. But with the new deal done, the only movement from the government is a promise to re-examine cricket's status before the next television contract is negotiated in four years' time.

A closed market is the last thing the ECB wants and should cricket become 'protected' once again as a direct result of this contract, how ironic it would be that the board would pay the price apparently for having had money as its sole motivating force. It is true that, last autumn, the ECB had no idea that cricket's popularity would soar to this extent. But one has to wonder if enough consideration really was given to the incalculable value of cricket being shown on terrestrial television, and free to all.

None of this is a criticism of BSkyB's coverage of cricket. Since 1990, it has televised all of England's overseas tours, and many hours of county cricket and women's matches are broadcast every summer. But no satellite or cable company would attract the number of casual viewers – up to 8 million in total – that sat, gripped, as they watched the Ashes possibly for the first time.

What will happen to these new converts? One thing is for sure: 45 minutes of highlights on Channel Five, which clash with *Coronation Street* and *EastEnders*, is not the answer.

New initiatives are to be announced soon, we are told by the ECB, but even with its tremendous recent success – or, possibly, because of it – the fact is that English cricket now faces its greatest challenge. Only time will tell, but come 2009, the impact of this new arrangement might have undone all the hard work of the past few years, and the glorious opportunity that has now presented itself will have been wasted.

Judging by the advances it has made over the past two years, the England team should be the best in the world in 2009. Some would say that it is already. But for England to be in that position, and remain there, careful planning will be required by Duncan Fletcher and his successor. Above all, ruthless decisions must be taken about the make-up of the team to prevent old age from striking in the way that the Australians were found out this summer.

Cricket is played at too fast a pace these days for sentimentality to cloud judgement. Personal milestones, landmarks and emotional ties must be utterly irrelevant to selection. A measured turnover of personnel keeps a team vibrant and fresh, and it is the only way to extend a period of superiority. Happily, however, this current England side is a young team, and it might be two or three years before the scalpel is required. But if the selectors then shy away from what will, inevitably, be difficult and unpopular decisions, they will not be doing English cricket any favours.

Their job was proved to be a difficult one this summer when just one injury – to Simon Jones – revealed a desperate lack of quality support. This was also true when David Graveney, the chairman of selectors, announced this winter's squad to tour

The winner of the 2005 General Election meets the winner of the 2005 Ashes – one of whom might be asking the other: 'What's it like to be the most popular man in the country?'

Pakistan. An out-of-sorts James Anderson, averaging 31 in county cricket, was considered to be the best of the bunch for The Oval while Shaun Udal, aged 36, was called up to support Ashley Giles in Pakistan. The lack of bowling resources in county cricket remains a real concern – but no mystery either.

Every year on these pages, Mark Baldwin and I argue against two divisions in the county championship and we will continue to do so until the administrators see sense. Rather than improve competition on the field – Yorkshire have gained promotion to the first division on the back of 10 drawn games out of 15 – the consequence of two divisions has been the flood of imported, so-called Kolpak players. Most are bowlers of very average quality – they would be playing, or trying to play Test cricket for their countries if they were better – but they are an instant, short-term fix in order to gain promotion or avoid relegation. Their presence seriously undermines county cricket, and hinders the development of the next generation of Test players.

These are wildly exciting times for English cricket, and we heartily congratulate everyone who has played a part in the success of 2005. But this is not the time to relax or become complacent. As one of cricket's newest supporters said just before he won the 2005 General Election, 'There is still so much to do.'

Jonathan Agnew, Leicestershire, September 2005

CHELTENHAM & GLOUCESTER MAN OF THE YEAR AWARD

There could really only be one winner of the C&G Man of the Year award for 2005: the man who brought home the Ashes for England. MICHAEL VAUGHAN, who succeeds 2004 winner Andrew Flintoff and 2003's inaugural winner Alec Stewart, is profiled here by JONATHAN AGNEW.

A quick glance at Michael Vaughan's record with the bat in the last 12 months reveals that England's most notable winning streak for decades coincided with the captain's least productive period in the team. But for a big hundred against Bangladesh, indeed, Vaughan would have just one century to show for his year, and he averaged only 31 in the series against South Africa and Australia.

There were moments, of course. A battling 82 not out in the dark at the Wanderers, and a two-hour fight in the second innings at Centurion as South Africa, trying to level the rubber, threw everything at England on the last afternoon of the series. Vaughan's beautiful 166 in the third Ashes Test at Old Trafford, meanwhile, was a reminder of how lucky we have been to see him at his fluent best in the past – combined, of course, with the hope that those days will come again soon.

But Vaughan's contribution to English cricket in this same period has been immeasurable, and although he would certainly have preferred to score more runs, the value of his captaincy outweighed any number of silky cover drives and effortless pulls over square leg. Thrust into the leadership when Nasser Hussain suddenly resigned in 2003, it has taken only two years for Vaughan to mould a promising and increasingly determined team into what many would now consider to be the best in the world.

He has had help, of course. Duncan Fletcher, the coach, plotted and schemed the potential downfall of every Australian batsman last summer, and Vaughan's bowlers implemented those plans to perfection. Andrew Flintoff's all-round efforts, in particular, have been quite staggering. But it needs a leader, and a man entirely trusted and respected by his peers, to make a team function successfully. You can be blessed with as many brilliant individuals as you like, but without team spirit and leadership they will not produce results.

Vaughan's style has surprised many people. Essentially a genial, friendly man, there had been little evidence in his early days of the tough streak that has now emerged, albeit restricted, as it is, to dressing rooms and team talks. Because his leadership record is so impressive, Vaughan has not yet had to deal with a hostile or, even, questioning media, and the captain's public face is always charming and polite. I remember travelling on the train to Lord's with him on the

Vaughan cover drives with trademark elegance during his magnificent 166 against Australia at Old Trafford. But it is his captaincy style, and his record (P31, W19, L5, D7 at the end of the Ashes series), which has been even more impressive.

day he was appointed England captain. It struck me then how much he wanted to know about the media, and how it worked. He also talked determinedly about the image that he wanted his team to present. There have been times since then when he has given interviews when he did not need to, and I have never heard him grumble about the ever-mounting commitments he is expected to fulfil.

A sign of the effect Vaughan's leadership has had on this team came in the second Test of the series against South Africa at Durban last Christmas. England faced certain defeat – and nine times out of ten the team of old would have lost in three days. But not only did his batsmen dig impressively deep to save the game – they almost won it.

Vaughan and his exhausted fielders sat on the outfield as bad light saved South Africa on that last afternoon, and they watched as Graeme Smith's team celebrated their lucky escape in the dressing rooms. Eight Tests later, at Old Trafford, there was a similar scene as the Australians hugged and congratulated each other after holding out for a draw on the desperately tense final day of the third Ashes Test.

In a moment of inspirational leadership – coming at a time of crushing disappointment – Vaughan called his team together into one of their huddles on the outfield. 'Look at them,' he urged. 'See how happy they are just to draw a game against us.'

It was brilliant captaincy, revealing skills far beyond field placements or bowling changes, and without any prompting from the coach. To be robbed of victory can sometimes be as damaging as defeat, and Vaughan seized the chance to galvanise his team, rather than have them leave the arena wracked with frustration.

But hands-on captaincy does come at a price. It is remarkably convenient, for the purpose of this comparison, that Vaughan has now played in 62 Test matches – 31 as captain and, before that, 31 merely as a batsman. The figures make interesting, if not entirely surprising reading. He averaged 51 from his first 31 Tests, and scored nine centuries. Since becoming captain, his average has dropped to 37. From the same number of Tests, Vaughan has scored three fewer hundreds.

He is aware of the comparison, and it annoys him that his form appears to have suffered. It is true, for instance, that Brian Lara's batting average is higher as captain than when he is not, but his input, effort and success as a leader falls a country mile short of Vaughan's. And that is the point. While Vaughan is contributing so heavily and, in particular, so successfully as a captain, his frustration is misplaced. It is inevitable that with so much energy being devoted to leadership that something has to give. Although many international batsmen would be more than satisfied with an average of 37, Vaughan is better than that and one day, when his enthusiasm for the captaincy is spent, he can return to the ranks and the centuries will surely flow from his bat with their former regularity.

But, until then, it is as an outstanding and inspirational leader that his real value to England lies.

Andrew Flintoff is perhaps Vaughan's greatest asset.

Mr Cool on the outside … but emotions are revealed naturally whenever success occurs.

THE YEAR IN PICTURES

There's no doubting the score: it's either 111, 222, 333 etc. as umpire David Shepherd hops on one leg. The much-loved 'Shep' retired from international umpiring during the final NatWest Challenge match at The Oval on 12 July – and from first-class cricket too, at Bristol, at the end of the domestic summer on Sunday 25 September.

The first fortnight of February 2005 belonged to Kevin Pietersen, who chose England's one-day series against the country of his birth and upbringing to announce his arrival as an international batsman of stunning power. At first, South Africa's crowds booed and baited him; within those incredible two weeks, however, they were standing to applaud him.

Saturday 18 June, 2005, and Mohammad Ashraful kisses the Cardiff pitch as he reaches a breathtaking 100 against Australia in the NatWest Series. Moments later, and despite Ashraful's almost immediate dismissal, Bangladesh complete a historic victory ... and the dancing on the streets of Dhaka begins.

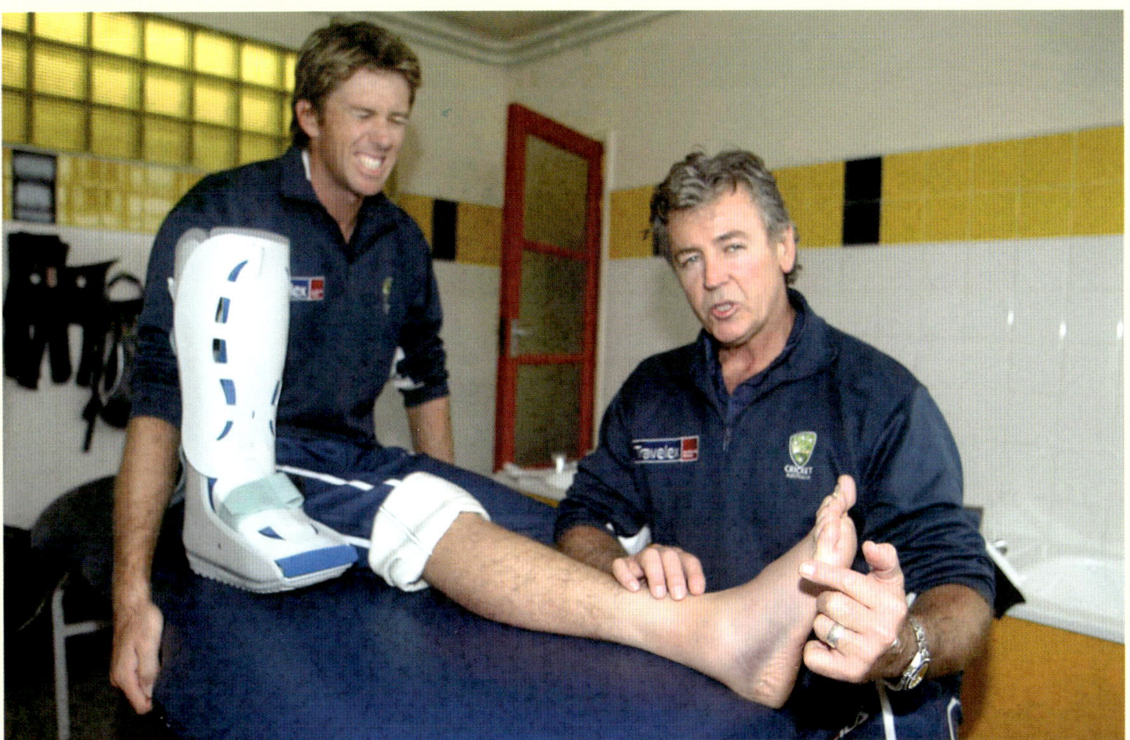

Does it hurt here? Glenn McGrath's badly twisted ankle, suffered in a freak pre-match accident at Edgbaston on 4 August, was for many commentators the biggest turning point of the entire Ashes series. McGrath is pictured here with Errol Alcott, the long-serving Australia team physiotherapist.

The moment that Edgbaston – and millions more watching and listening on both sides of the world – held its collective breath. Is Edgbaston 2005 the greatest Test match of all time, and part of the greatest Test series ever played?

A new slant on an iconic image: as Andrew Flintoff crouches down to congratulate a disconsolate Brett Lee on his heroic but ultimately unavailing resistance, the rest of the England team are busy celebrating their gut-wrenching two-run victory at Edgbaston.

It is the Saturday of the Old Trafford Test and, for Australia, the crock of gold at the end of the rainbow is that the time lost to rain ultimately enables them to save the game.

Closing in for the kill: England employ six slips as tension mounts at Old Trafford, but the Australians hang on for the draw.

Everyone already knew that Shane Warne was one of the greatest bowlers who has ever lived. What the Ashes series of 2005 revealed, however, was new depths of pride, heart, skill and sportsmanship from the bleached-blond former beach bum. After securing his 600th Test wicket at Old Trafford, Warne was increasingly feted everywhere he went by admiring English audiences. And he had the grace to laugh at most of the ribald comments that tumbled down from the terraces, too.

The master of the microphone: Richie Benaud, former Australian captain and iconic cricket commentator, takes his leave of English television audiences at The Oval in September's deciding Ashes Test.

It is late afternoon on Monday 12 September, 2005, and the capacity fifth-day crowd at The Oval does its best to drown out the roars of Michael Vaughan and his ecstatic England team as – at last – the Ashes urn is lifted by an English leader again.

The ticker-tape flies like autumn leaves in a storm as, on a calm and beautiful 13 September, England's Ashes heroes are honoured beneath Nelson's Column as tens of thousands of people attend the Trafalgar Square victory celebrations.

The new OCS Stand provides a dramatic backdrop for the final Ashes Test of 2005 on 8–12 September, while the legend on the gasometer reflects the entreaty of a nation. The historic Oval at Kennington staged England's first ever home Test, in 1880, and its 125th anniversary match wasn't a bad occasion either.

There is joy and sprayed champagne galore for Nottinghamshire as, on Saturday 17 September, they become Frizzell County Championship winners with a controversial victory against Kent at Canterbury.

ENGLAND

AUSTRALIA IN ENGLAND
TWENTY20 INTERNATIONAL
NATWEST TRIANGULAR ONE-DAY SERIES
NATWEST CHALLENGE
BANGLADESH IN ENGLAND

AUSTRALIA IN ENGLAND
By Jonathan Agnew

npower FIRST TEST
21–24 July 2005 at Lord's

In completing an emphatic victory well within four days, Australia appeared to have shrugged off their early tour problems. Indeed, being staged so late in the summer, a widespread feeling of gloom immediately descended over English cricket because the onset of the football season now seriously threatened to condemn the Ashes series to oblivion.

There were some, however, who spotted a chink or two in Australia's armoury as they recovered from the indignity of being hustled out for only 190 half an hour before tea on the opening day. In a furious burst of pace bowling – his best in the series, as it turned out – Steve Harmison hit Justin Langer, Ricky Ponting and Matthew Hayden. It was noticeable that none of England's fielders showed the slightest concern – an attitude that, rightly, upset the traditionalists but which also delivered a firm message to the Australians. England were not to be bullied and, taking lunch on 97 for 5, the visitors were rueing their decision to bat first.

Adam Gilchrist added 39 with Simon Katich, and Shane Warne made a bullish 28, but Harmison wrapped up the innings to finish with his first five-wicket haul at Lord's – and the ground was buzzing. By the close of the first day, however, reality had struck and England were reeling on 92 for 7. Not for the first time, Glenn McGrath expertly exploited the famous Lord's slope and, nagging away at the off stump, claimed five wickets for two runs in 31 balls. It was a mesmeric spell of bowling which, when he dismissed Marcus Trescothick for 4, included his 500th Test wicket. Seventeen wickets had fallen on the first day for 282 runs!

On the second morning, the English public were treated for the first time to a Kevin Pietersen Test innings. There had been great debate about whether the young South African-born batsman should take over from Graham Thorpe in the middle order, with more worries about his technique than his temperament or natural ability.

When he launched his counter-attack against McGrath – who he smashed straight into the pavilion – and Warne, who disappeared into the Grand Stand, it was immediately clear that this was the first appearance of a prodigious talent. It was only a brilliant catch by Damien Martyn at full speed on the deep midwicket boundary when he had scored 57 that spared the Australians further punishment, but Harmison and Simon Jones continued the fun with a last wicket stand of 33, which brought England to within 35 runs of Australia's first innings total.

England needed to strike early and, with the score on 18, Pietersen swooped to run out Langer from cover. Hayden was unsettled by Flintoff's aggression and pulled a short ball into his stumps for 34 and Ponting was caught by the substitute, James Hildreth, at point for 42. It was not the only time in the series that Ponting was to fall foul of an England substitute.

But England were then thwarted by a match-winning partnership of 155 between Martyn and the exciting Michael Clarke – who was dropped by Pietersen on 21. They were dismissed with consecutive deliveries for 65 and 91 respectively – Martyn to a scuttler from Harmison. Gilchrist fell to Flintoff for the second time in the game, and when Warne was caught in the gully off Harmison to the last ball of the day, Australia were 279 for 7, which gave them an overnight lead of 314.

Clearly, Australia were in the better position as the third day dawned, but with so much time remaining, any reasonable target was achievable. Brett Lee was run out by Giles when only ten further runs had been added, but then England's fielding fell apart as particularly Geraint Jones – but also Flintoff – squandered opportunities to wrap up Australia's innings. Jason Gillespie scored 13 out of a stand of

52 with Katich. And McGrath, who was dropped twice, was 20 not out when Katich was held at third man by Simon Jones for 67.

It all looked horribly familiar, and left England with a total of 420 to win – two more runs than the highest-ever fourth innings score to win a Test match. They began brightly with Trescothick and Strauss putting on an opening stand of 80. Lee then dived to take an athletic catch off his own bowling to dismiss Strauss for 37 and, within 13 overs, England were 119 for 5 and facing defeat. Trescothick was taken by Hayden at slip off Warne for 44, Vaughan was bowled by a full, straight ball for the second time in the game and, apparently rooted to the spot, Ian Bell played no stroke and was lbw to Warne for 8. After Flintoff was caught behind off Warne for 3, Pietersen and Jones managed to put on 37 before the close.

Heavy rain fell during the whole of the fourth morning and, not so long ago, would have washed

England's end is nigh as Hoggard becomes yet another victim of Glenn McGrath at Lord's.

FIRST TEST – ENGLAND v. AUSTRALIA
21–24 July 2005 at Lord's

AUSTRALIA

	First Innings		Second Innings	
JL Langer	c Harmison b Flintoff	40	run out	6
ML Hayden	b Hoggard	12	b Flintoff	34
RT Ponting (capt)	c Strauss b Harmison	9	c sub (JC Hildreth) b Hoggard	42
DR Martyn	c Jones GO b Jones SP	2	lbw b Harmison	65
MJ Clarke	lbw b Jones SP	11	b Hoggard	91
SM Katich	c Jones GO b Harmison	27	c Jones SP b Harmison	67
*AC Gilchrist	c Jones GO b Flintoff	26	b Flintoff	10
SK Warne	b Harmison	28	c Giles b Harmison	2
B Lee	c Jones GO b Harmison	3	run out	8
JN Gillespie	lbw b Harmison	1	b Jones SP	13
GD McGrath	not out	10	not out	20
Extras	b 5, lb 4, w 1, nb 11	21	b 10, lb 8, nb 8	26
	(40.2 overs)	190	(100.4 overs)	384

	First Innings				Second Innings			
	O	M	R	W	O	M	R	W
Harmison	11.2	0	43	5	27.4	6	54	3
Hoggard	8	0	40	1	16	1	56	2
Flintoff	11	2	50	2	27	4	123	2
Jones SP	10	0	48	2	18	1	69	1
Giles	-	-	-	-	11	1	56	0
Bell	-	-	-	-	1	0	8	0

Fall of Wickets
1-35, 2-55, 3-66, 4-66, 5-87, 6-126, 7-175, 8-178, 9-178
1-18, 2-54, 3-100, 4-255, 5-255, 6-274, 7-279, 8-289, 9-341

ENGLAND

	First Innings		Second Innings	
ME Trescothick	c Langer b McGrath	4	c Hayden b Warne	44
AJ Strauss	c Warne b McGrath	2	c & b Lee	37
MP Vaughan (capt)	b McGrath	3	b Lee	4
IR Bell	b McGrath	6	lbw b Warne	8
KP Pietersen	c Martyn b Warne	57	not out	64
A Flintoff	b McGrath	0	c Gilchrist b Warne	3
*GO Jones	c Gilchrist b Lee	30	c Gillespie b McGrath	6
AF Giles	c Gilchrist b Lee	11	c Hayden b McGrath	0
MJ Hoggard	c Hayden b Warne	0	lbw b McGrath	0
SJ Harmison	c Martyn b Lee	11	lbw b Warne	0
SP Jones	not out	20	c Warne b McGrath	0
Extras	b 1, lb 5, nb 5	11	b 6, lb 5, nb 3	14
	(48.1 overs)	155	(58.1 overs)	180

	First Innings				Second Innings			
	O	M	R	W	O	M	R	W
McGrath	18	5	53	5	17.1	2	29	4
Lee	15.1	5	47	3	15	3	58	2
Gillespie	8	1	30	0	6	0	18	0
Warne	7	2	19	2	20	2	64	4

Fall of Wickets
1-10, 2-11, 3-18, 4-19, 5-21, 6-79, 7-92, 8-101, 9-122
1-80, 2-96, 3-104, 4-112, 5-119, 6-158, 7-158, 8-164, 9-167

Umpires: Aleem Dar & RE Koertzen
Toss: Australia
Test debut: KP Pietersen
Man of the Match: GD McGrath

Australia won by 239 runs

out the day altogether. But, amazingly, just 45 minutes after the rain had stopped, play began and within an hour, Australia had won the game. It was a ghastly performance by England's lower order – only Pietersen, who finished unbeaten on 64, actually managed to score a single run! McGrath and Warne ran through the tail as England lost five wickets for 24 – Pietersen scored 22 of those – to complete a victory by 239 runs. Those, including McGrath, who had forecast a 5-0 whitewash by Australia, had no reason to alter their opinion.

npower SECOND TEST
4–7 August 2005 at Edgbaston

The second match of this series must come under serious consideration as the greatest Test of all time. In terms of crucial elements, it had the lot: entertainment, brilliance, high drama and, at the end, excruciating tension. It was a wonderful cricket match that England managed to win when all seemed lost. The country ground to a halt as, on the Sunday morning, Australia's last wicket pair added 59 runs, taking them to within just three runs of completing an astonishing victory. Michael Kasprowicz then gloved a lifting delivery from Harmison down the leg side where Geraint Jones took a tumbling catch. It was the moment that brought the Ashes alive.

England's preparations for the game had been dominated by the overwhelming disappointment of their defeat at Lord's. Wisely, the selectors held sway and announced the same squad – with the caveat from the chairman, David Graveney, that he expected a much-improved performance. Michael Vaughan and Duncan Fletcher held a meeting during which they agreed that England needed to play a much more positive game – especially against Shane Warne. But while the Aussies enjoyed a day or two at Goodwood races, followed by a pleasant warm-up at New Road, Worcester, England's players were restricted by the Twenty20 Cup tournament and, indeed, Flintoff's only cricket between the Tests was a quick thrash for Lancashire on the event's finals day.

Early arrivals at Edgbaston witnessed another defining moment in this series when Glenn McGrath trod on a stray ball during warm-ups, and sprained his right ankle. It was immediately obvious that he was out of the game, but Ponting – in a move that surely he now deeply regrets – decided to stick to the Australians' original plan regardless, and put England in to bat. Rumours of a serious difference of opinion between Warne and Ponting quickly surfaced and, indeed, it was a decision that

SECOND TEST – ENGLAND v. AUSTRALIA
4–7 August 2005 at Edgbaston

ENGLAND

	First Innings		Second Innings	
ME Trescothick	c Gilchrist b Kasprowicz	90	c Gilchrist b Lee	21
AJ Strauss	b Warne	48	b Warne	6
MP Vaughan (capt)	c Lee b Gillespie	24	(4) b Lee	1
IR Bell	c Gilchrist b Kasprowicz	6	(5) c Gilchrist b Warne	21
KP Pietersen	c Katich b Lee	71	(6) c Gilchrist b Warne	20
A Flintoff	c Gilchrist b Gillespie	68	(7) b Warne	73
*GO Jones	c Gilchrist b Kasprowicz	1	(8) c Ponting b Lee	9
AF Giles	lbw b Warne	23	(9) c Hayden b Warne	8
MJ Hoggard	lbw b Warne	16	(3) c Hayden b Lee	1
SJ Harmison	b Warne	17	c Ponting b Warne	0
SP Jones	not out	19	not out	12
Extras	lb 9, w 1, nb 14	24	lb 1, nb 9	10
	(79.2 overs)	407	(52.1 overs)	182

	First Innings				Second Innings			
	O	M	R	W	O	M	R	W
Lee	17	1	111	1	18	1	82	4
Gillespie	22	3	91	2	8	0	24	0
Kasprowicz	15	3	80	3	3	0	29	0
Warne	25.2	4	116	4	23.1	7	46	6

Fall of Wickets
1-112, 2-164, 3-170, 4-187, 5-290, 6-293, 7-342, 8-348, 9-375
1-25, 2-27, 3-29, 4-31, 5-72, 6-75, 7-101, 8-131, 9-131

AUSTRALIA

	First Innings		Second Innings	
JL Langer	lbw b Jones SP	82	b Flintoff	28
ML Hayden	c Strauss b Hoggard	0	c Trescothick b Jones SP	31
RT Ponting (capt)	c Vaughan b Giles	61	c Jones GO b Flintoff	0
DR Martyn	run out	20	c Bell b Hoggard	28
MJ Clarke	c Jones GO b Giles	40	b Harmison	30
SM Katich	c Jones GO b Flintoff	4	c Trescothick b Giles	16
*AC Gilchrist	not out	49	c Flintoff b Giles	1
SK Warne	b Giles	8	(9) hit wkt b Flintoff	42
B Lee	c Flintoff b Jones SP	6	(10) not out	43
JN Gillespie	lbw b Flintoff	7	(8) lbw b Flintoff	0
MS Kasprowicz	lbw b Flintoff	0	c Jones GO b Harmison	20
Extras	b 13, lb 7, w 1, nb 10	31	b 13, lb 8, w 1, nb 18	40
	(76 overs)	308	(64.3 overs)	279

	First Innings				Second Innings			
	O	M	R	W	O	M	R	W
Harmison	11	1	48	0	17.3	3	62	2
Hoggard	8	0	41	1	5	0	26	1
Jones SP	16	2	69	2	5	1	23	1
Flintoff	15	1	52	3	22	3	79	4
Giles	26	2	78	3	15	3	68	2

Fall of Wickets
1-0, 2-88, 3-118, 4-194, 5-208, 6-262, 7-273, 8-282, 9-308
1-47, 2-48, 3-82, 4-107, 5-134, 6-136, 7-137, 8-175, 9-220

Umpires: BF Bowden & RE Koertzen
Toss: Australia
Man of the Match: A Flintoff

England won by 2 runs

Right: Brett Lee celebrates the wicket of Marcus Trescothick as Australia fight back at the start of England's second innings.

stunned the Edgbaston groundstaff who, despite torrential rain in the days before the game, had produced a flat, slow pitch.

England's opening batsmen set off at breakneck speed. Indeed, the whole of the first day was played at an incredible rate that saw 407 runs scored from less than 80 overs. Ten sixes and 54 fours were struck as Australia's bowlers were put to the sword in front of a crowd consumed by ecstasy. The opening stand of 112 in 26 overs set the standard for the day – with a flat-batted six off Warne by Trescothick serving notice of what was to follow. Strauss was bowled by a huge leg spinner for 48, Trescothick edged behind for 90 from 102 deliveries, Bell nicked his third ball and when Vaughan threw his wicket away on 24, pulling Gillespie to long leg, England were 187 for 4.

Throughout the one-day series, we had wondered how Pietersen and Flintoff would bat together. A tabloid story that suggested Flintoff was miffed by the possibility of being outshone by Pietersen's big hitting did Freddie little justice as the pair now joined forces. Pietersen, too, was quite happy to play second fiddle as they added 103 massively entertaining runs from only 105 balls. Flintoff's 68 came from 62 balls, and included five sixes, before he edged the third ball after tea to give Gillespie his 250th Test wicket. Jones made only 1, but Giles supported Pietersen who now went for his shots and reached 71 from 76 balls before falling in the deep. Even the tail went for their shots – the last two wickets added 58 before Warne wrapped up the innings.

Lee was struck for 14 fours and five sixes from his 17 overs, while Warne's 25 overs conceded 13 fours and four sixes. Australia had played 493 Tests since the last time they conceded 400 runs on the opening day – going back, in fact, to the Lord's Test of 1938.

Langer held Australia's reply together as they lurched to 208 for 5. His grafting 82 was scored in more than four and a half hours before he became one of Giles' three victims. Gilchrist was 49 not out at the end – it was to be his highest score in a disappointing series – as Flintoff and Jones secured a first innings lead of 99.

Typically for this series, the game was dramatically turned on its head on the third morning when Lee snatched three wickets for 4 runs from 11 balls.

England were on the run at 75 for 6 at lunch as Warne applied the pressure. Flintoff remained England's only hope and despite a damaged shoulder, he responded magnificently with 73 from 86 balls, including a last wicket stand of 51 with Simon Jones. This ended when Flintoff became Warne's sixth victim and, at the time, no one was to appreciate the true value of that last partnership, which helped to set Australia 282 to win.

Langer and Hayden put on 47 for the first wicket and looked well set. Vaughan turned to his talisman, Flintoff, who responded with an outstanding opening over of bruising pace. He bowled Langer with the second ball and, having softened him up, ripped out Ponting four balls later for a duck. Trescothick pulled off a magnificent catch at slip to see the back of Hayden for 31 and England continued to chip away until, with the final ball of the third day, Harmison produced a perfect slower ball that utterly deceived the dangerous Clarke and bowled him for 30.

This left Australia requiring 107 more runs to win with only two wickets remaining and, as the Sunday crowd quickly filled Edgbaston, the feeling was that the game would quickly be over. But nine overs passed before England made a breakthrough, and 45 runs had been added when Warne finally stepped back into his own wicket for 42.

The tension was starting to bite, though, as the last pair – Lee and Kasprowicz – painstakingly and, apparently with little bother, compiled vital runs. Slowly but surely they inched their way towards their target. Simon Jones put down a difficult chance at third man off Kasprowicz with only 15 needed to win, and it seemed that Australia were destined to complete a famous victory.

When the target became single figures, England's fielders became increasingly desperate. Vaughan's face was twisted in agony as the batsmen pushed and ran comfortable singles. Four byes flew to the boundary and suddenly just an edge, or a lusty blow, was all that was needed. The game seemed up, but Kasprowicz then unluckily gloved Harmison and England had completed one of the great escape acts.

As the fielders celebrated in wild jubilation, the enduring memory will be of Flintoff comforting a devastated Lee who had slumped to his knees at the non-striker's end. It was the image that illustrated the true spirit of Ashes cricket, and the one that helped to capture an enormous new following. The nation was now truly gripped – and more high drama would quickly follow.

At the start of the over which, according to Michael Vaughan, turned the Ashes battle England's way, Andrew Flintoff bowls Justin Langer.

npower THIRD TEST
11–15 August 2005 at Old Trafford

The third Test followed hard on the heels of the second, and barely had the country regained its breath before another cliffhanger enthralled us all once again. Australia escaped with a draw – with their last pair at the crease – and saved a match they would certainly have lost had rain not washed out virtually all of the third day.

The big surprise was that McGrath was passed fit to play, despite a gloomy prognosis at Edgbaston that had the pessimists ruling him out of the remainder of the series. He was not 100 per cent, and was a shadow of his usual self, but such was Australia's desperation to have him in the team that they were prepared to risk both him and Lee, who had been hospitalised between the Tests with an infected knee. How ironic then, that it should be those two who were hanging on grimly at the end of the game, staving off defeat.

It was a crucial toss to win because England did not want to be facing Warne in the fourth innings, and although Strauss was deceived by Lee's slower ball and was bowled for 6 in the tenth over, England were soon rattling along with Trescothick and Vaughan – who had vowed to score a century in his pre-match press conference – adding 137 for the second wicket.

Warne was made to wait until the fifth ball of his fifth over for the wicket he needed to become the first bowler in the history of Test cricket to claim 600 victims – Trescothick was caught by Gilchrist off the back of his bat for 63 – and Vaughan rode some early luck. He was dropped by Gilchrist off McGrath on 41 and clean bowled by the very next delivery, only to be spared by the call of 'no ball'. As Bell settled in, he also survived a caught and bowled chance off McGrath, but his was a secondary role as Vaughan built on the fluent form he had shown briefly at Edgbaston, and recorded his third highest score against Australia with a typically silky 166.

Vaughan was disappointed with his dismissal – caught in the deep off the part-time wrist spinner, Katich, with the score on 290 – and England slipped at the end of the day, losing Pietersen and Hoggard to the second new ball.

Bell was caught hooking on the second morning without adding to his overnight score of 59, leaving England on 346 for 6 and having lost four wickets for 56. Flintoff and Jones – who bat superbly together – added 97, but they fell in successive overs and shortly after lunch on the second day England were dismissed for 444. Again it was a good total, but not as large as it ought to have been.

Hayden and Langer looked well set as they put on an opening stand of 58, but they were separated by an outstanding reflex catch at short leg by Bell to dismiss Langer off Giles for 31. At tea, Australia were 73 for 1, still 371 runs behind. Then Ponting fell for 7 to the very first ball after the break when Jones found some extra bounce, Bell taking another catch – this time at point. It was the start of a disastrous session for Australia who lost 6 for 141 before the close with Jones, Flintoff and Giles amongst the wickets despite all the batsmen reaching double figures.

It would have been far worse had it not been for a spirited and typically unorthodox innings by Warne. With Gillespie – and riding some luck – Warne added 86 in 24 overs, Gillespie scoring just 13 of them. Warne was missed twice by wicketkeeper Jones off Giles, who also put down a

Jumping to it: Ricky Ponting is airborne as he fights to keep out England's attack at Old Trafford.

difficult caught and bowled chance, and he seemed destined to reach his maiden Test century until he pulled Simon Jones to deep square leg for 90. No one has scored more Test runs that Warne without having scored a hundred. Gillespie's stubborn resistance ended when he became Jones' sixth victim, and Australia had conceded a substantial lead of 142 with a day and three quarters remaining.

It was now up to England to make up for the lost time on the previous day, and score runs as quickly as possible. Ideally, they wanted to get Australia back at the crease again before the close, and this they managed to do thanks to a fine hundred from Strauss and a second half-century by Bell.

Jones made amends for his flawed wicketkeeping with a timely reminder of his worth with the bat – his 27 from 12 balls included two big legside sixes off a chastened McGrath, and Vaughan was able to declare with a lead of 422 forty minutes before the end of the fourth day. Langer and Hayden survived until stumps, and the final day was perfectly set up.

Ten thousand unlucky spectators were turned away from Old Trafford next morning as we saw for the first time the effect this series was having on the cricketing public. Queues snaked right around the ground and, when England's bowlers appeared for the warm-ups, they received a standing ovation. It was an amazing atmosphere – and quite unprecedented for Test cricket in this country.

Hoggard was clearly stirred – he had Langer caught behind with his first ball of the day, but it was not until the 20th over that England struck again when Hayden lost his leg stump to a magnificent reverse-swinger from Flintoff for 36.

Lunch was taken with Australia needing to survive for a further 70 overs with eight wickets in hand, but Martyn was unlucky to be given out lbw to Harmison shortly after the break when umpire Bucknor failed to detect a big inside-edge. With Michael Clarke still nursing a back injury he had picked up on the opening day of the game, Katich joined his captain but made only 12 before Giles took the catch of his life at third slip off Flintoff. Gilchrist's wicket is always crucial, and it was Flintoff – in the same Herculean spell from the Statham End – who removed him via a catch by Bell in the gully for 4.

All this time Ponting stood firm and, although Clarke was inconvenienced by his back problem, the pair stayed together for an hour either side of tea, adding 81. It was brilliant cricket in that Ponting gave the impression, at least, of attempting to chase the target despite Australia needing five runs per over to win and with only five wickets left.

THIRD TEST – ENGLAND v. AUSTRALIA
11–15 August 2005 at Old Trafford

ENGLAND

	First Innings		Second Innings	
ME Trescothick	c Gilchrist b Warne	63	b McGrath	41
AJ Strauss	b Lee	6	c Martyn b McGrath	106
MP Vaughan (capt)	c McGrath b Katich	166	c sub b Lee	14
IR Bell	c Gilchrist b Lee	59	c Katich b McGrath	65
KP Pietersen	c sub b Lee	21	lbw b McGrath	0
MJ Hoggard	b Lee	4		
A Flintoff	c Langer b Warne	46	(6) b McGrath	4
*GO Jones	b Gillespie	4	(7) not out	27
AF Giles	c Hayden b Warne	0	(8) not out	0
SJ Harmison	not out	10		
SP Jones	b Warne	0		
Extras	b 4, lb 5, w 3, nb 15	27	b 5, lb 3, w 1, nb 14	23
	(113.2 overs)	444	(6 wkts dec 61.5 overs)	280

	First Innings				Second Innings			
	O	M	R	W	O	M	R	W
McGrath	25	6	86	0	20.5	1	115	5
Lee	27	6	100	4	12	0	60	1
Gillespie	19	2	114	1	4	0	23	0
Warne	33.2	5	99	4	25	3	74	0
Katich	9	1	36	1	–	–	–	–

Fall of Wickets
1-26, 2-163, 3-290, 4-333, 5-341, 6-346, 7-433, 8-434, 9-438
1-64, 2-97, 3-224, 4-225, 5-248, 6-264

AUSTRALIA

	First Innings		Second Innings	
JL Langer	c Bell b Giles	31	c Jones GO b Hoggard	14
ML Hayden	lbw b Giles	34	b Flintoff	36
RT Ponting (capt)	c Bell b Jones SP	7	c Jones GO b Harmison	156
DR Martyn	b Giles	20	lbw b Harmison	19
SM Katich	b Flintoff	17	c Giles b Flintoff	12
*AC Gilchrist	c Jones GO b Jones SP	30	c Bell b Flintoff	4
SK Warne	c Giles b Jones SP	90	(9) c Jones GO b Flintoff	34
MJ Clarke	c Flintoff b Jones SP	7	(7) b Jones SP	39
JN Gillespie	lbw b Jones SP	26	(8) lbw b Hoggard	0
B Lee	c Trescothick b Jones SP	1	not out	18
GD McGrath	not out	1	not out	5
Extras	b 8, lb 7, w 8, nb 15	38	b 5, lb 8, w 2, nb 19	34
	(84.5 overs)	302	(9 wkts 108 overs)	371

	First Innings				Second Innings			
	O	M	R	W	O	M	R	W
Harmison	10	0	47	0	22	4	67	2
Hoggard	6	2	22	0	13	0	49	2
Flintoff	20	1	65	1	25	6	71	4
Jones SP	17.5	6	53	6	17	3	57	1
Giles	31	4	100	3	26	4	93	0
Vaughan	–	–	–	–	5	0	21	0

Fall of Wickets
1-58, 2-73, 3-86, 4-119, 5-133, 6-186, 7-201, 8-287, 9-293
1-25, 2-96, 3-129, 4-165, 5-182, 6-263, 7-264, 8-340, 9-354

Umpires: BF Bowden & SA Bucknor
Toss: England
Man of the Match: RT Ponting

Match drawn

On 39, Clarke played no stroke to Jones and lost his off stump and in the following over, Hoggard trapped the obdurate Gillespie lbw for a duck. With 31 overs remaining, England's hopes soared again and with the crowd now baying encouragement to every bowler, Warne fought tooth and nail while Ponting moved into three figures and continued to strike boundaries.

They seemed to have broken England's spirit when, with nine overs left, Geraint Jones took a brilliant reflex catch off Flintoff to remove Warne for 34. The ball rebounded off Strauss at second slip, and the wicketkeeper flung himself low and to his right to take the catch inches from the ground. Australia had two wickets left, but Ponting looked immovable.

Simon Jones, who Vaughan brought back at the Stretford End, was now forced from the field with cramp and replaced by Harmison who, for the second time in successive matches, trapped a vital wicket off the glove down the leg side. This time it was Ponting who, with just four overs to go, was finally dismissed for a heroic 156. He had defied England for nearly seven hours, but now the last pair were together and England were one wicket away from taking a 2-1 lead.

With the crowd on their feet and roaring, Flintoff and Harmison – who bowled the final over – had 12 balls each with which to dislodge Lee and McGrath. Despite some near misses, they could not do it. The last delivery from Harmison was a legside full toss that Lee flicked to the boundary. The desolate figure at Edgbaston now flung his arms around McGrath as England – shattered both mentally and physically – were immediately drawn into a huddle by their captain. 'Look at their balcony', Vaughan told his players as the Australians celebrated ecstatically. 'That's what it means to them to draw a game against us.'

One each, with two to play.

Steve Harmison shows his frustration as England strive to break Australia's spirited resistance at Old Trafford.

Finally it's over, and Australian last pair Brett Lee and Glenn McGrath can celebrate the escape with a draw.

npower FOURTH TEST
25–28 August 2005 at Trent Bridge

It still seems scarcely believable that, following two tense and exciting Tests, we should be treated to a third in succession. The fate of the fourth match of the series was, like the third, decided by two tail-end batsmen. But, this time, England's Ashley Giles and Matthew Hoggard managed to eke out the 13 runs they needed against a rampant Shane Warne to secure a three-wicket victory, and a 2-1 lead.

When a team is down on its luck – and especially one that is on tour – it seems that events deliberately conspire against it. For the second time, Ricky Ponting found himself without the services of Glenn McGrath who, this time, was forced out of the game with an elbow injury. With Jason Gillespie and Mike Kasprowicz struggling for form, Ponting had little option but to draft in Shaun Tait, the young South Australian tearaway, to make his debut. Gillespie was dropped while England, on the other hand, were able to choose the same team for the fourth consecutive match.

Vaughan won the toss and England were quickly cashing in on McGrath's absence by scoring at five runs per over. Strauss fell just before lunch for 35, caught by Hayden at slip as he swept Warne, and Trescothick became Tait's first Test victim when he was bowled by the first ball after a rain break for 65.

Bell is fast gaining a reputation for being a 'good nicker' – a batsman who is unlucky enough to find the edge early in his innings, rather than play and miss. This was the case again as he fell to Tait for 3, and England's good start was beginning to unravel. Vaughan had been missed on 30, but he and Pietersen added 67 before the captain fell to Ponting's occasional medium pace for 58. The look of utter disbelief on Vaughan's face as he trooped off

Simon Jones produces the perfect outswinger to knock back Michael Kasprowicz's off stump at Trent Bridge.

was a picture, but the loss of his wicket gave Australia the upper hand at the end of a truncated first day in which only 60 overs were possible.

The stage was set for another Flintoff/Pietersen extravaganza, but Pietersen was caught behind for 45 in the fifth over of the day, further boosting Australia's hopes of dismissing England for a controllable total. But as we have seen a number of times in the recent past, Flintoff and Geraint Jones bat superbly together and they now added 177 in their vastly contrasting styles. Jones is cruelly misleading in that he appears happily to be handing the strike to Flintoff, and yet he scores at a rate of knots himself. He might have been caught behind off the first ball after lunch for 34 – the snickometer was inconclusive – but Flintoff reached his first century against Australia from 121 deliveries, including one six and 14 fours. Moments later he was gone, adjudged lbw to Tait for 102 and England were 418 for 6.

Jones was caught and bowled by Kasprowicz for 85 from 149 balls and England were dismissed at tea on the second day for 477. By the close, thanks to Matthew Hoggard's new ball swing, Australia were 99 for 5 – including the loss of three wickets in 11 balls – and in real trouble. For the second time in the series, too, Harmison dismissed Clarke in the last over of the day, this time lbw for 36 to end a stand of 41 with Katich.

England's seam bowling was simply too good throughout the series for Australia to escape at any time, and after Simon Jones had removed Katich in the ninth over of the third morning for 45, Australia's only resistance came from Lee who twice hit Harmison clean out of the ground at deep midwicket in a wonderfully entertaining thrash worth 47 from 44 balls. Jones got him in the end to finish with 5 for 44 and Vaughan enforced the follow-on with Australia 259 runs behind – the first time that particular ignominy had been imposed on Australia in 17 years.

As is usually the case, a batting team in that situation make a better fist of the second innings and, at tea on the third day, Australia were 115 for 1 with Ponting and Langer going well. We were then treated to what was arguably

the turning point in this Ashes series: a moment of brilliance that earned cult status for a little-known cricketer from Durham called Gary Pratt.

There was, apparently, growing unhappiness in the Australian camp of the use, by England, of specialist fielders as substitutes whenever a player left the field. The fact that this has become a long-standing arrangement for home teams – including Australia – seemed to pass Ponting's team by. In truth, it appeared to be more of a grumble about the number of times England's bowlers left the field for what the umpires were told were toilet breaks than anything else, so when Ponting was spectacularly run out by a superb direct hit from cover by the swooping Pratt – who was substituting for Simon Jones – the Australian captain saw red.

As he waited for the third umpire to give him out, he remonstrated with some of England's players. But it was as he stormed up the steps and through the startled members that he really exploded, bellowing expletives at the coaching staff on the England balcony. What compounded Ponting's predicament was that Jones was actually in hospital at the time, receiving a scan for an ankle injury that was to rule him out of the rest of the series.

Ponting was duly fined 75 per cent of his match fee and he was joined, next day, by Katich who showed dissent when harshly given out lbw for 59. He was fined 50 per cent. It had been a brave innings of

Our hero: Gary Pratt is hoisted high by England's players after running out Ricky Ponting with a brilliant pick-up and throw from cover.

FOURTH TEST – ENGLAND v. AUSTRALIA
25–28 August 2005 at Trent Bridge

ENGLAND

	First Innings		Second Innings	
ME Trescothick	b Tait	65	c Ponting b Warne	27
AJ Strauss	c Hayden b Warne	35	c Clarke b Warne	23
MP Vaughan (capt)	c Gilchrist b Ponting	58	c Hayden b Warne	0
IR Bell	c Gilchrist b Tait	3	c Kasprowicz b Lee	3
KP Pietersen	c Gilchrist b Lee	45	c Gilchrist b Lee	23
A Flintoff	lbw b Tait	102	b Lee	26
*GO Jones	c & b Kasprowicz	85	c Kasprowicz b Warne	3
AF Giles	lbw b Warne	15	not out	7
MJ Hoggard	c Gilchrist b Warne	10	not out	8
SJ Harmison	st Gilchrist b Warne	2		
SP Jones	not out	15		
Extras	b 1, lb 15, w 1, nb 25	42	lb 4, nb 5	9
	(123.1 overs)	477	(7 wkts 31.5 overs)	129

	First Innings				Second Innings			
	O	M	R	W	O	M	R	W
Lee	32	2	131	1	12	0	51	3
Kasprowicz	32	3	122	1	2	0	19	0
Tait	24	4	97	3	4	0	24	0
Warne	29.1	4	102	4	13.5	2	31	4
Ponting	6	2	9	1	-	-	-	-

Fall of Wickets
1-105, 2-137, 3-146, 4-213, 5-241, 6-418, 7-450, 8-450, 9-454
1-32, 2-36, 3-57, 4-57, 5-103, 6-111, 7-116

AUSTRALIA

	First Innings		Second Innings	
JL Langer	c Bell b Hoggard	27	c Bell b Giles	61
ML Hayden	lbw b Hoggard	7	c Giles b Flintoff	26
RT Ponting (capt)	lbw b Jones SP	1	run out	48
DR Martyn	lbw b Hoggard	1	c Jones GO b Flintoff	13
MJ Clarke	lbw b Harmison	36	c Jones GO b Hoggard	56
SM Katich	c Strauss b Jones SP	45	lbw b Harmison	59
*AC Gilchrist	c Strauss b Flintoff	27	lbw b Hoggard	11
SK Warne	c Bell b Jones SP	0	st Jones GO b Giles	45
B Lee	c Bell b Jones SP	47	not out	26
MS Kasprowicz	b Jones SP	5	c Jones GO b Harmison	19
SW Tait	not out	3	b Harmison	4
Extras	lb 2, w 1, nb 16	19	b 1, lb 4, nb 14	19
	(49.1 overs)	218	(124 overs)	387

	First Innings				Second Innings			
	O	M	R	W	O	M	R	W
Harmison	9	1	48	1	30	5	93	3
Hoggard	15	3	70	3	27	7	72	2
Jones SP	14.1	4	44	5	4	0	15	0
Flintoff	11	1	54	1	29	4	83	2
Giles	-	-	-	-	28	3	107	2
Bell	-	-	-	-	6	2	12	0

Fall of Wickets
1-20, 2-21, 3-22, 4-58, 5-99, 6-157, 7-157, 8-163, 9-175
1-50, 2-129, 3-155, 4-161, 5-261, 6-277, 7-314, 8-342, 9-373

Umpires: Aleem Dar & SA Bucknor
Toss: England
Test debut: SW Tait
Man of the Match: A Flintoff

England won by 3 wickets

nearly four and a half hours, and Warne's 45 helped to push Australia to 387, setting England 129 to win with 41 overs remaining on the fourth day.

Chasing small targets is a pressurised business, and England wanted to break the back of their task as quickly as possible. Trescothick and Strauss reached 31 in only six overs, but Warne was already in the attack and he produced what must rank as one of his finest spells. Trescothick was taken by Ponting at silly point for 27 and, in his next over, Warne had Vaughan caught at slip for a duck. Six overs later, Strauss was held at leg slip for 23 and when Bell was caught at long leg for 3, hooking at Lee, England had slipped to 57 for 4, and their target suddenly seemed a long way off. Pietersen and Flintoff added 46, and the unbearable tension around Trent Bridge appeared to have eased, only for Lee to find Pietersen's outside edge and, next over, to clean bowl Flintoff with an Exocet to leave England floundering on 111 for 6.

Thirteen more runs were needed when Jones then lofted Warne to mid-off, and Hoggard trudged out to join Giles. It was anybody's match now and, had Ponting been able to call up McGrath to support Warne, Australia might well have won it.

But Hoggard came up with an imperious (for him) cover drive for four off a Lee full toss to release the pressure, and Giles finally turned Warne through midwicket for the winning runs. Australia now had to win the final Test at The Oval to retain the Ashes.

npower FIFTH TEST
8–12 September 2005 at The Oval

After 16 years of Australian domination, England regained the Ashes in the final Test of the series, which ended in the most bizarre of circumstances. Bad light had stopped play late on the final afternoon with the game locked in stalemate. With the final hour of the match still technically to start, but with a crowd of 23,000 desperate to party, the umpires took the sensible decision of abandoning play early. The Oval then erupted in celebration.

The elements did their best to conspire against Australia, who had to win the game in order to retain the Ashes. The third and fourth days were both hit by the weather and bad light but, even so, England were by no means confident of their position until midway through the final afternoon, when Kevin Pietersen's 158 crushed any lingering Australian hopes.

The pitch was dreadfully flat and, with the promise of spin later in the game, England badly needed to win the toss. This they duly did and the openers were soon romping along at their customary five runs per over.

For those people – including Richie Benaud in his final Test in an English commentary box – who thought he had been at his best at Trent Bridge, Shane Warne turned in a performance of heroic proportions to keep his team in the game. He took four of the first five wickets to fall in conditions that did not help him one bit. Trescothick was brilliantly caught at slip by Hayden for 43, Vaughan casually flicked to midwicket for 11, Bell was lbw for 0 and Pietersen was beautifully deceived and bowled for 14 when Warne went wide of the crease.

Strauss stood firm, however, and finally found an ally in Flintoff who enthralled the first day crowd with a typically belligerent innings of 72. The pair added 143 for the fifth wicket, and were ramming home England's advantage when three late wickets – including Strauss for 129 from 210 balls – handed the first day to Australia. At 82 for no wicket and 274 for 4, England had been perfectly placed to bury Australia, and take complete control of the game. It was not the way of this series, however, and, at 319 for 7 at the close, Ponting was very satisfied.

Although Jones, Giles and Harmison extended England's total to 373, the second day also belonged to Australia. Thanks to an unbeaten stand of 112,

Above: Shane Warne bellows in triumph after catching Flintoff on the tense final morning.

Below: Kevin Pietersen hits Warne into the Oval crowd for six on his way to an epic, Ashes-clinching 158.

they were still 261 runs behind, but their aim of batting well beyond England and then letting Warne loose on a wearing pitch was still very much alive.

Frustratingly for Australia, they were able to add only 165 runs on the third day as Langer and Hayden extended their partnership to 185. Harmison bowled Langer off the edge for 105, and although Ponting sliced a catch to gully off Flintoff for 35, Hayden kept grinding away. This was comfortably his most significant contribution to what had otherwise been a bitterly disappointing series and he was never in a position to cut loose. After Martyn had failed again – caught at square leg – on the fourth morning, Hayden was finally trapped lbw by Flintoff after nearly seven hours at the crease for 138. England's bowlers ran through the lower order and, from being 323 for 3, Australia lost seven wickets for 44 in 15 overs.

But in bowling Australia out so quickly, England had left themselves exposed to the threat of being dismissed a second time and thus lose the match. It took a while for this to dawn on the crowd, which had been whipped up into wild hysteria as the Australian wickets tumbled. Strauss was immediately caught at short leg off Warne for 1 and, at 3.40pm, the umpires offered the batsmen the light. When they accepted and walked off, the full house roared its approval: another first, surely, in this remarkable series.

England were now 34 for 1, which gave them a slender lead of 40. Going into the final day of the series, it was still anybody's match, and Australia appeared to tighten their grip in the morning session as McGrath removed Vaughan and Bell with successive deliveries, and England lost four wickets – including Flintoff for 8.

At lunch, with half the side out, England's lead was only 133. Pietersen, dropped twice early in his innings, had clung on before the interval in the face of a furious spell from Lee, but he then ran amok in a brief but frenetic passage of play, which snatched the Ashes from Ponting's hands. Lee was hit for 55 runs from 48 balls, including two sixes over deep square leg. Collingwood, watching anxiously from the other end, was the perfect foil as he scored just 10 in more than an hour, and although Warne dismissed him, and Jones was bowled by Tait, Pietersen and Giles made absolutely sure that there were no further twists with a stand of 109. Pietersen was eventually bowled by McGrath for 158: an innings of the highest quality in terms of technique and entertainment. He returned to the dressing room a national hero – another young cricketer who, in this amazing summer, had become a household name.

Harmison bowled four balls at Langer, all vicious lifters wildly acclaimed, before the umpires offered the light and Vaughan became the first English captain for 20 years to lift the Ashes urn on home soil.

FIFTH TEST – ENGLAND v. AUSTRALIA
8–12 September 2005 at The Oval

ENGLAND

	First Innings		Second Innings	
ME Trescothick	c Hayden b Warne	43	lbw b Warne	33
AJ Strauss	c Katich b Warne	129	c Katich b Warne	1
MP Vaughan (capt)	c Clarke b Warne	11	c Gilchrist b McGrath	45
IR Bell	lbw b Warne	0	c Warne b McGrath	0
KP Pietersen	b Warne	14	b McGrath	158
A Flintoff	c Warne b McGrath	72	c & b Warne	8
PD Collingwood	lbw b Tait	7	c Ponting b Warne	10
*GO Jones	b Lee	25	b Tait	1
AF Giles	lbw b Warne	32	b Warne	59
MJ Hoggard	c Martyn b McGrath	2	not out	4
SJ Harmison	not out	20	c Hayden b Warne	0
Extras	b 4, lb 6, w 1, nb 7	18	b 4, w 7, nb 5	16
	(105.3 overs)	**373**	(91.3 overs)	**335**

	First Innings				Second Innings			
	O	M	R	W	O	M	R	W
McGrath	27	5	72	2	26	3	85	3
Lee	23	3	94	1	20	4	88	0
Tait	15	1	61	1	5	0	28	1
Warne	37.3	5	122	6	38.3	3	124	6
Katich	3	0	14	0	–	–	–	–
Clarke	–	–	–	–	2	0	6	0

Fall of Wickets
1-82, 2-102, 3-104, 4-131, 5-274, 6-289, 7-297, 8-325, 9-345
1-2, 2-67, 3-67, 4-109, 5-126, 6-186, 7-199, 8-308, 9-335

AUSTRALIA

	First Innings		Second Innings	
JL Langer	b Harmison	105	not out	0
ML Hayden	lbw b Flintoff	138	not out	0
RT Ponting (capt)	c Strauss b Flintoff	35		
DR Martyn	c Collingwood b Flintoff	10		
MJ Clarke	lbw b Hoggard	25		
SM Katich	lbw b Flintoff	1		
*AC Gilchrist	lbw b Hoggard	23		
SK Warne	c Vaughan b Flintoff	0		
B Lee	c Giles b Hoggard	6		
GD McGrath	c Strauss b Hoggard	0		
SW Tait	not out	1		
Extras	b 4, lb 8, w 2, nb 9	23	lb 4	4
	(107.1 overs)	**367**	(0 wkts 0.4 overs)	**4**

	First Innings				Second Innings			
	O	M	R	W	O	M	R	W
Harmison	22	2	87	1	0.4	0	0	0
Hoggard	24.1	2	97	4	–	–	–	–
Flintoff	34	10	78	5	–	–	–	–
Giles	23	1	76	0	–	–	–	–
Collingwood	4	0	17	0	–	–	–	–

Fall of Wickets
1-185, 2-264, 3-281, 4-323, 5-329, 6-356, 7-359, 8-363, 9-363

Umpires: BF Bowden & RE Koertzen
Toss: England
Man of the Match: KP Pietersen
Men of the Series: A Flintoff and SK Warne

Match drawn

SERIES AVERAGES
England v. Australia

ENGLAND

Batting	M	Inns	NO	Runs	HS	Av	100	50	c/st
KP Pietersen	5	10	1	473	158	52.55	1	3	–/–
ME Trescothick	5	10	0	431	90	43.10	–	3	3/–
A Flintoff	5	10	0	402	102	40.20	1	3	3/–
AJ Strauss	5	10	0	393	129	39.30	2	–	6/–
SP Jones	4	6	4	66	20*	33.00	–	–	1/–
MP Vaughan	5	10	0	326	166	32.60	1	1	2/–
GO Jones	5	10	1	229	85	25.44	–	1	15/1
AF Giles	5	10	2	155	59	19.37	–	1	5/–
IR Bell	5	10	0	171	65	17.10	–	2	8/–
SJ Harmison	5	8	2	60	20*	10.00	–	–	1/–
PD Collingwood	1	2	0	17	10	8.50	–	–	1/–
MJ Hoggard	5	9	2	45	16	6.42	–	–	–/–

Bowling	Overs	Mds	Runs	Wkts	Av	Best	5/inn	10m
SP Jones	102	17	378	18	21.00	6-53	2	–
A Flintoff	194	32	655	24	27.29	5-78	1	–
MJ Hoggard	122.1	15	473	16	29.56	4-97	–	–
SJ Harmison	161.1	22	549	17	32.29	5-43	1	–
AF Giles	160	18	578	10	57.80	3-78	–	–

Also bowled: PD Collingwood 4-0-17-0, IR Bell 7-2-20-0, MP Vaughan 5-0-21-0.

AUSTRALIA

Batting	M	Inns	NO	Runs	HS	Av	100	50	c/st
JL Langer	5	10	1	394	105	43.77	1	2	2/–
RT Ponting	5	9	0	359	156	39.88	1	1	4/–
MJ Clarke	5	9	0	335	91	37.22	–	2	2/–
GD McGrath	3	5	4	36	20*	36.00	–	–	1/–
ML Hayden	5	10	1	318	138	35.33	1	–	10/–
SK Warne	5	9	0	249	90	27.66	–	1	5/–
SM Katich	5	9	0	248	67	27.55	–	2	4/–
B Lee	5	9	3	158	47	26.33	–	–	2/–
AC Gilchrist	5	9	1	181	49*	22.62	–	–	18/1
DR Martyn	5	9	0	178	65	19.77	–	1	4/–
MS Kasprowicz	2	4	0	44	20	11.00	–	–	3/–
SW Tait	2	3	2	8	4	8.00	–	–	–/–
JN Gillespie	3	6	0	47	26	7.83	–	–	1/–

Bowling	Overs	Mds	Runs	Wkts	Av	Best	5/inn	10m
RT Ponting	6	2	9	1	9.00	1-9	–	–
SK Warne	252.5	37	797	40	19.92	6-46	3	2
GD McGrath	134	22	440	19	23.15	5-53	2	–
B Lee	191.1	25	822	20	41.10	4-82	–	–
SW Tait	48	5	210	5	42.00	3-97	–	–
SM Katich	12	1	50	1	50.00	1-36	–	–
MS Kasprowicz	52	6	250	4	62.50	3-80	–	–
JN Gillespie	67	6	300	3	100.00	2-91	–	–

Also bowled: MJ Clarke 2-0-6-0.

Overleaf: Two final images of England's unforgettable Ashes summer – Vaughan with the precious Ashes urn and Ashley Giles and Duncan Fletcher reflecting on a job well done. England's triumph was followed, the next day, by scenes of joy in London as the players were taken by open-top bus to a special celebration in Trafalgar Square. For weeks afterwards, too, it seemed as if cricket dominated the nation's consciousness as Vaughan and his team were feted as true sporting heroes.

Left: England's celebration party is about to start as Michael Vaughan raises the Ashes urn in triumph.

SHANE WARNE

SHANE WARNE became the first man to take 600 Test wickets during an Ashes series that was made all the more unforgettable because of his presence. But, amid the glory, 2005 also brought personal and professional heartache, as he tells RICHARD HOBSON of *The Times.*

When he reflects on the special summer of 2005 Shane Warne will recall some of the highest highs and lowest lows of his life and career. He claimed a record haul of wickets for Australia in a five-match series against England – but lost the Ashes. He was also Hampshire's leading Championship wicket-taker – but his county had to settle for second place. And all this after the high-profile breakdown of his marriage which left his three young children to follow his progress from the other side of the world.

It was quite a season, in quite a career. Already established as an all-time great, his standing as a player rose even further. And, as the challenging months slowly passed, he also became the great Test match captain who never was. For an Ashes turning point, try the moment in 2000 when the Australian Cricket Board sacked him as vice-captain, effectively leaving him out of contention to replace Steve Waugh. Would Warne, like Ricky Ponting, have bowled first with a McGrath-less attack at Edgbaston? Now there was a turning point.

His words are often dismissed as gamesmanship, but he was proved right time after time. Ponting once joked – not quite through tears – that it was Warne who picked Kevin Pietersen for England with his constant praise when the selectors were unsure. 'He is the most destructive player in England, Freddie Flintoff included,' Warne wrote in one of his columns in *The Times.* 'Selectors cannot mess around with a special talent like that. If England don't want him, I'd be overjoyed to see him bat for Hampshire.'

He proved equally sound in assessing England's prospects. While Glenn McGrath was happy to talk up a 5-0 whitewash, Warne took a more guarded approach. He advised England supporters not to get carried away with early success in the one-day series. Then, after Australia's emphatic victory in the first Test at Lord's, he cautioned his own followers. 'England are not the second best team in the world for nothing and they have three or four match-winners,' he said. Crystal balls, cricket balls ... Warne is clearly skilled with both.

He had bowled more overs than any of his Hampshire colleagues when he joined the Australia squad after the NatWest Series. Meanwhile Simone, his wife, had decided to separate after a kiss-and-tell story in a tabloid newspaper. Warne admitted that his life changed at that moment and he suffered some lonely, confused moments in the weeks ahead.

But whatever his personal difficulties, he has always managed to perform on the field. He spoke to his children on the phone most days, sometimes twice, before and after they went to school back home. And there was nothing like the Ashes to concentrate the mind.

A meeting with Terry Jenner at a function three days before the first Test set him up for the serious cricket. Jenner, a former Australia leg-spin bowler, was in England to help with an ECB spin-bowling programme at Loughborough. He is a long-time mentor of Warne and agreed to work with him on the Tuesday before Lord's. 'The ball was coming out of my hand beautifully but the alignment of my action was not quite right,' Warne said. 'I knew if I could get it right I would spin the ball more than ever. I just needed to get higher and straighter in my action. After that I probably bowled as well as ever. I don't think I could have batted or bowled much better through the series.'

One of Warne's biggest disappointments of 2005 was this stroke: on 90, and in sight of the maiden Test hundred he wants so much, he pulls Simon Jones straight to deep midwicket.

Wickets began to tumble, 40 in all with at best moderate support from the other end. That figure is all the more remarkable because England batted first in four of the five matches, before spin should really play a major part. He bowled Andrew Strauss on the Friday evening at Edgbaston with a ball turning full across an outstretched front pad to hit leg stump. Then, at The Oval, he spun one back almost square into an alarmed Marcus Trescothick; had it been a drop goal it would have screwed away for a lineout to guffaws from the crowd.

Like many judges, Warne does not think the series can be bettered. 'Every now and then you get a great Test match but not three or four in a row like that,' he said. 'Even at The Oval, although England batted it out and the end was a bit of a farce because of bad light, there was a long period on the final day where it looked like we were on for a chase against the clock.

'It is disappointing for me to say it was a thoroughly good series because I hate losing. But removing myself as an Australian cricketer for a moment, it was.'

He described the Edgbaston Test as the most topsy-turvy of his career, finding an inopportune moment to be out 'hit wicket' for the first time on the nail-biting Sunday morning. His batting became an issue at Old Trafford, too, when he seemed certain to complete a maiden Test hundred only to hole out to deep midwicket on 90. Again, he was forced into rearguard service second time around. This time, Australia narrowly hung on. But at Trent Bridge, where Warne's sheer force of personality almost pulled off a reversal of Headingley 1981 proportions, they could not quite recover lost ground.

'Looking back, we actually played some brilliant cricket in the series but we kept giving ourselves too much to do,' he said. 'At 7 for 137 [chasing 282] in the second innings at Edgbaston most people wouldn't have given us a prayer, and if I'm being honest we probably didn't think we could do it ourselves. In the end it was a fantastic effort to get within three runs of winning. Then, at Old Trafford, we scored 371 on the final day which was another great performance – we hadn't even thought of the target but we were only 52 short. And at Trent Bridge I reckon we were only 20 or so away.'

By a cruel piece of irony it was Warne, having done more than anybody to keep Australia alive, who was the man to spill Pietersen early in his career-defining innings at The Oval which gave England the draw required. 'There is no point dwelling on the "ifs" and "buts",' he said. 'We dropped Pietersen three times but would we have won the game if we held one of those catches? Who knows? When you cut through everything the plain fact is that England outplayed us through the series. I am not ashamed or embarrassed to say that because there is no disgrace in losing to a better side when you have given your all.'

A familiar sight on English cricket grounds in the summer of '05: the great Shane Warne acknowledging the crowd's applause.

On a personal level, of course, perhaps the biggest highlight was his 600th Test wicket, that of Trescothick at Old Trafford. It was also an emotional occasion as he kissed a wristband bearing the word 'STRENGTH' which was given to him by his eldest daughter, Brooke, before she returned to Australia.

Warne's mind was spinning like one of his leggies, but he also recalls a handshake from Michael Vaughan, who broke into the celebrations to offer congratulations. For Warne, that gesture epitomised the spirit of the series. He said, 'It was a privilege to be involved in something that kids in the grounds will be telling their grandchildren about 50 years from now. They were some of the hardest games I have been involved in but the one thing I will take is the respect between the sides. I hope it becomes a landmark series from that point of view, and that a few other countries have noted the way both sides clapped or shook hands when a player reached a landmark.'

His last Test appearance in England behind him, Warne intends to play for Hampshire for at least three more years. His shoulder, remarkably, is holding up well, although his back is causing problems. His commitment to Hampshire should not be underestimated. He enjoys the captaincy challenge and few celebrations were as vivid as the leap in the air which followed his hundred against Kent at Canterbury in May. Nor was criticism much stronger than Warne's blast at David Fulton when the Kent captain opened the way for Nottinghamshire to secure the Championship with a generous declaration in the penultimate round of games. At 36, his competitive streak burns deeper than ever.

11 June 2005 at Leicester
Australia 321 for 4 (50 overs) (ML Hayden 107,
A Symonds 92*, DR Martyn 85)
Leicestershire 226 for 8 (50 overs) (OD Gibson 50)
Australia won by 95 runs

Australia enjoyed a gentle start to their tour,
hammering a woeful Leicestershire by 95 runs.
Matthew Hayden was immediately into his
belligerent stride, thumping two sixes and 13 fours
in a 96-ball 107 and, although Adam Gilchrist and
Ricky Ponting went cheaply, both Damien Martyn
and Andy Symonds also made hay. Martyn's 85 was
all elegance, and Symonds' 59-ball unbeaten 92,
with three sixes and 10 fours, all raw power.
Leicestershire's reply was in tatters at 120 for 6, but
at least Paul Nixon and Ottis Gibson regained some
respectability with a seventh wicket stand of 94.

15 June 2005 at Taunton
Australia 342 for 5 (50 overs) (RT Ponting 80,
ML Hayden 76, MJ Clarke 63*, MEK Hussey 51)
Somerset 345 for 6 (46.5 overs) (GC Smith 108,
ST Jayasuriya 101)
Somerset won by 4 wickets

After their crushing defeat by England in the
Twenty20 International at the Rose Bowl, the
Australians were humbled again by Somerset on a
belter of a pitch. It may have been two established
overseas internationals who inflicted most of the
damage – Graeme Smith and Sanath Jayasuriya
both hitting memorable centuries and having a ball
in an opening stand of 197 in just 23 overs – but it
was two young Englishmen, James Hildreth and
Carl Gazzard, who held their nerve at the end with
an unbroken partnership of 54 in a mere 26 balls.
That took Somerset past Australia's 50-over total of
342 for 5 with as many as 19 balls to spare, and the
four-wicket win was celebrated joyously by a
raucous capacity crowd. Somerset had only ever
defeated the Australians once before, when a young
Ian Botham was at the forefront of the 1977 victory
at Bath. Mike Kasprowicz conceded 89 runs from
his eight overs, and Shane Watson 72 from 8.5.
Australia's only mitigation was that both Matthew
Hayden and Ricky Ponting had been retired out
when they were rattling along on 76 and 80

respectively to allow others the chance to bat.
'I am pretty embarrassed,' said Australian captain
Ponting, who played for Somerset in 2004. 'We
shall sit down and talk about why we were not good
enough or smart enough to defend a total of 342.
We'll have our work cut out against Bangladesh on
Saturday the way we are playing.'

15–17 July 2005 at Leicester
Leicestershire 217 (55.2 overs) (CJL Rogers 56,
B Lee 4 for 53) & 363 for 5 (79.4 overs)
(CJL Rogers 209, DDJ Robinson 81,
SCG MacGill 4 for 122)
Australia 582 for 7 dec (125 overs) (DR Martyn 154*,
RT Ponting 119, JL Langer 115, ML Hayden 75)
Match drawn

James Hildreth, one of English cricket's brightest young
batting talents, held his nerve as Somerset beat the
Australians at Taunton.

For two days all went well for the Australians, as they finalised their preparations for the opening Ashes Test. With Brett Lee firing, they tumbled out Leicestershire for 217 on the first day, and on the second day converted their overnight 169 for 2 into a mammoth 582 for 7. Justin Langer, who had put on 131 with Matthew Hayden for the first wicket, was joined as a century-maker by Ricky Ponting and Damien Martyn. They had added a further 201 for the fourth wicket, and Martyn's unbeaten 154 from 240 balls had featured 14 elegant fours. In an ineffective county attack only young Stuart Broad had stood up to the mauling well – and Australia seemed set to complete a morale-boosting victory on the final day. They had reckoned without the skill and ambition, however, of one of their own. Chris Rogers, the 27-year-old Western Australian taken on as a temporary overseas player in place of India's Dinesh Mongia, was joined in an opening partnership of 247 by the solid if unspectacular Darren Robinson, and suddenly it began to dawn on the Australians that they faced a long, unwanted day in the field. Robinson eventually fell for 81, after helping to establish the highest opening stand ever made by a county team against the touring Australians, and the left-handed Rogers went on to a career-best 209. He struck two sixes and 32 fours and, at the close, Leicestershire had won themselves a most honourable draw at 363 for 5.

30 July–1 August 2005 at Worcester
Australia 406 for 9 dec (98 overs) (BJ Haddin 94, ML Hayden 79, JL Langer 54, JN Gillespie 53*) & 161 for 2 (38 overs) (MJ Clarke 59, RT Ponting 59*)
Worcestershire 187 (44 overs) (SC Moore 69, MS Kasprowicz 5 for 67)
Match drawn

Just one over was possible on the first day before rain set in, Justin Langer driving Kabir Ali's first ball for four, but the Australians went smoothly along to 406 for 9 declared on day two with Langer, Matthew Hayden, Brad Haddin and Jason Gillespie all passing 50. Haddin's 95-ball 94 was particularly entertaining, and the Australians could later have enforced the follow-on after bundling out a spineless Worcestershire side for just 187 – with Mike Kasprowicz taking 5 for 67. But the tourists, unsurprisingly, opted for a little more batting practice, before the draw was completed, with both Michael Clarke and Ricky Ponting taking advantage of the opportunity in an opening stand of 80.

RICHIE BENAUD

The final Ashes Test at The Oval marked the last cricket commentary in England by Richie Benaud. Here, JONATHAN AGNEW adds his own personal tribute.

It would not be possible to reflect on 2005 without paying tribute to the doyen of cricket commentators, Richie Benaud. For 45 years – predominately with the BBC who trained him while he was still playing for Australia, and latterly Channel 4 – Richie became the most popular, and certainly the best television commentator cricket has known. Each word he delivered was chosen precisely and meticulously, and the all-important timing was perfect. Even when under pressure to talk more because of adverts at the end of each over, Richie never said anything that did not add to the picture.

I was very lucky to work with him during the 1999 World Cup when, with the exception of Richie, all the regular BBC TV commentators had joined either Channel 4 or BSkyB. With the cupboard bare, I was asked to present the television coverage: a completely new and terrifying experience. The hardest part of presentation, I found, was the absolute need to talk to time, with a woman's voice in my earpiece, counting down each second until the end of the programme. Thanks to Richie, we quickly found the answer.

I would ask him a question with about a minute to go and, as he listened to the countdown, he would talk until there were exactly eight seconds left. I then had just enough time to say thank you and good night!

Commentary is one thing, but viewers probably do not appreciate that calm, smooth and unflustered presentation is the toughest aspect of television – and Richie is King!

18 August 2005 at The Grange
Scotland v. **Australia**
Match abandoned

There was huge disappointment at the Grange in Edinburgh when rain washed out Scotland's intended one-day fixture against the Australians. A sell-out crowd waited around more in hope than anticipation, but the match was formally abandoned soon after 4pm.

20–21 August 2005 at Northampton
Australia 374 for 6 dec (96 overs) (ML Hayden 136, MJ Clarke 121) & 226 for 2 (58 overs) (JL Langer 86*, SM Katich 63)
Northamptonshire 169 (50.1 overs)
Match drawn

Against his former county, Matthew Hayden struck a mighty 136, with four sixes and 20 fours, to pull Australia up after an initial slide to 69 for 3 in a two-day, drawn practice match. Hayden was joined in a fourth wicket stand of 206 by Michael Clarke, who caught the mood to end up with 121 himself, from 177 balls and with five sixes and 15 fours. Northants, 29 for 2 overnight in reply to the Australians' 374 for 6 declared, were soon 42 for 4 as Shaun Tait ripped out Usman Afzaal and David Sales, while also causing opener Tim Roberts to retire hurt on 18. A shortish ball did not bounce as much as the batsman expected, bursting through the grille of his helmet and producing a cut above his left eye nasty enough to require five stitches. Northants only reached 169 thanks to the late strokeplay of Ben Phillips, who felled Tait with one thunderous straight drive which hit him on the inside of his left knee, but there was still time for Simon Katich and Justin Langer to cash in during Australia's second innings progress to 226 for 2.

3–4 September 2005 at Chelmsford
Essex 502 for 4 dec (105 overs) (AN Cook 214, RS Bopara 135, WI Jefferson 64)
Australia 561 for 6 (95 overs) (BJ Hodge 166, ML Hayden 150, JL Langer 87, SM Katich 72, BJ Haddin 59)
Match drawn

Fresh from collecting the 2005 Young Cricketer of the Year Award at the Cricket Writers' Club annual dinner at

Shaun Tait, Australia's young fast bowling hope, did some damage to Northamptonshire's batting at Wantage Road.

London's Hotel Intercontinental the evening before, Alastair Cook played the innings of his young life at Chelmsford. It is not every day that a young player gets to score 214 against Australia. The morning after the night before found 20-year-old Cook inspired by the experience of receiving the award from Tony Greig, who won it in 1967, and also getting the chance to chat with Greig's fellow former winners Derek Underwood, Mike Brearley, Paul Parker, Rob Bailey and Neil Foster. Cook's first hundred came off 107 balls, his 200 off 232 balls with 30 fours and a six. He added three more boundaries before being caught off Mike Kasprowicz, one of six suffering Aussie bowlers. With Ravi Bopara, also 20, impressing alongside Cook with 135 of his own, and Will Jefferson opening up with 64, Essex were propelled towards a remarkable final total of 502 for 4 – the first time an Australian team, indeed, had conceded more than 500 runs in a day. A capacity Chelmsford crowd were in raptures as Cook figured in stands of 140 with Jefferson and then an exhilarating 270 for the second wicket with Bopara.

Those who mischievously wondered if Essex captain Ronnie Irani, due to be next in, would opt to bat on into the second day, were disappointed at the overnight declaration but now it was the Australians' turn to have fun in the early September sunshine. Only Adam Gilchrist of the top six failed to reach at least 59, with Matthew Hayden being retired out on 150 – with 18 fours and seven sixes – and Brad Hodge plundering his first hundred of the tour from 119 balls and going on to 166. The Australians went past Essex's total and finished up on 561 for 6

declared, but this drawn match will always be remembered for the batting of Cook and Bopara. 'All in all, it's been a fantastic few days,' said Cook. 'I'm honoured to have received the Young Cricketer of the Year award the night before the game, especially as there are so many incredible cricketers who have won it in the past, and then I was fortunate to bat well on a flat wicket. It's a dream.'

From prizewinner to Aussie slayer: Alastair Cook hits 214 against the Australians after a night out in London to collect the 2005 Young Cricketer of the Year Award.

TWENTY20 INTERNATIONAL AND NATWEST TRIANGULAR ONE-DAY SERIES
(Australia, Bangladesh and England)

By Jonathan Agnew

Just days after arriving in England and, in the case of the majority of Australians, having not picked up a bat or ball for several weeks, the tourists were hijacked at the Rose Bowl in the first international Twenty20 match to be staged in this country. The match was ridiculously one-sided, but the crowd was left ecstatic as Australia – set 180 to win in 20 overs – collapsed to 31 for 7 in the sixth over. It was heady stuff – literally unbelievable – and, at the end of the summer, Duncan Fletcher attributed much of England's Ashes success to this game.

The tourists took their thrashing in good heart, and the occasion provided a first for an entire cricketing generation – the sight of an Australian team being mocked and ridiculed as they fumbled about, dropping catches and losing wickets. At the time, though, we did not really believe it would last for long. And yet, a few days later, Australia were beaten by Bangladesh, the worst team in the world, who England had just thrashed by ten wickets in the opening match of the NatWest Series.

Cardiff was the venue for one of sport's greatest upsets and, indeed, this was such a remarkable and unprecedented occasion that it scarcely seemed possible. Mohammad Ashraful's brilliant century took Bangladesh to within 23 runs of overhauling their target of 250 and, with 17 balls remaining, it seemed that Australia – who had bowled and fielded miserably – might get away with it. But Aftab Ahmed and Mohammad Rafique steered Bangladesh home with four balls to spare.

If Ricky Ponting had hoped his team could shrug off this amazing defeat, they were sorely disappointed next day in Bristol when they were defeated by England by three wickets and with 15 balls to spare. Alarm bells were now sounding loudly in the Australian dressing room, and there was also little doubt that the majority of the team were struggling with poor form. Add to this the disciplinary measures taken against Andrew Symonds for breaking a team curfew the night before the Bangladesh defeat and, clearly, problems were brewing. Jason Gillespie, in particular, looked a shadow of his former self, and he bore the brunt of an amazing onslaught by Kevin Pietersen which won England the game. Pietersen, continuing on from where he left off in South Africa,

smashed 91 from only 65 balls in a perfectly paced one-day innings after England had lost Vaughan for 57, at that stage needing 103 to win from 87 balls.

Much capital was made of the NatWest Series table, which had Australia now lying in third place, below Bangladesh, but the remainder of the tournament produced few surprises. Mohammad Ashraful – the hero of Cardiff – produced some entertaining innings for Bangladesh, the most notable being 94 from 52 balls against England at Trent Bridge. But with a win, a defeat and a washout from their three previous meetings in the competition, England and Australia duly lined up for what turned out to be a memorable final.

Put into bat on a cloudy morning, Australia struggled to 196 all out from 48.5 overs. None of the batsmen really got going after Hayden and Gilchrist posted 50 for the first wicket. Flintoff (3 for 23) and Harmison (3 for 27) were both outstanding, and England's target should have been a formality. But in 10 crazy overs, England slumped to 33 for 5, with all the big guns having been dismissed by McGrath and Lee.

Collingwood and Geraint Jones initially set out merely to bat out the rest of the overs, and they added 116 to take England to within 50 of victory with six overs remaining. In the next over, Jones fell for 71, and the Australians were clearly favourites once again. But Giles and Gough cashed in on the four overs bowled by Hussey to score 32 from 29 balls, and leave England needing three to win off the last ball. As tension gripped Lord's, they scampered two leg byes off a furious McGrath to snatch a tie.

TWENTY20 INTERNATIONAL

13 June 2005 at The Rose Bowl
England 179 for 8 (20 overs)
(ME Trescothick 41, PD Collingwood 46)
Australia 79 (14.3 overs) (J Lewis 4 for 24)
England won by 100 runs

NATWEST TRIANGULAR ONE-DAY SERIES

Match One
16 June 2005 at The Oval
Bangladesh 190 (45.2 overs)
(Aftab Ahmed 51, SJ Harmison 4 for 39)
England 192 for 0 (24.5 overs) (ME Trescothick 100*,
AJ Strauss 82*)
England (6pts) won by 10 wickets

Match Two

18 June 2005 at Cardiff
Australia 249 for 5 (50 overs)
(DR Martyn 77, MJ Clarke 54)
Bangladesh 250 for 5 (49.2 overs)
(Mohammad Ashraful 100)
Bangladesh (5pts) won by 5 wickets – Australia (1pt)

Match Three

19 June 2005 at Bristol
Australia 252 for 9 (50 overs)
(MEK Hussey 84, SJ Harmison 5 for 33)
England 253 for 7 (47.3 overs)
(KP Pietersen 91*, MP Vaughan 57)
England (5pts) won by 3 wickets – Australia (1pt)

Match Four

21 June 2005 at Trent Bridge
England 391 for 4 (50 overs) (AJ Strauss 152,
PD Collingwood 112*, ME Trescothick 85)

Bangladesh 223 (45.2 overs)
(Mohammad Ashraful 94, Javed Omar 59,
PD Collingwood 6 for 31, CT Tremlett 4 for 32)
England (6pts) won by 168 runs

Match Five

23 June 2005 at The Riverside
Australia 266 for 5 (50 overs)
(A Symonds 73, DR Martyn 68*)
England 209 for 9 (50 overs)
Australia (6pts) won by 57 runs

Match Six

25 June 2005 at Old Trafford
Bangladesh 139 (35.2 overs)
(Mohammad Ashraful 58,
A Symonds 5 for 18)
Australia 140 for 0 (19 overs)
(AC Gilchrist 66*, ML Hayden 66*)
Australia (6pts) won by 10 wickets

Mohammad Ashraful plays another beautifully executed stroke on the way to his match-winning century against Australia at Cardiff.

Match Seven

26 June 2005 at Headingley
Bangladesh 208 for 7 (50 overs)
(Javed Omar 81, A Flintoff 4 for 29)
England 209 for 5 (38.5 overs)
(AJ Strauss 98)
England (6pts) won by 5 wickets

Match Eight

28 June 2005 at Edgbaston
Australia 261 for 9 (50 overs)
(A Symonds 74)
England 37 for 1 (6 overs)
Match abandoned – 3pts each

Match Nine

30 June 2005 at Canterbury
Bangladesh 250 for 8 (50 overs) (Shahriar Nafees 75,
Khaled Mashud 71*)
Australia 254 for 4 (48.1 overs) (MJ Clarke 80*,
RT Ponting 66)
Australia (5pts) won by 6 wickets – Bangladesh (1pt)

	P	W	L	T	NR	RR	Pts
England	6	4	1	0	1	1.38	26
Australia	6	3	2	0	1	0.88	22
Bangladesh	6	1	5	0	0	-2.00	6

AUSTRALIA

*AC Gilchrist	c Pietersen b Flintoff	27
ML Hayden	c Giles b Gough	17
RT Ponting (capt)	c Jones GO b Harmison	7
DR Martyn	c Jones GO b Harmison	11
A Symonds	c Strauss b Collingwood	29
MJ Clarke	lbw b Jones SP	2
MEK Hussey	not out	62
GB Hogg	c Jones GO b Harmison	16
B Lee	c Jones GO b Flintoff	3
JN Gillespie	c Jones GO b Flintoff	0
GD McGrath	c Collingwood b Gough	0
Extras	b 4, lb 5, w 7, nb 6	22
	(48.5 overs)	**196**

	O	M	R	W
Gough	6.5	1	36	2
Jones SP	8	2	45	1
Flintoff	8	2	23	3
Harmison	10	2	27	3
Collingwood	8	0	26	1
Giles	8	0	30	0

Fall of Wickets
1-50, 2-54, 3-71, 4-90, 5-93, 6-147, 7-169, 8-179, 9-179

ENGLAND

ME Trescothick	c Ponting b McGrath	6
AJ Strauss	b Lee	2
MP Vaughan (capt)	b McGrath	0
KP Pietersen	c Gilchrist b Lee	6
A Flintoff	c Hayden b McGrath	8
PD Collingwood	run out	53
*GO Jones	lbw b Hogg	71
AF Giles	not out	18
SP Jones	b Hussey	1
D Gough	run out	12
SJ Harmison	not out	0
Extras	b 2, lb 12, w 3, nb 2	19
	(9 wkts 50 overs)	**196**

	O	M	R	W
Lee	10	1	36	2
McGrath	10	4	25	3
Gillespie	10	0	42	0
Symonds	10	2	23	0
Hogg	6	0	25	1
Hussey	4	0	31	1

Fall of Wickets
1-11, 2-13, 3-19, 4-19, 5-33, 6-149, 7-161, 8-162, 9-194

Umpires: BF Bowden & DR Shepherd
Toss: England
Man of the Match: GO Jones
Man of the Series: A Symonds

<u>Match tied</u>

Left: Ashley Giles hits out as the NatWest Series final reaches
its frantic closing stages.

Far left: Fetch that! Another big hit from Kevin Pietersen
sails away over the legside boundary.

NATWEST CHALLENGE

England v. Australia

In a cynical move aimed solely at making money, the ECB scheduled a further three one-day matches between England and Australia before the long-awaited Test series could finally begin. Even the players were becoming fed up with this apparently never-ending circus, and although the games were well attended, and duly did make money, enough was enough.

It was fitting, therefore, that this meaningless series should be the first in which substitutes were introduced. There can never have been a more absurd and badly thought-through concept ever introduced to cricket. The toss determined the outcome of each game. Not surprising, really, when the winner of the toss could field first on a fresh pitch, and then strengthen his batting by dropping the worst batsman for the run chase. At least Michael Vaughan was honest enough to condemn the ten-month experiment at the end of the series.

England thrashed Australia by nine wickets at Headingley, with Trescothick making 104, only for Australia to win the second game by seven wickets and with more than five overs to spare thanks to Ricky Ponting's 111.

The final match was even more one-sided as Australia cruised to their target of 229 in only 35 overs. The Australians were now unrecognisable from the team that had endured such a calamitous start to their tour and, this time, Gilchrist scored a century to leave all the main Australian batsmen, except Hayden, in prime form.

Match One
7 July 2005 at Headingley
Australia 219 for 7 (50 overs)
(PD Collingwood 4 for 34)
England 221 for 1 (46 overs) (ME Trescothick 104*,
MP Vaughan 59*)
England won by 9 wickets

Match Two
10 July 2005 at Lord's
England 223 for 8 (50 overs) (A Flintoff 87,
B Lee 5 for 41)
Australia 224 for 3 (44.2 overs)
(RT Ponting 111)
Australia won by 7 wickets

Match Three
12 July 2005 at The Oval
England 228 for 7 (50 overs) (KP Pietersen 74,
VS Solanki 53*)
Australia 229 for 2 (34.5 overs) (AC Gilchrist 121*)
Australia won by 8 wickets

Up and over: Ricky Ponting manufactures another thrilling stroke during his match–winning 111 at Lord's.

BANGLADESH IN ENGLAND
By Jonathan Agnew

10–12 May 2005 at Fenner's
Bangladesh 381 (109.1 overs) (Javed Omar 167,
Mohammad Ashraful 102) & 246 for 4 dec (64 overs)
(Habibul Bashar 75, Shahriar Nafees 50)
British Universities 238 (67.5 overs) (JP Knappett 73,
LC Parker 65, Shahadat Hossain 4 for 33)
Match drawn

Hundreds from Javed Omar and Mohammad
Ashraful ensured that the Bangladeshis enjoyed their
opening fixture of the tour, against a British
Universities side. The pair added 167 for the fourth
wicket, with Javed reaching a career-best score of 167
and the precocious Ashraful 102. The Universities
were 82 for 5 in reply until Luke Parker was joined
by wicketkeeper Josh Knappett in a stand of 134.
Shahadat Hossain took four wickets and impressed
with his pace, while Habibul Bashar, the captain,
took advantage of a second innings by hitting 75
before the draw was confirmed.

15–17 May 2005 at Hove
Sussex 549 for 7 dec (116.5 overs) (MH Yardy 257,
TR Ambrose 78, CD Hopkinson 64, MJ Prior 51)
Bangladesh 127 (47 overs) & 196 (63.2 overs)
(Mushfiqur Rahim 63, MH Yardy 5 for 83)
Sussex won by an innings and 226 runs

Mike Yardy and the rest of the Sussex top order
brought Bangladesh down to earth with a nasty
bump on a hard, bouncy pitch at Hove. The
tourists' bowling attack became mere cannon
fodder to Yardy, whose 257 was the highest
individual innings made by a Sussex batsman
against a touring team. It was, not unexpectedly, a
career-best, featuring two sixes and 35 fours, and
Yardy then followed up his batting exploits by
returning the best bowling figures of his career,
too, as the Bangladeshis were sent spinning to a
morale-sapping innings defeat. Sussex's faster
bowlers undermined them first time around, after
Yardy and Tim Ambrose had put on 176 for the
fourth wicket to help to propel the county to 549
for 7 declared. But the Bangladesh batsmen hardly
did any better in their second innings, although
16-year-old diminutive wicketkeeper Mushfiqur
Rahim certainly enhanced his reputation with a
classy 63 as Yardy showcased his experimental slow
left-arm spin to double his first-class wicket tally
with 5 for 83.

20–22 May 2005 at Northampton
Northamptonshire 230 for 6 dec (49 overs)
(BM Shafayat 76, Anwar Hossain Monir 4 for 113)
Bangladesh 309 for 7 dec (70 overs)
(Mushfiqur Rahim 115*, Mohammad Rafique 54)
Match drawn

Rain hampered Bangladesh's final preparations for
the opening Test against England, washing out day
two of their match at Northampton and also allowing
just 34.1 overs to be bowled on the opening day.
Bilal Shafayat continued his fine early-season form
with 76 off 89 balls, with 14 boundaries, and
Northants declared on the third morning to allow
the tourists a turn with the bat. They responded well,
despite initially faltering at 53 for 4, with the 5ft 4in
Mushfiqur Rahim living up to the impact he had
made in the previous game at Hove. In only his fifth
first-class match, and ninth innings, Mushfiqur
dominated the second string Northants attack to
reach his second first-class century. The highly
talented 16-year-old struck a six and 15 fours, from
167 balls, and received good support from the
experienced Mohammad Rafique.

npower FIRST TEST
26–28 May 2005 at Lord's

Not a great deal was expected of Bangladesh, and it
was no real surprise, therefore, when they delivered
nothing. Much of the build-up to their opening
match at Lord's – and their first in England – was
spent debating their worth as a Test-playing nation.
Their record spoke volumes in that having played 36
Tests, they had only one victory to their name (over
a hopelessly under-strength Zimbabwe) and of their
31 defeats, 20 had been by the margin of an innings.

In the narrow context of this summer, I could see
nothing but good coming from England's opportunity
to warm up for the Ashes against the worst team in
the world. What a chance for England's players to get
together after a break of three months, get runs and
wickets by the bagful and go into the series against
Australia with morale high.

This is entirely a myopic view, and offers little to
the wider debate about Bangladesh's status. However,
a cricket-mad country of 145 million people does
suggest great potential in the years to come. The
trouble is that, unlike Sri Lanka in 1982 for example,
Bangladesh simply do not have enough players
capable of immediately making the transition to Test
cricket and offering the competition and interest that
sponsors, spectators and the media demand.

To make matters worse for Bangladesh, they were invited to tour in May and in conditions that were entirely foreign to them. This does not necessarily incite sympathy – touring Bangladesh is a vastly different challenge that England's cricketers must cope with – but however cheerfully their cricketers went about their business, Habibul Bashar's men always looked frozen!

Eight weeks to the day that Michael Vaughan would be walking to the middle of Lord's to toss the coin with Australia's Ricky Ponting, the England captain inserted Bangladesh and exposed their batsmen's fallible techniques to the full. Within 39 overs they had been bundled out for 108 with only three batsmen reaching double figures. Easily the worst example was shown by Bashar himself who, having been hit on the head in a warm-up match against Sussex, played a ghastly slog which would not have looked out of place in a Twenty20 match.

With his confidence clearly shattered, the No. 3 aimed to pull a delivery from Hoggard that he

FIRST TEST – ENGLAND v. BANGLADESH
26–28 May 2005 at Lord's

BANGLADESH

	First Innings		Second Innings	
Javed Omar	c Trescothick b Jones SP	22	c Thorpe b Jones SP	25
Nafees Iqbal	c Trescothick b Harmison	8	c Flintoff b Hoggard	3
Habibul Bashar (capt)	c Jones GO b Hoggard	3	c Hoggard b Jones SP	16
Aftab Ahmed	c Strauss b Flintoff	20	lbw b Hoggard	32
Mohammad Ashraful	lbw b Flintoff	6	c Harmison b Flintoff	2
Mushfiqur Rahim	b Hoggard	19	c Jones GO b Flintoff	3
*Khaled Mashud	lbw b Hoggard	6	c Thorpe b Flintoff	44
Mohammad Rafique	run out	1	c Jones GO b Harmison	0
Mashrafe Mortaza	b Harmison	0	b Harmison	0
Anwar Hossain Monir	not out	5	c Trescothick b Jones SP	13
Shahadat Hossain	c Jones GO b Hoggard	4	not out	2
Extras	b 1, lb 1, nb 12	14	b 1, lb 4, nb 14	19
	(38.2 overs)	108	(39.5 overs)	159

	First Innings				Second Innings			
	O	M	R	W	O	M	R	W
Hoggard	13.2	5	42	4	9	1	42	2
Harmison	14	3	38	2	10	0	39	2
Flintoff	5	0	22	2	9.5	0	44	3
Jones SP	6	4	4	1	11	3	29	3

Fall of Wickets
1-31, 2-34, 3-65, 4-65, 5-71, 6-89, 7-94, 8-98, 9-98
1-15, 2-47, 3-57, 4-60, 5-65, 6-96, 7-97, 8-97, 9-155

ENGLAND

	First Innings	
ME Trescothick	c Khaled Mashud b M Rafique	194
AJ Strauss	lbw b Mashrafe Mortaza	69
MP Vaughan (capt)	c Khaled Mashud b M Mortaza	120
IR Bell	not out	65
GP Thorpe	not out	42
A Flintoff		
*GO Jones		
GJ Batty		
MJ Hoggard		
SJ Harmison		
SP Jones		
Extras	b 4, lb 11, w 3, nb 20	38
	(3 wkts dec 112 overs)	528

	First Innings			
	O	M	R	W
Mashrafe Mortaza	29	6	107	2
Shahadat Hossain	12	0	101	0
Anwar Hossain Monir	22	0	110	0
Mohammad Rafique	41	3	150	1
Aftab Ahmed	8	1	45	0

Fall of Wickets
1-148, 2-403, 3-415

Umpires: K Hariharan & DJ Harper
Toss: England
Test Debuts: Mushfiqur Rahim & Shahadat Hossain
Man of the Match: ME Trescothick

England won by an innings and 261 runs

Ian Bell got the nod from England's selectors for the Bangladesh series ... and cashed in with runs at Lord's and a maiden Test hundred at Chester-le-Street.

might almost have played off the front foot. Coming in at the fall of the first wicket, it was a dreadful shot by the captain, a bad example to set and one that his teammates then appeared to follow as absurdly expansive strokes accounted for the majority of the wickets. Hoggard finished with 4 for 42, while Harmison and Flintoff – whose heel looked comfortable after surgery – claimed two each. By the close of the first day's play, England already led by 80 runs.

Much of the second day was like watching a benefit match as Trescothick – who scored 194 – and Vaughan with 120 caned the bowling at will. They added 255 in 52 overs, although Vaughan offered the slow bowler, Rafique, an easy caught and bowled opportunity on eight. When Vaughan was eventually caught behind, Ian Bell – who was preferred to either Rob Key or Kevin Pietersen – scored his second fifty in two innings. Thorpe, who only the day before the Test, had controversially announced that he would be coaching in Australia this winter rather than touring with England, batted positively for his 42 not out and, 20 minutes after tea on the second day, England declared on 528 for 3: a lead of 420.

Bangladesh fared little better in the second innings. In the 16th over, they slumped to 65 for 5, giving rise to the possibility that England might finish them off in two days. But Ahmed and Mashud clung on until the close, with a stand of 25 in six overs, to deny Vaughan the opportunity to claim an extra half-an-hour's play.

But it needed only 17 overs and five balls to finish the task on the third morning. In fact, three wickets fell in the first nine balls as Harmison, Jones and Flintoff polished off a somewhat reluctant lower order. The margin of victory – an innings and 261 runs – was England's third largest in Test history.

npower SECOND TEST
3–5 June 2005 at Chester-le-Street

The second Test, which broke with tradition and started on a Friday, was in almost every other respect a carbon copy of the first. Bangladesh were thrashed again almost within two days, and England's top order batsmen ran riot.

Vaughan won the toss again, too. I wonder – later in the summer – if he might wish he could trade in these two successes to enable him to take the initiative against the Australians? But on a chilly, windswept morning at the Riverside, he chose to insert Bangladesh for a second time, and we all knew what would happen from there.

The tourists made four runs fewer than at Lord's and, again, failed to bat for 40 overs. Their total of 104 was a feeble effort, and only two batsmen – Javed Omar Belim and Khaled Mashud – reached double figures. Steve Harmison, who for the first time in months truly resembled the towering giant of a fast bowler who won so many matches for England in 2004, produced the most notable bowling figures. He found the length that had been so elusive in South Africa and he proved to be more than a handful for the small Bangladeshi batsmen. Harmison finished with 5 for 38 and although Strauss missed out, falling lbw to Mortaza for eight, England pulled into the lead shortly after tea at which point Vaughan – who had batted quite beautifully – edged another good ball from Mortaza for 44. The stand with Trescothick stood at 87 from only 12 overs, but the Somerset left-hander then went berserk, cutting loose after he had reached his century. His last 50 runs came from only 29 balls as, with Bell watching from the non-striker's end, he lambasted the Bangladesh bowlers. It got to a stage where Trescothick appeared to be trying to get himself out and, finally, he slogged a catch to long off for 151 from 148 balls. His partnership with Bell was worth 155 in 105 minutes but, even more remarkable, was the fact that in the final session of the day, 223 runs were scored from 35 overs! By the close, England already had a lead of 165 and many people believed that would prove to be enough.

First, though, Vaughan gave Bell the chance to register his first Test century. A composed, compact right-hander with an excellent technique, Bell looked quite at home when he made his debut against West Indies last summer. He reached 70 on that occasion in rather more testing circumstances and made 65 not out at Lord's. Now, on the second morning, he became the first English batsman since Les Ames in 1935 to score 100 runs before lunch. He pulled, drove and cut with great authority and, using Trescothick's innings as an example, he set about the bowling once he had reached his century from 132 balls. His last 62 runs came from only 36 balls and, with Thorpe quietly fiddling his way to 66 not out in his hundredth Test, Vaughan generously decided to call a halt to the carnage at lunchtime.

This was the cue for a two-day victory but, happily, Bangladesh's batsmen finally showed some of the discipline that had been so obviously lacking from the previous efforts. They were not helped by the decidedly dodgy dismissal of Nafees Iqbal whose edge from Flintoff appeared to drop short of the diving Geraint Jones who, nonetheless, claimed the catch. There were fielders in the slip cordon who would have seen from an ideal vantage point that the ball had appeared to bounce, but they kept quiet and although Nafees made a bid to return to the crease, the umpires dispatched him a second time.

The captain, Habibul, was dropped to No. 5 in the order and although he came in at 101 for 3, there did appear to be more of a solid structure to the line-up. Javed stood out again, converting his promising starts in his previous outings into a very good 71. Habibul, moreover, played an astonishingly cavalier knock of 63 from 52 balls as he and Mashud added 70, but a clatter of wickets enabled England to claim the extra half-hour, needing to take a further three wickets to win the game.

In fact, they managed only one. So, with Bangladesh needing a further 46 to make England bat again, an exhausting day on which the most runs (475) were scored in all Test cricket for 51 years came to an end.

Any hopes the tourists had of avoiding their 22nd innings defeat in 38 Tests were snuffed out within 23 balls on the third morning as Hoggard who, by his own admission bowled poorly, mopped up to finish with 5 for 73 and the Man-of-the-Match award. 'Bell was robbed,' he said from the podium a little later and indeed he was. Let us hope this puts an end to the demeaning, money-grabbing procedure employed by BSkyB television of allowing their viewers to vote for the prestigious award by text.

10 June 2005 at Derby
Bangladesh 189 (46.1 overs)
Derbyshire 190 for 4 (38.1 overs) (J Moss 72)
Derbyshire won by 6 wickets

Beginning their warm-up for the NatWest Series, the Bangladeshis were overpowered by a near full-strength Derbyshire side. Steve Stubbings, with 45 from 43 balls, Jon Moss with a fine 72, and Luke Sutton, with an unbeaten 42, were chiefly responsible for guiding Derbyshire to a comfortable six-wicket win. Bangladesh had earlier recovered partially to 189 after slipping initially to 19 for 3. Tushar Imran and Habibul Bashar added 80 for the fourth wicket in 19 overs, before Mohammad Rafique hit a spirited late 36.

12 June 2005 at New Road
Worcestershire 168 (44.1 overs)
Bangladesh 169 for 6 (36 overs)
Bangladesh won by 4 wickets

At last, Bangladesh could celebrate a first tour victory as a weakened Worcestershire were beaten by four wickets at New Road. At 24 for 3, in reply to Worcestershire's below-par 168, Bangladesh were wobbling, but Javed Omar was joined by Mohammad Ashraful in a match-winning stand of 82 in 12 overs for the fourth wicket. Ashraful hit five fours in 10 balls from Shoaib Akhtar, who was making his Worcestershire debut, but his sparkling 40 ended when he was brilliantly held by Stephen Peters at backward point. Javed also fell for 43, but Habibul Bashar saw his side home with an unbeaten 26.

If any of Bangladesh's bowlers emerged from the two-Test series against England with credit, it was fast bowler Mashrafe Mortaza.

SECOND TEST – ENGLAND v. BANGLADESH
3–5 June 2005 at The Riverside

BANGLADESH

	First Innings		Second Innings	
Javed Omar	c Jones GO b Hoggard	37	c Jones GO b Harmison	71
Nafees Iqbal	c Strauss b Harmison	7	c Jones GO b Flintoff	15
Habibul Bashar (capt)	b Harmison	6	(5) lbw b Flintoff	63
Mohammad Ashraful	c Jones GO b Jones SP	3	c Hoggard b Batty	12
Rajin Saleh	c Thorpe b Flintoff	2	(3) c Strauss b Flintoff	7
Aftab Ahmed	c Jones GO b Harmison	6	(7) not out	82
*Khaled Mashud	c Jones GO b Harmison	22	(6) lbw b Hoggard	25
Mohammad Rafique	c Batty b Hoggard	9	b Hoggard	2
Tapash Baisya	c Jones GO b Hoggard	0	(10) c Jones GO b Hoggard	18
Mashrafe Mortaza	c Jones GO b Harmison	1	(11) c Trescothick b Hoggard	0
Anwar Hossain Monir	not out	0	(9) c Thorpe b Hoggard	0
Extras	lb 2, w 5, nb 4	11	lb 6, w 1, nb 14	21
	(39.5 overs)	104	(72.5 overs)	316

	First Innings				Second Innings			
	O	M	R	W	O	M	R	W
Hoggard	12	6	24	3	15.5	3	73	5
Harmison	12.5	2	38	5	17	1	86	1
Jones SP	8	2	26	1	10	1	49	0
Flintoff	7	3	14	1	15	2	58	3
Batty	-	-	-	-	15	2	44	1

Fall of Wickets
1-17, 2-27, 3-34, 4-42, 5-59, 6-69, 7-87, 8-87, 9-93
1-50, 2-75, 3-101, 4-125, 5-195, 6-235, 7-245, 8-251, 9-311

ENGLAND

	First Innings	
ME Trescothick	c M Ashraful b Aftab Ahmed	151
AJ Strauss	lbw b Mashrafe Mortaza	8
MP Vaughan (capt)	c Khaled Mashud b M Mortaza	44
IR Bell	not out	162
GP Thorpe	not out	66
A Flintoff		
*GO Jones		
GJ Batty		
SP Jones		
MJ Hoggard		
SJ Harmison		
Extras	b 1, lb 10, w 2, nb 3	16
	(3 wkts dec 78 overs)	447

	First Innings			
	O	M	R	W
Mashrafe Mortaza	22	4	91	2
Tapash Baisya	15	2	80	0
Mohammad Rafique	18	0	107	0
Anwar Hossain Monir	15	1	102	0
Aftab Ahmed	8	0	56	1

Fall of Wickets
1-18, 2-105, 3-260

Umpires: DJ Harper & AL Hill
Toss: England
Man of the Match: MJ Hoggard
Men of the Series: Javed Omar & ME Trescothick

England won by an innings and 27 runs

SERIES AVERAGES
England v. Bangladesh

ENGLAND

Batting	M	Inns	NO	Runs	HS	Av	100	50	c/st
ME Trescothick	2	2	0	345	194	172.50	2	-	4/-
MP Vaughan	2	2	0	164	120	82.00	1	-	-/-
AJ Strauss	2	2	0	77	69	38.50	-	1	3/-
IR Bell	2	2	2	227	162*	-	-	1	1	-/-
GP Thorpe	2	2	2	108	66*	-	-	1	4/-
A Flintoff	2	0	0	0	0	-	-	-	1/-
MJ Hoggard	2	0	0	0	0	-	-	-	2/-
SP Jones	2	0	0	0	0	-	-	-	-/-
SJ Harmison	2	0	0	0	0	-	-	-	1/-
GJ Batty	2	0	0	0	0	-	-	-	1/-
GO Jones	2	0	0	0	0	-	-	-	13/-

Bowling	Overs	Mds	Runs	Wkts	Av	Best	5/inn	10m
MJ Hoggard	50.1	15	181	14	12.92	5-73	1	-
A Flintoff	36.5	5	138	9	15.33	3-44	-	-
SJ Harmison	53.5	6	201	10	20.10	5-38	1	-
SP Jones	35	10	108	5	21.60	3-29	-	-
GJ Batty	15	2	44	1	44.00	1-44	-	-

BANGLADESH

Batting	M	Inns	NO	Runs	HS	Av	100	50	c/st
Aftab Ahmed	2	4	1	140	82*	46.66	-	1	-/-
Javed Omar	2	4	0	155	71	38.75	-	1	-/-
Khaled Mashud	2	4	0	97	44	24.25	-	-	3/-
Habibul Bashar	2	4	0	88	63	22.00	-	1	-/-
Mushfiqur Rahim	1	2	0	22	19	11.00	-	-	-/-
Tapash Baisya	1	2	0	18	18	9.00	-	-	-/-
Anwar Hossain Monir	2	4	2	18	13	9.00	-	-	-/-
Nafees Iqbal	2	4	0	33	15	8.25	-	-	-/-
Shahadat Hossain	1	2	1	6	4	6.00	-	-	-/-
Mohammad Ashraful	2	4	0	23	12	5.75	-	-	1/-
Rajin Saleh	1	2	0	9	7	4.50	-	-	-/-
Mohammad Rafique	2	4	0	12	9	3.00	-	-	-/-
Mashrafe Mortaza	2	4	0	1	1	0.25	-	-	-/-

Bowling	Overs	Mds	Runs	Wkts	Av	Best	5/inn	10m
Mashrafe Mortaza	51	10	198	4	49.50	2-91	-	-
Aftab Ahmed	16	1	101	1	101.00	1-56	-	-
Mohammad Rafique	59	3	257	1	257.00	1-150	-	-

Also bowled: Tapash Baisya 15-2-80-0, Shahadat Hossain 12-0-101-0,
Anwar Hossain Monir 37-1-212-0.

GRAHAM THORPE

DEREK PRINGLE, cricket correspondent for the *Daily Telegraph*, was a senior player on the England A tour of Kenya and Zimbabwe in early 1990 – Graham Thorpe's very first tour in England colours. Here he looks back on those first impressions of Thorpe and profiles a batsman who will be remembered as one of the very best England have produced.

England's finest all-round batsman of the last ten years, Graham Thorpe, retired soon after making his 100th Test appearance against Bangladesh at Chester-le-Street in early June. His going, two months short of his 36th birthday, was not entirely of his own volition, but as he had been overlooked by selectors for the Ashes series in favour of Kevin Pietersen and Ian Bell he felt there was little point in carrying on.

Having made runs on good tracks and bad, in defence and attack, his was a career held aloft by sporting excellence and gritty resolve. Yet remarkable powers of recovery were needed, too, following a stormy private life starkly revealed in his recent autobiography *Rising from the Ashes*. Without that disruptive episode, which saw him withdraw from international cricket for 14 months, left-hander Thorpe might well have been England's second most-capped Test player after Alec Stewart, who managed 133 caps over a 14-year international career.

His parting wave was not a genial one and there was a spat between him and England's chairman of selectors, David Graveney, mostly played out in the media. The gist of it seemed to be that Graveney wanted Thorpe to keep on playing for Surrey and be on standby in case of injury but could not guarantee he would definitely be picked ahead of players, like Robert Key, also waiting in the wings. Thorpe found the ambiguity unacceptable and promptly announced his retirement.

To those who saw him play from Barbados to Brisbane, Thorpe's batting, while understated, always exuded class. Like Australia's left-handed legend Allan Border, he was compact in defence and used just a few well-oiled strokes. Knowing one's limitations and then playing within them is how it is often described, though both Border and Thorpe could expand their palette when the situation demanded. Mostly they relied on engaging the brain before the heart and channelling their aggression and adrenalin, rather than becoming overwhelmed by it.

But how difficult is it to spot a 100-cap Test player like Thorpe in the raw? Former Essex and England captain Keith Fletcher had few doubts. In his autobiography, Fletcher says he felt sure that the 15-year-old he saw in a schools match in 1985 would play for his country. Later, perhaps in determination to fulfil that judgement, Fletcher would push for him to be on every England A tour until he made his senior England debut against Australia in 1993 at Trent Bridge, a call-up he celebrated with a fine hundred.

My first encounter with Thorpe was on a tour of Kenya and Zimbabwe with the England A team in 1990. At 20, he was the baby of a squad that mixed ageing nous with energetic promise. Fifteen-year-old memories can play tricks, but he didn't appear to stand out until a cricket bat was placed in his hands. Then, all shyness fell away to be replaced by an authority that verged on the arrogant.

Some cricketers are flattered by first impressions and spend the rest of their careers trying to live up to them. Although his quiet rebellious streak never left him, the young Thorpe was blessed with a comforting solidity shorn of youthful extravagance and dodgy bravado. It didn't change on the cricket

Thorpe sweeps in the murk of Karachi 2000 – in one of his and England's greatest triumphs of modern times.

The very best of Thorpe? England's nuggety left-hander is pictured during his 113 against Sri Lanka in 2001.

The pugnacity and supporting role he showed then summed up his batting too, though as a distinctly unflashy player his contributions were often appreciated rather than lauded. He made 114 on his Test debut against Australia at Trent Bridge in 1993, a match in which another promising youngster, Mark Lathwell, also made his debut. Lathwell played one more Test for England, Thorpe another 99. But while the difference in their respective abilities was never of that magnitude, the gap in their mental toughness probably was.

Thorpe made sixteen Test hundreds and scored 6,744 Test runs, his average of 44.66 well over the 40 benchmark that separates the great from the good. Although his only double century came against a decent New Zealand side in Christchurch, arguably his best innings was the unbeaten 113 he scored against Sri Lanka in Colombo in 2001. In heat that turned tarmac to treacle, Thorpe kept his team in the game on a pitch produced to give Muttiah Muralitharan and the other spinners maximum assistance. To place his achievement and the difficulty of the conditions into context, he also made an unbeaten 32 in the second innings, which was the next highest score in the match for England. As a knock, his hundred was both brilliantly conceived and executed, and one that helped England to win a particularly hot-tempered Test series.

Always a master at pacing an innings to finish off a match, none was better timed than his 64 in the pitch black of Karachi in 2000, to bring about Pakistan's historic first Test defeat there. Afterwards, he put his ability to pick up the ball in the gloom down to his years playing as a youngster for Wrecclesham in the Flora Doris Cup, an evening league played in near-darkness in rural Surrey.

As one who has endured some of life's more painful slings and arrows, his outlook on life and cricket has changed. Settled with a new partner and baby daughter, he is this winter to join New South Wales as a trainee coach and administrator. It may not provide the buzz of batting in a Test match, but it is a challenge – and that is exactly what Thorpe relishes.

field, though an acrimonious divorce from his first wife meant he takes less for granted now than he once did.

Michael Atherton and Richard Blakey were the main run-scorers on that trip to Africa, though the run-rate in the three unofficial Tests against Zimbabwe was under two runs an over – too slow for Thorpe who, bored with the cat and mouse tactics on slow pitches, played a couple of brilliant cameos. As the only bowler to strike Zimbabwe's star off-spinner John Traicos over the top, he stood out as a batsman keen to set the agenda even if it meant taking risks. Fifteen years later there can be little doubt, even in Atherton's mind, which of the three has been the best Test player.

Although not easy to lead anyone astray in a Zimbabwe feeling the pinch of inflation (drinks costing Z$10 one day were Z$20 the next), he still blames me for the hangover (due I'm certain to him mixing his drinks) that brought him a first rollocking from Keith Fletcher, our coach on that tour. All I will say in my defence is, as Tommy Mitchell once retorted to Douglas Jardine when Harold Larwood turned up feeling rough during the Bodyline series, 'You can lead a horse to water, skipper, but you can't make him drink.'

He liked to mix it in another sense too, and when a drunken white farmer decided to pick a fight with the African attendant outside our dressing room in Mutare, he was quick to offer David 'Syd' Lawrence a hand in ejecting him. Not that big Syd needed one, dragging said boor through an ice bath before flinging him out into the twilight like a rag doll dismissed from the cot.

ENGLAND DOMESTIC SEASON INTRODUCTION
By Mark Baldwin

To the wider audience, the 2005 English cricket season ended in an orgy of Ashes celebration and a genuine feelgood atmosphere in which the old summer game had dramatically re-asserted itself as a major focus of the nation's affections. In the background, however, was the acrimonious and unhappy 'climax' of the County Championship.

Accusations of stupidity and farce, and of bringing the game into disrepute, flew around as Nottinghamshire emerged as the Frizzell champions and Hampshire finished as the sorest of runners-up. Sussex, in third place, weren't best pleased either. It was, in truth, the best advertisement for two conferences and for an end-of-season Championship play-off final as there could be.

It had all seemed so promising, initially. What long-serving Sussex captain Chris Adams called 'the best and most competitive championship I can remember' was for many months building itself up into a potential dog-fight of a finish with Nottinghamshire, Hampshire, Sussex, Kent and 2004 champions Warwickshire all fancying their chances of the title.

The last round of matches simply added to the intrigue: Hampshire to play Nottinghamshire at the Rose Bowl, and Sussex to take on historic rivals Kent at Hove.

And then Notts met Kent, at Canterbury. Being mid-September, it also rained, and much of the second day was lost. Part of the luck of the draw, you may say, and you might be right. But also part of any County Championship season is a dodgy deal or two, and if it happens in early May it is often forgotten in the final shake-up. What happened at the St Lawrence Ground, however, was a deal which – at a stroke – merely resulted in a potentially dazzling finish turning into a damp squib.

Notts were not bothered. Given a sudden chance to clinch championship glory that day by Kent captain David Fulton's agreement to serve up some declaration bowling and then chase a highly unlikely 420 in 70 overs, they grabbed victory and cracked open the champagne. Fulton was not overly bothered, either. Kent's own fast-fading hopes of the title had depended on forcing a win against Notts: he had little option but to go for broke.

Kent, once their top-order batting had fallen in the suicidal chase, did try to hang on for the draw. But Notts, with Andrew Harris outstanding, showed that they had the bowling firepower of worthy champions by dismissing Kent with more than 17 overs in hand.

Shane Warne, Hampshire's captain, was furious. 'I don't like to sledge other players, but what Dave Fulton did was absolutely stupid,' he said. 'It has put a real dampener on what could have been a great finish. Fulton gave himself no chance of winning that game, and brought the game into disrepute.' Fulton replied, 'I don't care about Hampshire – I only care about Kent', while Notts captain Stephen Fleming observed, 'He just wants to win games – just like Shane Warne down at Hampshire.'

When Notts picked a weakened team for the by then academic last match at Hampshire, however, and compounded that controversial decision by becoming the first side all season to win the toss at the Rose Bowl and put the opposition into bat, it was the turn of Sussex's Adams to explode. Adams' side were in the process of trouncing Kent, but their ambitions of finishing in second place were scuppered when Hampshire ran up a mammoth 714 for 5 declared against a side suddenly with nothing tangible to play for. Hampshire, indeed, soon completed the innings victory which took them to within two and a half points of the champions in the final table.

'It has all ended in farce,' complained Adams. 'No one puts the other side into bat at the Rose Bowl, but that's what Stephen Fleming did. It was the second worst decision in the history of the County Championship. The worst came the week before when Kent agreed to chase 420 in 70 overs against Notts.'

So there you have it: upset all round, unless you happen to be a Nottinghamshire fan. Like England, their success was based upon the cutting edge of four fast bowlers – one of whom, Mark Ealham, who could be described in county terms as a genuine all-rounder – a solid opening partnership, effective stroke-making middle-order batsmen, a decent spinner, and a run-scoring wicketkeeper. Notts supporters, indeed, would claim Chris Read as being superior to Geraint Jones in most respects – while the team as a whole was pulled together by Fleming, perhaps the one captain in world cricket to have the edge on Michael Vaughan in terms of experience, and to be the equal of him in shrewdness, temperament, tactical awareness and man-management.

Hampshire's consolation was their victory in the Cheltenham & Gloucester Trophy final at Lord's, against Warwickshire, although it is a symbol of a growing concern within English cricket circles that their line-up that day included (in addition to their two overseas players, the Australians Shane Watson and Andy Bichel) five players born and raised in southern Africa (Sean Ervine, Greg Lamb and Nic Pothas, in addition to the England-qualified Kevin Pietersen and Kevin Latouf) plus another wholly-Australia raised cricketer in Dimitri Mascarenhas. Another South African with a British passport, Jono McLean, was in the squad.

Besides official overseas signings, there were 40 'Kolpak' or EU-qualified non-Englishmen registered by the 18 first-class counties at the start of the 2005 season. While it has been argued before in these pages that the presence of more foreign players has contributed to a general raising of standards in county cricket, and therefore the added filtering of genuine young English talent by the system, it is a situation which demands careful policing. The England and Wales Cricket Board, in conjunction with the counties, must reach an accord to control the numbers of non-England qualified cricketers – over and above the new agreement which will see up to £100,000 per county of central income being distributed from 2006 onwards in 'performance-related' payments to those clubs who give most opportunity to home-grown players.

A change in the structure of domestic cricket will see, from next April, the C&G Trophy becoming a two-conference affair with a Lord's final, the totesport League reduce from a 45 to a 40-overs per side competition, and the County Championship adopt a two-up and two-down policy in the two divisions. There will also be a more 'block-like' look to the fixture list. The C&G conference stage will be played in early summer, the Twenty20 Cup will again occupy the mid-summer slot, and the totesport will be concentrated at the back-end of the season. There will also be a play-off for the third promotion place between the seventh-placed team in Division One and the third in Division Two.

Tinkering therefore continues, but quality young players like Alastair Cook, Ravi Bopara, Mike Yardy, Liam Plunkett, Monty Panesar, Luke Wright, Tim Bresnan, Alex Loudon, Bilal Shafayat, Samit Patel, Stuart Broad, Tom Smith, Steven Davies and Moeen Ali are now coming through in increasing strength and depth. Despite those end-of-season rows, there is much that is going right.

Mark Baldwin, a former cricket correspondent of the Press Association, has written on county cricket for The Times *since 1998.*

WEATHER EYE

KEEPING A WEATHER EYE
By Andrew Hignell

Time lost (in hours) in Frizzell County Championship matches – 2005

Derbyshire	44.25
Durham	57.75
Essex	57.25
Glamorgan	39.00
Gloucestershire	30.75
Hampshire	50.75
Kent	40.50
Lancashire	57.00
Leicestershire	64.25
Middlesex	39.50
Northamptonshire	67.00
Nottinghamshire	70.75
Somerset	73.00
Surrey	65.75
Sussex	49.50
Warwickshire	25.00
Worcestershire	45.50
Yorkshire	64.50

* This data is derived from estimates of time lost, based on the number of overs bowled each day in Frizzell County Championship matches.

* The ECB guidelines state that a minimum of 104 overs must be bowled on the first three days of a game, with 96 on the final day. Two overs are also lost for a change of innings, so by comparing the close of play situation with the one from the previous day, it is possible to produce a viable estimate of any overs lost on each day as a result of rain, bad light or other adverse conditions.

* This estimate of overs lost each day can then be converted into time lost, once again using the ECB guideline of one over per 3.75 minutes, which equates to 4 overs for 15 minutes, 8 overs for 30 minutes, 12 overs for 45 minutes and 16 overs per hour.

MCC v. WARWICKSHIRE

8–11 April 2005 at Lord's

A sleet shower ruled out any possibility of play on the opening day just as the players were coming out on to the field to prepare for a 5pm start, but the following three days provided much interesting cricket as the 2005 first-class season was kicked off by MCC's seven-wicket victory against Warwickshire, the champion county.

The match was a triumph in particular for Alastair Cook, the 20-year-old Essex opener who was also to end the summer being presented with the Cricket Writers' Club Young Cricketer of the Year Award on the evening before he took a double-hundred off the Australians at Chelmsford on 3 September. Cook's 120 and 97 gave the national selectors more evidence of the talent of a batsman who was good enough to play in Essex's Second XI at the age of 15, and who also distinguished himself at Bedford School and as captain of England Under 19s. His first innings hundred was predominantly watchful, but second time around he played more freely and struck 13 fours while launching MCC's attempt to score 296 in 62 overs so well that, in the end, they got home with eight overs to spare.

Andy Flower, with an effortless 110 not out from 114 balls, was later joined by another Essex youngster, Mark Pettini, in an unbroken partnership which swept MCC to their target and maintained their unbeaten record in a fixture that has now been contested 24 times since its revival in 1970. Owais Shah and Matthew Prior, two of eight England A players in the MCC side, revealed eye-catching early form in first innings century partnerships with Cook.

Warwickshire's batsmen, however, also enjoyed the fine early-season pitch produced by Mick Hunt, the MCC groundsman, with Jonathan Trott playing two excellent innings after Nick Knight had won the toss and then hit the summer's first first-class hundred.

MCC v. WARWICKSHIRE – at The Rose Bowl

WARWICKSHIRE	First Innings		Second Innings	
NV Knight (capt)	c Pettini b Swann	115		
MA Wagh	c Harrison b Swann	66		
IR Bell	c Pettini b Harrison	14	b Swann	20
IJL Trott	c Powell b Harrison	75	not out	72
MJ Powell	c Swann b Harrison	28	(1) c Prior b Stephenson	32
AGR Loudon	not out	7	(2) lbw b Harrison	5
DR Brown	not out	27		
*T Frost			(5) c Swann b Shah	91
HH Streak				
NA Warren				
D Pretorius				
Extras	b 1, lb 6, nb 6	13	b 2, lb 1, nb 2	5
	(5 wkts dec 87 overs)	345	(4 wkts dec 58.3 overs)	225

Bowling
Lewis 19-7-41-0. Mahmood 13-0-71-0. Harrison 20-5-70-3. Swann 32-5-124-2. Stephenson 3-0-32-0.
Lewis 10-1-31-0. Harrison 10-2-32-1. Swann 14-5-42-1. Stephenson 11-1-42-1. Shah 8.3-0-49-1. Cook 5-0-26-0.
Fall of Wickets: 1-130, 2-183, 3-225, 4-303, 5-310.
1-14, 2-56, 3-64, 4-225

MCC	First Innings		Second Innings	
AN Cook	c Frost b Warren	120	c Powell b Trott	97
*MJ Prior	c Trott b Bell	70	c Frost b Streak	29
OA Shah	not out	78		
MJ Powell			(3) lbw b Brown	6
A Flower			(4) not out	110
ML Pettini			(5) not out	41
GP Swann				
JP Stephenson (capt)				
J Lewis				
DS Harrison				
SI Mahmood				
Extras	lb 4, w 1, nb 2	7	b 4, lb 3, nb 6	13
	(2 wkts dec 72.5 overs)	275	(3 wkts 58 overs)	296

Bowling
Streak 14-3-39-0. Pretorius 6-1-18-0. Warren 10.5-2-40-1. Brown 11-3-40-0. Bell 5-1-13-1. Loudon 19-3-80-0. Trott 7-1-27-0.
Streak 9-0-45-1. Warren 10-1-58-0. Brown 12-1-50-1. Bell 8-1-49-0. Loudon 11-0-74-0. Trott 4-0-13-1. Powell 4-0-14-0.
Fall of Wickets: 1-109, 2-275
1-39, 2-54, 3-235

MCC won by 7 wickets

Summer's first: Nick Knight, captain of 2004 champions Warwickshire, hits to leg on his way to the new season's first hundred.

FRIZZELL COUNTY CHAMPIONSHIP
By Mark Baldwin

Round One: 13–16 April 2005

Division One

Trust Shane Warne, at the start of an Ashes summer especially, to grab the limelight, as the County Championship got under way in a mid-April chill. The great Australian, captaining Hampshire once more and having underlined his future commitment to the club, played a leading role with both bat and ball as Gloucestershire were edged out by 48 runs in an exciting opening fixture at the Rose Bowl.

Without the injured Kevin Pietersen, England's new icon and a winter signing from Nottinghamshire, Hampshire's batting looked about to let them down for the second time in the match … before Warne appeared at No. 7 to inspire a third-morning revival that turned the game. The home side's lead was still not into three figures when Warne was joined by Sean Ervine, and in eight overs before the close they battled hard to take Hampshire to 111 for 6. As the third day dawned, however, it was Gloucestershire who were in the ascendancy and their hopes of victory soared when Ervine was dismissed following a stand of 51 with his captain. Chris Tremlett though

Warne's latest hat-trick: even a bobble hat can't disguise the world's greatest spin bowler.

Round One: 13–16 April 2005 Division One

HAMPSHIRE v. GLOUCESTERSHIRE – at The Rose Bowl

HAMPSHIRE	First Innings		Second Innings	
JHK Adams	c Adshead b Hardinges	22	b Kirby	16
MJ Brown	c Lewis b Averis	35	b Averis	32
SM Katich	not out	72	b Lewis	20
JP Crawley	c Hancock b Hardinges	4	c Kadeer Ali b Averis	0
DA Kenway	c Spearman b Lewis	0	c Adshead b Lewis	20
*N Pothas	c Hancock b Lewis	4	lbw b Kirby	0
SM Ervine	lbw b Kirby	11	b Lewis	25
SK Warne (capt)	c Hardinges b Kirby	22	c Hardinges b Gidman	62
CT Tremlett	lbw b Gidman	3	b Hardinges	64
RJ Logan	c Spearman b Hardinges	5	c Adshead b Hardinges	28
BV Taylor	c Hancock b Lewis	2	not out	4
Extras	lb 1, nb 16	17	lb 2, nb 2	4
	(60.5 overs)	197	(79.3 overs)	275

Bowling
Lewis 16.5-5-51-3. Kirby 16-2-64-2. Averis 10-4-20-1. Hardinges 12-4-40-3. Gidman 6-2-21-1.
Lewis 25-8-59-3. Kirby 22-6-71-2. Averis 11-1-58-2. Hardinges 10.3-1-43-2. Gidman 11-2-42-1.
Fall of Wickets : 1-63, 2-63, 3-72, 4-77, 5-85, 6-109, 7-157, 8-160, 9-190
1-44, 2-48, 3-48, 4-88, 5-89, 6-94, 7-145, 8-215, 9-265

GLOS	First Innings		Second Innings	
WPC Weston	b Ervine	66	(2) b Taylor	57
CM Spearman	lbw b Warne	34	(1) c Pothas b Taylor	66
Kadeer Ali	c Pothas b Ervine	33	lbw b Taylor	10
JMM Averis	c Kenway b Warne	4	(9) c Warne b Taylor	0
CG Taylor (capt)	c Pothas b Tremlett	3	(4) lbw b Warne	7
THC Hancock	c Katich b Warne	2	(5) c Katich b Warne	0
APR Gidman	b Taylor	5	(6) b Taylor	24
*SJ Adshead	c Kenway b Taylor	0	(7) c Pothas b Tremlett	18
MA Hardinges	c Kenway b Taylor	2	(8) lbw b Warne	2
J Lewis	c Pothas b Logan	40	not out	3
SP Kirby	not out	0	lbw b Taylor	0
Extras	b 1, lb 9, w 2, nb 20	32	lb 3, w 7, nb 6	16
	(73.1 overs)	221	(65.4 overs)	203

Bowling
Tremlett 17-2-51-1. Logan 10.1-1-34-1. Taylor 12-2-38-3. Warne 23-3-50-3. Ervine 11-3-38-2.
Tremlett 13-3-43-1. Logan 9-1-27-0. Taylor 14.4-3-45-6. Ervine 5-2-20-0. Warne 22-2-56-3. Adams 2-0-9-0.
Fall of Wickets: 1-80, 2-112, 3-126, 4-131, 5-140, 6-155, 7-155, 8-160, 9-209
1-129, 2-131, 3-144, 4-148, 5-148, 6-181, 7-197, 8-200, 9-201

Hampshire won by 48 runs – Hampshire (17 pts), Gloucestershire (4 pts)

WARWICKSHIRE v. GLAMORGAN – at Edgbaston

GLAMORGAN	First Innings		Second Innings	
MTG Elliott	b Giles	84	lbw b Bell	69
IJ Thomas	lbw b Warren	24	lbw b Brown	1
DL Hemp	c Trott b Brown	8	b Bell	96
MJ Powell	c Powell b Giles	31	b Streak	31
MP Maynard	c Piper b Warren	20	b Bell	0
*MA Wallace	b Giles	3	st Piper b Giles	11
RDB Croft (capt)	b Giles	7	c Bell b Streak	33
SD Thomas	lbw b Giles	9	c sub b Carter	46
AG Wharf	c Brown b Giles	1	st Piper b Giles	0
DS Harrison	c Piper b Warren	2	b Giles	23
SP Jones	not out	0	not out	0
Extras	b 1, lb 3, w 1, nb 4	9	b 1, lb 7, w 1, nb 4	13
	(63.3 overs)	198	(82 overs)	323

Bowling
Streak 14-3-45-0. Brown 9-4-23-1. Warren 11-1-40-3. Carter 4-0-24-0. Giles 17.3-1-44-6. Bell 8-3-18-0.
Brown 7-1-46-1. Streak 17-4-46-2. Warren 4-0-26-0. Giles 27-4-85-3. Bell 15-2-64-3. Carter 12-1-48-1.
Fall of Wickets: 1-67, 2-85, 3-138, 4-157, 5-163, 6-183, 7-185, 8-186, 9-196
1-7, 2-169, 3-178, 4-178, 5-217, 6-217, 7-292, 8-295, 9-317

WARWICKSHIRE	First Innings	
NV Knight (capt)	c Hemp b Jones	44
MA Wagh	c Wallace b Wharf	28
IR Bell	lbw b Croft	96
IJL Trott	c Wallace b Thomas SD	10
MJ Powell	c Powell b Jones	146
DR Brown	c Jones b Croft	122
AF Giles	c Maynard b Jones	20
HH Streak	not out	41
NM Carter	c Wallace b Thomas SD	39
NA Warren		
*KJ Piper		
Extras	lb 12, nb 6	18
	(8 wkts dec 151.4 overs)	564

Bowling
Jones 29-2-121-3. Harrison 29-4-107-0. Croft 46-13-121-2. Wharf 31-3-120-1. Thomas SD 16.4-0-83-2.
Fall of Wickets: 1-70, 2-72, 3-110, 4-263, 5-424, 6-466, 7-487, 8-564

Warwickshire won by an innings and 43 runs – Warwickshire (22 pts), Glamorgan (1 pt)

SURREY v. SUSSEX – at The Oval

SUSSEX	First Innings	
IJ Ward	c Clinton b Ormond	22
RR Montgomerie	c Batty b Clarke	22
MH Yardy	lbw b Clarke	111
MW Goodwin	c Batty b Akram	31
CJ Adams (capt)	b Ormond	5
*MJ Prior	c Salisbury b Ormond	59
TR Ambrose	c Salisbury b Azhar Mahmood	15
RSC Martin-Jenkins	b Clarke	40
Mushtaq Ahmed	c Clarke b Akram	14
RJ Kirtley	not out	23
JD Lewry	c Ramprakash b Clarke	5
Extras	b 4, lb 17, w 2	23
	(103.1 overs)	370

Bowling
Ormond 26-9-67-3. Akram 25-2-104-2. Clarke 22.1-2-91-4. Azhar Mahmood 18-5-59-1. Salisbury 12-1-28-0.
Fall of Wickets: 1-36, 2-51, 3-102, 4-119, 5-210, 6-274, 7-290, 8-316, 9-360

SURREY	First Innings	
SA Newman	b Kirtley	5
RS Clinton	c Prior b Lewry	10
MR R'kash (capt)	lbw b Lewry	152
GP Thorpe	c Adams b Mushtaq Ahmed	59
*JN Batty	c Montgomerie b Yardy	70
AD Brown	not out	74
R Clarke	not out	10
IDK Salisbury		
Azhar Mahmood		
M Akram		
J Ormond		
Extras	b 6, lb 13, w 1, nb 2	22
	(5 wkts 109.2 overs)	402

Bowling
Kirtley 31-14-65-1. Lewry 26-8-96-2. Martin-Jenkins 20-5-72-0. Mushtaq Ahmed 28.2-3-126-1. Yardy 4-0-24-1.
Fall of Wickets: 1-6, 2-34, 3-150, 4-272, 5-385

Match drawn – Surrey (12 pts), Sussex (9 pts)

stayed with Warne long enough for another 70 precious runs to be garnered, then went on to 64 with some bold attacking strokes. Warne's 62 had nevertheless provided the key resistance, and Gloucestershire's demoralisation in the field was indicated when Richard Logan went on to help Tremlett put on a further 50.

Hampshire's final second innings total of 275 meant that their visitors had to score 252 to win, and, as on the first evening, openers Phil Weston and Craig Spearman seemed more than equal to the task. The tall left-hander Weston added 57 to his earlier 66 and Spearman 66 to his first day 34, as the pair constructed a largely untroubled 129 for the opening wicket. Surely Gloucestershire could win from here? By the close of day three, however, they had crumbled to 149 for five, with Billy Taylor making the initial strikes and Warne – who else? – dismissing both Chris Taylor and Tim Hancock cheaply.

The following morning saw Alex Gidman and Steve Adshead briefly threatening a rally with a partnership of 33, but medium-pacer Taylor added three more wickets to finish with a career-best 6 for 45 to spearhead Hampshire's charge to victory. The last five Gloucestershire wickets fell for 22 runs inside 13 overs with Warne adding 3 for 56 to his first innings 3 for 50. Hampshire also owed much to their Australian batsman Simon Katich, who made an unbeaten first innings 72 from No. 3, while Jon Lewis made valuable all-round contributions for Gloucestershire.

Champions Warwickshire, meanwhile, got their own campaign off to a winning start at Edgbaston by employing exactly the same sort of tactics that brought them their 2004 glory. After Ashley Giles had spun Glamorgan out for 198 on the first day, taking 6 for 44 and bowling the Welsh county's top scorer Matthew Elliott through the gate, Warwickshire set about batting their opponents out of the game.

As so often the previous summer, they expertly built a huge first-innings total and, as a result, heaped pressure on Glamorgan's batsmen second time around. Nick Knight and Mark Wagh laid a solid base, and then Michael Powell joined Ian Bell in a fourth-wicket stand of 153. Bell was eventually deceived by the ever-determined Robert Croft when 96, but Powell went on to complete his 12th first-class hundred. His 146 was also his highest championship score and, with Dougie Brown also reaching three figures, Glamorgan were soon left staring at almost certain defeat. After Brown was out for 122, both Heath Streak and Neil Carter enjoyed themselves at the bowlers' expense by hitting five

sixes between them before a declaration 366 runs ahead. To their credit, Glamorgan fought hard in their second innings, reaching 323 in the end thanks mainly to fine knocks from Elliott and David Hemp, who was out just four short of a century against his former county.

A potentially fascinating contest between Surrey and Sussex at The Oval was ruined by bad weather. Only 13.3 overs were possible on the third day, leaving time merely for Surrey to chase batting bonus points on the final afternoon. Led by Mark Ramprakash, the acting captain in the absence of the injured Mark Butcher, the home side duly went past Sussex's 370 to reach a maximum five batting points themselves. Ramprakash, his 152 was his 74th first-class hundred, was joined in successive stands of 116, 122 and 113 by Graham Thorpe, Jon Batty and the familiarly aggressive Alistair Brown, whose unbeaten 74 occupied just 72 balls. The Sussex innings had been built upon a fine 111 by Mike Yardy, who struck 17 fours and impressed with his driving while compiling only his second first-class century ... and his second against Surrey.

Division Two

Worcestershire grabbed one of the two positive results in Division Two's opening round of matches, kicking off their bid for an immediate return to the top flight by routing Derbyshire by ten wickets at Derby. Graeme Hick, no longer in England's plans but still one of the best players in county cricket as he approached his 39th birthday, took only 119 balls to make 80 on the first day, and Worcestershire's eventual 350 for 9 declared was too much for the home side. Left-arm seamer, Alamgir Sheriyar, back at Worcestershire from Kent as the first 'on-loan' signing in English domestic cricket, took three prime wickets as Derbyshire collapsed initially to 135 all out in reply. Their second innings, which lasted from the second evening until the fourth day due to several weather interruptions, was a better effort – with opener Steve Stubbings battling six and a half hours for 58 – but Gareth Batty's 5 for 87, and a career-best 4 for 68 from pace bowler David Wigley, eventually enabled Worcestershire to chase only a modest last-innings target. Both teams, by the way, had agreed beforehand to use the new floodlights at the Racecourse Ground in the advent of bad light; it would have been a first for English first-class cricket if it had happened.

Durham's innings and 216-run demolition of Leicestershire at Grace Road gave the north-east county an uplifting start to the new season. Most encouraging too, was the contribution of Liam Plunkett, the highly rated 20-year-old with the ability to turn into a genuine fast-bowling all-rounder. Plunkett's first innings' 5 for 43 destroyed Leicestershire's initial reply to Durham's imposing 523 for 8 declared, completely overshadowing Steve Harmison on the England spearhead's much-anticipated return to domestic action. And, although Harmison followed up his 11 wicketless first-innings overs with a burst of three wickets in 15 balls – and 4 for 30 overall – in Leicestershire's second batting effort, Plunkett also played a big part himself with three more wickets of his own.

The home side's second-innings' slide to 184 meant that the game was over well before the end of the third day. Durham's morale-boosting victory was also a big moment for Australian batsman Mike Hussey, who made a majestic 253 in his first championship game as the county's new captain. Hussey, a compact left-hander with all the strokes, had made 5,194 runs at 76.69 in three previous seasons with Northamptonshire – but this was a start possibly beyond even his lofty ambitions. To cap a wonderful match for Durham, their 22-year-old batsman Gordon Muchall hit a commanding 82 in a 166-run, third-wicket stand with Hussey.

Essex had much the better of their season's opener against Yorkshire at Chelmsford, with Will Jefferson immediately underlining his international claims with a brilliant 149 from just 219 balls, but in the end the huge amount of time lost on the first three days mitigated against a positive result. Yorkshire, mind you, had already been forced to follow on when the clock saved them; indeed, at 90 for 7 in reply to an Essex total of 401 for 4 that had

Round One: 13–16 April 2005 Division Two

DERBYSHIRE v. WORCESTERSHIRE – at Derby

WORCS	First Innings		Second Innings	
SD Peters	c Sutton b Hunter	55	not out	39
SC Moore	run out	19	not out	26
GA Hick	lbw b Moss	80		
BF Smith	c Bassano b Moss	48		
VS Solanki (capt)	b Welch	0		
GJ Batty	c Stubbings b Welch	47		
DA Leatherdale	c Sutton b Hunter	14		
*DJ Pipe	c Welch b Walker	33		
MS Mason	c Moss b Walker	18		
DH Wigley	not out	7		
A Sheriyar	not out	3		
Extras	lb 11, w 1, nb 14	26	b 2, lb 1, nb 3	6
	(9 wkts 115.3 overs)	350	(0 wkts 13.5 overs)	71

Bowling
Hunter 30-4-92-2. Walker 17.3-0-63-2. Dean 22-5-80-0. Welch 23-8-51-2. Moss 16-7-38-2. Botha 7-2-15-0.
Hunter 4-0-28-0. Walker 4-1-13-0. Welch 3-0-7-0. Dean 2.5-0-20-0.
Fall of Wickets: 1-30, 2-150, 3-174, 4-175, 5-241, 6-267, 7-318, 8-319, 9-347

DERBYSHIRE	First Innings		Second Innings	
MJ Di Venuto	c Pipe b Mason	0	(2) st Pipe b Batty	111
SD Stubbings	c Batty b Wigley	5	(1) c Smith b Batty	58
J Moss	c Pipe b Mason	9	c Hick b Batty	7
Hassan Adnan	c Smith b Wigley	15	c Hick b Batty	0
CWG Bassano	c Pipe b Wigley	30	c Moore b Wigley	6
*LD Sutton (capt)	c Pipe b Batty	21	c Hick b Wigley	47
G Welch	b Leatherdale	9	c Pipe b Wigley	29
AG Botha	c Pipe b Sheriyar	16	c Peters b Mason	6
KJ Dean	c Solanki b Sheriyar	12	not out	6
ID Hunter	c Pipe b Sheriyar	2	c Hick b Batty	9
NGE Walker	not out	12	c Smith b Wigley	0
Extras	lb 3, w 1	4	b 1, lb 2, w 1, nb 2	6
	(59.5 overs)	135	(106 overs)	285

Bowling
Mason 10-6-6-2. Sheriyar 20.5-6-48-3. Wigley 15-2-53-3. Leatherdale 9-3-18-1. Batty 5-1-7-1.
Mason 24-11-30-1. Sheriyar 16-2-68-0. Batty 38-9-87-5. Wigley 20-6-68-4. Leatherdale 8-1-29-0.
Fall of Wickets: 1-0, 2-12, 3-20, 4-59, 5-62, 6-71, 7-101, 8-107, 9-114
1-150, 2-166, 3-166, 4-175, 5-215, 6-259, 7-264, 8-274, 9-284

Worcestershire won by 10 wickets –
Derbyshire (3 pts), Worcestershire (21 pts)

LEICESTERSHIRE v. DURHAM – at Leicester

DURHAM	First Innings	
MEK Hussey (capt)	c Habib b Masters	253
JJB Lewis	c Nixon b Maddy	50
PD Collingwood	c Ackerman b Gibson	18
GJ Muchall	run out	82
DM Benkenstein	lbw b Gibson	16
N Peng	lbw b Masters	39
GR Breese	lbw b Gibson	10
*P Mustard	st Nixon b Snape	28
LE Plunkett	not out	11
SJ Harmison		
M Davies		
Extras	lb 8, nb 8	16
	(8 wkts dec 161 overs)	523

Bowling
Gibson 44-10-121-3. DeFreitas 25-8-84-0. Masters 33-9-117-2. Maddy 16-4-59-1. Henderson 34-5-104-0. Snape 8-1-23-1. Maunders 1-0-7-0.
Fall of Wickets: 1-93, 2-148, 3-314, 4-343, 5-446, 6-479, 7-491, 8-523

LEICESTERSHIRE	First Innings		Second Innings	
DDJ Robinson	c Collingwood b Plunkett	14	c Hussey b Plunkett	19
DL Maddy	c Benkenstein b Plunkett	10	c Collingwood b Plunkett	2
A Habib	run out	15	b Harmison	8
JK Maunders	lbw b Plunkett	4	c Hussey b Benkenstein	50
HD Ackerman (capt)	lbw b Plunkett	7	lbw b Davies	0
JN Snape	b Davies	19	c Benkenstein b Harmison	23
*PA Nixon	not out	17	c Mustard b Davies	32
OD Gibson	run out	0	b Harmison	0
PAJ DeFreitas	c Hussey b Collingwood	0	b Harmison	0
DD Masters	c Breese b Davies	1	lbw b Plunkett	19
CW Henderson	c Benkenstein b Plunkett	22	not out	0
Extras	b 5, lb 5, nb 4	14	b 5, lb 1, w 2, nb 4	12
	(39 overs)	123	(75.3 overs)	184

Bowling
Harmison 11-0-36-0. Plunkett 14-1-43-5. Collingwood 6-1-15-1. Davies 8-4-19-2.
Harmison 19-7-30-4. Plunkett 18.3-4-55-3. Collingwood 8-3-15-0. Davies 13-5-34-2. Benkenstein 10-4-26-1. Breese 7-2-18-0.
Fall of Wickets: 1-28, 2-35, 3-41, 4-49, 5-75, 6-75, 7-80, 8-81, 9-88
1-10, 2-25, 3-38, 4-74, 5-130, 6-130, 7-131, 8-131, 9-184

Durham won by an innings and 216 runs –
Leicestershire (1 pt), Durham (22 pts)

ESSEX v. YORKSHIRE – at Chelmsford

ESSEX	First Innings	
WI Jefferson	lbw b Lumb	149
AN Cook	c Dawood b Harvey	11
GW Flower	c Lumb b Hoggard	65
RS Bopara	c Lumb b Hoggard	46
A Flower	not out	62
RC Irani (capt)	not out	56
*JS Foster		
GR Napier		
AJ Tudor		
AR Adams		
D Gough		
Extras	lb 11, w 1	12
	(4 wkts dec 126.5 overs)	401

Bowling
Hoggard 30-8-86-2. Kruis 30-6-108-0. Silverwood 21-0-72-0. Harvey 24-10-47-1. McGrath 9.5-1-35-0. Dawson 10-1-35-0. Lumb 2-0-7-1.
Fall of Wickets: 1-32, 2-220, 3-254, 4-301

YORKSHIRE	First Innings		Second Innings	
MJ Wood	lbw b Adams	29	c & b Tudor	0
PA Jaques	c Adams b Tudor	2	not out	67
A McGrath	c Foster b Tudor	4	lbw b Bopara	27
MJ Lumb	lbw b Napier	18	not out	11
IJ Harvey	b Adams	0		
C White (capt)	not out	59		
*I Dawood	lbw b Napier	6		
RKJ Dawson	c Foster b Gough	13		
CEW Silverwood	b Adams	57		
MJ Hoggard	c Flower A b Bopara	7		
GJ Kruis	c Jefferson b Bopara	3		
Extras	b 1, lb 6	7		0
	(55.2 overs)	205	(2 wkts 24 overs)	105

Bowling
Gough 16-6-44-1. Tudor 9-1-30-2. Adams 15-4-52-3. Napier 12-3-59-2. Bopara 3.2-0-13-2.
Tudor 4-0-16-1. Napier 5-0-31-0. Bopara 2-0-9-1. Gough 3-1-7-0. Adams 2-1-9-0. Flower G.W. 4-1-18-0. Cook 4-0-15-0.
Fall of Wickets: 1-8, 2-12, 3-45, 4-53, 5-53, 6-68, 7-90, 8-171, 9-197
1-0, 2-52

Match drawn – Essex (12 pts),
Yorkshire (5.5 pts)

LANCASHIRE v. SOMERSET – at Old Trafford

LANCASHIRE	First Innings		Second Innings	
IJ Sutcliffe	c Turner b McLean	34	c Turner b Caddick	0
PJ Horton	c Turner b Caddick	19	c Turner b Laraman	41
MB Loye	c Turner b Laraman	53	b Blackwell	92
SG Law	c Trescothick b Caddick	37	b Blackwell	10
MJ Chilton (capt)	c Turner b Blackwell	39	not out	31
KW Hogg	c Trescothick b Blackwell	3	c Trescothick b McLean	6
*WK Hegg	b Johnson	4	not out	4
DG Cork	c & b Caddick	65		
SI Mahmood	c Francis b Caddick	57		
G Keedy	not out	2		
JM Anderson	c Burns b Johnson	0		
Extras	lb 9, w 1	10	lb 7, w 2, nb 2	11
	(96.3 overs)	323	(5 wkts dec 61 overs)	195

Bowling
Caddick 26-6-78-4. McLean 17-4-69-1. Johnson 20.3-3-84-2. Laraman 15-2-39-1. Blackwell 18-5-44-2.
Caddick 19-4-50-1. McLean 7-2-21-1. Johnson 5-0-26-0. Laraman 11-1-28-1. Blackwell 19-1-63-2.
Fall of Wickets: 1-36, 2-99, 3-137, 4-149, 5-164, 6-170, 7-212, 8-306, 9-321
1-0, 2-94, 3-121, 4-169, 5-184

SOMERSET	First Innings		Second Innings	
MJ Wood	lbw b Cork	10	c Cork b Keedy	27
ME T'cothick (capt)	c Chilton b Cork	11	c Cork b Anderson	22
M Burns	c Law b Keedy	40	not out	5
JD Francis	c Hegg b Anderson	1		
JC Hildreth	c Anderson b Mahmood	14	(4) c Cork b Keedy	0
ID Blackwell	c Sutcliffe b Hogg	122	(5) not out	1
AW Laraman	st Hegg b Keedy	6		
*RJ Turner	c Sutcliffe b Mahmood	21		
RL Johnson	c Keedy b Hogg	27		
AR Caddick	not out	0		
NAM McLean	lbw b Mahmood	0		
Extras	b 8, lb 5, w 3, nb 4	20	b 6, lb 6, nb 2	14
	(89.1 overs)	272	(3 wkts 22.3 overs)	69

Bowling
Anderson 23-8-58-1. Cork 22-5-52-2. Mahmood 16.1-6-41-3. Hogg 12-4-40-2. Keedy 16-3-68-2.
Anderson 8-2-28-1. Cork 7-3-21-0. Keedy 4-3-2-2. Mahmood 3.3-0-6-0.
Fall of Wickets: 1-15, 2-22, 3-23, 4-53, 5-133, 6-152, 7-190, 8-271, 9-272
1-51, 2-61, 3-65

Match drawn – Lancashire (10 pts), Somerset (9 pts)

Liam Plunkett took eight wickets as Durham began their season by crushing Leicestershire.

taken until seven balls into the final day to compile, they were struggling to see out time for the draw. Craig White, however, was then joined by Chris Silverwood in a partnership of 81, and both made half-centuries – as did Phil Jaques after they had been bowled out for 205 in their first innings.

Ian Blackwell, seeking to resurrect in 2005 an international career that had been put on hold by England, continued his eye-catching start to the season by hitting the Lancashire attack for 122 which included three sixes and ten fours at Old Trafford. Blackwell, 26, had played the last of his 23 one-day internationals ten months earlier, but had gone into this first championship fixture on the back of a 138-ball 191 against the students of Durham UCCE. Loss of time eventually meant a draw in the match, with Somerset left wobbling rather uncertainly at 69 for 3 after being set a token target of 247 in 31 overs. Mal Loye struck a fine 92 in Lancashire's second innings, following up his first innings half-century, while combative fifties from both Dominic Cork and Sajid Mahmood helped to haul the home side beyond 300 early on the second day.

Round Two: 20–23 April 2005

Division One

Champions Warwickshire were sent tottering to the brink of defeat at Canterbury by Kent – the last side to beat them in the championship, at the same venue. But this time, a courageous rearguard action, led by wicketkeeper Tony Frost, saved them and – in the end – Warwickshire emerged with the same number of points as the frustrated home team. Frost batted for 244 minutes and faced 232 balls for his unbeaten 82, while No. 10 Neil Carter hung on for 49 minutes for his 9. At the death, though, it was last-man Nick Warren who kept Frost faithful company for the final five and a half overs.

Kent sent down 101 overs on the fourth day, with left-arm spinner Min Patel taking 4 for 32 from 32 overs, 20 of which were maidens. Instead of making an overnight declaration, though, perhaps home captain David Fulton could have given his bowlers at least 20 minutes at Warwickshire's top order the previous evening. The other main thorn in Kent's side on the last day was a particularly painful one: Alex Loudon. Having left Kent the previous autumn during the fall-out from the controversy surrounding his friend Ed Smith's acrimonious departure to Middlesex, the talented 24-year-old batted obstinately for a vital 64 while helping Frost to steady a badly-listing ship in a sixth-wicket stand worth 116. Amjad Khan, who had bowled superbly to take 6 for 73 in Warwickshire's first innings, after the visitors had moved initially to 179 for 1 as Nick Knight and Ian Bell blossomed, could not reproduce that same fire second time around and Kent's other seamers also struggled to make an impact.

Martin van Jaarsveld, by contrast, could hardly have made a bigger first impression on Kent's supporters. The South African Test batsman, having turned his back on international cricket during the winter and signed for Kent as a 'Kolpak' registration, became the first player to make two hundreds on his championship debut for the county. 'The most Test matches I played in a row was three,' said 30-year-old van Jaarsveld, who had appeared against England during the winter, 'but I never felt confident that the South African selectors were going to give me their full backing.' Darren Stevens, who Kent had signed from Leicestershire, also had a championship debut to remember by making a first-innings 88 for his new county, while

It was frustration for Amjad Khan, and Kent, as Warwickshire staged a successful rearguard action at Canterbury.

skipper Fulton began the new campaign solidly too with half-centuries in both innings.

A magnificent, evenly-balanced and fiercely fought contest at Hove ended in a dramatic draw as Hampshire captain Shane Warne decided to shut up shop instead of pressing on for a victory which was tantalisingly within their grasp at the end of a rain-shortened final day. It was a shame, in fact, that rain had prevented a start until 3.30pm on the last afternoon, with Hampshire starting out at 89 for 3 as they chased a win target of 285 in their second innings. Just another 40 overs were scheduled but a positive result, which would have been guaranteed but for the bad weather, still looked on. However, when Sean Ervine joined Kevin Pietersen in a thrilling stand of 113 it seemed as if Hampshire could get to the finishing line. Pietersen's 61 took him only 51 balls, with five fours and three massive sixes – two off Mushtaq Ahmed and the other off the ever-combative James Kirtley – while Ervine weighed in with a 78-ball 57. Then Pietersen skied a catch, with 42 runs still required from 59 balls, and the equation had come down to 29 from 34 deliveries with two wickets left and Warne decided to settle for the draw. With Hampshire's remaining

Round Two: 20–23 April 2005 Division One

KENT v. WARWICKSHIRE – at Canterbury

KENT	First Innings		Second Innings	
DP Fulton (capt)	c Frost b Giles	53	b Warren	75
RWT Key	c Trott b Streak	4	lbw b Giles	21
M van Jaarsveld	b Giles	118	c Bell b Carter	111
MJ Walker	c Streak b Giles	3	not out	54
DI Stevens	b Brown	88	b Giles	0
*GO Jones	c Frost b Giles	32	c Trott b Carter	3
MJ Dennington	c Frost b Carter	2	lbw b Giles	12
SJ Cook	b Giles	1	not out	14
MM Patel	run out	10		
A Khan	lbw b Streak	4		
SMJ Cusden	not out	6		
Extras	b 3, lb 2, w 9, nb 12	26	b 4, lb 7, w 3, nb 4	18
	(105.2 overs)	347	(6 wkts dec 96 overs)	308

Bowling
Streak 19.2-5-53-2. Brown 15-2-63-1. Bell 6-0-16-0. Carter 17-1-59-1.
Warren 10-2-32-0. Loudon 8-0-25-0. Giles 29-6-86-5. Trott 1-0-8-0.
Streak 14-0-49-0. Brown 19-5-39-0. Warren 15-3-48-1. Giles 25-2-71-3.
Loudon 1-0-4-0. Carter 18-4-69-2. Bell 4-0-17-0.
Fall of Wickets: 1-5, 2-138, 3-142, 4-238, 5-301, 6-304, 7-309, 8-330, 9-334
1-46, 2-201, 3-235, 4-245, 5-250, 6-272

WARWICKSHIRE	First Innings		Second Innings	
NV Knight (capt)	c Jones b Patel	100	lbw b Cook	0
MJ Powell	c Jones b Khan	4	lbw b Cusden	21
IR Bell	lbw b Patel	63	c Jones b Cook	9
IJL Trott	b Patel	19	c Dennington b Cusden	20
AGR Loudon	lbw b Khan	40	c Key b Patel	64
DR Brown	c Walker b Cusden	22	c Jones b Patel	13
*T Frost	lbw b Khan	5	not out	82
AF Giles	lbw b Khan	18	c Fulton b Patel	0
HH Streak	c Jones b Khan	12	b Patel	0
NM Carter	not out	6	c Jones b Khan	9
NA Warren	b Khan	0	not out	0
Extras	b 7, lb 9, w 4	20	b 4, lb 5, w 4, nb 2	15
	(105.5 overs)	309	(9 wkts 101 overs)	233

Bowling
Cook 24-7-62-0. Khan 22.5-7-73-6. Patel 35-8-90-3. Cusden 16-1-57-1.
Walker 1-0-2-0. Dennington 7-3-9-0.
Cook 22-11-51-2. Khan 19-6-42-1. Cusden 12-0-50-2. Dennington 7-1-23-0.
Patel 32-20-32-4. Stevens 3-1-8-0. van Jaarsveld 6-2-18-0.
Fall of Wickets: 1-16, 2-179, 3-180, 4-212, 5-239, 6-266, 7-279, 8-296, 9-303
1-0, 2-10, 3-43, 4-55, 5-73, 6-189, 7-189, 8-199, 9-229

Match drawn – Kent (10 pts), Warwickshire (10 pts)

SUSSEX v. HAMPSHIRE – at Hove

SUSSEX	First Innings		Second Innings	
IJ Ward	c Pothas b Tremlett	3	c Pothas b Katich	86
RR Montgomerie	c Pothas b Ervine	5	c Warne b Tremlett	7
MH Yardy	c Pothas b Tremlett	104	lbw b Ervine	13
MW Goodwin	b Taylor	87	b Taylor	28
CJ Adams (capt)	c & b Warne	29	not out	79
*MJ Prior	lbw b Warne	4	lbw b Warne	12
RSC M-Jenkins	c Pothas b Tremlett	2	lbw b Warne	0
MJG Davis	c Brown b Tremlett	5	c Pothas b Taylor	1
Mushtaq Ahmed	c Pothas b Tremlett	0	c Pothas b Ervine	36
RJ Kirtley	not out	1	lbw b Warne	17
JD Lewry	b Tremlett	2	b Warne	0
Extras	nb 10	10	b 10, lb 5, w 4, nb 14	33
	(77.5 overs)	252	(108 overs)	312

Bowling
Tremlett 17.5-4-44-6. Ervine 18-8-55-1. Taylor 10-0-36-1. Udal 7-0-29-0.
Warne 23-5-72-2. Adams 1-0-9-0. Pietersen 1-0-7-0.
Tremlett 25-6-69-1. Ervine 23-11-37-2. Taylor 30-6-86-2. Udal 3-0-8-0.
Warne 21-2-81-4. Katich 6-1-16-1.
Fall of Wickets: 1-8, 2-10, 3-182, 4-234, 5-242, 6-242, 7-245, 8-245, 9-250
1-13, 2-59, 3-121, 4-194, 5-210, 6-210, 7-211, 8-267, 9-312

HAMPSHIRE	First Innings		Second Innings	
JHK Adams	c Prior b Lewry	32	c Martin-Jenkins b Kirtley	35
MJ Brown	c Adams b Kirtley	7	lbw b Lewry	7
SM Katich	b Kirtley	39	b Mushtaq Ahmed	27
JP Crawley	c Prior b Martin-Jenkins	28	c Prior b Kirtley	22
KP Pietersen	lbw b Kirtley	0	(6) c Goodwin b M Ahmed	61
*N Pothas	c Goodwin b Mushtaq Ahmed	84	(9) not out	6
SM Ervine	c Prior b Kirtley	23	c Lewry b Mushtaq Ahmed	57
SK Warne (capt)	b Martin-Jenkins	34	b Kirtley	6
SD Udal	not out	20	(10) not out	4
CT Tremlett	lbw b Martin-Jenkins	0		
BV Taylor	c Montgomerie b M Ahmed	4	(5) c Ward b Kirtley	24
Extras	b 2, lb 3, p 5	10	b 6, lb 12	18
	(90 overs)	280	(8 wkts 74 overs)	267

Bowling
Kirtley 24-5-54-4. Lewry 19-1-62-1. Martin-Jenkins 18-8-51-3.
Mushtaq Ahmed 25-5-84-2. Davis 4-0-19-0.
Kirtley 27-3-88-4. Lewry 13-2-40-1. Mushtaq Ahmed 24-3-89-3.
Martin-Jenkins 10-3-32-0.
Fall of Wickets: 1-11, 2-71, 3-89, 4-89, 5-130, 6-201, 7-253, 8-255, 9-255
1-14, 2-74, 3-82, 4-130, 5-130, 6-243, 7-254, 8-256

Match drawn – Sussex (9 pts), Hampshire (9 pts)

MIDDLESEX v. NOTTINGHAMSHIRE – at Lord's

NOTTS	First Innings		Second Innings	
DJ Bicknell	c Scott b Richardson	56	c Hutton b Hutchison	111
JER Gallian	c Scott b Richardson	46	c Joyce b Richardson	8
A Singh	c Shah b Richardson	25	c & b Hayward	14
SP Fleming (capt)	c Scott b Richardson	0	b Hayward	1
DJ Hussey	b Richardson	118	c Scott b Hutchison	57
*CMW Read	c Hutton b Weekes	63	not out	9
MA Ealham	lbw b Richardson	47	not out	4
PJ Franks	not out	104		
GP Swann	c Scott b Richardson	9		
RJ Sidebottom	c Hutton b Weekes	31		
GJ Smith	b Weekes	9		
Extras	b 6, lb 22, nb 10	38	b 1, lb 7	8
	(155.2 overs)	546	(5 wkts dec 50 overs)	212

Bowling
Keegan 26-7-103-0. Hayward 25-3-91-0. Richardson 38-10-113-7.
Hutton 10-0-54-0. Hutchison 18-2-70-0. Weekes 37.2-8-83-3. Shah 1-0-4-0.
Richardson 9-1-36-1. Hayward 9-1-23-2. Keegan 14-1-45-0. Hutchison 11-0-59-2.
Weekes 7-0-41-0.
Fall of Wickets: 1-74, 2-127, 3-127, 4-144, 5-271, 6-372, 7-407, 8-425, 9-520
1-29, 2-79, 3-87, 4-192, 5-204

MIDDLESEX	First Innings		Second Innings	
AJ Strauss	b Sidebottom	4	b Hussey	2
BL Hutton (capt)	c Read b Smith	2	not out	76
ET Smith	c Read b Smith	39	run out	49
OA Shah	c Fleming b Smith	5	not out	19
EC Joyce	c Fleming b Sidebottom	192		
PN Weekes	c Read b Ealham	24		
*BJM Scott	lbw b Ealham	1		
CB Keegan	c Read b Swann	28		
PM Hutchison	b Swann	0		
A Richardson	lbw b Franks	15		
M Hayward	not out	12		
Extras	lb 7, nb 16	23	lb 9, w 1, nb 2	12
	(93.5 overs)	345	(2 wkts 57 overs)	158

Bowling
Smith 22-6-67-3. Sidebottom 17.5-2-85-2. Franks 16-3-59-1. Ealham 17-2-68-2.
Swann 21-6-59-2.
Smith 2-1-2-0. Sidebottom 2-1-6-0. Swann 20-7-43-0. Hussey 24-6-61-1.
Gallian 9-1-37-0.
Fall of Wickets: 1-3, 2-9, 3-38, 4-69, 5-143, 6-155, 7-212, 8-212, 9-268
1-9, 2-96

Match drawn – Middlesex (9 pts), Nottinghamshire (12 pts)

three batsmen of the calibre of Nic Pothas, Shaun Udal and Chris Tremlett, though, it was a slightly surprising decision by the great Australian.

It had still been a tremendous game of cricket, however, from which both sides emerged with great credit. There was also a spicy epilogue, too, with Warne and Sussex captain Chris Adams exchanging verbal jousts after the latter had accused the former of 'disrespecting' wicketkeeper Matt Prior with comments aimed at him on the field of play. Adams himself had won his cricketing tussle with Warne on the third day, as he led Sussex into a position of relative control with a typically pugnacious unbeaten 79 from 157 balls. At one stage, Adams hit Warne for five fours in successive overs, while Mushtaq also took a heavy toll on the Aussie leg-spinner during a punchy, and invaluable, 39-ball 36 as Sussex hauled themselves up to 312 in their second innings. At one stage Warne made seven bowling changes in 13 overs as he tried all he knew to prevent Sussex from stretching their overall lead to potentially match-winning proportions. Mushtaq, however, added 56 with Adams for the eighth wicket, while Kirtley then helped his captain to put on another 45 for the ninth.

The first day had seen fast-improving paceman Tremlett take a career-best 6 for 44, which brought Hampshire right back into the game as Sussex's last seven wickets fell for a mere 18 runs in 11 overs. That collapse undid a lot of the fine work done by Mike Yardy's 104 and Murray Goodwin's skilful 87, and Pothas' stylish 84 enabled Hampshire to win a slender first-innings advantage despite Pietersen falling for a second-ball duck in his championship debut innings for the county.

Any chance that Nottinghamshire had of forcing victory over a Middlesex side that, apart from the magnificent Ed Joyce, had been outplayed for three days, disappeared when heavy drizzle delayed the start of the final day's play at Lord's until 2.50pm. In the end, the contest fizzled out into a tame draw with Ben Hutton steering his team safely through the 52 overs that were then possible.

It was Irishman Joyce, however, who previously was single-handedly responsible for keeping Middlesex afloat. At the end of the second day Middlesex were 167 for 6 and staring at heavy defeat in the shadow of Notts' massive first innings total of 546. But Joyce, 68 not out overnight, ignored the lack of a regular partner to go on thrillingly to 192, hitting four sixes and 26 fours in an innings that would have had the

watching David Graveney, England's chairman of selectors, filling up his notebook. Joyce was to qualify for England, by residence, in three months' time. Stephen Fleming, the New Zealand captain, made just 0 and 1 on his Notts championship debut, but there was ample compensation elsewhere. David Hussey and Darren Bicknell both scored a century and a half-century in each innings, while Paul Franks reached an unbeaten 104 just before the Notts first innings finally came to a close. There were significant runs, too, for Chris Read while – in a Middlesex attack that too often lacked for purpose or control – the steady seam bowling of Alan Richardson (a winter signing from Warwickshire) stood out.

Division Two

Steve Harmison took Durham's first hat-trick in first-class cricket as Division Two's surprise early pacesetters brushed Worcestershire aside at Chester-le-Street. A seven-wicket win was completed inside two days with the Durham seam attack of Harmison, Mark Davies and Liam Plunkett carrying all before them. Davies, preferred beforehand to Michael Lewis, the Australian paceman who had just heard of his

Paul Collingwood hit a century of quality as Durham maintained their fine start to the season at home to Worcestershire.

inclusion in Australia's elite 25-man contracted squad for the coming year, shattered the Worcestershire first innings with 6 for 32. In 2004 Davies had been the first bowler to reach 50 wickets, before an intercostal muscle tear prematurely ended his season; this performance underlined the effectiveness of his winter rehabilitation.

Paul Collingwood then proceeded to put Durham in complete command with a century of real quality. Making light of the bowler-friendly conditions, he reached 88 not out in a home reply of 139 for 2 by the close of the opening day, and went on to 129 the next morning. Durham collapsed from 271 for 4 to 286 all out, to give Worcestershire at least a glimmer of hope, but Harmison and Plunkett soon extinguished that. Harmison, in his first home championship appearance for almost two years, took 5 for 61 to add to his first innings 3 for 25 – with his three hat-trick victims all bowled. Jamie Pipe was beaten for pace and lost his off stump, Matt Mason was yorked and Dave Wigley inside edged another express delivery into his leg stump. In his next over last-man Alamgir Sheriyar was also clean bowled and Harmison said, 'Before the hat-trick ball I was quite confident I could do it because I don't think they were too keen to hang around.'

Marcus Trescothick, Somerset's acting captain, was also unable to hang around at Headingley – but for quite a different reason. Having put Yorkshire in to bat after a rained-off opening day, Trescothick saw the home side reach 501 for 9 declared, with Ian Harvey smashing an unbeaten 209 from 234 balls, with 30 fours, and Tim Bresnan helping him to add 238 for the eighth wicket. Worse, from Somerset's point of view, was to follow, however, when news reached them that Trescothick's wife Hayley was going into labour. Rushing home to witness the subsequent birth of his first child – daughter Ellie – brought Trescothick understandable joy but, back in Leeds, Somerset were forced to bat twice without their England opener after Yorkshire had enforced the follow-on. John Francis, in particular, did his best to battle for the draw, but the 24-year-old's unbeaten 125 – making him the first Somerset player since Peter Roebuck in 1991 to carry his bat – was ultimately not quite enough. Aaron Laraman helped Francis to add 130 for the fifth wicket, but when Laraman went for 53 just after tea there was not enough further support as Yorkshire completed an innings victory.

The match began with Graeme Swann – a winter departure to Nottinghamshire – using a column in the local paper to accuse Northamptonshire of losing their local identity. This fixture, against Leicestershire at Wantage Road, was indeed the first time since 1997 (a span of 115 first-class matches) that Northants had not selected at least one player born within the county. But David Sales and Rob

<h2 align="center">Round Two: 20–23 April 2005 Division Two</h2>

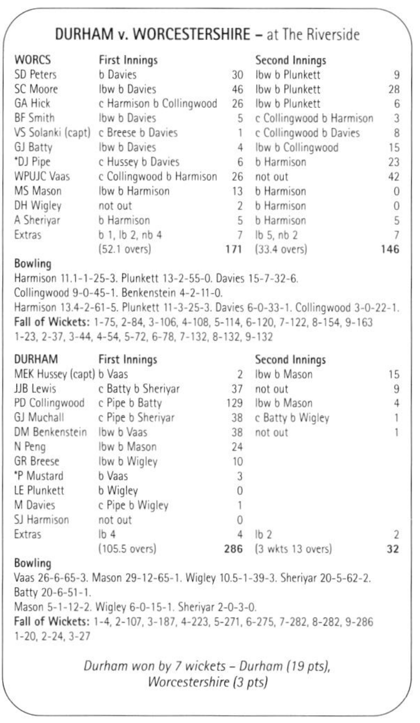

DURHAM v. WORCESTERSHIRE – at The Riverside

WORCS	First Innings		Second Innings	
SD Peters	b Davies	30	lbw b Plunkett	9
SC Moore	lbw b Davies	46	lbw b Plunkett	28
GA Hick	c Harmison b Collingwood	26	lbw b Plunkett	6
BF Smith	lbw b Davies	5	c Collingwood b Harmison	3
VS Solanki (capt)	c Breese b Davies	1	c Collingwood b Davies	8
GJ Batty	lbw b Davies	4	lbw b Collingwood	15
*DJ Pipe	c Hussey b Davies	6	b Harmison	23
WPUJC Vaas	c Collingwood b Harmison	26	not out	42
MS Mason	lbw b Harmison	13	b Harmison	0
DH Wigley	not out	2	b Harmison	0
A Sheriyar	b Harmison	5	b Harmison	5
Extras	b 1, lb 2, nb 4	7	lb 5, nb 2	7
	(52.1 overs)	171	(33.4 overs)	146

Bowling
Harmison 11.1-1-25-3. Plunkett 13-2-55-0. Davies 15-7-32-6. Collingwood 9-0-45-1. Benkenstein 4-2-11-0.
Harmison 13.4-2-61-5. Plunkett 11-3-25-3. Davies 6-0-33-1. Collingwood 3-0-22-1.
Fall of Wickets: 1-75, 2-84, 3-106, 4-108, 5-114, 6-120, 7-122, 8-154, 9-163
1-23, 2-37, 3-44, 4-54, 5-72, 6-78, 7-132, 8-132, 9-132

DURHAM	First Innings		Second Innings	
MEK Hussey (capt)	b Vaas	2	lbw b Mason	15
JJB Lewis	c Batty b Sheriyar	37	not out	9
PD Collingwood	c Pipe b Batty	129	lbw b Mason	4
GJ Muchall	c Pipe b Sheriyar	38	c Batty b Wigley	1
DM Benkenstein	lbw b Vaas	38	not out	1
N Peng	lbw b Mason	24		
GR Breese	lbw b Wigley	10		
*P Mustard	b Vaas	3		
LE Plunkett	b Wigley	0		
M Davies	c Pipe b Wigley	1		
SJ Harmison	not out	0		
Extras	lb 4	4	lb 2	2
	(105.5 overs)	286	(3 wkts 13 overs)	32

Bowling
Vaas 26-6-65-3. Mason 29-12-65-1. Wigley 10.5-1-39-3. Sheriyar 20-5-62-2. Batty 20-6-51-1.
Mason 5-1-12-2. Wigley 6-0-15-1. Sheriyar 2-0-3-0.
Fall of Wickets: 1-4, 2-107, 3-187, 4-223, 5-271, 6-275, 7-282, 8-282, 9-286
1-20, 2-24, 3-27

Durham won by 7 wickets – Durham (19 pts), Worcestershire (3 pts)

YORKSHIRE v. SOMERSET – at Headingley

YORKSHIRE	First Innings	
MJ Wood	c Turner b McLean	95
PA Jaques	b Johnson	27
A McGrath	c sub b Laraman	2
MJ Lumb	lbw b Caddick	21
IJ Harvey	not out	209
C White (capt)	c Trescothick b McLean	0
*I Dawood	c Burns b McLean	5
RKJ Dawson	c Blackwell b Caddick	21
TT Bresnan	b Laraman	74
MJ Hoggard	c McLean b Laraman	4
GJ Kruis	not out	16
Extras	b 3, lb 7, w 3, nb 14	27
	(9 wkts dec 122 overs)	501

Bowling
Caddick 22-3-95-2. McLean 18-3-107-3. Johnson 25-5-92-1. Laraman 30-3-100-3. Blackwell 20-4-70-0. Jayasuriya 7-0-27-0.
Fall of Wickets: 1-63, 2-82, 3-130, 4-177, 5-177, 6-189, 7-227, 8-465, 9-483

SOMERSET	First Innings		Second Innings	
ST Jayasuriya	c White b Hoggard	0	(2) c Dawson b Kruis	7
JD Francis	c Wood b Kruis	11	(1) not out	125
M Burns	c Dawood b Bresnan	23	c Dawood b Kruis	0
JC Hildreth	c Kruis b Bresnan	18	lbw b Kruis	0
ID Blackwell	c Dawood b Kruis	33	c Dawood b White	21
AW Laraman	c Wood b Kruis	21	c Lumb b Dawson	53
*RJ Turner	c Dawood b Bresnan	0	c Dawood b Harvey	24
RL Johnson	c McGrath b Harvey	15	b Dawson	11
AR Caddick	not out	23	c Jaques b Hoggard	13
NAM McLean	c White b Harvey	18	c Wood b Hoggard	0
ME T'cothick (capt)	absent		absent	
Extras	b 2, lb 16, nb 2	20	lb 9, nb 12	21
	(9 wkts 48.5 overs)	182	(9 wkts 101 overs)	275

Bowling
Hoggard 14-4-49-1. Kruis 12-3-39-3. Bresnan 13-2-50-3. McGrath 5-1-12-0. Harvey 4.5-1-14-2.
Hoggard 23-9-50-2. Kruis 14-4-41-3. Bresnan 16-4-46-0. White 5-1-21-1. Dawson 27-6-68-2. Harvey 13-5-29-1. Lumb 3-1-11-0.
Fall of Wickets: 1-0, 2-24, 3-59, 4-68, 5-102, 6-117, 7-127, 8-153, 9-182
1-10, 2-10, 3-10, 4-37, 5-167, 6-213, 7-243, 8-275, 9-275

Yorkshire won by an innings and 44 runs – Yorkshire (22 pts), Somerset (3 pts)

NORTHAMPTONSHIRE v. LEICESTERSHIRE – at Northampton

NORTHANTS	First Innings		Second Innings	
ML Love	lbw b Willoughby	50	not out	112
BM Shafayat	lbw b Gibson	59	c Nixon b DeFreitas	14
U Afzaal	c Nixon b DeFreitas	11	c Nixon b Gibson	5
DJG Sales (capt)	c Maunders b DeFreitas	113	c Habib b DeFreitas	79
RA White	c Nixon b DeFreitas	95	not out	22
*GL Brophy	not out	52		
DG Wright	lbw b DeFreitas	8		
BJ Phillips	not out	22		
J Louw				
PS Jones				
JF Brown				
Extras	b 2, lb 15, w 2, nb 4	23	lb 5, w 1	6
	(6 wkts dec 111 overs)	433	(3 wkts dec 49 overs)	238

Bowling
Willoughby 30-9-79-1. Gibson 31-4-123-1. DeFreitas 23-4-76-4. Henderson 19-4-86-0. Maddy 4-0-30-0. Snape 3-0-16-0. Maunders 1-0-6-0.
Willoughby 10-1-49-0. Gibson 13-2-48-1. DeFreitas 16-2-67-2. Henderson 10-0-69-0.
Fall of Wickets: 1-100, 2-132, 3-136, 4-328, 5-349, 6-361
1-50, 2-57, 3-172

LEICESTERSHIRE	First Innings		Second Innings	
DDJ Robinson	c Sales b Jones	100	retired hurt	6
DL Maddy	c Brophy b Jones	45	lbw b Jones	11
JK Maunders	c Brophy b Jones	5	lbw b Brown	14
A Habib	c Love b Brown	38	b Jones	2
HD Ackerman (capt)	lbw b Louw	16	not out	50
JN Snape	lbw b Afzaal	28	c Brophy b Phillips	31
*PA Nixon	b Wright	16	not out	1
OD Gibson	c Wright b Jones	18		
PAJ DeFreitas	c Brophy b Louw	19		
CW Henderson	not out	30		
CM Willoughby	c Sales b Phillips	9		
Extras	b 9, lb 2, nb 4	15		0
	(107.2 overs)	339	(4 wkts 47 overs)	115

Bowling
Wright 27-9-68-1. Louw 27-9-85-2. Jones 20-3-74-4. Brown 16-3-58-1. Phillips 15.2-6-33-1. Afzaal 2-0-10-1.
Wright 8-2-17-0. Louw 12-3-31-0. Jones 8-3-16-2. Brown 11-3-34-1. Phillips 5-1-12-1. Shafayat 3-0-5-0.
Fall of Wickets: 1-135, 2-143, 3-168, 4-198, 5-220, 6-262, 7-263, 8-286, 9-306
1-31, 2-31, 3-41, 4-110

Match drawn – Northamptonshire (12 pts), Leicestershire (9 pts)

White, both produced within the county system, played leading roles in Northants' first innings drive to 433 for 6 declared and, if bad weather had not caused the loss of almost 80 overs on day one, the home side might well have been able to force victory here. Darren Robinson's 100 enabled Leicestershire to build a solid enough first innings reply, but Martin Love's unbeaten 112 and a brutal 79 off 68 balls by Sales – including a six and 15 fours – at least enabled Northants to make a token effort to embarrass Leicestershire on the final afternoon. They lost four wickets, but Hylton Ackerman's 50 not out meant the visitors were ultimately able to negotiate their 47 overs in reasonable comfort.

Round Three: 27–30 April 2005

Division One

Warwickshire, having escaped with a draw against Kent in their previous match, stepped up the defence of their title by seeing off Middlesex by seven wickets at Edgbaston. The win, moreover, was built around the brilliance of batting starlet Ian Bell and the mature, all-round skills of Ashley Giles.

Bell's first innings 231, with 29 fours, was a masterpiece and it rescued Warwickshire from an unsteady start in reply to Middlesex's first-innings 298. Alex Loudon joined Bell in a fourth-wicket stand of 88, but it was Giles who provided the telling support. Coming in at 186 for 6, the England left-arm spinner scored 62 to help Bell to add a match-turning 167 for the seventh wicket. In the end, thanks to Bell's epic, Warwickshire won themselves a lead of 132. By the end of day three, Giles had followed up by taking two top-order wickets as the visitors struggled to 137 for three. Ed Joyce, in a rich vein of form, added a skilful 63 to his first innings 92, and the left-hander coped admirably with Giles bowling testingly into the rough outside his off stump. But, with Loudon supporting him ably with his off spin, Giles was good enough to finish with 6 for 91 – from 42.2 overs – and Middlesex's demise to 246 all out left Warwickshire with a simple win target. All that remained was for Bell – who else? – to guide them home with an unbeaten 47 that took his tally of first-class runs in April to a record 480.

Nottinghamshire buried Sussex beneath a deluge of runs at Trent Bridge, finally dismissing the 2003 champions for just 159 on the final day to emerge as ten-wicket winners. Only 36.3 overs were possible on day one, and Sussex reached 379 in their first innings thanks to half-centuries from Mike Yardy, Matt Prior

Young master: Ian Bell, whose brilliant 231 helped Warwickshire to beat Middlesex.

and Robin Martin-Jenkins. But Notts swept past that total with Jason Gallian and Stephen Fleming – the new captain and the man he had replaced – both hitting superb hundreds. Gallian struck a six and 26 fours but was eventually run out, cruelly, on 199. By then, however, David Hussey was adding further quick runs following Fleming's classy 111, and a punchy half-century from Chris Read enabled Notts to go past 500.

Ryan Sidebottom did much of the early damage in the Sussex second innings, before Graeme Swann continued the visitors' decline. Murray Goodwin and Martin-Jenkins were the only Sussex batsmen to shape up second time around, leaving Notts with a simple victory target.

Mark Wallace, the wicketkeeper, fought an almost lone hand of resistance for Glamorgan as Jimmy Ormond and Mark Ramprakash inspired Surrey to a confidence-boosting five-wicket win in Cardiff. The 23-year-old Wallace twice hooked Rikki Clarke for six as he reached an unbeaten 107-ball 86 in Glamorgan's first innings, but Ramprakash kept Surrey in contention with the 75th first-class hundred of his career. During his innings, Ramprakash uppercut a ball from Simon Jones for four to become only the second current player (after Graeme Hick) to reach 25,000 first-class runs. But it was Ormond's second innings 7 for 63, a career-best, which proved to be the difference between the two sides. Wallace did his best again for Glamorgan, hitting 55, but Ormond's fine display meant that Surrey required only 176 when they batted again. Scott Newman's aggressive 41-ball 48 gave them a flying start, but it was Ramprakash who steered his side past the winning post with a calm 68 not out.

In the end the loss of 72 overs to the weather on the first day, plus more time on subsequent days, condemned an attritional contest at Bristol to a draw. Jon Lewis and Simon Cook were the most impressive seamers on display but the best individual performances of the match came early on, when the ball was jagging around off the seam.

Kent, put in, lost two early wickets but Rob Key strengthened his England claims with an innings of 164. Supported by Matthew Walker in a stand worth 242 for the third wicket, Key made the most of being dropped early on the second day by going to successive fifties from 155, 94 and 58 balls. That statistic, alone, demonstrates the worth of his innings – and how batting became easier as the pitch dried out. Walker's 109 was also a fine effort, emphasised by the way Kent's innings fell away from 260 for 2 to 359 all out. Chris Taylor battled to a determined 66

Round Three: 27–30 April 2005 Division One

WARWICKSHIRE v. MIDDLESEX – at Edgbaston

MIDDLESEX	First Innings		Second Innings	
AJ Strauss	c Frost b Pretorius	13	c Trott b Loudon	37
BL Hutton (capt)	c Trott b Carter	7	b Giles	12
ET Smith	c Trott b Streak	0	lbw b Giles	30
OA Shah	c Frost b Brown	19	b Giles	54
EC Joyce	c Frost b Loudon	92	c Brown b Giles	63
SB Styris	c Bell b Pretorius	53	c Powell b Giles	6
PN Weekes	c Trott b Giles	11	c Powell b Loudon	14
*BJM Scott	lbw b Streak	37	c Frost b Brown	5
A Richardson	c Brown b Carter	10	not out	10
PM Hutchison	not out	26	c Brown b Loudon	2
M Hayward	b Carter	6	c Streak b Giles	1
Extras	b 2, lb 18, nb 4	24	b 6, lb 2, w 2, nb 2	12
	(87.1 overs)	298	(102.2 overs)	246

Bowling
Streak 18-6-64-2. Pretorius 15-1-60-2. Brown 15-5-40-1. Carter 13.1-6-37-3. Bell 1-0-6-0. Giles 12-3-31-1. Loudon 13-3-40-1.
Streak 11-3-18-0. Pretorius 12-1-35-0. Brown 13-2-27-1. Giles 42.2-9-91-6. Loudon 24-2-67-3.
Fall of Wickets: 1-21, 2-22, 3-44, 4-56, 5-141, 6-158, 7-253, 8-253, 9-280
1-47, 2-59, 3-102, 4-169, 5-179, 6-206, 7-224, 8-238, 9-245

WARWICKSHIRE	First Innings		Second Innings	
NV Knight (capt)	c Scott b Richardson	3	c & b Hutchison	29
MJ Powell	b Richardson	7	b Hayward	5
IR Bell	run out	231	not out	47
IJL Trott	lbw b Richardson	21	c Scott b Hutchison	11
AGR Loudon	c Hutton b Weekes	39	not out	8
DR Brown	c Scott b Hayward	12		
*T Frost	c Shah b Hayward	8		
AF Giles	c Hutchison b Richardson	62		
HH Streak	c Hutton b Weekes	17		
NM Carter	c Smith b Hutchison	7		
D Pretorius	not out	0		
Extras	b 5, lb 8, nb 10	23	b 1, lb 2, nb 12	15
	(118.4 overs)	430	(3 wkts 31.2 overs)	115

Bowling
Hayward 21-3-73-2. Richardson 27-2-87-4. Hutchison 17.4-0-83-1. Styris 17-2-62-0. Weekes 28-2-74-2. Hutton 8-1-38-0.
Richardson 7-4-11-0. Hayward 4-1-11-1. Hutton 1-0-4-0. Weekes 11-2-40-0. Hutchison 7-1-43-2. Shah 1.2-0-3-0.
Fall of Wickets: 1-10, 2-11, 3-51, 4-139, 5-168, 6-186, 7-353, 8-409, 9-430
1-16, 2-57, 3-83

Warwickshire won by 7 wickets –
Warwickshire (22 pts), Middlesex (5 pts)

NOTTINGHAMSHIRE v. SUSSEX – at Trent Bridge

SUSSEX	First Innings		Second Innings	
IJ Ward	lbw b Ealham	21	b Sidebottom	22
RR Montgomerie	c Fleming b Sidebottom	4	c Gallian b Smith	1
MH Yardy	c Read b Ealham	54	c Read b Smith	0
MW Goodwin	c Read b Smith	33	b Franks	41
CJ Adams (capt)	b Sidebottom	46	st Read b Swann	3
*MJ Prior	c Fleming b Franks	65	b Swann	0
RSC M-Jenkins	not out	66	c Read b Sidebottom	49
JJ van der Wath	c Read b Ealham	20	c Read b Swann	19
Mushtaq Ahmed	c Swann b Franks	12	c Fleming b Sidebottom	16
RJ Kirtley	c Singh b Swann	7	not out	0
JD Lewry	b Smith	17	c Hussey b Sidebottom	0
Extras	b 7, lb 12, w 9, nb 6	34	b 3, lb 3, nb 2	8
	(123.3 overs)	379	(53.4 overs)	159

Bowling
Smith 27.3-11-83-2. Sidebottom 30-12-73-2. Ealham 24-5-69-3. Franks 19-4-84-2. Swann 23-5-51-1.
Smith 14-4-56-2. Sidebottom 8.4-4-15-4. Swann 22-5-51-3. Franks 5-1-19-1. Ealham 4-0-12-0.
Fall of Wickets: 1-16, 2-38, 3-116, 4-143, 5-247, 6-250, 7-318, 8-336, 9-345
1-9, 2-11, 3-43, 4-56, 5-64, 6-72, 7-129, 8-158, 9-159

NOTTS	First Innings		Second Innings	
DJ Bicknell	lbw b Lewry	7	not out	17
JER Gallian	run out	199	not out	13
A Singh	lbw b van der Wath	7		
SP Fleming (capt)	run out	111		
DJ Hussey	b van der Wath	89		
*CMW Read	c Prior b Kirtley	51		
MA Ealham	b Mushtaq Ahmed	5		
GP Swann	not out	7		
PJ Franks	c Prior b Kirtley	8		
RJ Sidebottom				
GJ Smith				
Extras	b 10, lb 7, nb 8	25		0
	(8 wkts dec 124.4 overs)	509	(0 wkts 5.5 overs)	30

Bowling
Kirtley 24.4-2-96-2. Lewry 28-2-99-1. van der Wath 22-5-113-2. Mushtaq Ahmed 29-1-131-1. Martin-Jenkins 21-4-53-0.
Kirtley 3-0-15-0. Lewry 2.5-0-15-0.
Fall of Wickets: 1-33, 2-56, 3-242, 4-430, 5-447, 6-488, 7-499, 8-509

Nottinghamshire won by 10 wickets –
Nottinghamshire (22 pts), Sussex (6 pts)

GLAMORGAN v. SURREY – at Cardiff

GLAMORGAN	First Innings		Second Innings	
MTG Elliott	c Ramprakash b Ormond	0	c Batty b Akram	4
IJ Thomas	c Clarke b Doshi	29	c Batty b Ormond	1
DL Hemp	b Akram	60	c Clarke b Akram	24
MJ Powell	lbw b Murtagh	11	c Batty b Ormond	22
J Hughes	c Batty b Murtagh	0	c Batty b Ormond	0
*MA Wallace	c Clinton b Ormond	96	c Batty b Doshi	55
RDB Croft (capt)	c Batty b Akram	2	b Ormond	2
SD Thomas	c Ramprakash b Akram	15	c sub b Ormond	10
AG Wharf	b Akram	1	c Batty b Ormond	34
DS Harrison	c Batty b Clarke	3	not out	1
SP Jones	not out	7	c Ramprakash b Ormond	0
Extras	b 1, lb 3, nb 22	26	b 11, w 3, nb 6	20
	(64.1 overs)	250	(46.4 overs)	173

Bowling
Ormond 19.1-4-62-2. Akram 16.3-3-67-4. Murtagh 8.3-3-32-2. Clarke 13-2-64-1. Doshi 7-2-21-1.
Ormond 18.4-4-63-7. Akram 7.5-0-62-2. Clarke 4-1-14-0. Doshi 12-4-17-1. Clinton 4.1-0-6-0.
Fall of Wickets: 1-0, 2-60, 3-96, 4-100, 5-115, 6-125, 7-169, 8-182, 9-189
1-5, 2-9, 3-64, 4-64, 5-70, 6-75, 7-87, 8-167, 9-173

SURREY	First Innings		Second Innings	
SA Newman	b Wharf	44	lbw b Croft	48
RS Clinton	c Thomas IJ b Jones	7	c Elliott b Jones	1
MR R'kash (capt)	c Elliott b Jones	107	not out	68
GP Thorpe	b Thomas SD	5	lbw b Croft	5
*JN Batty	c Wallace b Wharf	18	c Wallace b Wharf	9
ND Doshi	b Thomas SD	0		
AD Brown	c & b Harrison	8	(6) c Powell b Wharf	34
R Clarke	b Thomas SD	35	(7) not out	5
J Ormond	b Thomas SD	0		
TJ Murtagh	not out	5		
M Akram	b Jones	0		
Extras	b 1, lb 12, nb 6	19	b 1, lb 5, nb 2	8
	(74.4 overs)	248	(5 wkts 36 overs)	178

Bowling
Jones 18.4-3-62-3. Harrison 17-5-52-1. Thomas SD 14-2-63-3. Wharf 19-4-52-3. Croft 6-3-6-0.
Jones 9-2-42-1. Harrison 7-0-31-0. Wharf 8-0-52-2. Croft 11-3-41-2. Thomas SD 1-0-6-0.
Fall of Wickets: 1-25, 2-66, 3-99, 4-162, 5-166, 6-195, 7-243, 8-243, 9-243
1-13, 2-63, 3-97, 4-114, 5-160

Surrey won by 5 wickets – Glamorgan (5 pts), Surrey (18 pts)

GLOUCESTERSHIRE v. KENT – at Bristol

KENT	First Innings		Second Innings	
DP Fulton (capt)	c Hancock b Lewis	2	c Spearman b Kirby	8
RWT Key	c Adshead b Kirby	164	c Lewis b Kirby	18
M van Jaarsveld	c Hancock b Lewis	2	b Averis	32
MJ Walker	c Adshead b Kirby	109	b Taylor	56
DI Stevens	run out	5	b Hancock	54
*GO Jones	lbw b Chandana	2	not out	36
MJ Dennington	b Lewis	13	not out	4
SJ Cook	not out	22		
MM Patel	c Chandana b Lewis	2		
A Khan	c Kadeer Ali b Chandana	4		
MJ Saggers	c Taylor b Lewis	6		
Extras	b 6, lb 7, w 1, nb 14	28	b 5, lb 7, w 1, nb 8	21
	(133 overs)	359	(5 wkts 68 overs)	229

Bowling
Lewis 34-9-57-5. Kirby 26-6-73-2. Averis 24-10-66-0. Gidman 11-1-45-0. Chandana 38-4-105-2.
Lewis 10-2-27-0. Kirby 10-1-38-2. Chandana 17-5-44-0. Averis 7-1-24-1. Taylor 8-1-26-1. Gidman 6-0-29-0. Hancock 5-2-14-1. Kadeer Ali 5-0-15-0.
Fall of Wickets: 1-2, 2-18, 3-260, 4-291, 5-295, 6-312, 7-341, 8-345, 9-350
1-30, 2-35, 3-95, 4-146, 5-224

GLOS	First Innings	
CM Spearman	c Jones b Dennington	35
WPC Weston	c van Jaarsveld b Cook	19
Kadeer Ali	c Fulton b Cook	3
CG Taylor (capt)	c Fulton b Patel	66
THC Hancock	c Jones b Cook	23
APR Gidman	c Fulton b Khan	43
*SJ Adshead	c Key b Patel	7
UDU Chandana	c van Jaarsveld b Khan	0
JMM Averis	lbw b Cook	22
J Lewis	c Patel b Cook	18
SP Kirby	not out	0
Extras	b 2, lb 5, w 5	12
	(108.1 overs)	248

Bowling
Saggers 19-7-32-0. Khan 20-7-55-2. Cook 25.1-9-57-5. Dennington 15-4-40-1. Patel 27-3-57-2. Stevens 2-2-0-0.
Fall of Wickets: 1-33, 2-45, 3-61, 4-129, 5-187, 6-207, 7-208, 8-211, 9-247

Match drawn – Gloucestershire (8 pts),
Kent (11 pts)

when Gloucestershire replied, and the last chance of a positive result disappeared when the home side – on 208 for 7 overnight – saved the follow-on in the second over of a rain-shortened final day.

Division Two

Andre Adams, Essex's New Zealander, bowled a hat-trick at Taunton as Somerset were beaten by nine wickets by Ronnie Irani's impressive-looking side. Adams' memorable triple strike came late on the third day, and was decisive in making sure that Essex would prevail. His victims were all top-order players, too, with Mike Burns being caught behind and both Sanath Jayasuriya and James Hildreth falling lbw. When Adams followed this up by having Ian Blackwell caught off the penultimate ball of the day, to give him overnight figures of 4 for 31 from 7.5 overs, Somerset were down and out at 128 for 5. John Francis, Rob Turner and the tail fought hard on the last day, hauling Somerset up to 313, but the result was never in doubt once Adams had produced his hat-trick and the weather held.

Somerset's first innings had been wrecked by the other mainline Essex seamers – Graham Napier, Alex Tudor and Darren Gough – and then three of the best young English batsmen in the country were responsible for giving the visitors a sizeable first-

A career-best 161 by Bilal Shafayat featured in a Northamptonshire opening stand of 297 against Derbyshire with Martin Love.

Round Three: 27–30 April 2005 Division Two

SOMERSET v. ESSEX – at Taunton

SOMERSET	First Innings		Second Innings	
ME Tcothick (capt)	c Adams b Tudor	4	c Middlebrook b Napier	18
JD Francis	lbw b Gough	35	c Irani b Middlebrook	64
M Burns	c Foster b Tudor	8	c Foster b Adams	3
ST Jayasuriya	c Foster b Napier	31	lbw b Adams	0
JC Hildreth	lbw b Napier	22	lbw b Adams	0
ID Blackwell	lbw b Napier	0	c Foster b Adams	38
AW Laraman	lbw b Gough	43	c Flower b Middlebrook	8
*RJ Turner	c Foster b Adams	20	not out	68
RL Johnson	c Tudor b Adams	18	c Foster b Gough	24
AR Caddick	c Napier b Gough	4	c Jefferson b Middlebrook	30
NAM McLean	not out	0	c Irani b Middlebrook	40
Extras	lb 3, nb 2	5	lb 5, w 1, nb 14	20
	(60.3 overs)	190	(87.5 overs)	313

Bowling
Gough 18.3-5-62-3. Tudor 18-6-48-2. Adams 15-4-52-2. Napier 9-2-25-3.
Gough 17-1-61-1. Tudor 9-2-24-0. Napier 16-2-82-1. Adams 20-6-67-4.
Middlebrook 22.5-5-60-4. Bopara 3-0-14-0.
Fall of Wickets: 1-5, 2-27, 3-60, 4-90, 5-90, 6-119, 7-164, 8-168, 9-190
1-57, 2-65, 3-65, 4-65, 5-128, 6-142, 7-151, 8-180, 9-243

ESSEX	First Innings		Second Innings	
WI Jefferson	c Trescothick b Caddick	11	not out	23
AN Cook	b Johnson	111	c Hildreth b McLean	25
RS Bopara	c Turner b Johnson	71	not out	22
A Flower	c Hildreth b Johnson	2		
RC Irani (capt)	c Francis b McLean	32		
*JS Foster	not out	78		
JD Middlebrook	c Hildreth b Caddick	26		
GR Napier	c Turner b Caddick	0		
AJ Tudor	run out	57		
AR Adams				
D Gough				
Extras	b 1, lb 14, w 2, nb 22	39	w 2, nb 6	8
	(8 wkts dec 126.5 overs)	427	(1 wkt 18.1 overs)	78

Bowling
Caddick 33.5-4-110-3. Johnson 30-6-98-3. McLean 13-3-50-1. Laraman 17-3-54-0.
Burns 6-0-31-0. Blackwell 22-6-51-0. Jayasuriya 5-0-18-0.
Johnson 4-1-17-0. McLean 7-0-39-1. Blackwell 6-2-12-0. Jayasuriya 1.1-0-10-0.
Fall of Wickets: 1-18, 2-199, 3-209, 4-224, 5-278, 6-320, 7-320, 8-427
1-39

*Essex won by 9 wickets – Somerset (2 pts),
Essex (22 pts)*

WORCESTERSHIRE v. LANCASHIRE – at Worcester

LANCASHIRE	First Innings		Second Innings	
MJ Chilton (capt)	c Pipe b Mason	26	b Mason	2
IJ Sutcliffe	b Vaas	14	lbw b Kabir Ali	21
MB Loye	c Hick b Kabir Ali	19	lbw b Vaas	40
SG Law	c Pipe b Kabir Ali	28	c Pipe b Mason	83
A Flintoff	c Hick b Kabir Ali	0	c Pipe b Moore	83
KW Hogg	c Solanki b Wigley	9	c Solanki b Vaas	0
*WK Hegg	not out	69	run out	29
DG Cork	lbw b Vaas	11	b Mason	57
SI Mahmood	b Vaas	1	c Pipe b Vaas	29
JM Anderson	lbw b Mason	18	not out	10
M Muralitharan	c Vaas b Mason	0	c Smith b Mason	0
Extras	lb 1	1	b 16, lb 1, nb 6	23
	(65 overs)	196	(95.3 overs)	377

Bowling
Vaas 22-8-49-3. Kabir Ali 17-3-70-3. Mason 14-6-22-3. Wigley 12-3-54-1.
Vaas 32-7-110-3. Mason 31.3-6-107-4. Batty 17-2-84-0. Kabir Ali 6-1-23-1.
Moore 9-0-36-1.
Fall of Wickets: 1-27, 2-50, 3-81, 4-81, 5-96, 6-97, 7-122, 8-130, 9-196
1-3, 2-52, 3-82, 4-221, 5-222, 6-264, 7-281, 8-359, 9-377

WORCS	First Innings		Second Innings	
SD Peters	c Hegg b Muralitharan	27	c Hegg b Anderson	0
SC Moore	lbw b Cork	0	lbw b Cork	1
GA Hick	c Muralitharan b Hogg	176	c Muralitharan b Cork	57
BF Smith	c & b Muralitharan	0	lbw b Cork	37
VS Solanki (capt)	c Flintoff b Cork	4	c Sutcliffe b Muralitharan	52
GJ Batty	lbw b Muralitharan	13	(7) c Law b Anderson	14
*DJ Pipe	c Hogg b Muralitharan	9	(8) c Flintoff b Muralitharan	7
WPUJC Vaas	lbw b Cork	22	(6) lbw b Cork	3
Kabir Ali	c Hogg b Muralitharan	21	c Flintoff b Muralitharan	2
MS Mason	b Anderson	18	not out	0
DH Wigley	not out	2	absent hurt	
Extras	lb 8, nb 6	14	b 4, lb 6, w 6, nb 2	18
	(76.2 overs)	306	(9 wkts 60.3 overs)	191

Bowling
Anderson 18-3-102-1. Cork 20-3-64-3. Muralitharan 26-5-69-5. Mahmood 4-0-35-0.
Hogg 8.2-1-28-1.
Anderson 12-3-52-2. Cork 16-4-51-4. Hogg 14-4-45-0. Muralitharan 18.3-5-33-3.
Fall of Wickets: 1-8, 2-66, 3-66, 4-71, 5-100, 6-130, 7-194, 8-227, 9-257
1-0, 2-24, 3-103, 4-116, 5-128, 6-178, 7-178, 8-186, 9-191

*Lancashire won by 76 runs –
Worcestershire (6 pts), Lancashire (17 pts)*

DERBYSHIRE v. NORTHAMPTONSHIRE – at Derby

NORTHANTS	First Innings	
ML Love	b Welch	168
BM Shafayat	lbw b Moss	161
U Afzaal	c Sutton b Walker	2
DJG Sales (capt)	c Welch b Hunter	39
RA White	not out	35
*GL Brophy	c Di Venuto b Welch	0
DG Wright	lbw b Welch	8
BJ Phillips	c Di Venuto b Welch	21
J Louw	not out	4
PS Jones		
JF Brown		
Extras	lb 7, nb 6	13
	(7 wkts dec 122 overs)	451

Bowling
Hunter 24-4-90-1. Dean 27-5-74-0. Walker 17-2-78-1. Welch 22-3-91-4.
Moss 22-7-63-1. Botha 8-1-41-0. Hassan Adnan 2-0-7-0.
Fall of Wickets: 1-297, 2-314, 3-373, 4-386, 5-386, 6-396, 7-446

DERBYSHIRE	First Innings		Second Innings	
MJ Di Venuto	c Sales b Phillips	25	(2) not out	55
SD Stubbings	c Sales b Louw	3	(1) not out	58
J Moss	b Louw	33		
Hassan Adnan	lbw b Jones	44		
CWG Bassano	lbw b Louw	76		
KJ Dean	lbw b Louw	4		
*LD Sutton (capt)	c Brophy b Wright	3		
G Welch	c Brophy b Phillips	8		
AG Botha	lbw b Louw	36		
ID Hunter	c Love b Louw	0		
NGE Walker	not out	0		
Extras	b 2, lb 7	9	b 2, lb 2, nb 2	6
	(109.5 overs)	241	(0 wkts 50 overs)	119

Bowling
Wright 29-10-57-1. Louw 30.5-10-71-6. Jones 13-3-39-1. Phillips 20-7-45-2.
Brown 17-8-20-0.
Wright 8-5-16-0. Louw 9-0-30-0. Jones 12-3-30-0. Phillips 5-3-2-0.
Brown 11-2-33-0. Afzaal 5-2-4-0.
Fall of Wickets: 1-6, 2-42, 3-85, 4-128, 5-145, 6-162, 7-175, 8-236, 9-236

*Match drawn – Derbyshire (7 pts),
Northamptonshire (12 pts)*

innings lead. Alastair Cook, the 20-year-old left-hander rated by Keith Fletcher as the best young batsman he has yet seen, scored 111 from 164 balls, with 14 boundaries, while Ravi Bopara – a week away from his 20th birthday – hit a maiden championship 50 and went on to 71. James Foster, just 25 and surely a Test wicketkeeper again in the future, was then joined by Tudor in an unbroken ninth-wicket stand of 107 that set up a declaration at 427 for 8.

Lancashire took advantage of an unfortunate injury and illness blight on the Worcestershire line-up to stage a fine recovery that brought them victory in the end by 76 runs at New Road. Things looked bleak for Lancashire, initially, with Graeme Hick taking their much-vaunted, international-class attack apart with a blistering 176 that included eight sixes and 20 fours. It was his 127th first-class ton and 97th for Worcestershire, and it gave his county a massive advantage as they tried to build a match-winning lead after bowling out Lancashire for 196 on day one. But no one could stay with Hick for very long and, with the next best score being 27, Worcestershire's lead had been held at 110. Worse, fast bowler Dave Wigley had broken a finger trying to fend off an accidental James Anderson beamer and the home side's attack was further depleted by Kabir Ali falling ill with tonsillitis and Matt Mason struggling with a hamstring problem.

Andy Flintoff, who had fallen for a fifth-ball duck on the opening day in his first first-class innings since the Centurion Test in January, was just the man to take a heavy toll on a wounded opponent. So it proved as the England all-rounder thumped 83 off 101 balls while dominating a fourth-wicket stand of 139 with Stuart Law. Flintoff straight drove Gareth Batty's first ball for six and, in all, plundered 31 from the off-spinner's opening three overs. Dominic Cork and Sajid Mahmood then put on 78 for the eighth wicket, as Worcestershire struggled to maintain any sort of control and, in the end, they found themselves needing a tricky 268 to win. Much depended, of course, on Hick, who was already 36 not out when they began the last day at 58 for 2. But when Hick spooned a catch to mid-on after making 57 off 92 balls, only some spirited resistance from Vikram Solanki lay between Lancashire and a 17-point win.

Bad weather allowed Derbyshire to escape with a draw against Northamptonshire at Derby, with no play at all being possible on the last day. At least Derbyshire had by that time made a better fist of their second innings, with Steve Stubbings and Michael Di Venuto having steered them to 119 without loss following a first-innings slide to 241 in which only Chris Bassano made significant headway against the Northants attack. The visitors' initial 451 for 7 declared, a big enough total to have condemned Derbyshire to following on, was based on a superlative opening stand of 297 between Martin Love and Bilal Shafayat. The pair had scored 292 of those runs on a first day shortened by 21 overs by a heavy downpour, which came one ball after Derbyshire's £200,000 floodlights had been turned on to combat poor light! Shafayat, who made 72 on his debut for Nottinghamshire at the age of 16 and was that county's youngest first-class century-maker at 18 in 2002, went on to a career-best 161, while Love finished with 168.

Round Four: 6–9 May 2005

Division One

Ball-tampering incidents scarred this round of matches in the first division. Unhappily, the names of several players were besmirched by events at The Oval and Cardiff and, in the case of Surrey, a great club found its own famous name being dragged through the dirt as a result of the actions of (allegedly) a small number of players.

Surrey were coming off distinctly second best against Nottinghamshire, in a game they eventually lost by an innings and 71 runs, when umpires Mervyn Kitchen and Nigel Llong reported them for illegally altering the condition of the ball, following an earlier warning. It was a transgression that spoke of either desperation or downright stupidity, and probably both. The first official warning from Kitchen and Llong came 35 overs into a Notts first innings reply to Surrey's own inadequate total of 217. Clearly unheeded, this was followed just before close of play on that first evening – sometime between the 47th and 52nd overs – by a second guilty verdict.

As a result, five penalty runs were added to the Notts score overnight and – after Darren Bicknell and Jason Gallian had built the foundations with an opening partnership of 178, Notts proceeded to amass a huge score on day two. Gallian, on 83 overnight, reached 141 before leaving the stage clear for Stephen Fleming, with a commanding 238 from 236 balls, and David Hussey to crush a humiliated Surrey team beneath the sheer weight of their runs. Fleming struck five sixes and 28 fours and, on the third morning, Mark Ealham and Paul Franks added a further unbroken stand of 72 for the eighth wicket before, at last, Notts declared on 692 for 7. Only Mark Ramprakash, who as stand-in captain found himself having to take responsibility for the ball-tampering affair, showed any sort of fight for survival – hitting 107 with three sixes and 12 fours to haul Surrey up to 404 in their second innings.

At Cardiff, on day three of Gloucestershire's seven-wicket win against Glamorgan, there was the strange but unedifying sight of the Welsh county's coach, John Derrick, walking out on to the field to complain about the alleged actions of fast bowler Steve Kirby. The Gloucestershire paceman had trotted into the car park to fetch the ball after David Hemp had hit one of three sixes in an explosive second innings of 57 that also contained seven boundaries. Derrick complained to the umpires, claiming that Kirby had deliberately roughed up the ball on the concrete before throwing it back. Derrick later contacted the ECB to voice his grievance, but the umpires confirmed that they had been happy with the condition of the ball. Kirby, nevertheless, was some weeks later found guilty of an inappropriate action and received a suspended sentence.

Glamorgan, meanwhile, could not recover in the game despite a fine century stand between Hemp and Matthew Elliott as they reached 345 in their second innings. The damage had been done first time around, with Alex Gidman's medium pace accounting for four wickets and three of Glamorgan's top five falling for ducks. A total of 239 meant

The storm before the storm: Chris Taylor hit 176 from only 185 balls in Gloucestershire's controversial clash with Glamorgan at Cardiff.

Round Four: 6–9 May 2005 Division One

SURREY v. NOTTINGHAMSHIRE – at The Oval

SURREY	First Innings		Second Innings	
SA Newman	c Sidebottom b Ealham	44	c Read b Sidebottom	17
*JN Batty	c Gallian b Franks	16	b Ealham	27
MR R'kash (capt)	c Read b Franks	0	b Swann	107
GP Thorpe	c Hussey b Ealham	9	b Ealham	0
AD Brown	lbw b Sidebottom	9	b Swann	21
R Clarke	c Hussey b Ealham	14	c Read b Swann	14
JGE Benning	lbw b Sidebottom	56	lbw b Franks	20
MP Bicknell	c Read b Swann	28	lbw b Ealham	59
J Ormond	run out	15	c Read b Swann	35
ND Doshi	c Read b Ealham	0	b Sidebottom	33
M Akram	not out	4	not out	27
Extras	b 2, lb 7, w 7, nb 6	22	b 9, lb 9, w 9, nb 12, p 5	44
	(49.1 overs)	**217**	(141.1 overs)	**404**

Bowling
Sidebottom 19-3-78-2. Franks 9-1-37-2. Ealham 14-4-53-4. Swann 7.1-1-40-1.
Sidebottom 37-12-82-2. Franks 18-3-72-1. Ealham 34-9-81-3. Patel 17-2-43-0.
Swann 33.1-8-94-4. Bicknell 1-0-2-0. Hussey 1-0-7-0.
Fall of Wickets: 1-58, 2-70, 3-70, 4-80, 5-95, 6-114, 7-190, 8-213, 9-213
1-42, 2-69, 3-69, 4-98, 5-150, 6-195, 7-296, 8-296, 9-353

NOTTS	First Innings	
DJ Bicknell	b Clarke	91
JER Gallian	c Akram b Ormond	141
A Singh	b Ormond	0
SP Fleming (capt)	b Bicknell	238
DJ Hussey	c Ramprakash b Benning	74
*CMW Read	c Batty b Akram	13
SR Patel	b Bicknell	2
MA Ealham	not out	57
PJ Franks	not out	26
GP Swann		
RJ Sidebottom		
Extras	b 11, lb 8, nb 26, p 5	50
	(7 wkts dec 134 overs)	**692**

Bowling
Bicknell 28-1-156-2. Ormond 21-1-88-2. Akram 34-1-155-1. Clarke 14-1-64-1.
Doshi 24-2-126-0. Benning 11-0-73-1. Ramprakash 2-0-6-0.
Fall of Wickets: 1-178, 2-179, 3-385, 4-561, 5-586, 6-589, 7-620

*Nottinghamshire won by an innings and 71 runs –
Surrey (3 pts), Nottinghamshire (22 pts)*

GLAMORGAN v. GLOUCESTERSHIRE – at Cardiff

GLOS	First Innings		Second Innings	
WPC Weston	lbw b Thomas SD	29	(2) lbw b Croft	23
CM Spearman	c Wallace b Cosker	73	(1) lbw b Cosker	18
Kadeer Ali	c Croft b Cosker	55	not out	20
CG Taylor (capt)	b Wharf	176	lbw b Cosker	15
THC Hancock	lbw b Wharf	0	not out	41
APR Gidman	run out	16		
*SJ Adshead	c Hughes b Harrison	59		
UDU Chandana	c Hemp b Croft	14		
ID Fisher	run out	16		
J Lewis	b Wharf	5		
SP Kirby	not out	6		
Extras	b 2, lb 8, w 1, nb 6	17	w 2	2
	(123.1 overs)	**466**	(3 wkts dec 44.3 overs)	**119**

Bowling
Harrison 16-4-77-1. Wharf 30.1-4-127-3. Thomas SD 21-3-66-1.
Cosker 29-6-79-2. Croft 27-3-107-1.
Harrison 4-0-14-0. Thomas SD 8-1-24-0. Cosker 17-3-43-2. Croft 15.3-6-38-1.
Fall of Wickets: 1-58, 2-126, 3-212, 4-213, 5-262, 6-392, 7-425, 8-439, 9-456
1-32, 2-44, 3-59

GLAMORGAN	First Innings		Second Innings	
MTG Elliott	c Spearman b Gidman	38	st Adshead b Fisher	123
IJ Thomas	b Gidman	18	b Chandana	40
DL Hemp	lbw b Lewis	0	c Adshead b Lewis	57
MJ Powell	b Gidman	0	c Taylor b Chandana	39
J Hughes	b Gidman	0	b Chandana	1
*MA Wallace	lbw b Chandana	52	c Adshead b Chandana	32
RDB Croft (capt)	b Chandana	31	b Fisher	8
SD Thomas	c Lewis b Kirby	17	b Fisher	21
AG Wharf	lbw b Kirby	35	b Fisher	0
DS Harrison	c Hancock b Chandana	12	lbw b Chandana	4
DA Cosker	not out	15	not out	0
Extras	b 4, lb 5, nb 12	21	lb 12, nb 8	20
	(66 overs)	**239**	(107.1 overs)	**345**

Bowling
Lewis 16-6-48-1. Kirby 14-1-50-2. Gidman 10-1-47-4. Chandana 21-2-73-3.
Fisher 5-2-12-0.
Lewis 12-3-34-1. Kirby 15-2-55-0. Chandana 36.1-9-117-5. Gidman 8-0-31-0.
Fisher 34-10-89-4. Taylor 2-0-7-0.
Fall of Wickets: 1-40, 2-43, 3-44, 4-48, 5-91, 6-137, 7-162, 8-176, 9-209
1-93, 2-196, 3-274, 4-280, 5-288, 6-309, 7-335, 8-340, 9-345

*Gloucestershire won by 7 wickets –
Glamorgan (4 pts), Gloucestershire (22 pts)*

HAMPSHIRE v. MIDDLESEX – at The Rose Bowl

HAMPSHIRE	First Innings		Second Innings	
JHK Adams	b Richardson	5	c Scott b Richardson	11
MJ Brown	c Scott b Styris	51	c Joyce b Styris	15
SM Katich	c Smith b Keegan	27	(4) b Weekes	28
JP Crawley	b Richardson	84	(5) b Styris	40
KP Pietersen	c Shah b Styris	0	(6) c Hutton b Styris	28
*N Pothas	c Weekes b Richardson	18	(7) lbw b Styris	65
SM Ervine	c Scott b Whelan	26	(8) c Shah b Whelan	30
AD Mascarenhas	b Styris	34	(9) not out	44
SK Warne (capt)	c Joyce b Styris	0	(10) c Richardson b Styris	12
CT Tremlett	not out	13	(11) c Smith b Styris	1
BV Taylor	c Scott b Richardson	0	(3) c Scott b Whelan	9
Extras	b 2, lb 12, w 1, nb 2	17	lb 9, w 2, nb 10	21
	(95.5 overs)	**275**	(100.5 overs)	**304**

Bowling
Keegan 25-7-78-1. Richardson 26.5-8-53-4. Whelan 14-4-58-1. Styris 22-8-45-4.
Weekes 3-0-10-0. Shah 1-0-4-0. Hutton 4-1-13-0.
Keegan 5-3-7-0. Richardson 31-9-90-1. Styris 29.5-8-73-6. Weekes 17-7-37-1.
Whelan 8-0-54-2. Hutton 10-0-34-0.
Fall of Wickets: 1-13, 2-91, 3-91, 4-92, 5-127, 6-182, 7-252, 8-252, 9-275
1-23, 2-27, 3-61, 4-114, 5-135, 6-156, 7-208, 8-281, 9-302

MIDDLESEX	First Innings		Second Innings	
AJ Strauss	c Adams b Ervine	6	b Warne	19
BL Hutton (capt)	c Pothas b Tremlett	6	c Pothas b Mascarenhas	24
ET Smith	lbw b Mascarenhas	11	b Warne	52
OA Shah	st Pothas b Warne	83	c Pothas b Tremlett	24
EC Joyce	c & b Warne	70	c Pietersen b Warne	20
SB Styris	lbw b Tremlett	33	c Brown b Tremlett	0
PN Weekes	c Pothas b Mascarenhas	13	b Mascarenhas	49
*BJM Scott	lbw b Mascarenhas	11	lbw b Warne	22
CB Keegan	lbw b Warne	17	c Katich b Tremlett	3
A Richardson	not out	1	c Katich b Tremlett	0
CD Whelan	b Tremlett	1	not out	9
Extras	b 8, lb 6, w 1, nb 12	27	b 4, lb 2, nb 8	14
	(93.2 overs)	**279**	(84 overs)	**236**

Bowling
Tremlett 22.2-8-41-3. Taylor 15-4-51-0. Mascarenhas 20-3-66-3. Ervine 9-2-34-1.
Warne 27-2-73-3.
Tremlett 19-6-59-4. Taylor 13-2-33-0. Warne 30-7-58-4. Mascarenhas 16-2-49-2.
Ervine 5-0-28-0. Katich 1-0-3-0.
Fall of Wickets: 1-13, 2-13, 3-27, 4-193, 5-196, 6-217, 7-241, 8-268, 9-278
1-39, 2-67, 3-125, 4-150, 5-151, 6-153, 7-203, 8-212, 9-212

Hampshire won by 64 runs – Hampshire (19 pts), Middlesex (5 pts)

Glamorgan had to follow on, Gloucestershire having earlier reached 466 largely through the brilliance of their captain, Chris Taylor. He hit a wonderful 176 from just 185 balls after Craig Spearman and Kadeer Ali had both laid foundations with half-centuries.

Hampshire's 64-run victory over Middlesex at the Rose Bowl was another triumph for Shane Warne, who shared eight wickets with the fast-improving Chris Tremlett to undermine the visitors' run chase. Scott Styris took ten wickets in the match for Middlesex with his often underrated seamers, but Warne and Tremlett also took three wickets apiece in the first innings to prevent Middlesex from building a significant lead on the back of fine knocks from Owais Shah and Ed Joyce.

Division Two

Durham secured their third successive win, and maintained their 100 per cent record, by withstanding an epic individual display from Andy Caddick at Stockton. The 36-year-old former England fast bowler took 12 wickets in the match, including a Herculean second innings effort which brought him 6 for 98 from 25 overs. That was the 67th haul of five wickets or more in his career, but it was not enough to stop Durham, who were guided to a tough win target by half-centuries from Mike Hussey and Dale Benkenstein, plus a superb unbeaten 79 by Gareth Breese.

Earlier Caddick had also starred with the bat for Somerset, hitting 54 (his seventh first-class half-century) to help boost his side's second innings from an ailing 177 for 8 to 288 all out. Caddick added 78 for the ninth wicket with Ian Blackwell,

Round Four: 6–9 May 2005 Division Two

DURHAM v. SOMERSET – at Stockton-on-Tees

SOMERSET	First Innings		Second Innings	
ME T'cothick (capt)	c Mustard b Harmison	21	c Breese b Harmison	20
JD Francis	c Benkenstein b Harmison	35	c Mustard b Harmison	4
M Burns	c Benkenstein b Davies	11	lbw b Harmison	34
ST Jayasuriya	b Davies	2	c Hussey b Collingwood	17
JC Hildreth	c Breese b Collingwood	70	b Plunkett	21
ID Blackwell	b Collingwood	48	c Plunkett b Harmison	87
AW Laraman	c Bridge b Plunkett	6	lbw b Davies	2
*RJ Turner	c Mustard b Collingwood	11	b Davies	5
RL Johnson	b Collingwood	8	c Mustard b Collingwood	4
AR Caddick	c Bridge b Collingwood	19	b Collingwood	54
SRG Francis	not out	5	not out	20
Extras	b 5, lb 9, nb 2	16	b 5, lb 9, nb 6	20
	(63.3 overs)	252	(71.1 overs)	288

Bowling
Harmison 18-2-72-2. Plunkett 19-3-53-1. Davies 12-3-49-2. Bridge 3-1-12-0.
Collingwood 11.3-1-52-5.
Harmison 26-6-84-4. Plunkett 17-3-78-1. Davies 12-3-40-2.
Collingwood 10.1-2-46-3. Breese 6-0-26-0.
Fall of Wickets: 1-26, 2-56, 3-64, 4-84, 5-187, 6-196, 7-208, 8-224, 9-243
1-9, 2-36, 3-71, 4-99, 5-125, 6-148, 7-166, 8-173, 9-251

DURHAM	First Innings		Second Innings	
MEK Hussey (capt)	c Trescothick b Caddick	47	c Turner b Caddick	51
JJB Lewis	c Turner b Laraman	36	b Caddick	7
PD Collingwood	c Turner b Caddick	6	lbw b Caddick	8
GJ Muchall	c Francis SRG b Johnson	12	c Francis SRG b Caddick	23
DM Benkenstein	c Turner b Caddick	6	c Turner b Caddick	51
GR Breese	c sub b Caddick	2	not out	79
*P Mustard	b Caddick	0	b Caddick	16
LE Plunkett	not out	74	not out	3
GD Bridge	c Turner b Caddick	6		
M Davies	b Jayasuriya	62		
SJ Harmison	lbw b Jayasuriya	0		
Extras	b 4, lb 8, w 1, nb 34	47	w 2, nb 4	6
	(80 overs)	298	(6 wkts 61 overs)	244

Bowling
Caddick 28-7-106-6. Johnson 17-3-66-1. Francis SRG 12-2-40-0.
Laraman 13-2-45-1. Blackwell 7-2-27-0. Jayasuriya 3-1-2-2.
Caddick 25-7-98-6. Johnson 16-2-52-0. Blackwell 12-1-56-0. Jayasuriya 3-1-13-0.
Laraman 5-1-25-0.
Fall of Wickets: 1-86, 2-102, 3-105, 4-113, 5-118, 6-118, 7-137, 8-160, 9-284
1-17, 2-31, 3-93, 4-98, 5-189, 6-217

Durham won by 4 wickets – Durham (19 pts), Somerset (5 pts)

ESSEX v. LEICESTERSHIRE – at Chelmsford

LEICESTERSHIRE	First Innings		Second Innings	
DDJ Robinson	b Gough	73	c Foster b Steyn	57
DL Maddy	lbw b Bopara	34	b Gough	6
D Mongia	c Foster b Adams	6	b Adams	39
A Habib	b Adams	2	c Foster b Napier	30
HD Ackerman (capt)	c Foster b Steyn	25	b Gough	93
*PA Nixon	b Gough	0	lbw b Gough	2
OD Gibson	c Adams b Steyn	4	c Jefferson b Steyn	22
PAJ DeFreitas	c Cook b Gough	20	c Irani b Napier	0
CW Henderson	c Jefferson b Steyn	6	b Adams	55
DD Masters	c Foster b Napier	27	not out	2
CM Willoughby	not out	2	c Irani b Gough	4
Extras	lb 3, nb 18	21	lb 5, w 1, nb 16	22
	(81 overs)	220	(94.1 overs)	332

Bowling
Gough 19-7-46-3. Adams 23-11-49-2. Steyn 17-3-69-3. Napier 14-3-34-1.
Bopara 8-1-19-1.
Gough 21.1-5-60-4. Adams 21-9-48-2. Steyn 21-3-102-2. Napier 16-5-49-2.
Bopara 5-0-31-0. Middlebrook 10-2-37-0.
Fall of Wickets: 1-98, 2-109, 3-113, 4-138, 5-138, 6-154, 7-161, 8-167, 9-216
1-15, 2-105, 3-125, 4-164, 5-183, 6-227, 7-228, 8-324, 9-326

ESSEX	First Innings		Second Innings	
WI Jefferson	c Mongia b DeFreitas	93	lbw b Gibson	13
AN Cook	c Ackerman b Gibson	28	c Nixon b DeFreitas	59
RS Bopara	b Masters	25	c Nixon b Masters	0
A Flower	c Nixon b Willoughby	10	not out	74
RC Irani (capt)	c Mongia b DeFreitas	46	lbw b Gibson	34
*JS Foster	c Robinson b DeFreitas	13	not out	0
JD Middlebrook	run out	40		
GR Napier	c Henderson b Gibson	34		
AR Adams	c Nixon b Gibson	27		
D Gough	not out	15		
DW Steyn	run out	0		
Extras	b 7, lb 2, nb 22	31	b 1, lb 3, w 3, nb 4	11
	(104.4 overs)	362	(4 wkts 44.2 overs)	191

Bowling
Willoughby 24.4-4-90-1. Gibson 30-3-118-3. Masters 16-3-60-1.
DeFreitas 21-6-68-3. Henderson 12-5-17-0. Mongia 1-1-0-0.
Gibson 12.2-1-38-2. Willoughby 8-1-48-0. Masters 7-2-26-1. DeFreitas 11-2-43-1.
Henderson 6-0-32-0.
Fall of Wickets: 1-68, 2-159, 3-159, 4-201, 5-232, 6-232, 7-289, 8-341, 9-345
1-32, 2-43, 3-94, 4-180

Essex won by 6 wickets – Essex (21 pts), Leicestershire (4 pts)

LANCASHIRE v. DERBYSHIRE – at Old Trafford

DERBYSHIRE	First Innings		Second Innings	
SD Stubbings	c Hodge b Cork	6	(2) c Chilton b Keedy	65
MJ Di Venuto	c Hegg b Chapple	28	(1) st Hegg b Keedy	40
J Moss	b Anderson	9	(4) c Loye b Muralitharan	12
Hassan Adnan	b Anderson	17	(5) b Chapple	1
*LD Sutton (capt)	run out	95	(6) b Keedy	4
JDC Bryant	c Law b Muralitharan	4	(7) lbw b Keedy	1
G Welch	c Hodge b Anderson	1	(8) c Chilton b Keedy	0
AG Botha	b Anderson	31	(9) not out	8
AKD Gray	run out	0	(3) b Anderson	28
ID Hunter	not out	20	b Keedy	2
NGE Walker	st Hegg b Muralitharan	0	st Hegg b Muralitharan	8
Extras	lb 2, nb 2	4	b 1, lb 5, nb 2, p 5	13
	(81.4 overs)	215	(78.1 overs)	182

Bowling
Anderson 21-4-62-4. Cork 20-7-31-1. Chapple 18-3-53-1.
Muralitharan 18.4-3-45-2. Keedy 4-1-22-0.
Anderson 16-4-60-1. Cork 5-4-10-0. Keedy 26-6-60-6. Muralitharan 26.1-17-31-2.
Chapple 5-1-10-1.
Fall of Wickets: 1-9, 2-36, 3-50, 4-70, 5-75, 6-80, 7-174, 8-174, 9-212
1-69, 2-106, 3-123, 4-124, 5-131, 6-142, 7-142, 8-171, 9-173

LANCASHIRE	First Innings	
MJ Chilton (capt)	b Welch	50
MB Loye	c Stubbings b Hunter	101
BJ Hodge	c Welch b Botha	65
SG Law	c Bryant b Moss	112
A Flintoff	b Botha	5
G Chapple	c Moss b Walker	41
*WK Hegg	c & b Botha	39
DG Cork	lbw b Botha	4
JM Anderson	b Botha	14
M Muralitharan	c Hassan Adnan b Botha	24
G Keedy	not out	1
Extras	b 7, lb 2, nb 4	13
	(137.3 overs)	469

Bowling
Hunter 21-0-98-1. Walker 17-3-54-1. Welch 25-3-61-1. Moss 20-4-81-1.
Botha 32.3-7-104-6. Gray 22-2-62-0.
Fall of Wickets: 1-126, 2-211, 3-241, 4-247, 5-349, 6-402, 7-406, 8-442, 9-449

Lancashire won by an innings and 72 runs – Lancashire (22 pts), Derbyshire (3 pts)

YORKSHIRE v. NORTHAMPTONSHIRE – at Headingley

NORTHANTS	First Innings		Second Innings	
ML Love	c Harvey b Hoggard	42	c Dawood b Kruis	4
BM Shafayat	c Harvey b Kruis	4	c Wood b Hoggard	25
U Afzaal	c Harvey b Kruis	0	c Hoggard b Kruis	19
DJG Sales (capt)	c McGrath b Kruis	33	b Bresnan	16
RA White	c Bresnan b Kruis	15	b Bresnan	5
*GL Brophy	b Kruis	0	absent hurt	
DG Wright	c Dawood b Hoggard	36	(6) c McGrath b Bresnan	15
BJ Phillips	not out	55	(7) c Dawood b Harvey	3
J Louw	c Jaques b McGrath	58	(8) lbw b Kruis	10
PS Jones	lbw b McGrath	13	(9) c & b Harvey	51
JF Brown	b McGrath	0	(10) not out	7
Extras	lb 9, w 2, nb 14	25	b 1, lb 8, w 1, nb 10	20
	(83.1 overs)	281	(9 wkts 55.3 overs)	175

Bowling
Hoggard 19-6-50-2. Kruis 19-7-59-5. Bresnan 16-2-51-0. Harvey 9-2-24-0.
Dawson 8-1-37-0. White 3-0-16-0. McGrath 9.1-0-35-3.
Hoggard 18-4-72-1. Kruis 14-5-30-3. Bresnan 16-2-48-3. Harvey 7.3-1-16-2.
Fall of Wickets: 1-34, 2-35, 3-70, 4-108, 5-108, 6-113, 7-156, 8-251, 9-277
1-9, 2-54, 3-58, 4-73, 5-84, 6-93, 7-97, 8-134, 9-175

YORKSHIRE	First Innings		Second Innings	
MJ Wood	c Sales b Wright	12	not out	56
PA Jaques	c Shafayat b Wright	176	not out	70
A McGrath	c Afzaal b Louw	26		
MP Vaughan	b Wright	12		
IJ Harvey	b Wright	0		
C White (capt)	lbw b Jones	12		
*I Dawood	c sub b Wright	51		
RKJ Dawson	c & b Wright	0		
TT Bresnan	c Love b Wright	5		
MJ Hoggard	b Wright	0		
GJ Kruis	not out	5		
Extras	b 8, lb 15, nb 6	29	lb 4, nb 2	6
	(98.4 overs)	328	(0 wkts 20 overs)	132

Bowling
Louw 21-3-72-1. Phillips 12-1-52-0. Jones 14-6-33-1. Wright 24.4-8-60-8.
Brown 25.1-3-81-0. Shafayat 1.5-0-7-0.
Wright 4-0-16-0. Louw 6-0-43-0. Jones 6-2-39-0. Phillips 4-0-30-0.
Fall of Wickets: 1-36, 2-95, 3-144, 4-144, 5-182, 6-297, 7-297, 8-303, 9-307

*Yorkshire won by 10 wickets –
Yorkshire (20 pts), Northamptonshire (5 pts)*

A Herculean effort with both ball and bat by Andy Caddick could not prevent a Somerset defeat at Durham.

whose 87 followed an equally pugnacious 48 in the first innings, while Simon Francis also contributed a spirited unbeaten 20 from No. 11. Paul Collingwood was a revelation with the ball in this game, taking eight wickets at low cost, while Steve Harmison included the vital early wicket of England colleague Marcus Trescothick in a crucial new-ball burst on the second evening. By then, Durham had needed to thank Liam Plunkett and Mark Davies for at last resisting the fiery Caddick and adding what proved to be a match-winning 124 for the ninth wicket.

Darren Gough, another former England Test fast bowler with powder left in his gun, spearheaded Essex's six-wicket success over Leicestershire at Chelmsford. He took seven wickets in the match, including Darren Maddy cheaply on the second evening. Darren Robinson fought hard against his former club, but Essex were always in control after Gough and Dale Steyn had undermined the visitors' first innings and Will Jefferson's 93 enabled Essex to build towards a sizeable lead.

Lancashire were expected to crush Derbyshire at Old Trafford but there was still much for the Red Rose county to be pleased about in terms of individual performances as the division's bottom side were blown away by an innings and 72 runs. James Anderson, for a start, had his best return for a year on the opening day, and Gary Keedy benefited hugely from Muttiah Muralitharan's presence at the other end to dismantle Derbyshire's second innings following initial stout resistance from Michael Di Venuto and Steve Stubbings. Luke Sutton, on the first day, was the only other visiting batsman to prosper, but for Lancashire there were promising early-season innings from Mal Loye and Stuart Law, with hundreds, Mark Chilton and Brad Hodge. Ant Botha plied his left-arm spin manfully on a third day that was so cold that pots of tea were brought out on to the field at a specially-convened 'drinks break'. Law also warmed the Derbyshire fielders' hands during an innings of 112 that contained two sixes and 13 fours.

Phil Jaques stood head and shoulders above all the other batsmen on view at Headingley, his brilliant first innings 176 and fluent unbeaten 70 on the final day doing more than anything to bring Yorkshire a comfortable 10-wicket win against Northamptonshire. Deon Kruis, the controversial Kolpak signing from South Africa, was the other 'Yorkshireman' to shine: the fast bowler included a spell of 3 for 4 in ten balls to send Northants plunging to 113 for 6 soon after lunch on the opening day, and then took his match haul to eight before celebrating victory on his 31st birthday.

An eighth-wicket stand of 95 between Ben Phillips and Johann Louw enabled Northants to stage some sort of first innings recovery, but Jaques' 176 from 254 balls, with a six and 24 fours, earned Yorkshire a lead. Tim Bresnan and Kruis then settled matters by reducing Northants from nine without loss to 115 for 7 on a third day on which only 36.5 overs were possible. The damage to the visitors, however, had been done.

Round Five: 10–14 May 2005

Division One

Only one first division match did not reach a positive conclusion in this round of games, but the single drawn affair was perhaps the most significant result – as well as by far the best game of cricket. No praise is too high for the fighting spirit which, ultimately, saw Kent survive 141 overs against

Hampshire – and Shane Warne, of course – to earn themselves four extra points at Canterbury and check their visitors' early-season charge.

The heroes were Min Patel and last man Amjad Khan, who kept out the final 22 deliveries from Warne and Chris Tremlett – but Kent's entire order deserves credit for a fine collective effort. Martin van Jaarsveld's four-hour 77 was the highest score, but everyone contributed and David Fulton, Darren Stevens and Matthew Dennington hit combative fifties. In the end, though, it was the stubbornness of Patel and Simon Cook, the ninth-wicket pair, who earned Kent their salvation. Cook's 37 occupied 76 balls, and 97 minutes, until he was defeated by a Warne leg-break, while Patel remained defiant on 41 after 102 minutes and 94 balls at the crease. Kent's 447 for 9 was the highest fourth-innings score in their history and, at one stage on an exciting final day, even their victory target of 485 looked possible.

On its first day the match had also featured a magical maiden first-class hundred for Warne, who counter-attacked thrillingly after coming to the wicket with his side in massive trouble at 130 for 7. With Tom Burrows, the 20-year-old wicketkeeper, keeping him courageous company on his debut, Warne set about the Kent bowlers and dominated an eighth-wicket stand of 131 in 19 overs. In his 321st first-class innings, and 15 years after his own debut, Warne blazed to a 72-ball century with 15 fours and three sixes. His previous best had been 99, made for Australia against New Zealand in the Perth Test of 2001, and no one had scored more than his 2,518 Test runs without making a first-class hundred. In reply Kent could not get past Hampshire's Warne-inspired 328. Simon Katich and

Round Five: 10–14 May 2005 Division One

KENT v. HAMPSHIRE – at Canterbury

HAMPSHIRE	First Innings		Second Innings	
JHK Adams	lbw b Saggers	0	c Jones b Saggers	1
MJ Brown	c Jones b Dennington	32	(4) b Patel	54
SM Katich	run out	56	st Jones b Patel	128
JP Crawley	c van Jaarsveld b Dennington	0	(2) run out	25
KP Pietersen	c van Jaarsveld b Dennington	1	c Key b Khan	125
SM Ervine	b Saggers	18	c Jones b Saggers	57
AD Mascarenhas	c Jones b Cook	9	c Jones b Khan	8
*TG Burrows	b Khan	42	c Cook b Khan	13
SK Warne (capt)	not out	107	not out	26
CT Tremlett	c Walker b Cook	35	lbw b Khan	4
RJ Logan	b Patel	4	not out	0
Extras	b 4, lb 12, w 2, nb 6	24	b 13, lb 3, nb 4	20
	(73.5 overs)	328	(9 wkts dec 109.2 overs)	461

Bowling
Saggers 19-4-64-2. Khan 15-2-82-1. Cook 16-4-62-2. Dennington 17-5-63-3.
Stevens 3-1-13-0. Patel 3.5-1-28-1.
Saggers 26-4-82-2. Khan 20-0-106-4. Cook 18-1-104-0. Dennington 6-0-25-0.
Patel 33.2-5-108-2. Stevens 6-1-20-0.
Fall of Wickets: 1-0, 2-61, 3-71, 4-79, 5-104, 6-121, 7-130, 8-261, 9-307
1-2, 2-97, 3-197, 4-248, 5-397, 6-411, 7-429, 8-446, 9-458

KENT	First Innings		Second Innings	
DP Fulton (capt)	c Burrows b Warne	74	c Burrows b Tremlett	37
RWT Key	b Ervine	20	c Pietersen b Warne	54
M van Jaarsveld	c Crawley b Tremlett	1	c Warne b Tremlett	77
MJ Walker	lbw b Logan	12	(5) c Burrows b Ervine	12
DI Stevens	c Burrows b Logan	68	(6) lbw b Ervine	58
*GO Jones	c Pietersen b Ervine	6	(7) b Warne	22
MJ Dennington	c Crawley b Tremlett	50	(8) b Tremlett	55
SJ Cook	b Warne	4	(9) b Warne	37
MM Patel	lbw b Warne	0	(10) not out	41
A Khan	not out	5	(11) not out	0
MJ Saggers	lbw b Logan	17	(4) c Burrows b Tremlett	23
Extras	b 1, lb 15, w 1, nb 31	48	b 16, lb 4, w 5, nb 6	31
	(80.3 overs)	305	(9 wkts 141 overs)	447

Bowling
Tremlett 14-2-61-2. Logan 15.3-3-59-3. Ervine 12-2-66-2. Mascarenhas 20-5-53-0.
Warne 19-3-50-3.
Tremlett 31-7-88-4. Logan 18-0-98-0. Ervine 30-4-104-2. Adams 2-1-7-0.
Mascarenhas 23-7-65-0. Warne 37-13-65-3.
Fall of Wickets: 1-54, 2-63, 3-93, 4-163, 5-226, 6-255, 7-271, 8-271, 9-283
1-56, 2-119, 3-177, 4-199, 5-243, 6-279, 7-366, 8-370, 9-441

Match drawn – Kent (10 pts), Hampshire (10 pts)

SURREY v. GLAMORGAN – at The Oval

SURREY	First Innings		Second Innings	
SA Newman	b Croft	117	c Croft b Davies	219
RS Clinton	c Wallace b Harrison	1	b Croft	24
MR R'kash (capt)	b Harrison	2	b Davies	97
R Clarke	c Wallace b Davies	84	lbw b Thomas SD	34
*JN Batty	c & b Cosker	25		
AD Brown	lbw b Cosker	122	(5) not out	42
JGE Benning	c Hughes b Harrison	57		
MP Bicknell	not out	17		
J Ormond	c Thomas IJ b Davies	2		
ND Doshi	b Davies	0		
M Akram	lbw b Croft	0		
Extras	lb 7, w 4, nb 6	17	lb 8, w 1	9
	(108.4 overs)	444	(4 wkts dec 91.3 overs)	425

Bowling
Harrison 20-6-72-3. Davies 24-4-121-3. Croft 29.4-3-116-2. Thomas SD 0.3-0-8-0.
Cosker 34.3-3-120-2.
Harrison 14-4-45-0. Davies 15-1-76-2. Croft 29-5-125-1. Cosker 20-1-87-0.
Thomas SD 13.3-1-84-1.
Fall of Wickets: 1-9, 2-25, 3-210, 4-210, 5-295, 6-409, 7-433, 8-443, 9-443
1-76, 2-330, 3-359, 4-425

GLAMORGAN	First Innings		Second Innings	
IJ Thomas	lbw b Bicknell	4	(2) c Newman b Bicknell	12
DD Cherry	lbw b Bicknell	47	(1) c Clarke b Bicknell	0
DL Hemp	lbw b Bicknell	24	c Batty b Akram	95
MJ Powell	b Ormond	43	c Bicknell b Ormond	93
J Hughes	b Clarke	30	b Clarke	6
*MA Wallace	c Batty b Bicknell	5	c sub b Akram	0
RDB Croft (capt)	c Batty b Akram	27	c Brown b Akram	7
SD Thomas	c Batty b Clarke	12	c Batty b Clarke	2
DS Harrison	not out	75	b Clarke	0
DA Cosker	c Batty b Bicknell	17	b Akram	12
AP Davies	b Bicknell	37	not out	0
Extras	b 1, lb 5, nb 18	24	lb 10, w 1, nb 10	21
	(74.5 overs)	345	(55.1 overs)	248

Bowling
Bicknell 19.5-3-74-6. Ormond 18-7-45-1. Clarke 9-0-61-2. Akram 17-3-98-1.
Doshi 9-2-32-0. Benning 2-0-29-0.
Bicknell 17-5-55-2. Ormond 12-3-47-1. Akram 12.1-1-63-4. Clarke 8-1-46-3.
Doshi 6-0-27-0.
Fall of Wickets: 1-4, 2-32, 3-125, 4-143, 5-165, 6-169, 7-191, 8-233, 9-301
1-4, 2-19, 3-190, 4-220, 5-224, 6-224, 7-227, 8-227, 9-233

Surrey won by 276 runs – Surrey (22 pts), Glamorgan (6 pts)

MIDDLESEX v. GLOUCESTERSHIRE – at Lord's

MIDDLESEX	First Innings		Second Innings	
AJ Strauss	c Lewis b Kirby	27	c Kadeer Ali b Averis	10
BL Hutton (capt)	c Chandana b Kirby	14	b Kirby	19
ET Smith	c Adshead b Lewis	13	c Adshead b Chandana	35
OA Shah	lbw b Chandana	63	not out	111
EC Joyce	c Hancock b Gidman	75	c Adshead b Averis	93
SB Styris	c Taylor b Gidman	16	c Hancock b Lewis	36
PN Weekes	b Kirby	69	c & b Gidman	1
*BJM Scott	c Adshead b Lewis	58	not out	13
CT Peploe	c Hancock b Lewis	8		
MM Betts	not out	12		
A Richardson	lbw b Lewis	4		
Extras	b 7, lb 5, w 1, nb 18	31	b 2, lb 9, w 3, nb 10	24
	(100.2 overs)	390	(6 wkts dec 101 overs)	342

Bowling
Lewis 24.2-6-82-4. Kirby 19-3-84-3. Gidman 20-1-89-2. Averis 13-2-49-0.
Chandana 24-6-74-1.
Lewis 23-6-48-1. Kirby 17.5-4-58-1. Averis 17-2-66-2. Chandana 32-5-104-1.
Gidman 11.1-0-55-1.
Fall of Wickets: 1-45, 2-60, 3-104, 4-167, 5-210, 6-238, 7-357, 8-373, 9-373
1-19, 2-65, 3-73, 4-226, 5-305, 6-306

GLOS	First Innings		Second Innings	
WPC Weston	c Scott b Richardson	24	(2) c Scott b Richardson	9
CM Spearman	c Strauss b Richardson	69	(1) b Betts	20
Kadeer Ali	c Scott b Richardson	0	b Betts	12
CG Taylor (capt)	c Strauss b Betts	17	c Weekes b Styris	46
THC Hancock	lbw b Styris	96	c Scott b Peploe	21
APR Gidman	c Hutton b Richardson	19	c Strauss b Betts	5
*SJ Adshead	b Betts	27	b Peploe	0
UDU Chandana	c Styris b Betts	2	lbw b Richardson	17
JMM Averis	c Shah b Richardson	21	b Betts	0
J Lewis	c Scott b Betts	0	c Hutton b Richardson	19
SP Kirby	not out	15	not out	4
Extras	b 4, lb 2, w 1, nb 12	19	lb 7	7
	(65.5 overs)	232	(42.4 overs)	160

Bowling
Richardson 19.5-8-32-5. Betts 15-0-86-4. Weekes 1-0-8-0. Peploe 17-5-49-0.
Styris 13-2-51-1.
Richardson 14.4-2-42-3. Betts 11-0-58-4. Peploe 10-4-35-2. Styris 7-1-18-1.
Fall of Wickets: 1-59, 2-59, 3-84, 4-105, 5-147, 6-156, 7-187, 8-200, 9-200
1-29, 2-33, 3-57, 4-113, 5-113, 6-113, 7-132, 8-137, 9-152

Middlesex won by 340 runs –
Middlesex (21 pts), Gloucestershire (4 pts)

SUSSEX v. WARWICKSHIRE – at Hove

SUSSEX	First Innings	
IJ Ward	c Loudon b Carter	3
RR Montgomerie	lbw b Pretorius	3
MH Yardy	lbw b Streak	88
MW Goodwin	c Streak b Carter	108
CJ Adams (capt)	run out	67
*MJ Prior	c Frost b Brown	4
RSC Martin-Jenkins	c Pretorius b Streak	21
RJ Kirtley	b Loudon	30
JJ van der Wath	c sub b Pretorius	34
Mushtaq Ahmed	not out	30
JD Lewry	c Carter b Pretorius	0
Extras	b 5, lb 17, nb 2	24
	(156.5 overs)	412

Bowling
Streak 28-8-50-2. Pretorius 25.5-4-88-3. Carter 31-10-60-2. Brown 34-10-71-1.
Bell 4-0-18-0. Giles 11-1-37-0. Trott 12-0-39-0. Loudon 11-2-27-1.
Fall of Wickets: 1-8, 2-35, 3-199, 4-226, 5-237, 6-280, 7-316, 8-361, 9-411

WARWICKSHIRE	First Innings		Second Innings	
NV Knight (capt)	lbw b Mushtaq Ahmed	45	b Kirtley	17
MJ Powell	b Lewry	45	c Yardy b van der Wath	13
IR Bell	lbw b Martin-Jenkins	1	c Prior b Mushtaq Ahmed	35
IJL Trott	c Prior b Lewry	29	b Mushtaq Ahmed	7
AGR Loudon	c & b Mushtaq Ahmed	6	b Lewry	13
DR Brown	b Lewry	9	(7) c Goodwin b Kirtley	18
*T Frost	lbw b Mushtaq Ahmed	7	(8) b Kirtley	23
AF Giles	not out	19	(9) c Goodwin b M Ahmed	0
HH Streak	c Adams b Mushtaq Ahmed	0	(10) not out	0
NM Carter	c Yardy b Lewry	1	(6) b Lewry	1
D Pretorius	b Lewry	1	b Mushtaq Ahmed	12
Extras	b 1, lb 13, nb 2	16	b 4, lb 3	7
	(62.2 overs)	179	(51.1 overs)	146

Bowling
Kirtley 6-0-16-0. Lewry 21.2-9-46-5. van der Wath 3-0-22-0.
Mushtaq Ahmed 24-4-73-4. Martin-Jenkins 8-5-8-1.
Kirtley 11-5-17-3. van der Wath 8-1-22-1. Martin-Jenkins 8-1-17-0.
Mushtaq Ahmed 17.1-2-65-4. Lewry 7-2-18-2.
Fall of Wickets: 1-75, 2-76, 3-111, 4-122, 5-141, 6-146, 7-158, 8-164, 9-165
1-26, 2-36, 3-59, 4-92, 5-92, 6-93, 7-129, 8-134, 9-134

Sussex won by an innings and 87 runs –
Sussex (21 pts), Warwickshire (2 pts)

Martin van Jaarsveld ... still in the early-season runs for Kent as he hits 77 against Hampshire.

Kevin Pietersen then treated the home attack with disdain to build what looked to be a match-winning second innings 461 for 9 declared, with Katich hitting five sixes in a 118-ball hundred and Pietersen sweeping Patel for successive sixes in his 83-ball ton. Rob Key's 54 on the third evening, though, was a sign of Kentish resistance to come and, the following morning, nightwatchman Martin Saggers hung on for more than a hour to play his part in the great escape.

Surrey bounced back from their ball-tampering episode to thrash Glamorgan by 276 runs at The Oval and send the Welsh county to their fourth defeat from four matches. Scott Newman, their highly-talented left-handed opener, now lies behind only Bobby Abel and Walter Read in the list of Surrey batsmen with the most runs scored in a first-class match. Newman made 117 and 219, setting Surrey on their way with a 185-run stand with Rikki Clarke early on the first day and adding 254 with Mark Ramprakash second time around. There were 28 fours and four sixes in his double hundred. Alistair Brown was also in a destructive mood, a 95-ball first-innings century giving him his 37th first-class ton and a brutal 22-ball 42 not out speeding Surrey to their second innings declaration.

In between, Martin Bicknell's 42nd haul of five wickets or more in an innings kept Glamorgan down at heel until David Harrison led a late flurry, and then Bicknell reached the milestone of 1,000 first-class wickets as he reduced the Welshmen to 19 for 2 on the third afternoon. David Hemp and Michael Powell offered attractive resistance, reaching 77 and 80 not out respectively at the end of a third day which brought 536 runs in all, but both were out early the next morning. Perhaps uniquely in the 2005 season, this championship match featured no overseas or Kolpak players.

The strokemaking qualities of Ed Joyce and Owais Shah shone out from Middlesex's 340-run humbling of Gloucestershire at Lord's, while the seam pairing of Alan Richardson and Mel Betts proved distinctly troublesome for the West Countrymen. Richardson, continuing his fine early form since a winter transfer from Warwickshire, and Betts both ended up with eight wickets as Gloucestershire subsided meekly. The only worrying note for Middlesex – and England, for that matter – was the continuing poor form of Andrew Strauss, who added 27 and 10 to a previous run of 4, 2, 13, 37, 6 and 19.

Warwickshire's first championship defeat for 20 months was a dispiriting experience for the champions at Hove. They lost 15 wickets for 184 runs in 64 overs on the third and final day to plunge to an innings and 87-run beating and, in truth, they were never in the match once Mike Yardy and Murray Goodwin had put on 164 for Sussex's third wicket. Chris Adams also batted well to take his side past 400, and then Jason Lewry and Mushtaq Mohammad got to work. James Kirtley played a part in Warwickshire's second-innings collapse, with Ashley Giles batting despite staying off the field on day two with a hip injury.

Division Two

Durham's magnificent early-season form claimed another notable scalp as Lancashire found themselves being well beaten by nine wickets at Old Trafford. Steve Harmison, who sent back Australia's Ashes squad batsman Brad Hodge twice in two days, wrapped up Durham's latest victory with a superb second innings haul of 6 for 52 – an analysis that also included the prize wicket of his great friend Andrew Flintoff. Harmison's third morning spell of 4 for 14 in 5.2 overs took his championship wickets to 27 in four matches. Lancashire's only real resistance, apart from Flintoff's second innings 55, was an unlikely ninth-wicket stand of 73 on the opening day between James Anderson, whose 37 not out was a career-best, and Gary Keedy. Mike Hussey, meanwhile, almost single-handedly took on and beat the much-vaunted Lancashire bowling line-up, although Phil Mustard also caught the eye by hitting Muttiah Muralitharan out of the attack during the 77 he made in a vital seventh-wicket partnership of 139 with his captain. Hussey, unbeaten on 144, carried his bat through Durham's first innings 338 and – fittingly – was also still at the crease when a famous victory was completed.

Yorkshire also completed a famous win at Leicester, with their magnificent fourth-innings 406 for 4 establishing a county record. Anthony McGrath, with a superb unbeaten 165 from 218 balls, with 20 boundaries, was the architect of a victory chase that eclipsed Yorkshire's previous highest fourth-innings winning score of 331 in 1910. There was even the rare sight of a Michael Vaughan championship half-century, and important runs from Ian Harvey and Craig White, but the win was a triumph for McGrath, who said he had felt horribly out of touch before walking to the wicket.

Leicestershire's defeat was tough on 36-year-old Ottis Gibson, who was chiefly responsible for Yorkshire being dismissed for just 151 first time around, but neither he nor any of the other home bowlers could make any impression on McGrath.

Dropped catches do not come much costlier than the one with which Michael Di Venuto let off Worcestershire opener Stephen Moore at New Road. On 12 at the time, when Di Venuto put him down at slip off Ian Hunter, Moore went on to score 246 and set his side well on the way to their eventual nine-wicket victory. Moore was joined by Jamie Pipe in what for Derbyshire was a particularly dispiriting ninth-wicket alliance, and Pipe finished unbeaten on 80. The Worcestershire seamers then got to work, with Chaminda Vaas, Kabir Ali and Matt Mason chipping away at Derbyshire's batsmen relentlessly either side of the follow-on. The end then came quickly as Graeme

Hick thumped 13 fours in a 48-ball 62 not out to rush Worcestershire to their modest target.

Johann Louw looked to be spearheading a Northamptonshire victory charge at Wantage Road, his first innings career-best of 6 for 52 forcing Essex

Round Five: 10–14 May 2005 Division Two

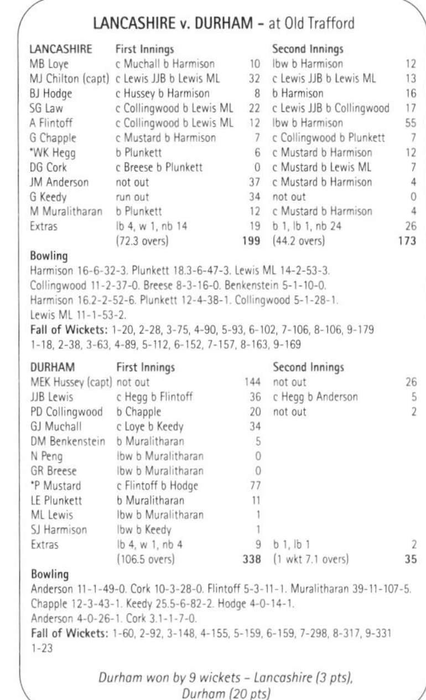

LANCASHIRE v. DURHAM – at Old Trafford

LANCASHIRE	First Innings		Second Innings	
MB Loye	c Muchall b Harmison	10	lbw b Harmison	12
MJ Chilton (capt)	c Lewis JJB b Lewis ML	32	c Lewis JJB b Lewis ML	13
BJ Hodge	c Hussey b Harmison	8	b Harmison	16
SG Law	c Collingwood b Lewis ML	22	c Lewis JJB b Collingwood	17
A Flintoff	c Collingwood b Lewis ML	12	lbw b Harmison	55
G Chapple	c Mustard b Harmison	7	c Collingwood b Plunkett	7
*WK Hegg	b Plunkett	6	c Mustard b Harmison	12
DG Cork	c Breese b Plunkett	0	c Mustard b Lewis ML	7
JM Anderson	not out	37	c Mustard b Harmison	4
G Keedy	run out	34	not out	0
M Muralitharan	b Plunkett	12	c Mustard b Harmison	4
Extras	lb 4, w 1, nb 14	19	b 1, lb 1, nb 24	26
	(72.3 overs)	199	(44.2 overs)	173

Bowling
Harmison 16-6-32-3. Plunkett 18.3-6-47-3. Lewis ML 14-2-53-3. Collingwood 11-2-37-0. Breese 8-3-16-0. Benkenstein 5-1-10-0.
Harmison 16.2-2-52-6. Plunkett 12-4-38-1. Collingwood 5-1-28-1. Lewis ML 11-1-53-2.
Fall of Wickets: 1-20, 2-28, 3-75, 4-90, 5-93, 6-102, 7-106, 8-106, 9-179
1-18, 2-38, 3-63, 4-89, 5-112, 6-152, 7-157, 8-163, 9-169

DURHAM	First Innings		Second Innings	
MEK Hussey (capt)	not out	144	not out	26
JJB Lewis	c Hegg b Flintoff	36	c Hegg b Anderson	5
PD Collingwood	b Chapple	20	not out	2
GJ Muchall	c Loye b Keedy	34		
DM Benkenstein	b Muralitharan	5		
N Peng	lbw b Muralitharan	0		
GR Breese	lbw b Muralitharan	0		
*P Mustard	c Flintoff b Hodge	77		
LE Plunkett	b Muralitharan	11		
ML Lewis	lbw b Muralitharan	1		
SJ Harmison	lbw b Keedy	1		
Extras	lb 4, w 1, nb 4	9	b 1, lb 1	2
	(106.5 overs)	338	(1 wkt 7.1 overs)	35

Bowling
Anderson 11-1-49-0. Cork 10-3-28-0. Flintoff 5-3-11-1. Muralitharan 39-11-107-5. Chapple 12-3-43-1. Keedy 25.5-6-82-2. Hodge 4-0-14-1.
Anderson 4-0-26-1. Cork 3.1-1-7-0.
Fall of Wickets: 1-60, 2-92, 3-148, 4-155, 5-159, 6-159, 7-298, 8-317, 9-331
1-23

Durham won by 9 wickets – Lancashire (3 pts),
Durham (20 pts)

LEICESTERSHIRE v. YORKSHIRE – at Leicester

LEICESTERSHIRE	First Innings		Second Innings	
DDJ Robinson	c Dawood b Bresnan	42	b Hoggard	6
DL Maddy	lbw b McGrath	53	lbw b Harvey	27
D Mongia	lbw b Harvey	0	c Dawood b Dawson	70
A Habib	b McGrath	41	lbw b Bresnan	16
HD Ackerman (capt)	not out	85	c Jaques b McGrath	30
*PA Nixon	c Wood b Dawson	0	b Kruis	68
OD Gibson	lbw b Kruis	6	c Dawson b Hoggard	9
PAJ DeFreitas	c Dawood b Kruis	6	lbw b Harvey	17
CW Henderson	b Bresnan	5	c McGrath b Dawson	10
DD Masters	c Dawood b Kruis	8	not out	9
CM Willoughby	b Hoggard	2		
Extras	lb 12, nb 18	30	lb 8, nb 6	14
	(102.5 overs)	278	(9 wkts dec 90.5 overs)	276

Bowling
Hoggard 20.5-1-57-1. Kruis 20-8-40-3. Dawson 6-1-18-1. Bresnan 17-6-38-2. Harvey 13-2-61-1. McGrath 26-7-52-2.
Hoggard 16-4-53-2. Kruis 13.5-3-45-1. Bresnan 12-4-32-1. Harvey 22-5-54-2. McGrath 15-1-42-1. Dawson 12-1-42-2.
Fall of Wickets: 1-62, 2-63, 3-151, 4-170, 5-199, 6-211, 7-223, 8-239, 9-259
1-20, 2-66, 3-107, 4-130, 5-170, 6-188, 7-226, 8-255, 9-276

YORKSHIRE	First Innings		Second Innings	
MJ Wood	c Nixon b Gibson	17	c Nixon b Maddy	48
PA Jaques	c Robinson b Gibson	14	lbw b DeFreitas	37
A McGrath	c Ackerman b Gibson	0	not out	165
MP Vaughan	lbw b Masters	9	b Henderson	53
IJ Harvey	b Gibson	1	b DeFreitas	47
C White (capt)	c Nixon b Masters	0	not out	34
*I Dawood	not out	62		
RKJ Dawson	c Robinson b Maddy	29		
TT Bresnan	c Nixon b Gibson	2		
MJ Hoggard	b Gibson	2		
GJ Kruis	c Habib b Henderson	4		
Extras	lb 6, w 1, nb 4	11	b 1, lb 8, w 7, nb 6	22
	(45.4 overs)	151	(4 wkts 96.1 overs)	406

Bowling
Gibson 17-3-56-6. Willoughby 8-1-18-0. Masters 8-1-28-2. DeFreitas 4-0-18-0. Maddy 2-0-6-1. Henderson 6.4-0-19-1.
Gibson 24.1-1-124-0. Willoughby 13-0-69-0. Masters 11-2-36-0. Maddy 18-2-70-1. DeFreitas 11-1-50-2. Henderson 16-5-41-1. Mongia 3-0-7-0.
Fall of Wickets: 1-27, 2-27, 3-44, 4-44, 5-45, 6-45, 7-106, 8-124, 9-134
1-94, 2-100, 3-184, 4-317

Yorkshire won by 6 wickets – Leicestershire (5 pts), Yorkshire (17 pts)

WORCESTERSHIRE v. DERBYSHIRE – at Worcester

WORCS	First Innings		Second Innings	
SD Peters	c Sutton b Hunter	2	c Hassan Adnan b Hunter	2
SC Moore	c Sutton b Hunter	246	not out	28
GA Hick	c Sutton b Havell	12	not out	62
BF Smith	c Moss b Hunter	0		
VS Solanki (capt)	c Hassan Adnan b Dean	27		
Z de Bruyn	c Sutton b Dean	25		
GJ Batty	c Botha b Dean	1		
WPUJC Vaas	c Sutton b Havell	45		
Kabir Ali	lbw b Welch	20		
*DJ Pipe	not out	80		
MS Mason	c Di Venuto b Havell	4		
Extras	lb 16	16	b 4, lb 2, nb 2	8
	(125.5 overs)	478	(1 wkt 16.2 overs)	100

Bowling
Hunter 26-1-108-3. Havell 24.5-4-106-3. Dean 29-3-93-3. Welch 28-8-77-1. Moss 7-0-36-0. Botha 11-1-42-0.
Hunter 4-0-30-1. Havell 4-0-18-0. Welch 3-0-18-0. Dean 3-0-16-0. Moss 1.2-0-2-0. Botha 1-0-10-0.
Fall of Wickets: 1-2, 2-17, 3-20, 4-83, 5-149, 6-151, 7-252, 8-300, 9-473
1-4

DERBYSHIRE	First Innings		Second Innings	
MJ Di Venuto	lbw b Vaas	0	(2) lbw b Kabir Ali	51
SD Stubbings	lbw b Kabir Ali	12	(1) lbw b Mason	7
J Moss	c Hick b Kabir Ali	25	c Kabir Ali b Batty	75
Hassan Adnan	lbw b Vaas	35	lbw b Vaas	6
CWG Bassano	c Solanki b Vaas	32	lbw b Vaas	0
*LD Sutton (capt)	c Hick b Kabir Ali	19	lbw b Mason	45
G Welch	c Solanki b Mason	29	lbw b Mason	63
AG Botha	c Kabir Ali b Batty	43	not out	29
KJ Dean	c Pipe b Mason	11	lbw b Batty	12
ID Hunter	c & b Kabir Ali	22	b Kabir Ali	4
PMR Havell	not out	2	c Hick b Vaas	0
Extras	b 5, lb 8, w 8, nb 12	33	b 6, lb 3, w 1, nb 12	22
	(83.3 overs)	263	(96.4 overs)	314

Bowling
Vaas 23-7-79-3. Kabir Ali 20.3-3-77-4. Mason 16-3-43-2. Batty 15-4-21-1. de Bruyn 9-2-30-0.
Vaas 23.4-2-85-3. Kabir Ali 16-2-69-2. Mason 18-6-34-3. Batty 25-8-61-2. de Bruyn 14-2-56-0.
Fall of Wickets: 1-0, 2-32, 3-59, 4-113, 5-122, 6-144, 7-206, 8-233, 9-235
1-31, 2-100, 3-107, 4-115, 5-179, 6-267, 7-268, 8-297, 9-303

Worcestershire won by 9 wickets – Worcestershire (22 pts),
Derbyshire (5 pts)

NORTHAMPTONSHIRE v. ESSEX – at Northampton

NORTHANTS	First Innings	
ML Love	b Napier	20
BM Shafayat	c sub b Redmond	153
RA White	lbw b Adams	21
DJG Sales (capt)	lbw b Phillips	20
U Afzaal	not out	168
*MH Wessels	lbw b Middlebrook	26
DG Wright	b Phillips	55
J Louw	c Cook b Phillips	15
BJ Phillips	not out	33
PS Jones		
JF Brown		
Extras	b 1, lb 16, w 1, nb 18, p 5	41
	(7 wkts dec 146.1 overs)	552

Bowling
Adams 33-7-95-1. Redmond 30-2-153-1. Napier 12-3-36-1. Bopara 11-3-33-0. Phillips 43-5-149-3. Middlebrook 17.1-1-64-1.
Fall of Wickets: 1-45, 2-100, 3-135, 4-269, 5-327, 6-437, 7-473

ESSEX	First Innings		Second Innings	
WI Jefferson	lbw b Phillips	38	c Wessels b Louw	11
AN Cook	c Sales b Louw	16	c Love b Phillips	195
RS Bopara	c Wessels b Wright	12	lbw b Phillips	79
A Flower	c Phillips b Brown	32	not out	142
RC Irani (capt)	c Love b Louw	36	b Phillips	1
*JS Foster	lbw b Brown	26	lbw b Brown	34
JD Middlebrook	b Louw	0	lbw b Brown	0
TJ Phillips	b Louw	0	not out	2
GR Napier	lbw b Louw	3		
AR Adams	lbw b Louw	0		
AJ Redmond	not out	1		
Extras	b 4, lb 10	14	b 21, lb 4, nb 6	31
	(66.5 overs)	178	(6 wkts 176 overs)	495

Bowling
Louw 14-4-51-6. Wright 14-4-36-1. Jones 14-4-30-0. Phillips 10-5-23-1. Brown 14.5-4-24-2.
Louw 31-7-95-1. Wright 20-2-73-0. Jones 28-7-90-0. Brown 56-15-110-2. Phillips 19-6-44-3. Afzaal 10-2-38-0. White 10-3-19-0. Shafayat 2-1-1-0.
Fall of Wickets: 1-33, 2-67, 3-67, 4-134, 5-152, 6-152, 7-152, 8-168, 9-168
1-12, 2-189, 3-419, 4-423, 5-482, 6-482

Match drawn – Northamptonshire (12 pts),
Essex (6 pts)

Durham's England star Steve Harmison was too quick for Lancashire at Old Trafford, taking nine wickets in the match.

to follow on in the face of the home side's massive 552 for 7 declared. But, led by the precocious talent of 20-year-old Alastair Cook, Essex batted through 176 overs to earn themselves a most creditable draw. Left-hander Cook, a player surely bound for a long Test career with England, stayed 513 minutes and 416 balls for his career-best 195, hitting 27 fours and being joined in a second-wicket stand of 177 by Ravi Bopara, himself just 20. Bopara's 79 was the fourth career-best performance of the match, while Andy Flower's determined unbeaten 142 in 435 minutes, ensured that the hard work of the two youngsters was not wasted. The first day, meanwhile, had witnessed yet another 20-year-old – Bilal Shafayat – showcasing his talent. Shafayat stroked 153 before Usman Afzaal took over centre stage to reach 168 not out, the highest score of his rejuvenated career.

Round Six: 20–23 May 2005

Division One

Hampshire went to the top of the championship table for the first time since 1992 when they overwhelmed Glamorgan by nine wickets to earn themselves maximum points at the Rose Bowl. 'I think we have the ability to win the championship,' said their captain, Shane Warne. The great Australian, for once, did not have much of an influence on the outcome. First, it was centuries from John Crawley and Kevin Pietersen which set up Hampshire's declaration at 401 for 8, and then it was the penetrative seam bowling of Chris Tremlett and Sean Ervine which proved to be too potent for the Welsh county's batting. In the end, not even the loss of Dimitri Mascarenhas with a back injury held up Hampshire's victory drive. Crawley's 106, by the way, was his first century in four years at the Rose Bowl, while Pietersen's 99-ball ton – and eventual 126 from 116 balls – was his first on home soil for his new county, and contained a six and 20 fours.

Kent captain David Fulton, meanwhile, was also talking up his team as potential champions after they knocked Nottinghamshire off top spot with a fine 196-run victory at Trent Bridge. Fulton continued his own consistent start to the season by hitting half-centuries in each innings, and Kent were always in control of the match despite Ryan Sidebottom's first innings 5 for 61 for Notts. Simon Cook was largely responsible for the home side's initial slide to 184, and a sizeable first innings deficit of 117, and after Andrew Hall and Min Patel had combined to send Notts tumbling to 146 for 9 second time around it was only a merry last-wicket stand of 73 between Sidebottom and Oliver Newby which held Kent up somewhat.

Division Two

Durham's bid to start their campaign with five straight wins was ruined by the weather at the Riverside, plus Yorkshire's determination in the field on a truncated final day. On the third evening, as Mike Hussey led his side to 53 without loss, a victory target of 245 looked to be well within Durham's reach. That score had become 105 for 2 on the final day, when rain began to fall. By the time the players were able to return to the field in mid-afternoon, the equation had come down to another 140 wanted from 32 remaining overs. Durham, bidding to become the first team to start a championship season with five wins on the bounce since Surrey in 1955 (who won nine!), then reached 150 for 3 and cut the target down to another 91 from the last 20. Then, however, wickets started to tumble as a succession of batsmen tried in vain to keep the scoreboard moving against excellent Yorkshire bowling, from Deon Kruis and Ian Harvey in particular. In the end, with 28 required from four overs, but with eight wickets down, Durham regretfully decided to shut up shop and ensure the four draw points instead.

The result, of course, still meant that Durham headed Yorkshire at the top of the table, but it was a shame that such a well-fought contest had not been allowed to reach a natural conclusion. Earlier, all three previous innings had featured gutsy fightbacks. Yorkshire's first innings had slumped to 179 for 9 before Kruis joined Richard Dawson in a partnership of 75. Dawson, who had come in at 107 for 6, reached 86 before falling one short of his career-best. Durham's own first innings was similarly struggling along at 146 for 6 before Phil Mustard helped Gareth Breese to add

Boot-iful plumage: Kevin Pietersen hit his first home Hampshire hundred against Glamorgan's battered attack.

Round Six: 20–23 May 2005 Division One

HAMPSHIRE v. GLAMORGAN – at The Rose Bowl

HAMPSHIRE	First Innings		Second Innings	
SM Katich	c Wallace b Davies	20	lbw b Croft	28
MJ Brown	c Wallace b Jones	16	not out	28
JP Crawley	c Croft b Jones	106	not out	24
GA Lamb	c Powell b Croft	42		
KP Pietersen	c Powell b Harrison	126		
*N Pothas	c Jones b Croft	21		
SM Ervine	c Wallace b Davies	34		
AD Mascarenhas	retired hurt	5		
SK Warne (capt)	not out	13		
CT Tremlett	c Elliott b Jones	4		
BV Taylor	not out	1		
Extras	b 7, lb 4, w 2	13		0
	(8 wkts dec 116 overs)	401	(1 wkt 14.4 overs)	80

Bowling
Jones 34-12-73-3. Harrison 20-5-63-1. Davies 26-8-76-2. Thomas 11-0-71-0. Croft 25-2-107-2.
Jones 3-0-24-0. Harrison 3.4-0-20-0. Croft 6-0-28-1. Davies 2-0-8-0.
Fall of Wickets: 1-37, 2-37, 3-115, 4-290, 5-314, 6-369, 7-381, 8-398
1-43

GLAMORGAN	First Innings		Second Innings	
MTG Elliott	lbw b Taylor	51	b Tremlett	15
DD Cherry	b Taylor	2	lbw b Warne	40
DL Hemp	c Pothas b Tremlett	38	c Pothas b Ervine	21
MJ Powell	b Tremlett	4	c Lamb b Ervine	68
J Hughes	c & b Tremlett	0	c Warne b Tremlett	17
*MA Wallace	b Warne	9	lbw b Tremlett	5
RDB Croft (capt)	b Katich	29	c Warne b Katich	30
SD Thomas	b Tremlett	63	c Brown b Ervine	13
DS Harrison	c Tremlett b Katich	0	lbw b Ervine	0
AP Davies	run out	4	not out	16
SP Jones	not out	12	c sub b Ervine	0
Extras	lb 3, nb 14	17	b 1, lb 6, w 1, nb 12, p 5	25
	(68.2 overs)	229	(84.4 overs)	250

Bowling
Tremlett 13-4-42-4. Ervine 10.2-1-30-0. Taylor 15-4-50-2. Warne 21-3-63-1. Lamb 4-0-16-0. Katich 5-0-25-2.
Taylor 19-2-48-0. Ervine 23.4-7-60-5. Tremlett 17-3-54-3. Warne 12-1-34-1. Katich 13-3-42-1.
Fall of Wickets: 1-12, 2-79, 3-85, 4-85, 5-110, 6-112, 7-199, 8-205, 9-215
1-36, 2-79, 3-99, 4-139, 5-147, 6-212, 7-226, 8-228, 9-247

Hampshire won by 9 wickets – Hampshire (22 pts), Glamorgan (3 pts)

NOTTINGHAMSHIRE v. KENT – at Trent Bridge

KENT	First Innings		Second Innings	
DP Fulton (capt)	c Read b Sidebottom	57	c Read b Sidebottom	51
RWT Key	c Hussey b Sidebottom	32	c Hussey b Newby	32
M van Jaarsveld	c Read b Sidebottom	0	b Clough	0
MJ Walker	lbw b Newby	51	c Read b Ealham	48
DI Stevens	lbw b Ealham	33	lbw b Patel	47
AJ Hall	c Gallian b Newby	0	lbw b Patel	0
*NJ O'Brien	c Read b Sidebottom	64	b Patel	8
SJ Cook	b Patel	0	c Ealham b Newby	38
MM Patel	c Read b Ealham	22	not out	37
A Khan	c Fleming b Sidebottom	19	not out	5
MJ Saggers	not out	12		
Extras	b 1, lb 9, w 1	11	b 19, lb 7, w 2, nb 4	32
	(102.2 overs)	301	(8 wkts dec 72 overs)	298

Bowling
Sidebottom 27.2-9-61-5. Newby 20-6-79-2. Ealham 24-5-69-2. Clough 17-2-45-0. Patel 14-2-37-1.
Sidebottom 14-4-35-1. Newby 15-1-78-2. Ealham 15-2-47-1. Clough 7-0-39-1. Patel 21-6-73-3.
Fall of Wickets: 1-81, 2-85, 3-126, 4-159, 5-167, 6-189, 7-192, 8-260, 9-271
1-77, 2-78, 3-136, 4-181, 5-188, 6-209, 7-216, 8-290

NOTTS	First Innings		Second Innings	
DJ Bicknell	run out	63	c van Jaarsveld b Hall	17
JER Gallian	c O'Brien b Cook	18	c Patel b Hall	36
A Singh	c Hall b Saggers	11	c Hall b Cook	11
SP Fleming (capt)	c Fulton b Khan	24	b Patel	20
DJ Hussey	c O'Brien b Cook	23	c O'Brien b Khan	26
*CMW Read	c van Jaarsveld b Cook	0	b Khan	0
SR Patel	c Khan b Hall	12	c Stevens b Hall	3
MA Ealham	c van Jaarsveld b Cook	0	c Hall b Patel	21
GD Clough	not out	14	lbw b Hall	0
RJ Sidebottom	c Cook b Khan	0	st O'Brien b Patel	31
OJ Newby	c Walker b Cook	11	not out	38
Extras	lb 1, w 1, nb 6	8	b 1, lb 11, w 2, nb 2	16
	(64 overs)	184	(73.2 overs)	219

Bowling
Saggers 17-3-66-1. Khan 12-1-38-2. Cook 18-5-44-5. Hall 16-3-33-1. Patel 1-0-2-0.
Saggers 15-7-38-0. Cook 9-2-30-1. Hall 18-5-42-4. Khan 11-3-36-2. Patel 20.2-6-61-3.
Fall of Wickets: 1-51, 2-80, 3-118, 4-134, 5-135, 6-146, 7-146, 8-166, 9-168
1-37, 2-56, 3-76, 4-114, 5-116, 6-116, 7-144, 8-144, 9-146

Kent won by 196 runs – Nottinghamshire (3 pts), Kent (20 pts)

126 for the seventh wicket, and Yorkshire looked to be down and out at 162 for 8 second time around – only for Chris Silverwood to thrash 80 from No. 10 and put on 108 for the ninth wicket with Anthony McGrath, who ended up unbeaten on 133.

A cussed three-and-a-half-hour 85 from Andy Flower could not save Essex from an eventual eight-wicket defeat to Worcestershire at Chelmsford. Gareth Batty turned the game irrevocably towards the visitors when, soon after tea on the third afternoon, he dismissed Flower and James Foster in a decisive spell of off spin. Batty had also made a useful 54 on the previous day, helping century-maker Ben Smith to build a first innings advantage that was stretched to match-winning proportions by a 71-run last-wicket stand between Kabir Ali and Matt Mason. The burly Mason, one of the most consistent quick bowlers on the circuit, also contributed seven wickets to the Worcestershire cause, while Graeme Hick celebrated his 39th birthday to speed them to victory with an unbeaten 76.

Persistent rain and drizzle allowed only 61 overs to be bowled on the first three days of Lancashire's visit to Taunton, leaving Somerset's first innings to stretch until lunchtime on the final day and the match to be condemned to a draw. Sanath Jayasuriya reached his fifty with a flat-batted six off Glen Chapple, before falling to his Sri Lankan team-mate Muttiah

Gareth Batty was at the heart of Worcestershire's win against Essex at Chelmsford.

Muralitharan – who ended up with his 16th haul of five wickets or more in only his 18th championship match for Lancashire spread over three spells with the county. Iain Sutcliffe and Brad Hodge at least enlivened a dull final afternoon with aggressive hundreds as Lancashire sought out as many batting points as they could muster. They added 161 for the third wicket, with opener Sutcliffe's 150 including two sixes and 22 fours.

Round Six: 20–23 May 2005 Division Two

DURHAM v. YORKSHIRE – at The Riverside

YORKSHIRE	First Innings		Second Innings	
MJ Wood	c Lewis ML b Plunkett	0	b Plunkett	8
PA Jaques	c Mustard b Lewis ML	12	c Benkenstein b Plunkett	1
A McGrath	lbw b Collingwood	18	not out	133
MJ Lumb	c Mustard b Davies	28	c Collingwood b Davies	27
IJ Harvey	c Breese b Plunkett	1	c Hussey b Davies	0
C White (capt)	c Mustard b Lewis ML	11	c Collingwood b Plunkett	12
*I Dawood	lbw b Davies	25	c Benkenstein b Lewis ML	12
RKJ Dawson	lbw b Lewis ML	86	c Hussey b Lewis ML	0
TT Bresnan	c Davies b Breese	7	c Collingwood b Lewis ML	5
CEW Silverwood	c Hussey b Lewis ML	2	b Lewis ML	80
GJ Kruis	not out	37	b Lewis ML	5
Extras	b 2, lb 11, w 2, nb 12	27	b 1, lb 8, nb 14	23
	(74.4 overs)	254	(68.2 overs)	306

Bowling
Lewis ML 21.4-7-77-4. Plunkett 21-6-67-2. Davies 14-3-32-2. Collingwood 11-2-39-1. Breese 7-1-26-1.
Lewis ML 21.2-3-80-5. Plunkett 19-2-93-3. Collingwood 11-1-43-0. Davies 13-2-48-2. Benkenstein 2-0-9-0. Breese 2-0-24-0.
Fall of Wickets: 1-1, 2-28, 3-51, 4-57, 5-70, 6-107, 7-124, 8-168, 9-179
1-8, 2-13, 3-72, 4-72, 5-103, 6-128, 7-128, 8-162, 9-270

DURHAM	First Innings		Second Innings	
MEK Hussey (capt)	b Bresnan	26	c Jaques b Kruis	61
JJB Lewis	lbw b Bresnan	23	c Harvey b Kruis	19
PD Collingwood	b Kruis	7	lbw b Kruis	0
GJ Muchall	c Dawood b Silverwood	48	b Harvey	47
DM Benkenstein	lbw b Harvey	21	not out	28
N Peng	c Dawood b Silverwood	13	c Wood b Bresnan	11
GR Breese	lbw b Lumb	64	(8) run out	13
*P Mustard	c McGrath b Dawson	78	(7) c White b Kruis	8
LE Plunkett	c Wood b Bresnan	16	lbw b Harvey	5
M Davies	not out	8	not out	7
ML Lewis	c Wood b Bresnan	2		
Extras	lb 4, w 2, nb 4	10	b 1, lb 12, nb 14	27
	(87 overs)	316	(8 wkts 69 overs)	226

Bowling
Kruis 24-7-97-1. Silverwood 14-2-63-2. Bresnan 20-2-69-4. Harvey 19-5-48-1. McGrath 1-0-5-0. Lumb 5-0-17-1. Dawson 4-0-13-1.
Kruis 30-4-96-4. Silverwood 8-2-23-0. Bresnan 16-5-62-1. Harvey 15-6-32-2.
Fall of Wickets: 1-45, 2-52, 3-60, 4-114, 5-137, 6-146, 7-272, 8-299, 9-304
1-53, 2-53, 3-132, 4-154, 5-168, 6-177, 7-208, 8-219

Match drawn – Durham (10 pts), Yorkshire (9 pts)

ESSEX v. WORCESTERSHIRE – at Chelmsford

ESSEX	First Innings		Second Innings	
WI Jefferson	b Kabir Ali	16	lbw b Vaas	42
AN Cook	c Hick b de Bruyn	39	c Pipe b Mason	46
RS Bopara	lbw b Mason	5	c Hick b Mason	4
A Flower	c Hick b Mason	4	c Hick b Batty	85
RC Irani (capt)	c & b Batty	85	c Pipe b Mason	21
*JS Foster	c Hick b Kabir Ali	22	c Pipe b Batty	39
JD Middlebrook	c Kabir Ali b Batty	37	c Pipe b Batty	0
D Gough	lbw b Mason	4	c Hick b Vaas	29
AP Cowan	c Hick b Mason	0	b Kabir Ali	27
AP Palladino	not out	0	not out	2
AJ Redmond	c Hick b Batty	0	b Kabir Ali	11
Extras	lb 4, nb 4	8	b 2, lb 17, nb 4	23
	(64.5 overs)	220	(100 overs)	329

Bowling
Vaas 12-4-33-0. Kabir Ali 14-2-55-2. Mason 14-1-48-4. de Bruyn 14-2-54-1. Batty 10.5-2-26-3.
Vaas 27-10-73-2. Kabir Ali 18-4-49-2. de Bruyn 18-2-71-0. Mason 23-6-66-3. Batty 14-2-51-3.
Fall of Wickets: 1-29, 2-45, 3-59, 4-69, 5-124, 6-187, 7-200, 8-200, 9-220
1-70, 2-82, 3-109, 4-159, 5-246, 6-246, 7-271, 8-312, 9-312

WORCS	First Innings		Second Innings	
SD Peters	c Bopara b Cowan	10	c Foster b Gough	0
SC Moore	b Bopara	39	not out	63
GA Hick	c Gough b Redmond	19	(4) not out	76
BF Smith	lbw b Gough	100		
VS Solanki (capt)	lbw b Middlebrook	31		
Z de Bruyn	c & b Middlebrook	0		
GJ Batty	st Foster b Middlebrook	54		
WPUJC Vaas	c Foster b Gough	10		
Kabir Ali	b Palladino	53		
*DJ Pipe	lbw b Middlebrook	3	(3) c Cowan b Redmond	11
MS Mason	not out	31		
Extras	lb 7, nb 26	33	b 4, lb 2, w 1, nb 10	17
	(89.1 overs)	383	(2 wkts 32.1 overs)	167

Bowling
Gough 19-1-72-2. Cowan 16-3-59-1. Palladino 7.1-1-38-1. Redmond 14-1-81-1. Bopara 6-0-37-1. Middlebrook 27-2-89-4.
Gough 11-2-33-1. Cowan 9-3-40-0. Redmond 8-1-53-1. Palladino 2.1-0-17-0. Bopara 2-0-18-0.
Fall of Wickets: 1-21, 2-62, 3-94, 4-170, 5-170, 6-258, 7-278, 8-298, 9-312
1-4, 2-21

Worcestershire won by 8 wickets – Essex (4 pts), Worcestershire (21 pts)

SOMERSET v. LANCASHIRE – at Taunton

SOMERSET	First Innings	
MJ Wood	lbw b Anderson	4
JD Francis	c & b Chapple	17
M Burns	lbw b Cork	87
ST Jayasuriya	c Sutcliffe b Muralitharan	73
JC Hildreth	c Loye b Muralitharan	4
ID Blackwell	c Loye b Muralitharan	3
AW Laraman	lbw b Anderson	2
*RJ Turner (capt)	c Sutcliffe b Chapple	45
GM Andrew	c Law b Muralitharan	32
RL Johnson	c Hegg b Muralitharan	0
M Parsons	not out	6
Extras	lb 17, nb 4	21
	(97.1 overs)	294

Bowling
Anderson 23-7-57-2. Cork 14-2-66-1. Chapple 19.1-7-50-2. Flintoff 15-3-48-0. Muralitharan 26-6-56-5.
Fall of Wickets: 1-4, 2-48, 3-187, 4-199, 5-200, 6-203, 7-205, 8-261, 9-261

LANCASHIRE	First Innings	
MJ Chilton (capt)	lbw b Jayasuriya	36
IJ Sutcliffe	c Jayasuriya b Andrew	150
MB Loye	c Johnson b Jayasuriya	11
BJ Hodge	not out	110
A Flintoff	not out	29
SG Law		
*WK Hegg		
G Chapple		
DG Cork		
JM Anderson		
M Muralitharan		
Extras	lb 2, w 3, nb 10	15
	(3 wkts 56.1 overs)	351

Bowling
Johnson 9-1-43-0. Parsons 9-1-47-0. Andrew 14.1-0-106-1. Jayasuriya 16-0-99-2. Laraman 8-0-54-0.
Fall of Wickets: 1-101, 2-123, 3-284

Match drawn – Somerset (7 pts), Lancashire (11 pts)

Round Seven: 25–29 May 2005

Division One

Kent's match against Surrey at Tunbridge Wells fizzled out, eventually, into a tame draw – but there were fireworks off the field on day three as Surrey's punishment for ball tampering was announced by the ECB. Remarkably, the Board's discipline committee, under Gerard Elias QC, decided merely to dock Surrey eight points for their misdemeanour against Nottinghamshire at The Oval on 6 May. The penalty did include another nine points, suspended until 31 May 2006, but the overall impression was that Surrey had got off lightly – especially as their own internal investigation into the affair had revealed no culprits. 'I think the eight-point penalty is a fair one,' said Surrey chief executive Paul Sheldon, 'but this incident is the most disappointing I have had in my ten years at Surrey. It is very disappointing, in particular, that the players have closed ranks over this.' With a maximum of 22 points the penalty for a sub-standard pitch, it seemed as if the Board was considering ball-tampering to be a lesser crime – a dangerous state of affairs, indeed.

On the pitch, and in front of fine crowds at one of the most beautiful grounds and most popular festival weeks on the county circuit, it seemed for long periods of the game that Kent would win comfortably and that Surrey would leave the Nevill Ground with fewer points in the championship table than when they arrived. Surrey had a chance to take control on day two, as Rikki Clarke and Ally Brown took them to 273 for 4 in reply to Kent's first

Round Seven: 25–28 May 2005 Division One

KENT v. SURREY – at Tunbridge Wells

KENT	First Innings		Second Innings	
DP Fulton (capt)	lbw b Bicknell	45	c Benning b Akram	18
RWT Key	c Newman b Benning	112	st Batty b Doshi	189
M van Jaarsveld	lbw b Bicknell	0	(4) b Benning	168
MJ Walker	b Bicknell	0	(6) not out	32
DI Stevens	c Batty b Bicknell	1		
JM Kemp	c Ramprakash b Benning	3	(5) not out	28
AJ Hall	c Ramprakash b Doshi	61		
*NJO'Brien	lbw b Benning	1		
SJ Cook	b Doshi	5		
MM Patel	c Clarke b Doshi	3		
MJ Saggers	not out	5	(3) c Clarke b Bicknell	19
Extras	b 2, lb 2, w 6, nb 16	26	b 4, lb 8, w 1	13
	(92.4 overs)	262	(4 wkts dec 113 overs)	467

Bowling
Bicknell 24-10-31-4. Akram 20-6-51-0. Doshi 13.4-1-58-3. Clarke 12-2-45-0. Benning 16-1-57-3. Salisbury 7-2-16-0.
Bicknell 17.4-3-74-1. Akram 17.2-3-55-1. Doshi 31-1-124-1. Salisbury 19-1-85-0. Benning 23-2-94-1. Clinton 5-1-23-0.
Fall of Wickets: 1-112, 2-112, 3-114, 4-118, 5-129, 6-229, 7-233, 8-251, 9-251
1-36, 2-80, 3-403, 4-407

SURREY	First Innings		Second Innings	
SA Newman	st O'Brien b Patel	21	c Stevens b Saggers	167
RS Clinton	b Saggers	33	c Fulton b Hall	105
MR R'kash (capt)	c van Jaarsveld b Patel	4		
R Clarke	c Cook b Patel	124	(5) not out	3
*JN Batty	c O'Brien b Patel	34	(6) not out	4
AD Brown	c Hall b Stevens	56	(3) st O'Brien b Patel	29
JGE Benning	lbw b Patel	14	(4) b Hall	3
MP Bicknell	b Patel	2		
IDK Salisbury	c O'Brien b Stevens	3		
ND Doshi	c Key b Stevens	16		
M Akram	not out	1		
Extras	b 6, lb 7, w 1, nb 2	16	b 8, lb 9, w 1, nb 4	22
	(91 overs)	324	(4 wkts 98.3 overs)	333

Bowling
Saggers 18-3-53-1. Hall 10-0-40-0. Cook 9-0-48-0. Patel 38-5-124-6. Kemp 3-0-24-0. Stevens 13-4-22-3.
Saggers 8-0-54-1. Patel 42.3-9-120-1. Stevens 10-1-34-0. Cook 7-2-16-0. Hall 17-1-64-2. van Jaarsveld 14-4-28-0.
Fall of Wickets: 1-57, 2-65, 3-67, 4-166, 5-273, 6-299, 7-302, 8-305, 9-323
1-280, 2-316, 3-324, 4-326

Match drawn – Kent (9 pts), Surrey (10 pts)

WARWICKSHIRE v. HAMPSHIRE – at Stratford

HAMPSHIRE	First Innings		Second Innings	
MJ Brown	c Frost b Tahir	15	(2) c Carter b Brown	49
JP Crawley	c Troughton b Tahir	34	(1) c Trott b Streak	3
CC Benham	b Brown	21	b Brown	4
GA Lamb	c Loudon b Carter	0	c Frost b Streak	2
KP Pietersen	b Brown	42	c Trott b Streak	0
*N Pothas	c Frost b Streak	1	c Westwood b Streak	0
SM Ervine	c Frost b Brown	16	lbw b Tahir	32
SK Warne (capt)	c Streak b Brown	0	b Brown	4
SD Udal	c Streak b Trott	34	c Loudon b Streak	0
RJ Logan	b Streak	5	not out	13
BV Taylor	not out	0	c Brown b Streak	12
Extras	b 4, lb 3, w 3, nb 6	16	lb 3, nb 2	5
	(61.5 overs)	184	(37 overs)	124

Bowling
Streak 17-6-39-2. Brown 14-3-59-4. Tahir 13-2-45-2. Carter 15-5-18-1. Trott 2.5-1-16-1.
Streak 13-5-31-6. Brown 13-0-51-3. Tahir 7-2-30-1. Carter 4-1-9-0.
Fall of Wickets: 1-48, 2-65, 3-68, 4-85, 5-94, 6-141, 7-145, 8-145, 9-176
1-12, 2-17, 3-24, 4-34, 5-34, 6-82, 7-87, 8-96, 9-106

WARWICKSHIRE	First Innings		Second Innings	
NV Knight (capt)	c Benham b Udal	51	not out	39
IJ Westwood	c Lamb b Taylor	68	not out	3
MJ Powell	c Pothas b Ervine	5		
NM Carter	b Taylor	6		
IJL Trott	lbw b Warne	28		
AGR Loudon	b Warne	18		
JO Troughton	b Warne	22		
DR Brown	b Warne	12		
*T Frost	c Pietersen b Warne	2		
HH Streak	c Pothas b Warne	22		
N Tahir	not out	5		
Extras	b 3, lb 9, nb 14	26	w 2	2
	(81.2 overs)	265	(0 wkts 4.4 overs)	44

Bowling
Logan 16-4-36-0. Taylor 14-4-54-2. Warne 24.2-2-88-6. Ervine 19-2-59-1. Udal 7-1-16-1. Pietersen 1-1-0-0.
Logan 2-0-22-0. Taylor 2-0-10-0. Lamb 0.4-0-12-0.
Fall of Wickets: 1-135, 2-140, 3-147, 4-150, 5-192, 6-205, 7-225, 8-227, 9-254

Warwickshire won by 10 wickets –
Warwickshire (19 pts), Hampshire (3 pts)

GLOUCESTERSHIRE v. NOTTINGHAMSHIRE – at Bristol

NOTTS	First Innings	
DJ Bicknell	c Gidman b Hardinges	48
JER Gallian	c Adshead b Gidman	46
A Singh	c Adshead b Hardinges	57
SP Fleming (capt)	lbw b Hardinges	92
DJ Hussey	not out	98
*CMW Read	c Gidman b Averis	23
MA Ealham	b Hardinges	27
SR Patel	c Weston b Greenidge	10
RJ Sidebottom	b Kirby	4
GJ Smith	b Chandana	26
OJ Newby	b Greenidge	0
Extras	b 4, lb 3, w 3, nb 28	38
	(117 overs)	469

Bowling
Kirby 20-5-70-1. Greenidge 21-4-104-2. Averis 23-3-65-1. Hardinges 25-4-115-4. Gidman 3-0-19-1. Chandana 25-2-89-1.
Fall of Wickets: 1-87, 2-127, 3-264, 4-265, 5-311, 6-387, 7-403, 8-410, 9-464

GLOS	First Innings		Second Innings	
WPC Weston	c Fleming b Sidebottom	45	c Read b Ealham	1
*SJ Adshead	c Hussey b Sidebottom	45	c Read b Sidebottom	2
Kadeer Ali	c Read b Smith	16	(4) c Hussey b Sidebottom	10
CG Taylor (capt)	lbw b Sidebottom	0	(5) c Fleming b Ealham	12
APR Gidman	c Gallian b Sidebottom	37	(6) c Gallian b Sidebottom	12
JA Pearson	c Read b Newby	15	(7) c Singh b Ealham	68
MA Hardinges	b Ealham	27	(8) c Read b Sidebottom	12
UDU Chandana	c Read b Ealham	17	(9) not out	49
JMM Averis	c Hussey b Ealham	4	(3) c Ealham b Patel	5
CG Greenidge	not out	20	c Read b Smith	7
SP Kirby	b Patel	8	c Bicknell b Smith	5
Extras	b 5, lb 5, nb 2	16	b 3, lb 4, w 1, nb 4	12
	(81.4 overs)	250	(67.3 overs)	192

Bowling
Sidebottom 25-6-65-4. Smith 15-2-55-1. Newby 12-3-66-1. Ealham 16-10-26-3. Patel 13.4-6-24-1.
Sidebottom 18-6-35-4. Ealham 19-4-64-3. Smith 18-5-41-2. Patel 11.3-1-41-1. Hussey 1-0-4-0.
Fall of Wickets: 1-100, 2-101, 3-101, 4-134, 5-162, 6-183, 7-202, 8-206, 9-225
1-3, 2-3, 3-18, 4-31, 5-36, 6-83, 7-160, 8-171, 9-181

Nottinghamshire won by an innings and 27 runs –
Gloucestershire (5 pts), Nottinghamshire (22 pts)

SUSSEX v. MIDDLESEX – at Hove

MIDDLESEX	First Innings		Second Innings	
ET Smith	c Adams b Lewry	41	c Prior b Lewry	29
BL Hutton (capt)	c Lewry b Kirtley	4	c Prior b Kirtley	7
OA Shah	b Martin-Jenkins	58	lbw b Lewry	20
EC Joyce	c Ward b Martin-Jenkins	82	c van der Wath b M Ahmed	6
SB Styris	c Goodwin b Kirtley	34	b Lewry	2
JWM Dalrymple	lbw b Kirtley	0	c Adams b Lewry	65
PN Weekes	c Prior b Kirtley	55	c Prior b Mushtaq Ahmed	71
*BJM Scott	c Prior b Kirtley	19	b Lewry	4
IK Pathan	c Prior b Kirtley	41	not out	13
MM Betts	not out	36	c Prior b Lewry	6
A Richardson	b Mushtaq Ahmed	10	b Mushtaq Ahmed	0
Extras	lb 12, w 1, nb 8	21	b 4, lb 7, w 2, nb 8	21
	(126.5 overs)	401	(63.3 overs)	244

Bowling
Kirtley 32-8-80-6. Lewry 27-3-92-1. van der Wath 18-6-54-0. Mushtaq Ahmed 30.5-3-117-1. Martin-Jenkins 18-1-45-2. Yardy 1-0-1-0.
Kirtley 12-2-37-1. van der Wath 7-2-25-0. Lewry 16-5-65-6. Mushtaq Ahmed 24.3-2-77-3. Martin-Jenkins 4-0-29-0.
Fall of Wickets: 1-9, 2-76, 3-125, 4-209, 5-209, 6-247, 7-290, 8-323, 9-368
1-18, 2-48, 3-63, 4-68, 5-72, 6-212, 7-218, 8-219, 9-243

SUSSEX	First Innings		Second Innings	
IJ Ward	b Pathan	6	c Scott b Pathan	24
RR Montgomerie	lbw b Pathan	6	c Hutton b Styris	52
MH Yardy	c Shah b Richardson	9	st Scott b Styris	5
MW Goodwin	c & b Styris	67	c Shah b Richardson	88
CJ Adams (capt)	b Styris	72	b Richardson	9
*MJ Prior	c Hutton b Richardson	41	c & b Styris	42
RSC Martin-Jenkins	c Scott b Pathan	25	b Richardson	32
JJ van der Wath	lbw b Richardson	0	lbw b Styris	6
Mushtaq Ahmed	c Shah b Weekes	57	c Styris b Richardson	0
RJ Kirtley	c & b Pathan	14	not out	4
JD Lewry	not out	12	not out	0
Extras	b 2, lb 11, nb 10	23	lb 7, nb 12, p 5	24
	(94 overs)	332	(9 wkts 90 overs)	286

Bowling
Pathan 25-5-81-4. Richardson 31-6-124-3. Betts 13-2-61-0. Styris 18-4-42-2. Dalrymple 4-2-4-0. Weekes 3-1-7-1.
Pathan 17-0-68-1. Richardson 23-8-40-4. Styris 29-4-83-4. Betts 8-1-40-0. Weekes 10-1-34-0. Dalrymple 3-1-9-0.
Fall of Wickets: 1-12, 2-19, 3-27, 4-157, 5-180, 6-232, 7-233, 8-252, 9-314
1-26, 2-33, 3-179, 4-193, 5-195, 6-263, 7-273, 8-274, 9-280

Match drawn – Sussex (10 pts), Middlesex (12 pts)

Hot Streak: Warwickshire's Heath blew away Hampshire at lovely Stratford-upon-Avon.

innings 262, but then Min Patel hauled his side back into the match. And, when Robert Key followed up his skilful first-day 112 with a high-class and often dismissive second innings knock of 189, with two sixes off Nayan Doshi and 19 fours, and during which he figured in a record Kent second-wicket partnership with Martin van Jaarsveld, whose 168 from 237 balls featured 21 boundaries, it looked as if there would be only one winner. But the pitch had, by now, lost any pace it once possessed and by mid-afternoon on the final day Surrey openers Scott Newman and Richard Clinton even looked to be manoeuvring their team into a winning position. In the end, though, after Newman was dismissed for 167 – his third championship hundred in four innings – and Clinton failed to press the accelerator hard enough, Surrey made merely a token effort through Brown and James Benning. 'It was very strange that they didn't really have a go for it,' said Kent captain David Fulton, who admitted he had been a worried man either side of the tea interval.

There was a two-day finish at Stratford-upon-Avon, to the disappointment even of Warwickshire supporters, who had seen their side thrash Hampshire by ten wickets on another lovely outground setting. The fact that Warwickshire County Council underwrote the match financially, however, meant that the host county did not lose out when refunds were paid to spectators and corporate guests who had purchased tickets for the lost third day.

Shane Warne responded to Hampshire's dismissal for only 184 on the first day by taking 6 for 88, but by then Warwickshire captain Nick Knight and his opening partner Ian Westwood had already seized the advantage for their side with a first-wicket stand of 135. Heath Streak's second innings new ball spell of 9-5-11-4 then further undermined Hampshire, and the Zimbabwean fast bowler ended up with 6 for 31 as he and Dougie Brown, who took seven wickets in the game, sent the visitors tumbling to 124 all out.

Nottinghamshire's innings and 27-run thumping of Gloucestershire at Bristol also maintained their own championship challenge, and Ryan Sidebottom's left-arm pace was at the heart of their success once the top-order batsmen had built a formidable first innings total of 469. Stephen Fleming's 98-ball 92 was a classy effort, featuring a six and 16 fours, but David Hussey also batted beautifully and was unlucky to be stranded on 98 not out when the innings ended. Gloucestershire's demise was spectacular, following a 100-run opening stand between Phil Weston and Steve Adshead, and by the close of the second day they were already following on and in dire straits at 3 for 2. The only real home resistance the next day came from 21-year-old James Pearson, in his first appearance for three years, who made a career-best 68 and went to 50 by pulling Samit Patel for six.

In many ways the best match in this division's round of games came at Hove, where Sussex came within 29 runs of beating Middlesex in a tense last day run chase before shutting up shop with nine wickets down. Richard Montgomerie and Murray Goodwin led the Sussex chase with fine half-centuries, but it was the fall of Matt Prior for 42 in the 82nd over of a possible 90 which scuppered the Sussex effort. Alan Richardson and Scott Styris bowled tenaciously for Middlesex on the last day, and this was a closely fought affair on a good cricket pitch from first ball to last.

James Kirtley's 6 for 80 prevented Middlesex from getting away from Sussex in their first innings, which featured a lovely 82 from Ed Joyce. Jason Lewry produced figures of 6 for 65 to give the home side their tantalising glimpse of possible victory after Sussex had fallen 69 runs short of their visitors on first innings. Middlesex, in fact, were in some difficulty at 72 for 5 in their second innings, before Jamie Dalrymple and Paul Weekes rallied them with a sixth-wicket partnership of 140.

Division Two

Somerset gained their first championship win of the season as a result of Northamptonshire's horrendous second innings collapse at Wantage Road. The home side had looked to be in command when Martin Love and Riki Wessels made first-innings hundreds and Jason Brown then snatched six first-innings Somerset wickets to earn a 52-run advantage. But then, against the swinging ball as purveyed by the medium pace trio of Gareth Andrew, Aaron Laraman and Mike Burns, Northants plunged to 100 all out in just 36.5 overs. A second-wicket partnership of 112 in 33 overs between Burns and John Francis then all but settled matters in Somerset's favour.

Love's 166 on day one was his fifth century in 11 championship innings for Northants, while the 19-year-old Wessels hit his maiden first-class hundred off only 116 balls. It was only his fifth

Darren Gough: a five-wicket haul and almost a hundred against his former county Yorkshire at Headingley.

Round Seven: 25–29 May 2005 Division Two

NORTHAMPTONSHIRE v. SOMERSET – at Northampton

NORTHANTS	First Innings		Second Innings	
ML Love	st Turner b Blackwell	166	lbw b Laraman	33
BM Shafayat	lbw b McLean	8	c Wood b Andrew	4
RA White	c Laraman b Johnson	49	(4) lbw b McLean	8
DJG Sales (capt)	c Hildreth b Johnson	0	(6) c Hildreth b Laraman	15
U Afzaal	c Wood b Johnson	0	lbw b Andrew	3
*MH Wessels	c Jayasuriya b Laraman	102	(7) c Blackwell b Burns	8
DG Wright	c Burns b Blackwell	9	(8) not out	14
BJ Phillips	b Laraman	5	(9) c Francis b Blackwell	3
J Louw	c Laraman b Andrew	37	(3) c Turner b Andrew	5
PS Jones	c Andrew b Jayasuriya	14	b Blackwell	0
JF Brown	not out	4	b Burns	0
Extras	lb 4, w 5, nb 5	14	b 4, lb 3	7
	(102.2 overs)	**408**	(36.5 overs)	**100**

Bowling
McLean 20-5-91-1. Johnson 17-3-54-3. Andrew 10.2-1-66-1. Blackwell 24-6-85-2. Jayasuriya 10-3-33-1. Laraman 13-2-56-2. Burns 8-1-19-0.
McLean 9-3-29-1. Andrew 12-4-31-3. Jayasuriya 1-1-0-0. Laraman 7-2-21-2. Burns 6.5-1-12-2. Blackwell 1-1-0-2.
Fall of Wickets: 1-21, 2-117, 3-117, 4-117, 5-302, 6-335, 7-344, 8-358, 9-400
1-12, 2-31, 3-40, 4-49, 5-72, 6-73, 7-85, 8-99, 9-99

SOMERSET	First Innings		Second Innings	
MJ Wood	c White b Brown	53	c Wessels b Wright	5
JD Francis	c Sales b Phillips	43	c Wessels b Brown	55
M Burns	c White b Wright	34	lbw b Louw	48
ST Jayasuriya	c Love b Brown	55	c Wright b Louw	22
JC Hildreth	c Wessels b Jones	20	not out	7
ID Blackwell	b Brown	59	not out	2
AW Laraman	lbw b Brown	16		
*RJ Turner (capt)	not out	27		
GM Andrew	b Brown	0		
RL Johnson	run out	32		
NAM McLean	c sub b Brown	0		
Extras	b 3, lb 6, nb 8	17	lb 3, w 9, nb 4	16
	(93.5 overs)	**356**	(4 wkts 46.1 overs)	**155**

Bowling
Louw 13-3-59-0. Wright 20-2-78-1. Jones 8-1-46-1. Brown 34.5-7-112-6. Phillips 18-4-52-1.
Wright 12-1-26-1. Louw 13-4-43-2. Brown 13.1-3-51-1. Phillips 3-0-15-0. Afzaal 5-1-17-0.
Fall of Wickets: 1-81, 2-121, 3-143, 4-183, 5-229, 6-271, 7-300, 8-300, 9-346
1-6, 2-118, 3-144, 4-144

Somerset won by 6 wickets –
Northamptonshire (8 pts), Somerset (21 pts)

YORKSHIRE v. ESSEX – at Headingley

ESSEX	First Innings	
WI Jefferson	lbw b Kruis	4
AN Cook	lbw b Kruis	42
GW Flower	lbw b Silverwood	0
RS Bopara	c Wood b McGrath	18
A Flower	c Silverwood b Bresnan	188
RC Irani (capt)	c Jaques b Bresnan	103
D Gough	c White b McGrath	93
*JS Foster	c McGrath b Dawson	92
JD Middlebrook	not out	44
AR Adams		
AJ Redmond		
Extras	b 1, lb 11, w 4, nb 22	38
	(8 wkts dec 184.3 overs)	**622**

Bowling
Kruis 32-8-93-2. Silverwood 29-13-80-1. Bresnan 32-6-101-2. Harvey 23-8-80-0. McGrath 20-4-58-2. Dawson 33.3-2-147-1. White 7-1-25-0. Lumb 8-1-26-0.
Fall of Wickets: 1-7, 2-12, 3-55, 4-76, 5-289, 6-429, 7-528, 8-622

YORKSHIRE	First Innings		Second Innings	
MJ Wood	c & b Adams	17	c Foster b Middlebrook	31
PA Jaques	c Foster b Adams	2	st Foster b Flower GW	89
A McGrath	lbw b Gough	35	c Foster b Jefferson	50
MJ Lumb	c Foster b Gough	33	c Bopara b Middlebrook	3
IJ Harvey	b Redmond	76	c & b Adams	15
C White (capt)	lbw b Bopara	60	not out	17
*I Dawood	lbw b Gough	21	not out	5
RKJ Dawson	c Cook b Gough	1		
TT Bresnan	c Jefferson b Redmond	70		
CEW Silverwood	b Gough	40		
GJ Kruis	not out	26		
Extras	b 3, lb 12, w 4, nb 8	27	b 7, lb 5, w 6, nb 10	28
	(135.2 overs)	**408**	(5 wkts 68 overs)	**238**

Bowling
Gough 29-6-85-5. Adams 39-11-96-2. Redmond 26.2-9-70-2. Bopara 7-0-43-1. Middlebrook 28-7-78-0. Flower GW 6-0-21-0.
Adams 9-0-38-1. Redmond 13-3-67-0. Middlebrook 29-8-75-2. Gough 5-2-13-0. Flower GW 5-2-8-1. Bopara 3-1-9-0. Jefferson 4-0-16-1.
Fall of Wickets: 1-13, 2-42, 3-79, 4-158, 5-201, 6-245, 7-247, 8-279, 9-370
1-94, 2-146, 3-149, 4-181, 5-223

Match drawn – Yorkshire (9 pts),
Essex (12 pts)

DERBYSHIRE v. LEICESTERSHIRE – at Derby

DERBYSHIRE	First Innings		Second Innings	
SD Stubbings	lbw b Willoughby	1	(2) lbw b Willoughby	32
MJ Di Venuto	c Masters b Maunders	76	(1) c & b Willoughby	73
JDC Bryant	c Nixon b Gibson	21	c Nixon b Gibson	61
Hassan Adnan	c Henderson b Masters	2	c Sadler b Henderson	16
J Moss	c & b Masters	4	b Maddy	5
*LD Sutton (capt)	c Nixon b Gibson	23	c Maddy b Henderson	8
G Welch	c Sadler b Maddy	42	lbw b Masters	13
AG Botha	c Nixon b Maddy	26	c Willoughby b Gibson	30
AKD Gray	not out	28	c Maddy b Gibson	14
ID Hunter	lbw b Henderson	9	st Nixon b Henderson	8
PMR Havell	not out	2	not out	0
Extras	b 1, lb 7, w 1, nb 8	17	b 4, lb 7, w 6, nb 8	25
	(9 wkts 103.3 overs)	**251**	(123 overs)	**285**

Bowling
Gibson 22-7-48-2. Willoughby 19-2-59-1. Masters 15-2-28-2. Maddy 12-3-26-2. Henderson 22.3-5-48-1. Mongia 4-0-11-0. Maunders 9-2-23-1.
Gibson 23-4-66-3. Willoughby 25-7-66-2. Henderson 38-9-76-3. Mongia 6-1-12-0. Maddy 18-8-25-1. Masters 11-3-22-1. Maunders 2-0-7-0.
Fall of Wickets: 1-3, 2-36, 3-51, 4-61, 5-106, 6-146, 7-201, 8-212, 9-245
1-81, 2-160, 3-191, 4-197, 5-208, 6-211, 7-259, 8-271, 9-285

LEICESTERSHIRE	First Innings		Second Innings	
DDJ Robinson	c Stubbings b Botha	110	c Sutton b Welch	14
DL Maddy	lbw b Moss	44	c Sutton b Havell	8
JK Maunders	c Gray b Welch	5	c Gray b Moss	23
D Mongia	c Sutton b Welch	51	b Gray	47
HD Ackerman (capt)	c Sutton b Welch	9	b Gray	57
JL Sadler	c Welch b Gray	13	not out	56
*PA Nixon	b Gray	0	c Hassan Adnan b Botha	33
OD Gibson	c Di Venuto b Botha	5	not out	4
CW Henderson	run out	6		
DD Masters	not out	25		
CM Willoughby	c Moss b Welch	6		
Extras	b 1, lb 2, nb 2	5	b 2, lb 8, nb 6	16
	(89.2 overs)	**279**	(6 wkts 85.1 overs)	**258**

Bowling
Hunter 14-5-47-0. Havell 9-2-41-0. Welch 18.2-4-48-4. Moss 18-7-42-1. Botha 13-3-41-2. Gray 17-2-57-2.
Hunter 8-1-34-0. Havell 12-0-45-1. Welch 24-7-52-1. Moss 14-7-22-1. Botha 9.1-0-54-1. Gray 18-5-41-2.
Fall of Wickets: 1-85, 2-96, 3-188, 4-206, 5-227, 6-232, 7-241, 8-241, 9-252
1-14, 2-42, 3-48, 4-143, 5-170, 6-254

Leicestershire won by 4 wickets –
Derbyshire (5 pts), Leicestershire (19 pts)

first-class innings, too, and after hitting a six and 17 fours the wicketkeeper-batsman son of Kepler Wessels, Northants' director of cricket, said he would one day like to represent England. His father, of course, played Test cricket both for Australia and then his native South Africa, but Riki Wessels said he did not feel South African because he was born and brought up largely in Australia. 'I'm still trying to find a home,' he said, 'and I hope it will be here in England.'

Yorkshire's hosting of Essex at Headingley was notable for one distinctive all-round performance – by former Yorkshire fast bowler Darren Gough. Sporting a new and severe haircut, the England one-day international veteran enjoyed himself immensely at his former team-mates' expense. After coming in as a nightwatchman towards the end of day one, Gough joined Andy Flower in an eventual sixth-wicket stand of 140 – dominating it with a bruising innings of 93 from 104 balls. He finally miscued an intended pull to cover, having hit three sixes and 11 fours, and as he walked back to an ovation from the Yorkshire faithful, one wag shouted out: 'Sign him up!' Gough was highly amused, and said later: 'That really made me chuckle.'

Gough, however, was not finished with the county he left amid some controversy at the end of the 2003 season. Replying to Essex's massive 622 for 8 declared, in which Ronnie Irani had also scored 103 and James Foster an accomplished 92, Yorkshire foundered on Gough's bowling, with only a ninth-wicket alliance of 91 between Tim Bresnan and Chris Silverwood eventually hauling them above 400. Gough finished with 5 for 85, but he only sent down five overs after Yorkshire had been asked to follow on. Phil Jaques, with a powerful 89 from 99 balls, steered the battered home side to the safety of a draw as the rest of the Essex attack could not match the effort of their ageing spearhead.

Leicestershire took the honours in the battle of the basement at Derby, rallying well from 48 for 3 on the last morning to reach a testing victory target. Derbyshire had begun that final day 243 runs ahead at 271 for 7, but their last three wickets only lasted five overs and suddenly Leicestershire were chasing 258 in a minimum of 89 overs. It was a better prospect than they would have expected at the beginning of the day but, after their early collapse, it still took batting of character and quality by Dinesh Mongia, Hylton Ackerman, John Sadler and Paul Nixon to see them home with, at the end, 23 balls to spare. Sadler's unbeaten 56 was especially valuable, while Darren Robinson's first innings 110

was another vital contribution in the context of a relatively low-scoring and attritional contest. Michael Di Venuto was the outstanding home batsman, with knocks of 76 and 73.

Round Eight: 1–4 June 2005

Division One

There was controversy at the Mote, Maidstone, when Kent were docked eight points for poor pitch preparation during the process of beating Gloucestershire by seven wickets. Kent subsequently appealed against the penalty, saying that bad batsmanship had contributed to wickets falling in conditions in which swing as much as seam movement had made survival a tricky proposition. The appeal was rejected, with the ECB upholding the decision made after Tony Pigott, the pitch liaison officer, had initially called in pitch inspector David Hughes on the opening day. They, in turn, had taken technical advice from Harry Brind, the ECB's pitches consultant and a former groundsman at The Oval. The surface of the pitch was damp when the game

A high-class 162 from Matthew Elliott saved Glamorgan from defeat against Sussex at Swansea.

began, but Kent argued that heavy rain in the days leading up to the game had hindered the pitch's preparation at a ground, ironically, with a tradition of being a batsman's paradise. Kent, in the end, were most unhappy at their treatment and captain David Fulton said, 'Surrey had eight points deducted for ball-tampering, which is deliberate cheating, and we receive the same penalty for a damp pitch. I feel that is harsh, and I have played on much worse pitches than this one.'

Gloucestershire reached 178 for 9 on a weather-shortened opening day, having been 92 for 7 at one stage – despite Matt Windows taking 17 off an Andrew Hall over. Kent's batsmen made little better progress in reply, but Darren Stevens followed up his top score of 35 with three cheap wickets as Gloucestershire slumped to 79 for 7 in their second innings by the close of day two. Kent's victory, albeit worth 10 points and not 18, did not take long in coming the following morning.

The never-say-die attitude of Shane Warne, who continually cajoled and encouraged his troops even when the situation seemed hopeless, inspired Hampshire to one of the most remarkable victories even the venerable County Championship has seen, against Nottinghamshire at Trent Bridge. The loss of the entire opening day to rain did not prevent Hampshire captain Warne, and his opposite number Stephen Fleming, from seeking to generate a positive result in a match that was vital to both sides' title aspirations. Two declarations meant that Notts were chasing 276 from 65 overs and, at 227 for 3, and later at 250 for 4, they seemed home and

Round Eight: 1–4 June 2005 Division One

KENT v. GLOUCESTERSHIRE – at Maidstone

GLOS	First Innings		Second Innings	
WPC Weston	b Hall	5	b Khan	0
*SJ Adshead	c Patel b Cook	2	c O'Brien b Hall	3
MGN Windows	lbw b Khan	39	c Kemp b Cook	15
CG Taylor (capt)	lbw b Cook	0	c O'Brien b Khan	18
APR Gidman	b Stevens	2	c Kemp b Stevens	13
JA Pearson	c O'Brien b Kemp	13	c Fulton b Stevens	0
MA Hardinges	c O'Brien b Khan	27	c O'Brien b Hall	19
UDU Chandana	c Kemp b Hall	7	c O'Brien b Stevens	1
ID Fisher	c O'Brien b Cook	39	c O'Brien b Hall	22
CG Greenidge	lbw b Khan	25	c O'Brien b Cook	0
SP Kirby	not out	4	not out	4
Extras	lb 6, w 1, nb 13	20	w 1, nb 2	3
	(60.3 overs)	183	(43.1 overs)	98

Bowling
Khan 11.3-2-31-3. Hall 16-4-47-2. Cook 19-6-54-3. Stevens 8-4-16-1. Patel 1-0-4-0. Kemp 5-2-25-1.
Khan 13-3-25-2. Hall 12.1-4-36-3. Cook 6-0-18-2. Stevens 11-2-19-3. Kemp 1-1-0-0.
Fall of Wickets: 1-5, 2-25, 3-25, 4-48, 5-54, 6-83, 7-92, 8-128, 9-170
1-0, 2-14, 3-26, 4-48, 5-52, 6-52, 7-56, 8-91, 9-92

KENT	First Innings		Second Innings	
DP Fulton (capt)	c Adshead b Hardinges	21	b Kirby	0
JL Denly	b Kirby	4	c Hardinges b Kirby	10
M van Jaarsveld	c Fisher b Greenidge	10	b Kirby	15
MJ Walker	b Hardinges	13	not out	19
DI Stevens	c & b Gidman	35	not out	23
JM Kemp	c Adshead b Hardinges	0		
AJ Hall	c Weston b Gidman	25		
*NJO'Brien	c Taylor b Hardinges	13		
SJ Cook	st Adshead b Fisher	23		
MM Patel	c Adshead b Hardinges	29		
A Khan	not out	11		
Extras	b 7, lb 6, w 1, nb 6	20	b 5, lb 6	11
	(67 overs)	204	(3 wkts 16.4 overs)	78

Bowling
Kirby 14-3-42-1. Greenidge 14-4-36-1. Hardinges 18-2-51-5. Gidman 9-2-28-2. Chandana 7-0-19-0. Fisher 5-1-15-1.
Kirby 8.4-2-38-3. Greenidge 3-1-6-0. Hardinges 5-0-23-0.
Fall of Wickets: 1-11, 2-43, 3-47, 4-71, 5-75, 6-125, 7-130, 8-157, 9-176
1-0, 2-26, 3-35

Kent won by 7 wickets – Kent (18 pts), Gloucestershire (3 pts)

NOTTINGHAMSHIRE v. HAMPSHIRE – at Trent Bridge

HAMPSHIRE	First Innings		Second Innings	
GA Lamb	c Hussey b Sidebottom	15	c Read b Hussey	75
MJ Brown	c Read b Harris	26	b Hussey	54
JP Crawley	b Ealham	39	b Hussey	6
KP Pietersen	lbw b Harris	0	c Harris b Hussey	41
CD McMillan	c Fleming b Harris	52	not out	26
*N Pothas	lbw b Harris	27		
SM Ervine	c Hussey b Harris	15	(6) not out	16
SK Warne (capt)	c Hussey b Sidebottom	46		
SD Udal	c Gallian b Swann	16		
CT Tremlett	not out	24		
RJ Logan	c Read b Harris	4		
Extras	b 1, lb 10, nb 2	13	w 2	2
	(81.4 overs)	277	(4 wkts dec 28.3 overs)	220

Bowling
Sidebottom 25-5-89-2. Smith 17-6-45-0. Harris 23.4-6-83-6. Swann 5-1-16-1. Ealham 11-4-33-1.
Gallian 10-1-71-0. Hussey 14-1-105-4. Bicknell 4.3-0-44-0.
Fall of Wickets: 1-34, 2-46, 3-50, 4-121, 5-162, 6-169, 7-206, 8-246, 9-250
1-90, 2-108, 3-172, 4-195

NOTTS	First Innings		Second Innings	
DJ Bicknell	c Brown b Ervine	4	c Lamb b Tremlett	13
JER Gallian	lbw b McMillan	17	c Crawley b Logan	20
A Singh	b McMillan	27	c Crawley b McMillan	18
SP Fleming (capt)	lbw b Ervine	7	c Ervine b Udal	105
DJ Hussey	c Udal b Tremlett	42	c Crawley b Tremlett	64
*CMW Read	not out	59	st Crawley b Warne	8
MA Ealham	not out	41	c Pothas b Tremlett	2
GP Swann			c Crawley b Tremlett	0
RJ Sidebottom			b Warne	0
GJ Smith			c Crawley b Tremlett	0
AJ Harris			not out	0
Extras	b 6, lb 4, w 3, nb 12	25	b 4, lb 9, w 4, nb 14	31
	(5 wkts dec 56.5 overs)	222	(63.2 overs)	261

Bowling
Tremlett 11.5-1-42-1. Ervine 15-5-36-2. Logan 8-0-50-0. Warne 7-0-26-0. McMillan 13-3-49-2. Udal 2-0-9-0.
Tremlett 16-1-80-5. Logan 8-2-22-1. Ervine 11-1-54-0. McMillan 11-1-36-1. Warne 12.2-1-37-2. Udal 5-0-19-1.
Fall of Wickets: 1-9, 2-57, 3-60, 4-64, 5-139
1-24, 2-53, 3-95, 4-227, 5-250, 6-258, 7-261, 8-261, 9-261

Hampshire won by 14 runs – Nottinghamshire (4 pts), Hampshire (17 pts)

SURREY v. WARWICKSHIRE – at Whitgift School

SURREY	First Innings		Second Innings	
SA Newman	c Frost b Streak	4	c Streak b Carter	37
RS Clinton	c Loudon b Brown	84	c Powell b Loudon	29
MR R'kash (capt)	b Carter	39	c Trott b Carter	18
R Clarke	c Frost b Tahir	12		
*JN Batty	not out	84	(4) c Frost b Tahir	31
AD Brown	b Loudon	40	(5) c Troughton b Tahir	14
MP Bicknell	c Knight b Streak	11	(6) c sub b Trott	58
TJ Murtagh	c Loudon b Carter	23	(7) not out	74
Harbhajan Singh	c Frost b Carter	0	not out	15
J Ormond	c Powell b Brown	9	(8) c Trott b Westwood	20
M Akram	hit wkt b Brown	4		
Extras	b 8, lb 13, w 1, nb 8	30	lb 10, nb 4	14
	(96 overs)	340	(7 wkts dec 81 overs)	310

Bowling
Streak 26-4-98-2. Brown 26-10-63-3. Carter 19-3-77-3. Tahir 9-1-42-1. Loudon 16-2-39-1.
Streak 12-4-37-0. Brown 11-1-38-0. Carter 14-4-43-1. Loudon 25-1-89-1. Tahir 8-0-28-3. Trott 8-2-35-1. Westwood 3-0-30-1.
Fall of Wickets: 1-8, 2-120, 3-140, 4-154, 5-223, 6-240, 7-284, 8-284, 9-324
1-66, 2-83, 3-103, 4-123, 5-150, 6-243, 7-273

WARWICKSHIRE	First Innings		Second Innings	
NV Knight (capt)	c Brown b Akram	37	c Batty b Ormond	35
IJ Westwood	c Clarke b Ormond	18	c Brown b Ormond	2
MJ Powell	c Newman b Akram	18	(4) not out	65
IJL Trott	c Batty b Akram	41	(3) c Brown b Harbhajan	37
AGR Loudon	c Batty b Ormond	58	not out	61
JO Troughton	run out	12		
DR Brown	c Batty b Akram	0		
*T Frost	c Clarke b Harbhajan	3		
HH Streak	c Newman b Harbhajan	19		
NM Carter	b Akram	0		
N Tahir	not out	0		
Extras	lb 3	3	b 8, lb 6, nb 8	22
	(57 overs)	209	(3 wkts 83 overs)	222

Bowling
Bicknell 7-1-40-0. Ormond 14-5-37-2. Harbhajan 20-4-57-2. Akram 12-4-51-5. Murtagh 4-0-21-0.
Bicknell 16-6-39-0. Ormond 23-4-68-2. Harbhajan 26-9-60-1. Akram 12-5-25-0. Murtagh 5-2-6-0. Clinton 1-0-10-0.
Fall of Wickets: 1-48, 2-67, 3-86, 4-168, 5-182, 6-184, 7-187, 8-197, 9-197
1-14, 2-69, 3-91

Match drawn – Surrey (10 pts), Warwickshire (8 pts)

GLAMORGAN v. SUSSEX – at Swansea

SUSSEX	First Innings	
IJ Ward	c Wallace b Harrison AJ	35
RR Montgomerie	not out	184
MH Yardy	lbw b Croft	38
MW Goodwin	c Wallace b Croft	158
CJ Adams (capt)	c Wallace b Davies	32
*MJ Prior	st Wallace b Cosker	30
JJ van der Wath	not out	9
RSC Martin-Jenkins		
Mushtaq Ahmed		
RJ Kirtley		
JD Lewry		
Extras	b 4, lb 2, w 1, nb 4	11
	(5 wkts dec 124 overs)	497

Bowling
Harrison DS 25-6-94-0. Davies 27-4-120-1. Croft 25-1-100-2. Harrison AJ 15-2-54-1. Ganguly 4-1-7-0. Cosker 28-2-116-1.
Fall of Wickets: 1-65, 2-133, 3-374, 4-450, 5-487

GLAMORGAN	First Innings		Second Innings	
MTG Elliott	lbw b Lewry	85	(2) c Kirtley b Yardy	162
DD Cherry	b Lewry	0	(1) b van der Wath	87
MJ Powell	b Kirtley	16	(4) not out	24
DL Hemp	b Lewry	128	(3) c & b Yardy	56
SC Ganguly	b Lewry	0	not out	15
*MA Wallace	lbw b Lewry	24		
RDB Croft (capt)	c Montgomerie b Lewry	9		
DS Harrison	lbw b Mushtaq Ahmed	1		
DA Cosker	not out	19		
AP Davies	c Goodwin b Mushtaq Ahmed	0		
AJ Harrison	b Mushtaq Ahmed	0		
Extras	b 1, lb 8, nb 10	19	lb 4, nb 6	10
	(61 overs)	301	(3 wkts 80 overs)	354

Bowling
Kirtley 11-1-49-1. Lewry 21-4-77-6. van der Wath 9-2-38-0. Mushtaq Ahmed 13-1-77-3. Yardy 1-0-5-0. Martin-Jenkins 6-0-46-0.
Kirtley 10-3-23-0. Lewry 11-1-42-0. Martin-Jenkins 6-0-28-0. van der Wath 12-0-73-1. Mushtaq Ahmed 15-0-92-0. Yardy 16-1-62-2. Adams 4-0-17-0. Montgomerie 5-0-13-0. Ward 1-1-0-0.
Fall of Wickets: 1-16, 2-37, 3-209, 4-209, 5-247, 6-267, 7-270, 8-294, 9-301
1-214, 2-296, 3-319

Match drawn – Glamorgan (8 pts), Sussex (12 pts)

dry. But, after David Hussey had gone for 64, Fleming himself holed out off Shaun Udal for 105 – a brilliant innings off 123 balls with three sixes and ten fours – and Warne suddenly smelt a chance of his own.

It was a Chris Tremlett hat-trick, though, which proved the decisive moments as Notts plunged to 261 all out and defeat by 14 runs. First, a fine Nic Pothas catch at deep square leg accounted for Mark Ealham, and then both Graeme Swann and Greg Smith fell first ball. With ten balls remaining, who else but Warne settled matters by bowling Ryan Sidebottom. Earlier Kevin Pietersen, in his first match back at Trent Bridge since leaving Notts, was trapped lbw for a second-ball duck by Andrew Harris – who went on to claim his first haul of five wickets or more since September 2002.

What otherwise was a gentle draw at Whitgift School was briefly enlivened when Surrey's Indian off-spinner Harbhajan Singh was called for a no-ball after bouncing a ball at Warwickshire's Mike Powell and sending it clean over the wicketkeeper's head. The umpires, Allan Jones and Peter Willey, would not confirm afterwards that Harbhajan had been called for throwing – saying they needed to seek 'clarification' from the ECB before commenting – but the bowler defused a potential incident by insisting he had not been no-balled for a throw.

Glamorgan might have been in trouble at Swansea after being forced to follow on early on the final day of a match against Sussex that had seen the whole of the first day washed out by rain. But Dan Cherry made a solid 87, Matthew Elliott a high-class 162 from just 171 balls, with 19 fours and two sixes, and David Hemp followed up his first innings 128 with another fluent 54-ball 56 to ensure a draw. Elliott had also batted beautifully in Glamorgan's first innings, but Jason Lewry had proved the pick of the bowlers on show to force the follow-on after big hundreds from Richard Montgomerie and Murray Goodwin had given Sussex early command.

Division Two

Bad weather meant no play on the opening day of three of the four matches in this round, but even at Chelmsford – where the rain largely held off – the match was drawn. With a touch more ambition, moreover, Derbyshire might have embarrassed Essex after earning themselves a significant first innings advantage largely through the all-round efforts of Graeme Welch. The first day featured a joyful moment for Leyton fast bowler Maurice Chambers,

17, who took his maiden first-class wicket in his fourth over when James Bryant cut hard to gully, but Steve Stubbings helped Derbyshire to gain early control and Welch, in seventh- and eighth-wicket stands with Ant Botha and Mo Sheikh, took the visitors to the rare heights of 462. It was only 33-year-old Welch's second first-class century but, by the close, he had added two new-ball scalps and a catch in the slips as Essex stumbled to 34 for 4. Led by Andy Flower and Ronnie Irani, and further bolstered by James Foster and James Middlebrook, Essex did recover some composure – but Welch still finished with 5 for 63 as he and the medium-pacer Sheikh put Derbyshire into a strong position.

Graeme Welch: an all-round performance of quality earned Derbyshire the best of their draw with Essex.

In 30 overs remaining on the third evening, though, Derbyshire's openers only managed 90 runs and the subsequent declaration on day four was delayed enough for the Essex target to be a stiff 379 from 63 overs. Derbyshire, it was clear, were not going to throw away the game – but, if they had given themselves a dozen or so more overs of bowling to dismiss Essex a second time, might Ravi Bopara and others have found it more difficult to save the match?

At Old Trafford it took a gutsy unbeaten 113 by their captain, opener Mark Chilton, to save Lancashire from defeat against Northamptonshire. In a low-scoring game, Lancashire finished on 188 for 8 after an aborted attempt to score 252 for victory on the last afternoon. Chilton hit four sixes and 12 fours, from 145 balls, staying to guide his side to the draw.

Ben Smith hit a fine 123 on a tricky pitch at New Road to rally Worcestershire from the depths of 121 for 7, in reply to Durham's 256. Each visiting batsman got into double figures before being dismissed early on the second morning, but conditions were illustrated by the fact that Phil Mustard's 39, made from No. 8, was the top score. Smith, dropped on 4, was eventually helped by Chaminda Vaas to rescue the Worcestershire reply after Mark Davies had got among the wickets. The eighth-wicket pair added 115 and a meaningless final afternoon allowed Paul Collingwood to reach a 155-ball century.

Leicestershire captain Hylton Ackerman hit his 21st first-class hundred and abject batting from Somerset briefly raised home hopes of victory at Oakham School. But John Francis, who batted for six and a

Round Eight: 1–4 June 2005 Division Two

ESSEX v. DERBYSHIRE – at Chelmsford

DERBYSHIRE	First Innings		Second Innings	
MJ Di Venuto	c Redmond b Bopara	23	not out	110
SD Stubbings	run out	92		
JDC Bryant	c Flower A b Chambers	0	(5) not out	9
BJ France	b Middlebrook	42	(2) b Flower GW	56
J Moss	c Cook b Bopara	38	(3) c & b Flower GW	29
*LD Sutton (capt)	c Flower A b Bopara	11		
G Welch	c Bopara b Flower GW	112		
AG Botha	lbw b Bopara	40		
MA Sheikh	c Flower A b Flower GW	45		
AKD Gray	not out	0		
NGE Walker	b Gough	11	(4) b Redmond	21
Extras	b 5, lb 5, w 4, nb 34	48	lb 4, w 3, nb 4	11
	(146.4 overs)	462	(3 wkts dec 63 overs)	236

Bowling
Gough 30.4-6-90-1. Redmond 28-8-78-0. Bopara 29-7-93-4. Chambers 15-1-73-1. Jefferson 6-2-19-0. Middlebrook 36-7-95-1. Flower GW 2-1-4-2.
Gough 8-4-8-0. Redmond 11-2-60-1. Middlebrook 18-1-64-0. Flower GW 19-0-64-2. Bopara 6-0-25-0. Chambers 1-0-11-0.
Fall of Wickets: 1-42, 2-53, 3-172, 4-182, 5-211, 6-269, 7-360, 8-439, 9-449
1-147, 2-196, 3-222

ESSEX	First Innings		Second Innings	
WI Jefferson	c Di Venuto b Welch	19	lbw b Welch	12
AN Cook	c Sutton b Sheikh	6	b Moss	59
GW Flower	c Welch b Sheikh	7	c Sutton b Welch	0
RS Bopara	lbw b Welch	0	not out	105
A Flower	b Welch	29	c Sutton b Walker	41
RC Irani (capt)	c Di Venuto b Welch	67		
*JS Foster	c France b Gray	67	(6) b Walker	15
JD Middlebrook	lbw b Sheikh	71	(7) not out	2
D Gough	c Botha b Sheikh	36		
AJ Redmond	c Sutton b Welch	0		
MA Chambers	not out	2		
Extras	b 4, lb 11, w 1	16	b 2, lb 8, w 1	11
	(99.5 overs)	320	(5 wkts 56 overs)	245

Bowling
Walker 10-0-51-0. Sheikh 26.5-10-67-4. Welch 20-5-63-5. Moss 15-5-51-0. Gray 21-3-53-1. Botha 7-3-20-0.
Welch 6-3-13-2. Sheikh 6-1-22-0. Walker 14-0-76-2. Gray 11-2-38-0. Botha 14-1-66-0. Moss 5-1-20-1.
Fall of Wickets: 1-8, 2-32, 3-34, 4-34, 5-136, 6-137, 7-276, 8-295, 9-296
1-14, 2-14, 3-141, 4-204, 5-232

Match drawn – Essex (9 pts), Derbyshire (11 pts)

LANCASHIRE v. NORTHAMPTONSHIRE – at Old Trafford

NORTHANTS	First Innings		Second Innings	
ML Love	c Sutcliffe b Anderson	0	lbw b Anderson	8
BM Shafayat	c Hodge b Cork	43	lbw b Cork	0
RA White	run out	34	c Loye b Muralitharan	23
U Afzaal	c Hegg b Cork	42	c Law b Anderson	48
DJG Sales (capt)	c Loye b Muralitharan	9	c Hodge b Cork	43
*MH Wessels	c Chilton b Muralitharan	15	b Chapple	23
DG Wright	hit wkt b Anderson	11	b Muralitharan	30
BJ Phillips	lbw b Muralitharan	6	not out	31
J Louw	c Sutcliffe b Anderson	0	c Loye b Muralitharan	0
C Pietersen	c Cork b Anderson	1	b Muralitharan	0
JF Brown	not out	1	c Loye b Keedy	1
Extras	lb 13	13	b 11, lb 7	18
	(66.5 overs)	175	(75.1 overs)	225

Bowling
Anderson 19.5-6-51-4. Cork 13-3-26-2. Chapple 8-2-16-0. Muralitharan 23-6-57-3. Keedy 3-1-12-0.
Anderson 12-3-40-2. Cork 19-5-43-2. Muralitharan 16-3-68-4. Chapple 13-2-27-1. Keedy 15.1-5-29-1.
Fall of Wickets: 1-2, 2-54, 3-115, 4-130, 5-138, 6-161, 7-172, 8-173, 9-173
1-8, 2-8, 3-60, 4-100, 5-148, 6-171, 7-210, 8-210, 9-212

LANCASHIRE	First Innings		Second Innings	
MJ Chilton (capt)	c Love b Wright	0	not out	113
IJ Sutcliffe	c Sales b Louw	2	c Wessels b Louw	0
MB Loye	c Wessels b Wright	0	lbw b Louw	6
BJ Hodge	c Pietersen b Louw	7	b Louw	25
SG Law	c Wessels b Pietersen	14	b Brown	7
G Chapple	c & b Wright	0	c Love b Brown	5
*WK Hegg	c Afzaal b Phillips	48	b Brown	14
DG Cork	c Afzaal b Louw	25	c White b Wright	12
JM Anderson	c Love b Brown	24	lbw b Brown	0
M Muralitharan	c Shafayat b Phillips	10		
G Keedy	not out	0	(10) not out	1
Extras	b 10, lb 3, nb 6	19	b 4, lb 1, nb 2	7
	(41.3 overs)	149	(8 wkts 43.5 overs)	190

Bowling
Wright 13-5-34-3. Louw 10-2-34-3. Pietersen 10-0-31-1. Brown 4.3-1-15-1. Phillips 4-0-22-2.
Wright 11-3-21-1. Louw 12.5-0-66-3. Brown 17-5-73-4. Pietersen 2-0-17-0. White 1-0-8-0.
Fall of Wickets: 1-0, 2-4, 3-12, 4-17, 5-27, 6-35, 7-88, 8-129, 9-141
1-0, 2-8, 3-67, 4-90, 5-112, 6-142, 7-165, 8-165

Match drawn – Lancashire (7 pts), Northamptonshire (7 pts)

WORCESTERSHIRE v. DURHAM – at Worcester

DURHAM	First Innings		Second Innings	
NJ Astle	lbw b Vaas	11		
JJB Lewis	lbw b Vaas	18	lbw b de Bruyn	49
PD Collingwood	c Vaas b Price	26	not out	103
GJ Muchall	c Pipe b Mason	32	not out	9
DM B'stein (capt)	b Kabir Ali	15		
N Peng	c Pipe b Mason	19	(1) c Solanki b Kabir Ali	5
GR Breese	run out	32		
*P Mustard	c Davies b Kabir Ali	39		
AA Noffke	c Hick b Vaas	18		
LE Plunkett	c Moore b Kabir Ali	37		
M Davies	not out	0		
Extras	b 1, lb 1, w 1, nb 6	9	b 1, lb 6, w 1, nb 6	14
	(81.5 overs)	256	(2 wkts 50 overs)	180

Bowling
Vaas 22-10-36-3. Kabir Ali 20.5-3-72-3. de Bruyn 5-0-37-0. Mason 13-5-49-2. Price 21-6-60-1.
Vaas 6-1-8-0. Kabir Ali 8-0-43-1. Price 9-1-36-0. Mason 11-5-25-0. de Bruyn 16-4-61-1.
Fall of Wickets: 1-14, 2-39, 3-91, 4-91, 5-117, 6-141, 7-185, 8-211, 9-246
1-7, 2-144

WORCS	First Innings	
SC Moore	c Mustard b Plunkett	16
SM Davies	c Mustard b Noffke	4
*DJ Pipe	c Breese b Noffke	12
GA Hick	c Breese b Davies	13
BF Smith	c Astle b Noffke	123
VS Solanki (capt)	c Collingwood b Davies	0
Z de Bruyn	lbw b Davies	2
Kabir Ali	lbw b Collingwood	7
WPUJC Vaas	lbw b Noffke	45
RW Price	c Davies b Collingwood	20
MS Mason	not out	0
Extras	lb 15, nb 10	25
	(83.5 overs)	267

Bowling
Noffke 25-8-75-4. Plunkett 19-1-83-1. Davies 17-6-43-3. Collingwood 12.5-5-29-2. Breese 10-1-22-0.
Fall of Wickets: 1-17, 2-41, 3-45, 4-80, 5-84, 6-104, 7-121, 8-236, 9-267

Match drawn – Worcestershire (9 pts), Durham (9 pts)

LEICESTERSHIRE v. SOMERSET – at Oakham School

LEICESTERSHIRE	First Innings	
DDJ Robinson	c Turner b Francis SRG	47
DL Maddy	c Hildreth b Laraman	42
JK Maunders	c Turner b Laraman	1
D Mongia	c Smith b McLean	26
HD Ackerman (capt)	c Smith b Francis SRG	117
JL Sadler	c Blackwell b McLean	0
*PA Nixon	c Francis SRG b Blackwell	17
OD Gibson	lbw b Blackwell	0
CW Henderson	c Turner b Laraman	50
SCL Broad	c Francis JD b Blackwell	17
CM Willoughby	not out	9
Extras	lb 2, w 2, nb 8	12
	(111.4 overs)	338

Bowling
McLean 12-3-29-2. Francis SRG 25-2-81-2. Andrew 16-2-58-0. Laraman 23-3-68-3. Burns 1-0-10-0. Blackwell 25.4-8-66-3. Jayasuriya 5-1-12-0. Smith 4-1-12-0.
Fall of Wickets: 1-91, 2-95, 3-95, 4-140, 5-140, 6-191, 7-191, 8-310, 9-314

SOMERSET	First Innings		Second Innings	
GC Smith	b Gibson	10	c Nixon b Willoughby	9
JD Francis	c Robinson b Willoughby	4	not out	104
M Burns	c Maddy b Broad	37	lbw b Broad	59
ST Jayasuriya	b Maddy	24	c Robinson b Henderson	9
JC Hildreth	c Maddy b Gibson	6	not out	25
ID Blackwell	c Maddy b Gibson	0		
*RJ Turner (capt)	c Sadler b Henderson	7		
AW Laraman	c Robinson b Willoughby	2		
GM Andrew	lbw b Henderson	8		
SRG Francis	not out	2		
NAM McLean	c & b Henderson	1		
Extras	lb 1, w 1, nb 2	4	b 7, lb 2, nb 10	19
	(50.3 overs)	105	(3 wkts 100 overs)	225

Bowling
Gibson 15-2-34-3. Willoughby 15-6-27-2. Broad 7-2-21-1. Maddy 6-3-9-1. Henderson 7.3-1-13-3.
Gibson 17-3-42-0. Willoughby 16-4-39-1. Maddy 9-3-21-0. Henderson 28-8-47-1. Broad 18-6-40-1. Mongia 7-1-18-0. Maunders 5-2-9-0.
Fall of Wickets: 1-14, 2-20, 3-52, 4-65, 5-65, 6-89, 7-93, 8-101, 9-103
1-22, 2-169, 3-184

Match drawn – Leicestershire (10 pts), Somerset (7 pts)

half hours and faced 302 balls for his unbeaten 104, saved the visitors' blushes on the last day – largely in alliance with the equally determined Mike Burns.

Round Nine: 8–13 June 2005

Division One

Kent, still smarting from their pitch penalty in the previous match, made short work of Glamorgan at Cardiff to step up their title challenge in impressive fashion. David Fulton was out to the first ball of the match, and Rob Key soon followed, but from then on Kent were never troubled as Martin van Jaarsveld underlined what a fine signing he had become by leading his new county to their highest total against Glamorgan. Van Jaarsveld eventually finished up unbeaten on 262, converting his fourth championship century of the season into something even more substantial. At one stage, on the opening day, he and Matthew Walker, plus both umpires and eight of the Glamorgan fielders, had to lie flat on the ground to allow a passing swarm of bees to fly overhead, but nothing seemed to faze van

Opposite: Ed Smith is a study in concentration as he takes advantage of a fine batting pitch at Lord's in the London derby between Middlesex and Surrey.

Jaarsveld as he reached 174 by the close and continued on to a career-best performance the next day. Darren Stevens hit an excellent 80 and Min Patel also produced an aggressive and entertaining 87 – another career-best – to help the South African to add 159 for the eighth wicket. Glamorgan looked a beaten team by the time Martin Saggers, the No. 11, also joined in the fun with 45, but at least David Hemp and Sourav Ganguly rallied the Welsh county from an initial 79 for 3 in reply to Kent's mammoth 568. Ganguly also hit a brilliant 142 when Glamorgan predictably followed on, from just 125 balls with five sixes and 15 fours, but Kent still had time to claim the extra half-hour and complete a 10-wicket win by 7.18pm on the third evening.

Warwickshire also produced a convincing victory, overpowering Gloucestershire by an innings and two runs at Gloucester with Heath Streak's 6 for 44 proving too much for the home side in their second innings. It was Neil Carter and Dougie Brown who struck the initial blows, however, sharing eight wickets as Gloucestershire were dismissed for 254 on the opening day. Jonathan Trott then played the most significant innings of the match, reaching 128 with a six and 28 fours, although both Ian Bell and Alex Loudon supported him well and Jim Troughton later hit 60 to ensure a healthy lead. Bell's 79 meant he had scored 306 first-class runs before being dismissed. At

Round Nine: 8–13 June 2005 Division One

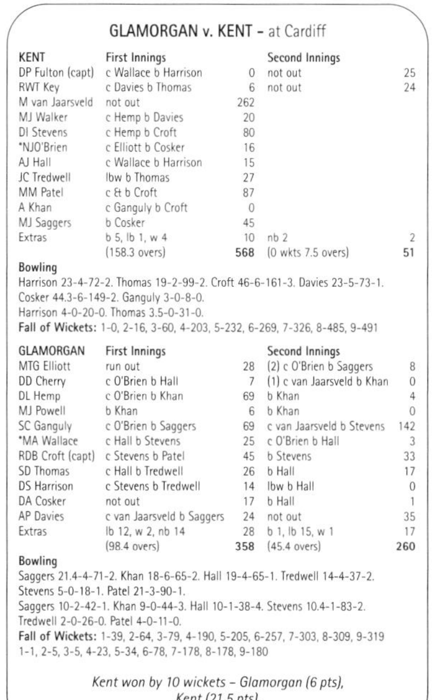

GLAMORGAN v. KENT – at Cardiff

KENT	First Innings		Second Innings	
DP Fulton (capt)	c Wallace b Harrison	0	not out	25
RWT Key	c Davies b Thomas	6	not out	24
M van Jaarsveld	not out	262		
MJ Walker	c Hemp b Davies	20		
DI Stevens	c Hemp b Croft	80		
*NJO'Brien	c Elliott b Cosker	16		
AJ Hall	c Wallace b Harrison	15		
JC Tredwell	lbw b Thomas	27		
MM Patel	c & b Croft	87		
A Khan	c Ganguly b Croft	0		
MJ Saggers	b Cosker	45		
Extras	b 5, lb 1, w 4	10	nb 2	2
	(158.3 overs)	**568**	(0 wkts 7.5 overs)	**51**

Bowling
Harrison 23-4-72-2. Thomas 19-2-99-2. Croft 46-6-161-3. Davies 23-5-73-1. Cosker 44.3-6-149-2. Ganguly 3-0-8-0.
Harrison 4-0-20-0. Thomas 3.5-0-31-0.
Fall of Wickets: 1-0, 2-16, 3-60, 4-203, 5-232, 6-269, 7-326, 8-485, 9-491

GLAMORGAN	First Innings		Second Innings	
MTG Elliott	run out	28	(2) c O'Brien b Saggers	8
DD Cherry	c O'Brien b Hall	7	(1) c van Jaarsveld b Khan	0
DL Hemp	c O'Brien b Khan	69	b Khan	4
MJ Powell	b Khan	6	b Khan	0
SC Ganguly	c O'Brien b Saggers	69	c van Jaarsveld b Stevens	142
*MA Wallace	c Hall b Stevens	25	c O'Brien b Hall	3
RDB Croft (capt)	c Stevens b Patel	45	b Stevens	33
SD Thomas	c Hall b Tredwell	26	b Hall	17
DS Harrison	c Stevens b Tredwell	14	lbw b Hall	0
DA Cosker	not out	17	b Hall	1
AP Davies	c van Jaarsveld b Saggers	24	not out	35
Extras	lb 12, w 2, nb 14	28	b 1, lb 15, w 1	17
	(98.4 overs)	**358**	(45.4 overs)	**260**

Bowling
Saggers 21.4-4-71-2. Khan 18-6-65-2. Hall 19-4-65-1. Tredwell 14-4-37-2. Stevens 5-0-18-1. Patel 21-3-90-1.
Saggers 10-2-42-1. Khan 9-0-44-3. Hall 10-1-38-4. Stevens 10.4-1-83-2. Tredwell 2-0-26-0. Patel 4-0-11-0.
Fall of Wickets: 1-39, 2-64, 3-79, 4-190, 5-205, 6-257, 7-303, 8-309, 9-319
1-1, 2-5, 3-5, 4-33, 5-34, 6-78, 7-178, 8-178, 9-180

Kent won by 10 wickets – Glamorgan (6 pts), Kent (21.5 pts).
Kent deducted 0.5 pts for slow over rate

GLOUCESTERSHIRE v. WARWICKSHIRE – at Gloucester

GLOS	First Innings		Second Innings	
WPC Weston	lbw b Brown	1	(2) b Brown	2
CM Spearman	b Carter	35	(1) c Trott b Streak	7
MGN Windows	c Trott b Brown	37	b Streak	3
CG Taylor (capt)	c Trott b Brown	13	b Brown	45
JA Pearson	c Streak b Loudon	52	c Powell b Streak	0
MA Hardinges	b Streak	21	lbw b Streak	0
*SJ Adshead	c Brown b Carter	43	b Streak	23
MW Alleyne	b Carter	16	lbw b Streak	51
ID Fisher	c Trott b Carter	8	c Frost b Carter	43
UDU Chandana	not out	0	b Loudon	19
CG Greenidge	c Streak b Brown	5	not out	4
Extras	b 5, lb 12, nb 6	23	b 7, lb 5, nb 8	20
	(102.5 overs)	**254**	(66.5 overs)	**217**

Bowling
Streak 22-7-42-1. Brown 24.5-7-51-4. Warren 10-5-16-0. Carter 21-6-57-4. Trott 9-1-23-0. Bell 5-2-18-0. Loudon 7-0-27-1. Troughton 4-3-3-0.
Streak 15.5-6-44-6. Brown 15-6-29-2. Carter 10-2-40-1. Warren 7-2-37-0. Loudon 15-1-33-1. Troughton 4-0-22-0.
Fall of Wickets: 1-13, 2-52, 3-81, 4-92, 5-147, 6-216, 7-229, 8-248, 9-249
1-10, 2-12, 3-16, 4-20, 5-20, 6-81, 7-98, 8-182, 9-209

WARWICKSHIRE	First Innings	
NV Knight (capt)	lbw b Alleyne	19
MJ Powell	c Spearman b Greenidge	1
IR Bell	c & b Fisher	79
IJL Trott	c Hardinges b Chandana	128
AGR Loudon	c Taylor b Fisher	47
JO Troughton	b Chandana	60
DR Brown	st Adshead b Fisher	20
*T Frost	c Fisher b Chandana	35
HH Streak	run out	28
NM Carter	c Fisher b Greenidge	20
NA Warren	not out	5
Extras	b 10, lb 5, w 4, nb 12	31
	(147.5 overs)	**473**

Bowling
Greenidge 23.5-4-78-2. Hardinges 22-3-82-0. Alleyne 24-3-84-1. Chandana 39-5-115-3. Fisher 39-12-99-3.
Fall of Wickets: 1-5, 2-33, 3-184, 4-287, 5-295, 6-354, 7-388, 8-432, 9-462

Warwickshire won by an innings and 2 runs – Gloucestershire (4 pts), Warwickshire (22 pts)

MIDDLESEX v. SURREY – at Lord's

MIDDLESEX	First Innings		Second Innings	
ET Smith	b Murtagh	60	c Batty b Thornely	88
BL Hutton (capt)	b Bicknell	44	c Brown b Ormond	10
OA Shah	c Batty b Bicknell	0	c Batty b Thornely	21
EC Joyce	lbw b Ormond	24	lbw b Harbhajan	60
SB Styris	lbw b Ormond	8	c Thornely b Bicknell	55
JWM Dalrymple	c Newman b Harbhajan	77	c Bicknell b Ormond	15
PN Weekes	b Ormond	39	not out	28
IK Pathan	b Harbhajan	68		
*BJM Scott	not out	64	(8) not out	61
CJC Wright	lbw b Bicknell	13		
A Richardson	lbw b Bicknell	19		
Extras	lb 14, w 1, nb 6	21	b 1, lb 9, w 1, nb 4	15
	(134.4 overs)	**437**	(6 wkts 82 overs)	**353**

Bowling
Bicknell 31.4-5-116-4. Ormond 30-6-98-3. Thornely 12-3-36-0. Murtagh 26-5-86-1. Harbhajan 35-10-87-2.
Bicknell 20-4-73-1. Ormond 15-2-67-2. Thornely 10-0-40-2. Murtagh 17-1-77-0. Harbhajan 10-2-37-1. Clinton 7-1-32-0. Newman 3-0-17-0.
Fall of Wickets: 1-100, 2-104, 3-118, 4-136, 5-148, 6-258, 7-282, 8-380, 9-409
1-30, 2-73, 3-173, 4-202, 5-253, 6-257

SURREY	First Innings	
SA Newman	c Hutton b Richardson	8
RS Clinton	c Hutton b Richardson	73
MR R'kash (capt)	retired hurt	28
GP Thorpe	c Scott b Richardson	4
*JN Batty	c Weekes b Richardson	45
AD Brown	not out	152
DJ Thornely	b Styris	81
MP Bicknell	lbw b Joyce	33
TJ Murtagh	c Joyce b Weekes	8
J Ormond	b Richardson	4
Harbhajan Singh	c Joyce b Richardson	0
Extras	b 1, lb 18, w 1, nb 4	24
	(9 wkts 126 overs)	**460**

Bowling
Pathan 23-3-73-0. Richardson 32-7-106-6. Wright 23-2-103-0. Styris 24-5-80-1. Hutton 5-2-20-0. Weekes 15-3-36-1. Dalrymple 2-0-7-0. Joyce 2-0-16-1.
Fall of Wickets: 1-11, 2-82, 3-158, 4-181, 5-365, 6-428, 7-447, 8-460, 9-460

Match drawn – Middlesex (12 pts), Surrey (12 pts)

20 for 5 in their second innings, Gloucestershire were left with little hope but at least Chris Taylor, Mark Alleyne and Ian Fisher put up some resistance.

The blandness of the pitch at Lord's, and the inability of both attacks to rise above it, condemned the televised London derby between Middlesex and Surrey to a dull draw. Alan Richardson, the Middlesex seamer, deserved praise for his six wickets but Ally Brown was in dominant form with an unbeaten 152 as Surrey made sure they got past the home side's first innings 437 and picked up maximum batting bonus points themselves. Ed Smith caught the eye for Middlesex with 60 and 88.

Division Two

A classic 240th Roses Match ended in a draw at Headingley, but only after Matthew Hoggard had showcased his vastly-improved batting skills by batting 41 overs for 64 not out to frustrate the Lancashire bowlers. Hoggard and Yorkshire last man Deon Kruis held on for 75 minutes in fading light to deny Lancashire, with Kruis facing 55 balls for his 13 not out and Hoggard hitting nine fours in a stay of 138 balls and 142 minutes. It was stirring stuff, after Yorkshire's chase after 382 to win in 90 overs had faltered in mid-innings. Lancashire's first innings of 379 was built around a beautifully constructed 153 from Iain Sutcliffe; his first 50 runs took him three and a half hours, but his second took only 84 balls and his last just 41 deliveries. Excellent batting from Phil Jaques, Michael Lumb and Craig White took Yorkshire to 335 in reply, but Sutcliffe hit another 52 and Mark Chilton made 112 before Stuart Law eased Lancashire towards their challenging declaration. Hoggard, however, had the final word on behalf of delighted Yorkshiremen everywhere.

Durham's fifth win in seven championship matches was a crushing innings and 19-run win against Essex at the Riverside. Centuries from Gordon Muchall and Dale Benkenstein underpinned their solid progress towards a first innings 506, and the visitors crumbled in reply – being bowled out for a mere 106 as Ashley Noffke and Mark Davies caused havoc. By the close of day two Davies had already dismissed Will Jefferson with the new ball as Essex, following on, slid to 12 for 1 – but at least on the following day they made Durham's bowlers work a little bit harder for their successes. Dale Steyn, the nightwatchman, clobbered 82 and, later in the innings, Andre Adams also enjoyed himself hugely by thumping 103 from 78 balls with five sixes and 11 fours. In between, James Foster stroked 78 but Durham, with Davies

Round Nine: 8–13 June 2005 Division Two

YORKSHIRE v. LANCASHIRE – at Headingley

LANCASHIRE	First Innings		Second Innings	
MJ Chilton (capt)	c Dawood b Hoggard	0	b Hoggard	112
IJ Sutcliffe	c Dawood b Kruis	153	lbw b Dawson	52
MB Loye	lbw b Harvey	67	c Lumb b Hoggard	43
BJ Hodge	c Dawood b Kruis	15	lbw b Hoggard	8
SG Law	c Dawood b Harvey	46	not out	53
G Chapple	b Harvey	2	c Bresnan b Kruis	13
*WK Hegg	lbw b Harvey	11	not out	32
DG Cork	c McGrath b Bresnan	31		
SI Mahmood	lbw b Bresnan	24		
JM Anderson	lbw b Bresnan	0		
G Keedy	not out	1		
Extras	b 4, lb 7, nb 18	29	b 4, lb 4, nb 16	24
	(103 overs)	379	(5 wkts dec 92 overs)	337

Bowling
Hoggard 20-6-80-1. Kruis 21-6-92-2. Dawson 18-2-52-0. Bresnan 19-2-76-3. Harvey 19-3-51-4. McGrath 6-2-17-0.
Hoggard 25-2-91-3. Kruis 19-4-64-1. Bresnan 9-2-44-0. Dawson 17-3-53-1. Harvey 6-0-31-0. McGrath 16-1-46-0.
Fall of Wickets: 1-0, 2-107, 3-124, 4-230, 5-285, 6-315, 7-319, 8-378, 9-378
1-100, 2-213, 3-223, 4-226, 5-262

YORKSHIRE	First Innings		Second Innings	
MJ Wood	run out	8	c Sutcliffe b Anderson	3
PA Jaques	c Cork b Chapple	97	(6) c Anderson b Keedy	44
A McGrath	c Cork b Chapple	4	c Chilton b Cork	3
MJ Lumb	c Hegg b Keedy	68	b Anderson	1
IJ Harvey	lbw b Anderson	14	c Hegg b Chapple	48
C White (capt)	c Sutcliffe b Anderson	71	(2) c Hegg b Mahmood	33
*I Dawood	lbw b Chapple	7	c Hodge b Chapple	4
RKJ Dawson	c Law b Keedy	9	b Chapple	28
TT Bresnan	c Hegg b Anderson	17	b Anderson	1
MJ Hoggard	c Hodge b Anderson	19	not out	64
GJ Kruis	not out	10	not out	13
Extras	b 3, lb 7, w 1	11	b 9, lb 12, nb 10	31
	(113.2 overs)	335	(9 wkts 92 overs)	273

Bowling
Anderson 25.2-3-97-4. Cork 22.2-7-44-0. Chapple 30-10-70-3. Mahmood 5.4-0-42-0. Keedy 22-2-65-2. Hodge 8-3-7-0.
Anderson 21-7-69-3. Cork 13-2-35-1. Chapple 18-5-45-3. Mahmood 20-4-56-1. Keedy 15-6-33-1. Hodge 5-0-14-0.
Fall of Wickets: 1-38, 2-47, 3-130, 4-165, 5-232, 6-243, 7-260, 8-300, 9-323
1-8, 2-23, 3-24, 4-100, 5-104, 6-109, 7-177, 8-182, 9-227

Match drawn – Yorkshire (10 pts), Lancashire (11 pts)

DURHAM v. ESSEX – at The Riverside

DURHAM	First Innings	
N Peng	c Cook b Adams	26
JJB Lewis	c Adams b Steyn	24
GJ Muchall	c Steyn b Adams	123
NJ Astle	c Flower GW b Bopara	15
DM B'stein (capt)	lbw b Adams	110
GR Breese	lbw b Steyn	63
*P Mustard	c Jefferson b Adams	17
AA Noffke	not out	25
M Davies	c Adams b Steyn	6
ML Turner	c Middlebrook b Westfield	18
N Killeen	c Foster b Thornicroft	23
Extras	b 4, lb 11, w 7, nb 33	55
	(140 overs)	505

Bowling
Adams 36-7-121-4. Thornicroft 22-6-70-1. Steyn 31-6-105-3. Westfield 18-0-90-1. Bopara 8-1-34-1. Middlebrook 11-1-42-0. Flower GW 8-2-18-0. Jefferson 6-3-10-0.
Fall of Wickets: 1-43, 2-69, 3-105, 4-272, 5-393, 6-415, 7-424, 8-438, 9-469

ESSEX	First Innings		Second Innings	
WI Jefferson	b Noffke	0	b Davies	2
AN Cook	c Mustard b Noffke	39	c Mustard b Turner	8
GW Flower	b Noffke	11	(4) c Lewis b Noffke	6
RS Bopara	c Muchall b Davies	9	(5) c Noffke b Davies	21
A Flower	b Davies	20	(6) c Lewis b Davies	24
*JS Foster (capt)	lbw b Noffke	2	(7) lbw b Killeen	78
JD Middlebrook	b Killeen	8	(8) b Benkenstein	37
AR Adams	c Benkenstein b Killeen	12	(9) b Davies	103
MS Westfield	c Breese b Davies	0	(10) lbw b Davies	0
ND Thornicroft	b Davies	0	(11) not out	4
DW Steyn	not out	0	(3) c Killeen b Noffke	82
Extras	lb 4, w 1	5	b 6, lb 1, nb 8	15
	(55 overs)	106	(104.1 overs)	380

Bowling
Noffke 15-9-19-4. Turner 13-2-36-0. Davies 12-6-15-4. Killeen 10-5-24-2. Breese 3-1-4-0. Astle 2-1-4-0.
Noffke 24-7-79-2. Davies 24-6-86-5. Turner 13-1-47-1. Killeen 14.1-2-46-1. Astle 11-3-20-0. Benkenstein 8-0-47-1. Breese 10-1-48-0.
Fall of Wickets: 1-1, 2-33, 3-46, 4-93, 5-146, 6-146, 7-202, 8-366, 9-376
1-7, 2-14, 3-41, 4-93, 5-146, 6-146, 7-202, 8-366, 9-376

Durham won by an innings and 19 runs – Durham (22 pts), Essex (3 pts)

SOMERSET v. WORCESTERSHIRE – at Bath

SOMERSET	First Innings		Second Innings	
GC Smith (capt)	c Batty b Vaas	55	b Mason	6
JD Francis	c Pipe b Mason	1	c Moore b Vaas	0
M Burns	c Hick b Malik	18	b Mason	49
ST Jayasuriya	c Price b Mason	66	b Mason	21
MJ Wood	c de Bruyn b Mason	127	c & b Price	10
ID Blackwell	c Smith b Batty	54	c Pipe b Malik	8
*RJ Turner	c Hick b Mason	8	c Smith b Mason	19
AW Laraman	c Vaas b Malik	11	(9) c Hick b de Bruyn	16
RL Johnson	c Pipe b Vaas	21	(8) c Davies b Mason	0
AR Caddick	b Vaas	19	b Vaas	11
SRG Francis	not out	5	not out	1
Extras	b 1, lb 14, w 1, nb 7	23	lb 1, w 2, nb 8	11
	(118 overs)	408	(76 overs)	152

Bowling
Vaas 30-5-88-3. Mason 27-7-82-4. Malik 26-3-87-2. de Bruyn 14-2-50-0. Batty 15-0-55-1. Price 6-1-31-0.
Mason 17-7-34-5. Vaas 18-4-53-2. Price 24-9-26-1. Malik 12-5-25-1. de Bruyn 5-1-13-1.
Fall of Wickets: 1-2, 2-40, 3-128, 4-157, 5-251, 6-280, 7-321, 8-358, 9-402
1-2, 2-10, 3-38, 4-63, 5-74, 6-112, 7-118, 8-121, 9-151

WORCS	First Innings		Second Innings	
SC Moore	c Smith b Blackwell	86	not out	66
SM Davies	c Smith b Caddick	1	c Smith b Caddick	1
GA Hick	c Smith b Caddick	55	c Burns b Caddick	17
BF Smith	lbw b Caddick	140	not out	39
Z de Bruyn	lbw b Johnson	30		
GJ Batty (capt)	retired hurt	16		
DKH Mitchell	lbw b Caddick	4		
WPUJC Vaas	b Blackwell	45		
*DJ Pipe	b Caddick	0		
RW Price	c Turner b Johnson	6		
MS Mason	c Turner b Johnson	2		
MN Malik	not out	3		
Extras	b 1, lb 11, w 1, nb 22	35	w 5, nb 10	15
	(9 wkts 115.5 overs)	423	(2 wkts 21.4 overs)	138

Bowling
Caddick 31-4-132-5. Johnson 31-9-93-3. Francis SRG 12-1-50-0. Laraman 13-1-43-0. Jayasuriya 5-0-16-0. Burns 4-0-19-0. Blackwell 19.5-2-58-2.
Caddick 6-0-49-0. Johnson 7-0-36-0. Blackwell 5-0-27-0. Laraman 1-0-14-0. Francis SRG 2.4-0-12-0.
Fall of Wickets: 1-3, 2-108, 3-220, 4-295, 5-366, 6-366, 7-387, 8-409, 9-417
1-10, 2-48

Worcestershire won by 8 wickets – Somerset (8 pts), Worcestershire (22 pts)

Famous name in a famous game: a Sutcliffe has often made runs in the Roses Match, and here Lancashire's Iain turns to leg while amassing a first innings 153 in a manner which would have delighted Yorkshire legend Herbert.

outstanding again with 5 for 86, were still happy enough at the end with maximum points.

A second-innings capitulation by sorry Somerset handed what had until then been a hard-fought contest at Bath to Worcestershire. Matt Mason took 5 for 34 and Chaminda Vaas also bowled well, but Somerset's slide to 151 for 9 by the end of day three was inexplicable after what had gone before.

Worcestershire, in reply to Somerset's first innings 408, had the unfair advantage of being able to bat 12 as a result of Gareth Batty's call-up into England's one-day team, but Andy Caddick's wholehearted bowling prevented them from gaining any more than a slender 15-run lead. Ben Smith's 140 cancelled out a fine earlier hundred from Matthew Wood, while Stephen Moore and Graeme Hick also made useful scores in reply to a Somerset innings which, besides Wood's 160-ball ton, had featured entertaining half-centuries from Graeme Smith, Sanath Jayasuriya and Ian Blackwell. When Somerset collapsed second time around, though, and were finished off for 152 fifteen balls into the final day, there could be only one winner. Caddick went down fighting, with the early wickets of Steven Davies and Hick, but Moore's unbeaten 66 soon saw Worcestershire to their modest victory target.

Round Ten: 15–18 June 2005

Division One

Kent, who heard during the game that their appeal to overturn an eight-point pitch penalty had failed, still went to the top of the Frizzell County Championship table by beating champions Warwickshire by an innings and 164 runs at Edgbaston. The emphatic margin of victory, in the last round of games before the mid-season block of Twenty20 Cup group fixtures, left Kent believing that their title challenge was a very real one. Their win also underlined the enduring quality of Min Patel, the left-arm spinner who at almost 35 was bowling as well as he had ever done despite a catalogue of injuries and operations.

Patel's second innings 6 for 53 swept Kent to victory after Andrew Hall had removed Michael Powell and Ian Bell with the new ball on the previous evening. Encouragingly for Kent, too, it had been Simon Cook and Amjad Khan who had done most of the damage to Warwickshire's first innings, with the home side doing well to recover from 116 for 8 to 252 thanks to some lusty blows from Neil Carter and Heath Streak. Kent's command of the game was soon apparent, however, with Rob Key and Martin van Jaarsveld building a base from which Matthew

Walker and Darren Stevens launched themselves at a Warwickshire attack which had lost Streak to injury after he had sent down just 4.1 overs. Walker hit two sixes and 14 fours in his 140 while Stevens' 163 from 258 balls, with a six and 22 fours, was a career-best.

Round Ten: 15–18 June 2005 Division One

WARWICKSHIRE v. KENT – at Edgbaston

WARWICKSHIRE	First Innings		Second Innings	
NV Knight (capt)	b Khan	8	b Patel	26
MJ Powell	c van Jaarsveld b Cook	49	b Hall	16
IR Bell	b Khan	1	b Hall	0
IJL Trott	c O'Brien b Cook	0	(5) lbw b Patel	12
AGR Loudon	c O'Brien b Cook	14	(6) b Patel	37
JO Troughton	c O'Brien b Hall	1	(7) c Walker b Patel	11
DR Brown	c Kemp b Khan	10	(8) b Khan	12
*T Frost	c Kemp b Stevens	23	(9) not out	7
HH Streak	lbw b Cook	51	(10) b Patel	4
NM Carter	lbw b Kemp	82	(11) b Khan	15
NA Warren	not out	2	(4) c O'Brien b Patel	4
Extras	lb 9, nb 2	11	b 3, lb 4, nb 2	9
	(84 overs)	252	(58.3 overs)	153

Bowling
Khan 18-4-64-3. Cook 23-5-79-4. Hall 24-12-39-1. Stevens 11-3-33-1.
Kemp 5-1-24-1. Patel 3-1-4-0.
Khan 15.3-4-52-2. Cook 6-0-23-0. Patel 25-10-53-6. Hall 11-3-14-2.
van Jaarsveld 1-0-4-0.
Fall of Wickets: 1-8, 2-10, 3-13, 4-34, 5-39, 6-52, 7-114, 8-116, 9-213
1-39, 2-39, 3-47, 4-54, 5-65, 6-87, 7-124, 8-128, 9-136

KENT	First Innings	
DP Fulton (capt)	c Trott b Brown	6
RWT Key	lbw b Bell	75
M van Jaarsveld	c Trott b Bell	62
MJ Walker	c Troughton b Carter	140
DI Stevens	c Frost b Loudon	163
JM Kemp	b Loudon	25
AJ Hall	c Bell b Warren	49
*NJO'Brien	not out	21
MM Patel	c sub b Loudon	0
SJ Cook	c Knight b Warren	1
A Khan	run out	0
Extras	b 2, lb 8, w 7, nb 10	27
	(167.1 overs)	569

Bowling
Streak 4.1-3-8-0. Brown 28-4-71-1. Carter 31.5-7-127-1. Bell 14-5-45-2.
Trott 15-2-37-0. Warren 24-2-104-2. Loudon 43.1-7-130-3. Troughton 7-0-37-0.
Fall of Wickets: 1-7, 2-145, 3-154, 4-461, 5-472, 6-517, 7-563, 8-564, 9-568

Kent won by an innings and 164 runs –
Warwickshire (3 pts), Kent (22 pts)

In his first full championship game as Surrey's captain Graham Thorpe led them to a thumping innings and 55-run win at the Rose Bowl over Hampshire, whose own title aspirations took a severe dent. Hampshire skipper Shane Warne was involved in a heated exchange of words with umpire Alan Whitehead on the opening day, which Surrey finished on 326 for 8. The incident was sparked off when Whitehead turned down an appeal for a catch at the wicket off Billy Taylor when Scott Newman, who went on to hit 111, was on just 14. Newman struck 13 fours in a vital innings, while Dominic Thornely's 73 later enabled Surrey to reach 361 after Warne and Whitehead had publicly shaken hands before play the following morning. Then it was Harbhajan Singh's turn to get into the action, taking 6 for 36 as Hampshire were swept aside for just 146 in reply. John Crawley made 67 after Hampshire followed on, but this time it was Mohammad Akram, with 5 for 41, and Jimmy Ormond, with three cheap wickets, who proved too potent for the home batsmen.

Glamorgan, desperate to stop a slide which had brought them six defeats out of their first seven matches back in Division One, decided to give Middlesex the opportunity of chasing a fourth-innings target on a superb batting pitch at Southgate. It was a plan that backfired spectacularly with the home side romping past the 406 they had been set in 80 overs. The win was also a personal

HAMPSHIRE v. SURREY – at The Rose Bowl

SURREY	First Innings	
SA Newman	c Pothas b Taylor	111
RS Clinton	c Lamb b Warne	30
GP Thorpe (capt)	c Lamb b Tremlett	10
R Clarke	c Adams b Ervine	16
*JN Batty	c and b Tremlett	10
AD Brown	lbw b Tremlett	28
DJ Thornely	b Tremlett	73
MP Bicknell	c Pothas b Taylor	26
J Ormond	c Lamb b Warne	7
Harbhajan Singh	b Ervine	25
M Akram	not out	2
Extras	b 5, lb 5, w 1, nb 12	23
	(81.4 overs)	361

Bowling
Tremlett 20-2-106-4. Taylor 11-3-39-2. Ervine 17.4-3-84-2. Warne 21-0-89-2.
Lamb 4-1-11-0. McMillan 8-2-22-0.
Fall of Wickets: 1-100, 2-117, 3-172, 4-184, 5-217, 6-222, 7-266, 8-303, 9-359

HAMPSHIRE	First Innings		Second Innings	
JHK Adams	b Bicknell	1	c Batty b Ormond	1
MJ Brown	c Ormond b Akram	34	c Harbhajan b Ormond	20
CC Benham	c Brown b Harbhajan	41	c Brown b Ormond	0
JP Crawley	c Clinton b Harbhajan	1	b Harbhajan	67
CD McMillan	st Batty b Harbhajan	17	c sub b Akram	4
GA Lamb	c Ormond b Harbhajan	5	c Clarke b Akram	11
*N Pothas	c Batty b Ormond	9	c Clarke b Harbhajan	4
SM Ervine	c Batty b Harbhajan	0	c Newman b Akram	11
SK Warne (capt)	b Harbhajan	3	c Harbhajan b Akram	14
CT Tremlett	not out	11	not out	12
BV Taylor	b Ormond	0	c Batty b Akram	0
Extras	b 4, lb 6, w 2, nb 8	20	lb 5, w 3, nb 12	20
	(49.5 overs)	146	(33.3 overs)	160

Bowling
Bicknell 7-1-20-1. Ormond 16.5-3-42-2. Thornely 3-1-11-0. Harbhajan 16-2-36-6.
Akram 7-3-27-1.
Bicknell 6-1-26-0. Ormond 7-2-20-3. Thornely 3-0-21-0. Akram 9.3-2-41-5.
Harbhajan 8-1-47-2.
Fall of Wickets: 1-12, 2-63, 3-79, 4-107, 5-115, 6-118, 7-121, 8-129, 9-131
1-1, 2-13, 3-39, 4-79, 5-104, 6-110, 7-128, 8-129, 9-148

Surrey won by an innings and 55 runs –
Hampshire (3 pts), Surrey (21 pts)

MIDDLESEX v. GLAMORGAN – at Southgate

GLAMORGAN	First Innings		Second Innings	
MTG Elliott	run out	59	(2) c Scott b Richardson	20
DD Cherry	c Smith b Weekes	226	(1) b Richardson	16
DL Hemp	c Shah b Betts	103	c Smith b Richardson	29
J Hughes	not out	134	not out	100
RN Grant	not out	22		
SC Ganguly			(5) not out	84
*MA Wallace				
RDB Croft (capt)				
DS Harrison				
AG Wharf				
DA Cosker				
Extras	b 13, lb 2, nb 25	40	lb 2, w 1, nb 4	7
	(3 wkts dec 133 overs)	584	(3 wkts dec 52 overs)	256

Bowling
Richardson 19-6-86-0. Pathan 19-4-66-0. Betts 20-5-80-1. Styris 19-0-100-0.
Weekes 22-1-103-1. Dalrymple 12-0-52-0. Shah 11-1-44-0. Joyce 4-1-13-0.
Hutton 7-0-25-0.
Pathan 5-1-36-0. Richardson 8-2-24-3. Betts 4-1-15-0. Dalrymple 12-2-43-0.
Weekes 10-0-57-0. Hutton 4-0-27-0. Joyce 6-0-36-0. Shah 3-1-16-0.
Fall of Wickets: 1-99, 2-274, 3-515
1-23, 2-65, 3-66

MIDDLESEX	First Innings		Second Innings	
ET Smith	b Cosker	92	c Elliott b Croft	145
BL Hutton (capt)	c Grant b Cosker	19	retired hurt	7
OA Shah	c Elliott b Harrison	49	c Harrison b Croft	155
EC Joyce	not out	155	not out	70
SB Styris	c Harrison b Wharf	85	run out	6
JWM Dalrymple	not out	14	b Cosker	4
IK Pathan			not out	4
PN Weekes				
*BJM Scott				
MM Betts				
A Richardson				
Extras	b 4, lb 3, w 2, nb 12	21	b 2, lb 6, w 5, nb 4	17
	(4 wkts dec 95.3 overs)	435	(4 wkts 77.5 overs)	408

Bowling
Harrison 15-1-85-1. Wharf 18.3-1-103-1. Cosker 34-4-133-2. Croft 25-2-95-0.
Elliott 3-0-12-0.
Harrison 9-1-59-0. Wharf 9-0-39-0. Cosker 25.5-1-123-1. Croft 25-0-141-2.
Ganguly 7-1-30-0. Elliott 2-0-8-0.
Fall of Wickets: 1-69, 2-170, 3-172, 4-407
1-288, 2-380, 3-391, 4-404

Middlesex won by 6 wickets – Middlesex (20 pts),
Glamorgan (6 pts)

SUSSEX v. NOTTINGHAMSHIRE – at Arundel Castle

SUSSEX	First Innings		Second Innings	
RR Montgomerie	run out	0	run out	16
*MJ Prior	c Read b Smith	103	b Harris	8
MH Yardy	c Read b Harris	31	b Swann	7
MW Goodwin	c Fleming b Swann	39	not out	102
CJ Adams (capt)	c Swann b Smith	58	not out	120
TR Ambrose	lbw b Smith	0		
RSC Martin-Jenkins	c Hussey b Harris	37		
LJ Wright	c Read b Harris	27		
Mushtaq Ahmed	c Read b Harris	11		
RJ Kirtley	not out	9		
JD Lewry	c Gallian b Harris	14		
Extras	lb 8, nb 18	26	lb 2, w 1	3
	(87.2 overs)	355	(3 wkts 56 overs)	256

Bowling
Sidebottom 4.4-3-6-0. Harris 28.2-3-131-5. Swann 13-2-55-1. Smith 27.2-3-116-3.
Ealham 14-5-39-0.
Smith 11-3-31-0. Harris 8-0-33-1. Swann 11-1-41-1. Ealham 5-1-18-0.
Gallian 11-2-72-0. Hussey 10-0-59-0.
Fall of Wickets: 1-0, 2-98, 3-183, 4-193, 5-195, 6-274, 7-300, 8-322, 9-335
1-19, 2-26, 3-40

NOTTS	First Innings	
DJ Bicknell	c Montgomerie b Kirtley	88
JER Gallian	b Kirtley	5
RJ Warren	b Wright	25
SP Fleming (capt)	lbw b Lewry	129
DJ Hussey	b Martin-Jenkins	13
AJ Harris	b Lewry	35
*CMW Read	not out	17
MA Ealham	b Lewry	13
GP Swann	b Lewry	11
GJ Smith	c Prior b Lewry	0
RJ Sidebottom	c Martin-Jenkins b Lewry	2
Extras	b 2, lb 8, w 3, nb 4, p 5	22
	(106.1 overs)	360

Bowling
Kirtley 28-7-87-2. Lewry 24.1-3-74-6. Martin-Jenkins 24-4-74-1.
Mushtaq Ahmed 22-4-71-0. Wright 8-2-39-1.
Fall of Wickets: 1-14, 2-85, 3-213, 4-243, 5-309, 6-326, 7-342, 8-354, 9-354

Match drawn – Sussex (11 pts),
Nottinghamshire (11 pts)

More runs for Robert Key as the Kent opener steps up his campaign to get back into the England Test side.

triumph for Ed Joyce, who hit 70 not out to add to his first innings unbeaten 155 to guide Middlesex home with 13 balls to spare. Joyce also became the first batsman to reach 1,000 first-class runs for the season during his second innings knock.

Middlesex's chase was built upon excellent hundreds from both Ed Smith and Owais Shah, whose 155 off 202 balls included four sixes and 12 fours. Smith's 171-ball 145, with 20 boundaries, made up for him narrowly missing out on a century in Middlesex's first innings when he was bowled by one of the few balls which gave the suffering bowlers hope of a more equal contest. Glamorgan put much faith in their two spinners on the final afternoon, but Robert Croft and Dean Cosker were plundered for 264 runs from their combined 50.5 overs.

At least Glamorgan's batsmen enjoyed themselves, with Dan Cherry turning a maiden first-class hundred into a massive 226, the highest score ever for Glamorgan against Middlesex, eclipsing the great Viv Richards' 224 in 1993. Cherry anchored the drive towards 584 for 3 declared, sharing in three-figure stands with Matthew Elliott, David Hemp – who struck a quite brilliant 103 – and Jonathan Hughes. The chunky left-handed opener faced 349 balls and struck two sixes and 32 fours, while Hughes followed up his first innings unbeaten 134 with another 100 not out as he and Sourav Ganguly sped Glamorgan to the third declaration of a match played in too-perfect batting conditions.

A frustrating sea mist hung over the Arundel Castle ground for much of the first two days of Sussex's match against Nottinghamshire, with just seven overs being possible on day two – in which Sussex advanced from 251 for 5 to 274 for 6. By the end of that second day, moreover, Sussex had lost a debilitating 623 overs to the weather during the season. There was no time left here, either, for a positive result to be reached, despite the efforts of Jason Lewry on the fourth morning.

Division Two

Derbyshire came agonisingly close to their first championship win at Derby since 2002, but their one-wicket defeat by Lancashire was their 25th match on the ground without success. Jon Moss and Ian Hunter almost bowled the home side to a famous victory, but in the end it was opener Iain Sutcliffe's determined 62 not out which saved Lancashire's blushes. Earlier Dominic Cork had been an inspiration for Lancashire, against his old county, following up a first innings 4 for 40 by hitting 64 to rally the visitors from 128 for 6 to 241 all out. Moss scored 51 as Derbyshire sought to set Lancashire as tricky a last innings target as possible, but Muttiah Muralitharan's six wickets meant that only 136 were needed. Even that, though, proved touch and go.

Dinesh Mongia trapped Nadeem Malik lbw to clinch a thrilling 12-run win for Leicestershire in another relatively low-scoring but close-fought affair at Grace Road. Mongia had also scored a first innings 66 but it was the second innings fighting qualities of Paul Nixon and Charl Willoughby, plus the youthful promise of 18-year-old seamer Stuart Broad, which ultimately made the difference for Leicestershire. Former Oakham School pupil Broad, the son of former England opener Chris Broad, took 4 for 64 on his home debut but could not prevent Worcestershire from establishing a 98-run first innings lead. When Leicestershire slipped to 149 for 8 in their second innings, the game looked up. But Nixon, first in a stand of 25 with Broad and then more significantly in a 64-run last-wicket alliance with Willoughby, gave his side renewed hope with a pugnacious 135-ball 85. Ottis Gibson then claimed the first three Worcestershire second innings wickets and Broad chipped in with 3 for 31 as the excitement mounted. Steven Davies, with 49, was the only visiting batsman to make any headway as the chase came up short at 128 all out.

Just 43 overs were bowled on the opening day at Northampton, and this time ultimately cost Durham the opportunity of putting added last-day pressure on the home side. As it was, Northants had little trouble in batting out 69 overs to claim the draw. A career-best 80 off 86 balls by 22-year-old wicketkeeper Phil Mustard enlivened Durham's second-day progress to 334, and Dale Benkenstein then followed up his own innings of 80 by taking 4 for 29 with his medium-pacers to leave Northants vulnerable. Benkenstein's unbeaten second innings 83 completed a fine all-round match, and Gareth Breese also hit 69 not out to add to his first innings 55, but Durham chose to err on the side of caution with their declaration.

Round Ten: 15–18 June 2005 Division Two

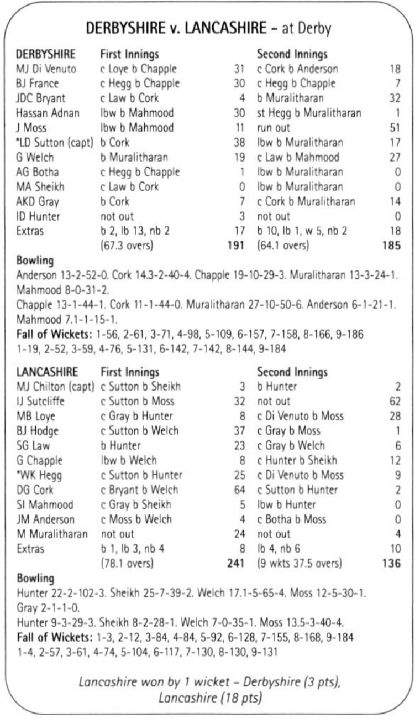

DERBYSHIRE v. LANCASHIRE – at Derby

DERBYSHIRE	First Innings		Second Innings	
MJ Di Venuto	c Loye b Chapple	31	c Cork b Anderson	18
BJ France	c Hegg b Chapple	30	c Hegg b Chapple	7
JDC Bryant	c Law b Cork	4	b Muralitharan	32
Hassan Adnan	lbw b Mahmood	30	st Hegg b Muralitharan	1
J Moss	lbw b Mahmood	11	run out	51
*LD Sutton (capt)	b Cork	38	lbw b Muralitharan	17
G Welch	b Muralitharan	19	c Law b Mahmood	27
AG Botha	c Hegg b Chapple	1	lbw b Muralitharan	0
MA Sheikh	c Law b Cork	0	lbw b Muralitharan	0
AKD Gray	b Cork	7	c Cork b Muralitharan	14
ID Hunter	not out	3	not out	0
Extras	b 2, lb 13, nb 2	17	b 10, lb 1, w 5, nb 2	18
	(67.3 overs)	191	(64.1 overs)	185

Bowling
Anderson 13-2-52-0. Cork 14.3-2-40-4. Chapple 19-10-29-3. Muralitharan 13-3-24-1. Mahmood 8-0-31-2.
Chapple 13-1-44-1. Cork 11-1-44-0. Muralitharan 27-10-50-6. Anderson 6-1-21-1. Mahmood 7.1-1-15-1.
Fall of Wickets: 1-56, 2-61, 3-71, 4-98, 5-109, 6-157, 7-158, 8-166, 9-186
1-19, 2-52, 3-59, 4-76, 5-131, 6-142, 7-142, 8-144, 9-184

LANCASHIRE	First Innings		Second Innings	
MJ Chilton (capt)	c Sutton b Sheikh	3	b Hunter	2
IJ Sutcliffe	c Sutton b Moss	32	not out	62
MB Loye	c Gray b Hunter	8	c Di Venuto b Moss	28
BJ Hodge	c Sutton b Welch	37	c Gray b Moss	1
SG Law	b Hunter	23	c Gray b Welch	6
G Chapple	lbw b Welch	8	c Hunter b Sheikh	12
*WK Hegg	c Sutton b Hunter	25	c Di Venuto b Moss	9
DG Cork	c Bryant b Welch	64	c Sutton b Hunter	2
SI Mahmood	c Gray b Sheikh	5	lbw b Hunter	0
JM Anderson	c Moss b Welch	4	c Botha b Moss	0
M Muralitharan	not out	24	not out	4
Extras	b 1, lb 3, nb 4	8	lb 4, nb 6	10
	(78.1 overs)	241	(9 wkts 37.5 overs)	136

Bowling
Hunter 22-2-102-3. Sheikh 25-7-39-2. Welch 17.1-5-65-4. Moss 12-5-30-1. Gray 2-1-1-0.
Hunter 9-3-29-3. Sheikh 8-2-28-1. Welch 7-0-35-1. Moss 13.5-3-40-4.
Fall of Wickets: 1-3, 2-12, 3-84, 4-84, 5-92, 6-128, 7-155, 8-168, 9-184
1-4, 2-57, 3-61, 4-74, 5-104, 6-117, 7-130, 8-130, 9-131

Lancashire won by 1 wicket – Derbyshire (3 pts), Lancashire (18 pts)

LEICESTERSHIRE v. WORCESTERSHIRE – at Leicester

LEICESTERSHIRE	First Innings		Second Innings	
DDJ Robinson	run out	31	c de Bruyn b Vaas	16
DL Maddy	b Price	49	lbw b Vaas	21
JK Maunders	c Pipe b Malik	19	c de Bruyn b Malik	3
D Mongia	b Malik	66	c de Bruyn b Malik	36
HD Ackerman (capt)	c Hick b Vaas	14	c Hick b Price	2
JL Sadler	c de Bruyn b Malik	22	c Hick b Price	19
*PA Nixon	c Hick b Price	11	run out	85
OD Gibson	c Davies b Price	6	c & b Price	5
CW Henderson	c Pipe b Malik	1	c Hick b Price	5
SCL Broad	not out	2	c Mitchell b Malik	14
CM Willoughby	c Smith b Malik	1	not out	16
Extras	lb 1, nb 2	3	b 8, lb 8	16
	(82.1 overs)	225	(73.2 overs)	238

Bowling
Mason 10-1-43-0. Vaas 18-6-37-1. Price 16-5-29-3. Malik 24.1-8-71-5. de Bruyn 14-3-44-0.
Mason 4-0-21-0. Vaas 26-10-63-2. Malik 16-4-74-3. Price 27.2-10-64-4.
Fall of Wickets: 1-49, 2-88, 3-112, 4-161, 5-200, 6-209, 7-219, 8-222, 9-222
1-34, 2-39, 3-53, 4-82, 5-98, 6-133, 7-143, 8-149, 9-174

WORCS	First Innings		Second Innings	
SC Moore	b Broad	41	b Gibson	3
SM Davies	c Nixon b Gibson	0	hit wkt b Gibson	49
GA Hick (capt)	b Gibson	13	c Maddy b Gibson	8
BF Smith	c & b Maddy	45	b Broad	14
Z de Bruyn	b Gibson	67	c Maddy b Willoughby	13
DKH Mitchell	not out	63	lbw b Mongia	10
WPUJC Vaas	c Sadler b Broad	20	c Ackerman b Broad	13
*DJ Pipe	b Willoughby	47	c Henderson b Broad	0
RW Price	c Robinson b Broad	5	run out	0
MS Mason	st Nixon b Henderson	4	not out	11
MN Malik	c Nixon b Broad	3	lbw b Mongia	3
Extras	lb 5, nb 10	15	b 2, lb 2	4
	(117.1 overs)	323	(45.1 overs)	128

Bowling
Gibson 25-1-101-3. Willoughby 29-10-56-1. Broad 17.1-2-64-4. Henderson 28-9-62-1. Maddy 11-2-22-1. Mongia 7-2-13-0.
Gibson 11-1-41-3. Willoughby 8-1-24-1. Henderson 9-1-15-0. Maddy 4-1-5-0. Broad 8-0-31-3. Mongia 5.1-1-8-2.
Fall of Wickets: 1-5, 2-27, 3-71, 4-129, 5-189, 6-213, 7-297, 8-313, 9-318
1-10, 2-26, 3-50, 4-68, 5-95, 6-107, 7-112, 8-113, 9-114

Leicestershire won by 12 runs – Leicestershire (18 pts), Worcestershire (6 pts)

NORTHAMPTONSHIRE v. DURHAM – at Northampton

DURHAM	First Innings		Second Innings	
N Peng	c Wessels b Louw	3	c Shafayat b Wright	16
JJB Lewis	c Love b Wright	6	c Love b Louw	52
GJ Muchall	c Wessels b Wright	4	c White b Brown	10
NJ Astle	c Wessels b Wright	32	c Pietersen b Wright	58
DM B'stein (capt)	c Love b Phillips	80	not out	83
GR Breese	lbw b Brown	55	not out	69
*P Mustard	c Sales b Wright	80		
AA Noffke	b Brown	65		
M Davies	b Louw	1		
ML Turner	not out	1		
N Killeen	lbw b Brown	0		
Extras	lb 3, w 4	7	lb 3, w 2	5
	(105.5 overs)	334	(4 wkts dec 91 overs)	293

Bowling
Wright 28-8-71-4. Louw 24-5-92-2. Phillips 19-5-46-1. Pietersen 6-1-30-0. Brown 28.5-6-92-3.
Wright 22-4-83-2. Louw 19-1-65-1. Brown 33-12-82-1. Phillips 10-2-31-0. Pietersen 7-0-29-0.
Fall of Wickets: 1-9, 2-9, 3-29, 4-73, 5-183, 6-185, 7-320, 8-321, 9-334
1-22, 2-35, 3-117, 4-168

NORTHANTS	First Innings		Second Innings	
ML Love	lbw b Davies	49	lbw b Benkenstein	62
BM Shafayat	lbw b Killeen	22	c Mustard b Davies	38
RA White	c Mustard b Benkenstein	13	c Astle b Breese	11
U Afzaal	c Muchall b Noffke	16	c Lewis b Breese	0
DJG Sales (capt)	not out	50	not out	23
*MH Wessels	lbw b Davies	3	not out	57
DG Wright	lbw b Turner	26		
BJ Phillips	b Benkenstein	24		
J Louw	c Mustard b Benkenstein	0		
C Pietersen	c Benkenstein b Breese	0		
JF Brown	c Mustard b Benkenstein	0		
Extras	b 1, lb 6, nb 4	11	b 6, lb 6, nb 2	14
	(66.4 overs)	214	(4 wkts 69 overs)	205

Bowling
Noffke 13-4-31-1. Turner 13-0-51-1. Davies 13-5-38-2. Killeen 13-6-31-1. Benkenstein 7.4-1-29-4. Astle 4-1-12-0. Breese 3-0-15-1.
Noffke 15-4-51-0. Turner 10-2-32-0. Killeen 11-4-37-0. Davies 7-4-5-1. Breese 17-2-45-2. Benkenstein 5-1-19-1. Astle 4-1-4-0.
Fall of Wickets: 1-54, 2-83, 3-98, 4-114, 5-121, 6-170, 7-210, 8-210, 9-211
1-89, 2-110, 3-120, 4-124

Match drawn – Northamptonshire (8 pts), Durham (10 pts)

Round 11: 8–13 July 2005

Division One

Hapless Glamorgan were once more the division's whipping boys as Nottinghamshire eased back to the top of the table with a comfortable ten-wicket victory at Trent Bridge. The omens were bad for the Welsh county even before the match began, with their Australian opener Matthew Elliott being ruled out for the rest of the season after tearing knee cartilage in fielding practice on the eve of the game.

Greg Smith's four wickets were largely responsible for Glamorgan's slide to 267 all out on the first day, despite the late boost of a 25-ball 41 from Andrew Davies, and by the close Nottinghamshire were poised to take complete control at 151 for 2. The second day saw Chris Read, with an unbeaten 103, David Hussey and Stephen Fleming take full advantage of the solid base laid down by Darren Bicknell's half-century of the evening before, and Glamorgan's only solace came in the shape of 18-year-old pace bowler Huw Waters. Fresh out of Monmouth School, he finished with 4 for 75 in a debut performance filled with rich promise for the future. Another young fast bowler, however, stole the honours on the third and final day: 19-year-old left-armer Mark Footitt ending his own debut match with figures of 4 for 45 as Glamorgan, struggling again on 108 for 4 overnight, subsided to 214 all out.

Kent, meanwhile, hardly displayed the stuff of potential champions at Canterbury, where Sussex came away with a 66-run win that was like gold dust for their own title hopes. At 321 for 5 in their first innings, in reply to Sussex's 378, Kent looked like

Round 11: 8–13 July 2005 Division One

NOTTINGHAMSHIRE v. GLAMORGAN – at Trent Bridge

GLAMORGAN	First Innings		Second Innings	
*MA Wallace	c Footitt b Smith	45	(2) c Read b Harris	12
DD Cherry	c Hussey b Smith	8	(1) b Footitt	27
DL Hemp	c Read b Ealham	44	lbw b Swann	12
J Hughes	lbw b Harris	5	c Bicknell b Footitt	20
SC Ganguly	c Hussey b Footitt	47	c Hussey b Smith	22
MJ Powell	b Smith	30	c Hussey b Harris	27
RN Grant	c Read b Ealham	8	c Hussey b Footitt	33
RDB Croft (capt)	c Ealham b Smith	4	b Footitt	20
DS Harrison	c Read b Harris	26	c Hussey b Ealham	21
AP Davies	not out	41	b Ealham	0
HT Waters	c Warren b Harris	3	not out	0
Extras	lb 5, w 1	6	b 8, lb 4, w 4, nb 4	20
	(61 overs)	267	(78.3 overs)	214

Bowling
Smith 17-4-64-4. Harris 14-2-62-3. Footitt 12-2-62-1. Ealham 15-1-58-2. Swann 3-0-16-0.
Smith 16-7-39-1. Harris 15-2-50-2. Swann 25-7-48-1. Footitt 14.3-4-45-4. Ealham 7-1-15-2. Hussey 1-0-5-0.
Fall of Wickets: 1-27, 2-64, 3-97, 4-107, 5-158, 6-171, 7-180, 8-205, 9-249
1-22, 2-40, 3-71, 4-76, 5-112, 6-132, 7-174, 8-211, 9-211

NOTTS	First Innings		Second Innings	
DJ Bicknell	run out	61	not out	20
JER Gallian	c Hemp b Harrison	21	not out	31
RJ Warren	c Hemp b Davies	34		
SP Fleming (capt)	c and b Ganguly	78		
DJ Hussey	c Wallace b Ganguly	81		
*CMW Read	not out	103		
MA Ealham	c Wallace b Waters	6		
GP Swann	lbw b Waters	0		
GJ Smith	lbw b Ganguly	4		
AJ Harris	c Wallace b Waters	10		
MHA Footitt	b Waters	16		
Extras	lb 10, w 1	11	b 4, lb 1, w 1	6
	(110 overs)	425	(0 wkts 17.4 overs)	57

Bowling
Harrison 22-1-83-1. Davies 26-2-107-1. Waters 23-2-75-4. Croft 23-3-82-0. Ganguly 16-0-68-3.
Harrison 4-1-17-0. Davies 2-0-10-0. Croft 6.4-4-15-0. Ganguly 3-2-5-0. Cherry 2-1-5-0.
Fall of Wickets: 1-48, 2-109, 3-157, 4-268, 5-289, 6-300, 7-300, 8-305, 9-324

Nottinghamshire won by 10 wickets –
Nottinghamshire (22 pts), Glamorgan (5 pts)

KENT v. SUSSEX – at Canterbury

SUSSEX	First Innings		Second Innings	
IJ Ward	c Fulton b Hall	100	c O'Brien b Saggers	3
RR Montgomerie	run out	21	lbw b Hall	17
MH Yardy	b Khan	6	c Hall b Khan	34
MW Goodwin	c O'Brien b Hall	63	c Stevens b Patel	26
CJ Adams (capt)	c O'Brien b Cook	83	b Patel	31
*TR Ambrose	b Cook	13	lbw b Hall	12
RSC Martin-Jenkins	c O'Brien b Saggers	2	c O'Brien b Patel	6
Naved ul-Hasan	c O'Brien b Patel	23	c O'Brien b Khan	6
Mushtaq Ahmed	c & b Stevens	7	c van Jaarsveld b Khan	4
RJ Kirtley	not out	21	b Khan	0
JD Lewry	c Saggers b Cook	4	not out	1
Extras	b 10, lb 14, w 3, nb 8	35	b 9, lb 1, w 1, nb 4	15
	(112.1 overs)	378	(55.3 overs)	155

Bowling
Saggers 20-1-65-1. Khan 15-1-65-1. Hall 24-1-73-2. Cook 24.1-11-57-3. Stevens 19-2-43-1. Patel 10-1-51-1.
Saggers 8-4-16-1. Khan 10.3-2-39-4. Hall 13-2-44-2. Cook 7-3-19-0. Patel 17-5-27-3.
Fall of Wickets: 1-65, 2-79, 3-210, 4-211, 5-235, 6-240, 7-291, 8-298, 9-370
1-14, 2-34, 3-87, 4-89, 5-116, 6-137, 7-144, 8-153, 9-154

KENT	First Innings		Second Innings	
DP Fulton (capt)	c Ambrose b Lewry	1	c Adams b Kirtley	4
RWT Key	c Adams b Lewry	74	c & b Naved-ul-Hasan	31
M van Jaarsveld	b Mushtaq Ahmed	32	lbw b Kirtley	4
DI Stevens	b Naved-ul-Hasan	50	(5) st Ambrose b Mushtaq Ahmed	0
AJ Hall	c Yardy b Kirtley	68	(6) c Ambrose b N-ul-Hasan	12
MJ Walker	c Ambrose b Naved-ul-Hasan	56	(4) c Goodwin b Mushtaq Ahmed	32
*NJO'Brien	b Martin-Jenkins	34	c Adams b Mushtaq Ahmed	10
MM Patel	b Mushtaq Ahmed	8	c Kirtley b Naved-ul-Hasan	2
SJ Cook	lbw b Naved-ul-Hasan	9	lbw b Mushtaq Ahmed	7
MJ Saggers	b Mushtaq Ahmed	6	not out	2
A Khan	not out	0	c & b Naved-ul-Hasan	8
Extras	lb 8, nb 2	10	lb 3, w 4	7
	(102.1 overs)	348	(44.2 overs)	119

Bowling
Kirtley 19-6-73-1. Lewry 19-5-63-2. Martin-Jenkins 11-2-24-1. Naved-ul-Hasan 19.1-1-46-3. Mushtaq Ahmed 34-2-134-3.
Kirtley 10-3-20-2. Lewry 7-3-10-0. Mushtaq Ahmed 15-3-58-4. Naved-ul-Hasan 12.2-3-28-4.
Fall of Wickets: 1-9, 2-102, 3-142, 4-187, 5-264, 6-321, 7-326, 8-336, 9-348
1-4, 2-14, 3-69, 4-69, 5-85, 6-93, 7-102, 8-105, 9-110

Sussex won by 66 runs – Kent (6 pts), Sussex (21 pts)

MIDDLESEX v. HAMPSHIRE – at Southgate

HAMPSHIRE	First Innings		Second Innings	
MJ Brown	lbw b Betts	15	b Richardson	1
CC Benham	c Shah b Richardson	20	b Betts	15
GA Lamb	c Shah b Styris	7	run out	51
JP Crawley	c Hutton b Peploe	62	st Scott b Dalrymple	14
CD McMillan	c Scott b Styris	7	b Dalrymple	15
*N Pothas	c Dalrymple b Peploe	26	c Shah b Peploe	19
SM Ervine	c Weekes b Peploe	33	lbw b Peploe	8
AD Mascarenhas	c Shah b Styris	39	c Joyce b Dalrymple	35
SK Warne (capt)	c Shah b Betts	101	c Smith b Peploe	4
SD Udal	c Scott b Betts	24	b Dalrymple	1
BV Taylor	not out	2	not out	3
Extras	lb 7, nb 12	19	b 5, lb 5, nb 16	26
	(80.2 overs)	355	(65.4 overs)	192

Bowling
Richardson 22-2-97-1. Betts 18.2-5-62-3. Styris 17-1-61-3. Hutton 4-1-14-0. Peploe 14-2-85-3. Joyce 2-0-13-0. Weekes 3-0-16-0.
Richardson 11-3-30-1. Betts 9-0-22-1. Peploe 27-6-77-3. Dalrymple 18.4-2-53-4.
Fall of Wickets: 1-19, 2-44, 3-50, 4-61, 5-130, 6-176, 7-189, 8-289, 9-342
1-6, 2-49, 3-78, 4-102, 5-129, 6-139, 7-154, 8-160, 9-161

MIDDLESEX	First Innings		Second Innings	
ET Smith	c Benham b Mascarenhas	22	b Udal	60
BL Hutton (capt)	c Udal b Warne	42	c Brown b Warne	5
OA Shah	lbw b Mascarenhas	16	c Warne b Udal	60
EC Joyce	c Mascarenhas b Taylor	54	run out	35
SB Styris	c Brown b Ervine	15	c Crawley b Lamb	3
JWM Dalrymple	c Lamb b Udal	62	(7) c Warne b Lamb	24
PN Weekes	c Mascarenhas b Warne	6	(8) not out	39
*BJM Scott	c Warne b Mascarenhas	2	(9) c Udal b Warne	14
CT Peploe	c Pothas b Udal	12	(10) not out	0
MM Betts	st Pothas b Udal	0		
A Richardson	not out	4	(6) c Brown b Udal	16
Extras	b 9, lb 9, nb 14, p 5	37	b 11, lb 5, nb 6	22
	(86.3 overs)	272	(8 wkts 79.4 overs)	278

Bowling
Taylor 21-2-71-1. Ervine 14-3-53-1. Mascarenhas 15-5-38-3. McMillan 4-1-12-0. Warne 23-4-57-2. Udal 9.3-4-18-3.
Taylor 7-2-10-0. Ervine 5-2-17-0. Mascarenhas 6-1-18-0. Warne 29.4-4-108-2. McMillan 3-0-19-0. Udal 21-5-60-3. Lamb 8-0-30-2.
Fall of Wickets: 1-24, 2-58, 3-144, 4-148, 5-191, 6-204, 7-215, 8-232, 9-238
1-20, 2-114, 3-151, 4-163, 5-198, 6-199, 7-255, 8-270

Middlesex won by 2 wickets – Middlesex (19 pts),
Hampshire (7 pts)

GLOUCESTERSHIRE v. SURREY – at Bristol

SURREY	First Innings		Second Innings	
SA Newman	c Adshead b Kirby	82	c Averis b Kirby	6
RS Clinton	c Adshead b Kirby	66		
GP Thorpe (capt)	b Averis	73	(5) not out	3
R Clarke	c Gidman b Averis	17	b Kirby	17
*JN Batty	c Adshead b Hardinges	55		
AD Brown	b Hardinges	7	(3) not out	18
Azhar Mahmood	run out	89	(2) c Spearman b Kirby	26
MP Bicknell	b Hardinges	76		
Harbhajan Singh	b Fisher	84		
J Ormond	b Kirby	33		
ND Doshi	not out	0		
Extras	lb 7, w 4, nb 10	21	b 1, lb 8, w 2, nb 3	14
	(138.1 overs)	603	(3 wkts 11 overs)	84

Bowling
Kirby 30.1-3-130-3. Averis 27-4-138-2. Hardinges 29-6-100-3. Fisher 32-4-149-1. Gidman 17-0-69-0. Taylor 3-0-10-0.
Kirby 6-0-30-3. Averis 3-0-32-0. Hardinges 2-0-13-0.
Fall of Wickets: 1-136, 2-167, 3-200, 4-295, 5-306, 6-321, 7-459, 8-535, 9-603
1-20, 2-54, 3-76

GLOS	First Innings		Second Innings	
CM Spearman	c Brown b Clarke	29	(2) c Clinton b Doshi	47
WPC Weston	c Azhar Mahmood b Bicknell	10	(1) c Batty b Ormond	52
MGN Windows	b Clarke	30	lbw b Ormond	6
JA Pearson	c Clarke b Harbhajan Singh	0	c Brown b Harbhajan Singh	34
APR Gidman	c Clarke b Harbhajan Singh	93	c Brown b Harbhajan Singh	142
*SJ Adshead	c Bicknell b Clarke	2	c Batty b Clarke	93
MA Hardinges	b Ormond	33	(8) b Azhar Mahmood	24
ID Fisher	lbw b Azhar Mahmood	36	(9) lbw b Ormond	22
CG Taylor (capt)	c Batty b Harbhajan Singh	21	(7) c Azhar Mahmood b Clarke	18
JMM Averis	c Newman b Harbhajan Singh	6	not out	29
SP Kirby	not out	0	lbw b Ormond	2
Extras	b 5, lb 10, w 3, nb 10	28	b 8, lb 14, w 3	25
	(88.1 overs)	288	(157.2 overs)	494

Bowling
Bicknell 15-5-51-1. Ormond 12-5-31-1. Azhar Mahmood 12-2-46-1. Clarke 17-4-74-3. Harbhajan Singh 23.1-6-51-4. Doshi 9-2-20-0.
Bicknell 17-4-57-0. Ormond 31.2-9-89-4. Azhar Mahmood 18-4-81-1. Doshi 24-11-48-1. Harbhajan Singh 49-8-142-2. Clarke 18-2-55-2.
Fall of Wickets: 1-17, 2-70, 3-71, 4-79, 5-83, 6-140, 7-230, 8-279, 9-287
1-85, 2-102, 3-109, 4-156, 5-391, 6-405, 7-419, 8-442, 9-486

Match drawn – Gloucestershire (8 pts),
Surrey (12 pts)

justifying their captain David Fulton's somewhat controversial decision to field first on day one – citing the presence of moisture in the pitch following several days of poor weather. Sussex, however, had finished the opening day on 357 for 8, with Ian Ward scoring his first hundred since the previous August and both Murray Goodwin and Chris Adams going past the half-century mark. Adams, indeed, was only dismissed on the second morning, for 83, but a steady Kent batting effort, led by Rob Key's careful 74, looked like tipping the balance in their favour.

Late on day two, though, Robin Martin-Jenkins breached the defences of Niall O'Brien and, from 323 for 6 overnight with Matthew Walker on 55, the home side could only reach 348. Even then, however, Sussex contrived to allow Kent back into the game as they slipped to 155 all out in their second innings on a blameless pitch. Yet the third-day drama did not end there. Needing just 186 to win, Kent collapsed themselves to 97 for 6 by the close after Key and Walker initially looked to be building a match-winning partnership. The end, too, came quickly on the final morning, with the Pakistan Test bowlers Mushtaq Ahmed and Naved-ul-Hasan claiming four Kentish scalps apiece.

Hampshire's title prospects took a dent when a second innings collapse against the spin of Middlesex's Jamie Dalrymple and Chris Peploe led to a two-wicket defeat in a tense finish at Southgate. The visitors looked to be in command after Shane Warne, back from a two-week break in Spain to try to repair his marriage, came in at 189 for 7 on the opening day and hit his second first-class century of the season – and his career. Warne initially added 100 in just 75 balls with Dimitri Mascarenhas, reaching his own half-century from 33 deliveries, and by the close he was unbeaten on 93 and his side's total had reached 331 for 8. The Warne hundred was duly completed the following

Graham Thorpe, under pressure to show England's selectors that he was fit enough to play in the opening Ashes Test, hit a first innings 73 for Surrey against Gloucestershire at Bristol.

morning, and Hampshire then earned themselves an 83-run first innings lead by bowling out Middlesex for 272 despite 50s from Dalrymple and Ed Joyce. The surrender of the initiative in their second innings, however, gave Middlesex a glimpse of victory and fine 60s from both Ed Smith and Owais Shah left them poised at 168 for 4 at the end of the third day. Joyce's needless run out cranked up the pressure on the Middlesex lower middle-order on the final morning, but Paul Weekes held his nerve and, eventually, pulled a Warne long hop for four to seal the win.

Alex Gidman and Steve Adshead were the heroes at Bristol as Gloucestershire defied Surrey with a magnificent rearguard action, after being forced to follow on. Both Gidman's 142 and Adshead's 93 were career-bests and their fifth-wicket stand raised 235 to frustrate the highly-rated Surrey attack. Even Indian off-spinner Harbhajan Singh found himself neutered by the Gloucestershire resistance, and the slowness of the Nevil Road surface, and ended up with just 2 for 142 from 49 overs as the home side reached 494 second time around. The match ended when Surrey, needing 180 from just 18 remaining overs, called off the chase at 84 for 3 after 11.

It was an excellent result for Gloucestershire, whose captain Chris Taylor had dislocated a shoulder in the field. Gidman, meanwhile, had hit a fine first innings 93 to hold together a faltering Gloucestershire reply of 288 to Surrey's mammoth first innings total of 603. Seven Surrey players passed 50, without going on to three figures and the Gloucestershire bowlers could make little impact. One of the run-getters on the opening day was Graham Thorpe, who scored a season's best 73 and hoped that it would be good enough to persuade England's selectors that he was fully fit for the opening Ashes Test.

Division Two

A remarkable, belligerent and high-class career-best 311 from Graeme Smith, their inspirational new captain, helped to sweep Somerset to a morale-boosting ten-wicket win against Leicestershire at Taunton. Showing his continued liking for the County Ground's true pitches, Smith ripped the Leicestershire bowling to shreds as he thumped 11 sixes and 27 fours in an innings which occupied just 255 balls. He was at the crease for a shade under six and a half hours and was joined in stands of 203 in 36 overs for the second wicket by Matthew Wood and of 114 for the fifth wicket by Ian Blackwell. Such was the rate of scoring that, after bowling out Leicestershire for 330 half an hour into the second day, Somerset were 203

A brilliant triple-hundred by Graeme Smith overwhelmed Leicestershire's bowlers at Taunton.

runs ahead by the close! They eventually totalled 566, after batting on for 5.3 overs on the third morning, and were left to make a token second innings score to complete victory after dismissing their visitors for 253. Andy Caddick, Charl Langeveldt and Blackwell all picked up three wickets.

Danish Kaneria undermined the Northamptonshire second innings with his leg-breaks and googlies, taking 6 for 74 as they collapsed from 202 for 2 to 261 all out. Essex thus completed a highly satisfactory three days by taking maximum points from a ten-wicket victory which had been built on their determined first innings progress to 506 all out. Monty Panesar's career-best 7 for 181, from 56.3 overs of hard toil, could not stop Essex from reaching a position of towering strength on a surface which became more spin-friendly as the match wore on. Off-spinner James Middlebrook then picked up four wickets as Northants failed to compile any sort of competitive

reply, and there were even three wickets for the part-time off-breaks of Alastair Cook after Bilal Shafayat's initial second innings resistance. Cook had Usman Afzaal lbw playing no stroke to his first ball – a maiden first-class wicket claimed in some style – as Northants lost their last eight wickets in 65 minutes.

Well-judged aggressive strokeplay from Richard Dawson, who finished unbeaten on 51, provided the final and decisive action in a hard-fought contest between Worcestershire and Yorkshire at New Road. The home side were left rueing the absence of the injured Shoaib Akhtar on a surface which favoured the quicker bowlers. Matthew Hoggard, confirming his readiness for the Ashes series, Tim Bresnan and Kabir Ali were always testing enough, but Shoaib's express pace might well have proved a match-winning ingredient. As it was, Worcestershire made Yorkshire fight all the way to their victory target of 268, with only Dawson's late thrust denying them. Richard Pyrah's first innings 78 for Yorkshire was a career-best.

Division Two leaders Durham were cut down to size by Lancashire at the Riverside, being bowled out for just 167 and 135 as the Red Rose county moved to within just 11 points of their opponents at the top of the table. Durham, indeed, took only a single point from the match, with Lancashire running up a huge 530 themselves to show that there was nothing at all wrong with the pitch. Mal Loye hit 30 fours in his magnificent 280-ball 200, and Dominic Cork also enjoyed himself immensely while reaching an

Round 11: 8–13 July 2005 Division Two

SOMERSET v. LEICESTERSHIRE – at Taunton

LEICESTERSHIRE	First Innings		Second Innings	
DDJ Robinson	c Durston b Parsons	33	lbw b Langeveldt	19
DL Maddy	c Gazzard b Langeveldt	8	c Francis SRG b Caddick	7
JK Maunders	run out	30	c Durston b Langeveldt	67
CJL Rogers	c Gazzard b Caddick	48	lbw b Caddick	0
HD Ackerman (capt)	c Francis SRG b Blackwell	35	c Francis JD b Caddick	51
JL Sadler	b Langeveldt	52	c Hildreth b Langeveldt	18
*PA Nixon	not out	62	not out	36
OD Gibson	lbw b Parsons	0	c Gazzard b Francis SRG	13
CW Henderson	c Smith b Caddick	25	c Francis JD b Blackwell	8
SCL Broad	c Gazzard b Caddick	0	c Francis JD b Blackwell	7
CM Willoughby	lbw b Langeveldt	3	b Blackwell	0
Extras	b 2, lb 11, w 1, nb 20	34	b 1, lb 1, w 3, nb 22	27
	(109.1 overs)	330	(75.2 overs)	253

Bowling
Caddick 30-9-83-3. Langeveldt 23.1-9-67-3. Francis SRG 14-2-69-0. Parsons 14-5-18-2. Blackwell 16-4-42-1. Durston 5-0-21-0. Smith 7-3-17-0. Caddick 19-8-46-3. Langeveldt 20-3-67-3. Blackwell 20.2-2-59-3. Francis SRG 7-1-34-1. Durston 4-1-21-0. Parsons 4-0-19-0. Hildreth 1-0-5-0.
Fall of Wickets: 1-14, 2-79, 3-81, 4-160, 5-182, 6-257, 7-262, 8-313, 9-319
1-38, 2-38, 3-38, 4-148, 5-173, 6-189, 7-219, 8-231, 9-253

SOMERSET	First Innings		Second Innings	
GC Smith (capt)	c Rogers b Henderson	311	not out	14
JD Francis	c Rogers b Willoughby	0	not out	4
MJ Wood	c Nixon b Willoughby	74		
JC Hildreth	c Rogers b Maddy	18		
WJ Durston	lbw b Maddy	0		
ID Blackwell	b Maddy	59		
KA Parsons	c Rogers b Maddy	6		
*CM Gazzard	b Broad	24		
AR Caddick	c Henderson b Broad	23		
CK Langeveldt	not out	18		
SRG Francis	c Ackerman b Broad	13		
Extras	b 8, lb 5, w 1, nb 6	20		0
	(101.3 overs)	566	(0 wkts 6 overs)	18

Bowling
Gibson 18-0-104-0. Willoughby 23-2-130-2. Maddy 14-1-65-4. Broad 20.3-0-119-3. Henderson 23-1-109-1. Maunders 3-0-26-0. Maddy 3-0-9-0. Henderson 3-0-9-0.
Fall of Wickets: 1-12, 2-215, 3-260, 4-260, 5-374, 6-394, 7-489, 8-522, 9-544

Somerset won by 10 wickets – Somerset (22 pts), Leicestershire (6 pts)

ESSEX v. NORTHAMPTONSHIRE – at Chelmsford

ESSEX	First Innings		Second Innings	
WI Jefferson	b Brown	48	not out	4
AN Cook	c Love b Brown	66	not out	0
GW Flower	b Panesar	55		
RS Bopara	b Wright	87		
A Flower	c Love b Panesar	72		
AP Palladino	b Panesar	3		
RC Irani (capt)	c Shafayat b Panesar	47		
*JS Foster	c Love b Panesar	11		
JD Middlebrook	b Panesar	42		
AR Adams	not out	29		
Danish Kaneria	c Sales b Panesar	22		
Extras	b 9, lb 12, w 1, nb 2	24		0
	(160.3 overs)	506	(0 wkts 0.2 overs)	4

Bowling
Wright 23-8-52-1. Jones 21-2-77-0. Phillips 13-2-39-0. Brown 47-13-136-2. Panesar 56.3-15-181-7.
Panesar 0.2-0-4-0.
Fall of Wickets: 1-108, 2-117, 3-220, 4-342, 5-349, 6-353, 7-389, 8-440, 9-462

NORTHANTS	First Innings		Second Innings	
ML Love	c & b Danish Kaneria	21	c Flower A b Danish Kaneria	32
BM Shafayat	lbw b Danish Kaneria	9	st Foster b Cook	84
TW Roberts	b Middlebrook	44	c Flower A b Danish Kaneria	0
U Afzaal	st Foster b Middlebrook	43	lbw b Cook	47
DJG Sales (capt)	c Cook b Middlebrook	0	c & b Danish Kaneria	12
*MH Wessels	lbw b Middlebrook	3	c Flower A b Cook	0
BJ Phillips	c Adams b Palladino	58	c Cook b Danish Kaneria	35
DG Wright	not out	53	c Cook b Adams	11
PS Jones	c Adams b Palladino	0	b Danish Kaneria	0
MS Panesar	lbw b Palladino	0	not out	0
JF Brown	run out	0	c Middlebrook b Danish Kaneria	0
Extras	b 8, lb 5, w 1, nb 2	16	b 19, lb 12, w 3, nb 6	40
	(82.2 overs)	247	(83.4 overs)	261

Bowling
Adams 10.2-1-41-0. Palladino 8-2-24-3. Danish Kaneria 31-9-83-2. Middlebrook 28-12-72-4. Flower GW 5-1-14-0.
Palladino 8-2-13-0. Adams 16-4-56-1. Danish Kaneria 32.4-10-74-6. Bopara 5-1-7-0. Middlebrook 16-3-48-0. Flower GW 3-0-19-0. Cook 3-1-13-3.
Fall of Wickets: 1-32, 2-33, 3-112, 4-114, 5-122, 6-141, 7-236, 8-236, 9-236
1-73, 2-73, 3-202, 4-203, 5-207, 6-227, 7-246, 8-253, 9-261

Essex won by 10 wickets – Essex (22 pts), Northamptonshire (3 pts)

WORCESTERSHIRE v. YORKSHIRE – at Worcester

WORCS	First Innings		Second Innings	
SC Moore	c Dawood b Dawson	74	c Dawood b Bresnan	26
SM Davies	c Wood b Hoggard	59	c Dawood b Hoggard	5
GA Hick	c Wood b Hoggard	8	c Sayers b Bresnan	22
BF Smith	c Jaques b Dawson	38	(5) c Jaques b Bresnan	1
Z de Bruyn	b Kruis	2	(6) c & b Kruis	41
DKH Mitchell	c Dawood b Hoggard	20	(7) c Jaques b McGrath	0
GJ Batty (capt)	c Dawson b Kruis	57	(8) c Dawood b Hoggard	29
Kabir Ali	c Wood b Bresnan	57	(9) not out	20
*DJ Pipe	c Dawson b Pyrah	10	(4) c McGrath b Kruis	32
MS Mason	c Hoggard b Bresnan	4	b Bresnan	24
MN Malik	not out	1	b Bresnan	0
Extras	b 1, lb 6, nb 8	15	b 4, lb 12, nb 6	22
	(92.1 overs)	345	(58 overs)	222

Bowling
Hoggard 22-6-68-3. Kruis 22-4-94-2. Dawson 16-3-63-2. Bresnan 17.1-3-78-2. McGrath 12-3-26-0. Pyrah 3-1-9-1.
Hoggard 21-3-76-2. Kruis 16-2-59-2. Bresnan 16-1-42-5. McGrath 5-0-29-1.
Fall of Wickets: 1-98, 2-120, 3-178, 4-181, 5-187, 6-247, 7-302, 8-329, 9-337
1-13, 2-44, 3-73, 4-79, 5-111, 6-111, 7-166, 8-166, 9-220

YORKSHIRE	First Innings		Second Innings	
MJ Wood	c Pipe b Kabir Ali	14	c Hick b Kabir Ali	9
JJ Sayers	c Hick b Malik	14	c Batty b Mason	24
A McGrath	b Batty	29	c Pipe b Kabir Ali	41
PA Jaques	c Kabir Ali b de Bruyn	38	b Batty	67
RM Pyrah	c Moore b Kabir Ali	78	lbw b Kabir Ali	0
C White (capt)	c Mason b Kabir Ali	56	c Pipe b Kabir Ali	27
*J Dawood	c Pipe b Mason	14	c Pipe b Mason	5
RKJ Dawson	c Pipe b Malik	0	not out	51
TT Bresnan	c Pipe b Malik	19	not out	9
MJ Hoggard	c de Bruyn b Mason	20		
GJ Kruis	not out	0		
Extras	b 4, lb 12, nb 2	18	b 13, lb 10, w 3, nb 10	36
	(91.2 overs)	300	(7 wkts 74.5 overs)	269

Bowling
Mason 23.2-5-60-2. Kabir Ali 22-4-59-3. Malik 22-5-79-3. de Bruyn 7-0-41-1. Batty 17-4-45-1.
Mason 22.5-6-61-2. Kabir Ali 22-6-70-4. Malik 12-2-53-0. de Bruyn 5-0-28-0. Batty 13-2-34-1.
Fall of Wickets: 1-28, 2-36, 3-99, 4-113, 5-233, 6-257, 7-257, 8-257, 9-284
1-16, 2-67, 3-115, 4-115, 5-194, 6-198, 7-230

Yorkshire won by 3 wickets – Worcestershire (6 pts), Yorkshire (20 pts)

DURHAM v. LANCASHIRE – at The Riverside

DURHAM	First Innings		Second Innings	
JJB Lewis	lbw b Chapple	36	absent hurt	
GM Scott	c Chilton b Cork	29	b Chapple	19
GJ Muchall	c Sutcliffe b Keedy	0	(1) b Cork	20
NJ Astle	b Chapple	58	(3) lbw b Chapple	23
DM Benkenstein (capt)	c Law b Anderson	1	(4) b Chapple	8
N Peng	b Anderson	4	(5) lbw b Anderson	17
GR Breese	lbw b Cork	0	(6) lbw b Chapple	1
*P Mustard	c Chilton b Keedy	15	(7) b Anderson	32
AA Noffke	c Hegg b Keedy	4	(8) b Cork	3
LE Plunkett	not out	0	(9) b Cork	0
M Davies	c Hegg b Chapple	1	(10) not out	0
Extras	lb 17, nb 2	19	b 5, lb 7	12
	(62.3 overs)	167	(9 wkts 44.1 overs)	135

Bowling
Anderson 16-4-65-2. Cork 16-5-35-2. Crook 4-1-9-0. Chapple 13.3-4-24-3. Keedy 13-6-17-3.
Anderson 15-5-47-2. Cork 9.1-1-30-3. Crook 5-1-19-0. Chapple 12-4-18-4. Keedy 3-1-9-0.
Fall of Wickets: 1-72, 2-73, 3-87, 4-92, 5-96, 6-109, 7-158, 8-158, 9-166
1-33, 2-51, 3-61, 4-80, 5-84, 6-116, 7-129, 8-135, 9-135

LANCASHIRE	First Innings	
MJ Chilton (capt)	lbw b Plunkett	52
IJ Sutcliffe	c Benkenstein b Breese	48
MB Loye	lbw b Davies	200
BJ Hodge	b Noffke	39
SG Law	b Plunkett	27
SP Crook	lbw b Noffke	5
DG Cork	not out	102
G Chapple	c Mustard b Davies	6
*WK Hegg	c Mustard b Davies	11
JM Anderson	b Breese	4
G Keedy	c Mustard b Davies	5
Extras	b 12, lb 9, w 2, nb 8	31
	(147.1 overs)	530

Bowling
Noffke 34-6-89-2. Plunkett 28-4-116-2. Davies 30.1-6-109-4. Benkenstein 13-3-47-0. Breese 21-3-80-2. Astle 14-2-40-0. Scott 7-1-28-0.
Fall of Wickets: 1-77, 2-155, 3-241, 4-305, 5-318, 6-463, 7-485, 8-511, 9-519

Lancashire won by an innings and 228 runs – Durham (1 pt), Lancashire (22 pts)

unbeaten 102. Durham's cause was not helped when Jon Lewis fractured a collarbone in the field, but this was a performance they immediately wanted to forget.

Round 12: 20–24 July 2005

Division One

For 24 hours, Nottinghamshire moved to the top of the division with a ten-wicket dismantling of champions Warwickshire at Edgbaston, but then Kent's incredible four-wicket triumph against Surrey at Guildford kept them in pole position. The championship race, indeed, was at this point of the season developing into one of the closest and most exciting for many years.

Kent's win at Guildford, on a pitch made for batting and on an outfield like glass, was a reward for their never-say-die spirit on the final day. Surrey had begun it on 173 for 2, a lead of only 43, but with Mark Ramprakash and Graham Thorpe at the crease and plenty of batting still to come the two batsmen relished the prospect of another chance to pepper the ground's short boundaries. Ramprakash and Thorpe, who had announced his retirement from international cricket the day before as a result of his non-selection for the Lord's Ashes Test, took their partnership to 98 but both fell just when it seemed that they were destined to score the centuries that had eluded them on the opening day. Kent captain David Fulton winkled out Thorpe when he introduced the part-time off-breaks of Martin van Jaarsveld before lunch, and the medium pace of Matthew Walker also gained Kent a precious wicket as they worked their way through the Surrey order. Min Patel's left-arm spin was again a telling factor for Kent, but the home side's eventual 350 total meant that 231 runs were still required for victory in just 35 remaining overs.

Fulton and Rob Key provided a rampaging start, however, and from 175 for 6 it was Justin Kemp and Niall O'Brien who came up with the partnership that won the game with five balls to spare. Kemp's unbeaten 47 from 37 balls completed a memorable match for him: his first innings 124 had featured in a 233-run stand in 53 overs with Walker, who made a brilliant 173, and put the cap on a

miserable start to the South African's Kent career in which his top score in all cricket for the previous two months had been 32. O'Brien's 23 not out, from 18 balls, was equally valuable in the tense final overs.

Nottinghamshire's victory in Birmingham was based on their all-round strengths: seam bowling on day one, top-order batting in the middle of the match and then Graeme Swann's off spin at the end. Excellent innings from Darren Bicknell, Jason Gallian and David Hussey enabled Notts to go significantly past Warwickshire's own first-innings score, despite a six-wicket return for Alex Loudon's off-breaks, and then Swann took advantage of the drying pitch to rout Warwickshire's batting in their second innings.

Hampshire, meanwhile, kept their own title-seeking momentum going by managing to escape a pitch penalty at the Rose Bowl, recover from two top-order batting collapses, and then deny Sussex's fourth innings run chase. The eventual margin of victory was 35 runs, but when Sussex reached 167 for 3 by the close of the third day it looked as if Hampshire would be beaten. The pitch had been reported by the umpires, and was the subject of scrutiny by the ECB pitch inspectors, but in the end no action was deemed necessary. The bowling of Dimitri Mascarenhas and Sean Ervine had also earned Hampshire a result that initially did not seem likely when they slid to 102 for 6 on the first day, with

The promise of 18-year-old seamer Huw Waters was again evident when Glamorgan met Middlesex.

Mascarenhas picking up 5 for 64 on the dramatic last morning and Ervine adding 4 for 54 to his first innings 5 for 73. Sussex were left kicking themselves. Not only had they allowed Hampshire to recover on the opening day, through Nic Pothas' fine century and 69 from the influential Ervine, but they also failed to finish off the home side second time around when they crumbled to 28 for 5. Shane Watson, with 82, and Pothas again, with 74, were chiefly responsible for Hampshire's second fighting recovery of the match, but Sussex's fate was ultimately sealed when last man Chris Tremlett was not prevented from thrashing his way to an unbeaten 44.

Glamorgan's members were not in the best of moods after seeing their team slump to the latest defeat of an unhappy return to the top flight: an innings and 23-run thumping by Middlesex at Cardiff. Their mood was not helped when it was announced that overseas batsman Sourav Ganguly would not be replaced for the remainder of the season – the Indian finishing his two-month stint at the county with a second innings 55 – and that Australian opener Matthew Elliott would be out for the rest of the summer with injury. Glamorgan's management, accepting that they were sure to be relegated, opted instead to use the last eight weeks of the season to blood younger players. One of those, 18-year-old seamer Huw Waters, impressed again with the ball despite his side being on the wrong end of Middlesex's advance to 534, and the youngster also hung around with the bat while skipper Robert Croft sped to 84 in a last-wicket stand of 60. That defiance, however, was not enough to prevent the follow-on and Scott Styris' five-wicket haul condemned the Welsh county to another heavy

Round 12: 20–24 July 2005 Division One

WARWICKSHIRE v. NOTTINGHAMSHIRE – at Edgbaston

WARWICKSHIRE	First Innings		Second Innings	
NV Knight (capt)	c Read b Ealham	57	c Fleming b Smith	11
IJ Westwood	c Read b Ealham	36	c Hussey b Sidebottom	33
IJL Trott	c Fleming b Harris	17	c Fleming b Swann	1
JO Troughton	b Sidebottom	24	c Warren b Swann	6
AGR Loudon	lbw b Harris	2	lbw b Swann	4
*T Frost	c Hussey b Sidebottom	4	b Swann	24
DR Brown	lbw b Harris	0	lbw b Ealham	17
LC Parker	not out	34	c Warren b Smith	18
NM Carter	c Warren b Smith	11	c Sidebottom b Swann	4
D Pretorius	lbw b Smith	22	c Harris b Swann	0
JE Anyon	c Read b Smith	0	not out	8
Extras	lb 10, nb 2	12	b 1, lb 4, nb 2	7
	(63 overs)	219	(59.1 overs)	133

Bowling
Sidebottom 14-4-41-2. Harris 15-3-48-3. Ealham 13-3-41-2. Smith 12-1-58-3. Swann 9-2-21-0.
Sidebottom 13-8-13-1. Harris 6-0-15-0. Swann 23-7-57-6. Smith 9.1-2-23-2. Ealham 8-1-20-1.
Fall of Wickets: 1-101, 2-104, 3-135, 4-139, 5-147, 6-152, 7-154, 8-168, 9-213
1-27, 2-30, 3-42, 4-58, 5-60, 6-97, 7-103, 8-108, 9-108

NOTTS	First Innings		Second Innings	
DJ Bicknell	b Carter	84	(2) not out	4
JER Gallian	c Carter b Loudon	62		
RJ Warren	c Westwood b Loudon	5		
SP Fleming (capt)	st Frost b Loudon	41		
DJ Hussey	c Pretorius b Loudon	77		
MA Ealham	b Pretorius	11		
GP Swann	c Pretorius b Loudon	19	(1) not out	8
RJ Sidebottom	c Frost b Brown	0		
GJ Smith	lbw b Brown	5		
*CMW Read	c Knight b Loudon	26		
AJ Harris	not out	1		
Extras	b 5, lb 3, nb 2	10		0
	(88.4 overs)	341	(0 wkts 1.4 overs)	12

Bowling
Pretorius 15-2-54-1. Brown 18-0-78-2. Anyon 6-1-34-0. Carter 20-7-59-1. Loudon 26.4-2-92-6. Troughton 3-0-16-0.
Carter 1-0-8-0. Pretorius 0.4-0-4-0.
Fall of Wickets: 1-123, 2-129, 3-195, 4-207, 5-243, 6-287, 7-288, 8-298, 9-339

Nottinghamshire won by 10 wickets –
Warwickshire (4 pts), Nottinghamshire (20 pts)

SURREY v. KENT – at Guildford

SURREY	First Innings		Second Innings	
*JN Batty	c Walker b Patel	50	c Walker b Hall	55
RS Clinton	c Kemp b Cook	0	c Fulton b Khan	45
MR R'kash (capt)	c O'Brien b Cook	97	c O'Brien b Cook	62
GP Thorpe	b Patel	95	c Stevens b van Jaarsveld	47
AD Brown	c O'Brien b Khan	107	b Walker	34
R Clarke	b Stevens	18	b Patel	7
Azhar Mahmood	lbw b Hall	41	c Fulton b Patel	25
IDK Salisbury	c O'Brien b Patel	15	c van Jaarsveld b Patel	20
J Ormond	not out	2	not out	2
ND Doshi	not out	4		
M Akram			c Stevens b Patel	0
Extras	b 7, lb 1, w 3, nb 16	27	b 25, lb 11, w 1, nb 12	49
	(8 wkts dec 118.4 overs)	452	(119.2 overs)	350

Bowling
Khan 21-4-92-1. Cook 17-3-78-2. Hall 21.4-4-73-1. Kemp 17-0-60-0. Patel 30-6-96-3. Stevens 11-0-40-1. Key 1-0-5-0.
Khan 20-2-86-1. Cook 15-3-37-1. Patel 47.2-8-110-4. Hall 15-5-22-2. Kemp 3-0-16-0. Walker 4-1-6-1. Stevens 13-0-25-0. van Jaarsveld 2-0-12-1.
Fall of Wickets: 1-4, 2-105, 3-238, 4-336, 5-382, 6-400, 7-449, 8-451
1-107, 2-142, 3-240, 4-269, 5-292, 6-301, 7-331, 8-344, 9-349

KENT	First Innings		Second Innings	
DP Fulton (capt)	c Brown b Azhar Mahmood	39	c Clinton b Salisbury	31
RWT Key	b Doshi	65	lbw b Akram	4
M van Jaarsveld	c Batty b Ormond	36	c Ramprakash b Doshi	25
MJ Walker	c Doshi b Akram	173	b Doshi	18
DI Stevens	lbw b Azhar Mahmood	0	c Clinton b Doshi	4
JM Kemp	b Azhar Mahmood	124	not out	47
AJ Hall	c Batty b Doshi	24	c Brown b Azhar Mahmood	47
*NJO'Brien	lbw b Salisbury	46	not out	13
MM Patel	st Batty b Doshi	27		
SJ Cook	c Batty b Salisbury	13		
A Khan	not out	1		
Extras	b 4, lb 6, nb 14	24	b 2, lb 9, w 1, nb 8	20
	(129.5 overs)	572	(6 wkts 34.1 overs)	232

Bowling
Akram 24-2-114-1. Ormond 28-1-109-1. Azhar Mahmood 24-2-104-3. Clarke 9-0-53-0. Doshi 30-3-111-3. Salisbury 14.5-0-71-2.
Ormond 9-0-68-0. Azhar Mahmood 8.1-0-40-1. Doshi 7-0-58-2. Salisbury 4-0-25-1. Akram 6-0-30-2.
Fall of Wickets: 1-58, 2-122, 3-201, 4-202, 5-435, 6-483, 7-495, 8-523, 9-571
1-83, 2-87, 3-121, 4-126, 5-140, 6-175

Kent won by 4 wickets – Surrey (8 pts), Kent (21 pts)

HAMPSHIRE v. SUSSEX – at The Rose Bowl

HAMPSHIRE	First Innings		Second Innings	
MJ Brown	c Prior b Naved-ul-Hasan	15	c Prior b Kirtley	16
CC Benham	c Prior b Kirtley	2	lbw b Mushtaq Ahmed	6
GA Lamb	lbw b Lewry	0	(4) b Kirtley	0
JP Crawley	lbw b Lewry	16	(5) c Yardy b Naved-ul-Hasan	5
SR Watson	c & b Kirtley	43	(6) st Prior b Mushtaq Ahmed	82
CD McMillan	c Prior b Naved-ul-Hasan	14	(7) c Montgomerie b Lewry	34
*N Pothas	lbw b Mushtaq Ahmed	135	(8) c Montgomerie b N-ul-Hasan	74
SM Ervine	c Ward b Naved-ul-Hasan	69	(9) c Prior b Kirtley	3
AD Mascarenhas	c Naved-ul-Hasan b Lewry	8	(3) lbw b Kirtley	1
SD Udal (capt)	lbw b Mushtaq Ahmed	0	(2) lbw b Kirtley	5
BV Taylor	not out	1		
CT Tremlett			(11) not out	44
Extras	lb 3, w 1, nb 2	6	b 4, lb 3	7
	(102.2 overs)	309	(76.4 overs)	277

Bowling
Kirtley 21-8-68-2. Lewry 26.2-8-50-3. Naved-ul-Hasan 26-7-82-3. Hopkinson 4-1-25-0. Mushtaq Ahmed 22-5-66-2. Yardy 3-0-15-0.
Kirtley 24-10-67-5. Naved-ul-Hasan 17.4-3-73-2. Mushtaq Ahmed 23-2-91-2. Lewry 12-2-39-1.
Fall of Wickets: 1-7, 2-16, 3-29, 4-51, 5-86, 6-102, 7-293, 8-305, 9-307
1-16, 2-17, 3-17, 4-28, 5-28, 6-111, 7-177, 8-188, 9-194

SUSSEX	First Innings		Second Innings	
IJ Ward	c Benham b Mascarenhas	27	b Ervine	60
RR Montgomerie	lbw b Ervine	64	b Ervine	1
MH Yardy	c Pothas b Watson	0	c Lamb b Tremlett	34
MW Goodwin	c Watson b Ervine	49	c Lamb b Mascarenhas	71
CJ Adams (capt)	c Pothas b Tremlett	41	b Mascarenhas	21
*MJ Prior	b Udal	24	c Udal b Mascarenhas	1
CD Hopkinson	c Watson b Ervine	25	c Crawley b Mascarenhas	0
Naved ul-Hasan	c Benham b Udal	39	c & b Ervine	25
Mushtaq Ahmed	not out	21	lbw b Ervine	3
RJ Kirtley	c Watson b Ervine	0	not out	0
JD Lewry	c Pothas b Ervine	5	c Ervine b Mascarenhas	1
Extras	lb 3, nb 18	21	lb 6, nb 4	15
	(76.5 overs)	316	(60.4 overs)	235

Bowling
Taylor 4-0-16-0. Ervine 19.5-4-73-5. Tremlett 15-0-70-1. Mascarenhas 15-5-25-1. Watson 11-2-49-1. McMillan 2-0-12-0. Udal 10-0-68-2.
Tremlett 11-0-56-1. Ervine 17-4-54-4. Mascarenhas 20.4-4-64-5. Watson 10-1-40-0. Udal 2-0-10-0.
Fall of Wickets: 1-53, 2-58, 3-136, 4-149, 5-219, 6-225, 7-289, 8-290, 9-290
1-10, 2-84, 3-124, 4-193, 5-195, 6-195, 7-216, 8-229, 9-232

Hampshire won by 35 runs – Hampshire (20 pts), Sussex (6 pts)

GLAMORGAN v. MIDDLESEX – at Cardiff

MIDDLESEX	First Innings	
ET Smith	b Waters	29
BL Hutton (capt)	c Hughes b Waters	73
OA Shah	c Wallace b Croft	101
EC Joyce	c & b Harrison	32
SB Styris	lbw b Waters	30
JWM Dalrymple	c Wharf b Harrison	108
PN Weekes	c Wallace b Croft	42
*BJM Scott	b Harrison	25
PD Trego	b Harrison	72
CT Peploe	not out	11
MM Betts	b Harrison	0
Extras	lb 5, nb 6	11
	(123.3 overs)	534

Bowling
Harrison 23.3-1-117-5. Wharf 28-4-143-0. Waters 26-4-75-3. Ganguly 5-0-30-0. Croft 38-1-146-2. Grant 3-0-18-0.
Fall of Wickets: 1-40, 2-149, 3-203, 4-267, 5-267, 6-336, 7-399, 8-521, 9-534

GLAMORGAN	First Innings		Second Innings	
*MA Wallace	c Hutton b Trego	23	(2) c Peploe b Dalrymple	64
DD Cherry	b Betts	14	(1) c Scott b Betts	4
DL Hemp	b Trego	22	b Betts	5
J Hughes	c Shah b Trego	7	b Peploe	41
SC Ganguly	run out	4	lbw b Styris	55
MJ Powell	lbw b Styris	18	c Joyce b Peploe	58
RN Grant	lbw b Styris	1	lbw b Styris	6
RDB Croft (capt)	c Peploe b Joyce	84	c Scott b Styris	25
AG Wharf	c Trego b Styris	21	c Scott b Styris	1
DS Harrison	b Dalrymple	5	c Smith b Styris	8
HT Waters	not out	1	not out	2
Extras	b 5, lb 14, w 5, nb 8	32	b 2, lb 2, w 4, nb 2	10
	(56.3 overs)	232	(88 overs)	279

Bowling
Betts 15-5-37-1. Trego 13-1-52-3. Hutton 4-3-4-0. Peploe 10-4-43-0. Styris 11-3-42-3. Dalrymple 3-0-31-1. Joyce 0.3-0-4-1.
Betts 16-2-44-2. Trego 9-2-37-0. Styris 17-4-57-5. Peploe 28-5-82-2. Dalrymple 13-1-46-1. Weekes 5-1-9-0.
Fall of Wickets: 1-40, 2-54, 3-76, 4-89, 5-103, 6-110, 7-117, 8-155, 9-172
1-14, 2-25, 3-105, 4-153, 5-208, 6-238, 7-262, 8-265, 9-270

Middlesex won by an innings and 23 runs –
Glamorgan (4 pts), Middlesex (22 pts)

defeat. Owais Shah and Jamie Dalrymple both hit hundreds in Middlesex's only innings, with Peter Trego celebrating the award of a contract at a third county (following his spells at Somerset and Kent) by striking three sixes and six fours in a 54-ball 72.

Division Two

Northamptonshire withstood the fire of Shoaib Akhtar at Wantage Road to go on to record their first win of the championship season. It was a battling performance by Northants, who were forced to concede an 82-run first innings deficit to Worcestershire after being dismissed on day one for 299 as Pakistan pace ace Shoaib took 6 for 47. In one single over, in fact, Shoaib clean bowled Martin Love, Riki Wessels and Damien Wright with vicious in-swingers. But, even after that, a brave 62-run partnership for the last wicket by Monty Panesar and Jason Brown illustrated the home team's fighting spirit. Steven Davies, with a career-best 95, and Vikram Solanki, with a stylish 80, then gave Worcestershire the advantage, before 84 from Bilal Shafayat and a gritty 102 from Wessels revived Northants' hopes again. By the close of the third day, indeed, a Northants win looked likely as the visitors struggled against the turning ball to 139 for 5, and when Ben Smith was out early the following morning, after adding just seven runs to his overnight 50 not out, it was left to Panesar – who

finished with 6 for 77 – to speed Northants home with his fast-improving left-arm spinners.

For the second time in two months, Yorkshire chased down a massive fourth innings target to stun Leicestershire and boost their promotion ambitions.

Round 12: 20–24 July 2005 Division Two

NORTHAMPTONSHIRE v. WORCESTERSHIRE – at Northampton

NORTHANTS	First Innings		Second Innings	
ML Love	b Shoaib Akhtar	74	c Davies b Price	27
BM Shafayat	c Hick b Kabir Ali	12	c Kabir Ali b Price	84
TW Roberts	c Price b Shoaib Akhtar	53	b Price	1
U Afzaal	lbw b Mason	0	lbw b Batty	21
DJG Sales (capt)	b Shoaib Akhtar	53	c Smith b Shoaib Akhtar	19
*MH Wessels	b Shoaib Akhtar	0	st Davies b Batty	102
DG Wright	b Shoaib Akhtar	4	b Kabir Ali	47
BJ Phillips	b Shoaib Akhtar	0	b Kabir Ali	17
J Louw	c de Bruyn b Mason	1	(10) b Batty	5
MS Panesar	not out	39	(9) lbw b Kabir Ali	0
JF Brown	c Hick b Kabir Ali	22	not out	0
Extras	lb 15, nb 26	41	b 4, lb 16, w 5, nb 16	41
	(75.4 overs)	299	(91.1 overs)	364

Bowling
Shoaib Akhtar 14-3-47-6. Kabir Ali 17.4-2-87-2. Mason 18-5-61-2. de Bruyn 9-2-36-0. Batty 15-3-51-0. Price 2-0-2-0.
Shoaib Akhtar 13-3-67-1. Kabir Ali 12-1-56-3. Mason 10-4-30-0. Batty 24.1-5-99-3. Price 32-6-92-3.
Fall of Wickets: 1-56, 2-150, 3-156, 4-166, 5-166, 6-170, 7-170, 8-173, 9-237
1-81, 2-105, 3-140, 4-168, 5-187, 6-291, 7-315, 8-315, 9-363

WORCS	First Innings		Second Innings	
SC Moore	c Shafayat b Panesar	20	c Afzaal b Panesar	17
*SM Davies	b Panesar	95	c Wessels b Brown	37
GA Hick	c Love b Panesar	10	c Shafayat b Panesar	0
BF Smith	c Love b Louw	27	c Love b Panesar	57
VS Solanki (capt)	c Love b Louw	80	c Sales b Panesar	22
Z de Bruyn	run out	10	(7) c Wessels b Louw	10
GJ Batty	c Louw b Wright	48	(8) not out	24
Kabir Ali	c Sales b Wright	24	(9) c Love b Panesar	7
RW Price	c Love b Wright	7	(6) c Shafayat b Louw	0
Shoaib Akhtar	not out	20	b Brown	1
MS Mason	b Louw	26	c Shafayat b Panesar	5
Extras	lb 12, nb 2	14	b 13, lb 7	20
	(110 overs)	381	(58.5 overs)	200

Bowling
Wright 18-1-80-3. Louw 16-1-77-3. Phillips 15-3-43-0. Panesar 29-5-91-3. Brown 29-7-65-0. Shafayat 3-0-13-0.
Wright 3-0-21-0. Louw 9-2-27-2. Panesar 26.5-3-77-6. Brown 20-3-55-2.
Fall of Wickets: 1-58, 2-70, 3-133, 4-201, 5-228, 6-289, 7-323, 8-335, 9-336
1-54, 2-56, 3-76, 4-129, 5-136, 6-146, 7-164, 8-188, 9-193

*Northamptonshire won by 82 runs –
Northamptonshire (19 pts), Worcestershire (7 pts)*

YORKSHIRE v. LEICESTERSHIRE – at Scarborough

LEICESTERSHIRE	First Innings		Second Innings	
DDJ Robinson	c Jaques b Dawson	26	b Bresnan	0
DL Maddy	lbw b Harvey	40	c Wood b Bresnan	0
JK Maunders	b Dawson	3	c Dawson b McGrath	48
CJL Rogers	st Dawood b Lawson	93	lbw b Dawson	35
HD Ackerman (capt)	lbw b Bresnan	20	c Jaques b McGrath	10
A Habib	lbw b McGrath	0	(7) b Dawson	26
*PA Nixon	b Kruis	10	(8) c Sayers b Dawson	22
OD Gibson	c Dawood b Kruis	91	(9) not out	33
CW Henderson	c Wood b Kruis	49	(6) c White b Bresnan	21
SCL Broad	not out	10	lbw b Dawson	2
CM Willoughby	c Jaques b Kruis	0	c Harvey b Kruis	4
Extras	lb 9, w 1, nb 14	24	lb 8, nb 8	16
	(110.5 overs)	366	(70.5 overs)	217

Bowling
Kruis 24.5-5-90-4. Bresnan 25-4-88-1. Dawson 28-4-70-2. Harvey 12-4-35-1. McGrath 10-2-30-1. Lawson 11-2-44-1.
Bresnan 16-4-44-3. Kruis 22.5-7-39-1. Harvey 6-1-21-0. Lawson 3-0-23-0. Dawson 13-0-54-4. McGrath 10-1-28-2.
Fall of Wickets: 1-60, 2-68, 3-96, 4-158, 5-165, 6-188, 7-226, 8-353, 9-366
1-0, 2-13, 3-78, 4-99, 5-100, 6-131, 7-173, 8-182, 9-194

YORKSHIRE	First Innings		Second Innings	
MJ Wood	lbw b Gibson	21	c Maunders b Henderson	70
JJ Sayers	c Robinson b Willoughby	5	c Maddy b Gibson	104
A McGrath	lbw b Gibson	4	c Ackerman b Willoughby	89
PA Jaques	c Henderson b Willoughby	22	c Nixon b Henderson	55
IJ Harvey	b Broad	4	not out	54
C White (capt)	c Nixon b Willoughby	33	not out	18
*I Dawood	c Nixon b Broad	45		
RKJ Dawson	lbw b Gibson	20		
TT Bresnan	lbw b Maddy	3		
MAK Lawson	not out	20		
GJ Kruis	c Gibson b Broad	0		
Extras	b 4, lb 2, w 4	10	b 4, lb 3, w 3	10
	(56.3 overs)	187	(4 wkts 126 overs)	400

Bowling
Gibson 18-4-36-3. Willoughby 17-2-55-3. Broad 8.3-1-35-3. Maddy 10-2-33-1. Henderson 3-1-22-0.
Gibson 28-7-82-1. Willoughby 25-6-88-1. Broad 14-0-60-0. Henderson 40-11-91-2. Maddy 13-1-44-0. Maunders 3-0-19-0. Rogers 3-0-9-0.
Fall of Wickets: 1-26, 2-26, 3-30, 4-44, 5-85, 6-98, 7-132, 8-147, 9-187
1-115, 2-269, 3-277, 4-356

Yorkshire won by 6 wickets – Yorkshire (17 pts), Leicestershire (7 pts)

DERBYSHIRE v. DURHAM – at Derby

DURHAM	First Innings		Second Innings	
MEK Hussey (capt)	lbw b Welch	10	not out	42
GM Scott	c Sutton b Welch	18	c France b Botha	28
PD Collingwood	c Moss b Walker	190	b Botha	12
GJ Muchall	c Moss b Walker	8	not out	0
DM Benkenstein	c Walker b Hunter	98		
GR Breese	lbw b Botha	11		
*P Mustard	c France b Welch	0		
AA Noffke	not out	10		
LE Plunkett	c Sutton b Walker	0		
M Davies	c Moss b Walker	4		
G Onions	c Friend b Hunter	4		
Extras	b 1, lb 12, w 3, nb 2	18	lb 1, w 6, nb 4	11
	(107.5 overs)	371	(2 wkts dec 36 overs)	93

Bowling
Hunter 19.5-3-79-2. Welch 23-8-51-3. Walker 20-4-69-4. Moss 18-5-47-0. Botha 14-0-74-1. France 8-2-33-0. Hassan Adnan 1-0-5-0.
Hunter 13-3-36-0. Welch 10-5-27-0. Moss 7-1-19-0. Botha 6-3-10-2.
Fall of Wickets: 1-23, 2-38, 3-59, 4-309, 5-350, 6-352, 7-352, 8-355, 9-359
1-70, 2-91

DERBYSHIRE	First Innings		Second Innings	
SD Stubbings	c Hussey b Noffke	14	(2) c Hussey b Onions	28
MJ Di Venuto	c Mustard b Davies	32	(1) c Breese b Benkenstein	203
BJ France	c Plunkett b Noffke	6	b Onions	0
Hassan Adnan	c Mustard b Plunkett	1	c Mustard b Plunkett	106
J Moss	b Davies	7	b Plunkett	0
*LD Sutton (capt)	lbw b Plunkett	29	c Muchall b Benkenstein	5
TJ Friend	c Hussey b Plunkett	3	c Onions b Breese	82
G Welch	c Mustard b Davies	40	not out	67
AG Botha	c Breese b Onions	13	not out	25
ID Hunter	not out	1		
NGE Walker	run out	0		
Extras	b 6, lb 1, nb 8	15	b 12, lb 7, nb 4	23
	(41.1 overs)	161	(7 wkts dec 149.5 overs)	539

Bowling
Plunkett 13-2-61-3. Noffke 14-0-61-2. Davies 6.1-5-4-3. Onions 8-0-28-1.
Plunkett 33-7-109-2. Onions 20-4-83-2. Collingwood 20-3-64-0. Davies 21.5-5-64-0. Breese 31-4-86-1. Benkenstein 18-2-84-2. Scott 1-0-7-0. Hussey 5-2-14-0.
Fall of Wickets: 1-29, 2-53, 3-55, 4-60, 5-69, 6-87, 7-124, 8-160, 9-160
1-82, 2-82, 3-354, 4-355, 5-356, 6-360, 7-495

Match drawn – Derbyshire (7 pts), Durham (11 pts)

LANCASHIRE v. ESSEX – at Old Trafford

ESSEX	First Innings	
WI Jefferson	c Horton b Cork	1
AN Cook	c Cork b Chapple	32
GW Flower	c Hegg b Keedy	115
RS Bopara	c & b Cork	17
A Flower	c Hegg b Crook	138
RC Irani (capt)	c Symonds b Chapple	59
*JS Foster	c Anderson b Cork	24
JD Middlebrook	c Chapple b Crook	64
AR Adams	b Crook	48
AP Palladino	not out	0
Danish Kaneria		
Extras	b 10, lb 21, w 1, nb 6	38
	(9 wkts dec 140 overs)	536

Bowling
Anderson 36-4-140-0. Cork 29-8-91-3. Chapple 30-13-55-2. Symonds 20-4-62-0. Keedy 15-0-86-1. Crook 10-2-71-3.
Fall of Wickets: 1-1, 2-57, 3-129, 4-225, 5-323, 6-363, 7-478, 8-505, 9-536

LANCASHIRE	First Innings	
MJ Chilton (capt)	c Foster b Adams	4
IJ Sutcliffe	c & b Bopara	66
MB Loye	c Cook b Flower GW	194
PJ Horton	c Adams b Flower GW	99
A Symonds	b Middlebrook	134
AR Crook	c & b Flower GW	43
DG Cork	not out	57
G Chapple	not out	19
*WK Hegg		
JM Anderson		
G Keedy		
Extras	b 12, lb 4, w 11, nb 12	39
	(6 wkts dec 220.3 overs)	655

Bowling
Palladino 16-4-45-0. Adams 19-6-65-1. Danish Kaneria 70.2-10-208-0. Bopara 18-3-64-1. Middlebrook 41.4-14-119-1. Cook 4-0-11-0. Flower GW 47.3-17-112-3. Jefferson 4-1-15-0.
Fall of Wickets: 1-15, 2-166, 3-376, 4-443, 5-525, 6-629

Match drawn – Lancashire (10 pts), Essex (9 pts)

At Grace Road in mid-May they reached 404, the county's record-winning fourth innings score; here they scored 397 to win. And with some ease, too, with Joe Sayers anchoring the effort with a 347-ball 104, and the likes of Anthony McGrath, Phil Jaques and Ian Harvey providing the strokemaking power. Matthew Wood's 70, in an opening stand of 115 with Sayers, was another important contribution – and it was all a far cry from Yorkshire's first innings demise to 187 all out. At that stage, indeed, they looked well beaten as Leicestershire had earlier totalled 366 in their first innings, thanks in the main to 93 from Chris Rogers and the unexpected bonus of a 127-run stand for the eighth wicket between Ottis Gibson, who made 91, and Claude Henderson. But

In his prime: Mal Loye continued his sparkling mid-summer form for Lancashire with a superb 194 against Essex.

Leicestershire could not press home their advantage, slipping to 106 for 5 in their second innings by the end of the second day, and Richard Dawson's four wickets helped to keep their score to an eventual 217 – and the victory target down to manageable proportions … for Yorkshire against these particular opponents, at least.

Derbyshire's hopes of only a fourth victory, achieved after being asked to follow on, were dashed by rain on the final day at Derby. Durham, set 330 after Derbyshire's courageous fightback, began the last day on 16 without loss but had declined to 93 for 2 when the rain began to fall just before lunch. It was a disappointing end to a fine contest, in which Durham had initially gained total command by reaching 371 on the back of Paul Collingwood's 255-ball 190 and then bowling out the home side for just 161. Collingwood hit two sixes and 28 fours and, joined by Benkenstein when Durham were 59 for 3, added 250 with his captain, who made 98. Mark Davies had the remarkable figures of 3 for 4 from 6.1 overs, five of them maidens, but it must have seemed like a different game once Michael Di Venuto and Hassan Adnan had got into their stride second time around. Derbyshire, 191 for 2 by the close of day two with Di Venuto already on 112, went on to a massive 539 for 7 declared as the Australian opener reached 203 and Adnan 106, before Travis Friend and Graeme Welch hit out to make the declaration possible. Di Venuto batted for 400 minutes, hitting 33 fours from the 298 balls he faced, while Adnan's five-hour resistance also enabled Friend later to thump 82 from 101 balls – with a six and 15 fours – and Welch a 116-ball unbeaten 67 against a tiring attack.

The story of the bore draw at Old Trafford can be told by the figures of Danish Kaneria, the world-class Pakistan leg-spinner. On a pitch which had almost nothing in it for any bowler, let alone the spinners, Kaneria finished with the barely-believable analysis of 70.2-10-208-0 – giving him the unwanted championship record for the most number of runs conceded by a wicketless bowler. Lancashire, not wanting to allow promotion rivals Essex back into the match, merely contented themselves with running up a huge total in reply to their visitors' initial 536 for 9 declared, in which both Flower brothers scored hundreds. Indeed, this was the first instance of two brothers achieving this in the same championship innings since Alan and Colin Wells for Sussex against Kent in 1987. James Anderson also ended up with dispiriting figures – but there were also four dropped catches in his 0 for 140. Mal Loye's 194 underlined his terrific mid-summer form, and in all he batted for

460 minutes and 416 balls, hitting two sixes and 25 fours. There was a career-best, meanwhile, for Peter Horton, which was only scant consolation for him being dismissed on 99, but in the end it was a relief to the few spectators still left on the ground when rain arrived minutes after Lancashire had finally declared on the stroke of tea. This was not entertainment.

Round 13: 26–29 July 2005

Division One

A surprise declaration by Surrey on the final afternoon of a rain-affected fixture at Trent Bridge almost brought about a positive result; but in the end Nottinghamshire, set 203 in 40 overs, were glad to hang on for the draw at 169 for 8 after a fitful chase. At 90 for 5, indeed, they might have shut up shop earlier, but Mark Ealham then breathed new life into the victory attempt by hitting 46 from 42 balls and adding 71 in 12 overs with David Alleyne. When Graeme Swann fell for a duck, though, Greg Smith and Ryan Sidebottom decided that discretion was the better part of valour and blocked out the remaining 34 balls. Ealham had scored 55 in the first innings, too, as Notts took initial command – despite Martin Bicknell's six-wicket haul – following their four-pronged seam attack's first day dismissal of Surrey for just 136. Bicknell's removal of elder brother Darren, by the way, was the third time in six championship innings that he had got him out. The match was possibly just in the home side's favour at the midway point, with Surrey on 93 for 3 in their second innings – but rain washed out day three and Rikki Clarke's unbeaten 127 from 210 balls then enabled Surrey to seize the initiative in an imaginative fashion.

There was a similarly tense finish at Hove, where Gloucestershire's ninth-wicket pair Ian Fisher and Jon Lewis batted out the final seven overs, despite the beseeching efforts of Mushtaq Ahmed, to claim the draw against Sussex. Mushtaq ended up with 3 for 25

Above right: Martin Bicknell again had the pleasure of dismissing elder brother Darren during Surrey's exciting draw against Nottinghamshire.

Round 13: 26–29 July 2005 Division One

NOTTINGHAMSHIRE v. SURREY – at Trent Bridge

SURREY	First Innings		Second Innings	
SA Newman	c Alleyne b Smith	15	c Swann b Smith	40
RS Clinton	lbw b Harris	8	lbw b Harris	15
MR R'kash (capt)	b Harris	42	b Sidebottom	7
R Clarke	lbw b Smith	0	not out	127
*JN Batty	c Alleyne b Smith	0	c Ealham b Smith	32
AD Brown	lbw b Sidebottom	28	c Alleyne b Ealham	18
Azhar Mahmood	b Sidebottom	19	b Smith	7
MP Bicknell	c Alleyne b Harris	0	not out	37
TJ Murtagh	b Ealham	7		
ND Doshi	not out	4		
M Akram	c Alleyne b Ealham	0		
Extras	b 5, lb 4, nb 4	13	lb 3, nb 6	9
	(48.5 overs)	136	(6 wkts dec 82 overs)	292

Bowling
Sidebottom 15-7-27-2. Harris 16-3-55-3. Ealham 9.5-5-12-2. Smith 8-2-33-3.
Sidebottom 20-2-73-1. Harris 16-2-82-1. Smith 19-4-57-3. Ealham 16-6-40-1.
Swann 7-2-21-0. Younis Khan 4-0-16-0.
Fall of Wickets: 1-12, 2-53, 3-53, 4-57, 5-92, 6-118, 7-119, 8-124, 9-136
1-30, 2-49, 3-75, 4-160, 5-214, 6-223

NOTTS	First Innings		Second Innings	
DJ Bicknell	c Newman b Bicknell	0	c Bicknell b Azhar Mahmood	17
JER Gallian (capt)	b Murtagh	37	b Bicknell	2
RJ Warren	c Azhar Mahmood b Murtagh	21	c Clarke b Akram	13
Younis Khan	c Clarke b Azhar Mahmood	10	c Clarke b Azhar Mahmood	0
DJ Hussey	lbw b Bicknell	29	b Akram	30
*D Alleyne	b Akram	6	c Azhar Mahmood b Doshi	40
MA Ealham	c Murtagh b Bicknell	55	run out	46
GP Swann	b Bicknell	29	b Azhar Mahmood	0
RJ Sidebottom	c Murtagh b Bicknell	4	not out	2
GJ Smith	c Newman b Bicknell	18	not out	0
AJ Harris	not out	1		
Extras	lb 6, nb 10	16	lb 1, nb 18	19
	(66 overs)	226	(8 wkts 40 overs)	169

Bowling
Bicknell 22-6-56-6. Azhar Mahmood 22-2-90-1. Akram 12-2-42-1. Murtagh 10-1-32-2.
Bicknell 3.4-0-13-1. Azhar Mahmood 12-2-65-3. Akram 10.2-1-37-2.
Murtagh 5-1-25-0. Clarke 2-0-22-0. Doshi 7-5-6-1.
Fall of Wickets: 1-0, 2-45, 3-74, 4-94, 5-112, 6-112, 7-162, 8-168, 9-219
1-7, 2-23, 3-25, 4-43, 5-90, 6-161, 7-161, 8-161

Match drawn – Nottinghamshire (8 pts), Surrey (7 pts)

SUSSEX v. GLOUCESTERSHIRE – at Hove

SUSSEX	First Innings		Second Innings	
RR Montgomerie	c Hardinges b Lewis	32	lbw b Kirby	0
MJ Prior	lbw b Kirby	6	c Adshead b Lewis	3
MH Yardy	c Adshead b Averis	20	c Weston b Fisher	106
MW Goodwin	c Fisher b Hardinges	16	c Hardinges b Kirby	43
CJ Adams (capt)	c Windows b Kirby	5	run out	61
*TR Ambrose	lbw b Lewis	31	c Gidman b Fisher	10
LJ Wright	c Sarwan b Lewis	0	c Fisher b Lewis	15
Naved ul-Hasan	c Sarwan b Lewis	13	c Adshead b Lewis	2
Mushtaq Ahmed	c Sarwan b Averis	4	lbw b Lewis	0
RJ Kirtley	not out	8	(11) not out	1
JD Lewry	c Gidman b Averis	23	(10) c Fisher b Lewis	6
Extras	b 4, lb 4, nb 25	33	b 3, lb 2, w 3, nb 12	20
	(46 overs)	191	(87.1 overs)	267

Bowling
Lewis 17-7-62-4. Kirby 13-2-55-2. Averis 10-3-54-3. Hardinges 6-2-12-1.
Lewis 27-2-88-5. Kirby 15-6-29-2. Averis 11-0-45-0. Hardinges 8-2-24-0.
Fisher 25.1-4-75-2. Sarwan 1-0-1-0.
Fall of Wickets: 1-8, 2-44, 3-81, 4-90, 5-106, 6-114, 7-145, 8-150, 9-156
1-3, 2-7, 3-83, 4-186, 5-208, 6-241, 7-244, 8-245, 9-263

GLOS	First Innings		Second Innings	
CM Spearman (capt)	lbw b Kirtley	48	(2) b Lewry	22
WPC Weston	b Lewry	7	(1) c Prior b Kirtley	21
RR Sarwan	c Adams b Naved-ul-Hasan	9	lbw b Wright	30
MGN Windows	c Prior b Wright	0	b Naved-ul-Hasan	28
APR Gidman	c Prior b Lewry	18	c Adams b Mushtaq Ahmed	1
MA Hardinges	b Naved-ul-Hasan	9	c Prior b Naved-ul-Hasan	23
*SJ Adshead	not out	28	lbw b Mushtaq Ahmed	5
ID Fisher	c Prior b Naved-ul-Hasan	0	not out	14
JMM Averis	b Wright	0	c Prior b Mushtaq Ahmed	15
J Lewis	c Prior b Naved-ul-Hasan	8	not out	5
SP Kirby	lbw b Kirtley	2		
Extras	lb 11, w 2	13	b 15, lb 9, nb 4	28
	(56 overs)	142	(8 wkts 74 overs)	192

Bowling
Kirtley 17-5-39-2. Lewry 14-4-30-2. Wright 12-4-36-2. Naved-ul-Hasan 13-5-26-4.
Kirtley 20-8-41-1. Naved-ul-Hasan 19.4-8-53-2. Lewry 6.2-2-16-1. Wright 9-0-33-1.
Mushtaq Ahmed 19-10-25-3.
Fall of Wickets: 1-11, 2-41, 3-42, 4-75, 5-85, 6-113, 7-113, 8-118, 9-131
1-48, 2-50, 3-93, 4-98, 5-130, 6-135, 7-154, 8-182

Match drawn – Sussex (7 pts), Gloucestershire (7 pts)

from 19 overs, but perhaps Sussex should have declared a little earlier after Mike Yardy's gutsy 106 had taken the home team into a position of some comfort. Lewis, besides his late batting heroics, picked up nine wickets in a match dominated by the bowlers, but also constantly interrupted by the weather. All in all, frustrating for Sussex.

Division Two

The positive result in this round of games was gained at Taunton, where Durham continued on their merry way at the head of the second division table by bowling out Somerset for 174 on a curious last afternoon. Time had been lost to the weather on days two and three, but when the last morning arrived Durham had still managed to manoeuvre themselves into a position from where it was unlikely they could lose. The in-form Paul Collingwood had just added a 73-ball second hundred of the match to his first innings 181, with ten fours and three sixes, when Durham declared to set Somerset 382 from 74 overs to win. At lunch, the home team were 50 for no wicket – and clearly dreaming of glory. Afterwards, a series of reckless strokes merely gave Durham the chance of victory themselves, and this they duly achieved as off-spinner Gareth Breese followed up his five first innings wickets with four more.

No play at all on the third day undoubtedly saved Derbyshire from heavy defeat against Yorkshire at Headingley. They had finished the second day at 247 for 7 in reply to Yorkshire's intimidating 570, but at least they took advantage of their good fortune with the weather to battle first to 350 all out when play resumed on the final day, before grafting to 173 for 5, and safety, in the time remaining. Steve Stubbings led the way with 34 in two and a half hours. Earlier, double-hundred maker Phil Jaques's 310-run stand with Anthony McGrath, which rallied their side from 29 for 2 in spectacular style, was just 13 runs short of the county's record third-wicket partnership.

Half of day two, and the whole of day three, was lost to rain at Leicester, and all that was left of interest on the final day was the considerable efforts of Aftab Habib against the county he had left the previous winter to rejoin Leicestershire. Essex's bowlers were powerless to stop Habib as he built his 21st first-class century and, in the end, reached 153 not out from 300 balls. He struck a six and 19 fours and, with Paul Nixon, added 178 in 50 overs for the seventh wicket to rescue Leicestershire from the depths of 123 for 6. Earlier, indeed, on the second day, Habib had put on 87 for the sixth wicket with John Maunders to resuscitate a team initially falling apart at 36 for 5. Ronnie Irani's first innings 97 for Essex, meanwhile, contained six sixes and five fours.

Round 13: 26–29 July 2005 Division Two

SOMERSET v. DURHAM – at Taunton

DURHAM	First Innings		Second Innings	
MEK Hussey (capt)	lbw b Caddick	63	c Parsons b Smith	27
GM Scott	c Parsons b Caddick	4	not out	61
PD Collingwood	lbw b Langeveldt	181	not out	105
GJ Muchall	c Johnson b Parsons	57		
DM Benkenstein	c Hildreth b Caddick	43		
GR Breese	c Hildreth b Johnson	51		
*P Mustard	lbw b Blackwell	20		
LE Plunkett	c Gazzard b Johnson	11		
M Davies	not out	7		
ML Lewis	c Caddick b Suppiah	4		
G Onions				
Extras	b 16, lb 7, nb 12	35	b 5, lb 2, w 2, nb 6	15
	(9 wkts dec 136.2 overs)	476	(1 wkt dec 39 overs)	208

Bowling
Caddick 36-6-130-3. Langeveldt 27-8-80-1. Johnson 21-4-76-2. Blackwell 28-7-90-1. Parsons 10-2-41-1. Smith 2-0-8-0. Suppiah 12.2-4-28-1.
Caddick 7-0-30-0. Langeveldt 5-0-25-0. Blackwell 4-1-15-0. Smith 7-0-34-1. Johnson 8-2-34-0. Suppiah 3-0-39-0. Parsons 5-0-24-0.
Fall of Wickets: 1-5, 2-147, 3-299, 4-346, 5-400, 6-427, 7-462, 8-465, 9-476
1-51

SOMERSET	First Innings		Second Innings	
GC Smith	b Davies	28	st Mustard b Breese	39
JD Francis	c Hussey b Plunkett	1	c Mustard b Davies	16
MJ Wood	b Breese	59	(4) lbw b Onions	2
JC Hildreth	c Lewis b Plunkett	86	(5) b Breese	3
AV Suppiah	c Collingwood b Breese	20	(6) st Mustard b Breese	2
ID Blackwell (capt)	c Mustard b Breese	59	(7) lbw b Lewis	8
KA Parsons	c Hussey b Davies	26	(8) c Hussey b Lewis	45
*CM Gazzard	c Mustard b Davies	2	(9) b Lewis	3
RL Johnson	c Hussey b Breese	0	(3) c sub b Breese	23
CK Langeveldt	b Breese	0	not out	9
AR Caddick	not out	0	lbw b Plunkett	10
Extras	b 8, lb 3, w 1, nb 10	22	b 4, lb 5, w 1, nb 4	14
	(68.3 overs)	303	(60 overs)	174

Bowling
Lewis 14-1-65-0. Plunkett 12-1-69-2. Davies 16.3-8-29-3. Breese 19-3-83-5. Onions 5-0-33-0. Scott 2-0-13-0.
Lewis 12-2-49-3. Plunkett 6-2-23-1. Breese 27-9-55-4. Davies 7-1-25-1. Onions 4-1-8-1. Collingwood 4-1-5-0.
Fall of Wickets: 1-8, 2-51, 3-183, 4-189, 5-230, 6-287, 7-303, 8-303, 9-303
1-56, 2-84, 3-86, 4-89, 5-93, 6-93, 7-137, 8-143, 9-150

Durham won by 207 runs – Somerset (5 pts), Durham (22 pts)

YORKSHIRE v. DERBYSHIRE – at Headingley

YORKSHIRE	First Innings	
MJ Wood	b Hunter	13
JJ Sayers	b Welch	8
A McGrath	c Walker b Botha	134
PA Jaques	c Moss b Welch	219
IJ Harvey	c Walker b Hunter	83
C White (capt)	not out	67
*I Dawood	c Di Venuto b Botha	0
RKJ Dawson	b Botha	18
TT Bresnan	lbw b Gray	7
CEW Silverwood	c & b Gray	1
GJ Kruis	c Hunter b Gray	4
Extras	b 2, lb 8, w 4, nb 2	16
	(128.5 overs)	570

Bowling
Welch 26-6-68-2. Hunter 23-1-127-2. Moss 17-3-74-0. Walker 17-1-92-0. Botha 35-2-143-3. Gray 10.5-1-56-3.
Fall of Wickets: 1-23, 2-29, 3-339, 4-421, 5-494, 6-495, 7-525, 8-548, 9-550

DERBYSHIRE	First Innings		Second Innings	
MJ Di Venuto	lbw b Dawson	79	(2) c Silverwood b Kruis	16
SD Stubbings	c Dawood b Kruis	2	(1) lbw b Kruis	34
Hassan Adnan	c Dawood b Silverwood	0	lbw b Kruis	0
J Moss	c Jaques b McGrath	52	c Silverwood b Dawson	50
*LD Sutton (capt)	c Sayers b Dawson	31	not out	43
TJ Friend	lbw b Bresnan	0	c Harvey b Silverwood	14
G Welch	c Sayers b Silverwood	42	not out	6
AG Botha	c Wood b Dawson	30		
AKD Gray	lbw b Silverwood	43		
ID Hunter	b Bresnan	40		
NGE Walker	not out	8		
Extras	b 6, lb 7, nb 10	23	lb 6, nb 4	10
	(108.2 overs)	350	(5 wkts 60 overs)	173

Bowling
Silverwood 18.2-3-73-3. Kruis 26-7-95-1. Bresnan 21-4-60-2. Harvey 13-6-18-0. McGrath 7-1-25-1. Dawson 23-3-66-3.
Silverwood 10-2-32-1. Kruis 18-5-51-3. Harvey 5-1-12-0. Dawson 15-5-34-1. Bresnan 6-0-24-0. McGrath 6-1-14-0.
Fall of Wickets: 1-26, 2-27, 3-126, 4-153, 5-154, 6-196, 7-226, 8-268, 9-338
1-20, 2-20, 3-106, 4-108, 5-150

Match drawn – Yorkshire (12 pts),
Derbyshire (11 pts)

LEICESTERSHIRE v. ESSEX – at Leicester

ESSEX	First Innings		Second Innings	
GW Flower	c Nixon b Masters	4	c Masters b Cummins	24
AN Cook	lbw b Willoughby	62	lbw b Masters	4
RS Bopara	c Cummins b Masters	17	not out	48
A Flower	c Maddy b Cummins	3	not out	0
RC Irani (capt)	b Masters	97		
*JS Foster	c Nixon b Cummins	32		
JD Middlebrook	c Nixon b Cummins	12		
AR Adams	c Ackerman b Henderson	36		
D Gough	c Mongia b Masters	2		
AP Palladino	lbw b Willoughby	17		
Danish Kaneria	not out	0		
Extras	b 6, lb 6, w 1, nb 2	15	b 1, lb 3	4
	(94.1 overs)	297	(2 wkts 29 overs)	80

Bowling
Willoughby 28.1-8-73-2. Masters 25-11-65-4. Cummins 12-2-49-3. Maddy 7-1-27-0. Henderson 13-3-32-1. Mongia 4-0-22-0. Maunders 5-0-17-0.
Willoughby 6-1-15-0. Masters 5-2-9-1. Henderson 9-1-33-0. Maddy 5-2-16-0. Cummins 4-2-3-1.
Fall of Wickets: 1-21, 2-54, 3-57, 4-113, 5-191, 6-213, 7-247, 8-253, 9-288
1-8, 2-72

LEICESTERSHIRE	First Innings	
DDJ Robinson	c Foster b Gough	5
DL Maddy	c Middlebrook b Gough	3
DD Masters	c Flower GW b Palladino	2
JK Maunders	c Middlebrook b Adams	46
D Mongia	lbw b Palladino	4
HD Ackerman (capt)	c Foster b Adams	9
A Habib	not out	153
*PA Nixon	c Foster b Danish Kaneria	85
CW Henderson	c Flower GW b Adams	36
RAG Cummins	not out	4
CM Willoughby		
Extras	b 3, lb 8, nb 24	35
	(8 wkts dec 115 overs)	382

Bowling
Gough 31-11-81-2. Palladino 25-6-80-2. Danish Kaneria 18-3-72-1. Adams 27-7-83-3. Bopara 5-0-21-0. Middlebrook 9-2-34-0.
Fall of Wickets: 1-9, 2-12, 3-14, 4-20, 5-36, 6-123, 7-301, 8-366

Match drawn – Leicestershire (11 pts),
Essex (8 pts)

Double-ton: more runs flowed from the prolific bat of Phil Jaques at Headingley ... 219 of them against Derbyshire.

Round 14: 3–7 August 2005

Division One

Warwickshire showed their willingness to fight to the end in their defence of the championship by completing a courageous three-wicket victory against Middlesex at Lord's. One of the stars of a remarkable fourth innings chase of 382 was Alex Loudon, at 24 one of the rising generation of highly-talented young English players; after seeing him finish on 95 not out, Loudon's captain, Nick Knight, said he was 'a very special cricketer'. A fast-developing off-spinner, Loudon is also a good enough batsman to warrant a top-order place – and he demonstrated his coolness under pressure to guide Warwickshire to their tough victory target. At the end, too, Loudon was joined by a younger and even less experienced partner, Luke Parker, in an unbroken stand of 63.

Parker, in fact, had popped up in the first innings too, hitting 43 and joining Dougie Brown, top scorer with 92, in a vital seventh-wicket partnership of 91 which kept Warwickshire in touch with Middlesex's first day 323. The hosts, however, were guilty of throwing away a near-impregnable position long before the heroics of Loudon, and those of Knight and Jim Troughton in a third-wicket stand of 187 in 31 overs which launched the run chase in spectacular style. At 281 for 3, Middlesex were 332 ahead and in total command, but when Ben Hutton got out for 92 there proved to be no one capable of staying with Owais Shah.

In the end, with Middlesex bowled out for just 330, a frustrated Shah was left high and dry on 156. Makhaya Ntini's five-wicket haul looked at first, though, to be in vain as Warwickshire slipped to 6 for 2. But then came Knight and Troughton, who completed a daring hundred in just 102 balls with four sixes and 11 fours, and later came Loudon, who struck 12 fours himself from 148 balls.

Hampshire kept up their championship challenge by bowling out Gloucestershire on the last day at Cheltenham. Traditionally, spin has always been the trump card at the gorgeous College Grounds – and so it proved once more as Shaun Udal produced a match-winning analysis of 6 for 61. Up until then, though, and apart from a decidedly dodgy Hampshire start on the opening morning, it had been the batsmen who had dominated proceedings before yet another big festival crowd. Hampshire, first finding themselves at 16 for 4 and then 81 for 7, were rescued by an astonishing, county record eighth-wicket stand of 256 in 60 overs between Nic Pothas and Andy Bichel. Gloucestershire's Sri Lankan leg spinner,

Malinga Bandara, must have wished the earth would swallow him up as Bichel went to 53 with 50 of his runs in boundaries, and then on to 138. Bandara had dropped him off his own bowling when Bichel was still to score. Pothas made 139, meanwhile, and Udal

Round 14: 3–7 August 2005 Division One

MIDDLESEX v. WARWICKSHIRE – at Lord's

MIDDLESEX	First Innings		Second Innings	
ET Smith	c Trott b Ntini	0	c Loudon b Ntini	21
BL Hutton (capt)	lbw b Loudon	49	c Frost b Pretorius	92
OA Shah	run out	63	not out	156
EC Joyce	lbw b Pretorius	13	c Frost b Brown	11
JWM Dalrymple	c Loudon b Ntini	9	c Frost b Ntini	17
PN Weekes	not out	92	c Knight b Loudon	1
*BJM Scott	c Loudon b Ntini	0	b Ntini	1
PD Trego	c Parker b Loudon	26	c Trott b Ntini	1
CT Peploe	c Frost b Ntini	23	c Knight b Ntini	7
SR Clark	c Carter b Pretorius	4	(11) lbw b Pretorius	6
MM Betts	c Trott b Brown	30	(10) c Carter b Loudon	1
Extras	lb 8, nb 6	14	b 1, lb 7, w 2, nb 6	16
	(78.1 overs)	323	(90 overs)	330

Bowling
Ntini 17-3-79-4. Pretorius 20-0-85-2. Brown 6.1-0-27-1. Carter 19-1-58-0. Loudon 16-0-66-2.
Ntini 22-1-69-5. Pretorius 16-2-56-2. Carter 14-0-67-0. Brown 9-2-31-1. Loudon 21-2-71-2. Troughton 2-0-10-0. Trott 6-0-18-0.
Fall of Wickets: 1-0, 2-117, 3-117, 4-139, 5-139, 6-139, 7-197, 8-247, 9-252
1-38, 2-189, 3-229, 4-281, 5-282, 6-287, 7-293, 8-304, 9-305

WARWICKSHIRE	First Innings		Second Innings	
NV Knight (capt)	b Clark	13	c Shah b Clark	75
IJ Westwood	lbw b Betts	0	c Weekes b Trego	5
IJL Trott	c Scott b Clark	6	c Hutton b Trego	0
JO Troughton	b Clark	7	c Joyce b Dalrymple	119
AGR Loudon	c Hutton b Clark	27	not out	95
*T Frost	c Scott b Clark	27	(7) c Smith b Betts	5
DR Brown	c Hutton b Weekes	92	(8) c Joyce b Peploe	19
LC Parker	c Scott b Betts	43	(9) not out	27
NM Carter	c Trego b Peploe	4	(6) c Smith b Clark	17
M Ntini	c Clark b Peploe	12		
D Pretorius	not out	21		
Extras	b 2, lb 7, w 1, nb 10	20	b 2, lb 11, nb 8	21
	(88.3 overs)	272	(7 wkts 84.1 overs)	383

Bowling
Clark 24-7-61-5. Betts 27-8-77-2. Trego 7-1-40-0. Peploe 23-6-54-2. Hutton 2-1-2-0. Weekes 4.3-0-25-1. Joyce 1-0-4-0.
Clark 21-3-68-2. Trego 4-0-33-2. Betts 18-5-71-1. Peploe 21-2-119-1. Dalrymple 20-0-77-1. Shah 0.1-0-2-0.
Fall of Wickets: 1-8, 2-15, 3-26, 4-33, 5-80, 6-85, 7-176, 8-189, 9-219
1-6, 2-6, 3-193, 4-236, 5-262, 6-279, 7-320

Warwickshire won by 3 wickets –
Middlesex (6 pts), Warwickshire (19 pts)

was particularly harsh on Jon Lewis as he thrashed an unbeaten 47 from 25 balls. By the close, indeed, Gloucestershire were 25 for 2 (one wicket to Bichel!) in reply to Hampshire's 385, and they did well in the circumstances to recover to 363 all out themselves as Alex Gidman, with 115, and Steve Adshead, 73, added 105 for the seventh wicket. John Crawley's elegant hundred, however, supported by half-centuries from Shane Watson, Jono McLean and Pothas, enabled Hampshire to set a target – and give Udal the opportunity he needed to spin Gloucestershire to defeat.

Sussex thoroughly deserved their five-wicket win over Surrey at Hove, even though they were making rather heavy weather of it before Matt Prior joined Mike Yardy to sweep them home on the third afternoon. This was a match in which the losers would be relegation favourites, alongside the already doomed Gloucestershire and Glamorgan, but Surrey's performance never really suggested a side willing to scrap to the last. When Mark Ramprakash was easing his way to a beautiful 97 on the first day, with three sixes and 13 fours, it looked as if Surrey might win the opening round, but he then cut Luke Wright's medium pace to backward point and, Azhar Mahmood's hitting apart, Surrey fell away alarmingly. Yardy's tenacity and technique, and Robin Martin-Jenkins' determination to make the most of his recall to first team colours, then ensured a hard-fought first innings advantage of 130 for

GLOUCESTERSHIRE v. HAMPSHIRE – at Cheltenham

HAMPSHIRE	First Innings		Second Innings	
MJ Brown	lbw b Lewis	1	lbw b Kirby	8
CC Benham	b Kirby	0	lbw b Lewis	8
JP Crawley	lbw b Kirby	11	(4) c Bandara b Fisher	120
SR Watson	c Bandara b Kirby	26	(5) b Bandara	52
JJ McLean	lbw b Lewis	0	(6) c Adshead b Bandara	68
*N Pothas	b Bandara	139	(7) not out	54
SM Ervine	b Bandara	6	(8) b Bandara	22
AD Mascarenhas	lbw b Bandara	0	(9) not out	16
AJ Bichel	c Hardinges b Bandara	138		
SD Udal (capt)	not out	47		
JTA Bruce	b Kirby	0		
CT Tremlett	(did not bat)		(3) c Spearman b Kirby	4
Extras	lb 12, w 1, nb 4	17	b 6, lb 4, w 8, nb 18	36
	(93.4 overs)	385	(7 wkts dec 107.5 overs)	388

Bowling
Lewis 20-5-112-2. Kirby 20.4-4-53-4. Hardinges 8-1-41-0. Bandara 30-4-110-4. Fisher 15-3-57-0.
Lewis 15-3-69-1. Kirby 10-3-24-2. Hardinges 13-1-52-0. Bandara 31.5-2-108-3. Fisher 34-2-108-1. Sarwan 4-0-17-0.
Fall of Wickets: 1-0, 2-12, 3-12, 4-16, 5-63, 6-81, 7-81, 8-338, 9-345
1-17, 2-22, 3-23, 4-143, 5-268, 6-319, 7-343

GLOS	First Innings		Second Innings	
CM Spearman (capt)	b Bichel	9	(2) b Bichel	34
WPC Weston	c Pothas b Bruce	22	(1) lbw b Udal	26
SP Kirby	lbw b Bruce	8	(11) lbw b Udal	4
RR Sarwan	c Pothas b Bruce	18	(3) c sub b Mascarenhas	48
MGN Windows	b Tremlett	33	(4) c Brown b Udal	50
APR Gidman	st Pothas b Udal	115	(5) lbw b Watson	17
MA Hardinges	lbw b Ervine	33	(6) c Benham b Udal	5
*SJ Adshead	b Watson	73	(7) not out	13
ID Fisher	c & b Bichel	19	(8) c Brown b Udal	12
CM Bandara	lbw b Watson	0	(9) b Watson	1
J Lewis	not out	24	(10) b Udal	0
Extras	b 1, lb 4, nb 4	9	b 5, lb 4, w 2, nb 11	22
	(98.1 overs)	363	(81.5 overs)	232

Bowling
Bichel 17.1-6-57-2. Bruce 12-1-42-3. Ervine 12-2-41-1. Mascarenhas 12-2-46-0. Tremlett 11-3-60-1. Udal 22-5-70-1. Watson 12-5-42-2.
Tremlett 12-3-37-0. Bichel 17-4-46-1. Ervine 8-2-28-0. Watson 17-4-35-2. Udal 22.5-5-61-6. Mascarenhas 5-1-16-1.
Fall of Wickets: 1-14, 2-25, 3-53, 4-58, 5-142, 6-191, 7-296, 8-332, 9-332
1-63, 2-77, 3-156, 4-195, 5-195, 6-202, 7-224, 8-225, 9-226

Hampshire won by 178 runs – Gloucestershire (7 pts), Hampshire (21 pts)

SUSSEX v. SURREY – at Hove

SURREY	First Innings		Second Innings	
SA Newman	lbw b Kirtley	1	lbw b Naved-ul-Hasan	74
RS Clinton	c Adams b Kirtley	0	c Wright b Kirtley	12
MR R'kash (capt)	c Goodwin b Wright	97	c Yardy b Naved-ul-Hasan	12
R Clarke	b Mushtaq Ahmed	34	lbw b Mushtaq Ahmed	75
*JN Batty	lbw b Martin-Jenkins	16	lbw b Martin-Jenkins	15
AD Brown	lbw b Martin-Jenkins	0	c & b Kirtley	1
Azhar Mahmood	not out	57	b Naved-ul-Hasan	41
TJ Murtagh	c Prior b Wright	6	c Adams b Mushtaq Ahmed	9
ND Doshi	b Wright	0	b Naved-ul-Hasan	0
M Akram	c Yardy b Mushtaq Ahmed	16	c & b Mushtaq Ahmed	9
JW Dernbach	lbw b Mushtaq Ahmed	1	not out	1
Extras	b 13, lb 3, w 2, nb 2	20	lb 4, w 1	5
	(69 overs)	248	(76 overs)	254

Bowling
Kirtley 16-5-52-2. Naved-ul-Hasan 16-2-62-0. Martin-Jenkins 15-5-52-2. Mushtaq Ahmed 11-1-33-3. Wright 11-3-33-3.
Kirtley 20-10-39-2. Naved-ul-Hasan 21-5-70-4. Mushtaq Ahmed 21-1-96-3. Martin-Jenkins 14-3-45-1.
Fall of Wickets: 1-2, 2-7, 3-95, 4-157, 5-157, 6-163, 7-181, 8-189, 9-237
1-64, 2-95, 3-130, 4-165, 5-166, 6-230, 7-234, 8-234, 9-245

SUSSEX	First Innings		Second Innings	
RR Montgomerie	c Batty b Azhar Mahmood	68	c Batty b Azhar Mahmood	4
CD Hopkinson	lbw b Doshi	24	c Azhar Mahmood b Akram	2
MH Yardy	c Brown b Murtagh	65	lbw b Akram	35
RJ Kirtley	c Brown b Murtagh	0		
MW Goodwin	c Dernbach b Azhar Mahmood	25	(4) c Batty b Azhar Mahmood	4
CJ Adams (capt)	c Batty b Azhar Mahmood	2	(5) c A Mahmood b Murtagh	5
*MJ Prior	c Batty b Azhar Mahmood	18	(6) not out	66
RSC M-Jenkins	b Akram	88	(7) not out	5
LJ Wright	c Clinton b Azhar Mahmood	26		
Naved-ul-Hasan	not out	26		
Mushtaq Ahmed	c Azhar Mahmood b Murtagh	14		
Extras	b 2, lb 6, nb 14	22	lb 2, nb 2	4
	(114.5 overs)	378	(5 wkts 28.1 overs)	125

Bowling
Akram 28-5-104-1. Azhar Mahmood 27-6-72-5. Murtagh 23.5-6-71-3. Doshi 18-5-45-1. Dernbach 17-2-69-0. Clinton 1-0-9-0.
Azhar Mahmood 6-1-16-2. Akram 8.1-0-21-2. Murtagh 6-1-22-1. Doshi 7-1-46-0. Dernbach 1-0-18-0.
Fall of Wickets: 1-67, 2-104, 3-108, 4-156, 5-160, 6-180, 7-260, 8-320, 9-345
1-6, 2-8, 3-20, 4-32, 5-115

Sussex won by 5 wickets – Sussex (21 pts), Surrey (4 pts)

KENT v. GLAMORGAN – at Canterbury

KENT	First Innings	
DP Fulton (capt)	c Wallace b Waters	15
RWT Key	b Wharf	35
M van Jaarsveld	b Wharf	41
MJ Walker	b Harrison	11
DI Stevens	c Wharf b Croft	208
JM Kemp	lbw b Cosker	39
AJ Hall	c & b Cosker	133
*NJO'Brien	c Croft b Cosker	0
MM Patel	c Hemp b Harrison	64
SJ Cook	c Hughes b Harrison	13
A Khan	not out	0
Extras	lb 3, w 1, nb 24	28
	(135.5 overs)	587

Bowling
Harrison 24.5-4-125-3. Wharf 24-5-93-2. Waters 18-1-83-1. Croft 39-5-160-1. Cosker 30-5-123-3.
Fall of Wickets: 1-46, 2-64, 3-99, 4-132, 5-233, 6-500, 7-500, 8-537, 9-587

GLAMORGAN	First Innings		Second Innings	
DD Cherry	b Khan	0	(2) b Patel	21
*MA Wallace	c Walker b Cook	0	(1) c O'Brien b Cook	10
DL Hemp	not out	171	(5) lbw b Hall	13
J Hughes	c Kemp b Khan	1	(3) b Khan	27
MJ Powell	lbw b Cook	23	(4) lbw b Hall	6
MPO'Shea	lbw b Hall	0	b Kemp	24
AG Wharf	c Stevens b Patel	21	lbw b Cook	5
RDB Croft (capt)	b Kemp	2	c Key b Kemp	12
DS Harrison	lbw b Khan	4	b Hall	19
DA Cosker	b Stevens	18	not out	7
HT Waters	c Stevens b Cook	34	lbw b Hall	0
Extras	b 4, lb 4, w 2, nb 22	32	b 1, lb 3, w 1, nb 8	13
	(95.5 overs)	306	(52 overs)	157

Bowling
Khan 20-0-96-3. Cook 13.5-5-35-3. Hall 15-4-36-1. Stevens 7-0-32-1. Patel 21-3-53-1. Kemp 13-1-38-1. van Jaarsveld 1-1-0-0. Fulton 2-0-5-0. Walker 3-0-3-0.
Cook 12-5-26-2. Hall 13-4-32-4. Khan 7-1-34-1. Kemp 9-2-23-2. Patel 8-1-26-1. Stevens 3-0-12-0.
Fall of Wickets: 1-2, 2-2, 3-17, 4-62, 5-63, 6-115, 7-127, 8-139, 9-188
1-14, 2-53, 3-61, 4-79, 5-92, 6-111, 7-125, 8-138, 9-157

Kent won by an innings and 124 runs –
Kent (22 pts), Glamorgan (5 pts)

'A very special cricketer' – Nick Knight's verdict on Alex Loudon (above) whose unbeaten 95 steered Warwickshire to a memorable victory at Lord's.

Sussex, and the bowling of Pakistani pair Naved-ul-Hasan and Mushtaq Ahmed kept the home side on top. Scott Newman, Rikki Clarke and Azhar, again, were the only Surrey batsmen who looked capable of holding up the Sussex victory march for long but, needing just 125, a nervy collapse to 32 for 4 left the visitors briefly dreaming of a late miracle. Prior, though, decided attack was the answer to the mini-crisis and he hit two sixes and ten fours in a 48-ball 66 not out.

Kent made sure they remained the team everyone else was chasing, however, with an innings win against Glamorgan at Canterbury completed with more than a day to spare. The home team were, in fact, only held up for any length of time by a last-wicket stand of 118 between David Hemp and Huw Waters, the fast bowler just out of Monmouth

School who looks destined to spend most of his county career in a higher position than No. 11. Hemp's magnificent unbeaten 171, scored from 231 balls and featuring a six and 20 fours, was a lone hand until Waters joined him at 188 for 9 in reply to Kent's first innings 587. Showing great spirit, Waters withstood 192 balls for his 34 until falling to Simon Cook, but his and Hemp's efforts could not prevent the follow-on from being enforced. Soon, with a clearly tired Hemp dropping down to No. 5 second time around and being dismissed cheaply, Glamorgan had been shot out again for 157 – with Waters this time bagging a duck and becoming the excellent Andrew Hall's fourth wicket of the innings. Hall had earlier hit a robust 133 as both he and Darren Stevens, with a brilliant 208, achieved career-best scores in a sixth-wicket stand worth 267. Min Patel then sped to a 32-ball 50 to rub salt into the Welsh county's gaping wounds.

Division Two

James Anderson's first five-wicket return of the season spearheaded Lancashire's emphatic 234-run victory against Leicestershire at Grace Road. Anderson's initial burst of 3-39 in ten overs on the third evening helped to reduce the home side to 78 for 5 overnight, and he then picked up two more scalps as the end came quickly the following morning. Lancashire's only wobble had come late on the second day when, after David Masters had added 77 for the ninth wicket with Aftab Habib to haul Leicestershire to within 30 runs of their opponents on first innings, they slipped to 38 for 3 overnight. But Andrew Symonds initially took charge on day three with a 155-ball 121, which included a six and 17 fours, before Glen Chapple and Warren Hegg took the game out of Leicestershire's reach in a 34-over eighth-wicket stand worth 121.

Iain Sutcliffe's first-day 93 against his former county was another notable Lancashire contribution, but a trio of Leicestershire players also took some good memories out of the game. Ryan Cummins, a 21-year-old seamer from Loughborough University, dismissed Mark Chilton with his first delivery in the Lancashire first innings, and then in his second spell took the wickets of Symonds and Sutcliffe in the space of five balls. Tom New, Leicestershire's 20-year-old reserve wicketkeeper, made an accomplished 50 as an opener, while Habib was just glad to continue to put behind him, with his first-innings 84, a season which had by then included a three-point penalty for dissent, a dislocated finger, being dropped to the second XI, and a broken left wrist.

A superb, skilful and calm unbeaten 132 by Andy Flower, compiled during 383 minutes and 278 balls at the crease, and including 11 fours, was the sole reason why Essex managed to overcome Durham by just two wickets in a finely-balanced contest at the new Garons Park venue in Southend. Alastair Cook's first innings 107 gave Essex the upper hand after the first day and a half, but then Durham hit back through Dale Benkenstein's determined 124, following a punchy 46 from only 58 balls by Paul Collingwood. Essex were 129 for 2 at the start of the final day, with Flower on 48, and even though Ronnie Irani hit 48 it always looked as if the home side's chances would revolve around the former Zimbabwe captain. Andre Adams provided vital support from No. 9, scoring 17, but this result was all about the unflustered Flower.

Graeme Hick recorded the very first pair of his prolific 21-year Worcestershire career as the home side were beaten by 137 runs by Northamptonshire at New Road. Even a first-day fast-bowling blitz by Shoaib Akhtar – the Pakistani speedster reacting to being plundered for 28 in two overs by Rob White by storming back to take 5 for 55 – could not knock Northants off their stride. Stephen Moore went past 1,000 first-class runs for the season during his first innings 62 but Johann Louw, Ben Phillips and Damien Wright limited the damage with their disciplined seam bowling and then, from the depths of 64 for 5 in their second innings, David Sales successfully took on Shoaib and the Worcestershire attack to the astounding tune of 190 from just 172

Round 14: 3–7 August 2005 Division Two

LEICESTERSHIRE v. LANCASHIRE – at Leicester

LANCASHIRE	First Innings		Second Innings	
MJ Chilton (capt)	c Mongia b Cummins	19	b Gibson	0
IJ Sutcliffe	lbw b Cummins	93	b Masters	3
MB Loye	b Gibson	22	lbw b Gibson	19
SG Law	c Habib b Masters	32	c New b Henderson	47
A Symonds	lbw b Cummins	45	lbw b Maunders	121
PJ Horton	b Henderson	13	lbw b Maunders	11
DG Cork	c New b Henderson	8	c Nixon b Maunders	4
G Chapple	b Gibson	22	b Cummins	60
*WK Hegg	c New b Masters	9	not out	77
SJ Marshall	not out	17	c Maunders b Gibson	9
JM Anderson	c Maunders b Gibson	0		
Extras	b 4, lb 3, nb 4	11	b 6, lb 8, w 1, nb 2	17
	(98.3 overs)	291	(9 wkts dec 100.3 overs)	368

Bowling
Gibson 17.3-0-80-3. Masters 21-9-38-2. Henderson 33-6-69-2. Cummins 10-2-32-3. Maddy 5-1-22-0. Maunders 7-2-33-0. Mongia 5-1-10-0.
Gibson 22.3-1-101-3. Masters 9-5-28-1. Maddy 14-0-47-0. Cummins 16-3-52-1. Henderson 20-2-72-1. Maunders 11-1-37-3. Mongia 8-2-17-0.
Fall of Wickets: 1-43, 2-83, 3-133, 4-219, 5-220, 6-231, 7-252, 8-271, 9-289
1-0, 2-10, 3-22, 4-133, 5-182, 6-192, 7-218, 8-339, 9-368

LEICESTERSHIRE	First Innings		Second Innings	
TJ New	lbw b Chapple	50	c Hegg b Anderson	20
DL Maddy	b Chapple	20	lbw b Cork	4
JK Maunders	c Hegg b Symonds	1	c Hegg b Anderson	17
D Mongia	lbw b Symonds	0	c Hegg b Anderson	31
HD Ackerman (capt)	lbw b Chapple	41	b Anderson	2
A Habib	c Chapple b Cork	84	(7) c Hegg b Chapple	22
*PA Nixon	lbw b Marshall	2	(8) c Hegg b Anderson	0
OD Gibson	c Hegg b Anderson	9	(9) lbw b Cork	23
CW Henderson	b Anderson	0	(6) c Hegg b Chapple	0
DD Masters	c Sutcliffe b Cork	36	not out	29
RAG Cummins	not out	1	lbw b Marshall	1
Extras	b 4, lb 3, nb 10	17	b 4, lb 4, w 5, nb 2	15
	(93.5 overs)	261	(44.3 overs)	164

Bowling
Anderson 17-3-61-2. Cork 20.5-5-44-2. Marshall 18-2-46-1. Chapple 19-2-60-3. Symonds 19-4-43-2.
Anderson 19-4-79-5. Cork 13-4-41-2. Chapple 9-4-28-2. Marshall 3.3-1-8-1.
Fall of Wickets: 1-69, 2-70, 3-70, 4-78, 5-149, 6-160, 7-183, 8-183, 9-260
1-12, 2-36, 3-70, 4-72, 5-73, 6-105, 7-109, 8-109, 9-153

*Lancashire won by 234 runs –
Leicestershire (5 pts), Lancashire (19 pts)*

ESSEX v. DURHAM – at Southend

DURHAM	First Innings		Second Innings	
MEK Hussey (capt)	c Foster b Adams	8	c Irani b Adams	0
GM Scott	c Bopara b Adams	19	c Flower A b Adams	1
GJ Muchall	c Foster b Middlebrook	37	(4) b Middlebrook	34
DM Benkenstein	c Foster b Adams	36	(5) c Adams b Napier	124
N Peng	c Foster b Adams	0		
GR Breese	c Flower A b Danish Kaneria	24	c Bopara b Middlebrook	42
*P Mustard	st Foster b Danish Kaneria	17	lbw b Middlebrook	20
LE Plunkett	b Danish Kaneria	7	run out	20
M Davies	c Cook b Napier	5	c sub b Danish Kaneria	17
ML Lewis	c Palladino b Adams	20	lbw b Danish Kaneria	10
G Onions	not out	0	not out	9
PD Collingwood			(3) c Adams b Middlebrook	46
Extras	b 1, lb 4, nb 18	23	b 7, lb 3, w 4, nb 10	24
	(69.1 overs)	196	(115.3 overs)	347

Bowling
Palladino 6-0-23-0. Adams 25.1-11-60-5. Bopara 3-1-6-0. Napier 9-1-47-1. Danish Kaneria 19-9-30-3. Middlebrook 7-1-25-1.
Palladino 3-1-31-0. Adams 29-9-83-2. Danish Kaneria 40.3-7-103-2. Middlebrook 34-7-92-4. Napier 9-2-28-1.
Fall of Wickets: 1-23, 2-80, 3-80, 4-86, 5-133, 6-158, 7-163, 8-174, 9-174
1-1, 2-13, 3-73, 4-94, 5-186, 6-232, 7-276, 8-313, 9-334

ESSEX	First Innings		Second Innings	
GW Flower	c Mustard b Lewis	15	(7) c Mustard b Plunkett	1
AN Cook	c Plunkett b Breese	107	c Mustard b Davies	44
RS Bopara	c Mustard b Lewis	11	(1) c sub b Plunkett	9
A Flower	c Scott b Benkenstein	14	(3) not out	132
RC Irani (capt)	c Scott b Lewis	4	(4) c Hussey b Collingwood	48
*JS Foster	c Muchall b Lewis	8	(5) c Collingwood b Lewis	2
AP Palladino	c Hussey b Davies	17	(10) not out	1
JD Middlebrook	run out	0	(6) b Breese	8
GR Napier	lbw b Breese	51	(8) c sub b Lewis	10
AR Adams	c Plunkett b Breese	6	(9) c Benkenstein b Breese	17
Danish Kaneria	not out	0		
Extras	lb 4, nb 8	12	b 4, lb 8, nb 15	27
	(69.2 overs)	245	(8 wkts 100.1 overs)	299

Bowling
Lewis 20-4-69-4. Plunkett 11-2-45-0. Davies 11-4-17-1. Onions 11-2-54-0. Benkenstein 3-1-7-1. Breese 7.2-1-22-3. Collingwood 6-1-27-0.
Lewis 33-3-85-2. Plunkett 16-4-74-2. Onions 7-0-30-0. Davies 5-2-9-1. Breese 32.1-6-73-2. Collingwood 7-2-16-1.
Fall of Wickets: 1-18, 2-40, 3-71, 4-80, 5-102, 6-133, 7-134, 8-220, 9-226
1-13, 2-85, 3-192, 4-203, 5-231, 6-240, 7-264, 8-289

Essex won by 2 wickets – Essex (18 pts), Durham (3 pts)

WORCESTERSHIRE v. NORTHAMPTONSHIRE – at Worcester

NORTHANTS	First Innings		Second Innings	
ML Love	c Kabir Ali b Malik	53	b Kabir Ali	14
BM Shafayat	c Solanki b Shoaib Akhtar	1	c Pipe b Kabir Ali	7
RA White	b Mason	30	c Hick b Mason	12
U Afzaal	st Pipe b Batty	41	b Mason	6
DJG Sales (capt)	b Shoaib Akhtar	31	c Batty b Malik	190
*MH Wessels	c Pipe b Shoaib Akhtar	13	c Batty b Malik	0
DG Wright	b Shoaib Akhtar	0	c Pipe b de Bruyn	85
BJ Phillips	c Pipe b Malik	5	c Hick b Batty	17
MS Panesar	c Moore b Malik	5	(10) b Shoaib Akhtar	5
J Louw	c Pipe b Shoaib Akhtar	0	(9) lbw b Shoaib Akhtar	27
JF Brown	not out	0	not out	5
Extras	lb 3, w 1, nb 6	10	b 1, lb 8, w 1, nb 8	18
	(49.2 overs)	189	(74.1 overs)	386

Bowling
Shoaib Akhtar 9.2-1-55-5. Kabir Ali 9-0-56-0. Mason 12-4-26-1. Malik 17-5-44-3. Batty 2-1-5-1.
Shoaib Akhtar 13.1-2-72-2. Kabir Ali 9-0-56-2. Mason 13-2-59-2. Malik 15-2-57-2. Batty 13-0-88-1. de Bruyn 11-1-45-1.
Fall of Wickets: 1-13, 2-65, 3-101, 4-147, 5-177, 6-177, 7-178, 8-187, 9-188
1-14, 2-33, 3-39, 4-59, 5-64, 6-252, 7-303, 8-372, 9-377

WORCS	First Innings		Second Innings	
VS Solanki (capt)	c Sales b Louw	17	c White b Louw	29
SC Moore	c Wessels b Phillips	62	c Wessels b Wright	8
GA Hick	lbw b Phillips	0	c Wessels b Louw	0
BF Smith	c Sales b Wright	38	b Panesar	92
Z de Bruyn	b Wright	6	lbw b Panesar	43
GJ Batty	c Sales b Louw	0	lbw b Phillips	2
Kabir Ali	c Shafayat b Wright	7	c Wessels b Phillips	5
*DJ Pipe	lbw b Phillips	4	lbw b Phillips	0
Shoaib Akhtar	b Louw	35	b Panesar	19
MS Mason	not out	30	b Panesar	5
MN Malik	b Louw	3	not out	0
Extras	b 1, lb 5, w 8	14	b 4, lb 4, w 5	13
	(66.1 overs)	216	(57.2 overs)	222

Bowling
Wright 23-8-87-3. Louw 22.1-7-66-4. Phillips 14-5-42-3. Panesar 4-0-8-0. Shafayat 3-1-7-0.
Wright 14-5-39-1. Louw 14-1-60-2. Phillips 14-3-56-3. Panesar 12.2-3-40-4. Shafayat 3-0-19-0.
Fall of Wickets: 1-29, 2-34, 3-95, 4-110, 5-127, 6-138, 7-143, 8-147, 9-190
1-13, 2-14, 3-83, 4-154, 5-161, 6-173, 7-175, 8-198, 9-211

*Northamptonshire won by 137 runs –
Worcestershire (4 pts), Northamptonshire (17 pts)*

DERBYSHIRE v. SOMERSET – at Derby

SOMERSET	First Innings		Second Innings	
MJ Wood	lbw b Hunter	4	b Hunter	10
JD Francis	c Sutton b Welch	19	c Sutton b Havell	34
AV Suppiah	c Sutton b Hunter	123	b Havell	14
JC Hildreth	c Welch b Botha	73	c Sutton b Hunter	30
WJ Durston	not out	146	c Sutton b Botha	44
ID Blackwell (capt)	c Sutton b Welch	18	not out	88
KA Parsons	c Stubbings b Welch	14	not out	15
*CM Gazzard	lbw b Welch	7		
RL Johnson	b Botha	35		
CK Langeveldt	lbw b Gray	0		
AR Caddick	c Friend b Gray	0		
Extras	b 4, lb 1, nb 16	21	lb 4, nb 6	10
	(128.5 overs)	460	(5 wkts dec 82 overs)	245

Bowling
Hunter 28-3-113-2. Havell 17-1-105-0. Welch 25-5-82-4. Moss 11-3-32-0. Botha 28-7-70-2. Gray 19.5-4-53-2.
Hunter 12-5-46-2. Havell 15-2-70-2. Welch 11-7-14-0. Botha 31-12-68-1. Gray 13-3-43-0.
Fall of Wickets: 1-6, 2-31, 3-176, 4-288, 5-341, 6-377, 7-401, 8-453, 9-454
1-30, 2-63, 3-76, 4-117, 5-207

DERBYSHIRE	First Innings		Second Innings	
SD Stubbings	b Blackwell	31	c Durston b Johnson	55
BJ France	c Gazzard b Caddick	1	lbw b Blackwell	7
Hassan Adnan	b Blackwell	74	(5) c & b Blackwell	48
J Moss	lbw b Caddick	24	c Johnson b Blackwell	106
*LD Sutton (capt)	c Gazzard b Caddick	1	(6) run out	19
TJ Friend	b Langeveldt	20	(7) b Caddick	1
G Welch	b Langeveldt	72	(8) run out	1
AG Botha	b Caddick	91	(3) c Caddick b Durston	4
AKD Gray	not out	77	c Wood b Blackwell	0
ID Hunter	not out	2	b Caddick	0
PMR Havell			not out	6
Extras	b 10, lb 18, w 7, nb 10	45	b 3, lb 4, nb 8	15
	(8 wkts dec 149 overs)	438	(43.4 overs)	262

Bowling
Caddick 40-10-102-4. Langeveldt 32-7-78-2. Johnson 22-5-63-0. Blackwell 41-5-105-2. Durston 8-2-39-0. Parsons 3-0-14-0. Suppiah 3-1-9-0.
Caddick 13-0-66-2. Langeveldt 6-1-35-0. Blackwell 15.4-1-86-4. Durston 4-0-33-1. Johnson 5-0-35-1.
Fall of Wickets: 1-11, 2-61, 3-141, 4-147, 5-148, 6-225, 7-264, 8-434
1-32, 2-49, 3-111, 4-206, 5-247, 6-249, 7-250, 8-253, 9-255

Somerset won by 5 runs – Derbyshire (7 pts), Somerset (21 pts)

There was joy for Ian Blackwell, against his former county, as Somerset won a remarkable match against Derbyshire.

balls to wrest the game his team's way. The powerful Sales struck eight sixes and 27 fours in his great innings, and Wright's 72-ball 85 was no less exciting to watch as the pair added a match-turning 188 in 27 overs for the sixth wicket.

Shoaib went for 65 runs in nine overs towards the end of the second day, with Wright thumping a six and 14 fours. Ben Smith made 92 as Worcestershire made a forlorn last-day chase, and shared in partnerships of 69 and 71 with Vikram Solanki and Zander de Bruyn, but Monty Panesar wheeled out four batsmen with his left-arm spin and the dependable Phillips again took important wickets.

One of the most remarkable finishes of the season, though, took place at Derby where – to the intense disappointment and frustration of the home side – Somerset held their nerve in the field to win by five

runs. Derbyshire, seeking a first home championship win for 27 games – and three years and 67 days – lost theirs as they crumbled from 247 for 4 to 262 all out. Set to get 268 in 44 overs, Derbyshire looked home and dry when they needed just another 21 runs from 26 balls. But Jon Moss, their inspiration with a fine 88-ball 106, top-edged a sweep at Ian Blackwell's left-arm spin and the last six wickets fell in a heap in 24 balls. The defeat was sealed when Luke Sutton, the captain, was run out by Matthew Wood's throw to the wicketkeeper as he tried to complete a second run from the third ball of the final over. 'We are setting new standards in disappointment,' said Dave Houghton, Derbyshire's director of cricket.

It was a triumph, though, for former Derbyshire player Blackwell, who took 4 for 86 to add to his second innings unbeaten 88 – and for two uncapped Somerset players, Arul Suppiah and Wes Durston. Both scored maiden first-class hundreds as Somerset totalled 460 in their first innings. Derbyshire, however, replied with an excellent 438 for 8 declared themselves, with the lower order in particular showing up well. Andy Caddick did his best to impress England selector Geoff Miller, with a wholehearted 4 for 102 from 40 overs as several younger men fell away.

Round 15: 10–15 August 2005

Division One

Hampshire and Kent fought out a fascinating and exciting draw at the Rose Bowl, but in the end the result was what neither side really wanted as they chased domestic cricket's main prize. Kent seemed to be in control for much of the first three days, totalling 446 in their first innings and then winning themselves a sizeable lead by dismissing the home team for 325. The visitors, however, then lost their way in a second innings slide to 153 for 7 on the third evening, and the subsequent fall of the last three wickets inside 11 overs on the final morning left Hampshire with an outside opportunity of knocking off the 307 needed for victory in what turned out to be 83 overs. At tea, taken on 158 for 3, Hampshire required another 149 from 32 overs, but a steady decline then left Kent pressing for a win instead. Nic Pothas, surviving a hard chance in the slips off Amjad Khan, finished up playing the decisive defensive innings. Earlier, Darren Stevens' first-day hundred – containing a six and 13 fours – took him past 1,000 runs for the first time in his career, while Hampshire's first innings owed much to a 138-run stand between Andy Bichel and Pothas for the eighth wicket.

Glamorgan announced a £6 million redevelopment of their Sophia Gardens headquarters in Cardiff

Round 15: 10–15 August 2005 Division One

HAMPSHIRE v. KENT – at The Rose Bowl

KENT	First Innings		Second Innings	
DP Fulton (capt)	c Brown b Mascarenhas	45	c Pothas b Mascarenhas	25
RWT Key	c Brown b Udal	88	lbw b Ervine	36
M van Jaarsveld	c Watson b Mascarenhas	1	(4) lbw b Watson	24
MJ Walker	c Brown b Tremlett	9	(5) b Bichel	21
DI Stevens	c Ervine b Mascarenhas	101	(6) lbw b Watson	22
JM Kemp	lbw b Bichel	69	(8) c Watson b Bichel	3
AJ Hall	b Bichel	23	(9) c Watson b Bichel	31
*NJO'Brien	c Mascarenhas b Bichel	9	(3) c McLean b Mascarenhas	7
MM Patel	not out	54	(10) b Mascarenhas	1
SJ Cook	c Pothas b Bichel	4	(7) c Crawley b Udal	0
A Khan	c & b Udal	33	not out	7
Extras	b 2, lb 8	10	b 3, lb 3, nb 2	8
	(118 overs)	446	(50.3 overs)	185

Bowling
Bichel 27-3-122-4. Tremlett 22-1-78-1. Mascarenhas 25-8-77-3. Ervine 11-0-56-0. Watson 14-0-43-0. Udal 18-4-51-2. Lamb 1-0-9-0.
Bichel 15.3-1-56-3. Watson 8-2-33-2. Mascarenhas 14-4-33-3. Tremlett 1-0-9-0. Ervine 5-0-29-1. Udal 7-0-19-1.
Fall of Wickets: 1-80, 2-90, 3-101, 4-201, 5-282, 6-336, 7-350, 8-357, 9-381
1-37, 2-45, 3-76, 4-114, 5-140, 6-141, 7-141, 8-158, 9-159

HAMPSHIRE	First Innings		Second Innings	
MJ Brown	c O'Brien b Hall	19	c Fulton b Hall	11
SM Ervine	lbw b Patel	74	c O'Brien b Kemp	69
JP Crawley	c Stevens b Hall	24	b Khan	46
SR Watson	c Walker b Khan	16	c Fulton b Kemp	30
JJ McLean	c O'Brien b Khan	0	c van Jaarsveld b Cook	19
*N Pothas	not out	74	not out	15
GA Lamb	c Hall b Kemp	8	(8) lbw b Cook	12
AD Mascarenhas	c O'Brien b Patel	4	(9) b Hall	6
AJ Bichel	c Hall b Cook	87	(7) c van Jaarsveld b Cook	2
SD Udal (capt)	lbw b Hall	2	not out	6
CT Tremlett	c Key b Patel	0		
Extras	b 1, lb 12, nb 4	17	b 6, lb 11, w 2, nb 6	25
	(83.4 overs)	325	(8 wkts 82.5 overs)	241

Bowling
Khan 20-3-89-2. Cook 21-2-74-1. Hall 19-3-62-3. Stevens 4-0-29-0. Patel 11.4-4-28-3. Kemp 8-1-30-1.
Khan 16-2-43-1. Hall 19-4-57-2. Patel 17-1-54-0. Cook 17-6-32-3. Walker 1-0-4-0. Kemp 12.5-3-34-2.
Fall of Wickets: 1-33, 2-99, 3-138, 4-140, 5-144, 6-167, 7-172, 8-310, 9-314
1-44, 2-139, 3-148, 4-189, 5-189, 6-191, 7-207, 8-231

Match drawn – Hampshire (10 pts), Kent (12 pts)

GLAMORGAN v. WARWICKSHIRE – at Colwyn Bay

GLAMORGAN	First Innings		Second Innings	
*MA Wallace	c Loudon b Pretorius	3	(2) lbw b Brown	68
DD Cherry	c Frost b Carter	21	(1) c Brown b Carter	24
DL Hemp	b Carter	31	(4) lbw b Carter	19
J Hughes	b Brown	7	(5) c Carter b Ntini	10
MJ Powell	b Pretorius	26	(6) not out	72
MPO'Shea	b Brown	4	(7) b Loudon	14
AG Wharf	lbw b Brown	0	(8) c Troughton b Carter	1
RDB Croft (capt)	not out	66	(9) lbw b Trott	33
SD Thomas	c Frost b Carter	16	(11) b Troughton	7
DS Harrison	b Brown	19	b Trott	25
DA Cosker	c Knight b Ntini	22	(3) c Trott b Ntini	23
Extras	b 9, lb 4, w 5, nb 6	24	lb 4, nb 8	12
	(58.1 overs)	239	(88.1 overs)	308

Bowling
Ntini 13.1-2-49-1. Pretorius 11-2-46-2. Carter 16-4-69-3. Brown 17-2-58-4. Loudon 1-0-4-0.
Ntini 13-2-59-2. Brown 17-3-54-1. Carter 22-4-73-3. Loudon 21-5-57-1. Pretorius 5-0-18-0. Troughton 6.1-1-24-1. Trott 4-0-19-2.
Fall of Wickets: 1-11, 2-37, 3-64, 4-64, 5-76, 6-76, 7-117, 8-168, 9-196
1-90, 2-99, 3-136, 4-147, 5-154, 6-175, 7-188, 8-269, 9-299

WARWICKSHIRE	First Innings		Second Innings	
NV Knight (capt)	b Harrison	36	not out	2
IJ Westwood	lbw b Croft	106	not out	0
IJL Trott	c O'Shea b Cosker	152		
JO Troughton	c Cosker b Croft	68		
AGR Loudon	c Cosker b Wharf	42		
*T Frost	c Harrison b Croft	3		
DR Brown	c Hughes b Wharf	64		
NM Carter	not out	36		
LC Parker	not out	19		
M Ntini				
D Pretorius				
Extras	b 1, lb 6, nb 12	19	lb 1	1
	(7 wkts dec 126 overs)	545	(0 wkts 2.2 overs)	3

Bowling
Harrison 26-4-101-1. Thomas 14-0-76-0. Croft 37-3-126-3. Wharf 22-3-129-2. Cosker 27-5-106-1.
Harrison 1.2-1-1-0. Wharf 1-0-1-0.
Fall of Wickets: 1-76, 2-259, 3-363, 4-380, 5-401, 6-464, 7-500

Warwickshire won by 10 wickets – Glamorgan (3 pts), Warwickshire (22 pts)

GLOUCESTERSHIRE v. SUSSEX – at Cheltenham

SUSSEX	First Innings		Second Innings	
RR Montgomerie	c Sarwan b Fisher	25	c Ball b Bandara	37
CD Hopkinson	lbw b Bandara	59	c Adshead b Bandara	35
MH Yardy	run out	13	not out	59
MW Goodwin	lbw b Bandara	51	c Adshead b Bandara	5
CJ Adams (capt)	st Adshead b Bandara	66	c Sarwan b Bandara	8
*MJ Prior	c Bandara b Rudge	52	lbw b Kadeer Ali	109
RSC M-Jenkins	c Ball b Fisher	35		
Naved-ul-Hasan	c Weston b Fisher	6	(7) not out	8
MJG Davis	c Gidman b Bandara	24		
Mushtaq Ahmed	c sub b Rudge	22		
RJ Kirtley	not out	0		
Extras	b 5, lb 5, nb 2	12	lb 1, nb 2	3
	(92.1 overs)	365	(5 wkts dec 63 overs)	264

Bowling
Kirby 4.3-1-15-0. Rudge 15.1-4-75-2. Fisher 24.3-5-93-3. Ball 25-1-108-0. Bandara 23-4-64-4.
Rudge 7-1-53-0. Kadeer Ali 5-2-12-1. Ball 21-6-70-0. Bandara 26-3-112-4. Fisher 4-0-16-0.
Fall of Wickets: 1-40, 2-58, 3-143, 4-186, 5-259, 6-292, 7-310, 8-319, 9-365
1-67, 2-86, 3-102, 4-112, 5-253

GLOS	First Innings		Second Innings	
WPC Weston	lbw b Mushtaq Ahmed	46	absent hurt	
Kadeer Ali	c Prior b Naved-ul-Hasan	3	c M-Jenkins b N-ul-Hasan	6
RR Sarwan	lbw b Naved-ul-Hasan	26	(1) b Naved-ul-Hasan	117
MGN Windows	c Hopkinson b Mushtaq Ahmed	33	(3) b Naved-ul-Hasan	0
APR Gidman (capt)	lbw b Mushtaq Ahmed	7	(4) lbw b Kirtley	7
*SJ Adshead	c N-ul-Hasan b M Ahmed	39	(5) lbw b Mushtaq Ahmed	6
ID Fisher	c Yardy b Mushtaq Ahmed	15	(6) lbw b Mushtaq Ahmed	13
MCJ Ball	b Naved-ul-Hasan	7	(7) b Naved-ul-Hasan	0
CM Bandara	c M-Jenkins b N-ul-Hasan	20	(8) b Naved-ul-Hasan	16
WD Rudge	lbw b Mushtaq Ahmed	7	(9) not out	0
SP Kirby	not out	0	(10) b Mushtaq Ahmed	6
Extras	b 14, lb 6, w 1	21	b 3, lb 5	8
	(72.1 overs)	224	(9 wkts 45.3 overs)	179

Bowling
Kirtley 9-1-25-0. Naved-ul-Hasan 15.1-3-53-4. Martin-Jenkins 9-5-8-0. Mushtaq Ahmed 23-2-65-6. Davis 16-2-53-0.
Kirtley 8-2-32-1. Naved-ul-Hasan 15-1-81-5. Mushtaq Ahmed 15.3-1-46-3. Martin-Jenkins 7-2-12-0.
Fall of Wickets: 1-8, 2-69, 3-92, 4-108, 5-151, 6-185, 7-190, 8-203, 9-224
1-34, 2-34, 3-51, 4-88, 5-146, 6-150, 7-160, 8-168, 9-179

Sussex won by 226 runs – Gloucestershire (4 pts), Sussex (21 pts)

NOTTINGHAMSHIRE v. MIDDLESEX – at Trent Bridge

MIDDLESEX	First Innings		Second Innings	
ET Smith	b Ealham	128	c Gallian b Ealham	25
BL Hutton (capt)	lbw b Harris	0	lbw b Ealham	31
OA Shah	c Harris b Ealham	27	not out	173
EC Joyce	lbw b Smith GJ	5	st Read b Younis Khan	101
JWM Dalrymple	c Hussey b Smith GJ	60	lbw b Younis Khan	45
PN Weekes	lbw b Swann	38		
*BJM Scott	not out	20		
PD Trego	c Hussey b Harris	1		
CJC Wright	lbw b Harris	0		
A Richardson	c Hussey b Smith GJ	25		
MM Betts	c Smith WR b Harris	13		
Extras	b 1, lb 3, w 2, nb 2	8	lb 6, nb 4	10
	(89.3 overs)	325	(4 wkts dec 94.5 overs)	385

Bowling
Sidebottom 15-4-41-0. Harris 21.3-4-86-4. Ealham 17-3-66-2. Smith GJ 18-3-68-3. Swann 12-1-40-1. Younis Khan 6-0-20-0.
Sidebottom 15-7-28-0. Harris 16-0-107-0. Ealham 17-3-61-2. Swann 10-0-43-0. Smith GJ 15-2-60-0. Younis Khan 16.5-1-67-2. Hussey 5-1-13-0.
Fall of Wickets: 1-2, 2-49, 3-59, 4-198, 5-250, 6-266, 7-269, 8-269, 9-308
1-51, 2-70, 3-295, 4-385

NOTTS	First Innings		Second Innings	
DJ Bicknell	lbw b Trego	33	b Richardson	62
JER Gallian (capt)	c Hutton b Trego	11	not out	56
WR Smith	c Weekes b Trego	6	not out	5
Younis Khan	b Trego	7		
DJ Hussey	b Betts	9		
*CMW Read	lbw b Richardson	10		
MA Ealham	c Scott b Richardson	26		
GP Swann	c Wright b Trego	53		
RJ Sidebottom	c Scott b Richardson	0		
GJ Smith	not out	6		
AJ Harris	b Trego	0		
Extras	b 2, lb 7, w 1, nb 10	20	lb 2, w 1, nb 2	5
	(55 overs)	181	(1 wkt 42 overs)	128

Bowling
Betts 11-6-23-1. Richardson 16-3-54-3. Trego 17-3-59-6. Wright 10-1-31-0. Hutton 1-0-5-0.
Richardson 10-4-24-1. Trego 6-2-18-0. Wright 5-0-25-0. Hutton 2-1-10-0. Dalrymple 10-2-24-0. Weekes 9-1-25-0.
Fall of Wickets: 1-36, 2-62, 3-65, 4-70, 5-82, 6-97, 7-146, 8-154, 9-180
1-115

Match drawn – Nottinghamshire (7 pts), Middlesex (10 pts)

Left: Ramnaresh Sarwan was a lone Gloucestershire success against Sussex.

during the visit of champions Warwickshire to Colwyn Bay, but the county's optimism off the field was not matched by events on it as the Welsh side's championship fortunes continued to take a dive. Warwickshire won eventually by ten wickets after rolling Glamorgan over for just 239 on the opening day and then cruising to 545 for 7 declared in reply. It was the third match in succession that Glamorgan had conceded 500 runs in an innings, with Jon Trott and Ian Westwood (who reached a maiden first-class century) the main beneficiaries. Jim Troughton struck Dean Cosker for three sixes as the visitors motored towards a declaration, and Dougie Brown weighed in with 64 off only 47 balls. Mike Powell and Mark Wallace resisted stubbornly second time around, but Warwickshire were left with merely a token target after bowling out Glamorgan for 308. The planned Cardiff redevelopment was scheduled to lift the ground's capacity from 6,000 to 13,500 in the next 12 months, and to 16,000 by 2008.

Pakistani bowling power was at the heart of Sussex's 226-run win over Gloucestershire at Cheltenham. Both Naved-ul-Hasan and Mushtaq Ahmed finished with nine wickets in the match as the home side were brushed aside. Only Ramnaresh Sarwan, Gloucestershire's recruit from the West Indies, came to terms with Naved's rapid swingers and Mushtaq's subtle variations of spin and flight as he hit a second innings 117 – out of 146 while he was at the crease. Otherwise, this was a straightforward victory for Sussex, inside three days, once they had rallied from 59 for 4 on the opening morning. Steve Kirby, the Gloucestershire fast bowler, limped off with a thigh injury after bowling his fifth over and four batsmen passed 50 as Sussex ran up 365. Malinga Bandara's leg spin showed up well enough, but Matthew Prior hit a second innings 109 to go with his first-day 52 as Sussex raced to their second innings declaration with 136 runs being added in just 15 overs on the third morning.

Nottinghamshire were lucky that a virtual last day washout at Trent Bridge prevented them from having to bat all day to save the game against Middlesex. Notts looked far from championship contenders as Peter Trego skittled them out for 181 on day two. Owais Shah and Ed Joyce then built still further on an advantage which Ed Smith's first innings 128 had also won for Middlesex, both adding fluent and attractive hundreds to their burgeoning season's run-tally.

Division Two

Yorkshire maintained their unbeaten record in the second division, but they were fortunate at Taunton that only 6.5 overs were possible on the final day. At 173 for 4 overnight, just two runs behind Somerset overall, the visitors were still confident of batting long enough to secure the draw, but it was a shame in particular for the home team's Matthew Wood that the bad weather brought with it the need for such speculation. The 24-year-old Wood, a quietly-spoken Devonian recently elevated to the vice-captaincy, batted nine hours and two minutes for his epic 297, the second-highest score ever made against Yorkshire – following WG Grace's unbeaten 318 against them in 1876. When he was at last caught at long on, only Viv Richards (322), Jimmy Cook (313 not out), Graeme Smith (311) and Harold Gimblett (310) had made higher individual scores for Somerset. The match was also something of a triumph for Andy Caddick, who became only the

Somerset's Matthew Wood: an epic 297 against Yorkshire put him up with some elite names.

sixth bowler still playing to take 1,000 first-class wickets when he had Joe Sayers caught at second slip from the second ball of the contest. Caddick finished the innings with 6 for 96, but even he could not make much impression on centurions Phil Jaques and Michael Lumb, whose 130 was a career-best and included a six and 21 fours.

Derbyshire looked to be gaining the upper hand against Northamptonshire at Wantage Road, ending the opening day at 135 for 4 after shooting the hosts out for 140. But then came the Northants fightback, led by Martin Love and with support chiefly from home captain David Sales. Monty Panesar's slow left-arm spin was also a decisive factor: he took eight wickets in the match and, after Northants' eventual second innings declaration at 466 for 6, teamed up with off spinner Jason Brown to put the skids under the Derbyshire second innings and ensure a 182-run win.

Durham's Mike Hussey continued his remarkable mastery over the Leicestershire bowling attack at the Riverside in which, ultimately, the weather was the only victor. In the time possible, Hussey's 146 and 61 not out took his championship run tally to 460 in just three innings against Leicestershire during the summer. For the visitors, however, Dinesh Mongia's 164 earned them a significant first innings advantage.

Round 16: 14–19 August 2005

Division One

Sussex pushed themselves up to the top of the first division table by overwhelming Middlesex by an innings and 232 runs at Lord's. It was a humiliating result for the home side, tumbled out for just 128 and 162 in reply to Sussex's astonishing 522. At one stage on day one, Sussex were languishing somewhat at 199 for 6, but then the increasingly impressive Mike Yardy was joined by Naved-ul-Hasan in a seventh-wicket stand worth 228 in double quick time. Naved's career-best 139 took him only 124 balls, and his strong-armed strokeplay brought him four sixes and 11 fours. Yardy went on to reach 179, from 229 balls, while Mark Davis enjoyed himself hugely at the end with an unbeaten 45-ball 50. Naved also starred with the ball, underlining what a magnificent late-season signing he had proved by taking seven wickets in the two Middlesex collapses. His second innings haul of four wickets all came in the same over! Mushtaq Ahmed, predictably, was also at the centre of things with nine wickets and a second innings analysis of 6 for 44, while Robin Martin-Jenkins also bagged four cheap Middlesex wickets in their first innings slide.

Nottinghamshire, however, remained just a single point behind Sussex after a thumping innings and

Round 15: 10–15 August 2005 Division Two

SOMERSET v. YORKSHIRE – at Taunton

YORKSHIRE	First Innings		Second Innings	
MJ Wood	c Gazzard b Caddick	34	c Parsons b Caddick	0
JJ Sayers	c Hildreth b Caddick	0	b Langeveldt	51
A McGrath	c Hildreth b Francis SRG	22	lbw b Langeveldt	68
PA Jaques	c Hildreth b Durston	106	b Caddick	14
MJ Lumb	lbw b Langeveldt	130	not out	19
C White (capt)	c Gazzard b Langeveldt	50	not out	9
GJ Kruis	c Gazzard b Caddick	0		
*I Dawood	lbw b Caddick	8		
RKJ Dawson	lbw b Caddick	15		
TT Bresnan	not out	4		
CEW Silverwood	b Caddick	0		
Extras	b 1, lb 11, w 3, nb 22	37	b 5, lb 5, nb 8	18
	(110.3 overs)	**406**	(4 wkts 61.5 overs)	**179**

Bowling
Caddick 29.3-7-96-6. Langeveldt 30-10-98-2. Francis SRG 13-1-79-1. Parsons 7-1-27-0. Blackwell 21-3-47-0. Durston 7-1-37-1. Suppiah 3-1-10-0.
Caddick 19.5-7-51-2. Langeveldt 18-5-42-2. Blackwell 12-4-32-0. Francis SRG 9-4-43-0. Durston 3-2-1-0.
Fall of Wickets: 1-1, 2-40, 3-109, 4-228, 5-368, 6-369, 7-371, 8-399, 9-406
1-4, 2-123, 3-140, 4-144

SOMERSET	First Innings	
MJ Wood	c Bresnan b Dawson	297
JD Francis	c Dawood b McGrath	30
AV Suppiah	c Dawood b McGrath	6
JC Hildreth	c Dawson b Bresnan	31
WJ Durston	c Sayers b Silverwood	16
ID Blackwell (capt)	c Jaques b Bresnan	62
KA Parsons	b Dawson	94
*CM Gazzard	c & b Dawson	0
AR Caddick	c Sayers b Dawson	5
SRG Francis	lbw b Silverwood	9
CK Langeveldt	not out	5
Extras	b 5, lb 11, w 2, nb 8	26
	(142 overs)	**581**

Bowling
Silverwood 29-5-94-2. Kruis 30-2-134-0. Bresnan 27-4-110-2. McGrath 22-2-93-2. Dawson 33-3-132-4. Lumb 1-0-2-0.
Fall of Wickets: 1-116, 2-130, 3-182, 4-215, 5-324, 6-525, 7-525, 8-543, 9-576

Match drawn – Somerset (12 pts), Yorkshire (11 pts)

NORTHAMPTONSHIRE v. DERBYSHIRE – at Northampton

NORTHANTS	First Innings		Second Innings	
ML Love	lbw b Sheikh	2	lbw b Sheikh	177
BM Shafayat	c Sutton b Hunter	1	c Hassan Adnan b Welch	22
RA White	lbw b Welch	25	c Sutton b Welch	0
U Afzaal	lbw b Hunter	9	lbw b Gray	59
DJG Sales (capt)	c Sutton b Sheikh	1	lbw b Gray	93
*MH Wessels	c Gray b Moss	17	not out	50
DG Wright	c Stubbings b Hunter	22	b Botha	43
BJ Phillips	b Welch	48		
J Louw	c Sutton b Hunter	0		
MS Panesar	lbw b Welch	0		
JF Brown	not out	0		
Extras	b 6, lb 7, nb 2	15	b 1, lb 8, w 5, nb 8	22
	(46.5 overs)	**140**	(6 wkts dec 104.3 overs)	**466**

Bowling
Hunter 15.5-3-50-4. Sheikh 15-7-24-2. Welch 10-4-21-3. Moss 5-1-21-1. Botha 1-0-11-0.
Hunter 13-0-91-0. Sheikh 17-2-63-1. Welch 18-6-63-2. Gray 30-4-130-2. Botha 21.3-1-87-1. Moss 5-1-23-0.
Fall of Wickets: 1-7, 2-7, 3-24, 4-27, 5-58, 6-70, 7-122, 8-140, 9-140
1-35, 2-43, 3-186, 4-353, 5-378, 6-466

DERBYSHIRE	First Innings		Second Innings	
MJ Di Venuto	lbw b Panesar	43	(2) c Shafayat b Panesar	47
SD Stubbings	c Wessels b Louw	44	(1) c Love b Brown	14
BJ France	c Wessels b Wright	0	c Shafayat b Panesar	11
Hassan Adnan	lbw b Phillips	24	c Love b Panesar	0
J Moss	c Love b Louw	0	c White b Brown	6
*LD Sutton (capt)	c Love b Panesar	32	c Afzaal b Brown	2
G Welch	c Sales b Panesar	14	b Brown	47
AG Botha	c Afzaal b Wright	11	c Love b Brown	24
MA Sheikh	lbw b Brown	14	c Love b Panesar	8
AKD Gray	not out	7	not out	8
ID Hunter	c Phillips b Panesar	20	b Wright	0
Extras	lb 8, nb 2	10	b 20, lb 12, nb 6	38
	(83.3 overs)	**219**	(99.2 overs)	**205**

Bowling
Wright 22-7-54-2. Louw 15-3-42-2. Phillips 13-3-39-1. Brown 9-2-20-1. Panesar 24.3-7-56-4.
Wright 9.2-7-10-1. Brown 45-22-61-5. Panesar 43-15-82-4. Louw 2-1-20-0.
Fall of Wickets: 1-81, 2-84, 3-107, 4-111, 5-135, 6-165, 7-178, 8-178, 9-198
1-40, 2-81, 3-81, 4-92, 5-94, 6-94, 7-162, 8-187, 9-201

Northamptonshire won by 182 runs – Northamptonshire (17 pts), Derbyshire (4 pts)

DURHAM v. LEICESTERSHIRE – at The Riverside

DURHAM	First Innings		Second Innings	
MEK Hussey (capt)	lbw b Masters	146	not out	61
JA Lowe	lbw b Willoughby	26	lbw b Gibson	14
PD Collingwood	c Maunders b Masters	39	lbw b Henderson	5
GJ Muchall	lbw b Masters	7	not out	22
DM Benkenstein	c Maunders b Masters	41		
GR Breese	lbw b Willoughby	0		
*P Mustard	b Masters	17		
LE Plunkett	c Maddy b Willoughby	5		
CD Thorp	b Willoughby	10		
ML Lewis	not out	7		
G Onions	c Habib b Masters	0		
Extras	lb 9, w 1, nb 2, p 5	17	lb 1	1
	(106.2 overs)	**315**	(2 wkts 37 overs)	**103**

Bowling
Gibson 22-7-48-0. Willoughby 31-9-92-4. Maddy 3-1-5-0. Masters 26.2-6-74-6. Henderson 20-4-61-0. Maunders 4-1-21-0.
Willoughby 4-0-16-0. Masters 5-0-16-0. Henderson 14-9-24-1. Gibson 8-3-27-1. Mongia 5-1-18-0. Robinson 1-0-1-0.
Fall of Wickets: 1-44, 2-99, 3-131, 4-260, 5-261, 6-269, 7-281, 8-297, 9-315
1-42, 2-47

LEICESTERSHIRE	First Innings	
DDJ Robinson	b Lewis	73
DL Maddy	b Plunkett	12
JK Maunders	lbw b Plunkett	22
D Mongia	st Mustard b Breese	164
HD Ackerman (capt)	b Breese	61
A Habib	c Collingwood b Breese	7
*PA Nixon	lbw b Lewis	26
OD Gibson	c Mustard b Breese	0
CW Henderson	not out	30
DD Masters	b Lewis	0
CM Willoughby	c Plunkett b Breese	10
Extras	lb 14, nb 24	38
	(102.4 overs)	**443**

Bowling
Lewis 22-4-83-3. Plunkett 22-4-100-2. Onions 12-1-73-0. Thorp 20-6-58-0. Collingwood 7-0-24-0. Breese 19.4-8-91-5.
Fall of Wickets: 1-34, 2-99, 3-191, 4-348, 5-373, 6-376, 7-378, 8-422, 9-422

Match drawn – Durham (10 pts), Leicestershire (12 pts)

151-run victory against Warwickshire at Trent Bridge. The defending champions were a pale imitation of their 2004 selves as they slumped to 156 all out on the first day and 207 all out on the third. Nottinghamshire's seamers held sway throughout the two innings, while in between the home team's batsmen also made hay. The chief destroyer was David Hussey, and the Australian's unbeaten 232 from 298 balls included six sixes. Hussey was joined by Chris Read, who made a very good 89, in a fifth-wicket partnership worth 148.

Surrey, at the other end of the table, were frustrated at The Oval when bad weather ruled out play on the final day of their match against Gloucestershire. The visitors were by no means out of the woods at 294 for 6 overnight – a lead of 181 – and Ramnaresh Sarwan was out for 99, made from 129 balls with 15 fours and a six. Alex Gidman, however, was still there on 40, having hit 84 off 118 balls first time around when he and Steve Adshead held up Surrey's bowlers with a fifth-wicket stand of 110. Adshead went on to reach his maiden first-class hundred and finished unbeaten on 148. Gloucestershire, having been 1 for 3 soon after the start, were more than pleased to reach 350, but this total was overhauled by the class of Mark Ramprakash, whose 192 swept him past 1,000 runs for the season. In his 77 first-class hundreds, Ramprakash had exceeded 150 on 23 occasions.

United in Surrey's cause are England's unwanted batsmen Mark Ramprakash (left) and Graham Thorpe.

Round 16: 14–19 August 2005 Division One

MIDDLESEX v. SUSSEX – at Lord's

SUSSEX	First Innings		
RR Montgomerie	c Scott b Trego	27	
CD Hopkinson	c Shah b Hayward	10	
MH Yardy	c Joyce b Peploe	179	
MW Goodwin	c Smith b Hayward	20	
CJ Adams (capt)	b Trego	17	
*MJ Prior	c Smith b Dalrymple	38	
RSC M-Jenkins	c Joyce b Dalrymple	8	
Naved-ul-Hasan	c Hutton b Joyce	139	
MJG Davis	c Scott b Clark	50	
Mushtaq Ahmed	c Shah b Weekes	7	
RJ Kirtley	not out	9	
Extras	lb 12, nb 6	18	
	(104.4 overs)	**522**	

Bowling
Clark 22.4-3-109-1. Trego 21-5-87-2. Hayward 15-1-65-2. Peploe 17-2-71-1. Hutton 1-0-10-0. Dalrymple 6-0-43-2. Weekes 15-2-75-1. Joyce 7-0-50-1.
Fall of Wickets: 1-27, 2-37, 3-78, 4-116, 5-185, 6-199, 7-427, 8-485, 9-492

MIDDLESEX	First Innings		Second Innings	
ET Smith	c Prior b Naved-ul-Hasan	13	b Mushtaq Ahmed	69
BL Hutton (capt)	c Prior b Naved-ul-Hasan	6	c Adams b Mushtaq Ahmed	21
OA Shah	c Yardy b Naved-ul-Hasan	4	lbw b Mushtaq Ahmed	0
EC Joyce	c Adams b Mushtaq Ahmed	36	c Kirtley b Mushtaq Ahmed	0
JWM Dalrymple	lbw b Mushtaq Ahmed	10	c Prior b Naved-ul-Hasan	0
PN Weekes	c Montgomerie b M Ahmed	6	b Naved-ul-Hasan	0
*BJM Scott	b Martin-Jenkins	13	b Naved-ul-Hasan	0
PD Trego	b Martin-Jenkins	16	lbw b Naved-ul-Hasan	0
CT Peploe	c M Ahmed b Martin-Jenkins	16	c Yardy b Mushtaq Ahmed	42
SR Clark	c Adams b Martin-Jenkins	2	b Mushtaq Ahmed	14
M Hayward	not out	0	not out	1
Extras	b 2, lb 2, nb 2	6	b 9, lb 1, nb 5	15
	(41.4 overs)	**128**	(46.2 overs)	**162**

Bowling
Kirtley 7-0-27-0. Naved-ul-Hasan 9-1-42-3. Mushtaq Ahmed 14-5-24-3. Martin-Jenkins 11.4-2-31-4.
Kirtley 13-1-54-0. Naved-ul-Hasan 17-4-54-4. Mushtaq Ahmed 16.2-5-44-6.
Fall of Wickets: 1-10, 2-18, 3-27, 4-58, 5-72, 6-87, 7-110, 8-111, 9-113
1-45, 2-45, 3-45, 4-48, 5-48, 6-48, 7-48, 8-145, 9-153

*Sussex won by an innings and 232 runs –
Middlesex (3 pts), Sussex (22 pts)*

NOTTINGHAMSHIRE v. WARWICKSHIRE – at Trent Bridge

WARWICKSHIRE	First Innings		Second Innings	
NV Knight (capt)	b Sidebottom	5	absent hurt	
IJ Westwood	c Read b Sidebottom	49	b Sidebottom	17
IJL Trott	c Hussey b Sidebottom	31	c Read b Smith GJ	19
JO Troughton	c Hussey b Sidebottom	0	c Read b Smith GJ	16
AGR Loudon	c Swann b Ealham	8	c Read b Smith GJ	46
*T Frost	lbw b Ealham	2	c Sidebottom b Harris	10
DR Brown	not out	34	b Swann	6
LC Parker	c Read b Harris	17	(1) b Swann	37
NM Carter	lbw b Harris	0	(8) not out	45
M Ntini	c Read b Harris	4	(9) c Sidebottom b Younis Khan	0
JE Anyon	lbw b Harris	0	(10) c & b Younis Khan	2
Extras	lb 6	6	b 1, lb 2, nb 6	9
	(44.4 overs)	**156**	(9 wkts 60.2 overs)	**207**

Bowling
Sidebottom 17-4-41-4. Harris 9.4-0-41-4. Ealham 13-3-39-2. Smith GJ 5-0-29-0.
Sidebottom 16-6-34-1. Harris 9-1-33-1. Ealham 6-1-11-0. Smith GJ 15-3-64-3. Swann 10-2-41-2. Younis Khan 4.2-0-21-2.
Fall of Wickets: 1-6, 2-54, 3-64, 4-89, 5-99, 6-107, 7-146, 8-146, 9-156
1-29, 2-67, 3-89, 4-126, 5-149, 6-155, 7-183, 8-204, 9-207

NOTTS	First Innings	
DJ Bicknell	b Brown	11
JER Gallian (capt)	c Loudon b Brown	20
WR Smith	c Knight b Ntini	0
Younis Khan	c Trott b Carter	29
DJ Hussey	not out	232
*CMW Read	c Trott b Brown	89
MA Ealham	c Loudon b Anyon	36
GP Swann	c Frost b Carter	39
RJ Sidebottom	c sub b Carter	12
GJ Smith	b Brown	2
AJ Harris	c Frost b Brown	21
Extras	b 1, lb 2, w 4, nb 16	23
	(118.3 overs)	**514**

Bowling
Ntini 22-4-96-1. Brown 30.3-3-128-5. Carter 25-3-96-3. Anyon 16-0-86-1. Loudon 22-2-91-0. Trott 3-0-14-0.
Fall of Wickets: 1-26, 2-27, 3-45, 4-75, 5-223, 6-290, 7-398, 8-445, 9-460

*Nottinghamshire won by an innings and 151 runs –
Nottinghamshire (22 pts), Warwickshire (3 pts)*

SURREY v. GLOUCESTERSHIRE – at The Oval

GLOS	First Innings		Second Innings	
CM Spearman	lbw b Azhar Mahmood	1	c & b Azhar Mahmood	7
Kadeer Ali	c Thorpe b Akram	0	b Doshi	66
RR Sarwan	c & b Azhar Mahmood	0	c Brown b Saqlain Mushtaq	99
MGN Windows	c Batty b Akram	21	lbw b Doshi	38
APR Gidman (capt)	lbw b Azhar Mahmood	84	not out	40
*SJ Adshead	not out	148	c Murtagh b Doshi	0
MA Hardinges	c Batty b Murtagh	7	c Batty b Azhar Mahmood	14
ID Fisher	c Newman b Doshi	13	not out	2
CM Bandara	c Newman b Doshi	8		
JMM Averis	lbw b Saqlain Mushtaq	29		
WD Rudge	b Murtagh	15		
Extras	lb 2, nb 22	24	lb 6, nb 22	28
	(96 overs)	**350**	(6 wkts 77 overs)	**294**

Bowling
Akram 17-3-63-2. Azhar Mahmood 18-7-63-3. Murtagh 13-2-37-2. Saqlain Mushtaq 28-3-110-1. Doshi 20-5-75-2.
Akram 9.5-0-67-0. Azhar Mahmood 16.1-5-52-2. Saqlain Mushtaq 25-3-82-1. Murtagh 5-1-19-0. Doshi 21-5-68-3.
Fall of Wickets: 1-1, 2-1, 3-1, 4-59, 5-169, 6-184, 7-227, 8-253, 9-312
1-25, 2-176, 3-214, 4-248, 5-248, 6-273

SURREY	First Innings	
SA Newman	c Kadeer Ali b Averis	14
MA Butcher (capt)	c Kadeer Ali b Rudge	6
ND Doshi	c Gidman b Averis	10
MR Ramprakash	c Spearman b Rudge	192
GP Thorpe	c Windows b Rudge	36
*JN Batty	c Sarwan b Hardinges	56
AD Brown	c & b Bandara	35
Azhar Mahmood	lbw b Bandara	0
TJ Murtagh	b Hardinges	66
Saqlain Mushtaq	c Averis b Bandara	8
M Akram	not out	4
Extras	b 1, lb 8, w 7, nb 20	36
	(124.1 overs)	**463**

Bowling
Averis 27-6-96-2. Rudge 25-4-97-3. Hardinges 23-5-66-2. Bandara 27.1-4-88-3. Fisher 17-1-78-0. Kadeer Ali 2-0-11-0. Sarwan 3-0-18-0.
Fall of Wickets: 1-20, 2-40, 3-40, 4-138, 5-271, 6-339, 7-339, 8-432, 9-459

Match drawn – Surrey (12 pts), Gloucestershire (11 pts)

Division Two

Superb batting from Will Jefferson, Andy Flower and Ronnie Irani enabled Essex to hunt down their victory target of 337 in 88 overs against Derbyshire at Derby – despite being 127 for 4 at one stage. When they had scored 426 in their first innings, the home side must have thought that defeat was out of the equation, especially when Essex slipped to 113 for 4 in reply by the close of the second day. But Grant Flower's 61, Irani's 99 and an ebullient 51 from 38 balls by Darren Gough hauled the visitors up to 306, before the leg-spinning quality of Danish Kaneria brought Essex further back into the game.

Worcestershire made the highest total in their history at New Road, disposing of Somerset by an innings and 56 runs as a result of it. Ben Smith and Steven Davies put on 270 in 51 overs for the fourth wicket, against a young and increasingly dispirited Somerset attack, and at one stage Worcestershire were 618 for 3 before 'falling away' to 696 for 8 declared. Zander de Bruyn also made a big hundred and Worcestershire even claimed the extra half-hour on the third evening in a bid to finish Somerset off. To their credit, the outgunned visitors hung on for more than 30 overs on the final day – as well as surviving those extra 30 minutes – and Carl Gazzard added to his reputation as a promising young

Round 16: 14–19 August 2005 Division Two

DERBYSHIRE v. ESSEX – at Derby

DERBYSHIRE	First Innings		Second Innings	
SD Stubbings	c Jefferson b Middlebrook	64	(2) lbw b Napier	5
MJ Di Venuto	run out	27	(1) c Foster b Bopara	4
CWG Bassano	lbw b Bopara	30	lbw b Danish Kaneria	1
Hassan Adnan	lbw b Danish Kaneria	52	c Jefferson b Bopara	13
J Moss	b Danish Kaneria	21	b Danish Kaneria	74
*LD Sutton (capt)	c Middlebrook b Danish Kaneria	88	not out	46
G Welch	lbw b Danish Kaneria	4	c Middlebrook b Danish Kaneria	0
AG Botha	c Jefferson b Gough	39	b Danish Kaneria	22
MA Sheikh	lbw b Danish Kaneria	55	b Middlebrook	9
J Needham	not out	1	lbw b Danish Kaneria	6
NGE Walker	lbw b Danish Kaneria	4	b Napier	7
Extras	b 14, lb 8, w 3, nb 16	41	b 13, lb 1, w 2, nb 8, p 5	29
	(155.1 overs)	**426**	(59.2 overs)	**216**

Bowling
Gough 22.3-4-54-1. Napier 24-6-78-0. Danish Kaneria 60.1-16-111-6. Middlebrook 27.3-6-67-1. Bopara 17-2-73-1. Cook 2-0-15-0. Flower GW 2-1-6-0. Napier 9.2-0-25-2. Bopara 11-2-65-2. Danish Kaneria 26-6-65-5. Middlebrook 6-1-13-1. Flower GW 7-0-29-0.
Fall of Wickets: 1-50, 2-129, 3-162, 4-206, 5-217, 6-233, 7-292, 8-412, 9-422
1-11, 2-11, 3-23, 4-34, 5-155, 6-155, 7-181, 8-192, 9-205

ESSEX	First Innings		Second Innings	
WI Jefferson	run out	8	c Hassan Adnan b Moss	83
AN Cook	lbw b Sheikh	1	b Welch	14
GW Flower	c Sutton b Welch	61	lbw b Welch	0
RS Bopara	lbw b Welch	1	run out	10
A Flower	c Stubbings b Welch	22	c Welch b Botha	104
RC Irani (capt)	c Sutton b Walker	99	not out	88
*JS Foster	lbw b Welch	0	not out	22
JD Middlebrook	lbw b Needham	42		
GR Napier	c Sutton b Needham	0		
D Gough	c Bassano b Welch	51		
Danish Kaneria	not out	0		
Extras	lb 9, w 2, nb 10	21	b 7, lb 7, w 2	16
	(97.2 overs)	**306**	(5 wkts 84.4 overs)	**337**

Bowling
Welch 26-8-68-5. Sheikh 24-9-74-1. Walker 18.2-4-74-1. Botha 16-7-26-0. Needham 11-3-42-2. Moss 2-0-13-0.
Welch 21.4-5-77-2. Sheikh 13-2-45-0. Botha 27-3-97-1. Needham 4-1-26-0. Walker 10-2-55-0. Moss 9-2-23-1.
Fall of Wickets: 1-13, 2-13, 3-18, 4-78, 5-124, 6-124, 7-228, 8-228, 9-305
1-33, 2-51, 3-82, 4-127, 5-304

Essex won by 5 wickets – Derbyshire (6 pts), Essex (19 pts)

WORCESTERSHIRE v. SOMERSET – at Worcester

SOMERSET	First Innings		Second Innings	
MJ Wood	c Smith b Kabir Ali	21	b Price	72
JD Francis	lbw b Mason	2	c Smith b Mason	15
AV Suppiah	c Peters b Price	72	c Davies b Batty	34
JC Hildreth	c Mitchell b Kabir Ali	4	c Mitchell b Batty	12
WJ Durston	c Mitchell b Malik	3	c Smith b Price	26
ID Blackwell (capt)	st Davies b Batty	9	c Mitchell b Batty	5
KA Parsons	c Peters b Malik	34	c Peters b Batty	11
*CM Gazzard	lbw b Price	74	not out	44
RJ Woodman	not out	46	c Peters b Price	0
AR Caddick	c Price b Mason	6	c Davies b Price	39
SRG Francis	c de Bruyn b Malik	3	b Kabir Ali	29
Extras	b 12, lb 13, w 1, nb 18	44	b 14, lb 8, w 1, nb 12	35
	(97.3 overs)	**318**	(108.5 overs)	**322**

Bowling
Mason 18-6-56-2. Kabir Ali 20-9-51-2. Malik 16.3-3-63-3. Batty 19-2-65-1. de Bruyn 8-0-24-0. Price 16-3-34-2.
Kabir Ali 8.5-0-50-1. Mason 10-2-39-1. Malik 3-0-23-0. Price 44-21-67-4. Batty 43-8-121-4.
Fall of Wickets: 1-19, 2-31, 3-37, 4-48, 5-57, 6-121, 7-198, 8-287, 9-305
1-28, 2-138, 3-154, 4-159, 5-169, 6-191, 7-207, 8-209, 9-267

WORCS	First Innings	
SD Peters	lbw b Woodman	88
SC Moore	c Gazzard b Francis SRG	28
Z de Bruyn	c Blackwell b Durston	161
BF Smith	c Francis JD b Parsons	172
*SM Davies	c & b Parsons	148
DKH Mitchell	not out	23
GJ Batty (capt)	c sub b Parsons	3
Kabir Ali	c Francis SRG b Blackwell	25
RW Price	lbw b Blackwell	16
MS Mason		
MN Malik		
Extras	b 4, lb 9, w 3, nb 16	32
	(8 wkts dec 148.2 overs)	**696**

Bowling
Caddick 31-4-119-0. Woodman 14-0-79-1. Francis SRG 20-3-112-1. Parsons 18-3-81-3. Blackwell 38.2-9-146-2. Suppiah 6-1-38-0. Hildreth 5-0-15-0. Durston 16-1-93-1.
Fall of Wickets: 1-51, 2-227, 3-348, 4-618, 5-624, 6-634, 7-669, 8-696

Worcestershire won by an innings and 56 runs – Worcestershire (22 pts), Somerset (4 pts)

LANCASHIRE v. YORKSHIRE – at Old Trafford

YORKSHIRE	First Innings		Second Innings	
MJ Wood	c Symonds b Anderson	86	c Sutcliffe b Cork	54
JJ Sayers	c Law b Chapple	14	c Hegg b Keedy	48
A McGrath	c Hegg b Chapple	35	c Cork b North	57
PA Jaques	lbw b Symonds	14	lbw b Symonds	14
MJ Lumb	b Keedy	34	c Hegg b Anderson	1
C White (capt)	not out	110	not out	66
*I Dawood	c Law b North	28	c & b Chilton	28
RKJ Dawson	lbw b Chapple	27	not out	0
TT Bresnan	c Hegg b Keedy	11		
CEW Silverwood	b Anderson	6		
GJ Kruis	c Loye b Anderson	35		
Extras	b 4, lb 7, w 4, nb 2	17	b 16, lb 8, w 7, nb 24	55
	(125 overs)	**417**	(6 wkts 109 overs)	**323**

Bowling
Anderson 23-2-100-3. Cork 27-7-58-0. Chapple 23-2-78-3. Keedy 25-4-101-2. Symonds 20-5-53-1. North 7-2-16-1.
Anderson 14-3-48-1. Cork 14-1-61-1. Keedy 35-9-88-1. North 17-4-41-1. Chapple 14-2-34-0. Symonds 10-3-18-1. Chilton 5-1-9-1.
Fall of Wickets: 1-58, 2-118, 3-148, 4-176, 5-214, 6-268, 7-324, 8-350, 9-361
1-118, 2-146, 3-172, 4-173, 5-277, 6-322

LANCASHIRE	First Innings	
MJ Chilton (capt)	c Dawood b Kruis	130
IJ Sutcliffe	c Dawood b Bresnan	93
MB Loye	lbw b Bresnan	11
SG Law	c Dawood b Kruis	0
A Symonds	c Lumb b Bresnan	146
MJ North	c White b Kruis	2
DG Cork	c Wood b Kruis	52
G Chapple	c McGrath b Kruis	0
*WK Hegg	c Jaques b Dawson	68
JM Anderson	c Dawood b Bresnan	12
G Keedy	not out	0
Extras	b 2, lb 9, nb 12	23
	(157.1 overs)	**537**

Bowling
Silverwood 13-1-42-0. Kruis 34.9-1-102-5. Dawson 41.1-5-151-1. Bresnan 41-11-111-4. McGrath 19-3-63-0. Lumb 4-0-29-0. White 2-0-9-0. Jaques 3-0-19-0.
Fall of Wickets: 1-223, 2-243, 3-243, 4-244, 5-250, 6-366, 7-371, 8-508, 9-537

Match drawn – Lancashire (11 pts), Yorkshire (11 pts)

Left: Ben Smith is pictured during his fine 172 against Somerset at Worcester.

wicketkeeper-batsman by staying 163 balls for an unbeaten second innings 44. In the Somerset first innings recovery from 57 for 5, he had also made 74.

The second Roses Match of the summer, starting on the day after the pulsating Old Trafford Test had finished, attracted a 3,000 crowd on that opening morning. Unfortunately for the home supporters, it was Yorkshire who won the first-day honours, reaching 324 for 6 by the close and then going on to 417 with Craig White converting his overnight 71 into 110 not out. Mark Chilton and Iain Sutcliffe then replied with an opening partnership of 223, before Sutcliffe was out seven runs short of his century, and although Chilton could not add to his overnight 130, Lancashire powered on from 243 for 2 to 537 all out on day three. Andy Symonds' 146 was characteristically forthright, while both Dominic Cork and Warren Hegg entertained the crowd towards the end of the innings. The match, though, was going nowhere – a fact confirmed by the ease with which Yorkshire held out for a draw on the final day. There was a considerable sting in the tail for Yorkshire's players, however, as their successful resistance condemned them to a late-night arrival in Southampton that evening and a farcical level of non-preparation for the following day's Cheltenham & Gloucester Trophy semi-final against Hampshire.

Round 17: 24–28 August 2005

Division One

A fascinating, fluctuating contest at Edgbaston saw Warwickshire dramatically boost fading hopes of retaining their title, and Sussex all but wave goodbye to their chances of adding to their historic 2003 success. Needing what seemed to be an eminently gettable 228 for victory, and with almost the whole of the final day to do it, Sussex slipped from 55 for 2 to a hugely disappointing 126 all out – their lowest score of the season. James Anyon took a career-best 4 for 33 for Warwickshire, whose captain Nick Knight expressed surprise at the eventual comfort of the 101-run winning margin. Yet it was an impressive all-round performance in the field by the champions, with Neil Carter picking up two key wickets and both Makhaya Ntini and Alex Loudon also chipping in with a couple of scalps apiece.

Earlier in the match Ntini had followed up taking a wicket with his first championship delivery for Warwickshire, away against Middlesex at Lord's, by removing Richard Montgomerie with his first championship ball in a home fixture. A magnificent 210 from Jonathan Trott, the 24-year-old South African hoping to qualify for England, included a third six off Mushtaq Ahmed to take him to his double hundred, and enabled Warwickshire to post a sizeable first innings total. Sussex initially stumbled in reply, but then Murray Goodwin joined Mike Yardy in a third-wicket stand of 153, and Goodwin went on to a big hundred of his own as Chris Adams also stayed with him. Eventually, Sussex were just 47 runs in arrears, and soon right back in the game as the home side slid to 54 for 5 in their second innings. A partial recovery allowed them to claw up to 180, but the hostile seam bowling of Naved-ul-Hasan and James Kirtley looked to have made Sussex favourites. It was, sadly for them, just an illusion.

Kent's championship hopes were also hit hard at Canterbury, despite their last day ingenuity and determination in the face of the loss of 130 overs to rain in the first half of the contest. But for the

Future England batsman? Jonathan Trott, a South African hoping to qualify for England by residence, hit 210 against the much-vaunted Sussex attack.

weather, Middlesex would surely have been defeated as they collapsed in their second innings to 77 for 6 and only scrambled away with a draw thanks to a defiant seventh-wicket partnership between Paul Weekes and Peter Trego. Weekes followed up his first innings unbeaten 128 with a 96-ball 51, while Trego, the former Kent all-rounder, blocked out 98 balls in 92 minutes at the crease for his 3 not out. Min Patel had looked the likely match-winner, with four quick wickets, but Trego and Weekes defied him in that tense final hour or so.

Earlier in the day Kent, gamely attempting to wring a win out of their unappetising overnight position, raced from 290 for 2 to 549 for 6 declared in only 45 overs – building a lead of 149 in the process. Darren Stevens followed up the previous day's centuries from David Fulton and Rob Key with 106, featuring two sixes and 12 fours, while Justin Kemp crunched 57 and helped to add 98 in 11 overs. The pressure thus put on Middlesex almost brought Kent a memorable victory, but in the end 52 overs proved too few. Only 36 overs were possible on the opening day, and then 51 on the second, and it wasn't until the third morning that Middlesex's first innings was brought to a close by their declaration once maximum batting bonus points had been secured. Owais Shah was the game's first century-maker, with his cultured 105 including 14 fours and a legside six off Patel, while Trego thrashed 51 from 33 balls with three sixes. Fulton and Key, who scored his fourth championship ton of the season, were just 17 runs short of Kent's first-wicket record when they were finally parted at 283.

Glamorgan's first championship success of an otherwise wretched season was also the third biggest

Round 17: 24–28 August 2005 Division One

WARWICKSHIRE v. SUSSEX – at Edgbaston

WARWICKSHIRE	First Innings		Second Innings	
NV Knight (capt)	c Adams b Wright	69	c Prior b Naved-ul-Hasan	15
IJ Westwood	c Prior b Martin-Jenkins	29	c Hopkinson b Kirtley	8
IJL Trott	b Naved-ul-Hasan	210	c Wright b Naved-ul-Hasan	16
AGR Loudon	b Kirtley	32	b Kirtley	1
MJ Powell	c Hopkinson b Mushtaq Ahmed	3	c Adams b Wright	36
LC Parker	b Kirtley	4	c Adams b Naved-ul-Hasan	1
*T Frost	c Kirtley b Wright	22	lbw b Mushtaq Ahmed	40
DR Brown	c Adams b Kirtley	21	c Prior b Mushtaq Ahmed	34
NM Carter	c Kirtley b Mushtaq Ahmed	39	lbw b Naved-ul-Hasan	2
M Ntini	lbw b Mushtaq Ahmed	18	c Prior b Kirtley	9
JE Anyon	not out	0	not out	0
Extras	b 4, lb 20, w 2, nb 2	28	b 1, lb 6, w 1, nb 10	18
	(136.1 overs)	475	(59.1 overs)	180

Bowling
Kirtley 31-2-99-3. Naved-ul-Hasan 33.1-5-135-1. Martin-Jenkins 22-7-51-1. Wright 16-3-39-2. Mushtaq Ahmed 34-5-127-3.
Naved-ul-Hasan 17-2-55-4. Kirtley 12.1-2-27-3. Wright 9-2-24-1. Martin-Jenkins 9-1-30-0. Mushtaq Ahmed 12-1-37-2.
Fall of Wickets: 1-78, 2-130, 3-198, 4-205, 5-215, 6-273, 7-328, 8-391, 9-423
1-12, 2-36, 3-45, 4-53, 5-54, 6-108, 7-158, 8-161, 9-171

SUSSEX	First Innings		Second Innings	
RR Montgomerie	lbw b Ntini	0	c Frost b Ntini	11
CD Hopkinson	b Brown	4	c Frost b Carter	23
MH Yardy	c Frost b Anyon	75	c Trott b Ntini	9
MW Goodwin	c Frost b Anyon	150	c Frost b Carter	16
CJ Adams (capt)	c & b Brown	66	lbw b Anyon	8
*MJ Prior	c Frost b Brown	13	c & b Anyon	7
RSC Martin-Jenkins	c Frost b Ntini	43	not out	27
Naved-ul-Hasan	c Brown b Ntini	34	c Trott b Anyon	2
LJ Wright	c Frost b Carter	8	c Frost b Loudon	12
Mushtaq Ahmed	b Carter	5	c Brown b Loudon	0
RJ Kirtley	not out	10	c Knight b Anyon	6
Extras	b 2, lb 6, nb 12	20	b 4, lb 1	5
	(101.4 overs)	428	(46 overs)	126

Bowling
Ntini 24-2-115-3. Brown 22-2-89-3. Carter 26.4-4-95-2. Trott 11-0-57-0. Anyon 14-3-45-2. Loudon 4-0-19-0.
Ntini 12-3-45-2. Brown 9-4-19-0. Carter 7-2-13-2. Anyon 14-2-33-4. Loudon 4-0-11-2.
Fall of Wickets: 1-0, 2-4, 3-157, 4-294, 5-324, 6-330, 7-388, 8-405, 9-414
1-18, 2-32, 3-55, 4-68, 5-68, 6-79, 7-85, 8-106, 9-108

Warwickshire won by 101 runs – Warwickshire (22 pts), Sussex (8 pts)

KENT v. MIDDLESEX – at Canterbury

MIDDLESEX	First Innings		Second Innings	
ET Smith	b Khan	40	b Khan	2
BL Hutton (capt)	b Khan	10	lbw b Patel	5
OA Shah	c O'Brien b Patel	105	b Patel	13
EC Joyce	c Key b Khan	12	st O'Brien b Patel	27
JWM Dalrymple	lbw b Hall	4	c Stevens b Patel	0
PN Weekes	not out	128	lbw b van Jaarsveld	51
*DC Nash	lbw b Khan	12	c van Jaarsveld b Hall	0
PD Trego	c Fulton b Patel	51	not out	3
A Richardson	c Kemp b Patel	5		
SR Clark	not out	4	(9) not out	0
M Hayward				
Extras	b 3, lb 7, w 1, nb 18	29	b 4, lb 7, nb 2	13
	(8 wkts dec 109 overs)	400	(7 wkts 51.4 overs)	114

Bowling
Khan 20-6-83-4. Cook 18-4-60-0. Hall 22-3-98-1. Kemp 12-1-32-0. Patel 27-6-90-3. Stevens 10-0-27-0.
Khan 6-0-27-1. Cook 6-1-13-0. Patel 22.4-8-34-4. Stevens 3-2-1-0. Hall 8-2-21-1. van Jaarsveld 6-3-7-1.
Fall of Wickets: 1-31, 2-92, 3-120, 4-136, 5-274, 6-314, 7-385, 8-391
1-6, 2-14, 3-51, 4-55, 5-76, 6-77, 7-114

KENT	First Innings	
DP Fulton (capt)	c Joyce b Clark	110
RWT Key	run out	142
M van Jaarsveld	b Richardson	50
MJ Walker	c Hutton b Clark	12
DI Stevens	b Hayward	106
JM Kemp	c Smith b Clark	57
AJ Hall	not out	27
*NJO'Brien	not out	1
MM Patel		
SJ Cook		
A Khan		
Extras	b 14, lb 11, nb 14, p 5	44
	(6 wkts dec 117 overs)	549

Bowling
Clark 26-5-79-3. Richardson 27-4-95-1. Trego 15-1-82-0. Hayward 20-0-117-1. Dalrymple 22-0-115-0. Weekes 5-1-15-0. Hutton 2-0-16-0.
Fall of Wickets: 1-283, 2-290, 3-306, 4-408, 5-506, 6-540

Match drawn – Kent (11 pts), Middlesex (11 pts)

GLOUCESTERSHIRE v. GLAMORGAN – at Bristol

GLAMORGAN	First Innings		Second Innings	
*MA Wallace	c Gidman b Sillence	49	(2) b Rudge	0
DD Cherry	c Bandara b Lewis	166	(1) c Sarwan b Bandara	40
DL Hemp	c Kadeer Ali b Sillence	23	b Bandara	45
J Hughes	lbw b Bandara	21	b Sarwan	21
MJ Powell	c Hardinges b Bandara	8	c Adshead b Sarwan	26
RE Watkins	c Sarwan b Hardinges	1	lbw b Bandara	27
AG Wharf	c Sarwan b Bandara	40	(8) st Adshead b Kadeer Ali	28
RDB Croft (capt)	c Spearman b Hardinges	23	(9) not out	21
DS Harrison	c Rudge b Hardinges	8	(10) run out	15
DA Cosker	run out	23	c & b Bandara	52
HT Waters	not out	0	b Lewis	0
Extras	b 3, lb 8, w 1, nb 8	20	b 8, lb 7	15
	(114.2 overs)	382	(95 overs)	290

Bowling
Lewis 30.2-7-77-1. Rudge 13-1-68-0. Sillence 17-2-90-2. Hardinges 22-6-67-3. Kadeer Ali 4-1-8-0. Bandara 27-9-56-3. Sarwan 1-0-5-0.
Lewis 13-3-39-1. Rudge 6-0-36-1. Sillence 13-1-54-0. Hardinges 3-0-19-0. Bandara 37-9-85-4. Sarwan 18-5-38-2. Kadeer Ali 2-0-4-1.
Fall of Wickets: 1-72, 2-114, 3-163, 4-179, 5-184, 6-267, 7-317, 8-325, 9-382
1-0, 2-76, 3-91, 4-119, 5-148, 6-214, 7-231, 8-247, 9-290

GLOS	First Innings		Second Innings	
CM Spearman	c Wallace b Harrison	9	c Powell b Waters	39
Kadeer Ali	c Powell b Wharf	11	lbw b Wharf	2
RR Sarwan	c Powell b Harrison	0	b Waters	54
MGN Windows	c Wharf b Harrison	8	lbw b Cosker	6
APR Gidman (capt)	c Powell b Wharf	2	c Hughes b Wharf	56
*SJ Adshead	c & b Wharf	36	c Hughes b Croft	14
MA Hardinges	b Harrison	0	lbw b Wharf	4
CM Bandara	c Hemp b Wharf	14	c Hughes b Wharf	6
RJ Sillence	c Cherry b Wharf	12	b Wharf	0
J Lewis	not out	36	not out	9
WD Rudge	b Wharf	0	c Wallace b Harrison	13
Extras	lb 3, nb 2	5	b 4, lb 9, w 1	14
	(34 overs)	133	(68.3 overs)	217

Bowling
Harrison 16-2-59-4. Wharf 17-4-59-6. Watkins 1-0-12-0.
Harrison 10.1-2-24-1. Wharf 16-2-62-5. Waters 13-3-45-2. Croft 4.2-2-11-1. Watkins 7-0-38-0. Cosker 18-10-24-1.
Fall of Wickets: 1-20, 2-20, 3-30, 4-34, 5-36, 6-37, 7-54, 8-66, 9-133
1-9, 2-93, 3-106, 4-114, 5-172, 6-185, 7-191, 8-191, 9-196

Glamorgan won by 322 runs – Gloucestershire (3 pts), Glamorgan (21 pts)

SURREY v. HAMPSHIRE – at The Oval

SURREY	First Innings		Second Innings	
SA Newman	b Mascarenhas	71	c Pothas b Ervine	7
RS Clinton	c Lamb b Bichel	0	c Watson b Lamb	51
MR Ramprakash	lbw b Bruce	6	c Crawley b Udal	37
MA Butcher (capt)	c Pothas b Bruce	75	c sub b Udal	45
*JN Batty	run out	124	c Brown b Udal	33
AD Brown	c Ervine b Bruce	8	c Mascarenhas b Udal	42
Azhar Mahmood	c Lamb b Ervine	49	c Pothas b Bruce	0
TJ Murtagh	c Watson b Udal	24	not out	44
Saqlain Mushtaq	not out	4	c Pothas b Udal	2
ND Doshi	c Ervine b Udal	0	run out	26
M Akram	lbw b Udal	0	c Udal b Crawley	0
Extras	b 4, lb 8, w 1, nb 4	17	b 6, lb 4, w 3, nb 2	15
	(92 overs)	378	(93.5 overs)	302

Bowling
Bichel 13-2-49-1. Bruce 14-1-82-3. Mascarenhas 14-1-55-1. Watson 15-2-52-0. Udal 19-4-65-3. Ervine 17-3-63-1.
Bruce 14-3-50-1. Ervine 12-2-52-1. Mascarenhas 6-1-22-0. Watson 10-3-29-0. Udal 30-9-65-5. Lamb 19-4-67-1. Crawley 2.5-0-7-1.
Fall of Wickets: 1-1, 2-24, 3-95, 4-207, 5-215, 6-327, 7-360, 8-378, 9-378
1-7, 2-100, 3-100, 4-174, 5-188, 6-189, 7-238, 8-250, 9-301

HAMPSHIRE	First Innings	
MJ Brown	c Batty b Akram	0
SM Ervine	c Batty b Akram	2
JP Crawley	lbw b Saqlain Mushtaq	42
SR Watson	c Saqlain Mushtaq b Doshi	88
JJ McLean	lbw b Akram	32
*N Pothas	not out	100
GA Lamb	c Clinton b Doshi	20
AD Mascarenhas	not out	49
AJ Bichel		
SD Udal (capt)		
JTA Bruce		
Extras	lb 4, nb 24	28
	(6 wkts dec 107.3 overs)	361

Bowling
Akram 22-5-80-3. Azhar Mahmood 17-3-69-0. Saqlain Mushtaq 28-7-59-1. Murtagh 16-4-44-0. Doshi 24.3-3-105-2.
Fall of Wickets: 1-0, 2-5, 3-112, 4-169, 5-206, 6-232

Match drawn – Surrey (10 pts), Hampshire (11 pts)

win – in terms of runs – in their history. The margin in the end over fellow strugglers Gloucestershire was 322 runs, after Robert Croft decided against enforcing the follow-on. Alex Wharf, with 6 for 59, had teamed up with David Harrison to destroy the Gloucestershire first innings for 133, in reply to a Glamorgan total of 382 which owed almost everything to opener Dan Cherry's dedicated 166, but Croft opted to bat again. Cherry and David Hemp added 76 for the second wicket, and Dean Cosker hit a late-order 50 as Glamorgan ground their way mercilessly to 290. By the close of the third day, Gloucestershire were left looking anxiously at the skies on 184 for 5, but there was no help from the weather and when Alex Gidman soon fell for 56 – after adding just two runs to his overnight score – the end came swiftly. The rampant Wharf, hitting the pitch hard throughout the match, picked up another 5 for 62 to earn himself memorable career-best match figures of 11 for 121.

Rain prevented any play at all on the first day of Surrey's meeting with Hampshire at The Oval and, thereafter, the draw always looked the likeliest outcome. So it proved with Surrey initially totalling 378, Hampshire replying strongly, and then the home side deciding merely to bat out the final day. Scott Newman's first innings 71 was made out of 95, with his 50 taking just 40 balls, while Jon Batty hit a fine 124 and joined Mark Butcher in a fourth-wicket alliance of 112. Butcher scored a promising 75 and 45 in what were his second and third championship innings of the summer but, in between, Shane Watson and Nic Pothas ensured that Hampshire more than held their own.

Division Two

Essex captain Ronnie Irani's anxiety to force a victory in the weather-affected match against Somerset at Colchester – in order to increase their chances of promotion – ultimately cost his side defeat. Irani wanted to arrange a Somerset last day chase of around 340, on a still slow and blameless pitch, but the visitors (themselves without any promotion pretensions) insisted on an easier challenge. The result

was Irani casting caution to the winds, and Somerset coasting to a five-wicket win as James Hildreth hit a career-best 125 not out and Ian Blackwell weighed in with a belligerent 57 which featured three sixes. Somerset were 147 for 4 when the pair came together, but 109 runs later the match had been won and lost. Hildreth struck a six and 16 fours, from 186 balls, and there were all but 30 overs to spare when the game ended 20 minutes after tea. Irani had earlier passed 1,000 runs for the season during an aggressive 86 that included four sixes, adding 157 in 47 overs for the sixth wicket of Essex's first innings with James Foster, who himself went on to reach 107 not out.

Just three overs had been bowled on day one, which was time enough for Alastair Cook to fall to 18-year-old seamer Ryan Woodman, but Will Jefferson's sparkling 93 matched the bright morning sunshine of the second day. A massive downpour at tea, however, left the Castle Park outfield almost submerged by a flash flood, and Irani's response – after Essex had reached maximum batting points on the third day – was to forfeit his side's second

Ronnie Irani was a popular man in Somerset when he forfeited Essex's second innings at Colchester.

innings following Somerset's declaration on their overnight score of 112 for 2.

The pitch used at Blackpool had been re-laid at a cost of £9,000, but it represented money well spent for Lancashire who crushed Worcestershire by an innings and 73 runs to step up their promotion push. Mal Loye and Stuart Law set up a mammoth 562 for 8 by adding 249 for the third wicket on day one, and Loye's anchor role of 187 from 318 balls was followed by a thumping 82 off just 67 balls by Glen Chapple that included a six and 14 fours. Law's first day 143, meanwhile, had occupied only 189 balls, and Worcestershire's early order did not seem to be in the mood for a lengthy scrap when, finally, it was their turn to bat. West Indies batsman Chris Gayle, on championship debut, sped to 43 from 25 balls before being yorked by Dominic Cork, who also had Graeme Hick lbw for a fourth successive championship duck. Ben Smith did show some determination on day three, however, reaching 133 and receiving excellent support from Vikram Solanki. Cork and James Anderson shared eight Worcestershire first innings wickets, though, and then Chapple assumed the central bowling role, with 5 for 32, as the visitors subsided to 113 all out second time around. Just ten balls were required on the final day to wrap up an innings that had crumbled to 112 for 9 the previous evening.

Both Yorkshire and Durham were ultimately happy with a high-scoring draw in another match badly affected by the weather at Scarborough. A 3,000 crowd suddenly materialised on the first evening, to watch Durham cruise to 140 for 1 from 40 overs as lovely sunshine banished the memory of a wet start, but more interruptions on every other day never allowed the match to progress beyond a pursuit of batting bonus points. Mike Hussey, Dale Benkenstein and Phil Jaques all added to their prolific records in

Round 17: 24–28 August 2005 Division Two

ESSEX v. SOMERSET – at Colchester

ESSEX	First Innings		Second Innings
WI Jefferson	b Blackwell	93	forfeited
AN Cook	lbw b Woodman	0	
GW Flower	c Gazzard b Langeveldt	5	
RS Bopara	b Blackwell	42	
A Flower	lbw b Munday	14	
RC Irani (capt)	run out	86	
*JS Foster	not out	107	
JD Middlebrook	not out	42	
GR Napier			
Danish Kaneria			
A Nel			
Extras	b 1, lb 2, nb 8	11	
	(6 wkts dec 126.1 overs)	400	

Bowling
Langeveldt 33-12-71-1. Woodman 24-8-78-1. Parsons 16.1-4-56-0. Blackwell 38-10-105-2. Munday 14-0-77-1. Hildreth 1-0-10-0.
Fall of Wickets: 1-4, 2-33, 3-124, 4-156, 5-158, 6-315

SOMERSET	First Innings		Second Innings	
MJ Wood	b Nel	0	lbw b Nel	0
JD Francis	not out	31	c Nel b Danish Kaneria	51
AV Suppiah	lbw b Nel	0	lbw b Bopara	29
JC Hildreth	not out	76	not out	125
WJ Durston			c Foster b Nel	0
ID Blackwell (capt)			c Cook b Flower GW	59
KA Parsons			not out	12
*CM Gazzard				
CK Langeveldt				
RJ Woodman				
MK Munday				
Extras	lb 1, nb 4	5	b 5, lb 5, w 2, nb 4	16
	(2 wkts dec 35 overs)	112	(5 wkts 66.1 overs)	292

Bowling
Nel 6-2-12-2. Napier 6-3-13-0. Danish Kaneria 14-2-46-0. Bopara 4-0-20-0. Middlebrook 5-0-20-0.
Nel 17-1-76-2. Napier 6-1-21-0. Bopara 10-0-40-1. Danish Kaneria 24-4-80-1. Middlebrook 7.1-0-39-0. Flower GW 2-0-26-1.
Fall of Wickets: 1-0, 2-0
1-0, 2-49, 3-147, 4-147, 5-256

Somerset won by 5 wickets – Essex (5 pts), Somerset (16 pts)

LANCASHIRE v. WORCESTERSHIRE – at Blackpool

LANCASHIRE	First Innings	
MJ Chilton (capt)	c Moore b Mason	0
IJ Sutcliffe	c Davies b Price	12
MB Loye	c Hick b Malik	187
SG Law	c Solanki b Malik	143
A Symonds	b Price	1
MJ North	c Kabir Ali b Mason	60
DG Cork	b Kabir Ali	14
G Chapple	c Mason b Price	82
*WK Hegg	not out	8
SJ Marshall	not out	26
JM Anderson		
Extras	b 4, lb 5, nb 20	29
	(8 wkts dec 135 overs)	562

Bowling
Mason 24-3-101-2. Kabir Ali 24-3-107-1. Malik 24-0-136-2. Price 47-4-167-3. Gayle 14-2-30-0. Solanki 1-0-4-0. Moore 1-0-8-0.
Fall of Wickets: 1-0, 2-63, 3-312, 4-319, 5-423, 6-424, 7-515, 8-527

WORCS	First Innings		Second Innings	
SC Moore	b Anderson	40	c Cork b Anderson	0
CH Gayle	b Cork	43	c Law b Cork	8
GA Hick	lbw b Cork	0	c Hegg b Chapple	24
BF Smith	lbw b Anderson	133	b Chapple	8
VS Solanki (capt)	c Hegg b Cork	65	lbw b Chapple	7
*SM Davies	c Anderson b Symonds	35	c Hegg b Chapple	0
SD Peters	c Hegg b Symonds	6	b Symonds	6
Kabir Ali	c Law b Anderson	11	c Anderson b Chapple	14
RW Price	not out	1	lbw b Anderson	14
MS Mason	c Sutcliffe b Anderson	4	b Cork	11
MN Malik	lbw b Cork	2	not out	1
Extras	b 9, lb 13, nb 14	36	b 2, lb 10, nb 8	20
	(98.3 overs)	376	(40.4 overs)	113

Bowling
Cork 22.3-4-103-4. Anderson 19-3-61-4. Chapple 15-3-56-0. Marshall 18-2-63-0. Symonds 13-0-32-2. North 11-2-39-0.
Cork 7-2-20-2. Anderson 13-3-33-2. Chapple 13.4-4-32-5. Symonds 7-2-16-1.
Fall of Wickets: 1-59, 2-67, 3-106, 4-250, 5-330, 6-344, 7-365, 8-368, 9-372
1-3, 2-21, 3-49, 4-58, 5-58, 6-61, 7-77, 8-97, 9-110

Lancashire won by an innings and 73 runs – Lancashire (22 pts), Worcestershire (6 pts)

YORKSHIRE v. DURHAM – at Scarborough

DURHAM	First Innings	
MEK Hussey (capt)	lbw b Bresnan	92
GM Scott	c Guy b Kruis	14
PD Collingwood	c McGrath b Kruis	33
GJ Muchall	c Blain b Bresnan	64
DM Benkenstein	c Wood b Kruis	126
GR Breese	c Guy b Kruis	13
*P Mustard	c McGrath b Harvey	21
LE Plunkett	c Guy b Bresnan	0
CD Thorp	c Sayers b Kruis	10
N Killeen	not out	3
BA Williams	c McGrath b Bresnan	6
Extras	b 1, lb 9, w 2, nb 20	32
	(115.5 overs)	414

Bowling
Kruis 36-9-106-5. Blain 19-0-97-0. Bresnan 30.5-6-101-4. Harvey 17-5-54-1. McGrath 10-5-28-0. Dawson 3-1-18-0.
Fall of Wickets: 1-56, 2-140, 3-152, 4-319, 5-360, 6-388, 7-389, 8-402, 9-405

YORKSHIRE	First Innings	
MJ Wood	lbw b Collingwood	47
JJ Sayers	c Hussey b Collingwood	31
A McGrath	lbw b Plunkett	30
PA Jaques	c Thorp b Plunkett	172
IJ Harvey	c Benkenstein b Hussey	24
C White (capt)	c Thorp b Collingwood	29
TT Bresnan	not out	58
RKJ Dawson	not out	63
GJ Kruis		
*SM Guy		
JAR Blain		
Extras	b 1, lb 11, w 5, nb 4	21
	(6 wkts 129 overs)	475

Bowling
Williams 26-8-80-0. Plunkett 25-4-100-2. Killeen 18-2-61-0. Thorp 12-2-37-0. Collingwood 14-1-56-3. Breese 22-2-82-0. Hussey 7-0-36-1. Muchall 5-0-11-0.
Fall of Wickets: 1-73, 2-78, 3-148, 4-217, 5-295, 6-365

Match drawn – Yorkshire (12 pts), Durham (11 pts)

LEICESTERSHIRE v. NORTHAMPTONSHIRE – at Leicester

LEICESTERSHIRE	First Innings	
DDJ Robinson	c & b Baker	139
JK Maunders	b Wright	19
TJ New	c Shafayat b Wright	41
HD Ackerman (capt)	b Wright	6
A Habib	c Wessels b Phillips	32
DL Maddy	c Wessels b Wright	34
*PA Nixon	not out	36
OD Gibson	not out	74
DD Masters		
CW Henderson		
SCL Broad		
Extras	b 8, lb 9, w 1, nb 6	24
	(6 wkts dec 122.4 overs)	405

Bowling
Wright 32-10-87-4. Louw 21-4-81-0. Phillips 25.4-9-76-1. Baker 13-2-55-1. Panesar 26-3-80-0. Shafayat 5-0-9-0.
Fall of Wickets: 1-42, 2-161, 3-185, 4-234, 5-269, 6-292

NORTHANTS	First Innings	
ML Love	st Nixon b Henderson	67
BM Shafayat	lbw b Maunders	56
RA White	c Habib b Broad	26
U Afzaal	lbw b Maunders	6
DJG Sales (capt)	b Henderson	20
*MH Wessels	c Nixon b Masters	17
DG Wright	b Gibson	18
BJ Phillips	c Ackerman b Henderson	24
J Louw	c Maddy b Henderson	18
MS Panesar	not out	1
TM Baker	c Maddy b Henderson	0
Extras	b 5, lb 2, w 1	8
	(80.4 overs)	261

Bowling
Gibson 18-7-41-1. Masters 15-3-59-1. Broad 16-4-58-1. Maddy 2-0-11-0. Henderson 19.4-4-63-5. Maunders 10-5-22-2.
Fall of Wickets: 1-99, 2-142, 3-157, 4-158, 5-183, 6-213, 7-229, 8-250, 9-261

Match drawn – Leicestershire (12 pts), Northamptonshire (8 pts)

English domestic cricket, while the home-grown Tim Bresnan gave further notice of his all-round talents.

If poor weather afflicted Scarborough, then proceedings at Grace Road in Leicester were almost obliterated by rainstorms, thunder and – at one stage – hail. No play at all was possible on day one, and just 14.3 overs on the second day. By then, both Leicestershire and Northamptonshire had decided merely to concentrate on the garnering of bonus points – an activity from which Leicestershire emerged the stronger. This was mainly due to the batting of Darren Robinson and Ottis Gibson, who struck three sixes, and the slow left-arm spin of Claude Henderson, who gained his best figures of the season and passed 500 first-class career wickets as Northants were bowled out on the final afternoon.

Round 18: 30 August–2 September 2005

Division One

Nottinghamshire regained top spot by beating Glamorgan by eight wickets at Cardiff. Hampshire, who had briefly headed the first division when they completed their win against Warwickshire the previous day, lay in second place, 3.5 points behind Notts – although they had played a game more. In third position were Kent, who had played the same

Darren Bicknell went past 1,000 runs for the ninth season in his career during the match against Glamorgan.

Round 18: 30 August–2 September 2005 Division One

GLAMORGAN v. NOTTINGHAMSHIRE – at Cardiff

GLAMORGAN	First Innings		Second Innings	
*MA Wallace	c Gallian b Sidebottom	7	(6) c Read b Ealham	14
DD Cherry	c Read b Smith	10	(1) lbw b Harris	4
DL Hemp	c Hussey b Harris	21	c Younis Khan b Sidebottom	14
J Hughes	c Read b Sidebottom	3	b Smith	10
MJ Powell	c Younis Khan b Smith	62	lbw b Harris	96
RE Watkins	c Hussey b Sidebottom	1	(2) lbw b Sidebottom	12
AG Wharf	lbw b Ealham	22	c Hussey b Harris	113
RDB Croft (capt)	lbw b Ealham	5	lbw b Ealham	0
DA Cosker	not out	12	lbw b Ealham	10
DS Harrison	b Smith	0	b Ealham	13
HT Waters	lbw b Smith	0	not out	0
Extras	b 3, lb 3, nb 2	8	b 2, lb 15, nb 4	21
	(48 overs)	151	(90.4 overs)	307

Bowling
Sidebottom 10-1-31-3. Harris 10-3-57-1. Smith 17-10-28-4. Ealham 11-3-29-2.
Sidebottom 16-4-36-2. Harris 19.4-2-70-3. Swann 26-4-75-0. Younis Khan 6-0-27-0. Smith 6-1-32-1. Ealham 17-3-50-4.
Fall of Wickets: 1-16, 2-41, 3-43, 4-66, 5-76, 6-113, 7-135, 8-147, 9-147
1-13, 2-25, 3-34, 4-59, 5-94, 6-212, 7-215, 8-258, 9-278

NOTTS	First Innings		Second Innings	
DJ Bicknell	c Harrison b Cosker	123	c Hughes b Cosker	16
JER Gallian (capt)	c Wallace b Harrison	0	c Hughes b Croft	70
RJ Warren	c Powell b Watkins	51	not out	60
Younis Khan	c Wallace b Croft	53	not out	20
DJ Hussey	b Cosker	1		
*CMW Read	lbw b Croft	9		
MA Ealham	b Cosker	1		
GP Swann	c Cosker b Croft	0		
RJ Sidebottom	run out	12		
GJ Smith	b Cosker	17		
AJ Harris	not out	1		
Extras	b 7, lb 1, w 2, p 5	15	b 6, lb 2, w 1, nb 4	13
	(106.5 overs)	283	(2 wkts 53.1 overs)	179

Bowling
Harrison 14-2-51-1. Wharf 18-4-39-0. Waters 13-3-36-0. Croft 27-5-57-3. Cosker 22.5-5-57-4. Watkins 12-2-30-1.
Harrison 3-0-19-0. Wharf 5-0-23-0. Cosker 22-5-48-1. Croft 22.1-3-77-1. Cherry 1-0-4-0.
Fall of Wickets: 1-7, 2-124, 3-231, 4-233, 5-243, 6-251, 7-251, 8-251, 9-278
1-51, 2-145

*Nottinghamshire won by 8 wickets –
Glamorgan (3 pts), Nottinghamshire (19 pts)*

HAMPSHIRE v. WARWICKSHIRE – at The Rose Bowl

HAMPSHIRE	First Innings	
JHK Adams	c Trott b Brown	65
SM Ervine	c Trott b Brown	60
JP Crawley	c Loudon b Trott	60
SR Watson	not out	203
JJ McLean	c Frost b Trott	4
*N Pothas	lbw b Ntini	30
GA Lamb	c Brown b Ntini	2
AD Mascarenhas	not out	102
AJ Bichel		
SD Udal (capt)		
CT Tremlett		
Extras	b 4, lb 20, nb 26	50
	(6 wkts dec 151 overs)	576

Bowling
Ntini 35-9-98-2. Brown 30-7-111-2. Anyon 20-4-103-0. Tahir 17-1-71-0.
Loudon 28-3-93-0. Trott 17-2-65-2. Troughton 4-1-11-0.
Fall of Wickets: 1-104, 2-178, 3-279, 4-285, 5-326, 6-342

WARWICKSHIRE	First Innings		Second Innings	
NV Knight (capt)	lbw b Mascarenhas	116	b Ervine	24
IJ Westwood	c Adams b Tremlett	0	c Ervine b Udal	48
IJL Trott	lbw b Bichel	1	lbw b Watson	27
JO Troughton	c Pothas b Mascarenhas	11	c McLean b Udal	76
AGR Loudon	c Lamb b Tremlett	10	c Ervine b Bichel	16
MJ Powell	lbw b Bichel	13	c Lamb b Udal	1
*T Frost	c McLean b Mascarenhas	19	c Pothas b Tremlett	0
DR Brown	c Pothas b Watson	24	c Watson b Udal	2
N Tahir	c Adams b Udal	4	c Watson b Udal	14
M Ntini	not out	27	b Udal	4
JE Anyon	b Ervine	10	not out	0
Extras	b 1, lb 6, nb 16	23	b 8, lb 1, w 1, nb 10	20
	(72.2 overs)	258	(66 overs)	232

Bowling
Bichel 14-6-39-2. Tremlett 18-1-93-2. Mascarenhas 16-5-52-3. Udal 8-1-23-1. Ervine 7.2-3-17-1. Watson 9-2-27-1.
Bichel 17-3-72-1. Tremlett 7-0-49-1. Mascarenhas 8-3-12-0. Ervine 6-0-24-1. Udal 22-8-44-6. Watson 6-1-22-1.
Fall of Wickets: 1-20, 2-21, 3-64, 4-94, 5-155, 6-185, 7-216, 8-216, 9-235
1-50, 2-110, 3-110, 4-137, 5-154, 6-167, 7-182, 8-221, 9-232

*Hampshire won by an innings and 86 runs –
Hampshire (22 pts), Warwickshire (4 pts)*

GLOUCESTERSHIRE v. MIDDLESEX – at Bristol

GLOS	First Innings		Second Innings	
CM Spearman	lbw b Richardson	0	b Clark	10
Kadeer Ali	lbw b Dalrymple	46	c Shah b Peploe	61
RR Sarwan	b Clark	4	lbw b Dalrymple	26
MGN Windows	c Richardson b Dalrymple	28	lbw b Weekes	28
APR Gidman (capt)	c Scott b Weekes	57	lbw b Weekes	25
*SJ Adshead	b Richardson	59	c Joyce b Dalrymple	36
MA Hardinges	st Scott b Dalrymple	6	not out	58
CM Bandara	lbw b Dalrymple	70	c Hutton b Clark	29
MCJ Ball	c Shah b Richardson	1	c Dalrymple b Clark	1
J Lewis	not out	30	b Betts	2
WD Rudge	c Hutton b Richardson	0	lbw b Betts	0
Extras	b 1, lb 13, nb 18	32	b 1, lb 4, nb 6	11
	(92.2 overs)	333	(99.5 overs)	287

Bowling
Clark 13-3-38-1. Richardson 18.2-2-77-4. Betts 8-1-39-0. Dalrymple 19-2-84-4. Peploe 24-4-61-0. Weekes 10-0-20-1.
Richardson 15-4-29-0. Clark 14-1-57-3. Betts 10.5-1-33-2. Dalrymple 20-4-58-2. Peploe 25-5-73-1. Weekes 14-3-29-2. Shah 1-0-3-0.
Fall of Wickets: 1-13, 2-28, 3-95, 4-96, 5-184, 6-209, 7-270, 8-278, 9-323
1-13, 2-68, 3-126, 4-153, 5-157, 6-225, 7-276, 8-282, 9-287

MIDDLESEX	First Innings		Second Innings	
ET Smith	c Adshead b Rudge	70	c Adshead b Lewis	8
BL Hutton (capt)	c Adshead b Rudge	11	lbw b Ball	43
OA Shah	lbw b Rudge	26	lbw b Bandara	25
EC Joyce	run out	73	lbw b Ball	90
JWM Dalrymple	c Gidman b Bandara	14	not out	22
PN Weekes	lbw b Ball	5	not out	3
*BJM Scott	c Adshead b Bandara	2		
CT Peploe	lbw b Bandara	24		
MM Betts	lbw b Bandara	34		
A Richardson	lbw b Bandara	0		
SR Clark	not out	17		
Extras	b 7, lb 2, w 1, nb 11	21	b 7, lb 3, nb 2	12
	(99.1 overs)	297	(4 wkts 72 overs)	203

Bowling
Lewis 22-6-61-0. Rudge 18-6-75-3. Bandara 26.1-8-71-5. Hardinges 8-3-31-0. Kadeer Ali 6-1-19-0. Ball 19-7-31-1.
Lewis 10-5-20-1. Rudge 9-1-32-0. Bandara 22-3-65-1. Ball 26-6-56-2. Sarwan 5-0-20-0.
Fall of Wickets: 1-29, 2-71, 3-154, 4-178, 5-185, 6-200, 7-246, 8-248, 9-248
1-8, 2-49, 3-153, 4-196

Match drawn – Gloucestershire (10 pts), Middlesex (9 pts)

number of games as Notts and were 8.5 points adrift of the leaders. It was proving to be an exciting finish to the championship – especially as Notts' last two matches were both away from home – against Kent and Hampshire.

Notts took control of their fixture at Cardiff on the very first morning. Michael Powell's 62, with 11 fours, was the only worthwhile resistance as the Welsh county folded to 151 all out. Greg Smith and Ryan Sidebottom were the chief destroyers, sharing seven wickets, and by the close half-centuries from Darren Bicknell and Russell Warren had already taken Notts to 151 for 2 in reply. Bicknell went to 123 on a rain-reduced second day, and also past 1,000 first-class runs for the season for the ninth time in his career, and although Glamorgan spinners Robert Croft and Dean Cosker pegged Notts back, the visitors still won themselves a 132-run lead.

At 94 for 5 in their second innings, after another lamentable top-order batting display, Glamorgan looked out of the game, but Powell again batted aggressively and well for 96 and found in Alex Wharf an equally determined and forthright partner. They added 118 in 35 overs and, although Powell's dismissal led to the fall of several more Glamorgan wickets, Wharf reached his hundred just before the end of the third day's play. He added just another 13 runs the following morning, before being last man out, and Notts had Jason Gallian and Warren to thank for a relatively stress-free advance to their victory target.

Hampshire's innings and 86-run win over Warwickshire, completed inside three days, was based on Shane Watson's magnificent unbeaten double-hundred and Shaun Udal's enduring off-breaks. The top three all made good runs before Watson, on 91 at the end of the first day, pushed on in the company of Dimitri Mascarenhas. They added an unbroken 234 for the seventh wicket, with the declaration coming after Mascarenhas had reached three figures and Watson 203 not out – an innings which featured a six and 25 fours. Nick Knight fought bravely in Warwickshire's reply, holding it together with 116, but Udal was all but irresistible when the champions followed on. Jim Troughton hit an attractive and defiant 76 but the evergreen Udal ended up with 6 for 44. Both sides, meanwhile, were thankful of the unscheduled day off before they met each other at Lord's in the C&G Trophy final.

A dour, dull struggle at Bristol eventually ended in a draw, with Gloucestershire opting not to declare on the final morning – which they began on 261 for 6. Mark Hardinges, whose unbeaten 58 did much to ensure that Middlesex were left with little option but to bat out time on a truncated last day, accepted an offer of a new three-year Gloucestershire contract. There was not much for anyone else to celebrate, however, although Ed Joyce again batted nicely in both innings to keep up his prolific season's form and Malinga Bandara enjoyed a useful all-round match. Gloucestershire, by the way, had their inevitable relegation mathematically confirmed when Hardinges was stumped at 3.15pm on the opening day.

Division Two

A thrilling contest at the Riverside eventually came down to Derbyshire needing to score five runs from the last ball. They managed just two, and so the match was drawn and Durham's lead at the top of the division was eight points. Full marks, though, for bottom team Derbyshire for pushing them so close – although most neutrals would have said that the visitors should have won. Only a double-century second-innings partnership between Paul Collingwood and Dale Benkenstein had kept Durham in the game on the third day, after

Jason Brown: deadly spin bowling at Wantage Road humbled Lancashire.

Derbyshire's seamers – led by Ian Hunter – had put them in control on day one. Battling innings from Chris Bassano, Jon Moss and Luke Sutton had then won Derbyshire a 96-run first innings lead, only for Collingwood and Benkenstein to turn the match on its head again. Collingwood was out early on the final day, which Durham began 167 runs ahead at 263 for 3, but Benkenstein carried on to 162 not out before declaring to set a target of 280 in 66 overs. At tea Derbyshire were 89 without loss, but had used up 35 overs in building a solid base perhaps too carefully. Even then, however, after Steve Stubbings had accelerated to a brilliant 101, they reached the final three overs requiring just another 18 for victory. Liam Plunkett's fine over meant the equation eventually came down to 11 off the last six balls – and just eight were scored.

Northamptonshire made it four wins in five matches by trouncing Lancashire by 285 runs at Wantage Road. On a pitch that was inspected on the third day by Tony Pigott, one of the ECB's pitch liaison officers, but then reprieved, the Northants spinners Jason Brown and Monty Panesar decimated the Lancashire second innings. The visitors were tumbled out for just 103, although Northants had just declared their own second innings on 400 for 6. Brown's second five-wicket haul of the match – including the prized wicket of Stuart Law with the final ball before lunch – earned him the third ten-wicket match analysis of his career, while Panesar brought off a quite brilliant return catch to get rid of Andy Symonds. Northants captain David Sales was also in excellent form, adding a 68-ball 77 to his 66 of the first day, while Law – with a first innings 111 – was the only Lancashire batsman to master a surface which offered the seamers occasional sharp bounce and, later, turned appreciably for the spinners. Usman Afzaal and Bilal Shafayat had few problems with it on the third day, however, adding 183 for the third Northants second innings wicket. Afzaal went on to a commanding 147.

Leicestershire took the safety-first approach against Worcestershire at New Road, batting far too timidly on the third evening and – in the end, after collecting a further 58 runs in nine overs the following morning – setting their opponents an unlikely 371 in 85 overs. Chris Gayle briefly blazed away, as he had also done in the first innings, but when he was out the Worcestershire second innings became merely an exercise in survival. Ben Smith and Gareth Batty subsequently saw their side to the sanctuary of the draw. The opening day of this match, meanwhile, belonged to John Maunders, who scored 148 in five and three quarter hours of intense concentration as he tried to secure himself a new Leicestershire contract.

Round 18: 30 August–2 September 2005 Division Two

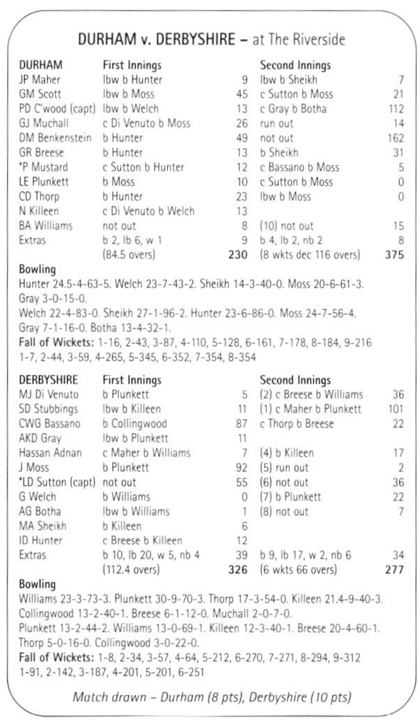

DURHAM v. DERBYSHIRE – at The Riverside

DURHAM	First Innings		Second Innings	
JP Maher	lbw b Hunter	9	lbw b Sheikh	7
GM Scott	lbw b Moss	45	c Sutton b Moss	21
PD C'wood (capt)	lbw b Welch	13	c Gray b Botha	112
GJ Muchall	c Di Venuto b Moss	26	run out	14
DM Benkenstein	b Hunter	49	not out	162
GR Breese	b Hunter	13	b Sheikh	31
*P Mustard	c Sutton b Hunter	12	c Bassano b Moss	5
LE Plunkett	b Moss	10	c Sutton b Moss	0
CD Thorp	b Hunter	23	lbw b Moss	0
N Killeen	c Di Venuto b Welch	13		
BA Williams	not out	8	(10) not out	15
Extras	b 2, lb 6, w 1	9	b 4, lb 2, nb 2	8
	(84.5 overs)	**230**	(8 wkts dec 116 overs)	**375**

Bowling
Hunter 24.5-4-63-5. Welch 23-7-43-2. Sheikh 14-3-40-0. Moss 20-6-61-3. Gray 3-0-15-0.
Welch 22-4-83-0. Sheikh 27-1-96-2. Hunter 23-6-86-0. Moss 24-7-56-4. Gray 7-1-16-0. Botha 13-4-32-1.
Fall of Wickets: 1-16, 2-43, 3-87, 4-110, 5-128, 6-161, 7-178, 8-184, 9-216
1-7, 2-44, 3-59, 4-265, 5-345, 6-352, 7-354, 8-354

DERBYSHIRE	First Innings		Second Innings	
MJ Di Venuto	b Plunkett	5	(2) c Breese b Williams	36
SD Stubbings	lbw b Killeen	11	(1) c Maher b Plunkett	101
CWG Bassano	b Collingwood	87	c Thorp b Breese	22
AKD Gray	lbw b Plunkett	11		
Hassan Adnan	c Maher b Williams	7	(4) b Killeen	17
J Moss	b Plunkett	92	(5) run out	2
*LD Sutton (capt)	not out	55	(6) not out	36
G Welch	b Williams	0	(7) b Plunkett	22
AG Botha	lbw b Williams	1	(8) not out	7
MA Sheikh	b Killeen	6		
ID Hunter	c Breese b Killeen	12		
Extras	b 10, lb 20, w 5, nb 4	39	b 9, lb 17, w 2, nb 6	34
	(112.4 overs)	**326**	(6 wkts 66 overs)	**277**

Bowling
Williams 23-3-73-3. Plunkett 30-9-70-3. Thorp 17-3-54-0. Killeen 21.4-9-40-3. Collingwood 13-2-40-1. Breese 6-1-12-0. Muchall 2-0-7-0.
Plunkett 13-2-44-2. Williams 13-0-69-1. Killeen 12-3-40-1. Breese 20-4-60-1. Thorp 5-0-16-0. Collingwood 3-0-22-0.
Fall of Wickets: 1-8, 2-34, 3-57, 4-64, 5-212, 6-270, 7-271, 8-294, 9-312
1-91, 2-142, 3-187, 4-201, 5-201, 6-251

Match drawn – Durham (8 pts), Derbyshire (10 pts)

NORTHAMPTONSHIRE v. LANCASHIRE – at Northampton

NORTHANTS	First Innings		Second Innings	
ML Love	c Hegg b Cork	44	c Hegg b Anderson	11
BM Shafayat	c Sutcliffe b Symonds	33	c North b Marshall	80
RA White	lbw b Marshall	41	lbw b Anderson	9
U Afzaal	b Chapple	38	c Hegg b Symonds	147
DJG Sales (capt)	c Hegg b Symonds	66	c North b Symonds	77
*MH Wessels	c Hegg b Anderson	18	not out	30
DG Wright	c Hegg b Chapple	5	c Law b Symonds	5
BJ Phillips	not out	18	not out	22
J Louw	lbw b Cork	3		
MS Panesar	c Anderson b Cork	0		
JF Brown	c Chilton b Cork	5		
Extras	b 8, lb 4, nb 6	18	b 5, lb 10, nb 4	19
	(107 overs)	**289**	(6 wkts dec 99 overs)	**400**

Bowling
Cork 17-9-27-4. Anderson 20-4-56-1. Chapple 19-5-45-2. Symonds 24-6-64-2. Marshall 12-2-39-1. North 15-2-46-0.
Cork 10-0-46-0. Anderson 28-2-108-2. Chapple 15-2-58-0. Symonds 23-4-80-3. North 6-0-34-0. Marshall 17-2-59-1.
Fall of Wickets: 1-83, 2-83, 3-166, 4-186, 5-224, 6-250, 7-266, 8-277, 9-277
1-15, 2-33, 3-216, 4-326, 5-345, 6-361

LANCASHIRE	First Innings		Second Innings	
MJ Chilton (capt)	lbw b Wright	0	lbw b Brown	38
IJ Sutcliffe	lbw b Brown	19	c White b Louw	4
MJ North	c Sales b Wright	30	(6) lbw b Brown	9
SG Law	c Afzaal b Brown	111	c Shafayat b Brown	3
A Symonds	c Love b Panesar	37	c & b Panesar	4
DG Cork	b Brown	11	(7) b Panesar	14
G Chapple	c Love b Wright	15	(8) c Love b Brown	0
MB Loye	c Love b Brown	38	(3) c Afzaal b Phillips	8
*WK Hegg	c Love b Wright	15	st Wessels b Panesar	12
SJ Marshall	c Shafayat b Brown	17	b Brown	0
JM Anderson	not out	1	not out	4
Extras	b 4, lb 3	7	b 4, lb 3	7
	(103.3 overs)	**301**	(47 overs)	**103**

Bowling
Wright 19-6-55-4. Phillips 13-6-26-0. Brown 36.3-9-113-5. Louw 2-1-12-0. Panesar 33-6-88-1.
Wright 6-2-21-0. Louw 7-3-21-1. Phillips 2-2-0-1. Brown 16-8-22-5. Panesar 16-3-32-3.
Fall of Wickets: 1-4, 2-36, 3-82, 4-146, 5-161, 6-199, 7-261, 8-265, 9-299
1-24, 2-37, 3-44, 4-55, 5-69, 6-82, 7-82, 8-86, 9-91

*Northamptonshire won by 285 runs –
Northamptonshire (19 pts), Lancashire (6 pts)*

WORCESTERSHIRE v. LEICESTERSHIRE – at Worcester

LEICESTERSHIRE	First Innings		Second Innings	
DDJ Robinson	c Smith b Kabir Ali	16	c Davies b Kabir Ali	11
JK Maunders	b Gayle	148	c Gayle b Kabir Ali	8
TJ New	b Price	31	b Kabir Ali	49
HD Ackerman (capt)	c Gayle b Kabir Ali	12	c Gayle b Price	16
A Habib	c Gayle b Kabir Ali	9	not out	90
DL Maddy	b Price	34	st Davies b Gayle	22
*PA Nixon	c Davies b Price	58	not out	28
DD Masters	c Smith b Gayle	0		
CW Henderson	b Kabir Ali	37		
SCL Broad	c Smith b Mason	31		
CM Willoughby	not out	1		
Extras	b 6, lb 3, w 1, nb 18	28	b 18, lb 1, nb 12	31
	(122.1 overs)	**405**	(5 wkts dec 72 overs)	**255**

Bowling
Shoaib Akhtar 15-4-43-0. Kabir Ali 24-5-95-4. Mason 22-7-88-1. Batty 29-3-91-0. Price 25.1-6-61-3. Gayle 7-2-18-2.
Mason 8-2-22-0. Kabir Ali 12-2-64-3. Shoaib Akhtar 7-0-34-0. Price 22-4-44-1. Batty 14-2-43-0. Gayle 9-0-29-1.
Fall of Wickets: 1-19, 2-113, 3-151, 4-173, 5-227, 6-301, 7-301, 8-346, 9-399
1-18, 2-25, 3-77, 4-126, 5-175

WORCS	First Innings		Second Innings	
SC Moore	c Nixon b Masters	23	c New b Broad	4
CH Gayle	c Nixon b Masters	51	c Robinson b Willoughby	57
GA Hick	c Nixon b Broad	38	b Henderson	19
BF Smith	c Nixon b Willoughby	13	not out	87
VS Solanki (capt)	c Nixon b Willoughby	44	c Masters b Willoughby	1
*SM Davies	b Masters	25	c Maddy b Masters	29
GJ Batty	lbw b Henderson	46	not out	52
Kabir Ali	not out	37		
Shoaib Akhtar	b Henderson	0		
RW Price	lbw b Henderson	4		
MS Mason	b Henderson	0		
Extras	lb 4, w 1, nb 4	9	b 2, lb 5, w 2	9
	(92 overs)	**290**	(5 wkts 75 overs)	**258**

Bowling
Willoughby 20-4-80-2. Masters 17-7-49-3. Broad 16-5-69-1. Henderson 34-8-72-4. Maddy 2-0-11-0. Maunders 3-0-5-0.
Masters 14-3-47-1. Broad 12-2-65-1. Willoughby 16-5-49-2. Henderson 26-5-70-1. Robinson 1-0-2-0. Maunders 3-0-13-0. Maddy 3-1-5-0.
Fall of Wickets: 1-75, 2-84, 3-124, 4-139, 5-183, 6-211, 7-286, 8-286, 9-290
1-5, 2-64, 3-85, 4-87, 5-133

Match drawn – Worcestershire (9 pts), Leicestershire (12 pts)

Round 19: 5–13 September 2005

Division One

Nottinghamshire stole a march on their closest rivals, especially Kent, by completing a crushing two-day victory against a dispirited Gloucestershire side in a match which thus finished even before the other first division games in this round had begun. When rain then affected Kent's match against Middlesex at Lord's – although by then Middlesex were very much in command anyway – Nottinghamshire's mood was even more joyful.

A brutal innings of 157 by David Hussey, with three sixes and 27 fours, set up Notts' win over Gloucestershire in cloudy, humid and therefore swinging conditions at Trent Bridge. At 43 for 3, after being put in, the home side were struggling, but Hussey's response was all-out attack. His withering strokeplay saw the Gloucestershire bowling attack

disintegrate, and with Russell Warren and Graeme Swann also playing useful innings, Notts were able to reach 336 by the end of a shortened opening day.

With overhead conditions much the same on day two, however, the Gloucestershire batsmen were no match for Notts' seamers – especially Mark Ealham. The former Kent all-rounder took nine wickets as Gloucestershire collapsed to 103 and 169 all out. Indeed, before Jon Lewis smashed a 26-ball 50 at the end of the second innings, Gloucestershire had lost 19 wickets for 213 runs in 64 overs of mayhem. Lewis' first 50 runs were made up entirely of boundary hits but Notts were happy enough: they had gone 28.5 points clear of Kent before their nearest rivals had even begun their game at Lord's.

Kent started the first day well, against Middlesex, by winning the toss and seeing Rob Key move to a fluent 94. But then came a slide to 249 for 9, and it was as well that they managed to end the day well too through a superb last-wicket stand of 135 in 27 overs between Justin Kemp and No. 11 Amjad Khan. No mug with the bat, Khan played beautifully and sensibly for his 58 not out, while Kemp continued his fine late-summer form by reaching 102.

Kent's mood, however, darkened on the second day as Ben Hutton and Owais Shah added 282 in 81 overs for the second wicket. It was purgatory for Kent, as Hutton matched the Test century being made across the Thames at The Oval by his best friend, Andrew Strauss, and Shah eased his way to a seventh championship hundred of the season.

Half-centuries from Jamie Dalrymple and Ed Joyce underlined Middlesex's batting mastery on the third day, and when play was halted at 3.30pm by a thunderstorm, Kent knew that this game was up. The championship hopefuls also heard, at around the same time, that the United Cricket Board of South Africa were recalling, ahead of schedule, both Kemp and Andrew Hall for a pre-season training camp. Kent protested that their two South African overseas players were under contract until 25 September, but it was to no avail. All in all, the events of Lord's were a blow to their title ambitions and, on a final day again affected by the

Owais Shah, on his way to a seventh championship hundred of a prolific season.

weather, it was as much as they could do to hold out for the draw. Kemp and Hall, ironically, were the players who steadied Kent from 118 for 5 with a stand of 48.

Sussex moved to within 10 points of the leaders, Notts, by trouncing Glamorgan by nine wickets inside two days at Hove. Chris Adams' side had at this stage played one game more than Notts, however, and Sussex supporters could have been forgiven for wishing that the season could last for another week or so, or that fast bowling all-rounder Naved-ul-Hasan had arrived at the club earlier than the first week of July. Naved teamed up with fellow Pakistani Mushtaq Ahmed to destroy the Glamorgan batting on the second afternoon – after Mushtaq had made a pretty good job of doing so on the previous day, too, in alliance with James Kirtley. David Hemp's 71 was the only real resistance in Glamorgan's first innings, while opener Dan Cherry deserves some plaudits at least for being the last man out in the Welsh county's second-day demise. The rest of the Glamorgan batting, though, was simply blown away by Naved's pace and swing, and Mushtaq's magic.

No play on the first day at Edgbaston, and only 58.1 overs on the second, ultimately condemned Warwickshire's meeting with Surrey to a draw. James Anyon impressed with four wickets as Surrey underachieved in their first innings, and Warwickshire assumed control of proceedings when Nick Knight's 117, and opening stand of 95 with Ian Westwood, was followed by half-centuries of poise from Alex Loudon and Mike Powell. Yet another hundred from Mark Ramprakash, however, and an unbeaten 76 from Jon Batty, earned Surrey the draw on the final day.

Round 19: 5–13 September 2005 Division One

NOTTINGHAMSHIRE v. GLOUCESTERSHIRE – at Trent Bridge

NOTTIS	First Innings	
DJ Bicknell	lbw b Lewis	13
JER Gallian (capt)	run out	0
RJ Warren	lbw b Lewis	60
Younis Khan	lbw b Kirby	12
DJ Hussey	c Adshead b Hardinges	157
*CMW Read	b Lewis	0
MA Ealham	c Gidman b Lewis	14
GP Swann	c Kadeer Ali b Kirby	38
RJ Sidebottom	not out	8
GJ Smith	b Hardinges	9
AJ Harris	c Adshead b Hardinges	0
Extras	lb 7, nb 18	25
	(82.4 overs)	336

Bowling
Lewis 19-2-80-4. Averis 15-0-75-0. Kirby 20-2-71-2. Hardinges 13.4-3-38-3. Bandara 15-3-65-0.
Fall of Wickets: 1-12, 2-16, 3-43, 4-179, 5-179, 6-203, 7-289, 8-322, 9-336

GLOS	First Innings		Second Innings	
CM Spearman	c & b Sidebottom	2	(2) c Read b Ealham	38
Kadeer Ali	not out	55	(1) c Read b Harris	1
RR Sarwan	b Harris	11	b Sidebottom	0
MGN Windows	c Warren b Smith	2	c Read b Sidebottom	8
APR Gidman (capt)	c Gallian b Ealham	0	c Younis Khan b Ealham	20
*SJ Adshead	b Ealham	0	b Ealham	3
MA Hardinges	lbw b Ealham	5	b Swann	10
CM Bandara	lbw b Smith	4	c Smith b Ealham	6
JMM Averis	b Smith	0	c Gallian b Swann	13
J Lewis	c Smith b Ealham	10	c Hussey b Smith	55
SP Kirby	b Ealham	7	not out	13
Extras	b 1, lb 5, w 1	7	lb 2	2
	(35 overs)	103	(36.1 overs)	169

Bowling
Sidebottom 7-3-18-1. Harris 8-4-15-1. Ealham 11-2-31-5. Smith 9-1-33-3.
Sidebottom 7-1-19-2. Harris 5-1-22-1. Smith 4.1-0-20-1. Ealham 10-2-44-4. Swann 10-3-62-2.
Fall of Wickets: 1-10, 2-34, 3-38, 4-39, 5-39, 6-53, 7-62, 8-62, 9-85
1-1, 2-2, 3-32, 4-62, 5-67, 6-80, 7-80, 8-98, 9-110

*Nottinghamshire won by an innings and 64 runs –
Nottinghamshire (20 pts), Gloucestershire (3 pts)*

MIDDLESEX v. KENT – at Lord's

KENT	First Innings		Second Innings	
DP Fulton (capt)	b Trego	16	c Shah b Richardson	9
RWT Key	c Shah b Richardson	94	c Joyce b Dalrymple	52
M van Jaarsveld	b Trego	0	st Scott b Golwalker	26
MJ Walker	c Scott b Trego	11	lbw b Dalrymple	0
DI Stevens	st Scott b Golwalker	43	lbw b Golwalker	15
JM Kemp	b Dalrymple	102	b Richardson	30
AJ Hall	c Joyce b Golwalker	16	not out	37
*NJO'Brien	c Hutton b Richardson	13	c Weekes b Golwalker	9
MM Patel	c Dalrymple b Golwalker	0	not out	0
SJ Cook	lbw b Richardson	0		
A Khan	not out	58		
Extras	lb 5, w 1, nb 25	31	b 1, lb 6, w 1, nb 6	14
	(103 overs)	384	(7 wkts 72.4 overs)	192

Bowling
Richardson 27-4-90-3. Betts 20-2-74-0. Trego 20-1-88-3. Golwalker 31-7-112-3. Dalrymple 5-0-15-1.
Trego 6-1-27-0. Richardson 16-6-38-2. Betts 5-1-16-0. Hutton 4-0-13-0. Golwalker 25.4-12-41-3. Dalrymple 16-1-50-2.
Fall of Wickets: 1-50, 2-56, 3-80, 4-172, 5-182, 6-198, 7-245, 8-248, 9-249
1-15, 2-90, 3-93, 4-104, 5-118, 6-166, 7-192

MIDDLESEX	First Innings	
ET Smith	b Khan	14
BL Hutton (capt)	c O'Brien b Hall	152
OA Shah	lbw b Patel	128
JWM Dalrymple	lbw b Stevens	76
EC Joyce	c Key b Stevens	68
PN Weekes	not out	26
PD Trego	lbw b Walker	28
*BJM Scott	b Kemp	4
MM Betts	c O'Brien b Kemp	4
YA Golwalker	c O'Brien b Kemp	3
A Richardson	not out	8
Extras	b 9, lb 16, w 2, nb 12	39
	(9 wkts dec 169 overs)	550

Bowling
Khan 24-3-106-1. Cook 19-2-59-0. Kemp 21-2-53-3. Hall 25-2-92-1.
Stevens 19-3-62-2. Patel 47-10-110-1. Walker 13-0-42-1. van Jaarsveld 1-0-1-0.
Fall of Wickets: 1-24, 2-306, 3-351, 4-475, 5-475, 6-512, 7-525, 8-529, 9-533

*Match drawn – Middlesex (12 pts),
Kent (9 pts)*

SUSSEX v. GLAMORGAN – at Hove

GLAMORGAN	First Innings		Second Innings	
DD Cherry	b Kirtley	8	c Kirtley b Mushtaq Ahmed	39
RE Watkins	c Naved-ul-Hasan b M Ahmed	30	b Naved-ul-Hasan	4
DL Hemp	b Kirtley	71	c Prior b Naved-ul-Hasan	1
J Hughes	lbw b Mushtaq Ahmed	32	c Prior b Naved-ul-Hasan	5
MJ Powell	lbw b Yardy	34	lbw b Mushtaq Ahmed	22
*MA Wallace	b Kirtley	4	b Naved-ul-Hasan	12
AG Wharf	c Yardy b Mushtaq Ahmed	11	lbw b Mushtaq Ahmed	0
RDB Croft (capt)	lbw b Kirtley	35	c Yardy b Mushtaq Ahmed	0
DA Cosker	c Montgomerie b M Ahmed	6	b Naved-ul-Hasan	0
DS Harrison	b Mushtaq Ahmed	1	lbw b Mushtaq Ahmed	0
HT Waters	not out	0	not out	0
Extras	b 8, lb 10, w 1, nb 4	23	b 3, lb 1, w 1, nb 8	13
	(77.3 overs)	255	(28 overs)	96

Bowling
Kirtley 15-4-42-4. Naved-ul-Hasan 19-5-51-0. Martin-Jenkins 3-0-18-0. Mushtaq Ahmed 25.3-3-89-5. Davis 11-2-22-0. Yardy 4-0-15-1.
Kirtley 8-0-22-0. Naved-ul-Hasan 11-1-41-5. Mushtaq Ahmed 9-0-29-5.
Fall of Wickets: 1-8, 2-62, 3-148, 4-154, 5-162, 6-187, 7-213, 8-253, 9-253
1-8, 2-10, 3-22, 4-52, 5-73, 6-74, 7-74, 8-77, 9-78

SUSSEX	First Innings		Second Innings	
IJ Ward	lbw b Wharf	48	c Harrison b Cosker	10
RR Montgomerie	lbw b Wharf	4	not out	18
MH Yardy	c Wharf b Cosker	22	not out	2
RJ Kirtley	c Wallace b Croft	12		
MW Goodwin	lbw b Waters	59		
CJ Adams (capt)	c Wharf b Watkins	84		
*MJ Prior	c Wallace b Wharf	15		
RSC Martin-Jenkins	not out	35		
Naved-ul-Hasan	b Watkins	19		
MJG Davis	b Croft	2		
Mushtaq Ahmed	c Harrison b Croft	7		
Extras	w 1, nb 4, p 5	10	lb 3, nb 2	5
	(96.4 overs)	317	(1 wkt 6.4 overs)	35

Bowling
Harrison 16-2-47-0. Wharf 21-3-75-3. Waters 7-2-18-1. Croft 26.4-2-97-3. Cosker 17-0-61-1. Watkins 9-3-14-2.
Wharf 3.4-0-8-0. Croft 2-0-17-0. Cosker 1-0-7-1.
Fall of Wickets: 1-16, 2-67, 3-79, 4-127, 5-171, 6-205, 7-275, 8-302, 9-309
1-25

*Sussex won by 9 wickets – Sussex (20 pts),
Glamorgan (5 pts)*

WARWICKSHIRE v. SURREY – at Edgbaston

SURREY	First Innings		Second Innings	
SA Newman	c Trott b Ntini	12	c Frost b Brown	15
MA Butcher (capt)	c Trott b Brown	30	c Westwood b Loudon	27
MR Ramprakash	c Powell b Carter	16	(4) c Frost b Troughton	126
R Clarke	c Brown b Anyon	63	(5) c Westwood b Brown	45
*JN Batty	c & b Anyon	3	(6) not out	76
AD Brown	lbw b Anyon	1		
Azhar Mahmood	c Ntini b Carter	24		
TJ Murtagh	c Knight b Brown	30		
Saqlain Mushtaq	c Frost b Anyon	31	(3) c Brown b Ntini	10
M Akram	c Westwood b Brown	12		
JW Dernbach	not out	0		
Extras	lb 3	3	b 1, lb 7, nb 6	14
	(60 overs)	225	(5 wkts dec 92.1 overs)	313

Bowling
Ntini 13-0-46-1. Brown 22-6-58-3. Carter 10-4-54-2. Anyon 15-1-64-4.
Ntini 21-3-65-1. Brown 16-3-41-2. Loudon 20-3-81-1. Carter 10-0-40-0. Anyon 13-2-44-0. Trott 9-3-15-0. Troughton 3.1-0-19-1.
Fall of Wickets: 1-22, 2-50, 3-76, 4-119, 5-121, 6-128, 7-153, 8-197, 9-225
1-39, 2-50, 3-70, 4-163, 5-313

WARWICKSHIRE	First Innings		Second Innings	
NV Knight (capt)	c Batty b Murtagh	117	not out	14
IJ Westwood	b Dernbach	45	not out	10
IJL Trott	b Dernbach	9		
JO Troughton	lbw b Azhar Mahmood	9		
AGR Loudon	b Saqlain Mushtaq	60		
MJ Powell	c Clarke b Saqlain Mushtaq	60		
*T Frost	c Newman b Saqlain Mushtaq	13		
DR Brown	c Batty b Saqlain Mushtaq	0		
NM Carter	c Brown b Azhar Mahmood	6		
M Ntini	c Batty b Azhar Mahmood	0		
JE Anyon	not out	1		
Extras	lb 10, nb 8	18	b 1, lb 1	2
	(86.5 overs)	338	(0 wkts 11 overs)	26

Bowling
Akram 11-2-42-0. Azhar Mahmood 18-4-70-3. Dernbach 12-1-66-2.
Murtagh 12-1-38-1. Saqlain Mushtaq 28.5-4-80-4. Clarke 5-0-32-0.
Clarke 6-0-10-0. Brown 5-0-14-0.
Fall of Wickets: 1-95, 2-117, 3-147, 4-247, 5-259, 6-291, 7-291, 8-306, 9-306

*Match drawn – Warwickshire (10 pts),
Surrey (8 pts)*

Division Two

Lancashire became the first county to be promoted to Division One when they defeated fourth-placed Essex by eight wickets at Chelmsford. Their victory was chiefly the work of one man – Indian slow left-arm spinner Murali Kartik, called up from Lancashire League club Ramsbottom to replace Australian batsman Marcus North – who was off to tour Pakistan with his country's A team – and, at the same time, stand in for the injured Gary Keedy. It proved to be an inspired signing, with Kartik becoming the first cricketer to take ten wickets in a match on his Lancashire debut. James Anderson's three wickets gave Kartik some support on the first day, and Sajid Mahmood took three cheap scalps when Essex batted a second time. But this was Kartik's match, with Iain Sutcliffe also impressing while going past 1,000 first-class runs for the season with a second innings unbeaten 80 to add to the 50 he made in an opening stand of 94 with Mark Chilton first time around. Lancashire's match-winning first innings lead was, however, chiefly the work of Andy Symonds' 98, featuring 15 fours and a six, and his 126-run seventh-wicket partnership with Glen Chapple, who struck three sixes and nine fours in his 70.

Yorkshire, meanwhile, were left cursing the bad weather at Headingley, where only five overs of play were possible on a last day that would have seen them romp home against Worcestershire. It was more than frustrating, too, for Anthony McGrath, who was in imperious form in this game – and looked to be sweeping Yorkshire to victory when the weather intervened. McGrath had made an unbeaten 173 in the first innings, going to his hundred with a six over extra-cover off Nadeem Malik and hitting three sixes and 22 fours in all.

Round 19: 5–13 September 2005 Division Two

ESSEX v. LANCASHIRE – at Chelmsford

ESSEX	First Innings		Second Innings	
WI Jefferson	lbw b Anderson	1	c Anderson b Kartik	35
AN Cook	lbw b Symonds	64	c Symonds b Anderson	19
GW Flower	c & b Anderson	0	b Kartik	13
RS Bopara	lbw b Chapple	20	c sub b Anderson	42
A Flower	b Kartik	22	c sub b Kartik	5
RC Irani (capt)	c Symonds b Kartik	15	c Law b Mahmood	10
*JS Foster	b Kartik	0	(8) c Chapple b Mahmood	24
JD Middlebrook	b Anderson	50	(9) b Mahmood	19
AR Adams	c Chilton b Kartik	38	(10) c Loye b Kartik	19
D Gough	st Horton b Kartik	15	(7) c sub b Kartik	15
Danish Kaneria	not out	19	not out	6
Extras	b 1, lb 2, nb 20	23	b 4, lb 4, nb 12	20
	(69.4 overs)	267	(63.2 overs)	227

Bowling
Anderson 14-0-56-3. Chapple 8-3-19-1. Mahmood 5-0-33-0. Symonds 19-4-63-1. Kartik 23.4-2-93-5.
Anderson 15-0-53-2. Chapple 7-2-42-0. Kartik 25.2-9-75-5. Symonds 10-1-28-0. Mahmood 6-0-21-3.
Fall of Wickets: 1-2, 2-2, 3-45, 4-101, 5-129, 6-130, 7-145, 8-231, 9-235
1-31, 2-63, 3-72, 4-84, 5-109, 6-134, 7-164, 8-202, 9-215

LANCASHIRE	First Innings		Second Innings	
MJ Chilton (capt)	b Adams	37	c Foster b Danish Kaneria	42
IJ Sutcliffe	lbw b Danish Kaneria	50	not out	80
MB Loye	b Danish Kaneria	10	b Danish Kaneria	16
SG Law	lbw b Gough	18	not out	13
JM Anderson	lbw b Adams	0		
A Symonds	c Flower A b Danish Kaneria	98		
PJ Horton	c Foster b Bopara	19		
G Chapple	c Adams b Middlebrook	70		
M Kartik	c Cook b Danish Kaneria	0		
SI Mahmood	b Middlebrook	0		
*WK Hegg	not out	0		
Extras	b 12, lb 16, w 2, nb 8	38	b 1, lb 1, nb 2	4
	(87.3 overs)	340	(2 wkts 51.5 overs)	155

Bowling
Gough 14-5-41-1. Adams 20-8-37-2. Bopara 9-2-46-1. Danish Kaneria 36-6-136-4. Middlebrook 8.3-0-52-2.
Gough 7-1-24-0. Adams 6-2-32-0. Danish Kaneria 23-4-61-2. Middlebrook 13.5-3-30-0. Bopara 2-0-6-0.
Fall of Wickets: 1-94, 2-106, 3-126, 4-126, 5-153, 6-214, 7-340, 8-340, 9-340
1-106, 2-126

Lancashire won by 8 wickets – Essex (5 pts), Lancashire (20 pts)

YORKSHIRE v. WORCESTERSHIRE – at Headingley

WORCS	First Innings		Second Innings	
SC Moore	c White b Bresnan	27	c McGrath b Kruis	30
CH Gayle	c Sayers b Kruis	29	c White b Kruis	4
GA Hick	c White b Bresnan	19	c Bresnan b Kruis	27
BF Smith	lbw b Harvey	27	c Guy b Cleary	0
VS Solanki (capt)	c Guy b McGrath	48	(4) not out	74
*SM Davies	c Guy b Bresnan	44	(5) run out	26
GJ Batty	c Guy b Kruis	14	c Guy b Cleary	7
Kabir Ali	c McGrath b Dawson	14	c Wood b Kruis	0
Shoaib Akhtar	c Guy b Cleary	1	c Kruis b Cleary	8
MS Mason	c & b Dawson	38	c Guy b Harvey	16
MN Malik	not out	21	c McGrath b Harvey	0
Extras	lb 10, nb 16	26	lb 9, nb 10	19
	(85 overs)	308	(43.4 overs)	211

Bowling
Kruis 22-7-88-2. Cleary 17-2-70-1. Bresnan 13-3-45-3. Harvey 11-3-25-1. McGrath 4-0-25-1. Dawson 18-5-45-2.
Cleary 12-1-65-3. Kruis 17-2-65-4. Bresnan 9-0-47-0. McGrath 1-0-4-0. Harvey 4.4-1-21-2.
Fall of Wickets: 1-41, 2-75, 3-92, 4-129, 5-204, 6-221, 7-246, 8-248, 9-250
1-14, 2-55, 3-74, 4-126, 5-130, 6-152, 7-155, 8-178, 9-211

YORKSHIRE	First Innings		Second Innings	
MJ Wood	c Batty b Kabir Ali	4	c Moore b Kabir Ali	8
JJ Sayers	c Smith b Malik	22	c Gayle b Malik	22
A McGrath	not out	173	not out	65
*SM Guy	c Shoaib Akhtar b Kabir Ali	7		
MJ Lumb	c Davies b Kabir Ali	3	(4) not out	16
IJ Harvey	c Kabir Ali b Malik	11		
C White (capt)	c Davies b Malik	5		
TT Bresnan	c Smith b Kabir Ali	6		
RKJ Dawson	retired hurt	49		
MF Cleary	c Hick b Batty	11		
GJ Kruis	c Gayle b Batty	4		
Extras	b 1, lb 3, w 2, nb 16	22	b 11, w 1, nb 2	14
	(9 wkts dec 68 overs)	317	(2 wkts 25 overs)	125

Bowling
Kabir Ali 16-1-79-4. Mason 13-1-73-0. Malik 16-1-71-3. Shoaib Akhtar 12-2-69-0. Gayle 3-2-1-0. Batty 8-1-20-2.
Kabir Ali 9-0-40-1. Mason 7-0-24-0. Malik 6-1-32-1. Shoaib Akhtar 3-0-18-0.
Fall of Wickets: 1-4, 2-91, 3-108, 4-122, 5-167, 6-181, 7-190, 8-313, 9-317
1-18, 2-70

Match drawn – Yorkshire (10 pts), Worcestershire (10 pts)

LEICESTERSHIRE v. DERBYSHIRE – at Leicester

LEICESTERSHIRE	First Innings	
DDJ Robinson	c & b Lungley	123
JK Maunders	c Hassan Adnan b Hunter	0
TJ New	c Sutton b Hunter	89
D Mongia	b Botha	71
HD Ackerman (capt)	lbw b France	125
A Habib	c Hunter b Botha	42
*PA Nixon	not out	50
OD Gibson	not out	19
DD Masters		
SCL Broad		
CM Willoughby		
Extras	b 10, lb 4, w 1, nb 18	33
	(6 wkts dec 166 overs)	552

Bowling
Welch 27-9-65-0. Hunter 22-2-93-2. Moss 23-4-56-0. Lungley 25-5-95-1. Botha 51-11-155-2. Hassan Adnan 10-0-37-0. France 8-1-37-1.
Fall of Wickets: 1-4, 2-221, 3-255, 4-348, 5-439, 6-506

DERBYSHIRE	First Innings	
SD Stubbings	lbw b Willoughby	25
BJ France	c Habib b Masters	0
CWG Bassano	c Nixon b Broad	29
Hassan Adnan	lbw b Willoughby	0
J Moss	lbw b Broad	14
PM Borrington	b Willoughby	4
*LD Sutton (capt)	c Robinson b Broad	18
G Welch	b Gibson	6
AG Botha	not out	34
T Lungley	b Masters	5
ID Hunter	lbw b Mongia	35
Extras	b 4, lb 13, w 1, nb 2	20
	(73.4 overs)	190

Bowling
Gibson 14-5-39-1. Masters 18-7-30-2. Willoughby 16-9-27-3. Broad 16-5-46-3. Maunders 6-1-13-0. Mongia 3.4-0-18-1.
Fall of Wickets: 1-0, 2-50, 3-59, 4-62, 5-68, 6-95, 7-98, 8-114, 9-127

Match drawn – Leicestershire (12 pts), Derbyshire (5 pts)

SOMERSET v. NORTHAMPTONSHIRE – at Taunton

SOMERSET	First Innings		Second Innings	
MJ Wood	c Wessels b Wright	58	lbw b Wright	4
JD Francis	lbw b Crook	8	b Wright	64
AV Suppiah	c sub b Panesar	91	c Sales b Wright	0
JC Hildreth	c Love b Brown	25	c Shafayat b Brown	50
WJ Durston	c Brown b Panesar	27	not out	36
ID Blackwell (capt)	c Panesar b Louw	98	not out	1
KA Parsons	lbw b Wright	31		
*CM Gazzard	run out	3		
GM Andrew	not out	10		
RL Johnson	c Shafayat b Panesar	0		
CK Langeveldt	b Panesar	6		
Extras	b 9, lb 17, w 3, nb 10	39	b 2, lb 2, nb 4	8
	(108.5 overs)	396	(4 wkts 54 overs)	163

Bowling
Wright 19-5-83-2. Louw 19-2-70-1. Crook 20-2-86-1. Brown 24-8-65-1. Panesar 26.5-7-66-4.
Wright 12-7-30-3. Louw 4-1-17-0. Panesar 17-3-58-0. Crook 5-0-21-0. Brown 16-7-33-1.
Fall of Wickets: 1-63, 2-80, 3-123, 4-190, 5-281, 6-353, 7-371, 8-382, 9-382
1-4, 2-4, 3-91, 4-159

NORTHANTS	First Innings	
ML Love	c Durston b Johnson	14
BM Shafayat	b Langeveldt	23
RA White	c & b Johnson	24
U Afzaal	b Parsons	112
DJG Sales (capt)	c and b Johnson	154
*MH Wessels	c Wood b Durston	0
DG Wright	c Gazzard b Johnson	71
SP Crook	not out	91
J Louw	c Parsons b Durston	64
MS Panesar	lbw b Andrew	0
JF Brown	b Andrew	2
Extras	lb 3, w 2, nb 14	19
	(140.2 overs)	574

Bowling
Langeveldt 21-4-74-1. Johnson 25-2-118-4. Andrew 21.2-2-105-2. Blackwell 37-5-118-0. Durston 17-0-82-2. Parsons 19-2-74-1.
Fall of Wickets: 1-23, 2-51, 3-76, 4-251, 5-252, 6-385, 7-426, 8-559, 9-560

Match drawn – Somerset (10 pts), Northamptonshire (12 pts)

Darren Robinson reached 1,000 runs for the second successive season.

Richard Dawson gave him staunch support before retiring hurt on 49 with a knuckle broken by a Shoaib Akhtar express. But Worcestershire's second innings collapse to 211 all out, despite Vikram Solanki's unbeaten 74, seemed to have set up Yorkshire for a straightforward win. McGrath had reached 65 not out, from just 55 balls and with 11 fours, after play on the final day had at last restarted at 3pm – but then poor light and more rain left Yorkshire 78 runs short of their target.

A career-best 89 from 20-year-old Tom New, plus three wickets on the last day for teenager Stuart Broad, at least provided Leicestershire with a clear sight of the youthful talent on their books as the game against Derbyshire fell foul of the weather. The entire third day was washed away, leaving Leicestershire with no hope of forcing the victory that their own first innings grind to 552 for 6 declared had looked to have set up. Darren Robinson, with 123, reached 1,000 runs for the second successive season for Leicestershire – after having failed to reach that landmark even once during his previous 11 summers with Essex.

At Taunton it was the final day that was a total washout, allowing Somerset to escape with a draw and denying Northamptonshire the chance to continue their late push for a promotion spot. David Sales was in prime form for Northants, hitting 154, while the threadbare home attack also felt the force of the strokes played by Usman Afzaal – who hit 117 himself in a stand of 175 with Sales – Damien Wright, Steven Crook, who made a career-best 91 not out, and Johann Louw. For Somerset, though, there was another promising innings from Arul Suppiah on the opening day, while James Hildreth later marked his 21st birthday with a second innings 50.

Round 20: 14–19 September 2005

Division One

Nottinghamshire clinched the championship amid much controversy at Canterbury after the two captains, Stephen Fleming and Kent's David Fulton, agreed a final morning deal aimed at breathing new life back into a match in which 88 overs had been lost to rain on the second day. Kent were desperate to win, because that represented their last chance at the championship title, and Fleming was equally keen to keep Kent interested because a win for his side would make their last week trip to Hampshire (the other side still in with a realistic chance of the title) irrelevant. Kent were due to start the last day on 237 for 5, in reply to Notts' huge 486 for 8 declared, but the deal that was done meant that Fulton immediately declared 251 runs behind. As agreed, Notts did not enforce the follow on but laid into some pre-arranged occasional bowling to thrash 170 for 3 from only 24 overs. Their declaration then left Kent to score an unlikely 420 from 70 overs.

It always seemed a target way out of Kent's reach, but if the home side thought that they could fall back to playing for a draw if their initial chase imploded then they were sadly mistaken. Andrew Harris, bowling with genuine pace and also gaining significant swing, was too hot for Kent's batsmen to handle and his 6 for 76 effectively clinched the championship for Notts. At 70 for 5, Kent's challenge was over, but Harris and the rest of the

Sweet taste: Stephen Fleming, captain of new county champions Nottinghamshire, drinks deep after the title is won in Canterbury.

Round 20: 14–19 September 2005 Division One

KENT v. NOTTINGHAMSHIRE – at Canterbury

NOTTS	First Innings		Second Innings	
DJ Bicknell	b Cook	64		
JER Gallian	run out	199	not out	74
RJ Warren	lbw b Khan	8	(4) c Saggers b Walker	16
SP Fleming (capt)	c Saggers b Khan	1	(5) not out	6
DJ Hussey	c Dexter b Stevens	11	(1) c O'Brien b Dexter	0
*CMW Read	c Fulton b Walker	75	(3) c Saggers b van Jaarsveld	63
MA Ealham	c Khan b Saggers	72		
GP Swann	c O'Brien b Cook	23		
RJ Sidebottom	not out	1		
GJ Smith	not out	9		
AJ Harris				
Extras	b 1, lb 9, w 3, nb 10	23	b 1, w 2, nb 8	11
	(8 wkts dec 131.5 overs)	486	(3 wkts dec 24 overs)	170

Bowling
Saggers 25.5-4-100-1. Khan 31-11-82-2. Cook 25-6-109-2. Dexter 10-1-55-0. Stevens 18-1-70-1. Patel 18-1-48-0. Walker 4-0-12-1.
Dexter 6-0-42-1. Stevens 3-0-19-0. Walker 9-0-95-1. van Jaarsveld 4-1-12-1. Saggers 2-1-1-0.
Fall of Wickets: 1-157, 2-174, 3-178, 4-194, 5-340, 6-420, 7-475, 8-477
1-0, 2-116, 3-163

KENT	First Innings		Second Innings	
DP Fulton (capt)	c Warren b Ealham	35	c Harris b Sidebottom	12
RWT Key	c Smith b Ealham	43	c Swann b Harris	6
M van Jaarsveld	c Read b Swann	9	c & b Smith	64
MJ Walker	lbw b Swann	11	c Gallian b Harris	3
DI Stevens	b Swann	0	c Gallian b Harris	11
NJ Dexter	not out	79	c Read b Ealham	4
*NJO'Brien	not out	56	c Ealham b Smith	28
MM Patel			b Harris	37
SJ Cook			b Harris	2
A Khan			lbw b Harris	15
MJ Saggers			not out	18
Extras	b 2, lb 2	4	lb 3, nb 2	5
	(5 wkts dec 80 overs)	237	(52.4 overs)	205

Bowling
Sidebottom 14-3-36-0. Harris 16-4-44-0. Swann 21-5-66-3. Smith 15-2-43-0. Ealham 14-2-44-2.
Sidebottom 8-1-28-1. Harris 17-0-76-6. Swann 14-3-55-0. Ealham 9-0-25-1. Smith 4.4-0-18-2.
Fall of Wickets: 1-66, 2-89, 3-99, 4-99, 5-108
1-10, 2-26, 3-30, 4-52, 5-70, 6-114, 7-156, 8-158, 9-180

Nottinghamshire won by 214 runs –
Kent (3 pts), Nottinghamshire (20 pts)

GLAMORGAN v. HAMPSHIRE – at Cardiff

HAMPSHIRE	First Innings		Second Innings	
JHK Adams	lbw b Croft	71		
SM Ervine	c Wallace b Davies	20	c Wharf b Cosker	75
JP Crawley	st Wallace b Cosker	17	lbw b Harrison	35
JJ McLean	c Wallace b Croft	52	(9) not out	0
*N Pothas	lbw b Harrison	26		
SM Katich	c Hemp b Cosker	50	(1) c Davies b Croft	49
AD Mascarenhas	c Wharf b Cosker	67	(6) not out	10
SK Warne (capt)	c Davies b Croft	24	(4) st Wallace b Croft	15
SD Udal	b Croft	9	(5) b Croft	28
RJ Logan	c Wharf b Croft	2	(8) c Wallace b Croft	0
JTA Bruce	not out	0	(7) st Wallace b Croft	2
Extras	b 3, lb 9	12	lb 4	4
	(95.4 overs)	350	(7 wkts dec 32 overs)	218

Bowling
Harrison 15-4-49-1. Wharf 15-3-39-0. Davies 14-4-38-1. Watkins 8-0-31-0. Cosker 18-4-78-3. Croft 25.4-2-103-5.
Harrison 5-0-43-1. Wharf 6-0-45-0. Davies 4-0-18-0. Croft 10-0-57-5. Cosker 7-0-51-1.
Fall of Wickets: 1-59, 2-90, 3-134, 4-178, 5-216, 6-280, 7-315, 8-346, 9-348
1-117, 2-125, 3-164, 4-186, 5-216, 6-218, 7-218

GLAMORGAN	First Innings		Second Innings	
DD Cherry	c Pothas b Logan	0	(6) lbw b Warne	23
RE Watkins	c Adams b Mascarenhas	41	c Pothas b Bruce	2
DA Cosker	b Bruce	39	(9) c Bruce b Mascarenhas	0
DL Hemp	run out	51	(5) b Ervine	14
RN Grant	c Katich b Warne	25	(7) c Crawley b Udal	8
MJ Powell	c & b Warne	7	(4) b Ervine	24
*MA Wallace	not out	31	(8) not out	33
AG Wharf	lbw b Warne	0	(3) b Bruce	19
RDB Croft (capt)	c sub b Ervine	20	(1) c Pothas b Ervine	90
DS Harrison	lbw b Warne	11	c Katich b Ervine	8
AP Davies	c Warne b Bruce	0	b Ervine	0
Extras	lb 6, w 8, nb 10	24	b 6, lb 5, nb 12	23
	(81 overs)	249	(62.4 overs)	244

Bowling
Logan 11-1-67-1. Bruce 14-3-38-2. Warne 22-5-50-4. Udal 19-3-42-0. Ervine 10-1-38-1. Mascarenhas 5-2-8-1.
Logan 10-1-36-0. Bruce 13-0-51-2. Mascarenhas 6-1-9-1. Udal 12-1-46-1. Warne 9-0-31-1. Ervine 12.4-1-60-5.
Fall of Wickets: 1-0, 2-66, 3-105, 4-151, 5-170, 6-178, 7-182, 8-227, 9-244
1-10, 2-44, 3-93, 4-113, 5-156, 6-185, 7-226, 8-227, 9-242

Hampshire won by 75 runs – Glamorgan (4 pts), Hampshire (21 pts)

Notts seamers made sure that the home side did not escape. Satisfyingly for him, too, it was Mark Ealham who took the catch to dismiss Niall O'Brien off Greg Smith which started the Notts celebrations. Ealham, who had left his native Kent at the end of the 2003 season in high dudgeon at the refusal of the county to offer him more than a one-year extension to his contract, had returned with a vengeance; he will also have taken much pleasure at Kent officials noticing that he was Notts' highest wicket-taker in the championship campaign with 56. Fleming afterwards defended the actions of Fulton and himself, saying that both sides were only doing what was in their best interests.

Fleming also paid tribute to the contribution of his predecessor as captain, Jason Gallian, who had acted as stand-in skipper when the New Zealander was away on international duty. Gallian, meanwhile, had an added reason to remember his county's title-clinching victory: he was run out on 199 for the second time in the campaign!

It was Notts' first championship since 1987 and it was Gallian and his fellow veteran opener Darren Bicknell who set them on the way to establishing an impregnable position against Kent by putting on 157 for the first wicket after Fleming had won the toss. Chris Read made 75, putting on 146 for the fifth wicket with Gallian, while Ealham also enjoyed himself with the bat, hitting 72. The only consolation for the home side was the batting of Neil Dexter, 21 the previous week, who marked his championship debut with an accomplished 79 not out. That rallied Kent's first innings from 108 for 5, in the company of O'Brien who scored an unbeaten 56.

Shane Warne was left fuming at what he saw as Kent's gift of victory to Nottinghamshire, especially after Hampshire had done their bit to set up what they hoped would be a potential showdown last match with Notts by defeating Glamorgan by 75 runs at Cardiff. Warne, struggling with a sore shoulder following his Ashes heroics, still managed to take a first innings 4 for 50 as Hampshire won themselves a 101-run lead. Simon Katich, also back from Australia duty, hit 50 and 49 in the match while there were excellent first innings half-centuries from Jimmy Adams, Jono McLean and Dimitri Mascarenhas and then an aggressive 73-ball 75 in the second innings from Sean Ervine.

Warne himself added to the overall sense of Hampshire urgency, following the first-day washout, by slugging Dean Cosker for 6, 6, 4, 6 off successive balls during his first innings cameo of 24. Robert Croft battled hard for his outgunned side, picking up ten wickets in the match with his off spin and then opting to open the Glamorgan second innings – when Warne set them 320 from 89 overs to win – and hitting a fine 90. With Ervine finishing with five for 60, however, it was not enough.

Division Two

Durham clinched promotion in their final match of the season, at home to nearest rivals Northamptonshire, but it was a bit of a struggle. In the end, Durham were fortunate that bad weather not only washed away the entire second day, but that bad light enabled them to come off and ensure the draw on a tense final afternoon. Set 246 in 44 overs by Northants, who earlier in the day had failed by just five runs to enforce the follow-on, Durham had slipped to 38 for 2 in 15 overs when they were offered the light. Gareth Breese and last man Brad Williams were the heroes who saved the day, adding 46 to frustrate the visitors. Breese, who made 78, had earlier been joined in a seventh-wicket stand of 94 by the promising Liam Plunkett but, overall, this was a disappointing way for Durham to earn their elevation into the top flight. Their bowling had also failed to make an impact on the opening day, when Northants cantered to 414 for 7 from 97.2 overs after Rob White had given them a flying start and Usman Afzaal, with his third hundred in successive games, had put on 185 for the fifth wicket with Riki Wessels. Not only did Wessels make a career-best 107 – he did it with a broken finger strapped up.

Like Durham, Yorkshire limped almost apologetically over the promotion line by gaining

Round 20: 14–19 September 2005 Division Two

DURHAM v. NORTHAMPTONSHIRE – at The Riverside

NORTHANTS	First Innings		Second Innings	
RA White	b Plunkett	84	c Killeen b Williams	22
BM Shafayat	lbw b Plunkett	13	c Killeen b Thorp	22
AR White	lbw b Plunkett	0	c Maher b Williams	6
U Afzaal	c Williams b Collingwood	119	(5) not out	21
DJG Sales (capt)	b Plunkett	11	(6) lbw b Plunkett	0
*MH Wessels	c Mustard b Williams	107	(7) c Mustard b Plunkett	0
DG Wright	b Plunkett	21	(8) c Plunkett b Thorp	1
SP Crook	not out	19	(4) b Thorp	10
J Louw	not out	5	not out	9
JF Brown				
C Pietersen				
Extras	b 4, lb 12, w 1, nb 18	35	lb 6, w 1, nb 3	10
	(7 wkts dec 97.2 overs)	414	(7 wkts dec 21 overs)	101

Bowling
Williams 15.2-1-88-1. Plunkett 24-4-86-5. Killeen 20-6-57-0. Thorp 11-1-43-0. Breese 18-1-79-0. Collingwood 9-0-45-1.
Plunkett 8-0-39-2. Williams 6-0-25-2. Thorp 4-1-10-3. Killeen 3-0-21-0.
Fall of Wickets: 1-63, 2-63, 3-140, 4-178, 5-363, 6-380, 7-404
1-36, 2-55, 3-70, 4-70, 5-71, 6-71, 7-80

DURHAM	First Innings		Second Innings	
JP Maher	lbw b Wright	0	b Wright	2
GM Scott	c Wessels b Louw	36	not out	12
PD C'wood (capt)	c Sales b Wright	22	b Louw	22
GJ Muchall	b Wright	2	not out	0
DM Benkenstein	c Wright b Brown	41		
GR Breese	c Shafayat b Crook	78		
*P Mustard	c Sales b Wright	2		
LE Plunkett	b Crook	46		
CD Thorp	b Crook	1		
N Killeen	b Wright	0		
BA Williams	not out	22		
Extras	b 5, lb 9, w 2, nb 4	20	lb 2	2
	(89.3 overs)	270	(2 wkts 15 overs)	38

Bowling
Wright 24-5-79-5. Louw 25-7-67-1. Pietersen 7-0-23-0. Crook 14.3-4-54-3. Brown 19-9-33-1.
Wright 5-2-13-1. Louw 7-5-13-1. Crook 2-0-7-0. Brown 1-0-3-0.
Fall of Wickets: 1-2, 2-30, 3-34, 4-100, 5-105, 6-115, 7-209, 8-217, 9-224
1-2, 2-35

Match drawn – Durham (8 pts), Northamptonshire (12 pts)

DERBYSHIRE v. YORKSHIRE – at Derby

DERBYSHIRE	First Innings		Second Innings	
SD Stubbings	c McGrath b Cleary	63	b Lawson	91
BJ France	c Kruis b Bresnan	17	c Guy b Bresnan	12
CWG Bassano	lbw b Harvey	16	lbw b Harvey	5
Hassan Adnan	lbw b Cleary	6	lbw b Kruis	42
J Moss	c McGrath b Kruis	19	lbw b Cleary	49
*LD Sutton (capt)	c White b Harvey	17	c McGrath b Lawson	10
G Welch	lbw b Harvey	19	c McGrath b Lawson	1
AG Botha	not out	28	not out	156
T Lungley	b Harvey	0	c Sayers b Lawson	36
NGE Walker	c Kruis b Cleary	4	lbw b Harvey	79
WA White	b Harvey	2	lbw b Lawson	6
Extras	b 12, lb 10, w 1, nb 2	25	b 11, lb 13, nb 12	36
	(63.4 overs)	216	(142 overs)	523

Bowling
Kruis 14-3-52-1. Cleary 14-3-46-3. Bresnan 15-5-44-1. Harvey 17.4-9-40-5. McGrath 3-0-12-0.
Kruis 30-4-107-1. Cleary 24-4-69-1. Harvey 20-5-51-2. Bresnan 22-3-93-1. Lawson 38-6-155-5. McGrath 8-1-24-0.
Fall of Wickets: 1-63, 2-103, 3-109, 4-120, 5-146, 6-167, 7-192, 8-192, 9-211
1-34, 2-41, 3-103, 4-203, 5-216, 6-220, 7-233, 8-373, 9-506

YORKSHIRE	First Innings		Second Innings	
MJ Wood	b Lungley	76	lbw b Welch	0
JJ Sayers	b Welch	46	not out	50
MAK Lawson	c Sutton b Walker	5		
A McGrath	c Stubbings b Botha	158	(3) c Sutton b White	13
MJ Lumb	c Sutton b Moss	9	(4) lbw b Moss	9
IJ Harvey	lbw b Lungley	103	c Sutton b Botha	7
C White (capt)	lbw b Botha	7	(5) c Hassan Adnan b Botha	1
TT Bresnan	b Walker	4	(7) b Walker	0
*SM Guy	c Moss b Botha	42	(8) not out	12
MF Cleary	c & b Botha	12		
GJ Kruis	not out	8		
Extras	b 8, lb 16, w 10, nb 16	50	b 10, lb 2, w 2, nb 8	22
	(142.3 overs)	520	(6 wkts 58.3 overs)	114

Bowling
Welch 31-3-87-1. Walker 18-2-84-2. Lungley 23-4-91-2. White 23-3-107-0. Moss 18-9-37-1. Botha 29.3-5-90-4.
Welch 11-3-29-1. White 6-1-16-1. Botha 23-12-20-2. Moss 12.3-6-19-1. Walker 6-1-18-1.
Fall of Wickets: 1-113, 2-130, 3-163, 4-214, 5-370, 6-389, 7-394, 8-484, 9-507
1-0, 2-25, 3-54, 4-57, 5-81, 6-82

Match drawn – Derbyshire (7 pts), Yorkshire (12 pts)

perhaps an undeserved draw against a gallant Derbyshire at Derby. At first it looked as if Yorkshire would earn themselves an emphatic win, with Ian Harvey grabbing 5 for 40 as the home sided were dismissed for just 216 on the first day. By the close, Yorkshire were already 117 for 1, and the next day they powered on to 520. Matthew Wood's 76 was followed by superb centuries from both Anthony McGrath and Harvey – McGrath taking his championship run tally to 835 from his last 11 innings with a 263-ball 158. He hit two sixes and 20 fours, but Harvey's 103 occupied an even more rapid 132 balls, with a six and 14 fours.

The upshot was that Derbyshire began their second innings in a seemingly hopeless position, but by the end of day three they had reached a fighting 366 for 7 and had succeeded, at least, in prolonging the match well into the fourth day. Steve Stubbings added 91 to his first innings 63, but the main resistance came from Ant Botha and Tom Lungley. They came together at 233 for 7, and Botha was on 98 not out by the close. The next morning saw Botha lose Lungley early, for 36, after a stand of 140, but then go on to a career-best 156 not out that was also his maiden first-class hundred. Nick Walker, in at 10, then thumped 79 as a further 133 were added for the ninth wicket – and suddenly Yorkshire were

facing a target of 220 in 59 overs. At 82 for 6 they looked as if they could even lose, but Simon Guy joined Joe Sayers and their stubborn seventh-wicket alliance saved the game. However, Sayers, finishing 50 not out, had been dropped four times.

Round 21: 21–24 September 2005

Division One

It was a good job Nottinghamshire had made sure of the championship title the previous week. After winning the toss at the Rose Bowl, skipper Stephen Fleming for some reason decided to bowl first – and then saw Hampshire, still much aggrieved at what had happened at Canterbury, rack up an enormous 714 for 5 declared. John Crawley finished just five runs short of Dick Moore's 1937 individual Hampshire record of 316, hitting four sixes and 33 fours in his 311 not out and once past 200 doing as he pleased with the battered Notts attack. Crawley took just 58 balls to score his third hundred, and his sixth-wicket stand with Dimitri Mascarenhas was worth 254 when Shane Warne called a halt.

Mascarenhas then added 5 for 55 to his unbeaten 103, and with Shaun Udal picking up four for 39, Notts were quickly rolled over for 213. They did exactly 100 runs better second time around, but a still furious Warne often set outrageously attacking fields in his bid to finish the game comfortably inside three days. Udal took another 4 for 70 and Warne, rationing his own overs because of various aches and pains, still had the pleasure of removing opposite number and good friend Fleming. Notts may have been champions, but this was a deeply embarrassing result for them.

Most eyes in this round of games were turned on to Surrey, who needed to beat Middlesex by a 15-point margin at The Oval to save themselves from relegation, and send their London rivals down instead. Once Middlesex had got past 400 on the opening day, however, to ensure maximum

Mark Ramprakash batted for 12 hours and 40 minutes but could not stop Surrey from being relegated.

batting points, they were in charge of the situation and had no hesitation in declaring straight away to allow Surrey just one bowling point. This meant that the home side had to reply by topping 400 themselves inside the first 130 overs, but also losing no more than two wickets in the process. It was a long shot, and at 59 for 2 by the close of day one, it looked a mission impossible.

When Scott Newman was lbw to Indian leg-spinner Yoginder Golwalkar for 51, early on the second day, Middlesex's players celebrated as if they had won the championship itself. From that moment on, the result of the match hardly mattered – although that should be no excuse for Middlesex's subsequent heavy beating. Taking advantage of more occasional bowling than usual, Mark Ramprakash and Azhar Mahmood helped themselves to a Surrey record fifth-wicket partnership of 318; Ramprakash batted 12 hours and 40 minutes, and faced 480 balls, for his 252 while Azhar's unbeaten 204 was a maiden double-hundred and took eight hours and 36 minutes. The Pakistan all-rounder faced 268 balls and struck three sixes and 24 fours to Ramprakash's two and 21. Then, with Saqlain Mushtaq and Ian Salisbury sharing six wickets as Middlesex were shot out for 243, despite Jamie Dalrymple's 87-ball 75, it looked on the surface to be just like old times for Surrey. Relegated by a single point, however, Surrey will not be able to challenge for the County Championship in 2006 for the first time in their 116-year history.

Sussex finished third by trouncing Kent by eight wickets at Hove. James Kirtley and Naved-ul-Hasan snatched four wickets each on day one as Kent were bowled out for 257, and then Mushtaq Ahmed hit an unlikely but hugely entertaining 90 not out from No. 10 to win Sussex a significant first innings lead.

Round 21: 21–24 September 2005 Division One

HAMPSHIRE v. NOTTINGHAMSHIRE – at The Rose Bowl

HAMPSHIRE	First Innings		
SM Ervine	b Harris	9	
JHK Adams	c Gallian b Swann	50	
JP Crawley	not out	311	
SM Katich	c Read b Footitt	53	
JJ McLean	c Fleming b Franks	67	
*N Pothas	b Harris	46	
AD Mascarenhas	not out	103	
SK Warne (capt)			
SD Udal			
JTA Bruce			
RJ Logan			
Extras	b 10, lb 13, w 14, nb 38	75	
	(5 wkts dec 146.3 overs)	**714**	

Bowling
Smith GJ 31-3-130-0. Harris 30-8-104-2. Footitt 17-0-153-1. Franks 20-1-89-1. Swann 39-5-145-1. Smith WR 9.3-0-70-0.
Fall of Wickets: 1-10, 2-107, 3-190, 4-352, 5-460

NOTTS	First Innings		Second Innings	
DJ Bicknell	c Pothas b Bruce	11	c Pothas b Udal	97
JER Gallian	c Pothas b Mascarenhas	26	lbw b Mascarenhas	5
WR Smith	c Crawley b Mascarenhas	13	c Pothas b Bruce	10
RJ Warren	c Crawley b Udal	8	c Pothas b Logan	29
SP Fleming (capt)	c Katich b Mascarenhas	42	c Adams b Warne	13
*CMW Read	c Bruce b Mascarenhas	34	c Adams b Udal	63
PJ Franks	not out	27	c Bruce b Mascarenhas	24
GP Swann	b Mascarenhas	9	c McLean b Udal	14
GJ Smith	c Pothas b Udal	7	c Adams b Udal	23
AJ Harris	c & b Udal	5	c Warne b Bruce	1
MHA Footitt	c Mascarenhas b Udal	0	not out	19
Extras	lb 9, w 2, nb 20	31	b 2, lb 7, w 1, nb 5	15
	(55.2 overs)	**213**	(67.5 overs)	**313**

Bowling
Bruce 7-1-19-1. Logan 9-2-35-0. Mascarenhas 14-2-55-5. Ervine 7.4-1-50-0. Udal 16.2-4-39-4. Warne 1.2-0-6-0.
Bruce 17-4-42-2. Logan 12-0-86-1. Mascarenhas 13-3-38-2. Udal 11.5-0-70-4. Warne 13-4-67-1. Adams 1-0-1-0.
Fall of Wickets: 1-14, 2-47, 3-56, 4-81, 5-150, 6-150, 7-170, 8-191, 9-199
1-24, 2-55, 3-120, 4-133, 5-189, 6-241, 7-261, 8-268, 9-269

*Hampshire won by an innings and 188 runs –
Hampshire (22 pts), Nottinghamshire (2 pts)*

SURREY v. MIDDLESEX – at The Oval

MIDDLESEX	First Innings		Second Innings	
ET Smith	c Salisbury b Akram	36	lbw b Akram	7
BL Hutton (capt)	st Batty b Saqlain Mushtaq	79	c Salisbury b Clarke	29
OA Shah	c Newman b Saqlain Mushtaq	58	(4) c sub b Saqlain Mushtaq	14
EC Joyce	c Brown b Salisbury	90	(6) c Newman b Salisbury	19
JWM Dalrymple	c Azhar Mahmood b Akram	0	c Murtagh b Salisbury	75
SB Styris	not out	100	(9) lbw b Saqlain Mushtaq	2
PN Weekes	not out	17	c Batty b Saqlain Mushtaq	14
*BJM Scott			(3) c Brown b Clarke	23
PD Trego			(8) c Brown b Salisbury	36
YA Golwalker			run out	2
A Richardson			not out	10
Extras	b 4, lb 2, nb 18	24	b 2, nb 10	12
	(5 wkts dec 84.1 overs)	**404**	(50.3 overs)	**243**

Bowling
Akram 19-0-99-2. Azhar Mahmood 11-1-57-0. Murtagh 12-2-53-0. Clarke 3-0-30-0. Saqlain Mushtaq 25-1-98-2. Salisbury 14.1-0-61-1.
Akram 9-1-44-1. Clarke 10-1-47-2. Saqlain Mushtaq 20-1-77-3. Salisbury 11.3-0-73-3.
Fall of Wickets: 1-40, 2-172, 3-199, 4-200, 5-374
1-8, 2-51, 3-70, 4-89, 5-155, 6-176, 7-215, 8-219, 9-224

SURREY	First Innings		
SA Newman	lbw b Golwalker	51	
MA Butcher (capt)	run out	5	
R Clarke	lbw b Styris	22	
MR Ramprakash	b Shah	252	
*JN Batty	c Scott b Shah	73	
Azhar Mahmood	not out	204	
AD Brown	not out	30	
IDK Salisbury			
TJ Murtagh			
Saqlain Mushtaq			
M Akram			
Extras	b 12, lb 2, w 11, nb 24	49	
	(5 wkts dec 177.3 overs)	**686**	

Bowling
Trego 13-4-53-0. Richardson 23-4-60-0. Styris 7-2-16-1. Golwalker 48-6-176-1. Dalrymple 30-2-109-0. Weekes 8-0-21-0. Shah 21.3-1-95-2. Joyce 10-0-68-0. Hutton 17-0-74-0.
Fall of Wickets: 1-7, 2-40, 3-139, 4-317, 5-635

*Surrey won by an innings and 39 runs –
Surrey (20 pts), Middlesex (6 pts)*

SUSSEX v. KENT – at Hove

KENT	First Innings		Second Innings	
DP Fulton (capt)	c Mushtaq Ahmed b Kirtley	6	c Yardy b Naved-ul-Hasan	13
RWT Key	lbw b Naved-ul-Hasan	8	c Prior b Martin-Jenkins	84
M van Jaarsveld	c Ambrose b Kirtley	11	(5) run out	17
MJ Walker	c Prior b Kirtley	34	(3) c Montgomerie b M Ahmed	33
DI Stevens	c Prior b Naved-ul-Hasan	26	(4) lbw b Mushtaq Ahmed	36
NJ Dexter	c Ambrose b Naved-ul-Hasan	34	c Ambrose b Naved-ul-Hasan	4
*NJO'Brien	c Adams b Kirtley	61	c Yardy b Mushtaq Ahmed	9
JC Tredwell	lbw b Naved-ul-Hasan	0	c Ambrose b Kirtley	15
MM Patel	c Wright b Mushtaq Ahmed	51	c Yardy b Kirtley	12
MJ Saggers	not out	16	c Ambrose b Kirtley	0
RH Joseph	c Adams b Mushtaq Ahmed	0	not out	0
Extras	lb 4, w 2, nb 4	12	b 4, lb 4, nb 4	12
	(78.4 overs)	**257**	(63.2 overs)	**238**

Bowling
Kirtley 19-5-53-4. Naved-ul-Hasan 20-0-83-4. Martin-Jenkins 7-1-25-0. Mushtaq Ahmed 27.4-5-81-2. Wright 5-0-11-0.
Kirtley 9.2-1-45-3. Naved-ul-Hasan 12-2-41-2. Wright 3-0-8-0. Mushtaq Ahmed 26-3-92-3. Yardy 6-1-22-0. Martin-Jenkins 7-2-22-1.
Fall of Wickets: 1-16, 2-27, 3-28, 4-80, 5-103, 6-169, 7-169, 8-201, 9-256
1-43, 2-122, 3-144, 4-182, 5-188, 6-194, 7-214, 8-234, 9-237

SUSSEX	First Innings		Second Innings	
RR Montgomerie	b Joseph	7	c Stevens b Patel	26
CD Hopkinson	run out	7	c O'Brien b Joseph	57
MH Yardy	b Patel	43	not out	55
TR Ambrose	lbw b Dexter	44	not out	3
CJ Adams (capt)	b Patel	41		
*MJ Prior	c Joseph b Patel	4		
RSC Martin-Jenkins	st O'Brien b Tredwell	20		
Naved-ul-Hasan	c Fulton b Patel	4		
LJ Wright	c Fulton b Patel	37		
Mushtaq Ahmed	not out	90		
RJ Kirtley	lbw b Joseph	17		
Extras	b 8, lb 3, w 8, nb 10, p 5	34	lb 7, w 3	10
	(90.5 overs)	**348**	(2 wkts 31 overs)	**151**

Bowling
Saggers 18-3-71-0. Joseph 18.5-4-69-2. Patel 25-4-81-5. Tredwell 11-3-38-1. Dexter 11-4-44-1. Stevens 7-0-29-0.
Joseph 6-0-33-1. Patel 10-3-34-1. Saggers 5-0-27-0. Tredwell 8-0-41-0. Dexter 2-0-9-0.
Fall of Wickets: 1-14, 2-14, 3-115, 4-117, 5-154, 6-184, 7-192, 8-192, 9-274
1-35, 2-144

*Sussex won by 8 wickets – Sussex (20 pts),
Kent (5 pts)*

WARWICKSHIRE v. GLOUCESTERSHIRE – at Edgbaston

WARWICKSHIRE	First Innings		Second Innings	
NV Knight (capt)	b Hardinges	6	(3) c Adshead b Ball	94
IJ Westwood	c Ball b Kirby	10	lbw b Bandara	55
IR Bell	c Ball b Kirby	2	(4) c Snell b Bandara	37
IJL Trott	b Lewis	9	(5) b Lewis	3
JO Troughton	c Spearman b Hardinges	84	(8) b Ball	57
AGR Loudon	c Hardinges b Kirby	19	(7) c Spearman b Ball	4
*T Frost	c Spearman b Bandara	27	(9) c Snell b Bandara	0
DR Brown	c Lewis b Bandara	10	c Hodnett b Bandara	16
NM Carter	b Bandara	18	(1) lbw b Lewis	21
N Tahir	c Ball b Bandara	18	not out	22
JE Anyon	not out	2	not out	6
Extras	lb 1, nb 2	3	lb 3, nb 2	5
	(90 overs)	**208**	(9 wkts dec 88 overs)	**320**

Bowling
Lewis 14-6-33-1. Kirby 15-10-23-3. Hardinges 12-3-48-2. Bandara 25-6-67-4. Ball 24-11-36-0.
Lewis 17-3-64-2. Kirby 10-1-51-0. Ball 34-7-99-3. Hardinges 3-1-13-0. Bandara 24-2-90-4.
Fall of Wickets: 1-12, 2-18, 3-18, 4-46, 5-90, 6-160, 7-160, 8-181, 9-190
1-32, 2-126, 3-191, 4-197, 5-239, 6-247, 7-274, 8-284, 9-296

GLOS	First Innings		Second Innings	
CM Spearman	b Brown	2	b Tahir	42
Kadeer Ali	lbw b Carter	1	c sub b Tahir	38
GP Hodnett	b Carter	49	b Carter	10
MGN Windows	c Trott b Carter	1	(5) not out	65
*SJ Adshead	c Troughton b Brown	14	(6) b Troughton	19
SD Snell	c Carter b Anyon	13	(7) c Bell b Loudon	3
MA Hardinges	lbw b Tahir	7	(8) c Bell b Loudon	15
CM Bandara	c Brown b Loudon	0	(9) c Troughton b Loudon	16
MCJ Ball	lbw b Carter	1	(10) c Trott b Loudon	0
J Lewis (capt)	c Westwood b Loudon	13	(11) c Anyon b Loudon	0
SP Kirby	not out	2	(4) b Loudon	15
Extras	b 4, lb 9, nb 2	15	lb 4, nb 2	6
	(55.3 overs)	**118**	(74 overs)	**229**

Bowling
Brown 16-10-27-2. Carter 16-6-30-4. Loudon 11.3-2-22-2. Anyon 7-2-16-1. Tahir 5-2-10-1.
Brown 16-4-58-0. Carter 14-4-48-1. Loudon 31-5-66-6. Tahir 11-3-38-2. Troughton 2-0-15-1.
Fall of Wickets: 1-10, 2-10, 3-19, 4-46, 5-69, 6-95, 7-96, 8-101, 9-116
1-80, 2-83, 3-100, 4-112, 5-154, 6-170, 7-202, 8-224, 9-229

*Warwickshire won by 181 runs –
Warwickshire (18 pts), Gloucestershire (3 pts)*

Until Mushtaq's innings, Sussex were languishing somewhat at 192 for 8, with Min Patel adding to his useful 51 of the day before by picking up another five-wicket haul. Rob Key replied on the second evening with a high-class 84, but when he fell in the day's final over, taken at slip off one that bounced from Robin Martin-Jenkins, the pendulum had swung back again towards Sussex. Resuming on 144 for 3, Kent slid unceremoniously to 238 all out, with Kirtley and Mushtaq sharing six wickets, and half-centuries from Carl Hopkinson and Mike Yardy then raced Sussex to their target ahead of threatened rain.

Alex Loudon celebrated his call-up for the Pakistan tour by showcasing his fast-developing off-spinning skills at Edgbaston. The victims were Gloucestershire batsmen who clearly found his variations difficult to deal with, and Loudon's second innings 6 for 66 was a season's best. It also swept Warwickshire to a 181-run victory, a result to which Jim Troughton had contributed scores of 84 and 57 and Nick Knight a second innings 94. Knight was unlucky to fall just six runs short of becoming the first Warwickshire batsman since Brian Lara in 1994 to score nine hundreds in all cricket. Malinga Bandara had a match haul of eight wickets for Gloucestershire, and 23-year-old Grant Hodnett battled to a gutsy 49 on his debut in an otherwise undistinguished first innings from the visitors, but Warwickshire were always in control of the contest, and Loudon's haul enabled the 2004 champions to sign off their 2005 campaign with a flourish.

Division Two

Pride of place in the last round of games in the second division should go to much-derided Derbyshire, who thrashed Somerset by an innings and 18 runs to prevent themselves suffering a first championship season since 1924 without a win. After their heroics in the previous match against Yorkshire, victory at Taunton was the least Luke Sutton's team deserved – and again they played excellently here to overwhelm their opponents. John Francis and James Hildreth made first-day half-centuries, but Somerset's 259 was hopelessly inadequate and something of a triumph, too, for 20-year-old fast bowler Wayne White, who finished with 4 for 77. By the close Derbyshire were 126 for 1 in reply, and the next day saw them move remorselessly to 549 for 9. Steve Stubbings continued his fine late-season form with 151 and Hassan Adnan's 191 was a career-best. Ant Botha and Jon Moss also chipped in with 50s and, eventually, after Sutton had made 53 and Graeme

Welch a violent 71-ball 99 not out, with four sixes, Derbyshire declared on 707 for 7. Francis had reached 107 not out by the close of day three, but Somerset had also lost two wickets. The opener fell for 108 early the following morning and Derbyshire were quite unmoved by the fact that Ian Blackwell earned himself the Walter Lawrence Trophy and a cheque for £5,000, for the fastest first-class hundred, by battering two sixes and 18 fours in his 67-ball ton. When he was out for 107, Derbyshire were almost there and it was fitting that their most consistent bowlers of the season – Welch, with five for 105, and Botha, with four for 93 – should take them to victory.

Lancashire had to endure an anxious wait, after going down to Leicestershire by only four runs at Old Trafford, for confirmation that they had finished as Division Two champions in any case. There was drama aplenty on the last day of Lancashire's season, though, with back injury victim Mal Loye bravely emerging to bat at No. 11 with 18 runs still required. Loye even managed a push through mid-on for three, despite the added pain, but after surviving 22 balls he found that his heroics were in vain as Leicestershire dismissed their opponents for 170 to clinch a thrilling win. Stuart Broad further impressed with three wickets in each Lancashire innings, but the home side were left to rue a sloppy first innings performance in which they allowed John Maunders to pick up 4 for 28 with his little-used medium pace. Glen Chapple and Murali Kartik had cut down Leicestershire's first innings, and there were four catches and a smart stumping on debut for 21-year-old Bury-born wicketkeeper Gareth Cross. James Anderson took 4 for 45 in Leicestershire's second innings, but Hylton Ackerman's 67 in the end proved just enough for the visitors.

It was, in fact, the confirmation of Yorkshire's defeat by an innings and 21 runs to Northamptonshire the following day which allowed Lancashire to celebrate the second division title. The home spinners, Monty Panesar and Jason Brown, were too much for Yorkshire's batsmen on a pitch which turned from the first morning at Wantage Road. Both Panesar and Brown had ten-wicket match hauls, but the young Yorkshire spin pairing of Mark Lawson and David Wainwright took a combined 1 for 236 as the Northants batsmen ran amok on the same surface. Martin Love hit an effortless 95 and Usman Afzaal a dominating 157. There was also a 76-run ninth-wicket stand between Steven Crook, who hit hard and high in his 97, and Panesar. Northants, in the end, finished in fourth place and just 6.5 points behind the side who they trounced here.

The long and gruelling championship season came to a highly exciting end at New Road, Worcester, where the home side failed by just four runs to chase down a target of 352 in 60 overs against Essex. Steven Davies was left needing to hit the last ball of the first-class summer for six to win the game, but he could only manage a single. Both Worcestershire and Essex, however, emerged with great credit from a contest dominated by the bat. There was a career-best 98 in Essex's first innings for Ryan ten Doeschate, who hit three sixes and ten fours in what was just his seventh first-class knock, and a second 99 of the season for Ronnie Irani. Will Jefferson hit a first-innings century, and Alastair Cook and Ravi Bopara added to the lustre of their breakthrough seasons with unbeaten innings of 117 and 58 respectively to set up Essex's last-day declaration.

For Worcestershire there was a fine debut return of five for 112 for 19-year-old seamer Stuart Wedge, from Wolverhampton, and brilliant first-innings hundreds for both Stephen Moore and Ben Smith. They added 333 in 74 overs, a record stand for Worcestershire against Essex, and Smith's 154 not out was his sixth hundred of the season. Moore, who had the rear window of his car smashed by one of the 16 sixes struck in Essex's first innings of 574, had his revenge with a 191 which included 35 fours and two sixes of his own. The innings which made Worcestershire supporters most happy, however, as they contemplated the 2006 season, was a return to form for Graeme Hick. After going 16 first-class innings without a fifty – the leanest spell of his prolific career – the 39-year-old Hick smashed 107 from just 96 balls, with four sixes and nine fours, to lead Worcestershire's brave bid for victory.

Round 21: 21–24 September 2005 Division Two

SOMERSET v. DERBYSHIRE – at Taunton

SOMERSET	First Innings		Second Innings	
MJ Wood	c Sutton b Welch	25	c Hassan Adnan b Walker	29
JD Francis	c Bassano b Lungley	54	c Welch b Botha	108
AV Suppiah	c Stubbings b Welch	0	b Welch	28
JC Hildreth	c Moss b Walker	84	b Botha	1
WJ Durston	c Sutton b Welch	25	lbw b Welch	0
ID Blackwell (capt)	c Welch b White	16	c & b Botha	107
KA Parsons	b White	20	not out	93
*CM Gazzard	not out	12	c Sutton b Botha	21
GM Andrew	b White	3	b Welch	15
RJ Woodman	lbw b Lungley	2	c Sutton b Welch	6
M Parsons	c Sutton b White	1	c Sutton b Welch	4
Extras	lb 8, w 3, nb 6	17	b 8, nb 10	18
	(64.5 overs)	259	(114.2 overs)	430

Bowling
Welch 15-3-42-3. White 12.5-1-77-4. Lungley 14-2-54-2. Walker 13-2-46-1. Botha 10-2-32-0.
Welch 31.2-4-105-5. White 17-3-80-0. Walker 10-1-64-1. Lungley 17-1-80-0. Botha 39-17-93-4.
Fall of Wickets: 1-50, 2-54, 3-133, 4-199, 5-199, 6-238, 7-240, 8-245, 9-252
1-89, 2-172, 3-173, 4-174, 5-174, 6-301, 7-359, 8-393, 9-414

DERBYSHIRE	First Innings	
SD Stubbings	c Durston b Andrew	151
CWG Bassano	c Suppiah b Durston	47
Hassan Adnan	run out	191
AG Botha	c Hildreth b Andrew	57
J Moss	c Gazzard b Andrew	53
PM Borrington	c Gazzard b Andrew	28
*LD Sutton (capt)	c Hildreth b Suppiah	53
G Welch	not out	99
T Lungley		
NGE Walker		
WA White		
Extras	b 7, lb 15, nb 6	28
	(7 wkts dec 171.5 overs)	707

Bowling
Woodman 28-3-111-0. Andrew 31-5-134-4. Parsons KA 16-2-74-0. Parsons M 18-2-88-0. Blackwell 31-9-70-0. Durston 28-1-122-1. Suppiah 15.5-1-67-1. Hildreth 4-0-19-0.
Fall of Wickets: 1-87, 2-370, 3-459, 4-470, 5-549, 6-554, 7-707

Derbyshire won by an innings and 18 runs –
Somerset (3 pts), Derbyshire (22 pts)

LANCASHIRE v. LEICESTERSHIRE – at Old Trafford

LEICESTERSHIRE	First Innings		Second Innings	
DDJ Robinson	c Cross b Chapple	14	b Kartik	33
JK Maunders	lbw b Kartik	40	c Sutcliffe b Kartik	34
TJ New	c Cross b Chapple	18	c Law b Mahmood	8
D Mongia	c Cross b Chapple	2	c Kartik b Symonds	14
HD Ackerman (capt)	c Law b Kartik	48	b Anderson	67
A Habib	b Symonds	6	lbw b Symonds	0
*PA Nixon	lbw b Kartik	11	b Chapple	0
OD Gibson	st Cross b Kartik	2	lbw b Anderson	6
DD Masters	not out	9	(11) not out	5
SCL Broad	c Cross b Chapple	7	(9) c Cross b Anderson	7
CM Willoughby	c & b Chapple	0	(10) b Anderson	1
Extras	b 1, lb 2, nb 6	9	b 4, lb 9, w 1, nb 6, p 5	25
	(68.5 overs)	165	(63.3 overs)	200

Bowling
Anderson 14-5-37-0. Chapple 14.5-4-22-5. Kartik 22-7-43-4. Mahmood 12-1-43-0. Symonds 6-1-17-1.
Chapple 15-0-52-1. Anderson 16.3-3-45-4. Kartik 19-3-49-2. Mahmood 7-1-28-1. Symonds 6-3-8-2.
Fall of Wickets: 1-19, 2-72, 3-74, 4-74, 5-89, 6-127, 7-137, 8-150, 9-165
1-63, 2-94, 3-94, 4-123, 5-123, 6-124, 7-147, 8-159, 9-171

LANCASHIRE	First Innings		Second Innings	
MJ Chilton (capt)	c Nixon b Broad	30	c & b Broad	36
IJ Sutcliffe	c Nixon b Masters	3	sub b Willoughby	16
PJ Horton	c Robinson b Broad	43	c Gibson b Broad	21
SG Law	c Nixon b Willoughby	6	b Broad	0
A Symonds	lbw b Maunders	27	c Nixon b Willoughby	10
G Chapple	c Ackerman b Maunders	33	c & b Mongia	20
*GD Cross	b Broad	14	lbw b Gibson	22
M Kartik	c Habib b Maunders	7	lbw b Willoughby	4
SI Mahmood	b Maunders	14	c Nixon b Maunders	9
JM Anderson	not out	5	c Robinson b Mongia	8
MB Loye	absent		not out	3
Extras	lb 7, nb 2	9	lb 3, w 6, nb 12	21
	(9 wkts 60 overs)	191	(51.3 overs)	170

Bowling
Gibson 16-3-52-0. Masters 8-5-7-1. Broad 14-1-57-3. Willoughby 11-3-27-1. Mongia 3-1-13-0. Maunders 8-0-28-4.
Gibson 14-4-35-1. Willoughby 10-1-32-3. Broad 10-3-49-3. Mongia 14.3-3-42-2. Maunders 3-1-9-1.
Fall of Wickets: 1-26, 2-54, 3-81, 4-85, 5-143, 6-148, 7-170, 8-172, 9-191
1-36, 2-73, 3-75, 4-78, 5-105, 6-118, 7-122, 8-155, 9-157

Leicestershire won by 4 runs –
Lancashire (3 pts), Leicestershire (17 pts)

NORTHAMPTONSHIRE v. YORKSHIRE – at Northampton

YORKSHIRE	First Innings		Second Innings	
MJ Wood	c White b Panesar	30	c Wright b Panesar	13
JJ Sayers	lbw b Brown	32	st Wessels b Panesar	6
A McGrath	c Shafayat b Brown	10	(4) c Love b Panesar	30
MJ Lumb	c Shafayat b Panesar	0	(5) lbw b Brown	36
IJ Harvey	lbw b Panesar	1	(7) c Shafayat b Brown	74
C White (capt)	c White b Brown	51	(8) c White b Brown	35
TT Bresnan	lbw b Brown	16	(6) c Shafayat b Panesar	23
*SM Guy	c Louw b Panesar	9	(9) c Shafayat b Panesar	12
DJ Wainwright	b Brown	0	(10) not out	4
MAK Lawson	st Wessels b Panesar	3	(3) c Love b Panesar	3
GJ Kruis	not out	0	st Wessels b Brown	4
Extras	b 10, lb 15, nb 2	27	b 17, lb 17, nb 4	38
	(82.5 overs)	177	(109.5 overs)	278

Bowling
Wright 5-1-23-0. Louw 7-3-9-0. Crook 9-2-23-0. Brown 34-10-65-5. Panesar 27.5-11-32-5.
Wright 5-2-8-0. Louw 3-2-5-0. Brown 50.5-14-95-5. Panesar 46-14-96-5. Crook 4-0-15-0. Afzaal 1-0-25-0.
Fall of Wickets: 1-66, 2-75, 3-76, 4-78, 5-102, 6-146, 7-163, 8-166, 9-177
1-19, 2-22, 3-43, 4-101, 5-113, 6-123, 7-202, 8-257, 9-262

NORTHANTS	First Innings	
RA White	c Lumb b Kruis	26
BM Shafayat	b Kruis	4
ML Love	c & b Harvey	95
U Afzaal	c Wood b Kruis	157
DJG Sales (capt)	c Lumb b Kruis	4
*MH Wessels	lbw b Kruis	2
DG Wright	c Wainwright b Lawson	11
SP Crook	lbw b Harvey	97
J Louw	c McGrath b Wainwright	16
MS Panesar	not out	25
JF Brown		
Extras	b 10, lb 14, w 1, nb 14	39
	(9 wkts dec 113.5 overs)	476

Bowling
Kruis 23-4-75-5. Bresnan 14-2-67-0. Wainwright 29-5-86-1. Lawson 30-1-150-1. McGrath 6-0-24-0. Sayers 5-0-26-0. Harvey 6.5-0-24-2.
Fall of Wickets: 1-17, 2-34, 3-254, 4-271, 5-281, 6-312, 7-356, 8-400, 9-476

Northamptonshire won by an innings and 21 runs –
Northamptonshire (22 pts), Yorkshire (3 pts)

WORCESTERSHIRE v. ESSEX – at Worcester

ESSEX	First Innings		Second Innings	
WI Jefferson	c Moore b Wedge	116	c Moore b Mitchell	20
AN Cook	c Mitchell b Kabir Ali	35	not out	117
RS Bopara	c Smith b Wedge	13	not out	58
RC Irani (capt)	c Price b Batty	99		
*JS Foster	c Smith b Wedge	0		
RN ten Doeschate	c Batty b Kabir Ali	98		
JD Middlebrook	c Wigley b Price	4		
TJ Phillips	c Hick b Wigley	89		
GR Napier	c Solanki b Wedge	55		
AR Adams	c Wigley b Wedge	38		
JS Ahmed	not out	14		
Extras	b 1, lb 4, w 2, nb 6	13	nb 6	6
	(155.2 overs)	574	(1 wkt dec 36 overs)	201

Bowling
Kabir Ali 25-4-92-2. Wigley 28.2-4-126-1. Wedge 31-5-112-5. Price 35-7-108-1. Batty 28-7-91-1. Mitchell 7-1-40-0. Moore 1-1-0-0.
Wigley 5-1-25-0. Wedge 6-1-31-0. Mitchell 8-0-59-1. Solanki 10-0-45-0. Smith 7-1-41-0.
Fall of Wickets: 1-55, 2-114, 3-227, 4-227, 5-324, 6-355, 7-387, 8-466, 9-537
1-68

WORCS	First Innings		Second Innings	
SC Moore	c Middlebrook b Bopara	191	b Bopara	45
DKH Mitchell	c Adams b Ahmed	6	c & b Bopara	53
GA Hick	b Adams	17	st Foster b Phillips	107
BF Smith	not out	154	c Napier b Phillips	76
VS Solanki (capt)	not out	24	c Jefferson b Phillips	15
*SM Davies			not out	26
GJ Batty			not out	10
Kabir Ali				
RW Price				
DH Wigley				
SA Wedge				
Extras	b 4, lb 6, w 1, nb 21	32	b 5, lb 5, w 2, nb 4	16
	(3 wkts dec 92 overs)	424	(5 wkts 60 overs)	348

Bowling
Adams 8-2-41-1. Ahmed 16-4-90-1. Bopara 10-0-50-1. Napier 13-1-73-0. Middlebrook 31-5-91-0. Phillips 14-2-69-0.
Adams 18-1-93-0. Ahmed 11-0-51-0. Napier 6-0-33-0. Bopara 15-2-95-2. Middlebrook 6-0-42-0. Phillips 4-0-24-3.
Fall of Wickets: 1-32, 2-49, 3-382
1-91, 2-119, 3-291, 4-298, 5-316

Match drawn – Worcestershire (11 pts), Essex (10 pts)

Division One Final Positions

	P	W	L	D	Bat	Bowl	Pts
Nottinghamshire	16	9	3	4	50	44	236.00
Hampshire	16	9	3	4	46	46	233.50
Sussex	16	7	3	6	57	45	224.00
Warwickshire	16	8	5	3	42	44	209.50
Kent*	16	6	3	7	57	42	202.50
Middlesex	16	4	5	7	56	42	181.50
Surrey†	16	4	3	9	53	44	180.50
Gloucestershire	16	1	10	5	26	46	104.00
Glamorgan	16	1	14	1	33	38	88.50

* Eight points deducted for a substandard pitch

† Eight points deducted for altering the condition of the ball

Slow Over Rate Deductions

Glos	0.50	v. Notts	(Bristol, 25 May)
Kent	0.50	v. Glamorgan	(Cardiff, 8 June)
Hampshire	0.50	v. Sussex	(The Rose Bowl, 20 July)
Surrey	0.50	v. Kent	(Guildford, 20 July)
Middlesex	0.50	v. Warks	(Lord's, 3 August)
Warks	0.50	v. Notts	(Trent Bridge, 14 August)
Glamorgan	0.50	v. Glos	(Bristol, 25 August)
Glos	1.50	v. Notts	(Trent Bridge, 5 Sept)

Division Two Final Positions

	P	W	L	D	Bat	Bowl	Pts
Lancashire	16	7	3	6	43	47	212.00
Durham	16	6	2	8	45	44	205.00
Yorkshire	16	5	1	10	49	42	200.50
Northants	16	5	3	8	45	46	193.00
Essex	16	5	4	7	51	36	185.00
Worcestershire	16	5	7	4	53	46	179.50
Leicestershire	16	3	6	7	45	45	159.50
Somerset	16	4	7	5	42	37	155.00
Derbyshire	16	1	8	7	31	43	116.00

Slow Over Rate Deductions

Yorkshire	0.50	v. Essex	(Chelmsford, 13 April)
Leicestershire	0.50	v. Essex	(Chelmsford, 6 May)
Worcestershire	2.00	v. Yorkshire	(Worcester, 8 July)
Worcestershire	0.50	v. Northants	(Northampton, 20 July)
Worcestershire	1.00	v. Northants	(Worcester, 4 August)
Worcestershire	2.00	v. Yorkshire	(Headingley, 7 Sept)

COUNTY CHAMPIONSHIP FEATURES 2005

INDIVIDUAL SCORES OVER 200

JP Crawley	311*	Hampshire v. Nottinghamshire	at The Rose Bowl
GC Smith	311	Somerset v. Leicestershire	at Taunton
MJ Wood	297	Somerset v. Yorkshire	at Taunton
M van Jaarsveld	262*	Kent v. Glamorgan	at Cardiff
MEK Hussey	253	Durham v. Leicestershire	at Leicester
MR Ramprakash	252	Surrey v. Middlesex	at The Oval
SC Moore	246	Worcestershire v. Derbyshire	at Worcester
SP Fleming	238	Nottinghamshire v. Surrey	at The Oval
DJ Hussey	232*	Nottinghamshire v. Warwickshire	at Trent Bridge
IR Bell	231	Warwickshire v. Middlesex	at Edgbaston
DD Cherry	226	Glamorgan v. Middlesex	at Southgate
SA Newman	219	Surrey v. Glamorgan	at The Oval
PA Jaques	219	Yorks v. Derbyshire	at Headingley
IJL Trott	210	Warwickshire v. Sussex	at Edgbaston
IJ Harvey	209*	Yorkshire v. Somerset	at Headingley
DI Stevens	208	Kent v. Glamorgan	at Canterbury
Azhar Mahmood	204*	Surrey v. Middlesex	at The Oval
SR Watson	203*	Hampshire v. Warwickshire	at The Rose Bowl
MJ Di Venuto	203	Derbyshire v. Durham	at Derby
MB Loye	200	Lancashire v. Durham	at The Riverside

BEST INNINGS BOWLING (6 WICKETS OR MORE)

DG Wright	8-60	Northants v. Yorkshire	at Headingley
J Ormond	7-63	Surrey v. Glamorgan	at Cardiff
A Richardson	7-113	Middlesex v. Nottinghamshire	at Lord's
MS Panesar	7-181	Northamptonshire v. Essex	at Chelmsford
HH Streak	6-31	Warwickshire v. Hampshire	at Stratford
M Davies	6-32	Durham v. Worcestershire	at The Riverside
Harbhajan Singh	6-36	Surrey v. Hampshire	at The Rose Bowl
AF Giles	6-44	Warwickshire v. Glamorgan	at Edgbaston
CT Tremlett	6-44	Hampshire v. Sussex	at Hove
HH Streak	6-44	Warwickshire v. Gloucestershire	at Gloucester
Mushtaq Ahmed	6-44	Sussex v. Middlesex	at Lord's
SD Udal	6-44	Hampshire v. Warwickshire	at The Rose Bowl
BV Taylor	6-45	Hampshire v. Gloucestershire	at The Rose Bowl
Shoaib Akhtar	6-47	Worcestershire v. Northamptonshire	at Northampton
M Muralitharan	6-50	Lancashire v. Derbyshire	at Derby
J Louw	6-51	Northamptonshire v. Essex	at Northampton
SJ Harmison	6-52	Durham v. Lancashire	at Old Trafford
MM Patel	6-53	Kent v. Warwickshire	at Edgbaston
OD Gibson	6-56	Leicestershire v. Yorkshire	at Leicester
MP Bicknell	6-56	Surrey v. Nottinghamshire	at Trent Bridge

BEST MATCH BOWLING

AR Caddick	12/204	Somerset v. Durham	at Stockton-on-Tees
AG Wharf	11/121	Glamorgan v. Gloucestershire	at Bristol
Danish Kaneria	11/176	Essex v. Derbyshire	at Derby
SB Styris	10/118	Middlesex v. Hampshire	at The Rose Bowl
Mushtaq Ahmed	10/118	Sussex v. Glamorgan	at Hove
MS Panesar	10/128	Northamptonshire v. Yorkshire	at Northampton
JF Brown	10/135	Northamptonshire v. Lancashire	at Northampton
RDB Croft	10/160	Glamorgan v. Hampshire	at Cardiff
JF Brown	10/160	Northamptonshire v. Yorkshire	at Northampton
M Kartik	10/168	Lancashire v. Essex	at Chelmsford
Mushtaq Ahmed	9/68	Sussex v. Middlesex	at Lord's
MA Ealham	9/75	Nottinghamshire v. Gloucestershire	at Trent Bridge

COUNTY CHAMPIONSHIP FEATURES 2005

BEST MATCH BOWLING (continued)

BV Taylor	9/83	Hampshire v. Gloucestershire	at The Rose Bowl
SJ Harmison	9/84	Durham v. Lancashire	at Old Trafford
M Davies	9/101	Durham v. Essex	at The Riverside
Mushtaq Ahmed	9/111	Sussex v. Gloucestershire	at Cheltenham
MS Mason	9/116	Worcestershire v. Somerset	at Bath
J Ormond	9/125	Surrey v. Glamorgan	at Cardiff
SM Ervine	9/127	Hants v. Sussex	at The Rose Bowl
AF Giles	9/129	Warwicks v. Glamorgan	at Edgbaston

HIGHEST TEAM TOTALS

714 for 5d	Hampshire v. Nottinghamshire	at The Rose Bowl
707 for 7d	Derbyshire v. Somerset	at Taunton
696 for 8d	Worcestershire v. Somerset	at Worcester
692 for 7d	Nottinghamshire v. Surrey	at The Oval
686 for 5d	Surrey v. Middlesex	at The Oval
655 for 6d	Lancashire v. Essex	at Old Trafford
622 for 8d	Essex v. Yorkshire	at Headingley
603	Surrey v. Gloucestershire	at Bristol
587	Kent v. Glamorgan	at Canterbury
584 for 3d	Glamorgan v. Middlesex	at Southgate
581	Somerset v. Yorkshire	at Taunton
576 for 6d	Hampshire v. Warwickshire	at The Rose Bowl
574	Northamptonshire v. Somerset	at Taunton
574	Essex v. Worcestershire	at Worcester
572	Kent v. Surrey	at Guildford
570	Yorkshire v. Derbyshire	at Headingley
569	Kent v. Warwickshire	at Edgbaston
568	Kent v. Glamorgan	at Cardiff
566	Somerset v. Leicestershire	at Taunton
564 for 8d	Warwickshire v. Glamorgan	at Edgbaston

LOWEST TEAM TOTALS

96	Glamorgan v. Sussex	at Hove
98	Gloucestershire v. Kent	at Maidstone
100	Northamptonshire v. Somerset	at Northampton
103	Lancashire v. Northamptonshire	at Northampton
103	Gloucestershire v. Nottinghamshire	at Trent Bridge
105	Somerset v. Leicestershire	at Oakham School
106	Essex v. Durham	at The Riverside
113	Worcestershire v. Lancashire	at Blackpool
118	Gloucestershire v. Warwickshire	at Edgbaston
119	Kent v. Sussex	at Canterbury
123	Leicestershire v. Durham	at Leicester
124	Hampshire v. Warwickshire	at Stratford
126	Sussex v. Warwickshire	at Edgbaston
128	Worcestershire v. Leicestershire	at Leicester
128	Middlesex v. Sussex	at Lord's
133	Warwickshire v. Nottinghamshire	at Edgbaston
133	Gloucestershire v. Glamorgan	at Bristol
135	Derbyshire v. Worcestershire	at Derby
135	Durham v. Lancashire	at The Riverside
136	Surrey v. Nottinghamshire	at Trent Bridge

COUNTY CHAMPIONSHIP FEATURES 2005

LEADING RUN SCORERS

Player	Runs	Matches
EC Joyce (Middlesex)	1668	16
OA Shah (Middlesex)	1650	16
MR Ramprakash (Surrey)	1568	14
RWT Key (Kent)	1556	15
BF Smith (Worcestershire)	1477	16
A McGrath (Yorkshire)	1425	16
MW Goodwin (Sussex)	1380	15
DL Hemp (Glamorgan)	1369	16
PA Jaques (Yorkshire)	1359	13
ML Love (Northamptonshire)	1345	15
SC Moore (Worcestershire)	1303	16
DI Stevens (Kent)	1277	16
AN Cook (Essex)	1249	16
JP Crawley (Hampshire)	1246	16
A Flower (Essex)	1239	15
DJ Hussey (Nottinghamshire)	1231	15
SA Newman (Surrey)	1230	15
ET Smith (Middlesex)	1228	16
MH Yardy (Sussex)	1217	16
MB Loye (Lancashire)	1198	16

MOST SIXES

Player	Sixes	Matches
DJ Hussey (Nottinghamshire)	23	15
RC Irani (Essex)	22	15
DJG Sales (Northamptonshire)	20	16
EC Joyce (Middlesex)	19	16
GA Hick (Worcestershire)	18	15
AD Brown (Surrey)	16	16
DL Hemp (Glamorgan)	16	16
DI Stevens (Kent)	15	16
ID Blackwell (Somerset)	15	16
SK Warne (Hampshire)	14	11
AR Adams (Essex)	14	12
MR Ramprakash (Surrey)	13	14
BF Smith (Worcestershire)	13	16
Azhar Mahmood (Surrey)	12	9
MEK Hussey (Durham)	12	10
SP Fleming (Nottinghamshire)	12	11
DG Cork (Lancashire)	12	14
OA Shah (Middlesex)	12	16
J Moss (Derbyshire)	12	16
GC Smith (Somerset)	11	4

COUNTY CHAMPIONSHIP FEATURES 2005

MOST FOURS

Player	Fours	Matches
BF Smith (Worcestershire)	214	16
RWT Key (Kent)	212	15
ML Love (Northamptonshire)	210	15
SC Moore (Worcestershire)	206	16
EC Joyce (Middlesex)	204	16
OA Shah (Middlesex)	196	16
PA Jaques (Yorkshire)	187	13
MR Ramprakash (Surrey)	184	14
MW Goodwin (Sussex)	182	15
ET Smith (Middlesex)	182	16
SA Newman (Surrey)	181	15
DJG Sales (Northamptonshire)	176	16
DL Hemp (Glamorgan)	174	16
DDJ Robinson (Leicestershire)	170	15
DI Stevens (Kent)	168	16
DJ Bicknell (Nottinghamshire)	164	16
MH Yardy (Sussex)	164	16
JER Gallian (Nottinghamshire)	162	16
A McGrath (Yorkshire)	162	16
AN Cook (Essex)	157	16

LEADING WICKET-TAKERS

Player	Wickets	Matches
Mushtaq Ahmed (Sussex)	80	16
GJ Kruis (Yorkshire)	64	16
JM Anderson (Lancashire)	60	16
MM Patel (Kent)	59	16
RJ Kirtley (Sussex)	59	16
G Welch (Derbyshire)	58	16
A Richardson (Middlesex)	57	13
MA Ealham (Nottinghamshire)	56	15
A Khan (Kent)	55	14
JF Brown (Northamptonshire)	55	15
Naved-ul-Hasan (Sussex)	54	9
DG Wright (Northamptonshire)	53	16
AR Caddick (Somerset)	52	10
LE Plunkett (Durham)	51	14
MS Mason (Worcestershire)	51	15
Kabir Ali (Worcestershire)	50	12
DR Brown (Warwickshire)	49	16
RJ Sidebottom (Nottinghamshire)	48	14
SK Warne (Hampshire)	47	11
AJ Harris (Nottinghamshire)	47	11

COUNTY CHAMPIONSHIP FEATURES 2005

LEADING CATCHES (EXCLUDING WICKETKEEPERS)

Player	Catches	Matches
ML Love (Northamptonshire)	36	15
GA Hick (Worcestershire)	35	15
IJL Trott (Warwickshire)	31	16
DJ Hussey (Nottinghamshire)	29	15
BL Hutton (Middlesex)	23	16
OA Shah (Middlesex)	22	16
CJ Adams (Sussex)	21	16
BM Shafayat (Northamptonshire)	21	16
A McGrath (Yorkshire)	20	16
DJG Sales (Northamptonshire)	20	16
MEK Hussey (Durham)	19	10
AD Brown (Surrey)	19	16
MJ Wood (Yorkshire)	19	16
SG Law (Lancashire)	18	15
BF Smith (Worcestershire)	18	16
M van Jaarsveld (Kent)	18	16
R Clarke (Surrey)	16	13
DP Fulton (Kent)	16	16
PD Collingwood (Durham)	15	13
IJ Sutcliffe (Lancashire)	15	14

LEADING DISMISSALS (WICKETKEEPERS)

Player	Dismissals	Matches
CMW Read (Nottinghamshire)	60	15
JN Batty (Surrey)	54	16
NJ O'Brien (Kent)	51	13
N Pothas (Hampshire)	51	15
LD Sutton (Derbyshire)	50	16
WK Hegg (Lancashire)	46	15
PA Nixon (Leicestershire)	44	16
BJM Scott (Middlesex)	42	15
DJ Pipe (Worcestershire)	41	10
T Frost (Warwickshire)	41	15
P Mustard (Durham)	41	16
SJ Adshead (Gloucestershire)	39	16
JS Foster (Essex)	39	16
MJ Prior (Sussex)	37	14
I Dawood (Yorkshire)	35	12
MA Wallace (Glamorgan	35	16
MH Wessels (Northamptonshire)	27	13
RJ Turner (Somerset)	22	8
CM Gazzard (Somerset)	15	8
GO Jones (Kent)	14	3

COUNTY CHAMPIONSHIP FEATURES 2005

MOST HUNDREDS

Player	Hundreds	Matches
OA Shah (Middlesex)	7	16
PD Collingwood (Durham)	6	13
MR Ramprakash (Surrey)	6	14
BF Smith (Worcestershire)	6	16
A Flower (Essex)	5	15
A McGrath (Yorkshire)	5	16
U Afzaal (Northamptonshire)	5	16
SP Fleming (Nottinghamshire)	4	11
PA Jaques (Yorkshire)	4	13
DDJ Robinson (Leicestershire)	4	15
ML Love (Northamptonshire)	4	15
MW Goodwin (Sussex)	4	15
RWT Key (Kent)	4	15
SA Newman (Surrey)	4	15
MB Loye (Lancashire)	4	16
DI Stevens (Kent)	4	16
DM Benkenstein (Durham)	4	16
MH Yardy (Sussex)	4	16
AN Cook (Essex)	4	16
M van Jaarsveld (Kent)	4	16

MOST FIFTIES (INCLUDING HUNDREDS)

Player	Fifties	Matches
EC Joyce (Middlesex)	16	16
OA Shah (Middlesex)	14	16
RWT Key (Kent)	12	15
MR Ramprakash (Surrey)	11	14
MW Goodwin (Sussex)	11	15
DJ Bicknell (Nottinghamshire)	11	16
DL Hemp (Glamorgan)	11	16
ID Blackwell (Somerset)	11	16
PA Jaques (Yorkshire)	10	13
RC Irani (Essex)	10	15
ML Love (Northamptonshire)	10	15
SD Stubbings (Derbyshire)	10	15
DJ Hussey (Nottinghamshire)	10	15
CJ Adams (Sussex)	10	16
BF Smith (Worcestershire)	10	16
A McGrath (Yorkshire)	10	16
DI Stevens (Kent)	10	16
MH Yardy (Sussex)	10	16
IJ Sutcliffe (Lancashire)	9	14
A Flower (Essex)	9	15

COUNTY CHAMPIONSHIP FEATURES 2005

LEADING DUCK-MAKERS

Player	Ducks	Matches
ND Doshi (Surrey)	6	10
M Akram (Surrey)	6	14
DS Harrison (Glamorgan)	6	16
JM Anderson (Lancashire)	6	16
MS Panesar (Northamptonshire)	5	8
AG Wharf (Glamorgan)	5	11
DD Cherry (Glamorgan)	5	13
MH Wessels (Northamptonshire)	5	13
OD Gibson (Leicestershire)	5	14
LE Plunkett (Durham)	5	14
JF Brown (Northamptonshire)	5	15
Hassan Adnan (Derbyshire)	5	15
J Louw (Northamptonshire)	5	15
PA Nixon (Leicestershire)	5	16
MJ Chilton (Lancashire)	5	16
AP Davies (Glamorgan)	4	6
KP Pietersen (Hampshire)	4	6
JMM Averis (Gloucestershire)	4	8
RL Johnson (Somerset)	4	10
GW Flower (Essex)	4	11

HUNDREDS IN EACH INNINGS

Name	For	Against	Venue	Date	1st	2nd
M van Jaarsveld	Kent	Warwicks	Canterbury	20 April	118	111
SA Newman	Surrey	Glamorgan	The Oval	11 May	117	219
RWT Key	Kent	Surrey	Tunbridge Wells	25 May	112	189
J Hughes	Glamorgan	Middlesex	Southgate	15 June	134*	100*
PD Collingwood	Durham	Somerset	Taunton	26 July	181	105*

FASTEST COUNTY CHAMPIONSHIP HUNDREDS

ID Blackwell	67 balls	Somerset v. Derbyshire	at Taunton	24 September
MJ Prior	72 balls	Sussex v. Glamorgan	at Hove	12 August
SK Warne	72 balls	Hampshire v. Kent	at Canterbury	11 May
PD Collingwood	73 balls	Durham v. Somerset	at Taunton	29 July
AR Adams	76 balls	Essex v. Durham	at The Riverside	11 June

ECB NATIONAL ACADEMY

PETER MOORES, who this winter has taken over from Rod Marsh as the ECB National Academy director, talks to BRUCE TALBOT about the challenge that lies ahead.

Peter Moores isn't someone given to bold statements or dramatic gestures. When he masterminded Sussex's improbable first championship success in 2003 he resisted all the efforts by his players to join them in their champagne-soaked reverie on the outfield, preferring instead to enjoy the greatest moment of his career blending into the background on the dressing room balcony at Hove.

There are a few pictures of Moores basking in the adulation of the Sussex faithful that day, but not many.

Fast forward two years to The Oval, 12 September 2005. As Michael Vaughan and his men celebrated recapturing the Ashes, it was England coach Duncan Fletcher playing the part of reluctant hero.

Both men share similar values and while Moores laughs at the suggestion that he is, like Fletcher, obsessed with the game, he recognises it as a compliment all the same. Perhaps it will be Moores, rather than Fletcher, blending quietly into the background when the Australians return in 2009. Not that Moores even allows himself such thoughts. He has more immediate priorities like ensuring the 'conveyor belt' of talent from the county game, which goes through the National Academy and into the England set-up, runs smoothly now that he has succeeded Rod Marsh as its director.

There can't be a better time to be involved in English cricket, a point not lost on Moores, who began work at Loughborough at the beginning of October. 'Our game is on an all-time high thanks to what happened this summer but the success we've had has been coming for the past four or five years,' said Moores. 'Central contracts have been a huge help but I've no doubt that a two-divisional championship has increased the intensity levels hugely. Once the intensity increased so did the skill factor and our domestic game has become much stronger as a result. You only have to look at how well guys like Andrew Strauss, Kevin Pietersen and Ian Bell have adapted to international cricket for evidence of that.'

The contrast between Moores and the man he is replacing couldn't be more marked. They were both wicketkeepers, but there the similarities end. While Moores was the epitome of the solid county pro – unostentacious but utterly reliable in a 13-year playing career – Marsh was one of the best glovemen of his generation who kept wicket for Australia in 96 Tests.

They share few similarities when it comes to coaching either, which isn't a bad thing of course. Moores sees himself as a facilitator – the man who can help his players get the best out of themselves and regards every one of them as a

Peter Moores – the man chosen to succeed Rod Marsh as director of the ECB National Academy.

different challenge. Discovering what makes an individual tick is almost as important to him as improving their skill levels. Whereas Marsh has been known to hurl water bottles across the dressing room when a wicket falls, Moores rarely rants and raves. But when he does raise his voice it invariably has the desired effect. The rollocking he administered halfway through the 2003 season, when he told the Sussex players 'to leave the land of bullshit and return to the land of reality', played a huge part in the success the county enjoyed.

But Moores has huge respect for the work Marsh has achieved with the Academy. 'He's done a fantastic job, simple as that,' said Moores. 'What I like is that Rod has instilled a very strong work ethic which is something I want to maintain. He has also made players aware that everything is there waiting for them if they want to grab it. It has come across pretty loud and clear that he feels it is in the players' hands. So do I. They have got to want to prepare properly and to work hard. That will give them the best possible opportunity to perform where it matters – on the pitch.'

Even as an impressionable youngster on the MCC groundstaff in 1982, Moores was always thinking how he might stay involved in cricket beyond any playing career. The boys were paid the princely sum of £32 and every payday coach Don Wilson would hold court in the indoor school bar at Lord's. Moores would invariably be the last to leave, happy to make sure that the coach's glass was always full as long as the stories and advice kept coming.

He took his first tentative steps into coaching just two years later, teaching the game to the well-heeled pupils of a private college in Zimbabwe. The following winter provided a far more daunting role with Free State Country in South Africa. 'It was a very good standard with eight or nine players with first-class experience. It was a heavy duty job for someone who was 20-plus and still a bit wet behind the ears.'

Virtually every winter over the next 15 years was spent in the dilapidated indoor nets at Hove. 'It was a great learning experience because one minute you would be teaching a group of kids and then the next it would be one-to-one sessions with a 60-year-old getting his eye in so he could play for his Sunday afternoon village team.'

Moores was the obvious choice as captain when the infamous revolution at Sussex in 1997 left the county shorn of experienced players and then as coach a year later when Desmond Haynes left Hove. He quickly established a reputation as a forward-thinking coach happy to integrate ideas from other sports. He introduced all-year contracts, used sports scientists and physiologists to improve fitness levels, and was the first county coach to embrace the video analysis system which logs every ball and provides a valuable tool in improving technical skills. And it wasn't long before his methods began to get noticed. He led England A to the West Indies in 2001 and three years later was short-listed for the job of West Indies' coach.

There were certainly more eye-catching candidates when the search for Marsh's successor began early in 2005, but Moores interviewed so well that there was only one choice. Fletcher, in particular, was deeply impressed. Moores admits it will be a big wrench to leave Hove after 20 years but Sussex cricket is in rude health as a result of his diligence. The county will play first division cricket in both competitions for the first time in 2006 and he has overseen the development of an exciting crop of young players. 'Sussex will always be a special place for me but I see the Academy as a new challenge and a very different one. I will bring the things I've learned in

Rod Marsh instilled a very strong work ethic during his years in charge of the Academy.

county cricket but I will learn a lot more from everyone I'll be working with which is exciting,' he said.

County commitments mean Moores has been restricted in watching potential candidates for this year's intake. The selectors, Marsh and other members of the Academy staff all had their own thoughts. But invariably the same names kept cropping up. As he looks ahead to the next stage of his career it isn't long before he starts warming to his theme. A cricket obsessive? As the Academy players are about to find out, once he's in full flow it's hard to stop him. 'For players coming into our Academy it's certainly all in place for them to succeed,' he insists. 'I'd like to think that when a player goes back to his county he is telling everyone that they have got to get there too because there is so much they can learn plus the opportunity to move their own game forward. It has to be a place where excellence is standard.

'The Academy bridges the gap from being a county player to an international player. You are looking to make players who have gone through your processes better in some way. It could be in little areas but they might make a big difference. For instance, it could be a bowler whose batting you've worked on for three or four months so that when he goes out in a Test match with seven to win he does it. A bit like Matthew Hoggard did at Trent Bridge last summer.

'Another challenge is dealing with players who are there because they are not in the main squad and who have to improve to get into it. Our job is to add that something to their game which will enable them to be picked.

'Slowly but surely you establish criteria and eventually you get outstanding people and outstanding performers and that means a winning side.

'We have set ourselves a challenge of being the best team in the world. Not for a few years but forever and part of that is developing players who have all the skills to thrive at the highest level. It's an enormous challenge but I'm going to love trying to meet it.'

Bruce Talbot is the cricket correspondent of the Brighton Evening Argus *newspaper.*

ECB National Academy squad 2005–06:

Gareth Batty (Worcestershire); Ravinder Bopara (Essex), Stuart Broad (Leicestershire), Rikki Clarke (Surrey), Alastair Cook (Essex), Jamie Dalrymple (Middlesex), Steven Davies (Worcestershire), Mark Footitt (Nottinghamshire), Ed Joyce (Middlesex), Robert Key (Kent), Sajid Mahmood (Lancashire), Liam Plunkett (Durham), Chris Read (Nottinghamshire), Owais Shah (Middlesex), Tom Smith (Lancashire), Luke Wright (Sussex), Mike Yardy (Sussex).

TOTESPORT LEAGUE
By Mark Baldwin

17 April 2005: Division One

at Old Trafford
Lancashire 160 for 8 (41.2 overs)
Glamorgan
Match abandoned – 2pts each

at The Rose Bowl
Hampshire 175 for 9 (45 overs)
Essex 69 for 2 (16 overs)
*Essex (4pts) won by 16 runs – DL Method: target 54
from 16 overs*

at Northampton
Worcestershire 211 for 4 (45 overs) (VS Solanki 119)
Northamptonshire 137 for 7 (32.5 overs)
*Worcestershire (4pts) won by 31 runs – DL Method:
target 169 from 32.5 overs*

at Trent Bridge
Nottinghamshire 173 (44.3 overs) (CB Keegan 6 for 33)
Middlesex 91 for 0 (21.3 overs) (PN Weekes 52*)
*Middlesex (4pts) won by 35 runs – DL Method: target 57
from 21.3 overs*

Simon Jones signed a new three-year deal with Glamorgan on
the understanding he would play more one-day cricket for them.

Glamorgan's defence of their trophy got off to a
damp start at Old Trafford, but before the game was
abandoned there was a promising glimpse of what
Simon Jones might offer his county – and his country
– in limited-overs cricket. The England fast bowler,
who had agreed to stay with his native county on a
new three-year contract, on the understanding that
he would play more one-day matches, tore into the
Lancashire top order to pick up figures of 3 for 19.

Kevin Pietersen was yorked for just 5 on his
Hampshire debut, by Essex slow left-armer Tim
Phillips, and a 2,000 crowd at the Rose Bowl were
also disappointed to see their side restricted to 175
for 9, and then beaten on the Duckworth-Lewis rule
as Will Jefferson made sure the visitors stayed ahead
of the required rate before the threatening rain
arrived to wash away the last scheduled 29 overs.

Vikram Solanki, Worcestershire's new captain,
took 119 off Northamptonshire's attack at Wantage
Road to drive his team towards their 45-over total of
211 for 4. Matt Mason's three-wicket new-ball spell
then put Northants further on to the back foot, and
when rain closed in they were 31 runs adrift of
Duckworth-Lewis requirements at 137 for 7.

There was a career-best return of 6 for 33 for Chad
Keegan at Trent Bridge, as Nottinghamshire were
blown away by Middlesex's South African-born
paceman with a remodelled action. After missing the
second half of the 2004 season with a serious double
stress fracture of the back, Keegan was forced to
change the way he bowls and said, 'At the moment it
feels like I'm bowling on someone else's legs.' It did
not seem to be affecting him too badly, however, as he
removed six of Notts' top seven. Middlesex were
cruising to victory at 91 without loss in reply when
rain simply confirmed their win by Duckworth-Lewis.

Division Two

at The Oval
Yorkshire 334 for 5 (45 overs) (MJ Wood 111,
IJ Harvey 69)
Surrey 291 (38.4 overs) (AD Brown 89, C White 4 for 14)
Yorkshire (4pts) won by 43 runs

at Leicester
Leicestershire 175 for 8 (45 overs) (DL Maddy 50)
Durham 85 for 3 (22 overs)
*Durham (4pts) won by 9 runs – DL Method: target 77
from 22 overs*

at Derby
Derbyshire 197 for 8 (45 overs) (J Moss 79)

Kent 9 for 0 (5 overs)
Match abandoned – 2pts each

at Edgbaston
Somerset 254 for 5 (45 overs) (M Burns 107,
JC Hildreth 54, KA Parsons 51)
Warwickshire
Match abandoned – 2pts each

Yorkshire had Craig White to thank for coming out
on top in a high-scoring thriller against Surrey at
The Oval. White took three wickets for no runs in
five overs, after bringing himself on as the seventh
bowler, to stop a courageous Surrey chase in its
tracks. His most important strike was the removal
of Alistair Brown with a searing yorker. Brown had
hit 89 from just 46 balls, with five sixes and nine
fours, and was making the pursuit of Yorkshire's
334 for 5 look far simpler than it had a right to be.
White's spell of 4 for 14 from four overs meant that
Surrey, after needing 74 off the last 12 overs with
five wickets in hand, collapsed from 261 for 5 to
263 for 8. Matthew Wood's 127-ball 111 had earlier
anchored Yorkshire's second-highest total in the
totesport League, with Ian Harvey launching it with
a 35-ball 50.

Durham were just ahead of Leicestershire on
Duckworth-Lewis when heavy rain helped them to
victory at Grace Road, but the weather caused the
points to be shared at Derby and at Edgbaston,
where Mike Burns made his first hundred in nine
seasons of trying against his former county
Warwickshire. Somerset's Burns received warm
applause from the Edgbaston crowd after hitting
107 from 134 balls.

22 April 2005: Division One

at Cardiff
Glamorgan v. **Essex**
Match abandoned – 2pts each

The wisdom, or lack of it, of scheduling a floodlit
match in the third week of April was fully exposed
when Glamorgan's home fixture against Essex –
potentially one of the most attractive of the season
in the division – was abandoned without a ball being
bowled due to rain.

24 April 2005: Division One

at Lord's
Middlesex 210 for 9 (45 overs) (JWM Dalrymple 81)

Lancashire 141 (37.2 overs)
Middlesex (4pts) won by 69 runs

at Bristol
Northamptonshire 202 for 7 (45 overs)
Gloucestershire 193 for 8 (45 overs) (APR Gidman 71)
Northamptonshire (4pts) won by 9 runs

Middlesex made it two wins from two matches by
defeating Lancashire by 69 runs at Lord's and overshadowing Andrew Flintoff's return to competitive
cricket after a three-month absence. Flintoff, who
did not bowl, scored just 17 and none of the
Lancashire batsmen could break the shackles
against some tidy seam bowling. The Middlesex
innings, however, had also been in some disarray at
37 for 6 in the 17th over before Jamie Dalrymple,
with support from the tail, turned the match on
its head with a superb and daring innings of 81
off 82 balls.

Dropped catches, questionable bowling changes
and some inconsistent bowling at crucial times lay
beneath Gloucestershire's nine-run home defeat to
Northamptonshire at Bristol. It was just not like
them, and not even a fine 71 from Alex Gidman
could pull them around.

Division Two

at The Riverside
Durham 224 for 8 (45 overs) (GJ Muchall 70*,
DM Benkenstein 63)
Surrey 86 (30.1 overs) (DM Benkenstein 4 for 16,
LE Plunkett 4 for 28)
Durham (4pts) won by 138 runs

at Headingley
Somerset 209 for 9 (45 overs) (TT Bresnan 4 for 25)
Yorkshire 213 for 5 (39.4 overs) (PA Jaques 84,
MJ Lumb 57)
Yorkshire (4pts) won by 5 wickets

at Hove
Sussex 254 for 8 (45 overs) (MJ Prior 74, IJ Ward 54)
Derbyshire 202 (32 overs) (Hassan Adnan 59)
*Sussex (4pts) won by 2 runs – DL Method: target 205
from 32 overs*

at Canterbury
Leicestershire 214 for 8 (45 overs) (D Mongia 62)
Kent 150 for 4 (33.5 overs) (M van Jaarsveld 69*)
*Kent (4pts) won by 6 runs – DL Method: target 145 from
33.5 overs*

Durham and Yorkshire shared the early lead in the second division table, both maintaining 100 per cent records at home to Surrey and Somerset respectively. Dale Benkenstein was the all-round inspiration behind Durham's 138-run thrashing of Surrey at the Riverside, first scoring 63 in a 100-run fifth wicket stand with Gordon Muchall and then taking four wickets for just 16 runs in a six-over spell which helped to close out the already faltering Surrey reply. Liam Plunkett, who had earlier removed Mark Ramprakash and Alistair Brown in the same over for ducks, finished with 4 for 28.

Yorkshire's five-wicket triumph at Headingley was built around Tim Bresnan's impressive four-wicket haul and a sumptuous 78-ball 84 from Phil Jaques. He dominated an 84-run stand for the third wicket with Michael Lumb, who then himself accelerated to a 53-ball half-century as Somerset struggled to stem the flow.

Graeme Welch almost pulled off an improbable win for Derbyshire against Sussex at Hove, hammering 41 from 24 balls to bring his side to within three runs of the target they had been set following mid-afternoon rain. Ian Ward and Matt Prior had batted well to set Sussex on course for their eventual 254 for 8, but Derbyshire's target was revised to 205 in 32 overs. Sussex seemed to be in control when Hassan Adnan fell for 59, but Welch struck three sixes and three fours before giving a catch in the penultimate over. Nine were needed from the last over, bowled by acting captain James Kirtley, who removed Ian Hunter's off stump with his fourth ball and then prevented Tom Lungley from hitting the final ball for six.

Kent just about deserved their six-run victory against Leicestershire, courtesy of Duckworth-Lewis, if only because their visitors to Canterbury should have totalled more than 214 for 8 and because Martin van Jaarsveld's unbeaten 69 was only matched for fluency by Darren Maddy's run-a-ball 40 at the start.

1 May 2005: Division One

at Lord's
Worcestershire 201 for 7 (44 overs) (DA Leatherdale 72*)
Middlesex 207 for 7 (43.4 overs) (PN Weekes 62)
Middlesex (4pts) won by 3 wickets – DL Method: target 202 from 44 overs

at Northampton
Northamptonshire 266 for 9 (45 overs)
(BM Shafayat 74, U Afzaal 54)
Hampshire 168 (39.1 overs) (BJ Phillips 4 for 48)
Northamptonshire (4pts) won by 98 runs

at Old Trafford
Lancashire 178 for 8 (43 overs) (SG Law 52)
Nottinghamshire 177 for 6 (43 overs) (SP Fleming 60, JER Gallian 53)
Lancashire (4pts) won by 1 run

An opening partnership of 104 between Paul Weekes and Ed Smith set Middlesex on the way to an exciting three-wicket victory over Worcestershire at Lord's. It made them, after three games, the only team with a 100 per cent record in the division. But, even with their fine start, Middlesex needed their No. 9, Chad Keegan, to stride to the wicket with seven more runs required off five balls. His first ball, from Chaminda Vaas, was smeared over point for four. His second went over mid-off's head for two,

Graeme Hick celebrates becoming the heaviest run–getter in one-day league history.

and the next ball – even though just one run was by now needed – saw Keegan smash a full toss straight for six. David Leatherdale had earlier hit an intelligently-paced 72 not out from 83 balls while Graeme Hick became the highest run-scorer in one-day league history with the boundary which took him to 29 and proved to be his final scoring shot. Hick was dismissed with 9,004 one-day league runs to his name, beating the previous record of 9,002 by Kim Barnett.

Northamptonshire went into second place by overwhelming Hampshire by 98 runs at Northampton. Bilal Shafayat scored 74 from 82 balls, after figuring in a 108-run opening stand with Martin Love, and then Usman Afzaal's 54 from 65 balls helped to push Northants on to 266 for 9. The home side's bowling and out-cricket then showed up that of their opponents, with Ben Phillips finishing with 4 for 48, including the prized scalps of Kevin Pietersen, for just 9, and Shane Warne.

Nottinghamshire failed to score 26 runs from the last six overs, with wickets in hand after Stephen Fleming and Jason Gallian had set them up with a second-wicket partnership of 65, and gifted Lancashire a one-run win at Old Trafford. The home side, for whom Stuart Law had opened up with 52, had needed a ninth-wicket stand of 34 between Warren Hegg and James Anderson, who later impressed with three wickets from his eight overs at a cost of just 18, to give them any sort of defendable total.

Division Two

at Headingley
Sussex 157 (42.2 overs)
Yorkshire 158 for 7 (41.3 overs)
Yorkshire (4pts) won by 3 wickets

at Taunton
Leicestershire 211 for 8 (45 overs)
Somerset 213 for 2 (44 overs) (KA Parsons 91*, JD Francis 73*)
Somerset (4pts) won by 8 wickets

at Edgbaston
Warwickshire 279 for 7 (45 overs) (NV Knight 122*)
Kent 260 (43.1 overs) (M van Jaarsveld 82, DP Fulton 57)
Warwickshire (4pts) won by 19 runs

at The Grange
Scotland v. **Durham**
Match abandoned – 2pts each

Yorkshire, like Middlesex in the division above, became the only team in their table to record a third win out of three by inching past Sussex's seemingly modest 157 on a sluggish surface at Headingley. Craig White took three wickets at the death for just six runs, from four overs, but Yorkshire were still indebted to a fifth-wicket stand of 63 in 18 overs between Anthony McGrath and Ian Harvey after sliding to 66 for 4.

Somerset's first win of the campaign arrived on the back of an unbroken partnership of 157 for the third wicket between John Francis and Keith Parsons, who was the chief aggressor with an unbeaten 91. Earlier, put in after morning rain and in muggy conditions, Leicestershire had struggled to reach 211 for 8 with Aaron Laraman taking 2 for 17 from his nine overs.

A spirited last-wicket partnership of 40 between Simon Cook and Martin Saggers narrowed the margin of victory, but Warwickshire were always in command at Edgbaston following a classy demonstation of limited-overs batsmanship by Nick Knight. The former England opener went in with the total 36 for 1, and walked off at the end with 122 not out to his name. His hundred came off 119 balls, with 11 fours, and he then struck a six and three more fours from the last six balls he faced. With support from a succession of partners, Knight's masterclass ensured a Warwickshire total of 279 for 7, and from 42 for 3 Kent did well to get as close as they did as Martin van Jaarsveld and David Fulton inspired a determined recovery.

2 May 2005: Division One

at The Rose Bowl
Gloucestershire 210 for 9 (45 overs) (WPC Weston 63)
Hampshire 150 (41.2 overs) (J Lewis 5 for 19)
Gloucestershire (4pts) won by 60 runs

at Trent Bridge
Glamorgan 204 for 4 (38 overs)
Nottinghamshire 217 for 8 (38 overs) (DJ Hussey 68)
Glamorgan (4pts) won by 4 runs – DL Method: target 222 from 38 overs

Jon Lewis was Gloucestershire's unlikely all-round hero at the Rose Bowl, even putting Shane Warne in his place as he had a day to remember with bat as much as ball. Lewis, normally a tailender, was promoted to No. 4 with orders to hit out after Matt Windows was forced to retire with hamstring problems in the 19th over, and with Gloucestershire also limping along on 50 for 1.

Lewis and Phil Weston immediately took 17 from Alan Mullally's fourth and last over, and Warne introduced himself for the 22nd over, with Gloucestershire now 74 for 1. Shaun Udal's off-breaks were also brought into the attack at the other end, but the first six overs of spin disappeared for 51. Warne, riled at being hit for a vast six over midwicket by Lewis, replied with a bouncer which the batsman calmly uppercut for another boundary. In the end Lewis was bowled by Warne, but his 28-ball 40 – a one-day best – had already served its purpose and, when Hampshire batted, it was noticeable that Gloucestershire captain Chris Taylor opted to keep a far tighter rein with his seamers. Lewis made two initial breakthroughs with the new ball before returning to finish off the innings and earn himself career-best one-day figures of 5 for 19.

Glamorgan, having had two no results, were helped by a rain break at Trent Bridge – their subsequent surge to 204 for 4 in an innings reduced to 38 overs meaning that Nottinghamshire had to score 222 themselves to win on Duckworth-Lewis calculations. That proved just beyond them, although David Hussey and Chris Read played well for 68 and 47 respectively after an initial plunge to 52 for 4, and Samit Patel hit the fourth and fifth balls of the final over, bowled by Darren Thomas, for six. That meant he could have won it for Notts with a third successive six, but this time Thomas produced a fine yorker and Patel managed merely to squeeze it for a single.

Division Two

at Taunton
Somerset 325 for 6 (44 overs) (KA Parsons 85, ST Jayasuriya 61, ME Trescothick 52)
Surrey 226 for 9 (44 overs) (AD Brown 65)
Somerset (4pts) won by 99 runs – DL Method: target 326 from 44 overs

at The Riverside
Sussex 182 for 7 (45 overs) (JJ van der Wath 80*, ML Lewis 5 for 48)
Durham 9 for 2 (7.3 overs)
Match abandoned – 2pts each

Somerset's record one-day league total at Taunton, 325 for 6, proved too potent for Surrey, for whom only Alistair Brown, with 65 off 37 balls, looked capable of matching up to the challenge of beating it. There were popular half-centuries for Marcus

Trescothick and Sanath Jayasuriya at the top end of the Somerset innings, but it was a late stand of 83 in only 42 balls between Keith Parsons (85 from 75 balls) and James Hildreth which took the match way out of Surrey's reach.

Johan van der Wath made an immediate impression for Sussex with an unbeaten 80, but the match with Durham at the Riverside became a victim of the weather before ten overs of the home side's reply could be bowled. Frustratingly for Sussex, the Durham innings had begun badly with openers Mike Hussey and Jon Lewis both falling to James Kirtley for 0, but only 7.3 overs were possible before the rain saved Durham.

8 May 2005: Division Two

at Hove
Sussex 283 for 7 (45 overs) (MJ Prior 144, MW Goodwin 79)
Warwickshire 153 for 7 (30 overs)
Sussex (4pts) won by 44 runs – DL Method: target 198 from 30 overs

at The Grange
Kent 227 for 6 (45 overs) (M van Jaarsveld 57, DI Stevens 51*)
Scotland 134 (32.2 overs) (DI Stevens 5 for 32)
Kent (4pts) won by 93 runs – DL Method: target 228 from 38 overs

The Duckworth-Lewis method was used to decide both second division games played at different ends of the country, at Hove and in Edinburgh. Sussex deservedly beat Warwickshire by 44 runs after Matt Prior had struck a brilliant 144 off 135 balls, with 19 fours and a six, and had been supported in a fourth-wicket stand of 209 by Murray Goodwin, who made 79. Rain reduced Warwickshire's task from 284 in a full allocation of overs to 198 off 30, but they lost wickets regularly. At the Grange, it was even easier for Kent after they had totalled 227 for 6 against the Scottish Saltires. Darren Stevens followed up his unbeaten 51 from 30 balls with a career-best one-day bowling return of 5 for 32.

11 May 2005: Division Two

at The Grange
Somerset 264 for 7 (45 overs) (ID Blackwell 86, AW Laraman 51)
Scotland 248 for 9 (45 overs) (CJO Smith 67)
Somerset (4pts) won by 16 runs

Scotland came within 16 runs of repeating their famous 2003 victory over Somerset in Edinburgh, but the county always seemed in control of affairs once Ian Blackwell's violent 86 – of which 64 runs came in boundaries – had boosted them to 264 for 7. Colin Smith, the Saltires wicketkeeper, kept his side's hopes alive with a fine 67 but in truth they never got within range.

15 May 2005: Division One

at Chelmsford
Glamorgan 216 for 7 (45 overs) (DL Hemp 62*)
Essex 217 for 5 (42.2 overs) (RS Bopara 96*)
Essex (4pts) won by 5 wickets

at Lord's
Hampshire 353 for 8 (45 overs) (SM Katich 85, KP Pietersen 80, AD Mascarenhas 50*)
Middlesex 248 (39 overs) (OA Shah 89, SD Udal 4 for 55)
Hampshire (4pts) won by 105 runs

at Old Trafford
Northamptonshire 215 for 7 (45 overs) (DJG Sales 57)
Lancashire 218 for 3 (36.4 overs) (MB Loye 94*, SG Law 54)
Lancashire (4pts) won by 7 wickets

at Worcester
Worcestershire 190 (44.5 overs) (Z de Bruyn 62, AJ Harris 4 for 41)
Nottinghamshire 174 (44.5 overs) (RW Price 4 for 21)
Worcestershire (4pts) won by 16 runs

Ravinder Bopara underlined his growing stature as a young cricketer with a big future by guiding Essex to a significant five-wicket victory over champions Glamorgan at Chelmsford. Essex were floundering at 31 for 4 in reply to the Welsh county's 216 for 7 when Bopara took charge in a manner mightily impressive for a 20-year-old. James Middlebrook joined him in a fifth-wicket stand of 122, and James Foster helped to add a further 64, but the stage belonged to Bopara. When the finishing line was crossed, he had 96 not out to his name from 113 balls, with ten fours.

Kevin Pietersen's 50-ball 80 was the centrepiece of Hampshire's highest score in the competition – 353 for 8 – and he hit six sixes to the short boundary at Lord's in front of the Grand Stand and Compton Stand. Simon Katich also struck four sixes in his 63-ball 85, as Hampshire built a score large enough to bring them victory in the end by 105 runs, but for Middlesex only Owais Shah, with three sixes and

nine fours in a commanding 89 from 64 balls, could match up to their rate of scoring.

A 29-ball blitz by Andrew Flintoff, which brought him 40 with two sixes and three fours, helped to speed Lancashire to a seven-wicket win over Northamptonshire at Old Trafford after Mal Loye and Stuart Law had laid the base for a comfortable canter to a target of 216. Loye finished 94 not out from 108 balls, while Law hit a sublime 54.

Nottinghamshire slipped to their fourth defeat in four matches, their batting malfunctioning after they had held Worcestershire to just 190 at New Road. Ray Price's slow left-arm spin and the swing and seam of Chaminda Vaas proved too potent a combination for Notts.

Division Two

at The Riverside
Durham 256 for 4 (45 overs) (MEK Hussey 66, N Peng 60, P Mustard 53*)
Yorkshire 205 (40.2 overs)
Durham (4pts) won by 51 runs

at Leicester
Leicestershire 194 for 9 (45 overs) (D Mongia 67)
Surrey 134 (40.1 overs) (D Mongia 4 for 15)
Leicestershire (4pts) won by 60 runs

Durham went top of the second division table by inflicting a first defeat of the season, in any competition, on Yorkshire. The player who most caught the eye at the Riverside was Phil Mustard, who smacked 53 not out from 26 balls and then pulled off three catches and a stumping. Nicky Peng also aided Durham's acceleration, after a slow start, with 60.

Surrey, relegated from Division One in 2004, stayed anchored to the bottom of the second division after suffering a fourth defeat out of four. What is more, they succumbed to Leicestershire on a sluggish surface at Grace Road without putting up much of a fight. Dinesh Mongia was the home star, scoring 67 from 86 balls and then taking four wickets with his left-arm spin.

20 May 2005: Division Two

at The Grange
Scotland 252 for 7 (45 overs) (JA Beukes 91)
Surrey 253 for 5 (38.3 overs) (GP Thorpe 69, AD Brown 65)
Surrey (4pts) won by 5 wickets

The calmness of Graham Thorpe helped Surrey to overcome a determined Scottish Saltires side in Edinburgh.

at Derby
Warwickshire 260 for 8 (45 overs) (JO Troughton 73, NV Knight 60)
Derbyshire 208 (40.4 overs) (J Moss 65)
Warwickshire (4pts) won by 52 runs

A canny 69 from Graham Thorpe, in a partnership of 111 with the more explosive Alistair Brown, saw Surrey finally get home by five wickets in a match against the Scottish Saltires which, for a long time, looked like it might have been running away from them. The Scots scored 252 for 7 for one thing, with Jonathan Beukes batting superbly for 91, and then Surrey lost three wickets for two runs, following the 88-run start which Scott Newman and James Benning had given them.

There was more gloom for Derbyshire, in front of their long-suffering supporters, as Warwickshire defeated them with some ease by 52 runs. Neil Carter's pinch-hitting brought 42 runs and then Nick Knight

and Jim Troughton both scored fluent half-centuries to ensure that Warwickshire reached a sizeable total.

22 May 2005: Division One

at Bristol
Middlesex 95 for 5 (21 overs) (OA Shah 50*)
Gloucestershire 40 for 2 (7 overs)
Match abandoned – 2pts each

In his last innings before the opening Test against Bangladesh, England opener Andrew Strauss continued his early-season struggles by only scoring 8 in a rain-affected match at Bristol which finally ended in an abandonment. Strauss, caught behind off a Jon Lewis outswinger, had at this stage scored just 168 runs from his first 12 innings of the season in all competitions. Owais Shah reached 50 not out in the original 21-overs per side game, in which Middlesex looked as if they had underperformed, but after more rain Gloucestershire themselves seemed to be struggling to reach a revised target of 87 in 13 overs when the soggy contest was put out of its misery by a final downpour.

27 May 2005: Division One

at Cardiff
Glamorgan 227 (45 overs) (DL Hemp 65*)
Worcestershire 174 (40.4 overs) (Z de Bruyn 51, DS Harrison 5 for 33)
Glamorgan (4pts) won by 53 runs

A warm evening blessed Glamorgan's second attempt to christen their new floodlights, following the washout of late April, and the Welsh county were also rewarded with a 53-run victory against Worcestershire. A total of 227 was built upon Matthew Elliott and Robert Croft's opening stand of 79 and later upon David Hemp's unbeaten 65, but it was David Harrison's three strikes with the new ball, and 5 for 33 overall, which meant that the visitors never recovered from being 40 for 4.

29 May 2005: Division Two

at Stratford
Warwickshire 113 (33 overs)
Scotland 116 for 9 (31.1 overs) (HH Streak 4 for 22)
Scotland (4pts) won by 1 wicket

at Tunbridge Wells
Durham 189 (44.5 overs) (N Peng 50)
Kent 188 for 9 (45 overs) (AJ Hall 72, MJ Walker 58)
Durham (4pts) won by 1 run

Stratford-upon-Avon is celebrated for its drama, but who could have written a finish like the one where Scotland's No. 11, Paul Hoffman, left the field to the swirling sound of bagpipes after heaving the winning six over extra cover to beat Warwickshire? Neil Carter was the bowler, and he had also been part of an earlier top-order collapse which saw the county team lose their first five wickets for just 17. Warwickshire's eventual total, 113, looked well within the Scottish compass as Dougie Lockhart and Jonathan Beukes took them to 70 for 1 in reply. But Heath Streak, Jonathan Trott and Carter then induced near panic in Scottish ranks by snatching 8 wickets for 38 runs in 12 overs. Hoffman, however, who had also taken three wickets earlier, proved more than equal to his task.

A crowd of 3,500 at Tunbridge Wells was left stunned as Durham maintained their unbeaten record at the top of Division Two by pulling off a remarkable one-run win against Kent. Yet no one in the ground would have been more devastated than Andrew Hall, who took three wickets earlier in the day and then hit a robust 72. Hall put on 97 in 21 overs with Matthew Walker, who was then joined in a further stand of 42 by David Fulton. But, from 170 for 3 in the 38th over, Kent contrived to make a complete hash of overhauling Durham's under-par 189. Full marks to Durham, who kept up the pressure superbly against a procession of new batsmen, but Kent's collapse was unworthy of a professional team.

30 May 2005: Division One

at Worcester
Middlesex 224 for 7 (44 overs) (ET Smith 93, SB Styris 80)
Worcestershire 192 for 9 (44 overs) (Z de Bruyn 55)
Middlesex (4pts) won by 32 runs

at Trent Bridge
Nottinghamshire 154 (43 overs) (D Gough 4 for 16)
Essex 158 for 4 (36 overs) (RC Irani 53)
Essex (4pts) won by 6 wickets

at Bristol
Gloucestershire 86 (33.2 overs) (DG Cork 4 for 14)
Lancashire 88 for 4 (21.3 overs)
Lancashire (4pts) won by 6 wickets

at The Rose Bowl
Hampshire 226 for 7 (45 overs) (GA Lamb 100*)
Northamptonshire 227 for 6 (43.2 overs)
Northamptonshire (4pts) won by 4 wickets

Scott Styris took an immediate liking to Gareth Batty, who had neither batted nor bowled in England's opening Test against Bangladesh, and the assault which brought the New Zealander four sixes and 36 runs in all off 22 balls from the off-spinner helped to propel Middlesex to 224 for 7. Styris' 80 came from 83 balls, and he added 140 with Ed Smith for the fourth wicket following an initial slump to 38 for 3. Moreover, Styris then dismissed Worcestershire's two top scorers, Vikram Solanki and Zander de Bruyn, as Middlesex emerged winners by 32 runs.

Darren Gough gave England's one-day selectors a last-minute reminder of his enduring quality, 24 hours ahead of the announcement of the NatWest Series squad, to spearhead Essex's stroll to a six-wicket win over Nottinghamshire at Trent Bridge. Gough was irresistible as he took four wickets for just 16 runs in eight overs of bustle and barrel-chested strut, and once Ronnie Irani had opened up with 53 it was easy for Essex.

Another England Test old boy, Dominic Cork, produced his best one-day figures for Lancashire – his 4 for 14 being even better than Gough's – as Gloucestershire were skittled for 86 at Bristol. Jon Lewis also enjoyed the bowler-friendly conditions when Lancashire replied, but his three wickets could not prevent a severe beating for the home team.

Greg Lamb's unbeaten 100, from the top of the order, bolstered Hampshire at the Rose Bowl, but

Scott Styris hits out for Middlesex during his excellent all-round contribution to their win against Worcestershire.

from 135 for 5 it was Northants who emerged unlikely victors. David Sales, their captain, was joined by Ben Phillips in a stand of 43 in five overs which sped the visitors home.

Division Two

at Derby
Leicestershire 146 (40.1 overs) (JL Sadler 50, KJ Dean 5 for 45)
Derbyshire 147 for 4 (41.3 overs)
Derbyshire (4pts) won by 6 wickets

at The Oval
Surrey 219 for 7 (38 overs) (JGE Benning 66, R Clarke 54)
Durham 176 (34.1 overs) (N Peng 63)
Surrey (4pts) won by 43 runs

at Headingley
Yorkshire 214 (44.5 overs) (A McGrath 57)
Scotland 154 (41.5 overs) (GM Hamilton 60)
Yorkshire (4pts) won by 60 runs

at Taunton
Somerset 297 for 6 (45 overs) (ID Blackwell 134*)
Sussex 298 for 8 (44.4 overs) (MJ Prior 77, JJ van der Wath 73*, CJ Adams 59, KA Parsons 4 for 34)
Sussex (4pts) won by 2 wickets

High-class swing bowling from Kevin Dean, back at something near his best following a knee operation in 2004, earned Derbyshire their first win of the season. Dean wrecked Leicestershire's hopes with 5 for 45, and was well-supported by Ant Botha's three cheap scalps. Derbyshire then took their time to reach their modest target, probably because they were savouring every minute of the success.

James Benning, Rikki Clarke and Tim Murtagh, three of Surrey's younger players, were at the forefront of the 43-run win at The Oval which ended Durham's unbeaten start to the season. Benning hit 66 from 84 balls, Clarke 54 off 67, and Murtagh followed up the unbeaten 31 from 21 balls which pushed Surrey on to 219 for 7 by taking three wickets in his first three overs without conceding a run.

Apart from Gavin Hamilton, who hit a satisfying 60 against his former county at Headingley, the Scottish Saltires could not find the batting performances to match their earlier work in the field. That restricted Yorkshire to 214, but the Scots fell away to a 60-run defeat.

It is not often that a player thumps an unbeaten 134 from only 71 balls and ends up on the losing

side. But that is just what happened to Somerset's Ian Blackwell against Sussex at Taunton. He struck Mushtaq Ahmed for four sixes in one memorable over, transforming a Somerset innings which had stuttered to 88 for 5 by the midway point. In all, Blackwell launched ten sixes and ten fours in a display of hitting that, in truth, will be remembered long after the result is forgotten. For the record, however, after Somerset totalled 297 for 6, Sussex romped home with two balls to spare as the youthful home attack found their inexperience exposed by the strokeplay of Matt Prior and Chris Adams – and then by the brutal striking of Johan van der Wath, whose 73 not out took him a mere 43 balls and decided the match.

5 June 2005: Division One

at Lord's
Middlesex 243 for 6 (45 overs) (SB Styris 71, PN Weekes 66)
Essex 245 for 9 (44.4 overs) (RN ten Doeschate 51*)
Essex (4pts) won by 1 wicket

at Old Trafford
Hampshire 200 (44.5 overs) (DA Kenway 65)
Lancashire 121 (38 overs)
Hampshire (4pts) won by 79 runs

at Swansea
Glamorgan v. **Nottinghamshire**
Match abandoned – 2pts each

Essex won the top-of-the-table clash at Lord's, with Middlesex paying a heavy price for not bowling their overs in the time allowed. Having gone past the 7.09pm cut-off before they were ready to deliver the final over, Middlesex found themselves being docked six penalty runs by the umpires. Suddenly, a 16-run requirement was down to ten for Essex, and Ryan ten Doeschate took full advantage to plunder two fours off Irfan Pathan and win the game with two balls to spare. Ten Doeschate, who earlier had seen his only over of the Middlesex innings – the 44th – smashed for 25 as Scott Styris lifted him for four sixes, thus gained his revenge with a 41-ball unbeaten 51.

Hampshire rid themselves of one of the more remarkable sequences in English cricket at Old Trafford, where their 79-run win ended a run of 18 consecutive one-day defeats to Lancashire. It was also their first victory over the Red Rose county in 28 matches in all competitions. Their total of 200, however, looked inadequate on a flattish pitch until Chris Tremlett and Sean Ervine quickly sent back the big guns of Loye, Law and Hodge and reduced Lancashire to 16 for 3. Mark Chilton did his best to hold his side together, with 47, but Lancashire threw away their wickets with even more disregard than Hampshire, and were soon all out for just 121.

Division Two

at Maidstone
Derbyshire 304 for 3 (45 overs) (MJ Di Venuto 116, SD Stubbings 66, JDC Bryant 53)
Kent 214 (38.4 overs) (AJ Hall 61)
Derbyshire (4pts) won by 90 runs

at Oakham School
Leicestershire 217 for 4 (45 overs) (D Mongia 75)
Somerset 146 (38.4 overs) (GC Smith 61, D Mongia 4 for 12)
Leicestershire (4pts) won by 71 runs

at Whitgift School
Warwickshire 309 for 8 (45 overs) (JO Troughton 69, NM Carter 58, AGR Loudon 54)
Surrey 260 (41.2 overs) (MR Ramprakash 89*, AD Brown 52)
Warwickshire (4pts) won by 49 runs

Derbyshire startled Kent at Maidstone by speeding to their highest total in the one-day league, with Michael di Venuto unfurling some magnificent back-foot shots on his way to 116 from 90 balls. Steve Stubbings, with 66 from 76 balls, provided ideal support in an opening stand worth 155 and both James Bryant and Jon Moss then weighed in with late cameos. Andrew Hall gave Kent a bright start, but Derbyshire's bowlers generally kept a tighter line than their opponents had and victory in the end came by 90 runs.

Dinesh Mongia was again the all-round inspiration for Leicestershire, hitting 75 from 72 balls and then mesmerising the Somerset reply at Oakham School with a spell of 4 for 12 in seven overs. At 85 without loss, after 20 overs, Somerset were in an excellent position to go on and win the game, but Mongia combined with fellow slow bowlers Jeremy Snape and Claude Henderson to snare all ten wickets (with one run out) for 61 runs.

Mark Ramprakash hit 89 not out, and put on 92 in 12 overs with Alistair Brown, but Surrey still finished up second best to Warwickshire at Whitgift School. Neil Carter and Nick Knight had put on 96

for the first wicket for the visitors, and then Jim Troughton and Alex Loudon both hit rapid half-centuries while adding 108 in 16 overs for the fourth wicket. A final total of 309 for 8 proved out of Surrey's reach.

10 June 2005: Division Two

at The Grange
Scotland 172 (44.5 overs) (CJO Smith 61)
Sussex 174 for 2 (28.3 overs) (MJ Prior 93*, IJ Ward 51)
Sussex (4pts) won by 8 wickets

Sussex eased themselves to a nine-wicket trouncing of the Scottish Saltires in Edinburgh, dismissing the hosts for 172 with some disciplined bowling and then seeing the openers, Ian Ward and Matt Prior, put the result beyond doubt with a century stand. After Ward was bowled for 51, and Mike Yardy run out for one, Prior went on to score 93 not out as he and Chris Adams closed out the game.

12 June 2005: Division One

at Northampton
Northamptonshire 283 for 1 (45 overs) (U Afzaal 122*, ML Love 111*)
Middlesex 284 for 8 (45 overs) (JWM Dalrymple 76, EC Joyce 74)
Middlesex (4pts) won by 2 wickets

at Trent Bridge
Nottinghamshire 249 for 8 (45 overs) (CMW Read 68*)
Lancashire 188 (41.3 overs)
Nottinghamshire (4pts) won by 61 runs

Usman Afzaal and Martin Love scored silky hundreds in a county record second-wicket stand of 227 unbroken for Northamptonshire, but it was Middlesex who took the points at Wantage Road on a run-filled day. Northants' 283 for 1 was a forbidding score, but Middlesex hunted it down remorselessly, with Ed Joyce and Jamie Dalrymple doing much to keep their side in a chase which came down to 108 from the final 15 overs. In the end, however, it all came down to a thrilling last-ball finish, and Mel Betts was more than equal to the task with a three struck to deep cover.

Chris Read, still overlooked by England, demonstrated his all-round talents with a 70-ball unbeaten 68 and three catches and a stumping as Nottinghamshire saw off Lancashire's challenge by 61 runs at Trent Bridge. Read struck four sixes and

Chris Read produced catches, a stumping and good runs as Nottinghamshire overwhelmed Lancashire at Trent Bridge.

five fours, sharing in partnerships of 72 in 13 overs with David Hussey and 86 in ten with Mark Ealham, who then also played his usual steady role with the ball as the Notts four-man pace attack sent Lancashire sliding to 126 for 8 on a pitch with good pace and bounce. From there, the visitors could only attempt to bat out time.

Division Two

at Leicester
Yorkshire 172 for 9 (45 overs)
(MJ Lumb 66*)
Leicestershire 176 for 3 (42.1 overs)
Leicestershire (4pts) won by 7 wickets

at Bath
Kent 319 for 5 (45 overs)
(M van Jaarsveld 114,
RWT Key 67, MJ Walker 56)
Somerset 245 (37.3 overs) (ID Blackwell 57,
JD Francis 56, JM Kemp 4 for 52)
Kent (4pts) won by 74 runs

Yorkshire did not make enough runs in their 45 overs at Grace Road, despite a fighting 66 not out from Michael Lumb, and Leicestershire's Dinesh Mongia built on a platform established by a second-wicket stand of 52 between Tom New and Hylton Ackerman to lead the subsequent cruise to a seven-wicket victory. Adam Warren, a New South Wales second XI fast bowler with an English mother, was controversially called up from league cricket with Bootle to play ahead of a number of Yorkshire's contracted reserve seamers, and took the wicket of Darren Maddy with his ninth ball.

Martin van Jaarsveld, motivated no doubt by the sight of his former national team captain leading the opposition, hit a blistering century to spearhead Kent's 74-run beating of Somerset at Bath. Van Jaarsveld might have felt he had a point to prove to South African captain Graeme Smith, after being discarded by his native country's national selectors during the previous winter's Test series against England, and if so he achieved it in some style. His 114 took him just 110 balls, with three sixes and 14 fours, while Rob Key and

Matthew Walker also shone with excellent half-centuries. Smith could only make 27 in reply, and Somerset's chase of a massive 320 fizzled out once Ian Blackwell, who hit three sixes and five fours in his 57, had run himself out.

13 June 2005: Division Two

at The Riverside
Derbyshire 82 (30.5 overs) (DM Benkenstein 4 for 17)
Durham 84 for 5 (29.4 overs)
Durham (4pts) won by 5 wickets – DL Method: target 83 from 39 overs

A poor pitch at the Riverside played into the hands of Durham's seamers, who tore through the Derbyshire batting with relish to dismiss them for just 82. Derbyshire then struck some quick blows of their own, reducing the hosts initially to 36 for 4, but steadying innings from Gordon Muchall and Gary Pratt saw them to a win that stretched their lead at the top of the division to six points.

17 June 2005: Division One

at Chelmsford
Essex 271 for 7 (45 overs) (A Flower 127*, RC Irani 67)
Gloucestershire 216 (41.1 overs) (WPC Weston 58)
Essex (4pts) won by 55 runs

Essex went joint top of the table after a wonderful unbeaten 127 by Andy Flower powered them to 271 for 7 against a Gloucestershire side now clearly past its considerable one-day best. Flower's innings took him just 93 balls, and included 15 fours, and was his highest in English domestic limited-overs cricket. Phil Weston was the only visitors' batsman to flourish, and when he was bowled by Danish Kaneria all Gloucestershire's fading hopes of hauling themselves off the bottom went with him.

Division Two

at Taunton
Scotland 232 for 6 (45 overs) (JA Beukes 92)
Somerset 217 (44.1 overs) (GC Smith 74)
Scotland (4pts) won by 15 runs

Somerset may have defeated the Australians in one-day cricket, but the Scottish Saltires were too good for Graeme Smith, Sanath Jayasuriya, Ian Blackwell et al when they visited Taunton. Jonathan Beukes' 92 was the basis of the Saltires' 232 for 6, and they had the perfect start in the field when Jayasuriya was caught for 0. Smith made 74, adding 66 with Matthew Wood and 82 with James Hildreth, but the Scots were not to be denied as South Africa's captain was run out and Hildreth dismissed one short of his half-century.

19 June 2005: Division One

at Worcester
Essex 203 for 9 (45 overs)
Worcestershire 164 (40.3 overs)
Essex (4pts) won by 39 runs

at Southgate
Middlesex 314 for 5 (45 overs) (PN Weekes 106, SB Styris 82)
Nottinghamshire 283 (44.4 overs) (SR Patel 82)
Middlesex (4pts) won by 31 runs

at Stowe School
Gloucestershire 215 for 9 (45 overs) (MA Hardinges 63)
Northamptonshire 219 for 5 (43.2 overs)
(BM Shafayat 97*, TW Roberts 90)
Northamptonshire (4pts) won by 5 wickets

at The Rose Bowl
Glamorgan 211 for 7 (45 overs) (RDB Croft 88)
Hampshire 212 for 3 (37.2 overs) (N Pothas 76)
Hampshire (4pts) won by 7 wickets

Essex and Middlesex kept well ahead of the rest at the head of the first division with wins of similar margins. Essex's 39-run victory over Worcestershire was possibly the more comfortable in a low-scoring affair at New Road. A two-paced pitch made batting tricky, but Essex worked hard for their total of 203 for 9 and then kept a tight hold on the home side's reply.

It was a different type of game altogether at the Walker Ground in Southgate, where a blameless surface and lightning-fast outfield had brought 1,683 runs and only 14 wickets in the preceding championship match and now proceeded to produce 601 more. Paul Weekes' skilful 106 and a bludgeoning 82 from 64 balls by Scott Styris saw Middlesex to 314 for 5, and from there it was only a matter of the home bowlers keeping some sort of check on the Nottinghamshire batsmen. Weekes struck two important early blows with his canny off-spin, but Samit Patel plundered 82 and figured in stands of 73 with David Hussey and 72 in just ten overs with Chris Read. Middlesex were just beginning to fret, but Alan Richardson popped up with the wickets of both Patel and Read, and the home side could celebrate.

Northamptonshire's first visit to the beautifully appointed, tree-lined Stowe School ground in Buckinghamshire was an unqualified success. More than 2,000 spectators turned up to enjoy the game, and the setting, and Northants also beat Gloucestershire by five wickets to send most spectators home even happier. Northants, indeed, were even thinking about the possibility of staging a future championship fixture at the venue by the time Bilal Shafayat and Tim Roberts were winning the game with an opening partnership of 166 in 29 overs. Roberts was the quicker scorer, his 90 taking just 85 balls, but Shafayat had gone on to 97 not out when the victory was confirmed.

Robert Croft opened up with 88 from 113 balls for Glamorgan, but after that the Welsh county did not have much more to offer as Hampshire ran out seven-wicket winners at the Rose Bowl. Shane Warne and Shaun Udal bowled their spinners with great control, before 76 from Nic Pothas and an unbroken stand of 78 in 12 overs between John Crawley and Craig McMillan sped Hampshire to their target.

Division Two

at Arundel Castle
Durham 195 (45 overs) (DM Benkenstein 57*, RJ Kirtley 4 for 29)
Sussex 196 for 3 (29.3 overs) (IJ Ward 93, CJ Adams 58*)
Sussex (4pts) won by 7 wickets

at Edgbaston
Warwickshire 217 for 6 (45 overs) (IJL Trott 93*,
AGR Loudon 51)
Leicestershire 218 for 3 (43.4 overs) (DL Maddy 107*)
Leicestershire (4pts) won by 7 wickets

at Derby
Derbyshire 220 for 8 (45 overs) (MJ Di Venuto 112)
Scotland 220 for 9 (45 overs) (DR Lockhart 88*)
Match tied – 2pts each

The battle of the division's top two seemed to be an
evenly fought affair as Durham gritted their teeth
against some testing Sussex bowling and made it to
195. Then Sussex batted. Durham's attack proved
simply incapable of maintaining the same sort of
control against the strokeplay, and know-how, of Ian
Ward and Chris Adams. Ward, in particular,
completely dominated against Liam Plunkett –
walking across his crease and down the pitch to put
the youngster off his line. He succeeded perhaps too
easily, with Plunkett spraying nine wides in a four-
over new-ball spell that cost him 46 runs. Ward's
50 took him just 28 balls, with 11 fours, and when
Adams joined him the Sussex captain moved from
29 to 49 with a dismissive assault on Graeme
Bridge's left-arm spin which brought two sixes and
two fours – the last one a reverse sweep – in the
same over. Ward was finally bowled by Nathan Astle
for 93, but Adams was 58 not out when the game
ended 15.3 overs early.

Darren Maddy paced his unbeaten 107 to perfection
to bring Leicestershire victory with eight balls to spare
against Warwickshire at Edgbaston. Earlier the home
side had slipped to 43 for 4 before Jonathan Trott
rescued them with a determined 93 not out.

The Scottish Saltires were involved in another
exciting last-ball finish at Derby, where Dougie
Lockhart made an heroic unbeaten 88 to snatch a tie.
A single was scrambled off the last ball, with the
floodlights on as a storm approached, and the Scots
were deserved sharers of the points after such a
battling performance with both bat and ball. Michael
Di Venuto earlier made a controlled 112 from 120 balls
for Derbyshire, but Scotland's attack kept chipping
away at the other end to limit the county to 220 for 8.

20 June 2005: Division Two

at Leicester
Leicestershire 208 for 7 (45 overs)
Scotland 188 (44 overs)
Leicestershire (4pts) won by 20 runs

Scotland's cricketers ran out of steam in their
third game in four days, going down by 20 runs
to Leicestershire at Grace Road. In their last
match in the competition before contesting the
ICC Trophy in Ireland, the Scots made a poor
start against the moving ball after doing well to
restrict Leicestershire to 208 for 7 from their
45 overs. They found the left-arm swing of Charl
Willoughby, who took 2 for 12 from his nine
overs, especially demanding and, at 27 for 3, they
faced a tough task. Regular wickets thereafter did
not help their cause, either, but even at 124 for 8
they did not give up – and some late hitting by
Gregor Maiden, who scored 35 from No. 10,
brought them closer than they had at one stage
thought possible.

8 July 2005: Division One

at Chelmsford
Northamptonshire 200 (43 overs)
Essex 201 for 5 (43.2 overs) (GW Flower 90*)
Essex (4pts) won by 5 wickets

Essex opened up a four-point lead at the top of the
league with a hard-working five-wicket victory
against third-placed Northamptonshire at
Chelmsford. Grant Flower was their main man,
following up three cheap wickets with his left-arm
spin by anchoring the successful chase with an
unbeaten 90. Wickets kept falling at the other end,
but Flower kept his head and, in the end, was joined
by Ryan ten Doeschate in a match-clinching
unbroken sixth-wicket stand of 52.

Division Two

at Hove
Kent 155 (44.3 overs)
Sussex 156 for 6 (41.3 overs) (MH Yardy 65)
Sussex (4pts) won by 4 wickets

Kent's one-day struggles reached a new low at
Hove where they reduced Sussex to 22 for 4 on a
seaming pitch – and still lost comfortably. Sussex's
four-wicket win was based on Mike Yardy's
excellent 65, and his 103-run alliance with Carl
Hopkinson for the fifth wicket, but Kent paid the
price for not having any adequate back-up for their
excellent new-ball pair Simon Cook and Andrew
Hall. Earlier, the home team had been held to 155
by Sussex's disciplined, and deeper in quality, five-
man attack.

9 July 2005: Division Two

at Edgbaston
Derbyshire 201 for 9 (45 overs) (SD Stubbings 69)
Warwickshire 205 for 5 (44.1 overs) (IR Bell 53)
Warwickshire (4pts) won by 5 wickets

Ian Bell's 53 from 79 balls was instrumental in
Warwickshire's five-wicket victory over Derbyshire
at Edgbaston. Steve Stubbings had anchored the
visitors' progress to 201 for 9 with a 108-ball 69, but
Warwickshire's reply was a steady one, with
Jonathan Trott and Trevor Penney taking them over
the finish line with an unbroken stand of 38.

13 July 2005: Division Two

at Headingley
Surrey 264 for 7 (45 overs) (R Clarke 90*,
JGE Benning 72)
Yorkshire 261 for 7 (45 overs) (PA Jaques 98,
MJ Lumb 56, A McGrath 54)
Surrey (4pts) won by 3 runs

Nayan Doshi defeated Tim Bresnan's wild swipe and
bowled him for a duck to secure a thrilling three-run
win for Surrey under the Headingley floodlights.
Yorkshire's chase had begun well, with Phil Jaques
hitting 98 from 111 balls and featuring in stands of
93 and 129 for the second and third wickets with
Michael Lumb and Anthony McGrath. But Surrey
held their nerve, no one more so than left-arm
spinner Doshi when four were required from that
final ball. Surrey, given a flyer by James Benning's 72
in an opening stand worth 111 with Jon Batty, had
Rikki Clarke to thank for reaching as many as 264.
Clarke, dropped twice before he had reached
double figures, blossomed to finish on 90 not out –
and plundering the lion's share of the 59 runs that
came from the last five overs of the innings.

17 July 2005: Division One

at Southgate
Middlesex 333 for 4 (45 overs) (PN Weekes 81,
JWM Dalrymple 60*, OA Shah 55, ET Smith 53)
Gloucestershire 335 for 6 (44.1 overs)
(CM Spearman 109, MGN Windows 87, WPC Weston 70,
PN Weekes 4 for 58)
Gloucestershire (4pts) won by 4 wickets

at Trent Bridge
Hampshire 240 for 8 (45 overs) (AD Mascarenhas 50)

Nottinghamshire 244 for 9 (44 overs) (SP Fleming 102*)
Nottinghamshire (4pts) won by 1 wicket

at Worcester
Worcestershire 273 for 3 (45 overs) (SC Moore 104,
VS Solanki 55, Z de Bruyn 54*)
Glamorgan 274 for 5 (44 overs) (MJ Powell 82,
SC Ganguly 53, DL Hemp 51*)
Glamorgan (4pts) won by 5 wickets

A magnificent run-fest at Southgate ended with
Gloucestershire making the highest totesport League
score by a team batting second to shock Middlesex.
The home fans were confident of their own side's
success after the Middlesex top five had run riot on
a flat pitch and scorched outfield. Jamie Dalrymple,
in at No. 5, scored his 60 not out off just 24 balls to
race Middlesex on to 333 for 4. Jon Lewis, an
England one-day bowler in the previous month,
conceded 86 from his nine overs ... but then so did
Mel Betts for Middlesex. Gloucestershire's
incredible chase was kick-started by Phil Weston's
46-ball 70. He dominated a 110-run first-wicket
partnership with Craig Spearman, which took just
14 overs, and Spearman went on to anchor the

**A fine hundred from Craig Spearman anchored a remarkable
Gloucestershire run chase at Southgate.**

innings by reaching 109 from 104 balls, with a six and 14 fours. But it was Matt Windows who injected the real surge into Gloucestershire's scoring rate: he struck four sixes in his 87 and although Paul Weekes came up with four wickets in quick succession the visitors still had enough left to complete victory with five balls in hand. The match, though, yielded a record aggregate of 668 runs, with 17 sixes.

Stephen Fleming's 102 not out took Nottinghamshire to the brink of victory against Hampshire at Trent Bridge. Then, with just three runs required from the last over, but with Fleming batting with the No. 11 Andrew Harris, the umpires decreed that Hampshire had failed to bowl their allotted 44 overs by the 7.12pm cut-off time and issued the six-run penalty which clinched the result for Notts. It was a win they badly needed, having achieved just one victory in their previous eight matches and it owed much to Fleming and his seventh-wicket stand of 75 with Mark Ealham.

Stephen Moore hit a maiden one-day hundred for Worcestershire at New Road, but with fast bowler Shoaib Akhtar misfiring again, to the chagrin of the locals, Glamorgan bounded home by five wickets on the back of a sparkling 110-run partnership between Mike Powell and Sourav Ganguly, and then an equally free-spirited 51 not out from David Hemp.

Division Two

at Derby
Surrey 260 for 8 (45 overs)
Derbyshire 264 for 5 (39.2 overs) (SD Stubbings 98, MJ Di Venuto 98)
Derbyshire (4pts) won by 5 wickets

at The Riverside
Durham 147 (44.3 overs) (DM Benkenstein 90)
Warwickshire 148 for 5 (34.4 overs) (AGR Loudon 51)
Warwickshire (4pts) won by 5 wickets

Steve Stubbings and Michael Di Venuto both scored 98 as their 217-run opening stand, in 32 overs, swept Derbyshire to a morale-boosting win at The Oval. Surrey looked a sorry bunch: none of their top five batsmen capitalised on good starts, and the bowling lacked any bite at all.

Dale Benkenstein rode his luck to lead Durham from 49 for 8 to 147 – courtesy, too, of the resistance of last man Neil Killeen in a tenth-wicket partnership which realised 77. But Warwickshire still won at a canter, after the Riverside crowd had briefly got excited at 29 for 2, with Alex Loudon scoring 51.

19 July 2005: Division One

at Old Trafford
Lancashire 154 for 8 (40 overs) (IJ Sutcliffe 54)
Essex 156 for 2 (32.5 overs) (GW Flower 66)
Essex (4pts) won by 8 wickets – DL Method: target 156 from 40 overs

Essex's lead at the top of the totesport table grew to eight points when Lancashire were thrashed on their own Old Trafford turf. In a match reduced to 40 overs per side due to rain, Essex won with more than seven overs to spare after restricting the hosts to 154 for 8. The five frontline Essex bowlers put in top-class performances, and then the Lancashire attack could impose no sort of control as Grant Flower masterminded the run chase with an authoritative 66 from 78 balls. Ravi Bopara also impressed with 45 not out.

20 July 2005: Division One

at Cardiff
Middlesex 284 for 9 (45 overs) (PN Weekes 72, EC Joyce 61, BL Hutton 61)
Glamorgan 173 (35.4 overs) (CT Peploe 4 for 38)
Middlesex (4pts) won by 111 runs

The two lower order 61s struck by Ed Joyce and Ben Hutton, the first off 46 balls and Hutton's off a mere 39, boosted Middlesex to a challenging 284 for 9 at Cardiff. Glamorgan began badly, with the run out of Robert Croft, and then faded to a 111-run defeat as Chris Peploe's left-arm spin brought him 4 for 38.

Division Two

at Derby
Derbyshire 223 for 8 (45 overs) (TJ Friend 52)
Durham 224 for 4 (43.4 overs) (MEK Hussey 97, GJ Muchall 70)
Durham (4pts) won by 6 wickets

Mike Hussey and Gordon Muchall built a masterly partnership of 224 for the third wicket to guide Durham to a comfortable six-wicket win against Derbyshire. The home team's total of 223 for 8 owed much to Travis Friend, with 52 off 55 balls, and Graeme Welch, whose unbeaten 37 took him only 24 deliveries. But Hussey was in control from the start, only falling three runs short of his century after facing 120 balls, while Muchall's 70 was an even more fluent innings that took Durham to within one run of victory.

24 July 2005: Division One

at Bristol
Gloucestershire 168 for 9 (30 overs) (MGN Windows 51)
Worcestershire 74 for 0 (12.4 overs)
Worcestershire (4pts) won by 20 runs - DL Method:
target 55 from 12.4 overs

at Trent Bridge
Northamptonshire 25 for 0 (4.2 overs)
Nottinghamshire
Match abandoned – 2pts each

Worcestershire were well on the way to victory
against Gloucestershire at Bristol anyway, with
Vikram Solanki and Stephen Moore adding an
unbroken 74 for the first wicket in just 12.4 overs,
when rain arrived again to bring them the result on
Duckworth-Lewis regulations. The points, however,
were shared at Trent Bridge, where just 26 balls
were bowled in the match between Nottinghamshire
and Northamptonshire.

Division Two

at Canterbury
Kent 90 for 6 (16 overs)
Somerset 95 for 2 (12.4 overs) (GC Smith 56*)
Somerset (4pts) won by 8 wickets

at The Grange
Scotland 166 for 9 (45 overs) (RR Watson 70)
Leicestershire 170 for 3 (36 overs) (DL Maddy 95*)
Leicestershire (4pts) won by 7 wickets

at Guildford
Sussex 219 for 9 (22 overs)
Surrey 171 (19 overs) (MR Ramprakash 63,
Mushtaq Ahmed 4 for 36)
Sussex (4pts) won by 48 runs

at Scarborough
Yorkshire 201 for 7 (45 overs) (MJ Lumb 57)
Warwickshire 202 for 3 (37.3 overs) (NM Carter 65,
IJL Trott 58*)
Warwickshire (4pts) won by 7 wickets

After early rain gave way to glorious late afternoon
sunshine, Kent found themselves losing the toss at
Canterbury and soon sliding to 38 for 5 against a
Somerset seam attack in which Andy Caddick and
Richard Johnson relished the conditions. After that,
in a 16-over contest, Kent had little hope of

Darren Maddy's scintillating batting display boosted
Leicestershire's promotion hopes in Division Two.

winning. Their total of 90 for 6 was, predictably,
overhauled with 20 balls to spare as Graeme Smith
enjoyed himself.

Leicestershire's promotion hopes were boosted as
Darren Maddy's unbeaten 100-ball 95 steered them
to an efficient seven-wicket win in Edinburgh. The
Scottish Saltires could make little headway against
an attack in which Maddy also took two wickets,
despite Ryan Watson's 70.

An entertaining 22-over match followed the rain
delay at Guildford, with Sussex scorching their way
to 219 for 9 as Matt Prior (37 off 18 balls), Luke
Wright (35 off 14 balls) and Murray Goodwin
(44 off 34) produced effervescent cameos. Surrey
could not live with their opponents, but reached
171 themselves with Mark Ramprakash hitting a
42-ball 63.

Two top-order wickets and a brutal 65 opening the
innings in his usual one-day manner made Neil
Carter the star of the show at Scarborough.
Yorkshire's 201 for 7 soon looked inadequate as
Carter blitzed five fours and six sixes in a 38-ball
assault which left Jonathan Trott and Jim Troughton
the fairly straightforward task of easing Warwickshire
home by seven wickets as early as the 38th over.

27 July 2005: Division One

at The Rose Bowl
Hampshire v. **Worcestershire**
Match abandoned – 2pts each

Rain caused Hampshire's fixture against Worcestershire to be abandoned without a ball being bowled.

Division Two

at Canterbury
Kent 177 for 9 (45 overs) (JM Kemp 84, D Pretorius 5 for 32)
Warwickshire 181 for 7 (44.1 overs) (AGR Loudon 73*)
Warwickshire (4pts) won by 3 wickets

The last thing Kent's supporters needed to see on one of their major floodlit nights at Canterbury, as their awful one-day form continued, was a brilliant match-winning innings of 73 by Alex Loudon – the highly-promising all-rounder who left the county at the end of the 2004 season as a result of dressing room disharmony. Loudon, however, drew generous applause from his former club's faithful after guiding Warwickshire to a tricky target after they had plunged to 62 for 6. Trevor Penney and Dougie Brown gave Loudon the full benefit of their experience in support, but it was an impressive, cool effort from the younger man. Kent's 177 for 9, meanwhile, had also been achieved despite an initial collapse against a new ball which darted around in conditions helpful to the bowlers. From 29 for 5, and then 99 for 7, they were rallied by a fine 84 from 93 balls by Justin Kemp.

31 July 2005: Division Two

at Headingley
Yorkshire 216 for 6 (45 overs) (MP Vaughan 116*)
Kent 218 for 5 (44.2 overs) (MJ Walker 56*)
Kent (4pts) won by 5 wickets

England captain Michael Vaughan emerged from a slump in batting form to bat through the Yorkshire innings for an unbeaten 116 at Headingley. Kent still won the game, though, an unbeaten 51-ball 56 from Matthew Walker guiding them home with four balls remaining. Vaughan also took two wickets in eight useful overs of off-spin, cutting short a promising 49 from youngster Joe Denly with a smart return catch and then having Darren Stevens lbw on the sweep.

1 August 2005: Division Two

at Hove
Sussex 266 for 3 (45 overs) (RR Montgomerie 132*, MJ Prior 62, MW Goodwin 50)
Somerset 255 for 9 (45 overs) (ID Blackwell 57, MH Yardy 4 for 26)
Sussex (4pts) won by 11 runs

Richard Montgomerie showed Sussex what they had been missing in the one-day arena when he hit Somerset's bowlers for an unbeaten 132, his highest limited-overs score, to spearhead an 11-run victory at Hove. Montgomerie, who had not been selected for any of Sussex's previous 23 one-day games, put on 132 for the first wicket with Matt Prior and another 97 for the third wicket with Murray Goodwin. In reply, Somerset were never quite on terms with the required rate, although they did have a chance while Ian Blackwell, who reached his 50 in 38 balls, was at the crease. When he was caught off Mike Yardy for 57, giving the bowler another success on his way to one-day best figures of 4 for 26, Sussex knew they were favourites.

2 August 2005: Division One

at Worcester
Northamptonshire 275 for 4 (45 overs) (U Afzaal 117, ML Love 76)
Worcestershire 237 for 9 (45 overs) (GA Hick 52, BM Shafayat 4 for 33)
Northamptonshire (4pts) won by 38 runs

Usman Afzaal's superb 117, and his 155-run second-wicket stand with Martin Love, proved too hot for Worcestershire to handle at New Road. As a result, Northamptonshire reached the challenging total of 275 for 4 and the home side's own final score was flattered by a last-wicket thrash by Shoaib Akhtar, the No. 11, and Jamie Pipe. They added 52, of which Shoaib claimed 36 not out, but Bilal Shafayat took the main honours with 4 for 33.

3 August 2005: Division Two

at Derby
Derbyshire 277 for 5 (45 overs) (MJ Di Venuto 87, LD Sutton 63*)
Somerset 262 for 9 (45 overs) (AV Suppiah 79, CM Gazzard 62, J Moss 4 for 60)
Derbyshire (4pts) won by 15 runs

Derbyshire lifted themselves into fifth place in the second division table with a hard-fought 15-run win over a predominantly youthful Somerset side under the Recreation Ground lights. Michael Di Venuto's 87 from 83 balls gave Derbyshire an ideal start, and skipper Luke Sutton contributed an intelligently-played unbeaten 63 against his former county to ensure a sizeable total. Carl Gazzard and Arul Suppiah courageously kept Somerset in the hunt with a second-wicket stand of 127 in 18 overs, but Ian Blackwell's run out for one was a major blow to the visitors' hopes and, in the end, an almost impossible 23 runs were required from the final over.

7 August 2005: Division One

at Southend
Essex 202 for 8 (45 overs) (RC Irani 61)
Middlesex 198 for 9 (45 overs) (PN Weekes 82, BJM Scott 50*)
Essex (4pts) won by 4 runs

at Cheltenham
Hampshire 186 (41.1 overs) (MA Hardinges 4 for 40)
Gloucestershire 188 for 5 (34.2 overs) (WPC Weston 72, MGN Windows 58)
Gloucestershire (4pts) won by 5 wickets

A dour struggle at Southend finished in a four-run victory for home side Essex, but it was a contest in which there was little to separate the leaders and their nearest challengers Middlesex. Ronnie Irani's 61 and a late 37-ball 44 not out from Ryan ten Doeschate, who added a crucial 56 in nine overs with James Foster, gave Essex something to defend – and they did so tigerishly on a slow surface. Danish Kaneria's leg spin, and Ravi Bopara's medium pace proved especially difficult to contend with, and only Paul Weekes' battling 82, from the top of the order, kept Middlesex's chase alive. There were still 13 runs needed when Darren Gough began the final over, and England's one-day spearhead was not about to give that situation away. Essex's win took them a decisive step closer to their first one-day league title for 20 years, and effectively ended Middlesex's hopes. Ben Hutton's side may have been still just eight points adrift, but they had played 12 games to Essex's 10.

A 5,000 crowd at Cheltenham College were delighted to see Gloucestershire not only move off the bottom of the table but also out of the relegation zone with a rollicking five-wicket win over Hampshire. The visitors made a decent enough

start, and were 78 for 1 at one stage, but then their innings fell away against excellent Gloucestershire bowling and fielding. Craig Spearman fell for 22, but then Phil Weston (72 off 78 balls) and Matt Windows (58 from 69) made victory a formality with a free-flowing partnership of 106.

Division Two

at Canterbury
Kent 211 (45 overs) (NC Saker 4 for 43)
Surrey 212 for 5 (41.2 overs) (JN Batty 82, AD Brown 65)
Surrey (4pts) won by 5 wickets

at The Grange
Scotland 203 for 9 (45 overs) (JA Beukes 78)
Yorkshire 207 for 5 (41.3 overs) (PA Jaques 57)
Yorkshire (4pts) won by 5 wickets

at Hove
Sussex 223 for 8 (45 overs) (CJ Adams 78, OD Gibson 4 for 37)
Leicestershire 227 for 4 (45 overs) (HD Ackerman 114*, DL Maddy 93)
Leicestershire (4pts) won by 6 wickets

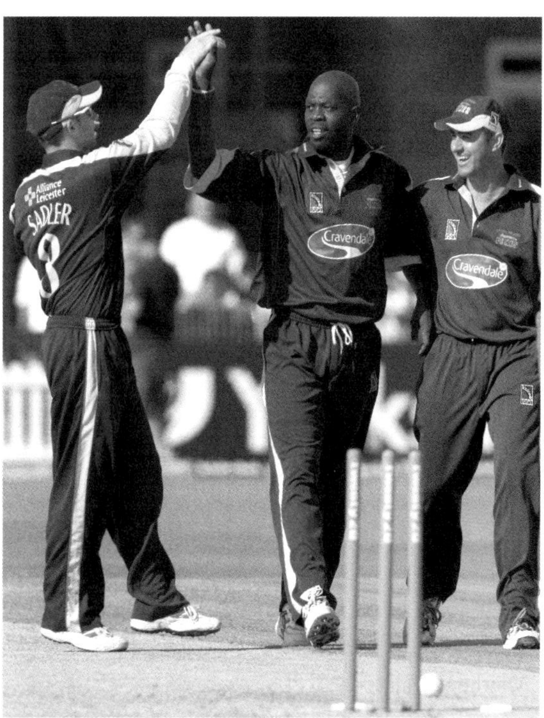

Leicestershire's Ottis Gibson took four wickets as Sussex were beaten at Hove.

Beer at Canterbury's St Lawrence Ground was being sold at just £1.50 a pint by Kent's chief sponsor, the brewers Shepherd Neame, in celebration of England's heart-stopping two-run win against Australia in the Edgbaston Test, but there was little else for the county's supporters to cheer about. A competition-best 82 from Jon Batty, and a 117-run stand between him and Alistair Brown, who made a typically cavalier 65, swept Surrey to a straightforward five-wicket win – even though Andrew Hall made three early strikes with the new ball. Kent's 211 had been a struggle from first to last, especially against the seam of Neil Saker and Tim Murtagh, who shared seven wickets.

Jonathan Beukes, Scotland's South African, hit 78 and took two wickets for 23 in seven overs, but the Saltires were still beaten in routine fashion by Yorkshire in Edinburgh. Phil Jaques' half-century, and 42 from Anthony McGrath, were the highlights of Yorkshire's stroll to a five-wicket win.

Hylton Ackerman hit an unbeaten 114, and was joined in a second-wicket partnership worth 185 by Darren Maddy, as Leicestershire made heavy weather of what was eventually a last-ball, six-wicket victory against Sussex at Hove. The visitors seemed to panic when Maddy was lbw for 93, but Sussex's pressure did not quite pay off. Earlier, Chris Adams struck 78 in a Sussex innings which was in danger of underachieving until Naved-ul-Hasan joined Robin Martin-Jenkins in a seventh-wicket stand of 67.

8 August 2005: Division One

at Northampton
Lancashire 236 for 9 (45 overs) (A Symonds 80, J Louw 4 for 39)
Northamptonshire 172 (40.5 overs)
Lancashire (4pts) won by 64 runs

A powerful 80 from Andrew Symonds was the basis of Lancashire's comfortable 64-run win over Northamptonshire at Wantage Road. Johann Louw bowled well for the hosts, but a total of 236 for 9 proved too much for Northants.

9 August 2005: Division One

at Cheltenham
Gloucestershire 87 (35.1 overs)
Nottinghamshire 88 for 2 (22 overs)
Nottinghamshire (4pts) won by 8 wickets

Younis Khan took three wickets with his little-used leg spin as Nottinghamshire inflicted a day to forget on Gloucestershire in front of a disgruntled Cheltenham crowd. Dismissed for just 87, after choosing to bat, Gloucestershire found Nottinghamshire's attack just too much for them. It took Notts just 22 overs to reach their modest target, with Pakistan Test star Younis finishing on 28 not out.

Division Two

at The Oval
Leicestershire 258 for 5 (45 overs) (HD Ackerman 78, A Habib 52)
Surrey 259 for 4 (39.3 overs) (AD Brown 108*, MR Ramprakash 69)
Surrey (4pts) won by 6 wickets

Surrey were in some trouble at 65 for 3 in the 17th over, in reply to Leicestershire's daunting 258 for 5, when Alistair Brown joined Mark Ramprakash. The result, once again, was a cricket match turned on its head by the power and sheer unorthodoxy of Brown's hitting. Ramprakash played his more classical part, too, but fell for 69 after a thrilling partnership of 166. Brown, however, whose 50 had taken 30 balls and his hundred a mere 57, finished on 108 not out after going to three figures with a straight six off Dinesh Mongia.

10 August 2005: Division One

at The Rose Bowl
Hampshire 251 for 5 (45 overs) (SR Watson 106*)
Lancashire 243 (43.3 overs) (A Symonds 86, MJ North 56)
Hampshire (4pts) won by 8 runs

In a match dominated by four Australians, with a couple of Zimbabweans chipping in, Hampshire beat Lancashire by an exciting eight-run margin at the Rose Bowl. Shane Watson hit a fine undefeated 106 to guide Hampshire to 251 for 5, Sean Ervine and Greg Lamb providing the chief support acts with 40 and 42 respectively. But then Andy Symonds, who had also taken two wickets, hit 86 and threatened to win the match for the visitors in alliance with fellow Aussie Marcus North, who scored 56. But Symonds' dismissal by the fourth Australian in this tale, Andy Bichel, who ended up with three vital wickets, did much to clinch the game for Hampshire.

14 August 2005: Division One

at Cheltenham
Gloucestershire 182 (44.1 overs) (MGN Windows 57)
Essex 122 (38.4 overs)
Gloucestershire (4pts) won by 60 runs

at Colwyn Bay
Glamorgan 173 (40.5 overs) (DG Cork 4 for 37)
Lancashire 176 for 2 (31.2 overs) (MB Loye 79*)
Lancashire (4pts) won by 8 wickets

The Essex sprint towards the totesport title was
rudely interrupted at Cheltenham, where a resurgent
Gloucestershire delved into their memory banks and
came up with a performance in the field reminiscent
of their recent glory days in limited-overs cricket.
After nine wins out of ten (the other game was
washed out), Essex plunged to their first defeat as
they were bundled out for 122. A dry, crumbling
pitch was hardly ideal for a one-day match, but it was
the same for both sides and Gloucestershire adapted
best to win by 60 runs. Even they had to recover first
from 118 for 8, though, with Malinga Bandara and
Martyn Ball adding 59 for the ninth wicket. Essex
were immediately in trouble against a Gloucestershire
attack missing both the injured Jon Lewis and Steve
Kirby. Jon Averis' eight overs brought him figures of
2 for 9 and wickets fell regularly until Andre Adams
offered some defiant blows in a quickfire 46.

Mal Loye swept Lancashire home by eight wickets
at Colwyn Bay, and his 79 not out made it look
increasingly likely that 2004 champions Glamorgan
would need to fight hard to stay out of the relegation
places 12 months on. The Welsh county were bowled
out for just 173, with Dominic Cork snatching 4 for 37.

Division Two

at Derby
Derbyshire 232 for 3 (45 overs) (MJ Di Venuto 129*)
Sussex 229 (45 overs) (RR Montgomerie 59)
Derbyshire (4pts) won by 3 runs

at Taunton
Somerset 345 for 4 (45 overs) (MJ Wood 129,
ID Blackwell 114)
Yorkshire 343 for 9 (45 overs) (PA Jaques 66,
I Dawood 57, MJ Wood 52)
Somerset (4pts) won by 2 runs

Michael Di Venuto's high-class 129 not out proved
just enough for Derbyshire as they later held their

nerve in the field to emerge with a valuable three-run
victory over Sussex in front of an appreciative
Recreation Ground crowd. At 104 for 1, Sussex
seemed set for a victory charge, but wickets kept
tumbling and in the end not even a rapid 30 by
Naved-ul-Hasan could get the visitors over the line.

There was an even closer, and more exhilarating,
contest at Taunton where Somerset raced to 345 for
4 on a batting paradise, but then found Yorkshire
making a brave bid to go past their record home
score in the competition. In the end the margin of
Somerset's victory was just two runs. Matthew Wood
had a particularly enjoyable day, the Somerset
version that is, especially so with a brilliant 129 from
105 balls, but the Yorkshire Wood did well too,
scoring 52 himself in an opening stand worth 121 in
16 overs with Phil Jaques. Ismail Dawood also hit an
excellent half-century, but the player who tipped the
balance most in Somerset's favour was Ian Blackwell,
whose 114 off a mere 61 balls included five sixes and
11 fours. If that was terrific entertainment, then so
was the Yorkshire chase. It finally came down to 23
from the last over, and then five off the last ball with
the visitors' No. 11 at the crease. Deon Kruis had 25
to his name by then, though, but could only strike
the final delivery for two.

15 August 2005: Division One

at Lord's
Northamptonshire 261 for 6 (45 overs)
(BM Shafayat 85*, RA White 57, ML Love 56)
Middlesex 247 for 9 (45 overs) (PN Weekes 111)
Northamptonshire (4pts) won by 14 runs

Bilal Shafayat's spectacular 85 from 46 balls put
Northamptonshire's total of 261 for 6 just out of
Middlesex's reach at Lord's. While the watching
crowd had as much interest, via their radios, in
England's heroic attempt to bowl out Australia in
the Old Trafford Test, Middlesex's ultimately
unsuccessful chase also vied for their full attention –
especially when Paul Weekes completed a gallant
hundred. When he fell for 111, however, another 34
runs were still required from 20 balls – an equation
which proved too much for the home side's tail.

16 August 2005: Division Two

at The Riverside
Leicestershire 113 (32.2 overs) (ML Lewis 4 for 13)
Durham 116 for 2 (26.2 overs) (PD Collingwood 51*)
Durham (4pts) won by 8 wickets

Durham's followers saw a far shorter game than they had bargained for at the Riverside, but they went home fairly happy anyway after seeing their side rout Leicestershire in helpful bowling conditions. Mick Lewis, Durham's popular Australian seamer, took four cheap wickets as the visitors were skittled for 113, and the home county's top order also struggled initially before Paul Collingwood emerged to thump a breezy unbeaten 51.

17 August 2005: Division One

at Northampton
Northamptonshire 201 (43.2 overs) (MH Wessels 80)
Glamorgan 203 for 5 (41.4 overs) (RDB Croft 81*)
Glamorgan (4pts) won by 5 wickets

Glamorgan hauled themselves out of the relegation zone by completing an excellent five-wicket victory at Northampton. David Harrison and the spinners, Robert Croft and Dean Cosker, were at the heart of Northants' troubled progress to 201 – and it was a total they would not have got near but for a fine innings of 80 from 19-year-old Riki Wessels. It was still not nearly enough in the conditions, however,

and the point was made most forcefully as Croft added a determined and occasionally belligerent undefeated 81 to his earlier two wickets.

21 August 2005: Division Two

at Leicester
Sussex 186 (45 overs) (MH Yardy 58, OD Gibson 4 for 39)
Leicestershire 190 for 5 (43.5 overs) (D Mongia 92*)
Leicestershire (4pts) won by 5 wickets

at Taunton
Durham 222 for 7 (45 overs) (DM Benkenstein 60*)
Somerset 226 for 5 (42.2 overs) (MJ Wood 76)
Somerset (4pts) won by 5 wickets

Sussex slipped to a third successive defeat, further throwing into doubt promotion hopes that had been buoyant when they lost just one of the first ten games. Leicestershire were the latest team to get the better of them, winning by five wickets at Grace Road after bowling well to restrict the division leaders to 186. Ottis Gibson took four wickets in an excellent team performance, and from 102 for 5 in reply it was the batting of Dinesh Mongia – well supported by the ever-combative Paul Nixon – which made the difference. Mongia had been dropped on 42, when Murray Goodwin put down a square slash at point off Robin Martin-Jenkins, and at 111 for 6 Leicestershire might have struggled. But, from then on, Mongia took complete control and finished with 92 not out from 93 balls.

Matthew Wood's mid-August love affair with the Taunton pitch continued as he added a fluent match-winning 76 against Durham to the 297 and 129 he had made in his previous two innings on the ground. Dale Benkenstein had scored 60 not out from 65 balls, but Durham's 222 for 7 was not enough; Wood got the home side off to the start they needed, and ultimately an unbroken stand of 83 between Keith Parsons and Wes Durston closed out the game.

An all-round performance of distinction by Robert Croft spearheaded Glamorgan's victory at Northamptonshire.

22 August 2005: Division One

at Old Trafford
Lancashire 267 for 7 (45 overs) (A Symonds 129,
MJ Chilton 59, SG Law 55, JMM Averis 4 for 40)
Gloucestershire 268 for 4 (43.4 overs) (RR Sarwan 118*,
MA Hardinges 111*)
Gloucestershire (4pts) won by 6 wickets

at Worcester
Worcestershire 185 for 7 (34 overs)
Hampshire 186 for 6 (33.2 overs) (JP Crawley 65,
SR Watson 65)
Hampshire (4pts) won by 4 wickets

at Chelmsford
Essex 53 for 2 (8 overs)
Nottinghamshire
Match abandoned – 2pts each

Three days after collapsing to defeat in the C&G
Trophy semi-finals, Lancashire were faced with more
bitter disappointment after losing to Gloucestershire
at Old Trafford in scarcely believable fashion. The
visitors were seemingly out of the match at 47 for 4,
following a three-wicket, new-ball burst by James
Anderson, as they replied to Lancashire's 267 for 7.
Andy Symonds' brilliant 129, in which he reached
three figures in just 88 balls, had been the catalyst of
Lancashire's innings, but even his effort was put into
the shade by Ramnaresh Sarwan and Mark
Hardinges. Their eventual unbroken fifth-wicket
partnership of 221 in 33 overs was a competition
record, and it left Lancashire and their supporters
stunned. Sarwan's first one-day hundred for the
county came from 105 balls and Hardinges' maiden
limited-overs century took him only 98 deliveries. A
tough asking rate of 100 runs from the last 12 overs
was made to look a stroll as Sarwan and Hardinges,
by now well into their stride, completed the chase
with eight balls still remaining.

John Crawley played the most significant innings
of 65 as Hampshire eased relegation worries with a
four-wicket victory at Worcester in a game reduced
to 34 overs per side. The result, however, kept
Worcestershire anchored to the foot of the Division
One table.

At the other end, meanwhile, Essex moved two
points nearer to the title when their fixture against
Nottinghamshire at Chelmsford was eventually
abandoned. Only eight overs of an intended 19-over
contest were possible, after a much-delayed start at
7.45pm, before more rain arrived.

Division Two

at The Oval
Surrey v. **Kent**
Match abandoned – 2pts each

at Leicester
Leicestershire v. **Warwickshire**
Match abandoned – 2pts each

Two second division matches, at The Oval and
Leicester, did not even see a ball bowled before they
were also abandoned.

23 August 2005: Division One

at Cardiff
Gloucestershire 194 for 9 (45 overs) (APR Gidman 62,
Kadeer Ali 56)
Glamorgan 197 for 6 (43 overs) (MJ Powell 69*)
Glamorgan (4pts) won by 4 wickets

David Harrison began the match with four
successive maidens, and Glamorgan stayed on top
from then on as Gloucestershire were beaten by
four wickets at Cardiff. Half-centuries from Kadeer
Ali and Alex Gidman enabled Gloucestershire to
reach 194 for 9, but Harrison's outstanding new-
ball spell of 9-4-16-2 had pegged them back so
much early on that it was a total always likely to be
overtaken. At 40 for 4, Glamorgan were struggling
however, and it took a calm unbeaten 69 from
Mike Powell, supported in stands of 79 and 73 by
Dan Cherry and Mark Wallace, to guide the
Welsh county home.

Division Two

at Edgbaston
Warwickshire 169 (42 overs) (MH Yardy 6 for 27)
Sussex 173 for 5 (40.5 overs) (MW Goodwin 86*)
Sussex (4pts) won by 5 wickets

Mike Yardy showed off his fast-improving slow-left
arm spin by taking a career-best 6 for 27 to surprise
Warwickshire at Edgbaston. The home side also
struggled against Naved-ul-Hasan's menace with the
new ball, and only determined knocks from Alex
Loudon and Michael Powell in the middle-order
enabled them to reach 169. Sussex lost two early
wickets to Makhaya Ntini, but Murray Goodwin's
fine unbeaten 86 anchored the visitors' floodlit
chase. At 91 for 5, however, the result was still in

some doubt, but Goodwin at last found reliable support in Robin Martin-Jenkins and the pair added an unbroken 82 to extend Sussex's lead at the top of the table.

24 August 2005: Division One

at Old Trafford
Lancashire 195 for 9 (45 overs) (SG Law 82)
Worcestershire 196 for 6 (39.1 overs) (CH Gayle 53, G Chapple 4 for 23)
Worcestershire (4pts) won by 4 wickets

Chris Gayle marked his debut for Worcestershire with a frisky 41-ball 53 which made a chase, after Lancashire's 195 for 9, that much easier at Old Trafford. It was Lancashire's third limited-overs defeat in five days, and not even an innings of 82 from Stuart Law at the head of their order, with a six and ten fours, could inspire the home side. Gayle also took two cheap wickets, and his runs meant that a bag of four wickets by the excellent Glen Chapple could not divert Worcestershire from their path.

26 August 2005: Division Two

at The Grange
Scotland 179 for 7 (38 overs) (DF Watts 71*)
Derbyshire 164 for 7 (31.3 overs) (SD Stubbings 75*)
Derbyshire (4pts) won by 3 wickets – DL Method: target 161 from 32 overs

Their first meeting of the season ended in a tie, but the return fixture between Derbyshire and the Scottish Saltires at Edinburgh produced an equally exciting finish. This time, in a game reduced by weather interruptions to a Duckworth-Lewis target, Derbyshire were left needing eight runs from the final over. They waltzed home with three balls to spare thanks to opener Steve Stubbings clubbing Ryan Watson for six to reach a superb unbeaten 75.

28 August 2005: Division One

at Colchester
Essex 222 for 9 (45 overs) (WI Jefferson 88)
Hampshire 210 for 8 (45 overs) (JP Crawley 84)
Essex (4pts) won by 12 runs

at Northampton
Nottinghamshire 207 (44 overs) (DG Wright 5 for 37)
Northamptonshire 208 for 6 (44.1 overs) (ML Love 59)
Northamptonshire (4pts) won by 4 wickets

At least England's Ashes heroes had the good grace, at Trent Bridge, to complete their nerve-shredding Fourth Test victory chase in time for Essex's followers, at Colchester, to be able to switch off their radios and concentrate on Ronnie Irani's side's exciting title-clinching win against Hampshire. At 173 for 3, in the 37th over, it seemed as if the visitors were going to make the runaway leaders wait for the moment that they could lift the totesport League trophy.

But Essex, spurred on by the buzz in the 4,000 Castle Park crowd in reaction to England's triumph, fought back tigerishly to ensure that their own 222 for 9, on a slow pitch, became a winning total. John Crawley, who had underpinned the Hampshire reply, was held off James Middlebrook, and Ravi Bopara then ran out Greg Lamb and bowled Kevin Latouf. Ultimately, Essex had tightened the noose so expertly that 18 were required from Andre Nel's final over – and the South African fast bowler marked his one-day debut for the county by virtually ensuring victory by bowling Dimitri Mascarenhas with the second ball. Cue champagne celebrations on the Essex dressing room balcony, with popular skipper Irani – in his sixth season as captain – telling the assembled throng below, 'This is our first trophy since 1998 but I want it to be the first in a new era. It is great to see so many of our fans celebrating again and this is like the good old days when I first came to the club and we always seemed to be winning something. But we now have some excellent young players, and I believe this could be the start of more success.'

Damien Wright picked up a career-best 5 for 37 as Northamptonshire dismissed Nottinghamshire for 207 and then knocked off the runs to win by four wickets. Johann Louw, with 3 for 27, supported Wright well, and a stylish 59 from Martin Love then made sure that Notts could not impose themselves on the Northants top order.

Division Two

at The Oval
Surrey 237 for 7 (45 overs) (JGE Benning 65)
Somerset 238 for 5 (39.5 overs) (ID Blackwell 88, JC Hildreth 75*)
Somerset (4pts) won by 5 wickets

at Scarborough
Yorkshire 219 for 8 (45 overs) (MJ Lumb 69, J Moss 4 for 28)

Derbyshire 221 for 5 (42.3 overs) (G Welch 58*,
AG Botha 56*)
Derbyshire (4pts) won by 5 wickets

at The Riverside
Durham 227 for 7 (45 overs) (GJ Muchall 79,
RR Watson 4 for 36)
Scotland 134 (35.2 overs)
(RR Watson 86)
Durham (4pts) won by 93 runs

Ian Blackwell was at his buccaneering best for
Somerset at The Oval, where his 88 from 53 balls
sped his side to five-wicket victory over a lacklustre
Surrey. The match, however, was still in the balance
when Blackwell entered the arena at 89 for 3 in the
19th over. It did not take long for that balance to be
shattered: Blackwell hit six sixes, and with James
Hildreth playing the perfect support act with a
63-ball half-century of his own, a stand of 120 in
just 16 overs ensued.

A sixth-wicket partnership of 102 between
Graeme Welch and Ant Botha meant that
Derbyshire maintained their position as promotion
possibles with a five-wicket victory at Scarborough.
Jon Moss's excellent 4 for 28 held Yorkshire to
219 for 8, but at 119 for 5 in reply Derbyshire were
still nervous about the outcome. They need not
have worried.

Ryan Watson played a lone hand with three sixes
and eight fours in a thumping 86 as Scotland
slumped to 134 all out and defeat by 93 runs to
Durham at the Riverside. Gordon Muchall made an
assured 79 in the county's solid 227 for 7.

30 August 2005: Division Two

at Canterbury
Yorkshire 164 (42.4 overs)
Kent 165 for 4 (31 overs) (DI Stevens 52)
Kent (4pts) won by 6 wickets

at Hove
Scotland 132 (44.5 overs) (JA Beukes 51,
Naved-ul-Hasan 5 for 30)
Sussex 133 for 3 (23.5 overs) (MJ Prior 69)
Sussex (4pts) won by 7 wickets

Poor batting by Yorkshire led to them being
defeated with 14 overs to spare by Kent at
Canterbury. A total of 164 was way below par in the
conditions, as Kent's batsmen then proceeded to
demonstrate. Andrew Hall, with 46, and Darren

Stevens, who hit an attractive half-century, took the
home side to the brink of victory – while Justin
Kemp provided some late fireworks under the
floodlights by scoring his unbeaten 42 from just 25
balls, including a straight six and seven fours.

The pace and swing of Naved-ul-Hasan was too
much for the Scottish Saltires at Hove, as Sussex
took another significant step towards the second
division title. The Pakistan fast bowler's 5 for 30
hastened the Scots to 132 all out, and Matt Prior's
50-ball 69 meant Sussex also lost little time in
reaching their victory target.

31 August 2005: Division Two

at Hove
Surrey 230 for 6 (45 overs)
Sussex 234 for 8 (45 overs) (CJ Adams 110*)
Sussex (4pts) won by 2 wickets

A brilliant match-winning 110 not out from their
captain, Chris Adams, took Sussex to the brink of
guaranteed promotion as Surrey were beaten off the
last ball. Mushtaq Ahmed struck the vital blow,
steering Azhar Mahmood's delivery past gully for
four with the scores level. Eleven had been needed
from the final over, but Adams had ignored the
regular loss of wickets at the other end to keep
Sussex on course for what was a challenging target
under lights. Alistair Brown and Rikki Clarke hit out
well towards the end of the Surrey innings, to ask
big questions of their opponents. Adams, who
batted for 125 balls and hit ten fours, answered
most of them himself.

1 September 2005: Division Two

at Canterbury
Kent 259 for 4 (45 overs) (JM Kemp 65*, AJ Hall 63)
Scotland 115 (33.1 overs) (JC Tredwell 4 for 16)
Kent (4pts) won by 144 runs

Kent overwhelmed the Scottish Saltires at
Canterbury, with spinners James Tredwell and Rob
Ferley taking the last seven wickets between them
after Andrew Hall had plucked out the top three.
Hall had earlier got Kent's batting effort off to a
fine start, too, with ten boundaries in his 63, and
the rest of the county's batsmen kept the
momentum going until Justin Kemp arrived at
No. 5 to thump 65 not out in 47 balls – including
four sixes and a four from successive balls in one
Cedric English over.

The roar of the Rawalpindi Express: Shoaib Akhtar's six wickets for just 16 runs at New Road gave him the new Worcestershire one-day league bowling figures.

4 September 2005: Division One

at Worcester
Gloucestershire 105 (36.3 overs)
(Shoaib Akhtar 6 for 16)
Worcestershire 106 for 2 (24.4 overs)
(CH Gayle 53*)
Worcestershire (4pts) won by
8 wickets

at Cardiff
Northamptonshire 282 for 7 (45 overs)
(DJG Sales 77, U Afzaal 64,
AP Davies 4 for 53)
Glamorgan 22 for 1 (5.3 overs)
Match abandoned – 2pts each

Shoaib Akhtar's 6 for 16 blew Gloucestershire away at New Road, where the heat of a beautiful early September Sunday was more than matched by the scorching speed of the 'Rawalpindi Express'. Four of his victims were clean bowled, defeated as much by pace as Shoaib completed Worcestershire's best individual bowling figures in a one-day league match. An unbeaten 53 from Chris Gayle then eased the home side to a win which took them out of the relegation places.

Glamorgan suffered their fourth abandonment of the totesport campaign, when rain intervened at Cardiff, but the Welsh county might have been glad to see the bad weather close in. They had already lost Robert Croft as they replied to Northamptonshire's intimidating 282 for 7, in which both David Sales and Usman Afzaal played outstanding innings.

Division Two

at Derby
Derbyshire 88 (39.1 overs) (TJ Murtagh 4 for 14)
Surrey 89 for 2 (16.1 overs) (JGE Benning 53)
Surrey (4pts) won by 8 wickets

at The Riverside
Kent 140 (44 overs) (MA Carberry 63)
Durham 144 for 2 (27.3 overs) (JP Maher 70)
Durham (4pts) won by 8 wickets

at Headingley
Leicestershire 253 for 8 (45 overs) (A Habib 65*,
DL Maddy 54)
Yorkshire 120 (35.3 overs)
Leicestershire (4pts) won by 133 runs

Fine new-ball bowling from Tim Murtagh and Azhar Mahmood shattered Derbyshire's hopes at Derby. The home side were 34 for 6 at one stage, after opting to bat first, and were eventually all out for 88 with Murtagh taking career-best one-day figures of 4 for 14 and Azhar picking up 3 for 20. Tim's younger brother Chris, 20, was making his county debut in this game and was at the crease on four not out when an eight-wicket win was completed.

Durham thrashed Kent by eight wickets, too, with Neil Killeen and Gareth Breese sharing six wickets and Jimmy Maher then hitting 70 in an opening stand of 123 with Gavin Hamilton. Another feature of the home side's win at the Riverside was when England's substitute fielder hero of the Trent Bridge Test, Gary Pratt, ran out Martin van Jaarsveld with a brilliant stop and throw from backward point.

Darren Maddy and Aftab Habib scored fine half-centuries as Leicestershire further improved their promotion chances with a commanding 133-run victory against Yorkshire at Headingley. There were three important early wickets, too, for Ottis Gibson before the rest of the Leicestershire attack throttled the home reply.

5 September 2005: Division One

at The Rose Bowl
Hampshire 227 for 6 (45 overs) (JP Crawley 92)
Middlesex 230 for 8 (43.1 overs) (OA Shah 96, JWM Dalrymple 57)
Middlesex (4pts) won by 2 wickets

Hampshire paraded the C&G Trophy at the Rose Bowl but then found their emotions dampened as Middlesex beat them by two wickets to leave them staring hard at the prospect of relegation. John Crawley's 92 from 122 balls had anchored steady progress to 227 for 6, but Middlesex had their own chances of the £22,000 runners-up prize boosted by a superb third-wicket stand of 139 in 20 overs between Owais Shah and Jamie Dalrymple. Shah included two sixes and 12 fours in his classy 92-ball 96, although Middlesex were guilty of middle-order panic once he had driven Chris Tremlett to extra cover. In the end, though, there were 11 balls in hand.

Division Two

at Taunton
Warwickshire 278 for 5 (45 overs) (IJL Trott 112*)
Somerset 281 for 6 (44 overs) (WJ Durston 58*, MJ Wood 53)
Somerset (4pts) won by 4 wickets

A dashing partnership of 94 from just 79 balls between John Francis and Wes Durston, who had come in at No. 8 with Somerset struggling at 187 for 6, meant further dejection for Warwickshire three days after their C&G Trophy final defeat. Durston finished unbeaten on 58, his half-century taking him just 33 balls, as Somerset were swept to an unlikely four-wicket win. Earlier, Jonathan Trott's 112 not out took Warwickshire to 278 for 5.

6 September 2005: Division Two

at Leicester
Leicestershire 164 for 8 (45 overs) (DDJ Robinson 61)
Derbyshire 168 for 4 (40 overs)
Derbyshire (4pts) won by 6 wickets

Derbyshire kept their own promotion ambitions alive, and also ensured that leaders Sussex would play in the totesport League's top division in 2006, by beating close rivals Leicestershire at Grace Road. A sluggish pitch meant for an attritional contest, rather than thrills and spills, but Derbyshire bowled and batted with great good sense to earn themselves their six-wicket success.

7 September 2005: Division One

at Chelmsford
Essex 273 for 6 (45 overs) (RN ten Doeschate 89*, GW Flower 63)
Lancashire 218 (41.2 overs) (D Gough 4 for 31)
Essex (4pts) won by 55 runs

Champions Essex set out to enjoy themselves in their floodlit fixture against Lancashire, and their supporters at Chelmsford had a ball too as the visitors were trounced by 55 runs. First there was some sparkling strokeplay by Ronnie Irani, Grant Flower and Ryan ten Doeschate, who confirmed his sudden emergence as a one-day striker of some substance with a career-best unbeaten 89 from 79 balls. Darren Gough then caught the mood, bounding in exuberantly to take 4 for 31 and spearhead Essex's dismissal of Lancashire for 218.

9 September 2005: Division One

at Trent Bridge
Gloucestershire 116 (28.5 overs) (SJ Adshead 52, MA Ealham 4 for 18)
Nottinghamshire 117 for 9 (28.4 overs) (JMM Averis 4 for 44)
Nottinghamshire (4pts) won by 1 wicket

A remarkable dogfight on a dodgy pitch, and against the swinging ball, ended with Nottinghamshire squeezing past Gloucestershire by just one wicket at Trent Bridge. Mark Ealham took 4 for 18 and Ryan

Sidebottom and Gareth Clough three apiece as Gloucestershire were skittled for 116. Only Steve Adshead, who opened and scored 52, made any headway and it was an eerily similar story when Notts replied. Anurag Singh, on his 30th birthday, was the opener who this time held the fort at one end while all around him was chaos – Singh making 41. James Averis took 4 for 44, and Mark Alleyne and Jon Lewis two each, and Gloucestershire even looked like winning until Greg Smith came in at No. 11 to hit an unbeaten 16 and put on a match-winning 19-run stand with Sidebottom.

11 September 2005: Division One

at Lord's
Middlesex 239 for 5 (45 overs) (OA Shah 66, PN Weekes 58)
Glamorgan 234 (43.4 overs) (MJ Powell 83*, SB Styris 4 for 56)
Middlesex (4pts) won by 5 runs

at Trent Bridge
Worcestershire 200 for 9 (45 overs) (BF Smith 58, AJ Harris 4 for 48)
Nottinghamshire 204 for 5 (41.2 overs) (SP Fleming 73)
Nottinghamshire (4pts) won by 5 wickets

Middlesex made sure of the runners-up spot as the last five Glamorgan wickets tumbled in the space of 16 balls at Lord's. It was an astonishing turn-around as Glamorgan, the only side who could have stolen second place from Middlesex, first recovered strongly from being 47 for 3 and then threw away a position of strength at 219 for 5 in the 42nd over. Michael Powell, who had batted beautifully, was left stranded on 83 not out as the Welsh county found themselves bowled out and beaten by five runs with eight balls still remaining. A second-wicket stand of 122 between Paul Weekes and Owais Shah had earlier been the basis of Middlesex's 239 for 5.

   Nottinghamshire won the battle of two relegation rivals by beating Worcestershire by five wickets at Trent Bridge. In a closely fought affair, the assured 73 of Notts' captain Stephen Fleming turned the match towards his side.

Division Two

at Headingley
Yorkshire 237 for 5 (45 overs) (A McGrath 68, MJ Lumb 52)

Durham 241 for 3 (43.2 overs) (GJ Muchall 101*)
Durham (4pts) won by 7 wickets

Gordon Muchall's 103-ball hundred took Durham to what was in the end a comfortable seven-wicket victory over Yorkshire at Headingley. Muchall shared an unbroken partnership of 109 in 17 overs with Gary Pratt, who had earlier run out Yorkshire's top-scorer Anthony McGrath for 68 with one of his trademark direct hits from point.

Long–serving New Zealand captain Stephen Fleming has also proved to be an inspirational leader of Nottinghamshire, and his 73 against Worcestershire was the decisive contribution.

13 September 2005: Division One

at Cardiff
Glamorgan 220 for 8 (45 overs) (MJ Powell 52)
Hampshire 69 (23.2 overs) (DS Harrison 4 for 28)
Glamorgan (4pts) won by 151 runs

A watching Shane Warne had to endure the sight of
Hampshire being dismissed for only 69 on his 36th
birthday as Glamorgan made sure of their first division
status at Cardiff. Michael Powell's 52 was the pick of a
number of useful contributions to Glamorgan's 220 for
8, but then David Harrison and Andrew Davies made
the most of the early-evening dew as Hampshire's
chase under the lights became a dismal procession.

14 September 2005: Division Two

at Derby
Yorkshire 171 for 9 (45 overs) (JJ Sayers 54*)
Derbyshire 172 for 5 (42.4 overs) (Hassan Adnan 57)
Derbyshire (4pts) won by 5 wickets

at Edgbaston
Warwickshire 292 for 8 (45 overs) (IJL Trott 101,
JO Troughton 82, NM Carter 51, R Clarke 4 for 49)
Surrey 224 (40.3 overs)
Warwickshire (4pts) won by 68 runs

Derbyshire moved into third place by
holding their nerve in a tricky run chase
under the Derby lights. Yorkshire had earlier
rallied from 66 for 7 to 171 for 9, with Joe
Sayers batting well for his unbeaten 54, but
Hassan Adnan and Luke Sutton also showed
grit with the bat to get their side home by
five wickets.

Jonathan Trott's second successive
totesport League hundred, plus his three
wickets, marked the day he received his
Warwickshire county cap at Edgbaston. Trott
was joined in a partnership of 144 in 22 overs
by Jim Troughton, who blazed 82 from 67
balls, while Neil Carter's 29-ball 51 at the
head of the order was another major factor in
the home side's rapid progress to 292 for 8.
This proved too big a task for Surrey, whose
steady decline to 224 all out was held up only
by a 12-minute floodlights power failure.

18 September 2005: Division One

at Chelmsford
Worcestershire 240 for 9 (45 overs) (VS Solanki 79)
Essex 243 for 6 (44.1 overs) (GW Flower 81, AN Cook 62)
Essex (4pts) won by 4 wickets

at Old Trafford
Middlesex 263 for 4 (45 overs) (ET Smith 71,
OA Shah 67, JWM Dalrymple 63*)
Lancashire 219 (44 overs) (G Chapple 71)
Middlesex (4pts) won by 44 runs

Grant Flower hit four sixes in his run-a-ball 81,
while youngsters Alastair Cook and Ravi Bopara also
batted attractively in Essex's four-wicket win over
Worcestershire at Chelmsford. The visitors badly
needed victory, as they struggled to avoid relegation,
but Essex were in no mood to let their title
celebrations fade away. Darren Gough and Danish
Kaneria underlined their quality as Worcestershire
were held to 240 for 9 on a good surface, and not
even the early loss of their captain Ronnie Irani
could deflect Essex from continuing their mastery of
the 45-over game.

An all-action display by Jamie Dalrymple inspired
Middlesex to a 44-run win at Lancashire, who were

In the thick of it: Jamie Dalrymple produced an
inspired all-round display to sweep Middlesex to
victory against Lancashire.

Fraser Watts scored a fine 88 for the Scottish Saltires, but it was not enough to prevent Warwickshire from taking the points at Edinburgh.

left teetering on the edge of relegation. Ed Smith and Owais Shah both scored excellent half-centuries, but it was Dalrymple's highly inventive 33-ball 63 not out which then propelled Middlesex to 263 for 4. In Lancashire's reply, Dalrymple then chalked up two direct-hit run outs, three catches and the wicket of Kyle Hogg. Glen Chapple tried to rescue Lancashire with five driven sixes, but his powerful 71 was not enough.

Division Two

at The Grange
Scotland 220 for 5 (45 overs)
(DF Watts 88, IM Stanger 65)

Warwickshire 221 for 5 (41.4 overs)
(NV Knight 104*, IJL Trott 54)
Warwickshire (4pts) won by 5 wickets

at Derby
Somerset 140 (43.4 overs)
Durham 141 for 5 (30.4 overs)
Durham (4pts) won by 5 wickets

at Canterbury
Sussex 230 for 9 (45 overs)
(RR Montgomerie 72)
Kent 169 (42.2 overs) (MA Carberry 51)
Sussex (4pts) won by 61 runs

Scotland's last match in the totesport League was ruined by Nick Knight, whose unbeaten 104 calmly steered Warwickshire to victory by five wickets with something to spare. Fraser Watts' 88 and an innings of 65 from Ian Stanger took the Saltires to a respectable total, but Knight's expertise told and the Scots had to accept defeat at the end of their three-year existence in the league.

Durham added promotion from the totesport second division to their elevation into the elite tier of the County Championship on a memorable day at the Riverside. Somerset's slump to 140 all out was a triumph in particular for Neil Killeen and Paul Collingwood, who shared six wickets, and the home side never looked in any danger of not reaching their modest target.

Kent's crash to 48 for 5 inside the first 15 overs left Sussex with a comparative stroll to the victory that made them odds-on favourites to lift the second division title. James Kirtley and Robin Martin-Jenkins picked up three wickets each as Kent then made it to 169 all out, mainly as a result of Michael Carberry's fighting 51. Earlier, Sussex's solid 230 for 9 was built upon by opener Richard Montgomerie's 72 from 82 balls.

20 September 2005: Division Two

at Edgbaston
Warwickshire 309 for 3 (45 overs)
(IR Bell 137, IJL Trott 94*)
Yorkshire 207 for 9 (45 overs) (MJ Wood 80)
Warwickshire (4pts) won by 102 runs

Class act: Warwickshire's Ian Bell celebrates his England winter tour selection by battering Yorkshire's attack for a brilliant 137 at Edgbaston.

Ian Bell celebrated his selection for England's winter tour of Pakistan, announced 24 hours earlier, by taking a heavy toll of Yorkshire's bowlers at Edgbaston. Jonathan Trott also weighed in with an unbeaten 94, but it was Bell's superb 137 which most caught the eye and also helped the young England batsman to put his Oval Test pair behind him. Matthew Wood fought hard in reply, but Yorkshire never threatened even to get close to Warwickshire's impressive total.

25 September 2005: Division One

at The Rose Bowl
Nottinghamshire 248 for 5 (45 overs) (DJ Hussey 75)
Hampshire 127 (19.5 overs)
*Nottinghamshire (4pts) won by 37 runs – DL Method:
target 165 from 20 overs*

at Worcester
Lancashire 186 for 8 (33 overs) (SG Law 67)
Worcestershire 111 (29.1 overs)
Lancashire (4pts) won by 75 runs

at Bristol
Glamorgan 262 for 6 (45 overs) (DL Hemp 84*)
Gloucestershire 263 for 7 (42.4 overs)
(CM Spearman 80)
Gloucestershire (4pts) won by 3 wickets

at Northampton
Northamptonshire 208 (44.3 overs) (ML Love 53,
DG Wright 51*)
Essex 209 for 3 (40.5 overs) (AN Cook 94, GW Flower 88*)
Essex (4pts) won by 7 wickets

Hampshire, pipped to the championship title by
Nottinghamshire, were also condemned by them to
the totesport League's second division as a result of
a 37-run defeat at the Rose Bowl. Notts first ran up
an excellent total of 248 for 5, in which David
Hussey's 53-ball 75 was the highlight, and then
needed to defend an adjusted target of 142 from 14
overs. This they did, despite a late 22-ball 36 from
Jono McLean, as Hampshire went down swinging.

In the battle for survival at New Road, it was
Lancashire who won the day as they bowled out
Worcestershire for 111 in a match reduced by rain to
33 overs per side. Stuart Law's 64-ball 67 included
four sixes, and Glen Chapple struck 41 from 40 balls
in their fifth-wicket partnership of 84 from 11 overs.

Spectators at Bristol finally got what they were
waiting for during Gloucestershire's exciting and
ultimately successful chase of Glamorgan's 262 for 6:
the scoreboard clicked around to the total 111 and
David Shepherd, the umpire and former local
favourite, duly gave the crowd one last 'Nelson' hop
and skip before retirement. Shepherd, who has
officiated in 92 Tests and 172 one-day internationals,
walked through a guard of honour provided by both
teams at the end of the match, and a reception was

**Young gun: Alastair Cook rounds off his breakthrough season by
hitting the Northants bowling for 94 in yet another Essex win.**

held at the ground later in the evening by the Gloucestershire club. There was also a home win for the Bristol crowd to applaud, with Craig Spearman's 71-ball 80 leading the way, but it was not enough to save Gloucestershire from relegation.

Alastair Cook, the 20-year-old batting prodigy from Essex, rounded off a triumphant season by scoring 94 at Northampton in only his fifth one-day league appearance to propel the totesport League champions to a remarkable 13th victory of a campaign in which they were only beaten once. Grant Flower helped Cook to add 168 in 34 overs for the third wicket, following the loss of two early wickets, and the Zimbabwean reached 88 not out himself to help set the seal on another memorable Essex display.

Division Two

at Hove
Yorkshire 99 (32 overs)
Sussex 102 for 2 (24.4 overs)
Sussex (4pts) won by 8 wickets

at The Oval
Scotland 212 for 9 (45 overs) (CM Wright 88*,
RO Hussain 52, JW Dernbach 4 for 36)
Surrey 204 for 2 (30.3 overs) (SA Newman 80*,
JN Batty 51)
*Surrey (4pts) won by 8 wickets – DL Method: target 203
from 42 overs*

at Taunton
Somerset 300 for 6 (45 overs) (ID Blackwell 75,
KA Parsons 75*, JD Francis 60)
Derbyshire 165 (33.3 overs) (Hassan Adnan 62,
ID Blackwell 5 for 26)
Somerset (4pts) won by 135 runs

at Leicester
Leicestershire 280 for 5 (45 overs) (HD Ackerman 78,
DL Maddy 51, D Mongia 50)
Kent 170 for 6 (33 overs) (DI Stevens 76,
M van Jaarsveld 59*)
*Leicestershire (4pts) won by 40 runs – DL Method:
target 211 from 33 overs*

at Edgbaston
Warwickshire 187 for 8 (45 overs)
Durham 154 for 2 (30.5 overs) (PD Collingwood 67*,
JP Maher 61)
*Durham (4pts) won by 8 wickets – DL Method: target
154 from 34 overs*

Seasoned howitzer: Ian Blackwell bludgeoned three more sixes in his 60–ball 75 against an overpowered Derbyshire at Taunton.

Essex, the runaway winners of the 2005 totesport League, are pictured celebrating the downfall of another opponent.

Peter Moores was given the perfect leaving present by his Sussex players at Hove: the totesport League second division title on the final day of his 20-year association with the club as player, captain, coach and director of cricket. Moores, now off to succeed Rod Marsh as the ECB National Academy director, saw Sussex pulverise Yorkshire by eight wickets.

Surrey chased a revised total of 203 from 42 overs to end their disappointing season with a win and send off the Scottish Saltires with the 14th defeat of their final totesport season. It could have been worse for the Scots: they were 57 for 6 in the 19th over before Craig Wright, the captain, was joined by Omer Hussain in a seventh-wicket stand worth 125 in 23 overs. Wright finished 88 not out, but Surrey sped to their target in the 31st over with Scott Newman leading the way with 80 not out.

Derbyshire only had a mathematical chance of promotion when they took on Somerset at Taunton, but the contest soon became academic as the home captain, Ian Blackwell, took command. Blackwell, entering at three after John Francis and Matthew Wood had put on exactly 100 for the first wicket, thumped three sixes and six fours in a 60-ball 75 that was the catalyst for a surge to 300 for 6. Keith

Parsons, who also made 75 – not out – added 83 for the fourth wicket with Blackwell, who then took five for 26 from his nine overs of left-arm spin, a career-best one-day return, as Derbyshire plummeted from 99 for 1 to 165 all out in reply.

Kent were well adrift of the asking rate, in reply to Leicestershire's 280 for 5, when rain confirmed the home side's victory at Grace Road. Hylton Ackerman, the home captain, made 78 and was well supported by Darren Maddy and Dinesh Mongia as Kent once again struggled to contain their opponents in the field. Darren Stevens, playing against his old club, gave Kent hope with a rapid 76 in a second-wicket stand of 106 with Martin van Jaarsveld, but the innings went into decline once he had fallen to the left-arm spin of Mongia. Stuart Broad again impressed with two for 35 from his seven overs.

Warwickshire secured promotion to the first division despite their eight-wicket defeat to Durham, who finished second, at Edgbaston. A crowd of 6,500 saw Warwickshire struggle to 187 for 8, boosted towards the end by a run-a-ball 48 from Dougie Brown, and then Durham move comfortably to their revised target following a rain interruption.

Final League Tables

totesport League – Division One

	P	W	L	T	NR	RR	Pts
Essex	**16**	**13**	**1**	**0**	**2**	**7.28**	**56**
Middlesex	16	10	5	0	1	5.54	42
Northants	16	7	7	0	2	-0.13	32
Glamorgan	16	6	6	0	4	-0.24	32
Nottinghamshire	16	6	7	0	3	5.83	30
Lancashire	16	6	9	0	1	-0.69	26
Gloucestershire	16	6	9	0	1	-8.39	26
Worcestershire	16	5	10	0	1	-2.53	22
Hampshire	16	5	10	0	1	-6.23	22

totesport League – Division Two

	P	W	L	T	NR	RR	Pts
Sussex	**18**	**13**	**4**	**0**	**1**	**13.93**	**54**
Durham	18	12	4	0	2	11.21	52
Warwickshire	18	10	6	0	2	6.00	44
Leicestershire	18	10	7	0	1	5.54	42
Derbyshire	18	9	7	1	1	-4.10	40
Somerset	18	9	8	0	1	0.85	38
Surrey	18	7	10	0	1	-5.08	30
Kent	18	6	10	0	2	0.67	28
Yorkshire	18	5	13	0	0	-8.63	20
Scotland	18	2	14	1	1	-16.67	12

FEATURES OF TOTESPORT LEAGUE 2005

HIGHEST TOTAL

353 for 8 (45 overs)	Hampshire v. Middlesex at Lord's	15 May

HIGHEST TOTAL BATTING SECOND

343 for 9 (45 overs)	Yorkshire v. Somerset at Taunton	14 August

LOWEST TOTAL

69 (45 overs)	Hampshire v. Glamorgan at Cardiff	13 September

BEST INDIVIDUAL SCORES

144	MJ Prior	Sussex v. Warwickshire at Hove	8 May

37 centuries were scored in the competition

SIX WICKETS IN AN INNINGS

6-16	Shoaib Akhtar	Worcs v. Glos at Worcester	4 September
6-27	MH Yardy	Sussex v. Warwickshire at Edgbaston	23 August
6-33	CB Keegan	Middlesex v. Notts at Trent Bridge	17 April

There were nine instances of five wickets in an innings

TIED MATCHES

Derbyshire tied with Scotland at Derby	19 June

WINNING BY ONE WICKET

Scotland beat Warwickshire at Stratford	29 May
Essex beat Middlesex at Lord's	5 June
Nottinghamshire beat Hampshire at Trent Bridge	17 July
Nottinghamshire beat Gloucestershire at Trent Bridge	9 September

WINNING BY MORE THAN 150 RUNS

151	Glamorgan beat Hampshire at Sophia Gardens	13 September

There were nine instances of a side winning by 100 runs or more

WINNING BY ONE RUN

Lancashire beat Nottinghamshire at Old Trafford	1 May
Durham beat Kent at Tunbridge Wells	29 May

NO PLAY POSSIBLE

Glamorgan v. Essex at Cardiff	22 April
Scotland v. Durham at The Grange	1 May
Glamorgan v. Nottinghamshire at Swansea	5 June
Hampshire v. Worcestershire at The Rose Bowl	27 July
Surrey v. Kent at The Oval	22 August
Leicestershire v. Warwickshire at Leicester	22 August

TOTESPORT LEAGUE: DIVISION ONE FEATURES 2005

BATTING: LEADING AVERAGES

	M	Inns	NO	Runs	HS	Av	100	50
DL Hemp (Glam)	14	12	5	400	84*	57.14	-	4
SR Watson (Hants)	6	6	1	277	106*	55.40	1	1
PN Weekes (Middx)	16	16	1	785	111	52.33	2	7
A Symonds (Lancs)	9	9	1	406	129	50.75	1	2
JWM Dalrymple (Middx)	15	15	5	481	81	48.10	-	5
U Afzaal (N'hants)	16	15	2	610	122*	46.92	2	2
AN Cook (Essex)	5	5	0	234	94	46.80	-	2
GW Flower (Essex)	12	12	2	466	90*	46.60	-	5
ML Love (N'hants)	15	15	2	579	111*	44.53	1	4
Z de Bruyn (Worcs)	9	8	1	306	62	43.71	-	4
MJ Powell (Glam)	14	12	2	432	83*	43.20	-	4
SP Fleming (Notts)	11	10	1	355	102*	39.44	1	2
AD Mascarenhas (Hants)	9	9	3	231	50*	38.50	-	2
A Flower (Essex)	13	13	5	307	127*	38.37	1	-
EC Joyce (Middx)	15	14	4	378	74	37.80	-	2
OA Shah (Middx)	16	15	1	527	96	37.64	-	6
MA Wallace (Glam)	14	10	5	188	33*	37.60	-	-
VS Solanki (Worcs)	14	14	1	468	119	36.00	1	2
JP Crawley (Hants)	14	14	1	466	92	35.84	-	3
BM Shafayat (N'hants)	15	15	3	425	97*	35.41	-	3
RS Bopara (Essex)	14	13	5	277	96*	34.62	-	1
CMW Read (Notts)	14	12	2	342	68*	34.20	-	1
MH Wessels (N'hants)	13	10	3	233	80	33.28	-	1
DJG Sales (N'hants)	16	14	1	417	77	32.07	-	2
AG Wharf (Glam)	11	10	1	286	42	31.77	-	-
ET Smith (Middx)	16	16	1	476	93	31.73	-	3
WI Jefferson (Essex)	10	10	1	283	88	31.44	-	1
SG Law (Lancs)	15	15	0	464	82	30.93	-	5
WPC Weston (Glos)	10	10	0	304	72	30.40	-	4
SB Styris (Middx)	12	12	0	363	82	30.25	-	3
RR Sarwan (Glos)	8	8	1	210	118*	30.00	1	-
SC Moore (Worcs)	15	15	1	420	104	30.00	1	-
SR Patel (Notts)	14	10	2	239	82	29.87	-	1
GA Lamb (Hants)	12	12	2	292	100*	29.20	1	-
SM Katich (Hants)	5	5	0	144	85	28.80	-	1
MJ Chilton (Lancs)	16	15	3	344	59	28.66	-	1
A Singh (Notts)	9	8	1	198	47	28.28	-	-
G Chapple (Lancs)	8	7	1	165	71	27.50	-	1
MGN Windows (Glos)	14	14	1	354	87	27.23	-	4
RDB Croft (Glam)	14	13	1	323	88	26.91	-	2
DJ Hussey (Notts)	15	13	0	339	75	26.07	-	2
KW Hogg (Lancs)	11	10	3	182	41*	26.00	-	-
RC Irani (Essex)	14	14	0	363	67	25.92	-	3

Qualification: averages 25 or above (minimum of five innings)

LEADING RUN SCORERS – TOP 20

Player	Runs	Inns
PN Weekes (Middx)	785	16
U Afzaal (Northants)	610	16
ML Love (Northants)	579	15
OA Shah (Middx)	527	15
JWM Dalrymple (Middx)	481	15
ET Smith (Middx)	476	16
VS Solanki (Worcs)	468	14
GW Flower (Essex)	466	12
JP Crawley (Hants)	466	14
SG Law (Lancs)	464	15
MJ Powell (Glam)	432	12
BM Shafayat (Northants)	425	15
SC Moore (Worcs)	420	15
DJG Sales (Northants)	417	14
A Symonds (Lancs)	406	9
DL Hemp (Glam)	400	12
EC Joyce (Middx)	378	14
SB Styris (Middx)	363	12
RC Irani (Essex)	363	14
SP Fleming (Notts)	355	10

BOWLING: LEADING AVERAGES

	O	M	Runs	W	Av	Best	4i	Econ
CB Keegan (Middx)	25	4	109	10	10.90	6-33	1	4.36
D Gough (Essex)	76.4	5	296	19	15.57	4-16	2	3.86
WPUJC Vaas (Worcs)	44.3	5	180	11	16.36	3-31	-	4.04
GW Flower (Essex)	67	0	283	17	16.64	3-21	-	4.22
Danish Kaneria (Essex)	79	4	278	16	17.37	3-24	-	3.51
RJ Sidebottom (Notts)	76.5	10	302	17	17.76	3-13	-	3.93
DS Harrison (Glam)	99.4	11	389	21	18.52	5-33	2	3.90
GD Clough (Notts)	60	5	292	15	19.46	3-22	-	4.86
JM Anderson (Lancs)	111	11	452	23	19.65	3-12	-	4.07
SD Udal (Hants)	112.5	5	502	25	20.08	4-55	1	4.44
J Lewis (Glos)	82.2	9	382	19	20.10	5-19	1	4.63
CT Peploe (Middx)	51	2	209	10	20.90	4-38	1	4.09
CT Tremlett (Hants)	86.2	5	481	23	20.91	3-30	-	5.57
SB Styris (Middx)	90.4	2	420	20	21.00	4-56	1	4.63
AJ Harris (Notts)	49.5	4	280	13	21.53	4-41	2	5.61
DG Wright (N'hants)	120	14	574	26	22.07	5-37	1	4.78
MCJ Ball (Glos)	83.3	5	333	15	22.20	3-44	-	3.98
JD Middlebrook (Essex)	102.3	2	421	18	23.38	3-30	-	4.10
Kabir Ali (Worcs)	88.3	9	492	21	23.42	3-42	-	5.55
RW Price (Worcs)	122	9	447	19	23.52	4-21	1	3.66
G Chapple (Lancs)	55	3	265	11	24.09	4-23	1	4.81
SK Warne (Hants)	58	1	276	11	25.09	2-34	-	4.75
DG Cork (Lancs)	92.3	9	383	15	25.53	4-14	2	4.14
J Louw (N'hants)	122	9	576	22	26.18	4-39	1	4.72
BL Hutton (Middx)	52	0	288	10	28.80	3-42	-	5.53
GP Swann (Notts)	81.3	1	349	12	29.08	3-46	-	4.28
AG Wharf (Glam)	83	3	495	17	29.11	3-71	-	5.96
PN Weekes (Middx)	79.4	1	386	13	29.69	4-58	1	4.84
JMM Averis (Glos)	85	9	424	14	30.28	4-40	2	4.98
SM Ervine (Hants)	78	6	397	13	30.53	3-32	-	5.08
DA Leatherdale (Worcs)	65.1	1	343	11	31.18	2-19	-	5.26
MN Malik (Worcs)	58	1	317	10	31.70	2-34	-	5.46
AD Mascarenhas (Hants)	66.1	2	332	10	33.20	2-32	-	5.01
DA Cosker (Glam)	101	1	491	14	35.07	3-31	-	4.86
MA Ealham (Notts)	82.5	4	400	11	36.36	4-18	1	4.82
GJ Smith (Notts)	83.2	4	418	11	38.00	3-49	-	5.01
AR Adams (Essex)	74.1	6	387	10	38.70	3-67	-	5.21

Qualification: averages of 38 or less (minimum of ten wickets)

LEADING WICKET-TAKERS – TOP 20

Player	W	O
DG Wright (Northants)	26	120
SD Udal (Hants)	25	112.5
CT Tremlett (Hants)	23	86.2
JM Anderson (Lancs)	23	111
J Louw (Northants)	22	122
Kabir Ali (Worcs)	21	88.3
DS Harrison (Glam)	21	99.4
SB Styris (Middx)	20	90.4
D Gough (Essex)	19	76.4
J Lewis (Glos)	19	82.2
RW Price (Worcs)	19	122
JD Middlebrook (Essex)	18	102.3
AG Wharf (Glam)	17	83
GW Flower (Essex)	17	67
RJ Sidebottom (Notts)	17	76.5
Danish Kaneria (Essex)	16	79
MCJ Ball (Glos)	15	83.3
DG Cork (Lancs)	15	92.3
GD Clough (Notts)	15	60
AP Davies (Glam)	15	109

FIELDING: LEADING DISMISSALS – TOP 20

JS Foster (Essex) - 21 (15ct, 6st); MA Wallace (Glam) - 20 (16ct, 4st); SJ Adshead (Glos) - 16 (13ct, 3st); N Pothas (Hants) - 16 (12ct, 4st); WK Hegg (Lancs) - 15 (13ct, 2st); CMW Read (Notts) - 15 (13ct, 2st); MJ Powell (Glam) - 14 (14ct); BJM Scott (Middx) - 14 (12ct, 2st); MH Wessels (Northants) - 12 (12ct); SG Law (Lancs) - 12 (12ct); BL Hutton (Middx) – 12 (12ct); VS Solanki – 10 (10ct); SM Davies (Worcs) - 9 (6ct, 3st); DJ Pipe (Worcs) - 9 (3ct, 6st); SP Fleming (Notts) – 9 (9ct); CM Spearman (Glos) – 9 (9ct); SD Snell (Glos) - 8 (8ct); JP Crawley (Hants) - 8 (8ct); RC Irani (Essex) - 8 (8ct); SD Udal (Hants) 8 (8ct)

TOTESPORT LEAGUE: DIVISION TWO FEATURES 2005

BATTING: LEADING AVERAGES

	M	Inns	NO	Runs	HS	Av	100	50
IJL Trott (Warks)	16	15	5	608	112*	60.80	2	4
RR Montgomerie (Sussex)	9	9	2	375	132*	53.57	1	2
DM B'stein (Durham)	17	13	5	411	90	51.37	-	4
R Clarke (Surrey)	12	9	3	306	90*	51.00	-	2
ID Blackwell (Somerset)	18	17	2	745	134*	49.66	2	5
CJ Adams (Sussex)	16	16	4	592	110*	49.33	1	3
MJ Di Venuto (Derbys)	17	17	1	753	129*	47.06	3	2
GJ Muchall (Durham)	17	14	4	462	101*	46.20	1	3
KA Parsons (Somerset)	18	17	4	558	91*	42.92	-	4
Hassan Adnan (Derbys)	7	7	1	256	62	42.66	-	3
DL Maddy (Leics)	17	17	2	621	107*	41.40	1	5
MJ Prior (Sussex)	17	17	1	660	144	41.25	1	5
SD Stubbings (Derbys)	14	14	1	524	98	40.30	-	4
AD Brown (Surrey)	17	15	1	561	108*	40.07	1	5
M van Jaarsveld (Kent)	17	16	2	549	114	39.21	1	4
PA Jaques (Yorks)	11	11	0	422	98	38.36	-	4
JL Sadler (Leics)	10	10	3	263	50	37.57	-	1
NV Knight (Warks)	17	16	2	520	122*	37.14	2	1
D Mongia (Leics)	15	15	2	481	92*	37.00	-	5
JA Beukes (Scotland)	14	14	0	513	92	36.64	-	4
AJ Hall (Kent)	9	9	0	324	72	36.00	-	3
JC Hildreth (Somerset)	18	17	5	427	75*	35.58	-	2
MJ Lumb (Yorks)	18	18	1	598	69	35.17	-	6
IJ Ward (Sussex)	9	9	0	313	93	34.77	-	3
DR Brown (Warks)	16	12	6	201	48	33.50	-	-
JO Troughton (Warks)	15	15	1	465	82	33.21	-	3
JD Francis (Somerset)	18	16	2	465	73*	33.21	-	3
HD Ackerman (Leics)	17	17	1	528	114*	33.00	1	2
MW Goodwin (Sussex)	16	15	2	425	86*	32.69	-	3
JGE Benning (Surrey)	17	17	0	553	72	32.52	-	4
AGR Loudon (Warks)	17	15	2	422	73*	32.46	-	4
PD Collingwood (Durham)	14	14	5	289	67*	32.11	-	2
MR R'kash (Surrey)	15	15	1	445	89*	31.78	-	3
MJ Wood (Somerset)	14	14	0	442	129	31.57	1	2
MEK Hussey (Durham)	9	9	0	280	97	31.11	-	2
PA Nixon (Leics)	17	12	4	248	47*	31.00	-	-
AV Suppiah (Somerset)	8	8	1	215	79	30.71	-	1
IR Bell (Warks)	9	8	0	245	137	30.62	1	1
A McGrath (Yorks)	18	18	1	517	68	30.41	-	3
N Peng (Durham)	10	10	1	269	63	29.88	-	3
J Moss (Derbys)	17	17	3	418	79	29.85	-	2
SA Newman (Surrey)	9	9	1	238	80*	29.75	-	1
I Dawood (Yorks)	11	10	4	175	57	29.16	-	1
G Welch (Derbys)	15	13	4	254	58*	28.22	-	1
DI Stevens (Kent)	17	16	2	385	76	27.50	-	3
NM Carter (Warks)	17	16	0	439	65	27.43	-	3
TJ New (Leics)	8	8	0	217	47	27.12	-	-
DP Fulton (Kent)	9	7	0	189	57	27.00	-	1
MJ Wood (Yorks)	17	17	0	451	111	26.52	1	2
MA Carberry (Kent)	10	9	2	185	63	26.42	-	2
JN Batty (Surrey)	17	17	1	422	82	26.37	-	2
CJO Smith (Scotland)	11	11	0	287	67	26.09	-	2
JJ Sayers (Yorks)	7	7	2	130	54*	26.00	-	1
CM Wright (Scotland)	13	12	5	181	88*	25.85	-	1

Qualification: averages 25 or above (minimum of five innings)

LEADING RUN SCORERS – TOP 20

Player	Runs	Inns
MJ Di Venuto (Derbys)	753	17
ID Blackwell (Somerset)	745	17
MJ Prior (Sussex)	660	17
DL Maddy (Leics)	621	17
IJL Trott (Warwicks)	608	15
MJ Lumb (Yorks)	598	18
CJ Adams (Sussex)	592	16
AD Brown (Surrey)	561	15
KA Parsons (Somerset)	558	17
JGE Benning (Surrey)	553	17
M van Jaarsveld (Kent)	549	16
HD Ackerman (Leics)	528	17
SD Stubbings (Derbys)	524	14
NV Knight (Warwicks)	520	16
A McGrath (Yorks)	517	18
JA Beukes (Scotland)	513	14
D Mongia (Leics)	481	15
JO Troughton (Warwicks)	465	15
JD Francis (Somerset)	465	16
GJ Muchall (Durham)	462	14

BOWLING: LEADING AVERAGES

Bowling	O	M	Runs	W	Av	Best	4i	Econ
C White (Yorks)	26	0	140	13	10.76	4-14	1	5.38
MH Yardy (Sussex)	32	0	173	15	11.53	6-27	2	5.40
ML Lewis (Durham)	36.2	3	156	13	12.00	5-48	2	4.29
HH Streak (Warks)	64.1	8	261	19	13.73	4-22	1	4.06
DM Benkenstein (Durham)	43	5	158	11	14.36	4-16	2	3.67
KJ Dean (Derbys)	42	4	198	11	18.00	5-45	1	4.71
D Pretorius (Warks)	41.3	3	188	10	18.80	5-32	1	4.53
LJ Wright (Sussex)	87	4	362	19	19.05	3-20	-	4.16
J Moss (Derbys)	117	8	516	27	19.11	4-28	2	4.41
RJ Kirtley (Sussex)	133	14	593	31	19.12	4-29	1	4.45
Naved-ul-Hasan (Sussex)	83.5	8	349	18	19.38	5-30	1	4.16
BA Williams (Durham)	49.2	4	221	11	20.09	3-52	-	4.47
TJ Murtagh (Surrey)	130	17	605	30	20.16	4-14	1	4.65
AJ Hall (Kent)	68.3	12	265	13	20.38	3-17	-	3.86
D Mongia (Leics)	73.3	4	318	15	21.20	4-12	2	4.32
N Killeen (Durham)	128	14	460	21	21.90	3-15	-	3.59
JC Tredwell (Kent)	65.2	3	294	13	22.61	4-16	1	4.50
AKD Gray (Derbys)	62.1	0	295	13	22.69	3-47	-	4.74
OD Gibson (Leics)	119	13	537	23	23.34	4-37	2	4.51
JW Dernbach (Surrey)	44	1	250	10	25.00	4-36	1	5.68
NM Carter (Warks)	128	14	608	24	25.33	3-28	-	4.75
JN Snape (Leics)	67.3	1	344	13	26.46	3-41	-	5.09
AG Botha (Derbys)	98.4	1	545	20	27.25	3-18	-	5.52
SJ Cook (Kent)	110	8	519	19	27.31	3-15	-	4.71
GR Breese (Durham)	91.5	2	445	16	27.81	3-30	-	4.84
RKJ Dawson (Yorks)	97	3	480	17	28.23	3-28	-	4.94
A Khan (Kent)	58.5	3	320	11	29.09	2-16	-	5.43
LE Plunkett (Durham)	117	9	553	19	29.10	4-28	1	4.72
IJL Trott (Warks)	64.5	3	351	12	29.25	3-46	-	5.41
PD Collingwood (Durham)	79.5	4	358	12	29.83	3-24	-	4.48
CW Henderson (Leics)	92.1	6	389	13	29.92	3-25	-	4.22
SRG Francis (Somerset)	83	6	456	15	30.40	2-25	-	5.49
DI Stevens (Kent)	69	4	344	11	31.27	5-32	1	4.98
DL Maddy (Leics)	74.3	8	315	10	31.50	2-14	-	4.22
Yasir Arafat (Scotland)	94.4	11	443	14	31.64	3-33	-	4.67
CM Willoughby (Leics)	115.5	18	412	13	31.69	2-12	-	3.55
Mushtaq Ahmed (Sussex)	127	3	635	20	31.75	4-36	1	5.00
CM Wright (Scotland)	89	9	413	13	31.76	2-10	-	4.64
RS Ferley (Kent)	77	0	393	12	32.75	3-36	-	5.10
GM Andrew (Somerset)	49.4	3	329	10	32.90	3-48	-	6.62
DR Brown (Warks)	115.5	10	521	15	34.73	3-49	-	4.49
RR Watson (Scotland)	98.3	2	488	14	34.85	4-36	1	4.95
RSC M-Jenkins (Sussex)	116	4	491	14	35.07	3-32	-	4.23
NC Saker (Surrey)	61	0	396	11	36.00	4-43	1	6.49
ID Hunter (Derbys)	101	5	555	15	37.00	2-23	-	5.49
ND Doshi (Surrey)	117	2	594	16	37.12	2-28	-	5.07
MJ Saggers (Kent)	111.3	9	499	13	38.38	3-29	-	4.47
GJ Kruis (Yorks)	122	11	504	13	38.76	3-27	-	4.13

Qualification: averages of 38 or less (minimum of ten wickets)

LEADING WICKET-TAKERS – TOP 20

Player	W	O
RJ Kirtley (Sussex)	31	133
TJ Murtagh (Surrey)	30	130
J Moss (Derbys)	27	117
NM Carter (Warwicks)	24	128
OD Gibson (Leics)	23	119
N Killeen (Durham)	21	128
Mushtaq Ahmed (Sussex)	20	127
AG Botha (Derbys)	20	98.4
HH Streak (Warwicks)	19	64.1
LJ Wright (Sussex)	19	87
SJ Cook (Kent)	19	110
LE Plunkett (Durham)	19	117
Naved-ul-Hasan (Sussex)	18	83.5
RKJ Dawson (Yorks)	17	97
ND Doshi (Surrey)	16	117
GR Breese (Durham)	16	91.5
ID Blackwell (Somerset)	16	131
SRG Francis (Somerset)	15	83
D Mongia (Leics)	15	73.3
DR Brown (Warwicks)	15	115.5

FIELDING: LEADING DISMISSALS – TOP 20

P Mustard (Durham) – 25 (22ct, 3st); PA Nixon (Leics) – 24 (18ct, 6st); LD Sutton (Derbys) – 22 (19ct, 3st); MJ Prior (Sussex) – 20 (16ct, 4st); T Frost (Warks) – 15 (10ct, 5st); JN Batty (Surrey) – 14 (11ct, 3st); I Dawood (Yorks) – 14 (10ct, 4st); CJO Smith (Scotland) – 12 (11ct, 1st); CM Gazzard (Somerset) – 12 (9ct, 3st); NJ O'Brien (Kent) – 11 (8ct, 3st); TL Penney (Warks) – 10 (10ct); AD Brown (Surrey) – 10 (10ct); MJ Wood (Yorks) – 10 (10ct); GR Breese (Durham) – 10 (10ct); M van Jaarsveld (Kent) – 10 (10ct); JC Tredwell (Kent) – 9 (9ct); DM Benkenstein (Durham) – 9 (9ct); KA Parsons (Somerset) – 9 (9ct); MH Yardy (Sussex) – 9 (9ct); AG Botha (Derbys) – 9 (9ct)

TOTESPORT LEAGUE COUNTY COLOURS: DIVISION ONE

For full county details, please refer to the form charts at the back of the book.

TOTESPORT LEAGUE COUNTY COLOURS: DIVISION TWO

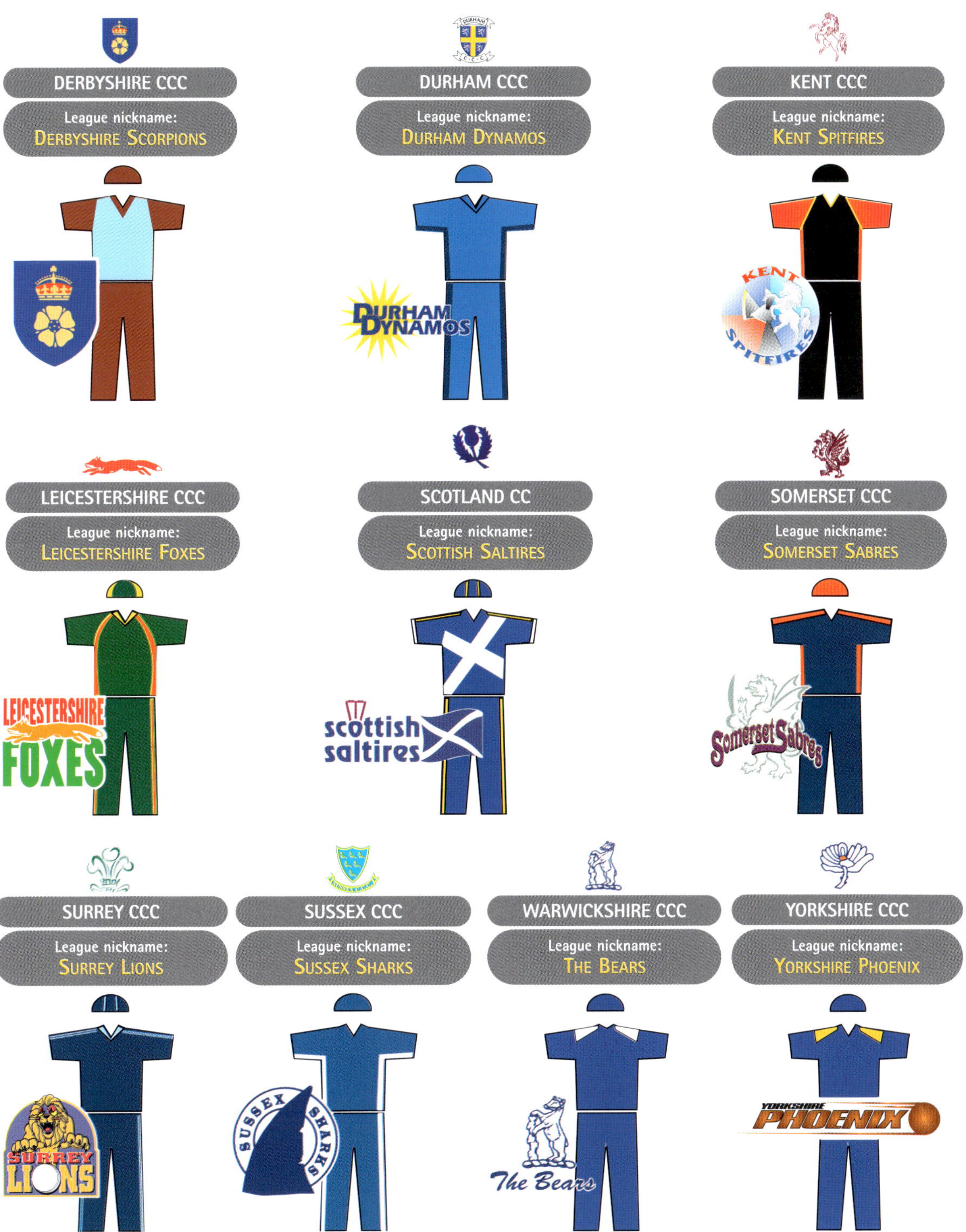

For full county details, please refer to the form charts at the back of the book.

TWENTY20 CUP
By Mark Baldwin

Of the four teams who travelled to The Oval to contest Finals Day on Saturday 30 July, three were the same as in 2004. It seemed as if the cream would always rise to the top, even in Twenty20. The eventual winners, however, were the outsiders in the quartet: Somerset, led with verve and huge enthusiasm by Graeme Smith, the young captain of South Africa. It was only their second title since the golden era of Botham, Richards and Garner ended trophy-wise in 1983, and it was achieved with a predominantly youthful side.

Twenty20 Cup cricket, in the third year of its existence, continued to win admirers. Its format had been expanded, with counties playing three more matches at the group stage to ensure a minimum of four home fixtures each. That, inevitably, meant aggregate attendances shot up from almost 300,000 in 2004 to half a million – staggering numbers for county cricket – but the most pertinent statistic was that the average crowd went up to nearly 7,000 per game: around 1,700 up on the figure for the competition's highly successful inaugural year in 2003.

As in 2004, the Middlesex-Surrey London derby match at Lord's drew a near-capacity crowd, of around 28,000, and there was a full house of 23,000 for the Finals Day at The Oval as well as 'ground full' signs for a significant number of group and quarter-final matches. People, of all ages, continued to be drawn to Twenty20 cricket not just because of all the attendant razzmatazz – which seemed to be toned down somewhat in 2005 anyway – but mainly because of the cricket itself. Like rugby sevens, cricket's short format merely highlights the skills needed to compete well in the longer and supposedly more serious form of the game. There is, in short, no hiding place. As Somerset's triumphant captain Smith himself said, 'A great benefit of Twenty20 is that you are put under pressure from ball one. In that sense it is useful because it closes the gap between domestic and international cricket.'

There was certainly a real intensity about the three matches which made up Finals Day, with some county cricketers experiencing for the first time what it is like to be put under extreme pressure in front of a big crowd by international-class players like Smith, Andy Symonds, Andy Caddick, and, released for the occasion by England head coach Duncan Fletcher, Ashes series stars Andrew Flintoff and Marcus Trescothick.

James Hildreth, the 20-year-old who stayed with Smith in Somerset's unbroken fourth-wicket stand of 53 in the final, and also hit the winning runs, said afterwards, 'Basically Graeme told me what to do out there. He was awesome.' Smith finished on 64 not out, from 47 balls, and would surely have scored heavily in the semi-final against Leicestershire, too, but for his dismissal to a wondrous flying catch by David Masters at deep mid-on.

Flintoff's heavy-duty bowling was a potent weapon for Lancashire throughout the day, but in Caddick and Richard Johnson there was also a real cutting edge for Smith to use when Somerset were in the field. Lancashire's batting, held together only by Stuart Law in a final reduced by rain to 16 overs per side, was too powerful a unit for a Surrey attack which was overdependent on Azhar Mahmood in the morning's semi-final. Flintoff gave many of the punters what they had come to see by crashing three sixes and four other boundaries in his 28-ball 49, while Symonds demonstrated his own brand of power-hitting to finish 52 not out from 30 balls. Law and Mal Loye had earlier given Lancashire a flying start with a stand of 56 in just five overs.

Surrey, however, had 93 on the board before James Benning was bowled in the ninth over – and Alistair Brown looked more than capable of going all the way. A 20-minute break for rain interrupted his flow, however, and his 32-ball 51 was ended – much to his disgust – by a run out after Mark Ramprakash had called him for a single.

When Rikki Clarke was bowled for a second-ball duck, missing a reverse sweep, Surrey were left requiring a further 114 from just 50 balls. Ramprakash and Azhar tried their best, with a partnership of 76 from 34 balls, but Flintoff returned to good effect and Lancashire had soon avenged their painful one-run defeat to Surrey at the same stage of this competition 12 months previously.

In the other semi-final Leicestershire, the defending champions, looked to be cruising – if any side can indeed feel as comfortable as that in the hurly-burly of Twenty20 – when Darren Maddy and Hylton Ackerman were posting 74 in 49 balls for the first wicket in pursuit of Somerset's 157 for 9. But Ackerman and Dinesh Mongia fell to Ian Blackwell and, unusually letting the pressure of the situation get to him, Maddy then gave Somerset's left-arm spinner the charge and was stumped.

Now it was a case of Smith, and Somerset, applying even more pressure on a team who had suddenly seen their biggest guns self-destruct. They did so with relish and skill, eventually earning themselves a four-run win – and the precious chance to shock Lancashire with the vibrancy of their performance in the field.

Somerset's celebrations afterwards were joyous, and Lancashire's misery was deep. It told everything about what winning, and losing, the Twenty20 Cup means.

North Division

22 June 2005

at Derby
Durham 130 for 7 (20 overs)
Derbyshire 134 for 4 (17.4 overs) (JDC Bryant 53*)
Derbyshire (2pts) won by 6 wickets

at Headingley
Yorkshire 165 for 7 (20 overs) (PA Jaques 72)
Lancashire 166 for 5 (16.5 overs) (BJ Hodge 64*, MB Loye 59)
Lancashire (2pts) won by 5 wickets

at Leicester
Nottinghamshire 143 for 8 (20 overs)
Leicestershire 147 for 5 (19.2 overs)
Leicestershire (2pts) won by 5 wickets

24 June 2005

at Derby
Leicestershire 137 (20 overs)
Derbyshire 105 for 3 (12.5 overs)
Derbyshire (2pts) won by 7 wickets – DL Method: target 103 from 14 overs

at Trent Bridge
Nottinghamshire 198 for 5 (20 overs) (SP Fleming 56)
Lancashire 106 (17.5 overs)
Nottinghamshire (2pts) won by 92 runs

26 June 2005

at Leicester
Leicestershire 150 for 9 (20 overs) (HD Ackerman 56)
Durham 147 for 5 (20 overs)
Leicestershire (2pts) won by 3 runs

at Trent Bridge
Nottinghamshire 170 for 8 (20 overs)
Yorkshire 174 for 8 (19.5 overs) (IJ Harvey 74)
Yorkshire (2pts) won by 2 wickets

27 June 2005

at Old Trafford
Leicestershire 146 for 7 (20 overs) (HD Ackerman 79*, M Muralitharan 4 for 19)
Lancashire 149 for 2 (16.1 overs) (SG Law 92*)
Lancashire (2pts) won by 8 wickets

28 June 2005

at Headingley
Derbyshire 195 for 8 (20 overs) (J Moss 83)
Yorkshire 198 for 4 (19 overs) (IJ Harvey 109)
Yorkshire (2pts) won by 6 wickets

at The Riverside
Nottinghamshire 179 for 9 (20 overs) (GR Breese 4 for 21)
Durham 180 for 4 (19.3 overs) (NJ Astle 64, GJ Muchall 64*)
Durham (2pts) won by 6 wickets

There were early runs in the competition for Brad Hodge, Lancashire's Australian batsman and a Twenty20 Cup winner in 2004 with Leicestershire.

29 June 2005

at Old Trafford
Lancashire 164 for 8 (20 overs)
Derbyshire 98 (17.3 overs) (BJ Hodge 4 for 17)
Lancashire (2pts) won by 66 runs

30 June 2005

at Trent Bridge
Leicestershire 150 for 4 (20 overs)
Nottinghamshire 129 for 8 (20 overs)
Leicestershire (2pts) won by 21 runs

at Headingley
Yorkshire 123 for 7 (20 overs)
Durham 124 for 8 (19 overs)
Durham (2pts) won by 2 wickets

1 July 2005

at Trent Bridge
Nottinghamshire 147 for 8 (20 overs)
(WR Smith 51)
Derbyshire 151 for 6 (19.4 overs) (LD Sutton 61*,
MJ Di Venuto 52)
Derbyshire (2pts) won by 4 wickets

at Old Trafford
Lancashire 207 for 6 (20 overs)
(SG Law 101)
Yorkshire 97 (15 overs)
Lancashire (2pts) won by 110 runs

at The Riverside
Leicestershire 154 for 7 (20 overs) (JL Sadler 73)
Durham 122 for 7 (20 overs)
Leicestershire (2pts) won by 32 runs

3 July 2005

at Headingley
Yorkshire 180 for 7 (20 overs) (PA Jaques 55)
Nottinghamshire 184 for 4 (19.4 overs)
(GP Swann 62, WR Smith 55)
Nottinghamshire (2pts) won by 6 wickets

at Old Trafford
Lancashire 208 for 4 (20 overs)
(MB Loye 100, BJ Hodge 68)
Durham 171 for 7 (20 overs)
(NJ Astle 55)
Lancashire (2pts) won by 37 runs

4 July 2005

at Derby
Lancashire 205 for 2 (20 overs) (BJ Hodge 90*, SG Law 67)
Derbyshire 106 for 7 (14.3 overs) (BJ Hodge 4 for 27)
*Lancashire (2pts) won by 50 runs – DL Method: target
157 from 14.3 overs*

at The Riverside
Yorkshire 171 for 7 (20 overs) (C White 55)
Durham 131 (17.1 overs) (DM Benkenstein 53)
Yorkshire (2pts) won by 40 runs

5 July 2005

at Leicester
Leicestershire v. **Derbyshire**
Match abandoned – 1pt each

6 July 2005

at The Riverside
Durham v. **Lancashire**
Match abandoned – 1pt each

at Derby
Nottinghamshire 139 for 5 (20 overs)
Derbyshire 142 for 1 (16.4 overs) (MJ Di Venuto 77*)
Derbyshire (2pts) won by 9 wickets

at Leicester
Yorkshire 177 for 5 (20 overs) (IJ Harvey 77)
Leicestershire 178 for 3 (18.3 overs) (DL Maddy 72*)
Leicestershire (2pts) won by 7 wickets

South Division

22 June 2005

at The Rose Bowl
Middlesex 210 for 6 (20 overs) (OA Shah 72)
Hampshire 192 for 7 (20 overs) (N Pothas 59)
Middlesex (2pts) won by 18 runs

at Hove
Essex 109 (16.3 overs) (Mushtaq Ahmed 5 for 11)
Sussex 110 for 1 (14.4 overs) (MJ Prior 66*)
Sussex (2pts) won by 9 wickets

at Beckenham
Kent 140 for 8 (20 overs) (M van Jaarsveld 51)
Surrey 141 for 3 (16 overs) (JGE Benning 66)
Surrey (2pts) won by 7 wickets

Take that: Alistair Brown, of Surrey, remained one of the most effective batsmen in Twenty20 cricket.

23 June 2005

at Lord's
Surrey 200 for 3 (20 overs) (DJ Thornely 67*,
AD Brown 64)
Middlesex 177 (19.3 overs) (OA Shah 78,
TJ Murtagh 6 for 24)
Surrey (2pts) won by 23 runs

24 June 2005

at The Rose Bowl
Hampshire v. **Sussex**
Match abandoned – 1pt each

at Chelmsford
Essex 132 for 6 (12 overs)
Kent 103 for 4 (12 overs)
Essex (2pts) won by 29 runs

25 June 2005

at Beckenham
Middlesex 189 for 8 (20 overs) (ET Smith 85)
Kent 169 for 5 (20 overs)
Middlesex (2pts) won by 20 runs

at The Oval
Surrey 118 (15.3 overs) (R Clarke 52, RJ Logan 4 for 37)
Hampshire 119 for 7 (17.5 overs)
Hampshire (2pts) won by 3 wickets

26 June 2005

at Chelmsford
Essex 151 for 5 (20 overs) (A Flower 59)
Sussex 108 (18.1 overs)
Essex (2pts) won by 43 runs

27 June 2005

at The Rose Bowl
Kent 154 for 9 (20 overs) (MA Carberry 56,
GA Lamb 4 for 28)
Hampshire 155 for 5 (20 overs) (N Pothas 58*)
Hampshire (2pts) won by 5 wickets

28 June 2005

at The Rose Bowl
Hampshire v. **Essex**
Match abandoned - 1pt each

at The Oval
Surrey 180 for 7 (20 overs)
Middlesex 78 for 4 (11 overs)
*Surrey (2pts) won by 22 runs – DL Method: target 101
from 11 overs*

29 June 2005

at Uxbridge
Kent 144 for 8 (20 overs)
Middlesex 145 for 4 (17.2 overs) (OA Shah 59*)
Middlesex (2pts) won by 6 wickets

at Chelmsford
Hampshire 151 for 9 (20 overs) (GA Lamb 67)
Essex
No result – 1pt each

at Hove
Sussex 139 for 6 (17 overs) (MJ Prior 51)

Surrey 116 for 5 (13 overs) (AD Brown 50)
*Surrey (2pts) won by 5 wickets – DL Method: target 114
from 13 overs*

1 July 2005

at Southgate
Middlesex 185 for 6 (20 overs) (OA Shah 79)
Essex 154 for 7 (20 overs) (JS Foster 62*,
IK Pathan 4 for 27)
Middlesex (2pts) won by 31 runs

at The Oval
Surrey 167 for 6 (15 overs) (SA Newman 52*)
Kent 144 for 8 (15 overs) (ND Doshi 4 for 27)
*Surrey (2pts) won by 23 runs – DL Method: target 168
from 15 overs*

at Hove
Sussex 99 for 5 (12 overs)
Hampshire 89 for 6 (12 overs)
Sussex (2pts) won by 10 runs

4 July 2005

at Hove
Middlesex 56 for 1 (7 overs)
Sussex
No result – 1pt each

5 July 2005

at Canterbury
Kent 91 for 1 (11 overs)
Sussex
No result – 1pt each

at Chelmsford
Essex 71 for 3 (5 overs)
Surrey 70 for 2 (5 overs)
Essex (2pts) won by 1 run

6 July 2005

at Richmond
Middlesex 174 for 7 (20 overs) (OA Shah 54)
Hampshire 178 for 4 (17.2 overs) (CD McMillan 65*)
Hampshire (2pts) won by 6 wickets

at Canterbury
Kent 154 for 4 (20 overs) (MA Carberry 59*)
Essex 149 for 7 (20 overs) (ML Pettini 60)
Kent (2pts) won by 5 runs

at The Oval
Surrey 144 for 8 (20 overs)
Sussex 148 for 7 (19.3 overs)
(IJ Ward 50)
Sussex (2pts) won by 3 wickets

Midlands/Wales/West Division

22 June 2005

at Worcester
Worcestershire 177 for 7 (20 overs)
(GA Hick 67)
Warwickshire 176 for 9 (20 overs)
Worcestershire (2pts) won by 1 run

at Campbell Park
Northamptonshire 224 for 5 (20 overs)
(DJG Sales 78*)
Gloucestershire 143 (17.2 overs)
(BJ Phillips 4 for 28)
Northamptonshire (2pts) won by 81 runs

at Cardiff
Somerset 183 (18.4 overs)
Glamorgan 183 for 8 (20 overs) (MJ Powell 68*)
Glamorgan (2pts) won by losing fewer wickets

23 June 2005

at Taunton
Somerset 210 for 6 (20 overs)
(MJ Wood 94)
Worcestershire 195 for 5 (20 overs)
(GA Hick 87)
Somerset (2pts) won by 15 runs

25 June 2005

at Swansea
Warwickshire 205 for 7 (20 overs)
Glamorgan 151 (18.2 overs)
(MTG Elliott 51, AGR Loudon 5 for 33)
Warwickshire (2pts) won by 54 runs

26 June 2005

at Bristol
Worcestershire 162 for 6 (20 overs)
(Z de Bruyn 76*)
Gloucestershire 166 for 5 (19.4 overs)
(WPC Weston 73*)
Gloucestershire (2pts) won by 5 wickets

27 June 2005

at Worcester
Northamptonshire 180 for 6 (20 overs)
(DJG Sales 59)
Worcestershire 143 for 8 (20 overs)
(SC Moore 53)
Northamptonshire (2pts) won by 37 runs

at Taunton
Somerset 212 for 3 (20 overs)
(JC Hildreth 71, KA Parsons 57*)
Glamorgan 123 (17.4 overs)
(ID Blackwell 4 for 26)
Somerset (2pts) won by 89 runs

28 June 2005

at Bristol
Warwickshire 44 for 1 (6.1 overs)
Gloucestershire
No result – 1pt each

29 June 2005

at Northampton
Northamptonshire 95 for 6 (12 overs)
Somerset 97 for 5 (12 overs)
Somerset (2pts) won by 5 wickets

30 June 2005

at Edgbaston
Warwickshire 169 for 9 (20 overs)
(JO Troughton 51)
Glamorgan 165 for 9 (20 overs)
Warwickshire (2pts) won by 4 runs

1 July 2005

at Bristol
Somerset 61 for 7 (13 overs)
Gloucestershire
No result – 1pt each

at Edgbaston
Worcestershire 141 (18.5 overs) (NM Carter 5 for 19)
Warwickshire 140 (20 overs) (HH Streak 59)
Worcestershire (2pts) won by 1 run

at Cardiff
Glamorgan v. **Northamptonshire**
Match abandoned – 1pt each

2 July 2005

at Worcester
Worcestershire 100 (18.4 overs)
Gloucestershire 102 for 1 (15 overs)
Gloucestershire (2pts) won by 9 wickets

at Taunton
Somerset 189 for 5 (20 overs) (GC Smith 105,
MJ Wood 54)
Northamptonshire 191 for 5 (19 overs) (ML Love 53)
Northamptonshire (2pts) won by 5 wickets

4 July 2005

at Edgbaston
Warwickshire 172 for 8 (20 overs)
Somerset 125 (17.3 overs)
Warwickshire (2pts) won by 47 runs

5 July 2005

at Northampton
Northamptonshire v. **Worcestershire**
Match abandoned – 1pt each

at Cardiff
Gloucestershire 128 (18.1 overs)
Glamorgan 129 for 0 (12.3 overs)
(RDB Croft 62*, MTG Elliott 52*)
Glamorgan (2pts) won by 10 wickets

6 July 2005

at Worcester
Worcestershire 223 for 9 (20 overs)
(BF Smith 105, GA Hick 59, RN Grant 4 for 38)
Glamorgan 186 for 5 (20 overs)
(MJ Powell 51)
Worcestershire (2pts) won by 37 runs

at Taunton
Somerset 228 for 5 (20 overs)
(GC Smith 53)
Gloucestershire 133 (16 overs)
(GM Andrew 4 for 22)
Somerset (2pts) won by 95 runs

at Edgbaston
Warwickshire 205 for 2 (20 overs)
(IR Bell 66*, NV Knight 61)
Northamptonshire 164 for 6 (20 overs)
Warwickshire (2pts) won by 41 runs

FINAL GROUP TABLES
NORTH

	P	W	L	T	NR	RR	Pts
Lancashire	8	6	1	0	1	1.77	13
Leicestershire	8	5	2	0	1	0.25	11
Derbyshire	8	4	3	0	1	-0.45	9
Yorkshire	8	3	5	0	0	-0.70	6
Durham	8	2	5	0	1	-0.87	5
Nottinghamshire	8	2	6	0	0	0.13	4

MIDLANDS/WEST/WALES

	P	W	L	T	NR	RR	Pts
Northamptonshire	8	4	2	0	2	1.17	10
Warwickshire	8	4	3	0	1	0.79	9
Somerset	8	4	3	0	1	1.08	9
Gloucestershire	8	3	3	0	2	-1.44	8
Worcestershire	8	3	4	0	1	-0.46	7
Glamorgan	8	2	5	0	1	-1.08	5

SOUTH

	P	W	L	T	NR	RR	Pts
Surrey	8	5	3	0	0	0.64	10
Middlesex	8	4	3	0	1	0.16	9
Sussex	8	3	2	0	3	0.13	9
Hampshire	8	3	2	0	3	0.20	9
Essex	8	3	3	0	2	-0.06	8
Kent	8	1	6	0	1	-1.02	3

18 July 2005: Quarter-finals

at Leicester
Leicestershire 159 for 6 (20 overs)
Middlesex 140 for 7 (20 overs) (SB Styris 73*)
Leicestershire won by 19 runs

at Old Trafford
Lancashire 189 for 7 (20 overs) (MB Loye 73, A Symonds 57*)
Derbyshire 172 (19.3 overs)
Lancashire won by 17 runs

at Northampton
Northamptonshire 154 for 8 (20 overs)
Somerset 155 for 6 (19.5 overs) (MJ Wood 58)
Somerset won by 4 wickets

at The Oval
Surrey 149 for 8 (20 overs)
Warwickshire 117 for 8 (15 overs)
Match tied – DL Method: Surrey won 4–3 in a stump bowling competition

30 July 2005: Semi-finals

at The Oval
Lancashire 217 for 4 (20 overs) (A Symonds 52*)
Surrey 195 for 7 (20 overs) (AD Brown 51)
Lancashire won by 22 runs

at The Oval
Somerset 157 for 9 (20 overs)
Leicestershire 153 for 8 (20 overs) (DL Maddy 56)
Somerset won by 4 runs

FINAL – LANCASHIRE v. SOMERSET
30 July 2005 at The Oval

LANCASHIRE

MB Loye	c Johnson b Caddick	5
SG Law	run out	59
A Flintoff	c Blackwell b Caddick	2
A Symonds	run out	12
DG Cork	c Trescothick b Johnson	1
G Chapple	b Johnson	0
MJ Chilton (capt)	b Blackwell	9
AR Crook	c Gazzard b Johnson	15
*WK Hegg	not out	6
JM Anderson		
G Keedy		
Extras	lb 2, w 3	5
	(8 wkts 16 overs)	114

	O	M	R	W
Caddick	4	0	21	2
Langeveldt	3	0	28	0
Johnson	3	0	26	3
Parsons	3	0	13	0
Blackwell	3	0	24	1

Fall of Wickets
1-6, 2-15, 3-40, 4-41, 5-41, 6-69, 7-101, 8-114

SOMERSET

GC Smith (capt)	not out	64
ME Trescothick	c Hegg b Flintoff	10
MJ Wood	b Flintoff	22
ID Blackwell	c Law b Keedy	3
JC Hildreth	not out	16
*CM Gazzard		
KA Parsons		
RL Johnson		
WJ Durston		
AR Caddick		
CK Langeveldt		
Extras	lb 1, w 2	3
	(3 wkts 14.1 overs)	118

	O	M	R	W
Cork	2	0	12	0
Anderson	1.1	0	14	0
Flintoff	4	0	33	2
Chapple	2	0	23	0
Keedy	3	0	21	1
Symonds	2	0	14	0

Fall of Wickets
1-28, 2-60, 3-65

Umpires: IJ Gould & P Willey
Toss: Lancashire
Man of the Match: GC Smith

Somerset won by 7 wickets

Left: Graeme Smith punches the air in triumph as Somerset score the winning runs in the Twenty20 Cup final against Lancashire at The Oval.

Below: Smith proudly holds the silverware as the Somerset players gather for the happiest of team photographs. Somerset are the new Twenty20 kings of England!

CHELTENHAM & GLOUCESTER TROPHY
By Mark Baldwin

First Round: 3–5 May 2005

at Svanholm
Denmark 56 (24.3 overs)
(C Pietersen 7 for 10)
Northamptonshire 59 for 2 (16.5 overs)
Northamptonshire won by 8 wickets

at South Wilts
Kent 160 (46.5 overs) (KJ Nash 4 for 46)
Wiltshire 151 (49.1 overs) (SJ Cook 4 for 22)
Kent won by 9 runs

at Reading
Gloucestershire 223 (49.3 overs)
(WPC Weston 80, CG Taylor 57)
Berkshire 138 (36.3 overs)
(UDU Chandana 4 for 27)
Gloucestershire won by 85 runs

at Rotterdam
Warwickshire 237 for 5 (50 overs)
(NV Knight 108, TL Penney 51*)
Holland 214 (49 overs) (DLS van Bunge 89,
HH Streak 4 for 27, NM Carter 4 for 34)
Warwickshire won by 23 runs

at Wormsley
Lancashire 370 for 4 (50 overs) (AR Crook 162*,
MB Loye 66, G Chapple 55*)
Buckinghamshire 39 for 2 (10.3 overs)
*Lancashire won by 51 runs – DL Method: target
91 from 10.3 overs*

at Leicester
Somerset 94 (29.1 overs)
(CM Willoughby 6 for 16)
Leicestershire 96 for 7 (29 overs)
Leicestershire won by 3 wickets

at Whitchurch
Shropshire 132 (42.5 overs)
Hampshire 133 for 3 (21.1 overs)
(KP Pietersen 76)
Hampshire won by 7 wickets

at Exmouth
Essex 264 for 5 (50 overs) (A Flower 69, RS Bopara 65*)
Devon 84 (34.2 overs)
Essex won by 180 runs

at Jesmond
Northumberland 206 for 8 (50 overs) (S Humble 88*)
Middlesex 210 for 0 (31.3 overs) (PN Weekes 106*,
ET Smith 96*)
Middlesex won by 10 wickets

at Belfast
Ireland 201 for 7 (50 overs) (EJG Morgan 59,
PG Gillespie 55, C White 4 for 43)
Yorkshire 202 for 4 (47.4 overs) (MP Vaughan 58,
IJ Harvey 57, PA Jaques 55*)
Yorkshire won by 6 wickets

at Swansea
Wales 119 (34.2 overs) (MA Ealham 4 for 28)
Nottinghamshire 121 for 4 (26.2 overs)
Nottinghamshire won by 6 wickets

There were six wickets for Charl Willoughby in a
thrilling low-scoring contest at Grace Road.

at Luton
Bedfordshire 143 for 9 (50 overs)
Sussex 146 for 2 (18.3 overs) (IJ Ward 65)
Sussex won by 8 wickets

at Leek
Staffordshire 186 (49.5 overs)
Surrey 192 for 7 (48.5 overs)
Surrey won by 3 wickets

at Bury St Edmunds
Glamorgan 320 for 5 (50 overs) (MTG Elliott 100*,
RDB Croft 56)
Suffolk 177 for 8 (50 overs)
Glamorgan won by 143 runs

at The Riverside
Durham 234 (50 overs) (PD Collingwood 82,
AG Botha 4 for 44)
Derbyshire 237 for 9 (50 overs) (CWG Bassano 57,
G Welch 50)
Derbyshire won by 1 wicket

at The Grange
Scotland 134 (46.5 overs) (RR Watson 53)
Worcestershire 138 for 0 (19.1 overs) (VS Solanki 74*,
SC Moore 57*)
Worcestershire won by 10 wickets

A sad consequence of the reorganisation of the Cheltenham & Gloucester Trophy, which comes into play in 2006, is that the competition's traditional – and popular – link between the first-class and recreational games is to be lost. Equally sad, as they took their leave, was that there was no 'cup upset' for a minor county, or non first-class team, to enjoy – and with which to say farewell.

Devon and Ireland had shocked Leicestershire and Surrey, respectively, at this stage in 2004 – but now Devon went down heavily by 180 runs against Essex at delightful Exmouth, and Ireland were beaten comfortably by six wickets in Belfast by Yorkshire, for whom England captain Michael Vaughan scored 58 in his first innings for 80 days. At least the Irish had a highly promising half-century from the 18-year-old schoolboy prodigy Eoin Morgan to cheer them, but Devon's plunge to 84 all out, after Darren Gough and Andre Adams had initially reduced them to 23 for 6 with three-wicket, new-ball spells apiece, made for a highly disappointing end to their own final cup adventure.

The best performance from the non first-class sides came from Holland, who gave Warwickshire a bit of a fright in Rotterdam before falling 23 runs short of the county's 237 for 5, in which Nick Knight made an excellent 108. Daan van Bunge, the 22-year-old former MCC Young Cricketers batsman, threatened to trump Knight's knock with a classy 89 from 104 balls, but from 124 for 5 not even his brave sixth-wicket partnership of 81 with the former Leicestershire all-rounder Billy Stelling could reignite the Dutch challenge brightly enough. Stelling hit 45 from 38 balls, but both he and van Bunge fell to Heath Streak in the same over and finishing off the task of scoring 92 from the final ten overs proved too much for the Holland tail.

Alex De La Mar, the chief executive of the Holland Cricket Board, spoke for every other non first-class team as much as for Dutch cricket itself when he said afterwards, 'It was a real blow for us when we found out that we wouldn't be in this competition any more. The C&G Trophy has been something for our players to work towards each year, as they need to face quality opposition to keep improving. Now their best chance of this will be to go to South Africa or India during the winter and that is expensive.'

Holland's rivals Denmark, meanwhile, came to an unhappy end on a damp pitch at the Svanholm Cricket Club in Brondby, being bowled out for just 56 in 24.3 overs by Northamptonshire. Charl Pietersen, a distant cousin of the England batsman Kevin Pietersen, wreaked havoc with his left-arm swing in a spell which finished with him the proud possessor of figures of 8-3-10-7. 'At least we were bowled out by someone with a Danish name,' said Claus Hansen, the chairman of the Denmark Cricket Federation. With the game all over by 2pm, in sunny if breezy conditions, it was an embarrassing end to Denmark's first competitive home match on a turf pitch against a professional team. The pity, of course, is that this will now prove to be the only chance they will have had to test and improve themselves in this competition.

The minor county that came closest to glory was Wiltshire, captained by 20-stone opener Russell Rowe. He hit 29, but his side could not quite get past Kent's poor total of 160, on an uneven Salisbury pitch, despite a mighty struggle. Simon Cook did most to spare Kentish blushes, with 4 for 22, while Michael Carberry's 41 from No. 7 was also vital; for Wiltshire, gas meter reader Keith Nash took 4 for 46.

Elsewhere, Kevin Pietersen also enjoyed himself. His 76 against Shropshire at Whitchurch, which swept Hampshire to a straightforward seven-wicket win, contained seven fours and six sixes. But the locals loved it, too, especially as a sizeable crowd had turned up to support their minor county against the likes of Pietersen and Shane Warne, who took three wickets but also provided a massive learning experience for 20-year-old Jono Whitney, who struck 39 off just 49 balls before being stumped attempting perhaps something too ambitious against the great Australian.

At 112 for 2, Berkshire were very much in their game against Gloucestershire at Reading, before collapsing against the leg-spin of the Sri Lankan Upul Chandana, while Suffolk also had their moments in a fixture with Glamorgan at Bury St Edmunds which did not begin until 3pm, because of rain, but which finished at 8.40pm after 497 runs had been scored in the full 100 overs. Glamorgan, in order to spare everyone coming back on the scheduled reserve day, delivered their last 32 overs, of spin, in 80 minutes. Who said modern-day over rates were pedestrian?

Worcestershire condemned Scotland to a ten-wicket thrashing at Edinburgh, going past the Scots' 134 in just 19.1 overs, but one of the two all-county fixtures, between Durham and Derbyshire at the Riverside, went all the way to the final ball. Paul Collingwood's 82 guided Durham to 234, but Ant Botha followed up his four wickets by turning the last ball, from Steve Harmison, to square leg for the winning run. Botha, who finished on 34, had been joined in an exciting tenth-wicket stand of 16 by Kevin Dean.

In the other all-county match, at Grace Road, another memorable contest developed after Charl Willoughby, the South African left-arm fast bowler, had decimated the Somerset top order with 6 for 16 – a Leicestershire one-day record. Somerset, 28 for 6 once Willoughby had finished with them, and 34 for 7 soon afterwards, had Ian Blackwell's 42-ball 40 to thank for reaching 94 – and then they almost succeeded in defending it. Richard Johnson, Simon Francis and Andy Caddick also proved a handful in conditions made for seam and swing, and at 70 for 7 Leicestershire were indebted to the tense unbroken stand between Ottis Gibson and Claude Henderson which inched them to a three-wicket victory.

Surrey were made to sweat at 47 for 4, in reply to Staffordshire's 186 at Leek, before recovering well but Wales, Buckinghamshire, Bedfordshire and Northumberland all felt the force of their first-class county opposition.

Second Round: 17–18 May 2005

at Derby
Kent 257 for 4 (50 overs) (GO Jones 70, MJ Walker 56*)
Derbyshire 130 (42.5 overs)
Kent won by 127 runs

at Cardiff
Glamorgan 214 (48.4 overs) (MJ Powell 56,
SM Ervine 5 for 50)
Hampshire 219 for 4 (39.1 overs) (N Pothas 114*,
KP Pietersen 69*)
Hampshire won by 6 wickets

at Bristol
Gloucestershire 230 for 8 (50 overs) (CG Taylor 74,
APR Gidman 58*)
Surrey 232 for 7 (49.3 overs) (MR Ramprakash 84,
R Clarke 62*)
Surrey won by 3 wickets

at Edgbaston
Warwickshire 235 for 9 (50 overs)
(NV Knight 69)
Leicestershire 152 (43.3 overs)
Warwickshire won by 83 runs

at Old Trafford
Essex 195 for 9 (50 overs) (A Flintoff 4 for 26)
Lancashire 196 for 4 (44 overs) (BJ Hodge 82)
Lancashire won by 6 wickets

at Headingley
Yorkshire 241 for 9 (50 overs) (A McGrath 74)
Worcestershire 227 for 8 (50 overs) (Z de Bruyn 82,
Kabir Ali 67)
Yorkshire won by 14 runs

at Lord's
Northamptonshire 238 (50 overs) (U Afzaal 75)
Middlesex 219 (49.3 overs) (PN Weekes 105,
DG Wright 4 for 38)
Northamptonshire won by 19 runs

at Hove
Nottinghamshire 195 for 9 (50 overs) (SR Patel 61*,
SP Fleming 50)
Sussex 197 for 6 (47 overs) (MW Goodwin 59,
CD Hopkinson 51)
Sussex won by 4 wickets

Gloucestershire suffered their first defeat in the C&G Trophy since July 2002 when they were beaten

Master at work: Mark Ramprakash whips the ball away against Gloucestershire leg spinner Upul Chandana as Surrey unseat the defending C&G Trophy champions at Bristol.

by three wickets in front of a stunned Bristol crowd by Surrey. Uncharacteristically for the side who had made success in 50-over cricket an art form, they allowed Surrey to wriggle off the hook.

After 11 straight wins in this competition, Gloucestershire looked like they would be able to defend a total of 230 when Surrey slipped to 110 for 4 in reply. But Rikki Clarke was dropped on 36 and proceeded to finish on 62 not out, after figuring in a stand of 82 with Mark Ramprakash, who played a captain's innings of 84 off 105 balls from No. 3. Martin Bicknell hit the first ball of the 49th over, from Jon Lewis, for six to bring down the runs required to one per ball, and Lewis then allowed the first ball of the final over to squirt through his legs so that Clarke was able to scamper four instead of the single that would have accrued had the fielder picked up the ball cleanly.

In command: Nick Knight displayed all his international-class one-day experience and skill to lead Warwickshire to quarter-final victory against Kent at Edgbaston.

Nic Pothas, contained four sixes and helped to sweep Hampshire to their six-wicket victory against Glamorgan at Sophia Gardens. Michael Vaughan made just 9 for Yorkshire at Headingley, but Craig White's three strikes with the ball – including the key wickets of Zander de Bruyn and Kabir Ali – earned his side a 14-run winning margin against Worcestershire.

Middlesex, however, blew a promising position against Northamptonshire at Lord's, losing by 19 runs after collapsing from 138 for 1. Andrew Strauss could make only 24, but his opening partner Paul Weekes was then joined by Ed Smith in a stand worth 90. Weekes was eventually out for 105 off 148 balls. But it was not enough as Damien Wright picked up four late wickets.

At Hove, meanwhile, in the single fixture scheduled for 18 May, Sussex overcame Nottinghamshire by four wickets to qualify for an away quarter-final at Lancashire – but, in the process, bizarrely denied themselves the chance to play the touring Australians on the same weekend. Some thought the victory may have cost the county around £50,000!

Graham Thorpe managed just 13 for Surrey, but England players were much to the fore elsewhere. Geraint Jones scored 70 as an opener as Kent overpowered Derbyshire by 127 runs, and Andrew Flintoff continued his rehabilitation as a bowler following ankle surgery by taking an impressive 4 for 26 in Lancashire's comfortable six-wicket win over Essex. Kevin Pietersen's 69 not out from 64 balls, in an unbroken partnership of 130 with century-maker

Quarter-finals: 15–16 July 2005

at The Oval
Surrey 358 for 6 (50 overs) (JN Batty 158*, JGE Benning 73, GP Thorpe 60)

Shane Watson powers another shot away during a brilliant match–winning 132 against Surrey.

Hampshire 359 for 8 (47.5 overs) (SR Watson 132)
Hampshire won by 2 wickets

at Edgbaston
Kent 259 for 6 (50 overs) (AJ Hall 62, RWT Key 53, MJ Walker 51)
Warwickshire 261 for 5 (46.1 overs) (NV Knight 112*, TL Penney 50*)
Warwickshire won by 5 wickets

at Old Trafford
Lancashire 249 for 8 (50 overs) (A Symonds 101)
Sussex 214 for 8 (50 overs) (MJ Prior 59)
Lancashire won by 35 runs

at Headingley
Yorkshire 270 (50 overs)
(MJ Lumb 89, IJ Harvey 74)
Northamptonshire 237 (48.1 overs)
(U Afzaal 57)
Yorkshire won by 33 runs

A fine limited-overs innings won for Hampshire one of the great one-day matches as they chased down Surrey's 358 for 6 with a remarkable 13 balls to spare at The Oval. Hampshire's match-winner was Shane Watson, the Australian all-rounder, who struck an astonishing 132 from 115 balls, with three sixes and 13 fours. Shaun Udal's

The former Australian all-rounder Ian Harvey was in commanding form with the bat as Yorkshire defeated Northamptonshire at Headingley to advance to the semi-finals.

unbeaten 44 was also a fine effort, but it was cruel in particular on Surrey's Jon Batty, who had batted through the innings to score an unbeaten 158 from 149 balls. Batty had added 142 for the first wicket with the fast-improving James Benning, while Graham Thorpe reacted to being left out of the opening Ashes Test by contributing a jaunty 53-ball 60.

The old heads of Nick Knight and Trevor Penney saw off Kent at Edgbaston, the pair adding an unbroken 82 in 14 overs to boost a Warwickshire chase that had seemed to be flagging at 179 for 5 in the 34th over. Kent, who had left out captain David Fulton against his own wishes, underachieved in reaching 259 for 6 from their 50 overs, but Justin Kemp's three wickets had made them slight favourites until Knight, who finished on 112 not out, and Penney, with a 43-ball unbeaten 50, turned the match back Warwickshire's way.

Lancashire's 35-run win against Sussex was almost entirely the work of Andy Symonds, their new overseas signing. He marked his debut with a century, four catches, the important wickets of Chris Adams and Murray Goodwin and a run out. Andrew Flintoff also took three wickets at a cost of just 30 runs from his nine overs, as Sussex slipped from 160 for 3, but there was only one choice for the man-of-the-match award.

Yorkshire, put in by David Sales in front of a 5,000 crowd at Headingley, delighted their supporters by reaching 270 and then defending that total astutely under the stand-in captaincy of 24-year-old Richard Dawson. Ian Harvey's 84-ball 74 gave Yorkshire a good start, and he added 93 in 14 overs with Michael Lumb, who then went on to 89 from 108 balls. Northants, despite reaching 163 for 2 at one stage, lost Usman Afzaal to Matthew Hoggard and could not keep up with the asking rate as Dawson applied the pressure.

Semi-finals: 20 August 2005

at The Rose Bowl
Yorkshire 197 for 9 (50 overs)
Hampshire 199 for 2 (39.5 overs) (SM Ervine 100,
N Pothas 73*)
Hampshire won by 8 wickets

at Edgbaston
Warwickshire 236 for 7 (50 overs)
Lancashire 137 (38 overs) (NM Carter 4 for 26)
Warwickshire won by 99 runs

Farce descended upon the C&G Trophy semi-finals when Yorkshire, who had travelled south from Manchester in a tortuous seven-hour coach journey the previous evening, following the end of a championship match against Lancashire, were late on parade for their semi-final tie against Hampshire at the Rose Bowl because the coach driver was not allowed to take them to the ground. His regulations stated that nine hours had to elapse before he could get behind his wheel again, and that meant 9.20am. The Yorkshire players, gathered sleepily in their hotel lobby at 8.30am, suddenly found themselves having to make other arrangements.

Craig White, the captain, decided to jog the three miles to the ground, but others tried to hitch lifts. Spectator traffic leading into the Rose Bowl, however, meant that most of them were so badly delayed that some were not even ready to start warm-ups at 9.30am – 45 minutes before the scheduled start.

The umpires decided, as a result of Yorkshire's plight, to put back the start until 10.30am, but White's team – put in after the toss was lost – never seemed to recover their composure. They struggled to 197 for 9, with White himself attempting a damage limitation exercise with an unbeaten 40, but it never looked enough. John Crawley went early, but Sean Ervine then joined Nic Pothas in a match-

Makhaya Ntini, Warwickshire's wholehearted overseas signing from South Africa, made the early breakthrough as Lancashire were overwhelmed at Edgbaston.

winning stand of 147. Pothas' 73 featured seven fours, but Ervine's strokeplay was more brutal: when he was finally dismissed for 100, he had faced just 99 balls and hit a six and 12 fours.

The moral for Yorkshire? Don't travel so far by road when time is short – go by air. The moral for the England and Wales Cricket Board? Don't schedule important knockout cup semi-finals the day after a round of County Championship games. Preparation should involve net practice and rest: there simply must be a free day inserted into the fixture list before important cup games.

Warwickshire's 99-run trouncing of Lancashire at Edgbaston was, by contrast, a dull affair. Lancashire, who had only had a short drive down the M6 to Birmingham the night before, underperformed horribly with the bat after restricting the home side to 236 for 7. Even that total had owed much to an unbroken eighth-wicket stand of 81 in 15 overs between Michael Powell and Tony Frost, but the Warwickshire seam attack then got to work with a vengeance. Makhaya Ntini made the first two strikes, but Neil Carter and James Anyon were also impressive as Lancashire's challenge unravelled.

Final: 3 September 2005 at Lord's

The transformation of Hampshire cricket, engineered under the ambitious chairmanship of lifelong fan and millionaire businessman Rod Bransgrove, found tangible expression on a sunlit day at Lord's as the county won their first trophy for 13 years.

Holding their nerve after Warwickshire's run chase faltered because of an unfortunate attack of cramp suffered by their England batsman Ian Bell, Hampshire squeezed the remaining life out of their opponents' challenge with some inspired out-cricket. Well-marshalled by Shaun Udal, again doing a fine job as captain in the absence of Shane Warne – who had somewhat small-mindedly been forced to stay in Chelmsford to watch the Australians' two-day match against Essex instead of being allowed to go to Lord's – Hampshire tightened the screw as Andy Bichel, Chris Tremlett and Shane Watson all bowled intelligent but aggressive spells.

Nick Knight, who had put on 122 for the second wicket with Bell, found himself powerless to prevent the momentum turning towards Hampshire as wickets tumbled regularly at the other end. Bell hit 54 from 82 balls, but perhaps should have left the field when first afflicted. He limped past 50, but

after some lengthy treatment decided to bat on. In some discomfort, he allowed the strike rate to dip before finally holing out, and none of his successors could give Knight the support he required. When Knight at last fell in the 48th over, having scored 118 from 127 balls with ten fours, the asking rate was above ten – and the Warwickshire tail found it beyond them as Hampshire's triumph was confirmed by 18 runs.

As in the semi-final win against Yorkshire, the second-wicket pair of Sean Ervine and Nic Pothas had come off spectacularly. This time, they added 134, following a fluent start provided by John Crawley and, although Pothas was dismissed for a 99-ball 68, Ervine underlined a talent and maturity rare in a 22-year-old to accelerate on to 104 from just 93 balls, with 12 fours.

Having played five Tests for his native Zimbabwe, Ervine has turned his back on his benighted country and travelled to Hampshire as a non-overseas player thanks to his Irish passport. Moreover, as he spends his winters trying to win a permanent place in the Western Australia side, he could yet qualify by residence to return to international cricket with either England or Australia. 'I'm just taking every opportunity that comes along,' he said. 'I want to play international cricket again; whether it's for England or Australia, we'll have to wait and see. But, at the moment, I'm having an amazing experience and this is the best day of my life.'

The make-up of the two sides in the final, meanwhile, brought into sharper relief the vexed question of the increasing numbers of 'non-English' cricketers in the county game. Ervine was one of nine players in the final born in southern Africa, but only one of them – Warwickshire's Makhaya Ntini – was classified as an overseas player. Add the two Australians (Hampshire's Watson and Bichel) and take away the England-qualified but Natal-born Kevin Pietersen and England Under-19 batsman Kevin Latouf, also South Africa-born, and that left nine players appearing in English county cricket's showpiece cup final who were ineligible to represent England.

Opposite: A Greek bearing a gift – Nic Pothas, the South African whose Greek ancestry and EU passport enables him to play for Hampshire as a non-overseas player, scored 68 in the C&G Trophy final at Lord's.

Right: Andy Bichel celebrates as Hampshire close in on C&G Trophy triumph.

Below: The Hampshire team, led by Shaun Udal (front right) pose for the cameras with the C&G Trophy.

Above: Sean Ervine was voted Man of the Match for his 104 from just 93 balls.

FINAL – HAMPSHIRE v. WARWICKSHIRE
3 September 2005 at Lord's

HAMPSHIRE

JP Crawley	c Frost b Carter	29
*N Pothas	c Frost b Carter	68
SM Ervine	c Troughton b Trott	104
KP Pietersen	c Giles b Trott	5
SR Watson	c Troughton b Trott	25
AD Mascarenhas	c Bell b Carter	8
AJ Bichel	c Bell b Carter	16
GA Lamb	run out	4
SD Udal (capt)	c Bell b Carter	0
KJ Latouf	not out	0
CT Tremlett	run out	7
Extras	lb 4, w 20	24
	(50 overs)	290

	O	M	R	W
Ntini	10	2	43	0
Brown	8	0	50	0
Carter	10	0	66	5
Bell	3	0	18	0
Giles	10	0	50	0
Loudon	4	0	24	0
Trott	5	0	35	3

Fall of Wickets
1-57, 2-191, 3-206, 4-249, 5-253, 6-265, 7-282, 8-282, 9-282

WARWICKSHIRE

NM Carter	run out	32
NV Knight (capt)	c Latouf b Bichel	118
IR Bell	c Tremlett b Watson	54
JO Troughton	b Bichel	10
TL Penney	c Pothas b Bichel	4
IJL Trott	run out	3
AGR Loudon	b Tremlett	7
DR Brown	b Watson	15
AF Giles	b Watson	6
*T Frost	not out	2
M Ntini	b Tremlett	0
Extras	b 1, lb 2, w 10, nb 2, p 6	21
	(49.2 overs)	272

	O	M	R	W
Bichel	10	0	57	3
Tremlett	9.2	0	48	2
Ervine	6	0	43	0
Mascarenhas	10	0	44	0
Udal	6	0	37	0
Watson	8	0	34	3

Fall of Wickets
1-44, 2-166, 3-198, 4-207, 5-215, 6-237, 7-251, 8-260, 9-265

Umpires: AA Jones & NA Mallender
Toss: Warwickshire
Man of the Match: SM Ervine

Hampshire won by 18 runs

Left: A delighted Shaun Udal parades the C&G Trophy after victory against Warwickshire at Lord's.

SOUTH AFRICA

ENGLAND IN SOUTH AFRICA

ENGLAND IN SOUTH AFRICA
By Jonathan Agnew

FIRST TEST
17–21 December 2004 at St George's Park, Port Elizabeth

All the talk before the opening Test of the five-match series was of England's apparent lack of preparation. A one-day beer match against Nicky Oppenheimer's XI and a solitary first-class match – which England lost – were deemed satisfactory. In the case of Steve Harmison, who opted out of touring Zimbabwe, this represented his only cricket for three months. It was not enough and Harmison, who experienced a miserable tour, paid the price for a serious miscalculation by the England management.

South Africa had just come off the back of a series defeat in India, and there was a general sense of discontent about the team and particularly the policy of selecting a given number of non-white players. It was always stated that this was an unofficial guide, but when Thami Tsolekile continued to be chosen in preference to Mark Boucher, it was hardly surprising that South African fans were muttering. Any form of experimental team selection can be forgiven so long as that team is winning. But when defeats outnumber victories, the entire process is undermined and it will not be long before the sponsors and television partners begin to apply pressure on the selectors simply to choose the best players.

In fact, South Africa had its remarkable home record to fall back on. Since returning to the international fold, only Australia had won a series in South Africa (twice) while the Proteas had lost only five out of 22 Tests on home soil. This was to change, of course, and England surprised many people by the manner in which they dominated the first Test, especially given their lack of cricket beforehand.

Graeme Smith won the toss; chose to bat and – second ball – was trudging back to the pavilion. AB de Villiers and Jacques Kallis – who failed to pick up a full toss from Harmison – also fell before lunch, but Jacques Rudolph and Boeta Dippenaar batted throughout the afternoon as 81 runs were added in 29 overs to leave South Africa on 164 for 3.

But after their stand had reached 112, Andrew Flintoff returned to find some extra bounce, and Rudolph edged to Geraint Jones for 93 from 192 balls. Zander de Bruyn, batting at No. 6, offered no stroke and was bowled by Flintoff for 6 and when Hoggard removed both Shaun Pollock and Andrew Hall before the close, South Africa were bitterly disappointed with their first day's efforts of 273 for 7. Dippenaar was still at the crease, having crawled to 79 from 193 balls and, on the second morning, he duly completed his century in six hours. After a stand of 63 with Tsolekile, Dippenaar drove at Simon Jones' third ball of the day and was taken by Marcus Trescothick at slip for 110. Tsolekile then showed his inexperience in the next over by having a wild slog at Ashley Giles and was caught for 22, and Giles wrapped it up for 337 when Dale Steyn was caught at short leg.

England were quickly in control of the match thanks to an opening stand of 152 between the left-handers, Trescothick and Strauss. Steyn eventually took his first Test wicket when Trescothick drove him to mid-off for 47, but although Mark Butcher looked horribly out of sorts, he and Strauss batted through to the end of the second day, with Strauss reaching his third Test century in eight Tests from 194 balls, and becoming the first batsman ever to score a hundred against the first three countries he played.

Pollock ended Strauss' innings in the fourth over of the third day when he was caught at point for 126 and this started a mini collapse as Vaughan for 10, and Thorpe for 4, fell in quick succession. Flintoff joined Butcher – who was still looking as if he had never held a bat in his life – and the pair added 79 to take England into the lead before Butcher tried to pull a full-length ball from Ntini and was caught behind for 79. Flintoff fell in Ntini's next over, rather casually flicking a catch to deep square leg for 35, Geraint Jones was caught in the covers for 2 and when Hoggard was caught behind for a duck at 358 for 8, England were squandering their excellent start.

Simon Jones then teamed up with Giles to add 36, and when Giles was caught at slip for 26, we were treated to a riotous last-wicket stand between Jones and Harmison, which was worth 31. Harmison was dropped twice and caught off a no-ball, and when Jones finally drove a return catch to Steyn for 24, England were 425 all out and 88 runs

FIRST TEST – SOUTH AFRICA v. ENGLAND
17–21 December 2004 at Port Elizabeth

SOUTH AFRICA

	First Innings		Second Innings	
GC Smith (capt)	c Strauss b Hoggard	0	(2) c Jones SP b Flintoff	55
AB de Villiers	lbw b Flintoff	28	(1) c & b Hoggard	14
JA Rudolph	c Jones GO b Flintoff	93	c Trescothick b Giles	28
JH Kallis	b Harmison	0	lbw b Jones SP	61
HH Dippenaar	c Trescothick b Jones SP	110	b Giles	10
Z de Bruyn	b Flintoff	6	c Trescothick b Flintoff	19
SM Pollock	c Trescothick b Hoggard	31	c Jones GO b Jones SP	0
AJ Hall	b Hoggard	6	run out	17
*TL Tsolekile	c Flintoff b Giles	22	b Jones SP	0
M Ntini	not out	2	lbw b Jones SP	4
DW Steyn	c Strauss b Giles	8	not out	2
Extras	lb 13, w 4, nb 14	31	b 4, lb 3, w 1, nb 6, p 5	19
	(110.4 overs)	337	(69.1 overs)	229

	First Innings				Second Innings			
	O	M	R	W	O	M	R	W
Hoggard	20	4	56	3	12	2	38	1
Harmison	25	2	88	1	14	1	54	0
Jones SP	16	4	39	1	13.1	3	39	4
Flintoff	22	4	72	3	15	2	47	2
Giles	27.4	8	69	2	15	2	39	2

Fall of Wickets
1-0, 2-63, 3-66, 4-178, 5-192, 6-253, 7-261, 8-324, 9-327
1-26, 2-64, 3-152, 4-168, 5-201, 6-201, 7-217, 8-218, 9-224

ENGLAND

	First Innings		Second Innings	
ME Trescothick	b Steyn	47	c Tsolekile b Pollock	0
AJ Strauss	c de Villiers b Pollock	126	not out	94
MA Butcher	c Tsolekile b Ntini	79	c Smith b Ntini	0
MP Vaughan (capt)	c Smith b Hall	10	b Steyn	15
GP Thorpe	b Smith	4	not out	31
A Flintoff	c Rudolph b Ntini	35		
*GO Jones	c Dippenaar b Ntini	2		
AF Giles	c Hall b Pollock	26		
MJ Hoggard	c Tsolekile b Hall	0		
SP Jones	c & b Steyn	24		
SJ Harmison	not out	15		
Extras	lb 21, w 1, nb 35	57	lb 3, nb 2	5
	(126.5 overs)	425	(3 wkts 40.4 overs)	145

	First Innings				Second Innings			
	O	M	R	W	O	M	R	W
Pollock	32	14	61	2	11	2	36	1
Ntini	28	6	75	3	6.4	1	24	1
Steyn	25.5	2	117	2	6	1	29	1
Hall	22	1	95	2	9	1	14	0
de Bruyn	9	1	31	0	-	-	-	-
Smith	10	3	25	1	8	0	39	0

Fall of Wickets
1-152, 2-238, 3-249, 4-267, 5-346, 6-353, 7-353, 8-358, 9-394
1-0, 2-11, 3-50

Umpires: DB Hair & SJA Taufel
Toss: South Africa
Test debuts: AB de Villiers, DW Steyn
Man of the Match: AJ Strauss

<u>England won by 7 wickets</u>

Far left: Andrew Strauss celebrates another personal triumph, his third Test hundred.

A controlled spell of seam and swing bowling from Simon Jones tipped the balance of the opening Test match England's way.

SECOND TEST
26–30 December 2004 at Kingsmead Ground, Durban

Although England enjoyed a slice of fortune with the elements in the previous Test, this time it was the South Africans who prospered when they were rescued by bad light on the final afternoon. With only two wickets left, and 15 overs remaining, an England victory was very much the likely result, and this represented a remarkable turn-around from the end of the second day when it appeared England would lose the match.

On a boiling Boxing Day morning, and with the world's attention focusing on the unfolding events in Asia triggered by the tsunami, Smith won the toss for a second time and decided to give his bowlers first use of a grassy, but dry pitch. They responded magnificently, bowling England out in only 58 overs for 139. England might have been bundled out for even less, but for a fighting 21 from Simon Jones who came in at No. 10. The re-jigged South African order looked much stronger than at Port Elizabeth.

Herschelle Gibbs returned to open the batting after injury, which moved de Villiers down to No. 7. In the event, Gibbs scored only 15, but Kallis made a methodical, if rather workmanlike 162 – his 18th Test century – from 264 balls. He added 87 with Pollock, who scored 43, and the last four wickets added 214 between them. Kallis was the last man out, giving South Africa a lead of 192 with 45 minutes still remaining on the second day.

The England of old might well have succumbed, but even this team, which has learned to fight itself out of trouble rather than capitulate, needed a good start. They knew that if they batted for two days, South Africa would be in trouble on the final day.

Strauss and Trescothick safely negotiated the 11 overs that remained, and were still together at tea on the third day. Strauss had been missed at third slip in the fifth over of the day, but other than that the two left-handers batted superbly. They took England into the lead, and the advantage stood at

in the lead. They had, however, lost nine wickets for 198 on the day and, by the close of the third day, South Africa had moved into the lead by 11 runs, having lost the wickets of de Villiers and Rudolph.

At lunch on the fourth day, the game was finely balanced with South Africa now 92 ahead but, having lost Smith, they were soon four wickets down and leaning heavily on Kallis, who was 49 not out. But it was after the break that England surged ahead with Simon Jones – who had been largely anonymous until now – taking 4 for 18 in 7.1 overs of controlled seam bowling. This included the wicket of Kallis for 61, and South Africa collapsed from 201 for 4 to 229 all out, setting England 142 to win.

Alarm bells rang when they were 11 for 2, with Trescothick and Butcher both falling for ducks, but the phlegmatic Strauss, who made an unbeaten 94, and Thorpe saw them home with a stand of 95 in the tenth over of the final day. Within two hours, a spectacular thunderstorm flooded the ground.

80 – and the partnership 273 – when Trescothick succumbed to the second new ball, edging Pollock to the wicketkeeper for 132. He had faced 261 balls and, as is so often the case, not only did the man who followed the partnership (Butcher) fail, but Strauss also managed to survive for just nine more overs before he was caught at third slip off the bowling of Ntini for 136, in the fifth over of the fourth day.

Vaughan was rather unluckily caught down the legside for ten, and this put England on the back foot once again with their lead standing at 113, but now with four wickets down. Thorpe had looked in no form at all up to this point, but showing great application, he settled down with Flintoff to shore up England's position. They added 114 for the fifth wicket, taking England's lead to the relative safety of 235, when Smith – bowling his speculative off spin – had Flintoff caught behind, cutting, for 60. This paved the way for Geraint Jones to remind everyone what a busy little batsman he is, as he scored 73 at virtually a run-a-ball in a stand with Thorpe worth 132. Thorpe duly reached his century from 197 balls, but when Giles – who had not been fit to bowl earlier in the game – was dismissed with 35 minutes of the fourth day remaining, Vaughan declared leaving South Africa the impossible target of 378 to win.

A draw was the best Smith's team could hope for, but England's prospects of a victory rose sharply when the captain fell lbw to Hoggard for 5 just before the close.

With low, grey cloud always threatening to have the final say, England's bowlers picked their way through the South African batsmen. Harmison claimed the important wicket of Kallis during the morning as lunch was taken at 104 for 4. Rudolph fell to Giles after a stand of 69 with van Jaarsveld, who edged Hoggard to slip for 49 four overs later. Hashim Amla had already completed a miserable first Test appearance on his home ground (1 and 0) and South Africa were now 183 for 7.

But England were frustrated by de Villiers and Pollock. With their backs to the wall, they added 85 but, far more importantly, batted for 27 crucial overs. Even when Pollock was run out, of all things, for 35, the cloud was already drifting over the

Graham Thorpe's fighting century at Kingsmead completed a superb second innings counter-attack by England in the second Test.

SECOND TEST – SOUTH AFRICA v. ENGLAND
26–30 December 2004 at Durban

ENGLAND

	First Innings		Second Innings	
ME Trescothick	c de Villiers b Ntini	18	c de Villiers b Pollock	132
AJ Strauss	c Ntini b Boje	25	c van Jaarsveld b Ntini	136
MA Butcher	b Steyn	5	c van Jaarsveld b Kallis	13
MP Vaughan (capt)	lbw b Ntini	18	c de Villiers b Ntini	10
GP Thorpe	lbw b Pollock	1	not out	118
A Flintoff	c Amla b Pollock	0	c de Villiers b Smith	60
*GO Jones	c Rudolph b Ntini	24	c Ntini b Boje	73
AF Giles	c Rudolph b Steyn	10	c de Villiers b Steyn	0
MJ Hoggard	not out	6		
SP Jones	b Pollock	21		
SJ Harmison	b Pollock	0		
Extras	lb 9, nb 2	11	b 3, lb 8, w 2, nb 15	28
	(57.1 overs)	139	(7 wkts dec 172.3 overs)	570

	First Innings				Second Innings			
	O	M	R	W	O	M	R	W
Pollock	15.1	7	32	4	36	16	79	1
Ntini	13	2	41	3	37	4	111	2
Steyn	13	4	26	2	25.3	2	122	1
Kallis	7	4	10	0	25	4	57	1
Boje	9	2	21	1	44	5	163	1
Smith	–	–	–	–	5	1	27	1

Fall of Wickets
1-21, 2-32, 3-53, 4-62, 5-64, 6-80, 7-93, 8-113, 9-139
1-273, 2-293, 3-306, 4-314, 5-428, 6-560, 7-570

SOUTH AFRICA

	First Innings		Second Innings	
GC Smith (capt)	c Flintoff b Harmison	9	lbw b Hoggard	5
HH Gibbs	b Hoggard	15	c Giles b Harmison	36
JA Rudolph	c Thorpe b Harmison	32	(4) c Strauss b Giles	61
JH Kallis	c sub b Hoggard	162	(5) c Jones GO b Harmison	10
M van Jaarsveld	b Flintoff	1	(6) c Trescothick b Hoggard	49
HM Amla	c Jones GO b Harmison	1	(7) lbw b Jones SP	0
*AB de Villiers	c Thorpe b Jones SP	14	(8) not out	52
SM Pollock	c Jones GO b Vaughan	43	(9) run out	35
N Boje	c sub b Hoggard	15	(3) c Thorpe b Flintoff	10
M Ntini	c Jones SP b Flintoff	22	not out	16
DW Steyn	not out	7		
Extras	lb 7, nb 4	11	b 8, lb 4, w 1, nb 3	16
	(102 overs)	332	(8 wkts 86 overs)	290

	First Innings				Second Innings			
	O	M	R	W	O	M	R	W
Hoggard	23	8	58	3	19	3	58	2
Harmison	28	3	91	3	19	4	62	2
Flintoff	23	5	66	2	14	5	38	1
Jones SP	18	1	81	1	14	4	36	1
Vaughan	10	2	29	1	1	1	0	0
Giles	–	–	–	–	19	1	84	1

Fall of Wickets
1-17, 2-48, 3-70, 4-80, 5-90, 6-118, 7-205, 8-243, 9-293
1-12, 2-33, 3-87, 4-103, 5-172, 6-173, 7-183, 8-268

Umpires: DB Hair & SJA Taufel
Toss: South Africa
Man of the Match: JH Kallis

Match drawn

ground once again. The floodlights were fired up, but under the new regulations – which lean too much in favour of play being suspended – the light was offered to the batsmen who, without a second thought, bolted for the safety of the dressing room. They never returned.

THIRD TEST
2–6 January 2005 at Newlands, Cape Town

Anticipating the third Test was an interesting exercise. England had come so close to winning the second that it seemed hard to imagine that their confidence could possibly have been knocked as a result – especially since their position at the end of the second day had seemed so desperate. But they were drained, and South Africa was clearly the happier team as the players all set off for Cape Town. Smith's men had almost lost, and would have trailed 2-0 in the series. Psychologically, the South Africans were noticeably boosted, and this was further enhanced by the knowledge that England had not won a Test at Newlands for nearly 50 years.

The tourists made one enforced change when Butcher injured his wrist in the nets before the game. It was an injury that would eventually finish his tour, and this gave Rob Key the chance to reclaim his position at No. 3 although, thanks to England's crazy preparation schedule, he had played only one game of cricket in three months.

Smith won the toss for the third time in the series – Vaughan's success rate with the coin in overseas Tests now stood at two out of 12 – and elected to bat having replaced van Jaarsveld with Dippenaar and Steyn with Charl Langeveldt. The captain, who had scored just 69 runs in the series so far, found some form and after the early losses of Gibbs and Rudolph, added 75 with Kallis to take South Africa to 145 for 2. Giles then had him smartly taken at slip by Trescothick for 74 to claim England's only success in the afternoon session. Giles bowled Dippenaar for a thoroughly tedious 29 with 12 overs remaining, but Kallis remained ominously poised on 81 at the close.

As expected, Kallis continued in his stately, but entirely methodical one-paced manner until he was eventually the eighth man out for 149, made from 334 balls. He is an attractive batsman to watch, but the fact that he seems unable to raise the scoring rate – especially when batting with the lower order – is a valid criticism. Because of this weakness, Kallis has been accused of selfishness in the past. By contrast,

THIRD TEST – SOUTH AFRICA v. ENGLAND
2–6 January 2005 at Cape Town

SOUTH AFRICA

	First Innings		Second Innings	
GC Smith (capt)	c Trescothick b Giles	74	lbw b Hoggard	2
HH Gibbs	b Hoggard	4	c Jones GO b Flintoff	24
JA Rudolph	c Jones GO b Jones SP	26	c Key b Jones SP	23
JH Kallis	c Jones GO b Flintoff	149	run out	66
HH Dippenaar	b Giles	29	c Vaughan b Flintoff	44
HM Amla	lbw b Hoggard	25	(7) c Jones GO b Jones SP	10
*AB de Villiers	b Giles	21	(8) c Giles b Harmison	10
SM Pollock	c Jones GO b Flintoff	4	(9) not out	3
N Boje	c Jones GO b Flintoff	76	(6) run out	4
M Ntini	c Vaughan b Flintoff	0	not out	0
CK Langeveldt	not out	5		
Extras	b 4, lb 15, w 3, nb 6	28	b 7, lb 12, w 10, nb 7	36
	(142.1 overs)	441	(8 wkts dec 69.3)	222

	First Innings				Second Innings			
	O	M	R	W	O	M	R	W
Hoggard	32	7	87	2	10	0	46	1
Harmison	26	6	82	0	19	3	55	1
Flintoff	31.1	7	79	4	18	1	46	2
Jones SP	18	0	69	1	9.3	4	15	2
Giles	35	3	105	3	13	2	41	0

Fall of Wickets
1-9, 2-70, 3-145, 4-213, 5-261, 6-308, 7-313, 8-417, 9-417
1-2, 2-62, 3-101, 4-184, 5-190, 6-203, 7-215, 8-219

ENGLAND

	First Innings		Second Innings	
ME Trescothick	c Gibbs b Ntini	28	c Amla b Pollock	0
AJ Strauss	b Ntini	45	lbw b Boje	39
RWT Key	c de Villiers b Pollock	0	st de Villiers b Boje	41
MP Vaughan (capt)	c de Villiers b Langeveldt	11	c Rudolph b Ntini	20
GP Thorpe	c Rudolph b Langeveldt	12	c de Villiers b Pollock	26
MJ Hoggard	c Smith b Ntini	1	(9) not out	7
A Flintoff	c Gibbs b Ntini	12	(6) c de Villiers b Pollock	20
*GO Jones	c Smith b Langeveldt	13	(7) c Kallis b Boje	38
AF Giles	not out	31	(8) c Kallis b Boje	25
SP Jones	b Langeveldt	0	c Kallis b Pollock	19
SJ Harmison	c Smith b Langeveldt	0	c Dippenaar b Ntini	42
Extras	b 4, lb 6	10	b 6, lb 3, w 6, nb 12	27
	(58 overs)	163	(123.4 overs)	304

	First Innings				Second Innings			
	O	M	R	W	O	M	R	W
Pollock	17	5	36	1	31	11	65	4
Ntini	19	6	50	4	24.4	6	49	2
Langeveldt	16	4	46	5	17	3	50	0
Boje	4	1	15	0	34	13	71	4
Kallis	2	1	6	0	15	4	49	0
Smith	-	-	-	-	2	0	11	0

Fall of Wickets
1-52, 2-55, 3-70, 4-95, 5-97, 6-109, 7-128, 8-141, 9-149
1-0, 2-68, 3-103, 4-105, 5-146, 6-158, 7-220, 8-225, 9-253

Umpires: SA Bucknor & DJ Harper
Toss: South Africa
Test debut: CK Langeveldt
Man of the Match: JH Kallis

South Africa won by 196 runs

Nicky Boje made an excellent 76 from 97 balls, and this helped to push South Africa to a total of 441.

By the close of the second day, England were already in trouble at 95 for 4 – having lost Trescothick, Strauss, Key and Vaughan – and still needing 147 to avoid the follow-on. Despite a swashbuckling 31 from 34 balls from Giles, they lost their remaining six wickets for only 68 in the first 20 overs of the third morning, and were bowled out for 163.

Smith might have enforced the follow-on but, instead, chose to build on his lead of 278. Kallis top scored again with 65 as South Africa looked to ram home their advantage and although they lost five wickets in 11 overs on the fourth morning, Smith declared an hour before lunch setting England 501 to win or, more realistically, a minimum of 167 overs in which to survive.

They suffered a dreadful blow when Trescothick drove a catch to short mid-off in the first over, but

Jacques Kallis hits a ball from Ashley Giles high to the legside boundary during his first innings 149 at Cape Town.

It was only delaying the inevitable, but No. 11 Steve Harmison's highly entertaining 42 at the end of England's second innings at Newlands earned him the team's top score.

they lost only one further wicket during the afternoon when Strauss was a little unfortunate to be adjudged lbw to Boje for 39. After recording a duck in the first innings, Key looked much more assured in the second and played very well until he had a moment of madness and advanced down the pitch to Boje and was stumped for 41. Vaughan and Flintoff both followed for 20 apiece, leaving England praying for another intervention by the weather on the final day.

On this occasion, however, another glorious Cape morning put paid to England's chances and ushered in their first defeat in 14 Tests. Pollock dismissed Thorpe in the sixth over for 26 and, after a stand of 62 between Giles and Geraint Jones, Boje removed both in successive overs. Harmison slogged his highest score – 42 – in an unlikely stand of 51 with the shotless Hoggard, but Ntini snaffled the last wicket to secure South Africa's victory by the not inconsiderable margin of 196 runs, and also to level what was becoming a very good series.

FOURTH TEST
13–17 January 2005 at The Wanderers, Johannesburg

A worrying injury to Flintoff – who picked up a side strain during the course of England's defeat at Cape Town – dominated the build-up to the match at the Wanderers. The options for England are always limited when Flintoff is unfit to bowl, and although the management ruled out dropping Giles so England could play four pace bowlers on what is usually the fastest pitch in South Africa, it must have been one of the few alternatives available. As it was, Flintoff was passed fit to play a full part in the game and, as usual, he responded wholeheartedly.

Finally, Vaughan won a toss, taking his overall tally to seven successes in 23 attempts, and England replaced Simon Jones with James Anderson in the hope that the ball would swing. Once again – as was the case with Key in Cape Town – it was a mixed blessing for the replacement who had played no cricket since the final one-day international in Zimbabwe more than two months earlier. South Africa, meanwhile, recalled Mark Boucher who became his team's third wicketkeeper in four Tests: a record, surely?

After losing Trescothick for 16, England's batsmen dominated the opening day to close on 263 for 4. Strauss completed his third century of the series, scoring an excellent 147 as he and Key added 182 for the second wicket. Key made 83 from 164 balls before being taken at first slip by Smith off Ntini and, as bad light – which was to become a feature of this game – descended, Strauss's fine innings came to an end when he was also caught in the slips for 147. Two overs later, Thorpe fell to a catch at third slip for a duck and, moments later, the batsmen were offered the light. The timing of Thorpe's dismissal and the bizarre regulations which now allow the fielding team to accept bad light when the floodlights are on, combined to frustrate Vaughan who, the following evening, was only very mildly critical of the umpiring in this regard and, outrageously, was fined a full 100 per cent of his match fee by the referee, Clive Lloyd. Perhaps he was wrong to criticise the umpires during the match, but he was right to point the finger at a stupid regulation which means there is always one team – either fielding or batting – that is behind in the game and, therefore, will always accept bad light. Once again, it is the paying public who are being cheated.

The second day was also grey and damp, but Vaughan played a truly outstanding innings to defy the conditions and, with help from Giles – who scored 26 – and Harmison with whom he added 82, England closed the day on 411 for 8 when South Africa's fielders accepted the offer of bad light. Vaughan was unbeaten on 82 but, the following day, he gambled and declared in the hope that his bowlers would enjoy the favourable conditions.

This was to be the nadir of Harmison's already disappointing tour. After two overs – in which virtually every delivery was wide of the leg stump – Vaughan took him off. It was a decision that was unthinkable only a couple of months before, but now summed up Harmison's plight. Immediately afterwards, the sun came out and Vaughan's brave and selfless act backfired as South Africa's batsmen then enjoyed the best conditions of the game. Hoggard toiled away, typically tirelessly, to finish with 5 for 144 but Anderson was out of sorts and Flintoff understandably wary of overstretching his side. And so it was that Gibbs took control of the day, scoring 161 from 307 deliveries. The tenacious

Boucher gave him excellent support as they added 120 and, just before lunch on the third day, South Africa were bowled out for 419, giving them a lead of eight runs.

Strauss recorded a rare failure when he was caught at third slip off Ntini for a duck, and when the fast bowler found the edge of Key's bat for 19, England were 51 for 2, only 43 runs ahead. But now we were treated to one of the most awesome innings in recent Test history from Marcus Trescothick. A thumping left-hander, Trescothick hit the ball with staggering power. He dominated the stand of 124 with Vaughan, who scored 54, and of the 60 runs added by England in the last nine overs, Trescothick struck 54 of them. His partnership with Harmison was worth 58, of which Harmison scored three! In all, Trescothick faced 248 balls in his 180, and he batted for a shade over six hours. His innings totally transformed the game and the South Africans were deflated to the point of being blown away. England declared on 332 for 9, leaving the home team to score 325 in 68 overs.

They might not win, but the locals were sure they could survive on what was still a good pitch.

They were hampered by a freak injury to Smith, who was hit on the head during fielding practice and was instructed not to bat. But as Hoggard began to tear into the South African batting line-up, taking the first six wickets to fall, Smith had little choice but to defy the doctor's orders. He batted with typical bravery and threatened to deny England their victory. But Hoggard, who finished with 7 for 61 – to give him match figures of 12 for 205 – returned to have Steyn caught behind to leave Smith stranded on 67 not out.

Makhaya Ntini shouts 'Catch it!' but Michael Vaughan's hook shot flew away for six as England's captain returned to form at the Wanderers.

FOURTH TEST – SOUTH AFRICA v. ENGLAND
13–17 January 2005 at Johannesburg

ENGLAND

	First Innings		Second Innings	
ME Trescothick	c Boucher b Steyn	16	c Boucher b Ntini	180
AJ Strauss	c Kallis b Pollock	147	c de Villiers b Ntini	0
RWT Key	c Smith b Ntini	83	c Kallis b Ntini	19
MP Vaughan (capt)	not out	82	c Boucher b Pollock	54
GP Thorpe	c Dippenaar b Ntini	0	c & b Kallis	1
MJ Hoggard	c de Villiers b Ntini	5	(9) c Boucher b Kallis	0
A Flintoff	c Smith b Ntini	2	(6) c Boucher b Pollock	7
*GO Jones	c Smith b Pollock	2	(7) c de Villiers b Pollock	13
AF Giles	c Gibbs b Steyn	26	(8) c Gibbs b Kallis	31
SJ Harmison	not out	30	not out	3
JM Anderson				
Extras	lb 13, nb 5	18	lb 7, w 6, nb 11	24
	(8 wkts dec 124 overs)	411	(9 wkts dec 81.1 overs)	332

	First Innings				Second Innings			
	O	M	R	W	O	M	R	W
Pollock	33	12	81	2	19	2	74	3
Ntini	34	8	111	4	20.1	2	62	3
Steyn	21	7	75	2	9	0	47	0
Kallis	22	2	79	0	21	5	93	3
Boje	14	2	52	0	12	0	49	0

Fall of Wickets
1-45, 2-227, 3-262, 4-263, 5-273, 6-275, 7-278, 8-329
1-2, 2-51, 3-175, 4-176, 5-186, 6-222, 7-272, 8-274, 9-332

SOUTH AFRICA

	First Innings		Second Innings	
GC Smith (capt)	lbw b Hoggard	29	(8) not out	67
HH Gibbs	c Hoggard b Anderson	161	lbw b Giles	98
JA Rudolph	c Giles b Hoggard	4	b Hoggard	2
JH Kallis	b Hoggard	33	c Trescothick b Hoggard	0
HH Dippenaar	c Trescothick b Flintoff	0	c Giles b Hoggard	14
AB de Villiers	c Giles b Hoggard	19	(1) lbw b Hoggard	3
*MV Boucher	c Strauss b Anderson	64	(6) c Jones b Hoggard	0
SM Pollock	lbw b Hoggard	0	(9) c Jones b Flintoff	4
N Boje	run out	48	(7) c & b Hoggard	18
M Ntini	b Giles	26	lbw b Flintoff	13
DW Steyn	not out	0	c Jones b Hoggard	8
Extras	b 9, lb 11, w 6, nb 9	35	b 2, lb 5, w 1, nb 12	20
	(118.1 overs)	419	(59.3 overs)	247

	First Innings				Second Innings			
	O	M	R	W	O	M	R	W
Hoggard	34	2	144	5	18.3	5	61	7
Harmison	12.5	4	25	0	14	1	64	0
Anderson	28	3	117	2	6	1	32	0
Flintoff	30.1	8	77	1	16	2	59	2
Giles	8.1	0	25	1	5	0	24	1
Trescothick	5	1	11	0	-	-	-	-

Fall of Wickets
1-64, 2-75, 3-138, 4-149, 5-184, 6-304, 7-306, 8-358, 9-399
1-10, 2-18, 3-18, 4-80, 5-86, 6-118, 7-163, 8-172, 9-216

Umpires: SA Bucknor & Aleem Dar
Toss: England
Man of the Match: MJ Hoggard

England won by 77 runs

FIFTH TEST
21–25 January 2005 at Supersport Park, Centurion

Now they were 2-1 down with only the final Test to play, South Africa had to do something dramatic. The result was an emerald green, damp pitch at Centurion Park where, whenever England visits, it rains. This year was no exception, and South Africa's prospects of winning the match virtually vanished on a first day that was entirely washed out.

The damp conditions, and the state of the pitch, made this a good toss to win and Vaughan surprised not least himself by calling correctly. Having put South Africa in to bat, he then called up Giles to

Simon Jones jumps into the arms of Matthew Hoggard after taking another first innings South African wicket at Centurion.

bowl before lunch: yet the truth was that the strip was not nearly as juicy as it had appeared.

AB de Villiers retained his position at the top of the order and Smith moved down to No. 5 as South Africa rang the changes once again. All-rounder Andrew Hall and Andre Nel – the wholehearted but idiotically behaved seamer – were drafted in to give Smith more options but, de Villiers (92) apart, the batsmen simply could not get going and South Africa were dismissed in the first over of the third morning for 247. It was hardly the sort of imposing total that was needed to put England under pressure, but credit must be given to Simon Jones who wrapped up the innings with a spell of 3 for 12 in five overs.

England's plan was made all the more simple because of South Africa's low total – they needed to bat for as long as possible, not merely to take time out of the game to prevent South Africa from winning, but also to build a substantial lead themselves. But when Vaughan was caught at square leg for 0 as he mis-pulled Pollock, England were 29 for 3, and the door remained open for Smith's team. Thorpe and Flintoff then set about shoring up England's position with a stand of 141 in three and a quarter hours. This took England into the lead by just eight runs at which point Thorpe was yorked by the aggressive Nel for 86. It had been a classic Thorpe innings – patient, and full of deflections and tucks off the pads – and Flintoff's demise came in the very next over when he edged Hall to Boucher for 77. Still South Africa felt they had a chance but Giles, who had an excellent series with the bat, dug in once again. With Geraint Jones playing in his usual busy fashion, 78 precious runs were added before Nel removed Jones for exactly 50, via an excellent low catch by Smith. Nel wrapped up the tail to finish with his best figures of 6 for 81, but England's lead was 112 with 19 overs remaining on the fourth day.

There was nothing else for South Africa to do but to put bat to ball on the final morning to set up a declaration that left them enough time to bowl England out. De Villiers reached his first Test century which, understandably, took some time to complete, but Kallis' innings once again sparked furious accusations of selfishness from within the local media. Instead of taking charge of the situation, South Africa's leading and most experienced batsman carefully compiled a century without any obvious reference to the team's requirements. After lunch – by which time Smith really ought to have declared – Kallis added 39 runs in 18 overs as England quite happily set defensive fields. The result was that Smith

Graham Thorpe pulls during his vital 86 in the final Test.

had no option but to wait until tea to declare which left England 185 runs to win but, more important to the state of the series, gave South Africa only 44 overs in which to bowl the tourists out.

Had England got away to a good start, they might have attacked the modest target but, as it was, wickets fell at an alarming rate. This only increased the level of criticism of Kallis, for after 12 overs England were 20 for 3, with Trescothick, Strauss and Key all back in the pavilion. For 16 overs, Thorpe and Vaughan took everything the South Africans could throw at them – or, in Nel's case, shout at them. Thorpe then edged Ntini to slip for 8, scored in 70 minutes, and England were 45 for 4 with 12 overs remaining. Vaughan and Flintoff made sure there were no further alarms and, fittingly in this weather-hit series, it was bad light that came to England's rescue after 41 of the 44 overs had been completed.

FIFTH TEST – SOUTH AFRICA v. ENGLAND
21–25 January 2005 at Centurion

SOUTH AFRICA

	First Innings		Second Innings	
AB de Villiers	lbw b Giles	92	c Hoggard b Jones SP	109
HH Gibbs	c Jones GO b Flintoff	14	c Jones GO b Flintoff	4
JA Rudolph	c Key b Hoggard	33	(6) b Harmison	2
JH Kallis	b Flintoff	8	not out	136
GC Smith (capt)	c Trescothick b Flintoff	25	c sub b Harmison	3
*MV Boucher	c Trescothick b Jones SP	25	(7) c Trescothick b Hoggard	6
SM Pollock	b Flintoff	0		
N Boje	c Thorpe b Jones SP	9		
AJ Hall	c Strauss b Jones SP	11	(3) b Flintoff	9
M Ntini	c Hoggard b Jones SP	6		
A Nel	not out	1		
Extras	lb 1, w 3, nb 19	23	b 2, lb 14, w 2, nb 9	27
	(75.3 overs)	**247**	(6 wkts dec 73 overs)	**296**

	First Innings				Second Innings			
	O	M	R	W	O	M	R	W
Hoggard	18	4	64	1	14	2	51	1
Harmison	17	2	79	0	16	2	59	2
Flintoff	19	6	44	4	13	2	46	2
Jones SP	15.3	3	47	4	19	2	74	1
Giles	6	1	12	1	11	1	50	0

Fall of Wickets
1-27, 2-114, 3-144, 4-187, 5-200, 6-200, 7-222, 8-237, 9-245
1-17, 2-29, 3-256, 4-267, 5-277, 6-296

ENGLAND

	First Innings		Second Innings	
ME Trescothick	run out	20	b Ntini	7
AJ Strauss	c Boucher b Nel	44	c Kallis b Ntini	0
RWT Key	c Boucher b Pollock	1	lbw b Pollock	9
MP Vaughan (capt)	c Rudolph b Pollock	0	not out	26
GP Thorpe	b Nel	86	c Gibbs b Ntini	8
A Flintoff	c Boucher b Hall	77	not out	14
*GO Jones	c Smith b Nel	50		
AF Giles	b Nel	39		
MJ Hoggard	c Kallis b Nel	1		
SP Jones	not out	0		
SJ Harmison	lbw b Nel	6		
Extras	b 1, lb 22, w 8, nb 4	35	lb 7, nb 2	9
	(123 overs)	**359**	(4 wkts 41.2 overs)	**73**

	First Innings				Second Innings			
	O	M	R	W	O	M	R	W
Pollock	21	11	30	2	7	3	9	1
Ntini	28	8	92	0	11	6	12	3
Nel	29	7	81	6	12	5	24	0
Hall	16	3	58	1	5.2	2	9	0
Boje	19	7	59	0	1	1	0	0
Kallis	2	0	5	0	2	0	4	0
Smith	8	2	11	0	3	1	8	0

Fall of Wickets
1-27, 2-29, 3-29, 4-114, 5-255, 6-257, 7-335, 8-351, 9-352
1-0, 2-16, 3-20, 4-45

Umpires: Aleem Dar & SA Bucknor
Toss: England
Man of the Match: AB de Villiers
Man of the Series: AJ Strauss

Match drawn

SERIES AVERAGES
South Africa v. England

SOUTH AFRICA

Batting	M	Inns	NO	Runs	HS	Av	100	50	c/st
JH Kallis	5	10	1	625	162	69.44	3	2	8/-
HH Gibbs	4	8	0	356	161	44.50	1	1	5/-
AB de Villiers	5	10	1	362	109	40.22	1	2	3/1
HH Dippenaar	3	6	0	207	110	34.50	1	-	3/-
JA Rudolph	5	10	0	304	93	30.40	-	2	6/-
GC Smith	5	10	1	269	74	29.88	-	3	9/-
N Boje	4	7	0	180	76	25.71	-	1	-/-
M van Jaarsveld	1	2	0	50	49	25.00	-	-	2/-
M V Boucher	2	4	0	95	64	23.75	-	1	8/-
SM Pollock	5	9	1	120	43	15.00	-	-	-/-
M Ntini	5	9	3	89	26	14.83	-	-	2/-
Z de Bruyn	1	2	0	25	19	12.50	-	-	-/-
DW Steyn	3	5	3	25	8	12.50	-	-	1/-
TL Tsolekile	1	2	0	22	22	11.00	-	-	3/-
AJ Hall	2	4	0	43	17	10.75	-	-	1/-
HM Amla	2	4	0	36	25	9.00	-	-	2/-
CK Langeveldt	1	1	1	5	5*	-	-	-	-/-
A Nel	1	1	1	1	1*	-	-	-	-/-

Bowling	Overs	Mds	Runs	Wkts	Av	Best	5/inn	10m
A Nel	41	12	105	6	17.50	6-81	1	-
CK Langeveldt	33	7	96	5	19.20	5-46	1	-
SM Pollock	222.1	83	503	21	23.95	4-32	-	-
M Ntini	221.3	49	627	25	25.08	4-50	-	-
DW Steyn	100.2	16	416	8	52.00	2-26	-	-
AJ Hall	52.2	7	176	3	58.66	2-95	-	-
GC Smith	36	7	121	2	60.50	1-25	-	-
N Boje	137	31	430	6	71.66	4-71	-	-
JH Kallis	96	20	303	4	75.75	3-93	-	-

Also bowled: Z de Bruyn 9-1-31-0.

ENGLAND

Batting	M	Inns	NO	Runs	HS	Av	100	50	c/st
AJ Strauss	5	10	1	656	147	72.88	3	1	5/-
ME Trescothick	5	10	0	448	180	44.80	2	-	1/-
GP Thorpe	5	10	2	287	118*	35.87	1	1	4/-
MP Vaughan	5	10	2	246	82*	30.75	-	2	2/-
A Flintoff	5	9	1	227	77	28.37	-	2	2/-
GO Jones	5	8	0	215	73	26.87	-	2	16/-
AF Giles	5	8	1	188	39	26.85	-	-	5/-
RWT Key	3	6	0	153	83	25.50	-	1	2/-
MA Butcher	2	4	0	97	79	24.25	-	1	-/-
SJ Harmison	5	7	3	96	42	24.00	-	-	-/-
SP Jones	4	5	1	64	24	16.00	-	-	2/-
MJ Hoggard	5	7	2	20	7*	4.00	-	-	5/-
JM Anderson	1	0	0	0	0	-	-	-	-/-

Bowling	Overs	Mds	Runs	Wkts	Av	Best	5/inn	10m
A Flintoff	201.2	42	574	23	24.95	4-44	-	-
MJ Hoggard	200.3	37	663	26	25.50	7-61	2	1
SP Jones	123.1	21	400	15	26.66	4-39	-	-
MP Vaughan	11	3	29	1	29.00	1-29	-	-
AF Giles	139.5	18	449	11	40.81	3-105	-	-
SJ Harmison	190.5	28	659	9	73.22	3-91	-	-
JM Anderson	34	4	149	2	74.50	2-117	-	-

Also bowled: ME Trescothick 5-1-11-0.

ONE-DAY INTERNATIONALS

Match One
30 January 2005 at Johannesburg
South Africa 175 for 9 (50 overs)
England 103 for 3 (25.1 overs)
England won by 26 runs – DL Method: target 78 from 25.1 overs

Match Two
2 February 2005 at Bloemfontein
England 270 for 5 (50 overs) (KP Pietersen 108*)
South Africa 270 for 8 (50 overs) (HH Gibbs 78, JH Kallis 63)
Match Tied

Match Three
4 February 2005 at Port Elizabeth
England 267 for 8 (50 overs) (VS Solanki 66)
South Africa 270 for 7 (49.1 overs) (GC Smith 105, HH Gibbs 50)
South Africa won by 3 wickets

Match Four
6 February 2005 at Cape Town
South Africa 291 for 5 (50 overs) (HH Gibbs 100, JH Kallis 71, JM Kemp 57)
England 183 (41.2 overs) (KP Pietersen 75)
South Africa won by 108 runs

Match Five
9 February 2005 at East London
South Africa 311 for 7 (50 overs) (GC Smith 115*, JM Kemp 80)
England 304 for 8 (50 overs) (KP Pietersen 100*, MP Vaughan 70)
South Africa won by 7 runs

Match Six
11 February 2005 at Durban
South Africa 211 (46.3 overs) (HH Gibbs 118)
England 7 for 2 (3.4 overs)
Match abandoned – no result

Match Seven
13 February 2005 at Centurion
England 240 (49.5 overs) (KP Pietersen 116)
South Africa 241 for 7 (49 overs) (AG Prince 62*)
South Africa won by 3 wickets

A one-sided series of seven matches was, curiously, dominated by a player from the losing team. England's Kevin Pietersen – who had previously appeared in four matches in Zimbabwe prior to this tour – scored three centuries in seven innings to achieve a remarkable aggregate of 454 runs at an average of 151. The irony of the situation was not lost on the South African public: Pietersen is South African born and bred and even represented South African Schools. But his mother comes from Kent and has a British passport, and having served out his qualification period at Nottinghamshire, Pietersen was clear to play for his adopted country.

A tall right-handed batsman, Pietersen is a natural and imposing one-day player. Strong through the

Return of the native: Kevin Pietersen salutes his first limited-overs century, at Bloemfontein, before going on to hit two more in a remarkable personal series.

legside, he hits the ball hard and in the air. It was a shame that Flintoff was not batting alongside him in this series to give England supporters a taste of what we can expect over the coming years – Flintoff had returned home to have an operation on his injured ankle – but many an appetite has been whetted after this amazing performance.

The weather was always a problem, and England's only success came in the rain-affected opener at Johannesburg where Vaughan's 44 steered his team to a winning position as determined by Messrs Duckworth and Lewis. There was high drama in the next encounter at Bloemfontein where Kabir Ali's final delivery of the match thwarted South Africa's effort to score the one run they needed to win. Geraint Jones – standing up – pulled off the stumping to dismiss Hall, so the match was tied with both teams having scored 270, and Pietersen recorded the first of his three hundreds.

It was now that the South Africans took control of the series. Pietersen managed only 33 in the following game in Port Elizabeth, and Smith's century saw his team ease past England's total of 267 for 8 in the final over.

There followed a much more convincing victory for South Africa at Cape Town, where, to the delight of the locals, Gibbs scored exactly 100 on his home ground. Set 292 to win, England fell woefully short to finish on 183 all out, despite 75 from 85 balls by Pietersen.

It became 3-1 with two games to play when South Africa pulled off a narrow win in East London. Once again, Smith led from the front with his second century of the series. The hard-hitting Kemp weighed in with 80 to post a target of 312 which, batting second under lights, was a formidable challenge. An astonishing innings of exactly 100 not out from only 69 balls by Pietersen – who came in at 117 for 3 – took England to within eight runs of victory.

The penultimate game at Durban was washed out as England had reached 7 for 2 chasing a target of 212, and the South Africans recorded their fourth win out of five games at Centurion despite another hundred from Pietersen. This time he scored 116 from 110 balls and took his boundary count in the series to 15 sixes and 36 fours. That equates to 234 of his 454 runs. Giles weighed in with 41 to set a target of 241. Smith made 47 and Kallis 36, but it was an innings of 62 from the middle-order batsman, Ashwell Prince, that, with Boucher's 44, saw South Africa home with an over to spare.

SOUTH AFRICA REPORT
By Telford Vice

Johannesburg's summer afternoons steam with the promise of intoxication, from the illicit to the illegal and even, in some sad minds, the immoral. The brassy heat shimmers deep into the city's generous soul and does strange things – some wonderful, some wicked, sometimes wonderfully wicked – to the people it finds there.

17 January 2005 was just such an afternoon. It will forever belong to Matthew Hoggard, who swung the ball as diabolically as the worm swirls in a bottle of tequila to complete a haul of 12 wickets. He took five after lunch on the last day of the fourth Test, and was able to savour the rare delight of removing Jacques Kallis first ball. The afternoon's other hero, Graeme Smith, stood tall amid the debris. Smith had to sneak past the team's medical staff to bat at No. 8 after being concussed during a warm-up session. His defiance lasted more than two hours and earned him a half-century. But it wasn't enough to stop England winning by 77 runs and taking what would prove a decisive 2-1 lead in the series.

It was the darkest of days for South Africans, who wrote off the duly lost Test series in India that preceded England's tour. One-day success against England smoothed brows that had been deeply furrowed during the Test series, and there were no surprises in the non-contest against Zimbabwe. A triumphant tour of the West Indies put the smiles back, but they were closer to expressions of relief than satisfaction.

The enduring memory of South Africa's 2004–05 season will be defeat by England, the first time this calamity had struck in the Republic for 40 years. For some, all manner of chickens had come home to roost. Every soapboxable issue, from Hansie Cronje's dealings with the devil to the seeming dearth of fast bowling depth to the United Cricket Board's inept or negligent (take your pick) administration, to its continued efforts to darken what remains a painfully white game in South Africa, was given fresh impetus.

The Indian series of two Test matches was South Africa's first under the rough-and-ready hand of Ray Jennings, the gung-ho caretaker coach. Mark Boucher was axed from the squad in favour of the talented and exciting Thami Tsolekile, whose fragile psyche and lack of the less-obvious skills required of a top-class wicketkeeper were cruelly exposed in India. Hashim Amla forced his way into the touring party by scoring four centuries in five first-class

Graeme Smith's bravery at the Wanderers was not enough to prevent his side going down to a series-deciding defeat against England.

However, there was no hiding behind gimmicks in the second Test in Kolkata, which India won by eight wickets. Kallis scored 121 and 55, but few teams, much less the spin-challenged South Africans, would have been able to survive Harbhajan Singh in the form he showed in the second innings as he collected seven for 87.

'Treat people softly and they'll become soft,' Jennings growled before the first Test against England in Port Elizabeth. So when England looked every inch the harder team as they went about winning the first Test by seven wickets, he looked more than a little silly.

The local media seemed more interested in Andrew Strauss' South African birth than in his innings of 126 and 94 not out, and Simon Jones fast-forwarded the match with his crucial four-wicket burst in the second innings.

Bad light saved South Africa in the Boxing Day Test in Durban, but the home side showed their quality by dismissing England for 139. South Africa's lead of 193 owed much to Kallis' 162, and England wrenched back the advantage when Marcus Trescothick and Strauss shared an opening stand of 273. A third century, by Graham Thorpe, saw England set South Africa a target of 378. They were 290 for 8 when bad light ended the match 15 overs early, but England were able to celebrate an unbeaten 2004.

Kallis' 149 followed by superb bowling by debutant Charl Langeveldt, who took 5 for 46, and Ntini earned South Africa the ascendancy in the New Year Test in Cape Town. Shaun Pollock and Nicky Boje then flummoxed England's wavering batsmen, and South Africa won by 196 runs.

Smith's team seemed the more bullish when the series arrived in Johannesburg. Boucher was back in

matches, and became the first South African of Asian descent to be named in a national squad. Oddly, Amla was left out for the first Test.

Jennings' influence could be seen in Boucher's, Tsolekile's and Amla's fate. But he had his moments. Like when he sent one of his favourites, Andrew Hall, to open the innings in the first Test at Kanpur. Almost ten hours later Hall was still there, and his 163 was the fulcrum around which South Africa's first innings of 510 for 9 declared slowly turned. The visitors were plainly in search of a draw, and they ensured that result by batting until the third morning.

True grit: the 13 wickets for 132 that Makhaya Ntini took in Port-of-Spain, in defiance of the sweltering conditions, brought him the best Test match analysis by a South African.

the side and England were unsure of the fitness of Andrew Flintoff. England declared before the start of the third day's play on 411 for 8, with Strauss' 147 the centrepiece. Herschelle Gibbs scored 161 as South Africa replied with 419, and the game was on.

England's lead was 189 at stumps on the fourth day, and Trescothick scored a masterful 180 – the innings of the series – to put the visitors 324 ahead. A draw would surely follow. Instead, Hoggard claimed his first ten-wicket haul. Even Jennings spoke sense, 'We didn't show enough mental toughness.'

Both teams knew the series had been decided, but first to Centurion. AB de Villiers, South Africa's find of the season, scored 92 and 109, his maiden century, Kallis crowned a fine series with 136 not out, and Andre Nel took 6 for 81 in the first innings. England did what they needed to, but no more. And then, the draw secured, they celebrated.

The one-day series, which South Africa won 4-1, will be remembered for the escalation of public abuse hurled at Kevin Pietersen, who flaunted his ersatz Englishness and made a point of antagonising the crowd.

Zimbabwe were swept aside with comical ease. They were thrashed in all three one-day internationals, and then crashed to their lowest Test score, 54, on their way to losing the first Test by an innings and 21 runs in two days. The second Test lasted a day longer, and South Africa won by an innings and 62 runs.

Blame and recrimination for the England defeat still smouldered two months later when South Africa embarked for the Caribbean. When Wavell Hinds and Shivnarine Chanderpaul scored 213 and 203 not out respectively in the first Test in Georgetown, the groans were almost audible across the oceans. South Africa were shot out for 188 in reply to the West Indies' 543 for 5 declared. But Kallis rode to the rescue by batting for the entire final day to score an unbeaten 109 and force a draw.

That was the last time South Africa looked the lesser team.

In Port of Spain, Brian Lara returned to West Indian ranks following a contractual dispute and played as fine an innings, a wondrous 196, as the game has surely seen. But Makhaya Ntini's 6 for 95 was the more valuable performance. Smith's gritty 148 garnered a lead of 51, and Ntini's 7 for 37 reduced the victory target to 144, which the visitors reached with eight wickets standing. Ntini's 12 for 132 was the best return by a South African, a fitting reward for this supreme athlete's relentlessness in extreme heat.

South Africa settled the series by winning the third Test in Bridgetown by an innings and 86 runs. Lara played another hand as brilliant as it was lone with his 176, but Smith and De Villiers negated that with an opening stand of 191. South Africa took a lead of 252, and Nel found bounce in a placid pitch to claim 6 for 32 and complete a haul of 10 for 88.

The drawn fourth Test at St John's wasn't short on records. The most significant among them was the fact that never before had a Test yielded eight centuries. Top of the pile was Chris Gayle, whose 317 made him the fourth West Indian to score a Test triple-century.

The match ended badly with accusations of on-field racism levelled at Smith by the West Indians. They were dismissed by match referee Jeff Crowe.

South Africa emphasised their superiority with a 5-0 sweep of the one-day series. Langeveldt ended the third match in Bridgetown with a sensational hat-trick to dismiss the West Indies and leave South Africa victors by a single run.

ONE-DAY INTERNATIONALS
v. Zimbabwe

Match One
25 February 2005 at Johannesburg
South Africa 301 for 7 (50 overs)
(AM Bacher 56, GC Smith 50, JA Rudolph 50)
Zimbabwe 136 (37.2 overs)
South Africa won by 165 runs

Match Two
27 February 2005 at Durban
South Africa 329 for 6 (50 overs)
(GC Smith 117, HH Gibbs 75, JM Kemp 53*)
Zimbabwe 198 for 7 (50 overs)
South Africa won by 131 runs

Match Three
2 March 2005 at Port Elizabeth
Zimbabwe 206 for 8 (50 overs)
(HH Streak 68)
South Africa 207 for 5 (46.3 overs)
(JM Kemp 78*)
South Africa won by 5 wickets

FIRST TEST – SOUTH AFRICA v. ZIMBABWE
4–5 March 2005 at Cape Town

ZIMBABWE

	First Innings		Second Innings	
S Matsikenyeri	c de Villiers b Ntini	12	c Rudolph b Ntini	13
BG Rogers	c Boucher b Pollock	1	c Boucher b Ntini	28
DD Ebrahim	b Ntini	3	lbw b Langeveldt	72
H Masakadza	lbw b Kallis	6	c Gibbs b Boje	46
BRM Taylor	c Boucher b Ntini	2	c Langeveldt b Boje	9
*T Taibu (capt)	c de Villiers b Kallis	7	c sub b Langeveldt	9
E Chigumbura	c Smith b Kallis	2	b Boje	0
HH Streak	c Boucher b Pollock	9	c Gibbs b Kallis	12
AM Blignaut	c Boje b Kallis	8	st Boucher b Boje	61
AG Cremer	c Kallis b Pollock	0	run out	2
CB Mpofu	not out	0	not out	0
Extras	nb 4	4	b 2, lb 7, w 2, nb 2	13
	(31.2 overs)	54	(75.2 overs)	265

	First Innings				Second Innings			
	O	M	R	W	O	M	R	W
Pollock	8	4	9	3	5	1	14	0
Ntini	10	2	23	3	16	2	68	2
Langeveldt	6	2	9	0	9.3	3	27	2
Kallis	7.2	3	13	4	17.3	7	40	1
Boje	-	-	-	-	26.2	5	106	4
Rudolph	-	-	-	-	1	0	1	0

Fall of Wickets
1-2, 2-13, 3-20, 4-22, 5-33, 6-36, 7-37, 8-50, 9-50
1-25, 2-59, 3-157, 4-173, 5-183, 6-186, 7-186, 8-214, 9-247

SOUTH AFRICA

	First Innings	
GC Smith (capt)	c Masakadza b Cremer	121
AB de Villiers	c Blignaut b Cremer	98
JA Rudolph	not out	49
JH Kallis	c Blignaut b Cremer	54
HH Gibbs	not out	8
AG Prince		
*MV Boucher		
SM Pollock		
N Boje		
M Ntini		
CK Langeveldt		
Extras	lb 1, w 1, nb 8	10
	(3 wkts dec 50 overs)	340

	First Innings			
	O	M	R	W
Streak	13	0	90	0
Mpofu	12	2	53	0
Blignaut	6	0	44	0
Chigumbura	8	0	53	0
Cremer	9	0	86	3
Matsikenyeri	1	0	6	0
Taylor	1	0	7	0

Fall of Wickets
1-217, 2-234, 3-328

Umpires: BF Bowden & B Doctrove
Toss: Zimbabwe
Man of the Match: JH Kallis

South Africa won by an innings and 21 runs

SECOND TEST – SOUTH AFRICA v. ZIMBABWE
11–13 March 2005 at Centurion

ZIMBABWE

	First Innings		Second Innings	
S Matsikenyeri	c Smith b Langeveldt	12	b Zondeki	5
BG Rogers	c Boucher b Nel	7	c Boucher b Zondeki	0
DD Ebrahim	b Kallis	37	c Smith b Nel	1
H Masakadza	c Smith b Zondeki	26	c Boucher b Zondeki	47
BRM Taylor	b Kallis	4	lbw b Zondeki	6
*T Taibu (capt)	c Gibbs b Zondeki	14	c Boucher b Zondeki	13
E Chigumbura	c sub b Kallis	0	(8) c Boucher b Boje	44
HH Streak	b Kallis	85	(7) c Gibbs b Kallis	16
AM Blignaut	c Smith b Zondeki	52	c Boucher b Kallis	0
AG Cremer	c Boucher b Nel	12	c Boucher b Zondeki	0
CB Mpofu	not out	1	not out	0
Extras	b 4, lb 8, w 4, nb 3	19	b 4, lb 10, nb 3	17
	(85 overs)	269	(59.3 overs)	149

	First Innings				Second Innings			
	O	M	R	W	O	M	R	W
Nel	12	7	17	2	16	6	42	1
Zondeki	21	7	66	3	14.3	2	39	6
Langeveldt	5	1	19	1	-	-	-	-
Kallis	13	4	33	4	12	5	20	2
Smith	7	2	39	0	-	-	-	-
Boje	18	1	62	0	15	7	25	1
de Villiers	7	0	16	0	-	-	-	-
Rudolph	2	0	5	0	2	1	9	0

Fall of Wickets
1-15, 2-22, 3-71, 4-80, 5-115, 6-115, 7-115, 8-191, 9-264
1-6, 2-13, 3-18, 4-29, 5-76, 6-85, 7-143, 8-147, 9-149

SOUTH AFRICA

	First Innings	
AB de Villiers	c Masakadza b Mpofu	47
GC Smith (capt)	c Rogers b Chigumbura	41
JA Rudolph	b Cremer	12
HH Gibbs	c Taibu b Streak	47
AG Prince	not out	139
*MV Boucher	c Masakadza b Cremer	18
JH Kallis	b Streak	58
N Boje	b Cremer	82
M Zondeki		
CK Langeveldt		
A Nel		
Extras	b 4, lb 5, w 5, nb 22	36
	(7 wkts dec 109.5 overs)	480

	First Innings			
	O	M	R	W
Streak	20	1	78	2
Mpofu	21	1	110	1
Chigumbura	25	1	97	1
Cremer	26.5	4	106	3
Blignaut	16	0	74	0
Taylor	1	0	6	0

Fall of Wickets
1-93, 2-106, 3-133, 4-197, 5-219, 6-338, 7-480

Umpires: B Doctrove & DJ Harper
Toss: South Africa
Man of the Match: M Zondeki
Man of the Series: JH Kallis

South Africa won by an innings and 62 runs

SERIES AVERAGES
South Africa v. Zimbabwe

SOUTH AFRICA

Batting	M	Inns	NO	Runs	HS	Av	100	50	c/st
N Boje	2	1	0	82	82	82.00	-	1	1/-
GC Smith	2	2	0	162	121	81.00	1	-	5/-
AB de Villiers	2	2	0	145	98	72.50	-	1	2/-
JA Rudolph	2	2	1	61	49*	61.00	-	-	1/-
JH Kallis	2	2	0	112	58	56.00	-	2	1/-
HH Gibbs	2	2	1	55	47	55.00	-	-	4/-
MV Boucher	2	1	0	18	18	18.00	-	-	12/1
AG Prince	2	1	1	139	139*	-	1	-	-/-
SM Pollock	1	0	0	0	0	-	-	-	-/-
M Ntini	1	0	0	0	0	-	-	-	-/-
A Nel	1	0	0	0	0	-	-	-	-/-
M Zondeki	1	0	0	0	0	-	-	-	-/-
CK Langeveldt	2	0	0	0	0	-	-	-	1/-

Bowling	Overs	Mds	Runs	Wkts	Av	Best	5/inn	10m
SM Pollock	13	5	23	3	7.66	3-9	-	-
JH Kallis	49.5	19	106	11	9.63	4-13	-	-
M Zondeki	35.3	9	105	9	11.66	6-39	1	-
M Ntini	26	4	91	5	18.20	3-23	-	-
CK Langeveldt	20.3	6	55	3	18.33	2-27	-	-
A Nel	28	13	59	3	19.66	2-17	-	-
N Boje	59.2	13	193	5	38.60	4-106	-	-

Also bowled: JA Rudolph 5-1-15-0, AB de Villiers 7-0-16-0, GC Smith 7-2-39-0.

ZIMBABWE

Batting	M	Inns	NO	Runs	HS	Av	100	50	c/st
H Masakadza	2	4	0	125	47	31.25	-	-	3/-
HH Streak	2	4	0	122	85	30.50	-	1	-/-
AM Blignaut	2	4	0	121	61	30.25	-	2	2/-
DD Ebrahim	2	4	0	113	72	28.25	-	1	-/-
E Chigumbura	2	4	0	46	44	11.50	-	-	-/-
T Taibu	2	4	0	43	14	10.75	-	-	1/-
S Matsikenyeri	2	4	0	42	13	10.50	-	-	-/-
BG Rogers	2	4	0	36	28	9.00	-	-	1/-
BRM Taylor	2	4	0	21	9	5.25	-	-	-/-
AG Cremer	2	4	0	14	12	3.50	-	-	1/-
CB Mpofu	2	4	4	1	1*	-	-	-	-/-

Bowling	Overs	Mds	Runs	Wkts	Av	Best	5/inn	10m
AG Cremer	35.5	4	192	6	32.00	3-86	-	-
HH Streak	33	1	168	2	84.00	2-78	-	-
E Chigumbura	33	1	150	1	150.00	1-97	-	-
CB Mpofu	33	3	163	1	163.00	1-110	-	-

Also bowled: S Matsikenyeri 1-0-6-0, BRM Taylor 2-0-13-0, AM Blignaut 22-0-118-0.

ZIMBABWE

ENGLAND IN ZIMBABWE

ENGLAND IN ZIMBABWE
By Jonathan Agnew

England's cricket tour of Zimbabwe in the autumn of 2004 had been threatening to be a highly contentious issue ever since Nasser Hussain's team boycotted their World Cup fixture in Harare in 2003. It was clear that the England and Wales Cricket Board was keen to avoid the tour from the outset, but pressure from the International Cricket Council, which supported Zimbabwe's cause, made it clear that if England were to pull out of the trip, then the ECB would face a substantial financial penalty, and even the possibility of suspension. The size of the fine was merely the subject of speculation, but the Chief Executive of ECB, Tim Lamb, suggested that the future of English cricket would be jeopardised as a result.

Meanwhile, the tour was downgraded during the summer of 2004 when a walkout by Zimbabwe's white players – who subsequently failed to persuade an ICC investigation team that they were the victims of racism – meant that Zimbabwe's Test team was simply not worthy of the name. This left England with the prospect of playing five one-day internationals against a weakened team in a country whose government has widely been accused of human rights abuse and whose President, Robert Mugabe, is the patron of Zimbabwe Cricket.

When the British government failed to make its opposition to the tour any more persuasive than merely a preference for it not to take place, the ECB claimed it had no choice but to stand against widespread public dismay, and undertake the trip.

There was a further twist when, with the team completing its warm-up in Namibia, Zimbabwean immigration officials announced that a number of British journalists – myself included – would not be allowed into the country to report on the tour. Suddenly the ECB had another means of wriggling off the hook, and this became the most likely option when, finally, the ICC switched its support to England. The players were now waiting in a hotel at Johannesburg airport, anticipating that rather than flying to Harare they would, in fact,

Ian Bell watches the ball intently, as does Tatenda Taibu behind the stumps, as the England batsman marks his one-day international debut by scoring 75 in the opening match of the series in Harare.

be returning home, when the remarkable and unprecedented climb-down by the Zimbabwe government was announced: the journalists were welcome, and the tour was back on – albeit reduced, on England's insistence, to four matches.

The cricket was irrelevant, of course. Having been told in no uncertain terms that our presence in Zimbabwe was tolerated only as long as we stayed away from the rural areas, we were otherwise allowed unfettered access to a part of the world in which reports from foreign journalists on the famine, petrol queues and rampant inflation are mainly carried out covertly. The longer we stayed in the country, the more we learned about the enormous hardship faced by the majority of the Zimbabwean people. I was also shown further documentary evidence of racism within the newly formed Zimbabwe Cricket, including a death threat made to a white official.

What we could not gauge until the cricket started was the reception the England cricket team would receive. The opening match, played in Harare on a Sunday, attracted a good, well-natured crowd. There were no demonstrations and no placards. The game was closer than anticipated, and to add further relief to the officials at Zimbabwe Cricket, their patron wisely chose to stay away.

Zimbabwe's young and hopelessly inexperienced team were reduced to 195, with the promising Elton Chigumbura scoring 52, and England lost five wickets before winning the game with 14 balls to spare. There then followed a grotesquely one-sided match in which Zimbabwe were bowled out for 102 chasing the small matter of 264 to win.

It became 3-0 in Bulawayo when Zimbabwe posted a decent total and set England 239 to win. Vikram Solanki's century ensured this was

Kevin Pietersen is dismissed during the final one–day international, at the Queens Sports Club in Bulawayo, to the delight of Tatenda Taibu and (right) Hamilton Masakadza.

completed with nearly seven overs to go and finally, in front of such a sparse crowd that one could only conclude that a spectators' boycott had taken place, England completed a clean sweep by defeating Zimbabwe by 75 runs.

To the great relief of the ECB, the tour was completed speedily and with the minimum of fuss. It was fascinating, meanwhile, to monitor what is clearly a thriving cricket development programme in the underprivileged areas of Harare – which I would not have believed had I not seen it with my own eyes. One can only hope that a radical change in the policies of the Zimbabwean government will, one day, give the talented, bare-footed youngsters I saw the chance to fulfil their undoubted cricket talent.

ONE-DAY INTERNATIONALS
v. England

Match One
28 November 2004 at Harare
Zimbabwe 195 (49.3 overs)
(E Chigumbura 52)
England 197 for 5 (47.4 overs)
(IR Bell 75, MP Vaughan 56)
England won by 5 wickets

Match Two
1 December 2004 at Harare
England 263 for 6 (50 overs)
(KP Pietersen 77*, GO Jones 66)
Zimbabwe 102 (36 overs)
(AG Wharf 4 for 24)
England won by 161 runs

Match Three
4 December 2004 at Bulawayo
Zimbabwe 238 for 7 (50 overs)
(S Matsikenyeri 73, DD Ebrahim 65)
England 239 for 2 (43.1 overs)
(VS Solanki 100, MP Vaughan 54*,
IR Bell 53)
England won by 8 wickets

Thank you, and goodbye: England's players, having won the series 4–0, are congratulated by their Zimbabwe opponents on return to the Bulawayo dressing rooms.

Match Four
5 December 2004 at Bulawayo
England 261 for 6 (50 overs)
(MP Vaughan 90*, GO Jones 80)
Zimbabwe 187 (48.4 overs)
(H Masakadza 66, D Gough 4 for 34)
England won by 74 runs

Zimbabwe captain Tatenda Taibu, who made 71 not out and 52 in the match, sweeps during the first innings of the opening Test against India, at Bulawayo.

ZIMBABWE REPORT
By Telford Vice

The kindest analysis of Zimbabwe's dive towards unplumbed depths of misery is to state, baldly, their results in the period under review. They played seven Test matches, losing six and drawing one. Of 16 one-day internationals, they won two and lost the rest.

If we could leave it there and fill the rest of these pages with a picture of Tatenda Taibu in the throes of one of his many doughty innings, all well and good. But, of course, that would be a dereliction of duty. It would not be as serious an offence as a national board offering its players contracts that mean nothing without the fairytale incentives attached to them; the same board that pays hefty salaries to employees fulfilling questionable functions – do marketing people need liaison people? – and splashes out on new vehicles and offices. It would not be as alarming as a high-ranking administrator telling the media clumsy lies, or a board co-opting and undermining the players'

association, or 'shutting the door' on players who stand up to its bullying.

But we would nonetheless be remiss if we did not describe Zimbabwe's trials and tribulations more fully. As if the mass of talented but woefully inexperienced players the country was left with in the wake of the rebel crisis wasn't damaging enough, Taibu's team was sideswiped by injuries in the second half of their season. Tinashe Panyangara, the most exciting Zimbabwean fast bowler to emerge for a generation and as such inspirational evidence that there is life after the current crop of players, was poleaxed by stress fractures. Two more of the brighter young things, Elton Chigumbura and Prosper Utseya, were also hampered, while injuries to Douglas Hondo and Mluleki Nkala further eroded the tiny base of Zimbabwean players who know their way around the international stage. Then Andy Blignaut broke down with shoulder and elbow problems.

Suddenly the second paragraph of this sad tale does not seem quite so damning. The Zimbabweans, bless them, were desperately short of reasons to be cheerful. They received none from England, who hurried to a 4-0 victory in a one-day series in Zimbabwe that was originally scheduled to last five games. One of the matches was scrapped when England debated whether to proceed with the tour after the Zimbabwean government said it would not accredit several media representatives. The government relented, and with that went England's last hope of avoiding the tour. Vikram Solanki scored the only century of the series, but Michael Vaughan was dependable and scored three half-centuries. A slick England never looked like stumbling.

Taibu's men must have hoped that success awaited them in Bangladesh. Alas, they became the vanquished in the home side's first Test victory. Their fate was sealed after lunch on the fifth day at Chittagong when Christopher Mpofu prodded a catch to silly point and Enamul Haque celebrated figures of 6 for 45, then the best by a Bangladeshi. Bangladesh, led by Habibul Bashar's 94 and three more half-centuries, scored 488. Zimbabwe might have sunk without trace were it not for Taibu's 92, but they were still dismissed 176 runs behind. Bashar scored another 55 in the second innings as Bangladesh set Zimbabwe a target of 381. Hamilton Masakadza's 56 and Brendan Taylor's 44 aside, the visitors were clueless against Haque and duly crashed to defeat by 226 runs.

Haque returned to the record-breaking trail in the second Test at Dhaka, taking 7 for 95 in the first innings and 12 for 105 in the match. But Bangladesh were denied a 2-0 series win by the obdurate Taibu, who batted for five hours for his undefeated 85 in the first innings and was last out for 153 in the second dig. Honest artisan Hondo claimed 6 for 59 as Zimbabwe earned a first innings lead of 87, and the visitors gave themselves a chance of squaring the rubber when they asked Bangladesh to chase 374. However, the home side were never in trouble after Javed Omar and Nafees Iqbal put on 133 for the first wicket, and Iqbal scored 121 in the inevitable draw.

The Zimbabweans were on the verge of revenge when they fought back hard to win the first two games in the five-match one-day series. But Bangladesh reeled in three consecutive wins by increasing margins to confirm their superior minnowhood.

Never again in the season were Zimbabwe competitive. South Africa were sweatless winners of all three one-day internationals before dismissing Zimbabwe for a record low of 54 on their way to an innings victory in a Cape Town Test that was over in two days. Another innings defeat followed in Centurion, this time in three days.

New Zealand hardly twitched a silver fern in winning in two days in Harare and in three days in Bulawayo, both times by an innings. No one gasped when Zimbabwe lost all of their matches in a home triangular series that saw New Zealand beat India in the final.

Then it was India's turn to administer some punishment. The first Test, in Bulawayo, remarkably lasted four days but Zimbabwe suffered their fifth consecutive innings defeat. There was some kind of hollow pleasure to be taken from the fact that they went down by a mere ten wickets in the second Test, but not much considering the match was completed in three days. The only casualty was Phil Simmons, who was replaced by Kevin Curran as Zimbabwe's coach after the series.

Taibu's shoulders drooped with each added thrashing, and there is real concern about this valuable young player's mental well-being.

Outside the corridors of power in Zimbabwe, that is.

Douglas Hondo's 6 for 59 in Dhaka restored a bit of Zimbabwean pride after their defeat by Bangladesh in the opening Test at Chittagong.

FIRST TEST – ZIMBABWE v. NEW ZEALAND
7–8 August 2005 at Harare

NEW ZEALAND

	First Innings		
JAH Marshall	c Taibu b Mahwire		5
L Vincent	c Carlisle b Mahwire		13
HJH Marshall	lbw b Mpofu		20
SP Fleming (capt)	c Carlisle b Mpofu		73
NJ Astle	c Taylor b Streak		23
SB Styris	run out		7
*BB McCullum	c Cremer b Mahwire		111
DL Vettori	b Streak		127
JEC Franklin	b Cremer		13
SE Bond	not out		41
CS Martin	not out		4
Extras	b 1, lb 7, w 2, nb 5		15
	(9 wkts dec 89 overs)		452

	First Innings			
	O	M	R	W
Streak	23.4	5	102	2
Mahwire	26	4	115	3
Mpofu	16.2	1	100	2
Cremer	22	0	113	1
Taylor	1	0	14	0

Fall of Wickets
1-21, 2-24, 3-63, 4-104, 5-113, 6-233, 7-309, 8-369, 9-432

ZIMBABWE

	First Innings		Second Innings	
NR Ferreira	c McCullum b Franklin	5	c Fleming b Franklin	16
BRM Taylor	run out	10	c Vettori b Franklin	0
DD Ebrahim	lbw b Franklin	0	b Martin	8
H Masakadza	lbw b Franklin	0	c & b Vettori	42
CB Wishart	b Bond	0	c Fleming b Bond	5
SV Carlisle	not out	20	c Fleming b Bond	0
*T Taibu (capt)	lbw b Martin	5	c Fleming b Martin	4
HH Streak	c McCullum b Martin	0	lbw b Vettori	3
NB Mahwire	lbw b Martin	4	not out	4
AG Cremer	c Martin b Vettori	1	c Marshall JAH b Vettori	3
CB Mpofu	st McCullum b Vettori	0	st McCullum b Vettori	0
Extras	lb 6, w 1, nb 7	14	lb 8, nb 6	14
	(29.4 overs)	59	(49.5 overs)	99

	First Innings				Second Innings			
	O	M	R	W	O	M	R	W
Bond	5	1	11	1	11	8	10	2
Franklin	5	0	11	3	10	2	19	2
Martin	10	1	21	3	8	5	16	2
Styris	7	4	9	0	2	0	3	0
Vettori	2.4	2	1	2	13.5	4	28	4
Astle	-	-	-	-	5	0	15	0

Fall of Wickets
1-9, 2-9, 3-10, 4-11, 5-28, 6-46, 7-46, 8-51, 9-53
1-5, 2-14, 3-53, 4-76, 5-80, 6-84, 7-90, 8-90, 9-99

Umpires: MR Benson & DB Hair
Toss: Zimbabwe
Test debut: NR Ferreira
Man of the Match: DL Vettori

New Zealand won by an innings and 294 runs

SECOND TEST – ZIMBABWE v. NEW ZEALAND
15–17 August 2005 at Bulawayo

ZIMBABWE

	First Innings		Second Innings	
DD Ebrahim	lbw b Bond	0	c Styris b Bond	2
BRM Taylor	c McCullum b Bond	37	c Vettori b Bond	77
SV Carlisle	lbw b Bond	1	run out	10
H Masakadza	c Martin b Bond	0	b Vettori	28
CB Wishart	c Astle b Franklin	30	run out	0
*T Taibu (capt)	c Vettori b Bond	76	lbw b Vettori	25
HH Streak	c McCullum b Bond	0	c McCullum b Bond	2
KM Dabengwa	b Martin	17	c McCullum b Bond	4
NB Mahwire	c Astle b Vettori	42	not out	50
AG Cremer	not out	7	lbw b Vettori	1
CB Mpofu	c Marshall JAH b Vettori	7	run out	3
Extras	lb 4, nb 10	14	lb 2, nb 3	5
	(79 overs)	231	(61.1 overs)	207

	First Innings				Second Innings			
	O	M	R	W	O	M	R	W
Bond	17	5	51	6	14	1	48	4
Franklin	12	3	43	1	10	3	24	0
Martin	13	4	42	1	12	2	47	0
Styris	4	2	9	0	3	0	20	0
Vettori	27	9	56	2	22.1	8	66	3
Astle	6	2	26	0	-	-	-	-

Fall of Wickets
1-0, 2-3, 3-7, 4-65, 5-74, 6-74, 7-123, 8-211, 9-217
1-4, 2-19, 3-69, 4-69, 5-146, 6-146, 7-153, 8-164, 9-173

NEW ZEALAND

	First Innings		
JAH Marshall	c Carlisle b Streak		10
L Vincent	b Streak		92
HJH Marshall	run out		13
SP Fleming (capt)	c Taibu b Mahwire		65
NJ Astle	b Streak		128
SB Styris	c Taibu b Mahwire		45
*BB McCullum	c Taylor b Dabengwa		24
DL Vettori	c Taibu b Dabengwa		48
JEC Franklin	lbw b Streak		19
SE Bond	b Mahwire		8
CS Martin	not out		0
Extras	b 6, lb 6, w 2, nb 18		32
	(111.1 overs)		484

	First Innings			
	O	M	R	W
Streak	22	6	73	4
Mahwire	25.1	2	121	3
Mpofu	15	1	80	0
Cremer	24	1	111	0
Dabengwa	25	2	87	2

Fall of Wickets
1-34, 2-48, 3-185, 4-205, 5-292, 6-346, 7-439, 8-475, 9-484

Umpires: MR Benson & DB Hair
Toss: Zimbabwe
Man of the Match: SE Bond
Player of the Series: SE Bond

New Zealand won by an innings and 46 runs

SERIES AVERAGES
Zimbabwe v. New Zealand

ZIMBABWE

Batting	M	Inns	NO	Runs	HS	Av	100	50	c/st
NB Mahwire	2	4	2	100	50*	50.00	-	1	-/-
BRM Taylor	2	4	0	124	77	31.00	-	1	2/-
T Taibu	2	4	0	110	76	27.50	-	1	4/-
H Masakadza	2	4	0	70	42	17.50	-	-	-/-
NR Ferreira	1	2	0	21	16	10.50	-	-	-/-
KM Dabengwa	1	2	0	21	17	10.50	-	-	-/-
SV Carlisle	2	4	1	31	20*	10.33	-	-	3/-
CB Wishart	2	4	0	35	30	8.75	-	-	-/-
AG Cremer	2	4	1	12	7*	4.00	-	-	1/-
DD Ebrahim	2	4	0	10	8	2.50	-	-	-/-
CB Mpofu	2	4	0	10	7	2.50	-	-	-/-
HH Streak	2	4	0	5	3	1.25	-	-	-/-

Bowling	Overs	Mds	Runs	Wkts	Av	Best	5/inn	10m
HH Streak	45.4	11	175	6	29.16	4-73	-	-
NB Mahwire	51.1	6	236	6	39.33	3-115	-	-
KM Dabengwa	25	2	87	2	43.50	2-87	-	-
CB Mpofu	31.2	2	180	2	90.00	2-100	-	-
AG Cremer	46	1	224	1	224.00	1-113	-	-

Also bowled: BRM Taylor 1-0-14-0.

NEW ZEALAND

Batting	M	Inns	NO	Runs	HS	Av	100	50	c/st
DL Vettori	2	2	0	175	127	87.50	1	-	4/-
NJ Astle	2	2	0	151	128	75.50	1	-	2/-
SP Fleming	2	2	0	138	73	69.00	-	2	4/-
BB McCullum	2	2	0	135	111	67.50	1	-	6/2
L Vincent	2	2	0	105	92	52.50	-	1	-/-
SE Bond	2	2	1	49	41*	49.00	-	-	-/-
SB Styris	2	2	0	52	45	26.00	-	-	1/-
HJH Marshall	2	2	0	33	20	16.50	-	-	-/-
JEC Franklin	2	2	0	32	19	16.00	-	-	-/-
JAH Marshall	2	2	0	15	10	7.50	-	-	2/-
CS Martin	2	2	2	4	4*	-	-	-	2/-

Bowling	Overs	Mds	Runs	Wkts	Av	Best	5/inn	10m
SE Bond	47	15	120	13	9.23	6-51	1	1
DL Vettori	65.4	23	151	11	13.72	4-28	-	-
JEC Franklin	37	8	97	6	16.16	3-11	-	-
CS Martin	43	12	126	6	21.00	3-21	-	-

Also bowled: NJ Astle 11-2-41-0, SB Styris 16-6-41-0.

FIRST TEST – ZIMBABWE v. INDIA
13–16 September 2005 at Bulawayo

ZIMBABWE

	First Innings		Second Innings	
BRM Taylor	c Gambhir b Khan	13	lbw b Pathan	4
T Duffin	lbw b Pathan	56	b Khan	2
H Masakadza	c Karthik b Khan	14	c Kumble b Pathan	2
DD Ebrahim	c & b Pathan	24	b Pathan	1
*T Taibu (capt)	not out	71	c Karthik b Kumble	52
HH Streak	c Dravid b Kumble	27	lbw b Pathan	0
CK Coventry	lbw b Kumble	2	c Gambhir b Harbhajan Singh	24
AM Blignaut	lbw b Khan	4	b Harbhajan Singh	26
KM Dabengwa	c Laxman b Pathan	35	lbw b Harbhajan Singh	16
GM Ewing	lbw b Pathan	0	lbw b Harbhajan Singh	34
NB Mahwire	b Pathan	4	not out	13
Extras	b 1, lb 7, w 1, nb 20	29	b 2, w 2, nb 7	11
	(98.5 overs)	279	(47.5 overs)	185

	First Innings				Second Innings			
	O	M	R	W	O	M	R	W
Pathan	18.5	3	58	5	12	4	53	4
Khan	22	5	74	3	8	1	28	1
Ganguly	1	1	0	0	-	-	-	-
Kumble	26	7	71	2	12	2	43	1
Harbhajan Singh	26	5	55	0	15.5	1	59	4
Sehwag	5	1	13	0	-	-	-	-

Fall of Wickets
1-25, 2-45, 3-119, 4-124, 5-193, 6-197, 7-210, 8-269, 9-269
1-4, 2-9, 3-9, 4-16, 5-18, 6-67, 7-110, 8-130, 9-138

INDIA

	First Innings	
G Gambhir	c Taylor b Mahwire	46
V Sehwag	b Mahwire	44
R Dravid	c Taylor b Mahwire	77
VVS Laxman	run out	140
SC Ganguly (capt)	c Duffin b Ewing	101
Yuvraj Singh	b Dabengwa	12
*KKD Karthik	c Taibu b Blignaut	1
IK Pathan	c and b Dabengwa	52
A Kumble	c Coventry b Dabengwa	17
Harbhajan Singh	c Coventry b Mahwire	37
Z Khan	not out	13
Extras	lb 7, w 3, nb 4	14
	(151.3 overs)	554

	First Innings			
	O	M	R	W
Streak	26	3	91	0
Mahwire	25.3	4	92	4
Blignaut	19	2	96	1
Dabengwa	39	7	127	3
Ewing	42	5	141	1

Fall of Wickets
1-88, 2-98, 3-228, 4-356, 5-372, 6-379, 7-476, 8-502, 9-522

Umpires: Aleem Dar & DJ Harper
Toss: Zimbabwe
Test debuts: CK Coventry, T Duffin
Man of the Match: IK Pathan

India won by an innings and 90 runs

SECOND TEST – ZIMBABWE v. INDIA
20–22 September 2005 at Harare

ZIMBABWE

	First Innings		Second Innings	
BRM Taylor	c Dravid b Pathan	4	lbw b Pathan	4
T Duffin	c Laxman b Pathan	12	c Dravid b Pathan	10
DD Ebrahim	c Karthik b Khan	14	c Yuvraj Singh b Khan	3
*T Taibu (capt)	c Karthik b Pathan	0	(5) c Kumble b Khan	1
H Masakadza	lbw b Pathan	27	(4) lbw b Pathan	71
HH Streak	c Gambhir b Harbhajan Singh	14	c Laxman b Khan	8
CK Coventry	c Dravid b Harbhajan Singh	37	c Ganguly b Pathan	25
AM Blignaut	c Karthik b Pathan	13	not out	84
KM Dabengwa	c Laxman b Pathan	18	c Karthik b Pathan	0
NB Mahwire	lbw b Pathan	1	b Kumble	0
W Mwayenga	not out	14	lbw b Khan	1
Extras	b 1, lb 3, w 1, nb 2	7	b 5, lb 6, w 2, nb 3	16
	(44.2 overs)	161	(55 overs)	223

	First Innings				Second Innings			
	O	M	R	W	O	M	R	W
Pathan	15.2	4	59	7	19	2	67	5
Khan	7	1	24	1	19	4	58	4
Ganguly	4	2	10	0	1	0	8	0
Kumble	7	1	19	0	11	3	52	1
Harbhajan Singh	11	3	45	2	5	0	27	0

Fall of Wickets
1-4, 2-31, 3-31, 4-31, 5-75, 6-83, 7-122, 8-136, 9-138
1-13, 2-18, 3-18, 4-21, 5-42, 6-85, 7-201, 8-201, 9-202

INDIA

	First Innings		Second Innings	
G Gambhir	c Taibu b Mahwire	97	not out	1
V Sehwag	c Taibu b Streak	44	not out	14
R Dravid	b Mahwire	98		
VVS Laxman	lbw b Streak	8		
SC Ganguly (capt)	c Taibu b Mwayenga	16		
Yuvraj Singh	b Streak	25		
*KKD Karthik	b Streak	1		
IK Pathan	c Coventry b Streak	32		
A Kumble	c Ebrahim b Streak	8		
Harbhajan Singh	not out	13		
Z Khan	c Taibu b Blignaut	3		
Extras	b 2, lb 11, nb 8	21	b 4	4
	(107.4 overs)	366	(0 wkts 2.2 overs)	19

	First Innings				Second Innings			
	O	M	R	W	O	M	R	W
Streak	32	10	73	6	-	-	-	-
Mahwire	26	5	86	2	1	0	9	0
Blignaut	19.4	1	80	1	1.2	0	6	0
Mwayenga	21	6	79	1	-	-	-	-
Dabengwa	9	1	35	0	-	-	-	-

Fall of Wickets
1-75, 2-198, 3-219, 4-245, 5-306, 6-306, 7-318, 8-342, 9-361

Umpires: Aleem Dar & DJ Harper
Toss: India
Test debut: W Mwayenga
Man of the Match: IK Pathan
Man of the Series: IK Pathan

India won by 10 wickets

SERIES AVERAGES
Zimbabwe v. India

ZIMBABWE

Batting	M	Inns	NO	Runs	HS	Av	100	50	c/st
AM Blignaut	2	4	1	127	84*	42.33	-	1	-/-
T Taibu	2	4	1	124	71*	41.33	-	2	5/-
H Masakadza	2	4	0	114	71	28.50	-	1	-/-
CK Coventry	2	4	0	88	37	22.00	-	-	3/-
T Duffin	2	4	0	80	56	20.00	-	1	1/-
KM Dabengwa	2	4	0	69	35	17.25	-	-	1/-
GM Ewing	1	2	0	34	34	17.00	-	-	-/-
W Mwayenga	1	2	1	15	14*	15.00	-	-	-/-
HH Streak	2	4	0	49	27	12.25	-	-	-/-
DD Ebrahim	2	4	0	42	24	10.50	-	-	1/-
BRM Taylor	2	4	0	25	13	6.25	-	-	2/-
NB Mahwire	2	4	1	18	13*	6.00	-	-	-/-

Bowling	Overs	Mds	Runs	Wkts	Av	Best	5/inn	10m
HH Streak	58	13	164	6	27.33	6-73	1	-
NB Mahwire	52.3	9	187	6	31.16	4-92	-	-
KM Dabengwa	48	8	162	3	54.00	3-127	-	-
W Mwayenga	21	6	79	1	79.00	1-79	-	-
AM Blignaut	40	3	182	2	91.00	1-80	-	-
GM Ewing	42	5	141	1	141.00	1-141	-	-

INDIA

Batting	M	Inns	NO	Runs	HS	Av	100	50	c/st
R Dravid	2	2	0	175	98	87.50	-	2	4/-
VVS Laxman	2	2	0	148	140	74.00	1	-	4/-
G Gambhir	2	3	1	144	97	72.00	-	1	3/-
SC Ganguly	2	2	0	117	101	58.50	1	-	1/-
V Sehwag	2	3	1	102	44	51.00	-	-	-/-
Harbhajan Singh	2	2	1	50	37	50.00	-	-	-/-
IK Pathan	2	2	0	84	52	42.00	-	1	1/-
Yuvraj Singh	2	2	0	37	25	18.50	-	-	1/-
Z Khan	2	2	1	16	13*	16.00	-	-	-/-
A Kumble	2	2	0	25	17	12.50	-	-	2/-
KKD Karthik	2	2	0	2	1	1.00	-	-	6/-

Bowling	Overs	Mds	Runs	Wkts	Av	Best	5/inn	10m
IK Pathan	65.1	13	237	21	11.28	7-59	3	1
Z Khan	56	11	184	9	20.44	4-58	-	-
Harbhajan Singh	57.5	9	186	6	31.00	4-59	-	-
A Kumble	56	13	185	4	46.25	2-71	-	-
V Sehwag	5	1	13	0	-	-	-	-
SC Ganguly	6	3	18	0	-	-	-	-

AUSTRALIA

AUSTRALIA REPORT
By Jim Maxwell

Adam Gilchrist's worst fears may come to haunt him unless Australia regain the Ashes in 2007. Gilchrist had said prior to the 2005 tour of England that he didn't want to finish his career losing the Ashes. Several careers have already concluded as a result of England's remarkable win, with Damien Martyn, Jason Gillespie and Michael Kasprowicz in limbo in the aftermath of Australia's momentous loss.

These issues, however, were way off the agenda when Australia set off for India in October 2004, hoping to bury a 35-year bogey. And it was Gilchrist who led the team, standing in for Ricky Ponting who had broken his thumb during the Champions Trophy semi-final loss to England on a cold September day at Edgbaston.

Significantly the four-match Test series stood alone, with no prior or post one-dayers included in the itinerary.

Michael Clarke's debut century in Bangalore received plenty of rave notices for dashing strokeplay, and alongside the free-scoring Gilchrist, who hit a run-a-ball hundred, their partnership was the cornerstone of a disciplined performance that grabbed the early initiative from India. Without Tendulkar, recovering from his tennis elbow injury, India's batting lacked authority, and the combined pace of McGrath, Gillespie and Kasprowicz strangled the scoring.

Sehwag's aggressive batting kept India buoyant in the Chennai Test, where Damien Martyn

Adam Gilchrist led Australia to a memorable victory in India as the injured Ricky Ponting's deputy.

Michael Clarke emerged in 2004–05 as a genuine new world-class star, scoring hundreds on Test debut both at home and away.

bowled out for 200. Australia chose not to enforce the follow-on at Nagpur, driven perhaps by the ghosts of Calcutta 2001 still being fresh in the memory, plus the awkward prospect of facing Kumble and Kartik in a fourth-innings chase. Gilchrist had always coveted the captaincy, and in an emotional, demonstrative reaction to Australia's long-awaited victory, led the celebrations.

Ponting returned for the Mumbai Test, but Warne cried off with a thumb fracture, sustained while batting in the nets. The Polly Umrigar-supervised pitch at the Wankhede Stadium, meanwhile, looked underprepared. Justin Langer's inquiries about why the practice pitches were firmer than the centre strip were met with the usual nonsense about 'It will play better than it looks,' and 'It will definitely last five days.' One of the shortest Test matches in history ended in 202 overs, and within three days. The pitch was a

steadied Australia, striking a century in a match unfortunately washed out on the final day, when the result was in the balance. Martyn's impressive, applied batting continued, following up with scores of 114 and 97 in the third Test. McGrath and Gillespie squeezed the life out of India in a showcase exhibition of precision bowling after lunch on the second day of that Nagpur Test.

Gillespie bowled Dravid with a magnificent delivery, bagging a rare five-wicket haul, which became nine for the match when India chased an improbable 543 in the fourth innings and were

farce, and if ever there was a charge of bringing the game into disrepute under the ICC's code of conduct regimen, Mumbai and its perpetrators should have copped a ban.

Australia's pathetic final innings batting, however, chasing only 107, did not help their condemnation of the pitch in the wash-up of a 'great Indian win' by 13 runs, and the folly of not having MacGill on tour as Warne's back-up was confirmed when Tendulkar took to inexperienced off spinner Nathan Hauritz, whose extravagance contrasted bizarrely alongside Michael Clarke's

Shane Warne and Ricky Ponting discuss tactics during the epic 2005 Ashes series in England.

absurd 6 for 9. Fortunately, the result did not change the destination of the Border-Gavaskar Trophy, and given the benefit of hindsight this was Australia's high watermark for 2004–05.

At home Michael Clarke repeated his century on debut performance, against New Zealand, while Gilchrist scored the first of four summer Test hundreds, taking toll of a Kiwi attack that lacked quality pace bowling and relied too much on Vettori's spin.

Australia were omnipotent against both New Zealand and Pakistan. Only a rain-affected draw in Wellington could break a run of overwhelming victories for Ponting's team; margins of an innings and 156 runs, 491 runs, and nine wickets on four occasions, contributed to seven resounding wins in

Glenn McGrath signalled his full recovery from a lengthy injury break by picking up 8 for 24, his Test-best figures, when Australia thrashed Pakistan in Perth.

easily achieved than his maiden Test 50 against New Zealand, where he featured in a century partnership with Jason Gillespie for the last wicket.

New Zealand's only succour was a win in the inaugural Chappell-Hadlee Trophy match, an annual contest designed to maintain continuity between the two countries, in the style of the regular Bledisloe Cup rugby matches. Alas, the series finished in a tie, because the third match was rained off after McGrath and Gillespie had rejoined the Australian team for an equalising win in game two.

One-day games are rarely memorable, so perhaps the individual effort from Kyle Mills should go on the record. He hit four sixes from four balls, providing some sting in the Kiwi tail as they lost by 17 runs in Sydney. Another sidelight that spawned public interest was Mark Richardson's sprint race against Darren Lehmann at the end of the Adelaide Test. Dressed in skin-tight lycra body suits, Green and Gold versus Biege, the battle of the slow men, in support of charity, was easily won by Richardson, who had announced his retirement from Test cricket during another one-sided Test.

Shoaib Akhtar created bursts of excitement, meanwhile, by hurling searing deliveries at the Australian batsmen, until he became reunited with a hamstring injury again after two matches. Pakistan's best chance came in the Boxing Day Test. Defending 341, they had held Australia to

eight matches, with New Zealand's horrible 76 in Brisbane eclipsed by Pakistan's inept 72 in Perth where McGrath recorded his Test best figures of 8 for 24. McGrath's performance was probably more

The match-winner: Damien Martyn's silky elegance brought him 142 against Pakistan at Melbourne.

5 for 171 before Martyn engineered the escape with his accomplice from Chennai, Jason Gillespie, who scored his second Test half-century to Martyn's skilful 142.

Pakistan were beset by an unhappy mix of touring problems; their captain Inzamam-ul-Haq missed two Tests through injury, Akhtar and Mohammad Sami broke down also through injury, there was a rape allegation against one of their players, and after being beaten 2-0 in the one-day finals by Australia, their coach Bob Woolmer came up with a 29-5 statistic of decisions that had gone against the touring team. Australia dropped plenty of slip catches, but the lapses were not costly because they created so many chances.

Across the Tasman, Australia won the first international Twenty20 match, roused by Ricky Ponting's powerful 98 from 55 balls at Eden Park, and the one-day caravan cruised along seamlessly by registering five straight wins. Lee bowled rapidly, menacingly, but still couldn't crack the Test team.

New South Wales tried in vain to get him back for the Pura Cup first-class final, and won somehow without him by one wicket as MacGill and Bracken scrambled to victory over Queensland at the Gabba. In addition, Queensland lost in the limited-overs final to Tasmania, who won their first domestic one-day competition since 1978–79.

Within three months, however, Australia's seemingly impregnable supremacy unravelled; Twenty20, Somerset, Bangladesh, England unlimited in one-day mode, and then, redefining nature, the Ashes were lost in the most sensational series that the game's oldest rivals have ever played.

FIRST TEST – AUSTRALIA v. NEW ZEALAND
18–21 November 2004 at Brisbane

NEW ZEALAND

	First Innings		Second Innings	
MH Richardson	c Ponting b Kasprowicz	19	c Gilchrist b McGrath	4
MS Sinclair	c Ponting b Gillespie	69	lbw b McGrath	0
SP Fleming (capt)	c Warne b Kasprowicz	0	c Langer b McGrath	11
SB Styris	c Gilchrist b Kasprowicz	27	lbw b Warne	7
NJ Astle	run out	19	c Warne b Kasprowicz	17
CD McMillan	c Gilchrist b Warne	23	lbw b Gillespie	9
JDP Oram	not out	126	c Hayden b Warne	8
*BB McCullum	st Gilchrist b Warne	10	c Gilchrist b Gillespie	8
DL Vettori	c Warne b Kasprowicz	21	c Hayden b Warne	2
KD Mills	c Hayden b Warne	29	not out	4
CS Martin	c Ponting b Warne	0	lbw b Warne	0
Extras	b 1, lb 2, w 3, nb 4	10	lb 2, nb 4	6
	(117.3 overs)	353	(36.2 overs)	76

	First Innings				Second Innings			
	O	M	R	W	O	M	R	W
McGrath	27	4	67	0	8	1	19	3
Gillespie	29	7	84	1	10	5	19	2
Kasprowicz	28	5	90	4	8	2	21	1
Warne	29.3	3	97	4	10.2	3	15	4
Lehmann	4	0	12	0	-	-	-	-

Fall of Wickets
1-26, 2-26, 3-77, 4-138, 5-138, 6-180, 7-206, 8-264, 9-317
1-6, 2-7, 3-19, 4-42, 5-44, 6-55, 7-69, 8-72, 9-72

AUSTRALIA

	First Innings	
JL Langer	lbw b Vettori	34
ML Hayden	lbw b Mills	8
RT Ponting (capt)	c Astle b Martin	51
DR Martyn	c McMillan b Martin	70
DS Lehmann	c McCullum b Vettori	8
MJ Clarke	b Vettori	141
*AC Gilchrist	c Styris b Martin	126
SK Warne	lbw b Vettori	10
JN Gillespie	not out	54
MS Kasprowicz	c Mills b Martin	5
GD McGrath	c Astle b Martin	61
Extras	b 1, lb 7, w 1, nb 8	17
	(153.5 overs)	585

	First Innings			
	O	M	R	W
Martin	39.5	7	152	5
Mills	26	8	99	1
Styris	8	1	33	0
Oram	25	4	116	0
Vettori	50	9	154	4
McMillan	5	1	23	0

Fall of Wickets
1-16, 2-85, 3-109, 4-128, 5-222, 6-438, 7-450, 8-464, 9-471

Umpires: SA Bucknor & Aleem Dar
Toss: New Zealand
Man of the Match: MJ Clarke

Australia won by an innings and 156 runs

SECOND TEST – AUSTRALIA v. NEW ZEALAND
26–30 November 2004 at Adelaide

AUSTRALIA

	First Innings		Second Innings	
JL Langer	c Oram b Vettori	215	lbw b Wiseman	46
ML Hayden	c & b Wiseman	70	c McCullum b Vettori	54
RT Ponting (capt)	st McCullum b Vettori	68	not out	26
DR Martyn	c Fleming b Wiseman	7	not out	6
DS Lehmann	b Wiseman	81		
MJ Clarke	lbw b Vettori	7		
*AC Gilchrist	c & b Vettori	50		
SK Warne	not out	53		
JN Gillespie	c Richardson b Vettori	12		
MS Kasprowicz				
GD McGrath				
Extras	b 4, lb 4, nb 4	12	lb 6, nb 1	7
	(8 wkts dec 155.2 overs)	575	(2 wkts dec 56 overs)	139

	First Innings				Second Innings			
	O	M	R	W	O	M	R	W
Martin	27	4	118	0	6	1	11	0
Franklin	17	2	102	0	5	0	18	0
Oram	24	7	55	0	5	1	17	0
Vettori	55.2	10	152	5	18	2	35	1
Wiseman	32	7	140	3	22	3	52	1

Fall of Wickets
1-137, 2-240, 3-261, 4-445, 5-457, 6-465, 7-543, 8-575
1-93, 2-119

NEW ZEALAND

	First Innings		Second Innings	
MH Richardson	b Kasprowicz	9	c Langer b Kasprowicz	16
MS Sinclair	c Warne b Gillespie	0	lbw b Gillespie	2
SP Fleming (capt)	c Gilchrist b McGrath	83	b McGrath	3
PJ Wiseman	lbw b Kasprowicz	11	(10) not out	15
NJ Astle	c Langer b McGrath	52	c Langer b Lehmann	38
JDP Oram	c Gilchrist b Gillespie	12	c Gilchrist b McGrath	40
*BB McCullum	lbw b Gillespie	10	lbw b Gillespie	36
DL Vettori	lbw b McGrath	20	c Gillespie b Lehmann	59
JEC Franklin	lbw b Warne	7	c Gilchrist b Kasprowicz	13
SB Styris	c Clarke b McGrath	28	(4) c Clarke b Warne	8
CS Martin	not out	2	c Ponting b Warne	2
Extras	b 3, lb 5, nb 9	17	b 1, lb 12, nb 5	18
	(88.1 overs)	251	(82.3 overs)	250

	First Innings				Second Innings			
	O	M	R	W	O	M	R	W
McGrath	20.1	3	66	4	12	2	32	2
Gillespie	19	4	37	3	16	5	41	2
Warne	28	5	65	1	27.3	6	79	2
Kasprowicz	16	3	66	2	14	4	39	2
Lehmann	5	2	9	0	13	0	46	2

Fall of Wickets
1-2, 2-44, 3-80, 4-153, 5-178, 6-183, 7-190, 8-213, 9-242
1-11, 2-18, 3-34, 4-34, 5-97, 6-150, 7-160, 8-206, 9-243

Umpires: SA Bucknor & DR Shepherd
Toss: Australia
Man of the Match: JL Langer
Man of the Series: GD McGrath

Australia won by 213 runs

SERIES AVERAGES
Australia v. New Zealand

AUSTRALIA

Batting	M	Inns	NO	Runs	HS	Av	100	50	c/st
JL Langer	2	3	0	295	215	98.33	1	-	4/-
AC Gilchrist	2	2	0	176	126	88.00	1	1	8/1
MJ Clarke	2	2	0	148	141	74.00	1	-	2/-
RT Ponting	2	3	1	145	68	72.50	-	2	4/-
JN Gillespie	2	2	1	66	54*	66.00	-	1	1/-
SK Warne	2	2	1	63	53*	63.00	-	1	4/-
GD McGrath	2	1	0	61	61	61.00	-	1	-/-
DS Lehmann	2	2	0	89	81	44.50	-	1	-/-
ML Hayden	2	3	0	132	70	44.00	-	2	3/-
DR Martyn	2	3	1	83	70	41.50	-	1	-/-
MS Kasprowicz	2	1	0	5	5	5.00	-	-	-/-

Bowling	Overs	Mds	Runs	Wkts	Av	Best	5/inn	10m
GD McGrath	67.1	10	184	9	20.44	4-66	-	-
JN Gillespie	74	21	181	8	22.62	3-37	-	-
SK Warne	95.2	17	256	11	23.27	4-15	-	-
MS Kasprowicz	66	14	216	9	24.00	4-90	-	-
DS Lehmann	22	2	67	2	33.50	2-46	-	-

NEW ZEALAND

Batting	M	Inns	NO	Runs	HS	Av	100	50	c/st
JDP Oram	2	4	1	186	126	62.00	1	-	1/-
KD Mills	1	2	1	33	29	33.00	-	-	1/-
NJ Astle	2	4	0	126	52	31.50	-	1	2/-
PJ Wiseman	1	2	1	26	15*	26.00	-	-	1/-
DL Vettori	2	4	0	102	59	25.50	-	1	1/-
SP Fleming	2	4	0	97	83	24.25	-	1	1/-
MS Sinclair	2	4	0	71	69	17.75	-	1	-/-
SB Styris	2	4	0	70	28	17.50	-	-	1/-
CD McMillan	1	2	0	32	23	16.00	-	-	1/-
BB McCullum	2	4	0	64	36	16.00	-	-	2/1
MH Richardson	2	4	0	48	19	12.00	-	-	1/-
JEC Franklin	1	2	0	20	13	10.00	-	-	-/-
CS Martin	2	4	1	4	2*	1.33	-	-	-/-

Bowling	Overs	Mds	Runs	Wkts	Av	Best	5/inn	10m
DL Vettori	123.2	21	341	10	34.10	5-152	1	-
PJ Wiseman	54	10	192	4	48.00	3-140	-	-
CS Martin	72.5	12	281	5	56.20	5-152	1	-
KD Mills	26	8	99	1	99.00	1-99	-	-

Also bowled: CD McMillan 5-1-23-0, SB Styris 8-1-33-0, JEC Franklin 22-2-120-0, JDP Oram 54-12-188-0.

ONE-DAY INTERNATIONALS
v. New Zealand

Match One
5 December 2004 at Melbourne
Australia 246 for 9 (50 overs) (AC Gilchrist 68, DS Lehmann 50)
New Zealand 247 for 6 (49.4 overs) (NJ Astle 70, HJH Marshall 50*)
New Zealand won by 4 wickets

Match Two
8 December 2004 at Sydney
Australia 261 for 7 (50 overs) (AC Gilchrist 60, DS Lehmann 52)
New Zealand 244 (47.1 overs) (CL Cairns 50)
Australia won by 17 runs

Match Three
10 December 2004 at Brisbane
Australia v. **New Zealand**
Match abandoned

FIRST TEST – AUSTRALIA v. PAKISTAN
16–19 December 2004 at Perth

AUSTRALIA

	First Innings		Second Innings	
JL Langer	c Younis Khan b Mohammad Sami	191	b Abdul Razzaq	97
ML Hayden	lbw b Shoaib Akhtar	4	b Shoaib Akhtar	10
RT Ponting (capt)	b Mohammad Sami	25	st Kamran Akmal b D Kaneria	98
DR Martyn	c Kamran Akmal b M Sami	1	not out	100
DS Lehmann	b Shoaib Akhtar	12	b Danish Kaneria	5
MJ Clarke	c Inzamam-ul-Haq b S Akhtar	1	c Inzamam-ul-Haq b M Sami	27
*AC Gilchrist	b Abdul Razzaq	69	not out	0
SK Warne	c Yousuf Youhana b A Razzaq	12		
JN Gillespie	c Kamran Akmal b S Akhtar	24		
MS Kasprowicz	lbw b Shoaib Akhtar	4		
GD McGrath	not out	8		
Extras	b 1, lb 14, w 5, nb 10	30	lb 15, w 2, nb 7	24
	(90.5 overs)	381	(5 wkts dec 85.2 overs)	361

	First Innings				Second Innings			
	O	M	R	W	O	M	R	W
Shoaib Akhtar	22	1	99	5	6.3	1	22	1
Mohammad Sami	25.5	3	104	3	14	1	55	1
Mohammad Khalil	16	0	59	0	9.2	0	38	0
Abdul Razzaq	12	0	55	2	12.3	1	48	1
Danish Kaneria	15	2	49	0	32	3	130	2
Imran Farhat	-	-	-	-	11	0	53	0

Fall of Wickets
1-6, 2-56, 3-58, 4-71, 5-78, 6-230, 7-253, 8-333, 9-362
1-28, 2-191, 3-271, 4-281, 5-360

PAKISTAN

	First Innings		Second Innings	
Salman Butt	c Gilchrist b Kasprowicz	17	c Hayden b McGrath	9
Imran Farhat	c Gilchrist b Gillespie	18	lbw b McGrath	1
Younis Khan	c Gillespie b Warne	42	c Warne b McGrath	17
Inzamam-ul-Haq (capt)	b Kasprowicz	1	(6) c Gilchrist b McGrath	0
Yousuf Youhana	c Gilchrist b Kasprowicz	1	(4) c Gilchrist b McGrath	27
Abdul Razzaq	b Warne	21	(5) c Gilchrist b McGrath	1
*Kamran Akmal	b Kasprowicz	2	c Clarke b McGrath	0
Mohammad Sami	c Clarke b Kasprowicz	29	b Kasprowicz	2
Mohammad Khalil	b Warne	0	(10) c & b Kasprowicz	5
Shoaib Akhtar	c Warne b McGrath	27	(9) c Lehmann b McGrath	1
Danish Kaneria	not out	6	not out	0
Extras	b 1, lb 3, w 7, nb 4	15	lb 7, w 2	9
	(77.3 overs)	179	(31.3 overs)	72

	First Innings				Second Innings			
	O	M	R	W	O	M	R	W
McGrath	19	7	44	1	16	8	24	8
Gillespie	14	2	43	1	12	3	37	0
Kasprowicz	16.3	6	30	5	3.3	2	4	2
Warne	21	9	38	3	-	-	-	-
Lehmann	4	2	5	0	-	-	-	-
Ponting	3	1	15	0	-	-	-	-

Fall of Wickets
1-32, 2-45, 3-55, 4-60, 5-108, 6-110, 7-110, 8-111, 9-171
1-5, 2-34, 3-43, 4-49, 5-49, 6-61, 7-64, 8-66, 9-72

Umpires: BF Bowden & RE Koertzen
Toss: Pakistan
Test debut: Mohammad Khalil
Man of the Match: JL Langer

Australia won by 491 runs

SECOND TEST – AUSTRALIA v. PAKISTAN
26–29 December 2004 at Melbourne

PAKISTAN

	First Innings		Second Innings	
Salman Butt	run out	70	c Kasprowicz b McGrath	0
Imran Farhat	c Ponting b Kasprowicz	20	c Martyn b Gillespie	5
Yasir Hameed	lbw b Gillespie	2	c Gilchrist b McGrath	23
Younis Khan	c Gilchrist b Gillespie	87	c Hayden b Kasprowicz	23
Yousuf Youhana (capt)	st Gilchrist b Warne	111	c Ponting b Warne	12
Shoaib Malik	c Ponting b Gillespie	6	c Gillespie b Warne	41
Abdul Razzaq	not out	4	(8) c Gilchrist b McGrath	19
*Kamran Akmal	c Gilchrist b McGrath	24	(9) lbw b Warne	0
Mohammad Sami	lbw b Warne	12	(7) lbw b Gillespie	11
Shoaib Akhtar	st Gilchrist b Warne	0	b McGrath	14
Danish Kaneria	run out	0	not out	9
Extras	lb 4, w 1	5	b 4, lb 1, nb 1	6
	(107.3 overs)	341	(64.2 overs)	163

	First Innings				Second Innings			
	O	M	R	W	O	M	R	W
McGrath	28	12	54	1	11.2	1	35	4
Gillespie	26	7	77	3	12	7	15	2
Kasprowicz	20	6	66	1	16	3	42	1
Warne	28.3	2	103	3	25	7	66	3
Clarke	3	0	24	0	-	-	-	-
Lehmann	2	0	13	0	-	-	-	-

Fall of Wickets
1-85, 2-93, 3-94, 4-286, 5-298, 6-301, 7-326, 8-341, 9-341
1-0, 2-13, 3-35, 4-60, 5-68, 6-98, 7-101, 8-140, 9-140

AUSTRALIA

	First Innings		Second Innings	
JL Langer	c Imran Farhat b Danish Kaneria	50	c Kamran Akmal b M Sami	5
ML Hayden	c Shoaib Malik b Shoaib Akhtar	9	not out	56
RT Ponting (capt)	c Shoaib Malik b Shoaib Akhtar	7	not out	62
DR Martyn	lbw b Danish Kaneria	142		
DS Lehmann	c Yasir Hameed b Shoaib Akhtar	11		
MJ Clarke	c Shoaib Akhtar b D Kaneria	20		
*AC Gilchrist	c Mohammad Sami b D Kaneria	48		
SK Warne	c & b Shoaib Akhtar	10		
JN Gillespie	not out	50		
MS Kasprowicz	c sub b Shoaib Akhtar	4		
GD McGrath	lbw b Danish Kaneria	1		
Extras	b 1, lb 2, w 5, nb 19	27	lb 2, nb 2	4
	(99.3 overs)	379	(1 wkt 27.5 overs)	127

	First Innings				Second Innings			
	O	M	R	W	O	M	R	W
Shoaib Akhtar	27	4	109	5	7	0	35	0
Mohammad Sami	23	2	102	0	5	0	22	1
Abdul Razzaq	7	0	27	0	-	-	-	-
Danish Kaneria	39.3	5	125	5	10.5	1	52	0
Imran Farhat	3	0	13	0	5	2	16	0

Fall of Wickets
1-13, 2-32, 3-122, 4-135, 5-171, 6-230, 7-254, 8-347, 9-368
1-11

Umpires: RE Koertzen & JW Lloyds
Toss: Pakistan
Man of the Match: DR Martyn

Australia won by 9 wickets

THIRD TEST – AUSTRALIA v. PAKISTAN
2–5 January 2005 at Sydney

PAKISTAN

	First Innings			Second Innings	
Salman Butt	c Gilchrist b McGrath	108		c Warne b MacGill	21
Yasir Hameed	c Clarke b Warne	58		lbw b Warne	63
Younis Khan	c McGrath b MacGill	46		lbw b Watson	44
Yousuf Youhana (capt)	c Warne b MacGill	8		b MacGill	30
Asim Kamal	c Gillespie b MacGill	10		c Ponting b Gillespie	87
Shahid Afridi	c McGrath b MacGill	12		run out	46
*Kamran Akmal	c Warne b McGrath	47		c Hayden b Warne	4
Naved-ul-Hasan	lbw b McGrath	0		lbw b Warne	9
Shoaib Akhtar	b McGrath	0		c Martyn b Warne	0
Danish Kaneria	c Gilchrist b MacGill	3		b MacGill	0
Mohammad Asif	not out	0		not out	12
Extras	b 6, lb 2, w 1, nb 3	12		b 4, lb 3, nb 2	9
	(86.4 overs)	304		(89.2 overs)	325

	First Innings				Second Innings			
	O	M	R	W	O	M	R	W
McGrath	16.4	5	50	4	16	2	53	0
Gillespie	14	3	47	0	13.2	2	39	1
Watson	10	3	28	0	9	2	32	1
Warne	24	4	84	1	26	2	111	4
MacGill	22	4	87	5	25	3	83	3

Fall of Wickets
1-102, 2-193, 3-209, 4-241, 5-241, 6-261, 7-261, 8-261, 9-280
1-46, 2-104, 3-164, 4-164, 5-238, 6-243, 7-261, 8-269, 9-270

AUSTRALIA

	First Innings			Second Innings	
JL Langer	b Naved-ul-Hasan	13		b Danish Kaneria	34
ML Hayden	b Danish Kaneria	26		not out	23
RT Ponting (capt)	b Naved-ul-Hasan	207		not out	4
DR Martyn	st Kamran Akmal b D Kaneria	67			
MJ Clarke	st Kamran Akmal b D Kaneria	35			
*AC Gilchrist	st Kamran Akmal b D Kaneria	113			
SR Watson	c Mohammad Asif b D Kaneria	31			
SK Warne	c Younis Khan b D Kaneria	16			
JN Gillespie	lbw b Naved-ul-Hasan	0			
GD McGrath	c Yousuf Youhana b D Kaneria	9			
SCG MacGill	not out	9			
Extras	b 6, lb 13, w 3, nb 20	42		nb 1	1
	(133.3 overs)	568		(1 wkt 9.3 overs)	62

	First Innings				Second Innings			
	O	M	R	W	O	M	R	W
Shoaib Akhtar	15	2	69	0	-	-	-	-
Naved-ul-Hasan	26	3	107	3	3	0	28	0
Mohammad Asif	16	3	72	0	2	0	16	0
Danish Kaneria	49.3	7	188	7	2.3	0	16	1
Shahid Afridi	27	3	113	0	2	0	2	0

Fall of Wickets
1-26, 2-83, 3-257, 4-318, 5-471, 6-529, 7-535, 8-537, 9-556
1-58

Umpires: BF Bowden & DR Shepherd
Toss: Pakistan
Test debuts: SR Watson, Mohammad Asif
Man of the Match: SCG MacGill
Man of the Series: DR Martyn

Australia won by 9 wickets

SERIES AVERAGES
Australia v. Pakistan

AUSTRALIA

Batting	M	Inns	NO	Runs	HS	Av	100	50	c/st
DR Martyn	3	4	1	310	142	103.33	2	1	2/-
RT Ponting	3	6	2	403	207	100.75	1	2	4/-
AC Gilchrist	3	4	1	230	113	76.66	1	1	12/2
JL Langer	3	6	0	390	191	65.00	1	2	-/-
JN Gillespie	3	3	1	74	50*	37.00	-	1	3/-
ML Hayden	3	6	2	128	56*	32.00	-	1	3/-
SR Watson	1	1	0	31	31	31.00	-	-	-/-
MJ Clarke	3	4	0	83	35	20.75	-	-	3/-
SK Warne	3	3	0	38	16	12.66	-	-	5/-
DS Lehmann	2	3	0	28	12	9.33	-	-	1/-
GD McGrath	3	3	1	18	9	9.00	-	-	2/-
MS Kasprowicz	2	2	0	8	4	4.00	-	-	2/-
SCG MacGill	1	1	1	9	9*	-	-	-	-/-

Bowling	Overs	Mds	Runs	Wkts	Av	Best	5/inn	10m
GD McGrath	107	35	260	18	14.44	8-24	1	-
MS Kasprowicz	56	17	142	9	15.77	5-30	1	-
SCG MacGill	47	7	170	8	21.25	5-87	1	-
SK Warne	124.3	24	402	14	28.71	4-111	-	-
JN Gillespie	91.2	24	258	7	36.85	3-77	-	-
SR Watson	19	5	60	1	60.00	1-32	-	-

Also bowled: RT Ponting 3-1-15-0, DS Lehmann 6-2-18-0, MJ Clarke 3-0-24-0.

PAKISTAN

Batting	M	Inns	NO	Runs	HS	Av	100	50	c/st
Asim Kamal	1	2	0	97	87	48.50	-	1	-/-
Younis Khan	3	6	0	259	87	43.16	-	1	2/-
Salman Butt	3	6	0	225	108	37.50	1	1	-/-
Yasir Hameed	2	4	0	146	63	36.50	-	2	1/-
Yousuf Youhana	3	6	0	189	111	31.50	1	-	2/-
Shahid Afridi	1	2	0	58	46	29.00	-	-	-/-
Shoaib Malik	1	2	0	47	41	23.50	-	-	2/-
Abdul Razzaq	2	4	1	45	21	15.00	-	-	-/-
Mohammad Sami	2	4	0	54	29	13.50	-	-	1/-
Kamran Akmal	3	6	0	77	47	12.83	-	-	3/4
Imran Farhat	2	4	0	44	20	11.00	-	-	1/-
Shoaib Akhtar	3	6	0	42	27	7.00	-	-	2/-
Danish Kaneria	3	6	3	18	9*	6.00	-	-	-/-
Naved-ul-Hasan	1	2	0	9	9	4.50	-	-	-/-
Mohammad Khalil	1	2	0	5	5	2.50	-	-	-/-
Inzamam-ul-Haq	1	2	0	1	1	0.50	-	-	2/-
Mohammad Asif	1	2	2	12	12*	-	-	-	1/-

Bowling	Overs	Mds	Runs	Wkts	Av	Best	5/inn	10m
Shoaib Akhtar	77.3	8	334	11	30.36	5-99	2	-
Danish Kaneria	149.2	18	560	15	37.33	7-188	2	-
Abdul Razzaq	31.3	1	130	3	43.33	2-55	-	-
Naved-ul-Hasan	29	3	135	3	45.00	3-107	-	-
Mohammad Sami	67.5	6	283	5	56.60	3-104	-	-

Also bowled: Imran Farhat 19-2-82-0, Mohammad Asif 18-3-88-0,
Mohammad Khalil 25.2-0-97-0, Shahid Afridi 29-3-115-0.

VB SERIES
(Australia, Pakistan and West Indies)

Match One
14 January 2005 at Melbourne
Australia 301 for 4 (50 overs)
(DR Martyn 95*, RT Ponting 78,
MJ Clarke 66)
West Indies 185 (46.2 overs)
(BC Lara 58, GB Hogg 5 for 32)
Australia won by 116 runs

Match Two
16 January 2005 at Hobart
Pakistan 272 for 7 (50 overs) (Inzamam-ul-Haq 68,
Salman Butt 61, Shahid Afridi 56*)
Australia 253 for 6 (43 overs) (MJ Clarke 97)
*Australia won by 4 wickets – DL Method: target 253
from 45 overs*

Match Three
19 January 2005 at Brisbane
West Indies 273 for 5 (50 overs)
(CH Gayle 82, RR Sarwan 76)
Pakistan 274 for 4 (47 overs)
(Kamran Akmal 124, Inzamam-ul-Haq 62*,
Shoaib Malik 60)
Pakistan won by 6 wickets

Match Four
21 January 2005 at Brisbane
West Indies 263 for 9 (50 overs)
(WW Hinds 107)
Australia 43 for 5 (11 overs)
Match abandoned – no result

Match Five
23 January 2005 at Sydney
Pakistan 163 (39.2 overs)
(Inzamam-ul-Haq 50)
Australia 167 for 1 (36.2 overs)
(MJ Clarke 103*)
Australia won by 9 wickets

Match Six
26 January 2005 at Adelaide
Australia 269 for 8 (50 overs)
(SM Katich 76, PT Collins 5 for 43)
West Indies 196 (44.5 overs)
(S Chanderpaul 55, B Lee 4 for 38)
Australia won by 73 runs

Match Seven
28 January 2005 at Adelaide
West Indies 339 for 4 (50 overs)
(BC Lara 156, S Chanderpaul 85)
Pakistan 281 for 9 (50 overs)
West Indies won by 58 runs

More runs for Ricky Ponting, as he reached 78 in
the first VB Series match against the West Indies
at Melbourne.

Ramnaresh Sarwan scored 76 and 87 against Pakistan in the VB Series, but the West Indies did not qualify for the final after winning just one of their six group matches.

Match Eight
30 January 2005 at Perth
Australia 265 (50 overs) (MJ Clarke 75*,
Abdul Razzaq 4 for 53)
Pakistan 268 for 7 (47.2 overs) (Yousuf Youhana 72,
Abdul Razzaq 63*)
Pakistan won by 3 wickets

Match Nine
1 February 2005 at Perth
Pakistan 307 for 8 (50 overs) (Yousuf Youhana 105,
Inzamam-ul-Haq 74)
West Indies 277 (48.1 overs) (RR Sarwan 87,
S Chanderpaul 58, Naved-ul-Hasan 4 for 29)
Pakistan won by 30 runs

First Final
4 February 2005 at Melbourne
Australia 237 (49 overs) (A Symonds 91,
DR Martyn 53)
Pakistan 219 for 9 (50 overs) (Shoaib Malik 66,
Inzamam-ul-Haq 51)
Australia won by 18 runs

Second Final
6 February 2005 at Sydney
Australia 239 for 9 (50 overs)
Pakistan 208 (45.4 overs) (Yousuf Youhana 51,
GD McGrath 5 for 27)
Australia won by 31 runs

	P	W	L	T	NR	RR	Pts
Australia	6	4	1	0	1	1.08	27
Pakistan	6	3	3	0	0	-0.29	17
West Indies	6	1	4	0	1	-0.71	10

BANGLADESH

BANGLADESH REPORT
By Qamar Ahmed

It was quite a year for Bangladesh, featuring a historic first Test win and, even more remarkably, a one-day victory over Australia that will reverberate for years and give cricket in the youngest Test nation a tremendous boost. Though bottom of the league of Test-playing nations, Bangladesh realised their dream of a victory in Test cricket when to their glee they managed to beat the visiting Zimbabweans by 226 runs at Chittagong. Later in that the series, too, they hung on for a draw in the Dhaka Test.

Their joy needed no prompting as their ecstatic supporters and countrymen celebrated their long-awaited first Test victory. The whole country came to a standstill as people sang and danced in the streets and congratulations poured in. Among the messages was one from their Prime Minister, Begum Khalida Zia. Their achievement was made even more memorable as, later during the Zimbabwe visit, Bangladesh also won their first one-day international series – beating the humbled Zimbabweans 3-2. Earlier, moreover, Bangladesh had also won a famous one-day international at home to India.

Whereas New Zealand had taken 26 years for their first win in a Test, and India 20 years, Bangladesh had achieved this feat within five years

of being accepted as a full member of the ICC. Since their elevation in 2000, Bangladesh had played 34 Tests. After 2-0 defeats against both New Zealand and India in previous Test series this year, this was a massive breakthrough for Bangladesh.

Their historic victory by 226 runs, at Chittagong, came after they had piled up an impressive 488 in

Habibul Bashar, the dedicated captain of Bangladesh and also their most consistent batsman.

the first innings to dominate a weakened Zimbabwe team whose Test programme had been suspended earlier in the year and who were playing in their first Test since being reinstated. Bangladesh's first innings score was based on a fine 94 by captain Habib-ul-Bashar and half-centuries from Nafis Iqbal (56), Rajin Saleh (89) and Mohammad Rafique (69).

Captain Tatenda Taibu's 92 and Elton Chigumbura's 71 in Zimbabwe's reply, however, did not stop Bangladesh taking a lead of 176 runs on the first innings. Bashar struck another neat 50 in the second knock to declare at 204 for 9 and set Zimbabwe 381 runs to win.

The tourists were bowled out for only 154 in the second innings as left-arm spinner Enamul Haque picked up six wickets for 45 runs. Zimbabwe, on 46 for 3 overnight, lost Hamilton Masakadza, Brendon Taylor and Taibu in the first session on the final day as Haque dented their ranks even further to clinch a memorable victory.

In the second Test, at Dhaka, Bangladesh needed 374 to win and were reduced to 206 for 5 with 26 overs remaining on the final day. But Rajin Saleh with 56, and Khalid Mashud (28) added 79 for the sixth wicket to earn a draw and with it the series. Nafis Iqbal's 121, his maiden century in a Test, was another bonus for Bangladeshi cricket, while the other features of the drawn Test were 153 by Taibu, his first hundred at that level and spinner Enamul Haque's bag of 12 wickets for 200 in the match.

Earlier in the season Bangladesh had lost both the Tests and the one-day series to the visiting New Zealanders and also had conceded the two-Test series to India and also the three-match one-day series – but not before they had won that one-day international against the Indians.

At Dhaka, against New Zealand, they lost the first Test by an innings and 99 runs. James Franklin, the medium-pace bowler, had destroyed them with 5 for 28 in the first innings and left-arm spinner Daniel Vettori was the chief destroyer with 5 for 28 in the second.

In the second Test the story was not much different as Stephen Fleming hammered a double-century (202) in New Zealand's first innings 545. After following on 363 runs behind, the home team were bowled out twice with Vettori helping himself with hauls of 6 for 70 and 6 for 100 to finish with 12 for 170 in the match. The margin of defeat was an innings and 101 runs.

The pattern of defeat was similar against India. The first Test at Dhaka was lost by an innings and 140 runs. After being bowled out for 184 in the first innings, they were punished by the Indian batsmen to the tune of 526 with Sachin Tendulkar making 248 with 35 fours to equal his compatriot Sunil Gavaskar's record of 34 centuries in Tests. Bangladesh, 342 runs in arrears, failed to perform any better after following on. They were out for 202 in the second innings as Irfan Pathan picked up six wickets for 51 to finish with 11 wickets for 96 runs in the match. Anil Kumble also reached a notable landmark, passing Kapil Dev's tally of 434 Test wickets.

In the second Test at Chittagong the tourists won by an innings and 83 runs. Gautum Gambhir (139) and Rahul Dravid (160) were the main contributors to India's 540 in the first innings. Bangladesh were rallied by Mohammad Ashraful's unbeaten 158, in which he struck 24 boundaries and three sixes, and replied with a respectable 333. But in their second innings they succumbed to Pathan to be out for 124 as the left-arm fast bowler grabbed five wickets for 32 to have a haul of 18 wickets in the series.

And so to the tour of England, and the incredible win against Australia in Cardiff, during the NatWest Series, which completed a roller-coaster ride of a year for Bangladesh cricket.

The capitulation in the two Tests played on their first tour to England was predictable in the early-summer English conditions, but any disappointment at that was more than compensated for by the scenes at Cardiff's Sophia Gardens – and in the wider Bangladeshi communities. Ashraful made a wonderful 100 from just 101 deliveries to win his country a historic five-wicket victory with just four balls to spare.

On the domestic front Dhaka retained the National first-class competition by gaining 43 points in ten matches and Rajshahi ended as the runners-up with 40 points in as many games.

Golam Rahman, of Sylhet, scored 825 runs at an average of 51.56 and was the most successful batsman in the first-class matches while Alamgir Kabir, with 45 wickets at an average of 18.80, was the top bowler.

In the national one-day league Rajshahi emerged as the champions and Sylhet the runners-up. Forhad Reza of Rajshahi made 340 runs at an average of 34 and Manjurul Islam of Khulna and Hasibul Hossain of Sylhet, with 17 wickets each, were the highest wicket-takers.

Overleaf: Bangladesh celebrate their momentous win over Australia at Cardiff in the NatWest Series.

FIRST TEST – BANGLADESH v. NEW ZEALAND
19–22 October 2004 at Dhaka

BANGLADESH

	First Innings			Second Innings	
Hannan Sarkar	c Fleming b Oram	0	(3) c & b Vettori	1
Javed Omar	b Franklin	1	c McCullum b Vettori	14
Nafees Iqbal	c McCullum b Oram	1	(1) run out	49
Rajin Saleh	c Oram b Franklin	41	c McCullum b Vettori	0
Mohammad Ashraful	c Astle b Vettori	67	c Styris b Vettori	26
Alok Kapali	c McCullum b Vettori	14	c McCullum b Wiseman	0
*Khaled Mashud (capt)	not out	23	c Styris b Wiseman	2
Manjural Islam Rana	c McCullum b Franklin	16	c Richardson b Vettori	1
Mohammad Rafique	c Styris b Franklin	0	c Fleming b Wiseman	24
Tapash Baisya	b Franklin	0	(11) not out	0
Tareq Aziz	c Astle b Oram	0	(10) lbw b Vettori	0
Extras	lb 7, w 1, nb 6	14	b 6, nb 3	9
	(98.5 overs)	177	(54.5 overs)	126

	First Innings				Second Innings			
	O	M	R	W	O	M	R	W
Oram	22.5	9	36	3	7	4	6	0
Franklin	17	7	28	5	5	1	14	0
Styris	2	1	4	0	-	-	-	-
Butler	12	3	34	0	4	1	8	0
Vettori	29	15	26	2	22	13	28	6
Wiseman	16	5	42	0	16.5	1	64	3

Fall of Wickets
1-0, 2-5, 3-5, 4-120, 5-124, 6-136, 7-165, 8-165, 9-165
1-27, 2-33, 3-41, 4-87, 5-88, 6-92, 7-101, 8-112, 9-122

NEW ZEALAND

	First Innings	
MH Richardson	c Khaled Mashud b M Rafique	15
MS Sinclair	lbw b M Rafique	76
SP Fleming (capt)	c K Mashud b M Islam Rana	29
SB Styris	c Rajin Saleh b M Islam Rana	2
NJ Astle	c M Islam Rana b M Rafique	11
JDP Oram	c M Islam Rana b M Rafique	23
*BB McCullum	c Alok Kapali b M Rafique	143
DL Vettori	c Nafees Iqbal b M Islam Rana	23
JEC Franklin	c Rajin Saleh b Tapash Baisya	23
PJ Wiseman	b Mohammad Rafique	28
IG Butler	not out	15
Extras	b 3, lb 5, w 4, nb 2	14
	(145.1 overs)	402

	First Innings			
	O	M	R	W
Tapash Baisya	28	4	112	1
Tareq Aziz	12	1	59	0
Mohammad Rafique	59.1	18	122	6
Manjural Islam Rana	42	12	84	3
Rajin Saleh	1	0	4	0
Alok Kapali	2	0	6	0
Mohammad Ashraful	1	0	7	0

Fall of Wickets
1-34, 2-97, 3-99, 4-122, 5-139, 6-223, 7-294, 8-351, 9-371

Umpires: MR Benson & DJ Harper
Toss: Bangladesh
Test debut: Nafees Iqbal
Man of the Match: BB McCullum

New Zealand won by an innings and 99 runs

SECOND TEST – BANGLADESH v. NEW ZEALAND
26–29 October 2004 at Chittagong

NEW ZEALAND

	First Innings	
MH Richardson	c M Rahman b Enamul Haque jnr	28
MS Sinclair	b Mohammad Rafique	23
SP Fleming (capt)	c M Rahman b Rajin Saleh	202
SB Styris	c & b Mohammad Rafique	89
NJ Astle	lbw b Mohammad Rafique	39
HJH Marshall	c T Baisya b Enamul Haque jnr	69
JDP Oram	not out	38
*BB McCullum	not out	17
DL Vettori		
JEC Franklin		
PJ Wiseman		
Extras	b 9, lb 11, w 2, nb 18	40
	(6 wkts dec 152 overs)	545

	First Innings			
	O	M	R	W
Tapash Baisya	17	0	82	0
Mushfiqur Rahman	15	1	68	0
Mohammad Rafique	55	12	130	3
Enamul Haque jnr	42	4	142	2
Rajin Saleh	19	0	81	1
Mohammad Ashraful	1	0	5	0
Alok Kapali	3	0	17	0

Fall of Wickets
1-49, 2-61, 3-265, 4-364, 5-447, 6-517

BANGLADESH

	First Innings			Second Innings	
Nafees Iqbal	c Styris b Vettori	13	b Wiseman	9
Javed Omar	c Sinclair b Wiseman	58	c and b Franklin	1
Aftab Ahmed	lbw b Vettori	20	b Vettori	28
Rajin Saleh	c Sinclair b Wiseman	2	c Sinclair b Vettori	35
Mohammad Ashraful	c Astle b Wiseman	0	c Styris b Vettori	0
Alok Kapali	c Fleming b Vettori	13	c Astle b Wiseman	13
*Khaled Mashud (capt)	lbw b Vettori	18	b Oram	51
Mushfiqur Rahman	c McCullum b Franklin	15	b Vettori	20
Mohammad Rafique	c Wiseman b Vettori	32	c Sinclair b Vettori	31
Tapash Baisya	c Sinclair b Vettori	0	st McCullum b Vettori	66
Enamul Haque jnr	not out	0	not out	0
Extras	b 4, lb 2, w 2, nb 3	11	b 4, lb 3, w 1	8
	(71.2 overs)	182	(70.2 overs)	262

	First Innings				Second Innings			
	O	M	R	W	O	M	R	W
Oram	5	0	20	0	10	4	33	1
Franklin	5	0	17	1	8	3	16	1
Vettori	32.2	12	70	6	28.2	9	100	6
Wiseman	27	5	68	3	24	4	106	2
Astle	2	1	1	0	-	-	-	-

Fall of Wickets
1-34, 2-66, 3-82, 4-82, 5-108, 6-128, 7-142, 8-181, 9-182
1-9, 2-25, 3-47, 4-51, 5-74, 6-123, 7-161, 8-183, 9-217

Umpires: MR Benson & DJ Harper
Toss: New Zealand
Test debut: Aftab Ahmed
Man of the Match: SP Fleming
Man of the Series: DL Vettori

New Zealand won by an innings and 101 runs

SERIES AVERAGES
Bangladesh v. New Zealand

BANGLADESH

Batting	M	Inns	NO	Runs	HS	Av	100	50	c/st
Khaled Mashud	2	4	1	94	51	31.33	-	1	2/-
Aftab Ahmed	1	2	0	48	28	24.00	-	-	-/-
Mohammad Ashraful	2	4	0	93	67	23.25	-	1	-/-
Tapash Baisya	2	4	1	66	66	22.00	-	1	1/-
Mohammad Rafique	2	4	0	87	32	21.75	-	-	1/-
Rajin Saleh	2	4	0	78	41	19.50	-	-	2/-
Javed Omar	2	4	0	74	58	18.50	-	1	-/-
Nafees Iqbal	2	4	0	72	49	18.00	-	-	1/-
Mushfiqur Rahman	1	2	0	35	20	17.50	-	-	2/-
Alok Kapali	2	4	0	40	14	10.00	-	-	1/-
Manjural Islam Rana	1	2	0	17	16	8.50	-	-	2/-
Hannan Sarkar	1	2	0	1	1	0.50	-	-	-/-
Tareq Aziz	1	2	0	0	0	0.00	-	-	-/-
Enamul Haque jnr	1	2	2	0	0*	-	-	-	-/-

Bowling	Overs	Mds	Runs	Wkts	Av	Best	5/inn	10m
Mohammad Rafique	114.1	30	252	9	28.00	6-122	1	-
Manjural Islam Rana	42	12	84	3	28.00	3-84	-	-
Enamul Haque jnr	42	4	142	2	71.00	2-142	-	-
Rajin Saleh	20	0	85	1	85.00	1-81	-	-
Tapash Baisya	45	4	194	1	194.00	1-112	-	-

Also bowled: Mohammad Ashraful 2-0-12-0, Alok Kapali 5-0-23-0, Tareq Aziz 12-1-59-0, Mushfiqur Rahman 15-1-68-0.

NEW ZEALAND

Batting	M	Inns	NO	Runs	HS	Av	100	50	c/st
BB McCullum	2	2	1	160	143	160.00	1	-	6/1
SP Fleming	2	2	0	231	202	115.50	1	-	3/-
HJH Marshall	1	1	0	69	69	69.00	-	1	-/-
JDP Oram	2	2	1	61	38*	61.00	-	-	1/-
MS Sinclair	2	2	0	99	76	49.50	-	1	5/-
SB Styris	2	2	0	91	89	45.50	-	1	5/-
PJ Wiseman	2	1	0	28	28	28.00	-	-	1/-
NJ Astle	2	2	0	50	39	25.00	-	-	4/-
DL Vettori	2	1	0	23	23	23.00	-	-	1/-
JEC Franklin	2	1	0	23	23	23.00	-	-	1/-
MH Richardson	2	2	0	43	28	21.50	-	-	1/-
IG Butler	1	1	1	15	15*	-	-	-	-/-

Bowling	Overs	Mds	Runs	Wkts	Av	Best	5/inn	10m
JEC Franklin	35	11	75	7	10.71	5-28	1	-
DL Vettori	111.4	49	224	20	11.20	6-28	3	1
JDP Oram	44.5	17	95	4	23.75	3-36	-	-
PJ Wiseman	83.5	15	280	8	35.00	3-64	-	-

Also bowled: NJ Astle 2-1-1-0, SB Styris 2-1-4-0, IG Butler 16-4-42-0.

ONE-DAY INTERNATIONALS
v. New Zealand

Match One
2 November 2004 at Chittagong
New Zealand 224 (49.2 overs) (CL Cairns 74, Nazmul Hossain 4 for 40)
Bangladesh 86 (31.5 overs) (KD Mills 4 for 14)
New Zealand won by 138 runs

Match Two
5 November 2004 at Dhaka
Bangladesh 146 (43.4 overs);
New Zealand 148 for 7 (44.4 overs) (MS Sinclair 62, Aftab Ahmed 5 for 31)
New Zealand won by 3 wickets

Match Three
7 November 2004 at Dhaka
New Zealand 250 for 7 (50 overs) (MS Sinclair 66, SB Styris 51, Mohammad Rafique 4 for 63)
Bangladesh 167 for 7 (50 overs)
New Zealand won by 83 runs

FIRST TEST – BANGLADESH v. INDIA
10–13 December 2004 at Dhaka

BANGLADESH

	First Innings		Second Innings	
Javed Omar	lbw b Pathan	4	lbw b Pathan	4
Nafees Iqbal	lbw b Pathan	20	lbw b Kumble	54
Habibul Bashar (capt)	c Tendulkar b Khan	8	c Khan b Pathan	12
Rajin Saleh	lbw b Pathan	0	lbw b Pathan	0
Mohammad Ashraful	not out	60	lbw b Pathan	0
*Khaled Mashud	c Karthik b Khan	8	c Karthik b Pathan	5
Manjural Islam Rana	c Karthik b Pathan	24	c Karthik b Khan	69
Mushfiqur Rahman	lbw b Pathan	0	c Dravid b Harbhajan Singh	6
Mohammad Rafique	lbw b Kumble	47	c Sehwag b Kumble	11
Tapash Baisya	c Dravid b Kumble	0	c Tendulkar b Pathan	29
Mashrafe Mortaza	run out	7	not out	0
Extras	lb 4, nb 2	6	lb 5, w 2, nb 5	12
	(57.5 overs)	184	(53.2 overs)	202

	First Innings				Second Innings			
	O	M	R	W	O	M	R	W
Pathan	16	5	45	5	15	5	51	6
Khan	15	2	51	2	13.2	2	60	1
Ganguly	4	2	16	0	-	-	-	-
Kumble	13.5	2	45	2	13	4	42	2
Harbhajan Singh	9	1	23	0	12	3	44	1

Fall of Wickets
1-8, 2-29, 3-29, 4-35, 5-50, 6-106, 7-106, 8-171, 9-171
1-4, 2-24, 3-24, 4-24, 5-36, 6-100, 7-117, 8-133, 9-202

INDIA

	First Innings	
G Gambhir	run out	35
V Sehwag	lbw b Tapash Baisya	13
R Dravid	b Mashrafe Mortaza	0
SR Tendulkar	not out	248
SC Ganguly (capt)	b Tapash Baisya	71
VVS Laxman	lbw b Mohammad Rafique	32
*KKD Karthik	c M Mortaza b M Rahman	25
IK Pathan	c M Rahman b M Rafique	5
A Kumble	b Mashrafe Mortaza	1
Harbhajan Singh	c Habibul Bashar b M Rahman	8
Z Khan	st Khaled Mashud b M Ashraful	75
Extras	b 2, lb 11	13
	(136.4 overs)	526

	First Innings			
	O	M	R	W
Tapash Baisya	29	4	114	2
Mashrafe Mortaza	31	8	125	2
Mushfiqur Rahman	24	4	104	2
Mohammad Rafique	40	9	113	2
Manjural Islam Rana	12	1	55	0
Mohammad Ashraful	0.4	0	2	1

Fall of Wickets
1-19, 2-24, 3-68, 4-232, 5-291, 6-339, 7-348, 8-368, 9-393

Umpires: Aleem Dar & JW Lloyds
Toss: India
Man of the Match: IK Pathan

India won by an innings and 140 runs

SECOND TEST – BANGLADESH v. INDIA
17–20 December 2004 at Chittagong

INDIA

	First Innings	
V Sehwag	c Habibul Bashar b M Mortaza	10
G Gambhir	b Nazmul Hossain	139
R Dravid	c Khaled Mashud b M Mortaza	160
SR Tendulkar	lbw b Mashrafe Mortaza	36
SC Ganguly (capt)	c Talha Jubair b M Rafique	88
VVS Laxman	c and b Mohammad Rafique	9
*KKD Karthik	c Khaled Mashud b M Rafique	11
IK Pathan	c Khaled Mashud b M Rafique	4
A Kumble	st Khaled Mashud b M Ashraful	23
Harbhajan Singh	c M Islam Rana b Nazmul Hossain	47
Z Khan	not out	0
Extras	b 5, lb 4, w 2, nb 2	13
	(148.2 overs)	540

	First Innings			
	O	M	R	W
Mashrafe Mortaza	26	5	60	3
Nazmul Hossain	25.5	4	114	2
Talha Jubair	19	1	95	0
Mohammad Rafique	50	2	156	4
Manjural Islam Rana	16.3	0	63	0
Aftab Ahmed	4	0	14	0
Mohammad Ashraful	7	0	29	1

Fall of Wickets
1-14, 2-273, 3-334, 4-371, 5-384, 6-402, 7-412, 8-465, 9-540

BANGLADESH

	First Innings		Second Innings	
Nafees Iqbal	c Gambhir b Harbhajan Singh	31	lbw b Pathan	0
Javed Omar	c Dravid b Kumble	10	c Karthik b Pathan	6
Mashrafe Mortaza	lbw b Kumble	4	(9) c Harbhajan Singh b Tendulkar	6
Habibul Bashar (capt)	st Karthik b Kumble	22	(3) lbw b Pathan	17
Mohammad Ashraful	not out	158	(6) lbw b Kumble	3
Aftab Ahmed	lbw b Kumble	43	(4) c Karthik b Pathan	4
Manjural Islam Rana	lbw b Khan	0	c Gambhir b Kumble	0
*Khaled Mashud	c Karthik b Khan	22	c Dravid b Harbhajan Singh	0
Mohammad Rafique	c Dravid b Pathan	4	(5) c Sehwag b Pathan	22
Talha Jubair	b Pathan	0	(11) c Pathan b Harbhajan Singh	31
Nazmul Hossain	run out	0	(10) not out	8
Extras	b 17, lb 8, w 3, nb 11	39	b 9, lb 7, w 7, nb 4	27
	(91 overs)	333	(26.4 overs)	124

	First Innings				Second Innings			
	O	M	R	W	O	M	R	W
Pathan	23	7	86	2	9	2	32	5
Khan	18	3	76	2	6	1	28	0
Kumble	26	9	55	4	4	2	2	2
Harbhajan Singh	22	5	79	1	4.4	0	19	2
Tendulkar	2	0	12	0	3	0	27	1

Fall of Wickets
1-48, 2-54, 3-54, 4-124, 5-239, 6-240, 7-300, 8-312, 9-312
1-0, 2-30, 3-34, 4-75, 5-76, 6-77, 7-78, 8-80, 9-84

Umpires: MR Benson & Aleem Dar
Toss: India
Test debut: Nazmul Hossain
Man of the Match: Mohammad Ashraful
Man of the Series: IK Pathan

India won by an innings and 83 runs

SERIES AVERAGES
Bangladesh v. India

BANGLADESH

Batting	M	Inns	NO	Runs	HS	Av	100	50	c/st
Mohammad Ashraful	2	4	2	221	158*	110.50	1	1	-/-
Nafees Iqbal	2	4	0	105	54	26.25	-	1	-/-
Aftab Ahmed	1	2	0	47	43	23.50	-	-	-/-
Manjural Islam Rana	2	4	0	93	69	23.25	-	1	1/-
Mohammad Rafique	2	4	0	84	47	21.00	-	-	1/-
Talha Jubair	1	2	0	31	31	15.50	-	-	1/-
Habibul Bashar	2	4	0	59	22	14.75	-	-	2/-
Tapash Baisya	1	2	0	29	29	14.50	-	-	-/-
Khaled Mashud	2	4	0	35	22	8.75	-	-	3/2
Nazmul Hossain	1	2	1	8	8*	8.00	-	-	-/-
Javed Omar	2	4	0	24	10	6.00	-	-	-/-
Mashrafe Mortaza	2	4	1	17	7	5.66	-	-	1/-
Mushfiqur Rahman	1	2	0	6	6	3.00	-	-	1/-
Rajin Saleh	1	2	0	0	0	0.00	-	-	-/-

Bowling	Overs	Mds	Runs	Wkts	Av	Best	5/inn	10m
Mohammad Ashraful	7.4	0	31	2	15.50	1-2	-	-
Mashrafe Mortaza	57	13	185	5	37.00	3-60	-	-
Mohammad Rafique	90	11	269	6	44.83	4-156	-	-
Mushfiqur Rahman	24	4	104	2	52.00	2-104	-	-
Tapash Baisya	29	4	114	2	57.00	2-114	-	-
Nazmul Hossain	25.5	4	114	2	57.00	2-114	-	-

Also bowled: Aftab Ahmed 4-0-14-0, Talha Jubair 19-1-95-0, Manjural Islam Rana 28.3-1-118-0.

INDIA

Batting	M	Inns	NO	Runs	HS	Av	100	50	c/st
SR Tendulkar	2	2	1	284	248*	284.00	1	-	2/-
G Gambhir	2	2	0	174	139	87.00	1	-	2/-
R Dravid	2	2	0	160	160	80.00	1	-	5/-
SC Ganguly	2	2	0	159	88	79.50	-	2	-/-
Z Khan	2	2	1	75	75	75.00	-	1	1/-
Harbhajan Singh	2	2	0	55	47	27.50	-	-	1/-
VVS Laxman	2	2	0	41	32	20.50	-	-	-/-
KKD Karthik	2	2	0	36	25	18.00	-	-	7/1
A Kumble	2	2	0	24	23	12.00	-	-	-/-
V Sehwag	2	2	0	23	13	11.50	-	-	2/-
IK Pathan	2	2	0	9	5	4.50	-	-	1/-

Bowling	Overs	Mds	Runs	Wkts	Av	Best	5/inn	10m
IK Pathan	63	19	214	18	11.88	6-51	3	1
A Kumble	56.5	17	144	10	14.40	4-55	-	-
SR Tendulkar	5	0	39	1	39.00	1-27	-	-
Harbhajan Singh	47.4	9	165	4	41.25	2-19	-	-
Z Khan	52.2	8	215	5	43.00	2-51	-	-

Also bowled: SC Ganguly 4-2-16-0.

ONE–DAY INTERNATIONALS
v. India

Match One
23 December 2004 at Chittagong
India 245 for 8 (50 overs) (M Kaif 80, R Dravid 53)
Bangladesh 234 for 8 (50 overs) (Habibul Bashar 65, Khaled Mashud 50*)
India won by 11 runs

Match Two
26 December 2004 at Dhaka
Bangladesh 229 for 9 (50 overs) (Aftab Ahmed 67)
India 214 (47.5 overs) (S Sriram 57)
Bangladesh won by 15 runs

Match Three
27 December 2004 at Dhaka
India 348 for 5 (50 overs) (V Sehwag 70, Yuvraj Singh 69, R Dravid 60, SC Ganguly 55)
Bangladesh 257 for 9 (50 overs) (Rajin Saleh 82, SR Tendulkar 4 for 54)
India won by 91 runs

FIRST TEST – BANGLADESH v. ZIMBABWE
6–10 January 2005 at Chittagong

BANGLADESH

	First Innings		Second Innings	
Javed Omar	c Taibu b Chigumbura	33	(7) c Masakadza b Chigumbura	15
Nafees Iqbal	c Sibanda b Nkala	56	c Taylor b Hondo	0
Habibul Bashar (capt)	c Taibu b Mpofu	94	c Masakadza b Chigumbura	55
Mohammad Ashraful	c Masakadza b Nkala	19	c Taibu b Mpofu	22
Rajin Saleh	c & b Matsikenyeri	89	(1) c & b Hondo	26
Aftab Ahmed	lbw b Mpofu	6	(5) c Cremer b Chigumbura	11
*Khaled Mashud	c Nkala b Cremer	49	(6) c Cremer b Hondo	23
Mohammad Rafique	c Taibu b Mpofu	69	not out	14
Mashrafe Mortaza	c Sibanda b Cremer	48	c Hondo b Chigumbura	19
Tapash Baisya	b Mpofu	6	c Sibanda b Chigumbura	1
Enamul Haque jnr	not out	0		
Extras	b 7, lb 3, w 6, nb 3	19	b 1, lb 8, nb 4, p 5	18
	(149.3 overs)	488	(9 wkts dec 51.1 overs)	204

	First Innings				Second Innings			
	O	M	R	W	O	M	R	W
Mpofu	29	3	109	4	12	1	47	1
Hondo	27	6	70	0	17	0	61	3
Chigumbura	28	6	79	1	16.1	3	54	5
Nkala	26	10	50	2	-	-	-	-
Cremer	16.3	1	86	2	-	-	-	-
Matsikenyeri	23	3	84	1	6	0	28	0

Fall of Wickets
1-91, 2-93, 3-153, 4-272, 5-283, 6-341, 7-410, 8-472, 9-480
1-7, 2-47, 3-83, 4-114, 5-145, 6-156, 7-176, 8-202, 9-204

ZIMBABWE

	First Innings		Second Innings	
S Matsikenyeri	c Habibul Bashar b T Baisya	28	b Enamul Haque jnr	20
BG Rogers	run out	5	c sub b Tapash Baisya	0
V Sibanda	lbw b Mohammad Rafique	12	lbw b Tapash Baisya	0
H Masakadza	b Mashrafe Mortaza	29	c & b Enamul Haque jnr	56
AG Cremer	lbw b Mohammad Rafique	0	(9) c Rajin Saleh b E Haque jnr	2
BRM Taylor	lbw b Mashrafe Mortaza	39	(5) lbw b Enamul Haque jnr	44
*T Taibu (capt)	lbw b Mohammad Rafique	92	(6) c Aftab Ahmed b E Haque jnr	0
E Chigumbura	c Khaled Mashud b M Rafique	71	(7) c K Mashud b M Mortaza	10
ML Nkala	c Khaled Mashud b M Rafique	23	(8) b Mashrafe Mortaza	5
DT Hondo	c Khaled Mashud b M Mortaza	1	not out	6
CB Mpofu	not out	0	c M Ashraful b Enamul Haque jnr	5
Extras	b 1, lb 1, w 1, nb 9	12	lb 1, w 1, nb 4	6
	(131.4 overs)	312	(64.2 overs)	154

	First Innings				Second Innings			
	O	M	R	W	O	M	R	W
Mashrafe Mortaza	31	12	59	3	17	4	45	2
Tapash Baisya	24	5	87	1	10	6	20	2
Mohammad Rafique	41.4	19	65	5	15	6	43	0
Enamul Haque jnr	26	9	55	0	22.2	5	45	6
Mohammad Ashraful	5	0	19	0	-	-	-	-
Rajin Saleh	4	0	25	0	-	-	-	-

Fall of Wickets
1-31, 2-48, 3-59, 4-59, 5-86, 6-152, 7-271, 8-308, 9-312
1-2, 2-2, 3-42, 4-112, 5-115, 6-126, 7-138, 8-143, 9-145

Umpires: Asad Rauf & TH Wijewardene
Toss: Bangladesh
Test debuts: AG Cremer, CB Mpofu, BG Rogers
Man of the Match: Enamul Haque jnr

Bangladesh won by 226 runs

SECOND TEST – BANGLADESH v. ZIMBABWE
14–18 January 2005 at Dhaka

ZIMBABWE

	First Innings		Second Innings	
S Matsikenyeri	b Enamul Haque jnr	51	lbw b Mashrafe Mortaza	14
BG Rogers	b Enamul Haque jnr	29	lbw b Mashrafe Mortaza	20
DD Ebrahim	lbw b Enamul Haque jnr	12	lbw b Mashrafe Mortaza	1
H Masakadza	c Aftab Ahmed b Tapash Baisya	43	c Rajin Saleh b M Rafique	1
BRM Taylor	lbw b Enamul Haque jnr	2	b Enamul Haque jnr	78
*T Taibu (capt)	not out	85	c Tapash Baisya b E Haque jnr	153
E Chigumbura	c M Ashraful b Tapash Baisya	34	c Khaled Mashud b M Ashraful	0
T Panyangara	c Khaled Mashud b M Mortaza	21	st Khaled Mashud b E Haque jnr	6
AG Cremer	b Enamul Haque jnr	1	lbw b Enamul Haque jnr	0
DT Hondo	b Enamul Haque jnr	9	c Aftab Ahmed b E Haque jnr	3
CB Mpofu	c M Ashraful b Enamul Haque jnr	0	not out	1
Extras	b 4, lb 6, nb 1	11	lb 2, nb 7	9
	(118 overs)	298	(103 overs)	286

	First Innings				Second Innings			
	O	M	R	W	O	M	R	W
Tapash Baisya	22	7	67	2	13.2	2	50	0
Mashrafe Mortaza	23	5	69	1	19.4	7	51	3
Mohammad Rafique	38	14	57	0	24	9	56	1
Enamul Haque jnr	35	9	95	7	37	8	105	5
Mohammad Ashraful	-	-	-	-	9	2	22	1

Fall of Wickets
1-65, 2-96, 3-107, 4-111, 5-171, 6-221, 7-257, 8-262, 9-298
1-30, 2-36, 3-37, 4-37, 5-187, 6-196, 7-212, 8-218, 9-285

BANGLADESH

	First Innings		Second Innings	
Javed Omar	c Taibu b Hondo	34	c Taylor b Cremer	43
Nafees Iqbal	c Taibu b Hondo	28	c Taylor b Panyangara	121
Habibul Bashar (capt)	b Hondo	10	c Masakadza b Panyangara	2
Mohammad Ashraful	lbw b Hondo	5	c Ebrahim b Cremer	3
Rajin Saleh	c Masakadza b Cremer	24	not out	56
Aftab Ahmed	c Matsikenyeri b Hondo	0	c Taibu b Panyangara	5
*Khaled Mashud	b Hondo	0	not out	28
Mohammad Rafique	c Ebrahim b Masakadza	56		
Mashrafe Mortaza	c Chigumbura b Panyangara	26		
Tapash Baisya	c Chigumbura b Cremer	13		
Enamul Haque jnr	not out	3		
Extras	lb 7, nb 5	12	b 13, lb 6, nb 8	27
	(78.4 overs)	211	(5 wkts 142 overs)	285

	First Innings				Second Innings			
	O	M	R	W	O	M	R	W
Panyangara	17	5	37	1	21	10	28	3
Mpofu	11	3	28	0	22	10	29	0
Hondo	22	7	59	6	21	7	37	0
Chigumbura	9	1	32	0	19	7	31	0
Cremer	12.4	1	32	2	34	9	61	2
Masakadza	7	1	16	1	10	3	11	0
Matsikenyeri	-	-	-	-	8	0	41	0
Taylor	-	-	-	-	4	0	11	0
Rogers	-	-	-	-	3	0	17	0

Fall of Wickets
1-58, 2-71, 3-84, 4-85, 5-103, 6-107, 7-132, 8-168, 9-203
1-133, 2-148, 3-153, 4-196, 5-206

Umpires: Nadeem Ghauri & MG Silva
Toss: Zimbabwe
Man of the Match: T Taibu
Man of the Series: Enamul Haque jnr

Match drawn

SERIES AVERAGES
Bangladesh v. Zimbabwe

BANGLADESH

Batting	M	Inns	NO	Runs	HS	Av	100	50	c/st
Mohammad Rafique	2	3	1	139	69	69.50	-	2	-/-
Rajin Saleh	2	4	1	195	89	65.00	-	2	2/-
Nafees Iqbal	2	4	0	205	121	51.25	1	1	-/-
Habibul Bashar	2	4	0	161	94	40.25	-	2	1/-
Khaled Mashud	2	4	1	100	49	33.33	-	-	6/1
Javed Omar	2	4	0	125	43	31.25	-	-	-/-
Mashrafe Mortaza	2	3	0	93	48	31.00	-	-	-/-
Mohammad Ashraful	2	4	0	49	22	12.25	-	-	3/-
Tapash Baisya	2	3	0	20	13	6.66	-	-	1/-
Aftab Ahmed	2	4	0	22	11	5.50	-	-	3/-
Enamul Haque jnr	2	2	2	3	3*	-	-	-	1/-

Bowling	Overs	Mds	Runs	Wkts	Av	Best	5/inn	10m
Enamul Haque jnr	120.2	31	300	18	16.66	7-95	3	1
Mashrafe Mortaza	90.4	28	224	9	24.88	3-51	-	-
Mohammad Rafique	118.4	48	221	6	36.83	5-65	1	-
Mohammad Ashraful	14	2	41	1	41.00	1-22	-	-
Tapash Baisya	69.2	20	224	5	44.80	2-20	-	-

Also bowled: Rajin Saleh 4-0-25-0.

ZIMBABWE

Batting	M	Inns	NO	Runs	HS	Av	100	50	c/st
T Taibu	2	4	1	330	153	110.00	1	2	7/-
BRM Taylor	2	4	0	163	78	40.75	-	1	3/-
H Masakadza	2	4	0	129	56	32.25	-	1	5/-
E Chigumbura	2	4	0	115	71	28.75	-	1	2/-
S Matsikenyeri	2	4	0	113	51	28.25	-	1	2/-
ML Nkala	1	2	0	28	23	14.00	-	-	1/-
T Panyangara	1	2	0	27	21	13.50	-	-	-/-
BG Rogers	2	4	0	54	29	13.50	-	-	-/-
DD Ebrahim	1	2	0	13	12	6.50	-	-	2/-
DT Hondo	2	4	1	19	9	6.33	-	-	2/-
V Sibanda	1	2	0	12	12	6.00	-	-	3/-
CB Mpofu	2	4	2	6	5	3.00	-	-	-/-
AG Cremer	2	4	0	3	2	0.75	-	-	2/-

Bowling	Overs	Mds	Runs	Wkts	Av	Best	5/inn	10m
T Panyangara	38	15	65	4	16.25	3-28	-	-
ML Nkala	26	10	50	2	25.00	2-50	-	-
DT Hondo	87	20	227	9	25.22	6-59	1	-
H Masakadza	17	4	27	1	27.00	1-16	-	-
AG Cremer	63.1	11	179	6	29.83	2-32	-	-
E Chigumbura	72.1	17	196	6	32.66	5-54	1	-
CB Mpofu	74	17	213	5	42.60	4-109	-	-
S Matsikenyeri	37	3	153	1	153.00	1-84	-	-

Also bowled: BRM Taylor 4-0-11-0, BG Rogers 3-0-17-0.

ONE-DAY INTERNATIONALS
v. Zimbabwe

Match One
20 January 2005 at Dhaka
Zimbabwe 251 for 8 (50 overs) (BRM Taylor 58, H Masakadza 54)
Bangladesh 229 (48.1 overs)
Zimbabwe won by 22 runs

Match Two
24 January 2005 at Chittagong
Zimbabwe 237 for 5 (50 overs) (BG Rogers 66, T Taibu 64*)
Bangladesh 206 (47.1 overs) (Nafees Iqbal 58)
Zimbabwe won by 31 runs

Match Three
26 January 2005 at Chittagong
Bangladesh 244 for 9 (50 overs) (Rajin Saleh 77)
Zimbabwe 204 (47.5 overs) (BG Rogers 51, Manjural Islam Rana 4 for 34)
Bangladesh won by 40 runs

Match Four
29 January 2005 at Dhaka
Bangladesh 247 for 9 (50 overs) (Nafees Iqbal 56, Khaled Mashud 51)
Zimbabwe 189 (47.2 overs) (S Matsikenyeri 50, Mohammad Rafique 4 for 33, Manjural Islam Rana 4 for 36)
Bangladesh won by 58 runs

Match Five
31 January 2005 at Dhaka
Zimbabwe 198 (49 overs) (BG Rogers 84)
Bangladesh 202 for 2 (33 overs) (Aftab Ahmed 81*, Mohammad Rafique 72)
Bangladesh won by 8 wickets

INDIA

INDIA REPORT
By Gulu Ezekiel

Indian cricket, which enjoyed one of its finest seasons ever in 2003–04, came crashing down to earth with a thud heard round the cricket world in 2004–05.

It was the season when Murphy's Law reigned supreme – everything that could go wrong just about did – leaving the once-proud and mighty side in tatters by April 2005, beaten, bruised and virtually rudderless.

After reaching the World Cup Final in 2003, then following up with magnificent performances in Australia and Pakistan, India finished eighth out of ten in the ICC ODI rankings by the time they had been crushed by Pakistan at home.

It is a strange irony that while Indian cricket has been compared to wine (they don't travel well) and have enjoyed a magnificent record at home – just two Test series defeats since 1987 – the roles should be so sharply overturned this time around. Australia won their first Test series here since 1969–70 and while Pakistan managed a draw, it was surely a moral victory for Inzamam-ul-Haq and his raw team. The final nail in the Indian coffin was driven in by the seemingly imperturbable 'Inzy' as Pakistan came storming back after losing the first two ODIs to win the series 4-2. It plunged the nation into collective despair.

India's woes were compounded by the shocking loss of form of Sourav Ganguly and his repeated run-ins with the ICC's long arm of the law. The man who had been the inspiration behind India's resurgence the previous season now became a laughing stock as the team crumbled around him. He went through the entire season without a century in either form of the game and by the time the Pakistanis came visiting at the end of the season, the captain was barely able to put bat to ball.

Fall from grace: Sourav Ganguly had an unhappy time of it as India's captain.

Anil Kumble was in outstanding form in the Chennai Test against Australia, taking 13 wickets.

The team's woes were compounded by yet another injury to Sachin Tendulkar and his disappointing form with the bat. The Indian maestro did reach two landmarks – his 34th Test century – equalling the world record of Sunil Gavaskar – and his 10,000th Test run. But a serious bout of 'tennis elbow' apparently played its part in slowing down his normally dominating form of batsmanship, leaving Indian fans struggling to reconcile themselves to their favourite son's new, defensive avatar.

His highest Test score of 248 not out against Bangladesh at Dhaka was his 34th century but also the lone three-figure knock in nine Test matches in the season. And, as the nation held its breath in anticipation of the new world record, the pressure seemed to tell on Tendulkar and the team as a whole. Similarly, in nine ODIs, Tendulkar had but one century, against Pakistan.

To top it all, former New Zealand captain John Wright, who had taken over as coach the same year as Ganguly was appointed captain (2000) – the unlikely pair had forged one of Indian cricket's most successful partnerships – retired at the end of the season, disconsolate to see all his good work laid to waste. Wright was succeeded shortly afterwards by Australian batting legend Greg Chappell.

The Indians struggled at the start of the new season in three ODI tournaments, first in the Netherlands in August, then the NatWest Challenge against England and finally in the ICC Champions Trophy in September. It was a shaky start from which they never recovered, and nine months later they were left scrambling for crumbs of comfort.

Australia were the first of three touring teams to visit during the season amidst tremendous media hype and expectations of another grand series. India alone had been able to halt the march of the all-conquering Aussies in recent years, beating them 2-1 at home in 2001 and holding them to a 1-1 draw in their own backyard the previous season.

But it was not to be. With Ricky Ponting injured for the first three Tests, it was left to Adam Gilchrist to achieve what no Aussie captain had managed since Bill Lawry: the conquest of the 'final frontier', as Steve Waugh described the Indian citadel at home.

The first Test at Bangalore turned out to be a rout with debutant Michael Clarke leading the charge with a dazzling century. The second at Chennai was set up for a pulsating finish with India requiring 210 to win with all their second innings wickets in hand when rain washed out the final day's play. Anil Kumble with 13 wickets was the outstanding performer.

There was plenty of drama leading up to the third Test at Nagpur, Glenn McGrath's 100th. It also marked Tendulkar's return after a gap of two months, confident that he had got over the worst of his elbow injury. There was also a shock on the morning of the match when Ganguly declared himself unfit. Team physio Andrew Leipus' comment, 'We don't know what the injury is at the moment,' only added to the mystery as the rumour mill swung into action.

The pitch at the VCA had rather more than the usual smidgen of green that one has come to associate with Indian tracks. The Indian team management voiced their protest but in vain. There may even have been a hint of sabotage involved, all tied up with the labyrinthine politics of Indian cricket. The local association was part of the group opposed to Indian cricket's major-domo Jagmohan Dalmiya, who just a month earlier had staged a coup by ensuring his man Ranbir Singh Mahendra replaced him as the outgoing president of the BCCI, while he got himself appointed as Patron-in-Chief.

Rahul Dravid took over the captaincy at short notice under stormy circumstances as there were by now rumblings within the team about their captain's last-minute decision.

The Aussie pace attack was meanwhile licking its lips in anticipation. And it hardly came as a surprise when India were routed by 342 runs, with McGrath and Jason Gillespie blocking all escape routes.

Gilchrist and his men were in seventh heaven but they came crashing down to earth a week later in the fourth Test at Mumbai. If the pitch at Nagpur had them jumping for joy, the dustbowl at the Wankhede stadium saw them fuming and cursing. Ponting was back to lead Australia but Ganguly was once again missing the action although he was present in Mumbai during the Test for a commercial photo-shoot! The match was all over in two days and a bit as Australia fell short by 13 runs when set 107 to win. The Indian spinners grabbed 18 of the 20 wickets but it was part-time left-arm spinner Michael Clarke's second innings analysis (6.2-0-9-6) that really showed up the pitch.

The season was meant to be a grand celebration of the BCCI's 75th anniversary. But the stormy elections and the legal wrangling that followed meant all that fell flat. So did the one-off ODI staged against Pakistan in November, which was meant to be part of the celebrations.

The only ones celebrating were the Pakistanis and to compound his woes, Ganguly was slapped with a two-Test match ban for India's tardy over rate. That was overturned by the ICC on appeal but the mood was still sour when the South Africans dropped by for two Test matches. The first at Kanpur was drawn while India won the second rather unconvincingly at Kolkata.

On their first full tour to Bangladesh India expectedly romped home in both Tests. What was hardly expected though was defeat in the second ODI at Dhaka, the first time Bangladesh had won a full international at home. And it occurred on the day the devastating tsunami struck South East Asia.

Pakistan's return visit to India, following India's tour the year before, was being predicted as the series that would bring the smiles back to the Indian team. As it turned out, captain Inzamam proved to be the master of all he surveyed as he expertly shepherded his young but determined squad.

India held all the aces going into the final day of the opening Test at Mohali. Pakistan were ahead by only 53 runs with four wickets in hand. All predictions pointed to the Indian bowlers polishing off the tail and then the batsmen racing to victory. Instead they came up against the determined resistance of Abdul Razzaq and Kamran Akmal whose 184-run partnership for the sixth wicket not only saved them the Test but also helped force home the point that the tourists would not be pushovers.

India duly won the second Test at Kolkata by 195 runs but still Inzamam maintained they could make it 1-1 by winning the third.

He was true to his word. His own 184 and a triple-century stand with his deputy Younis Khan (267) gave his side the upper hand from the first day at Bangalore. Still, India had all their wickets intact going into the final day, facing a target of 383. Preservation of wickets was the sole purpose and at 103 for one at lunch, there seemed little that could prevent a draw, giving the series to India. But in an astonishing capitulation, the final Indian wicket fell with just six overs remaining in the match as the batsmen wrapped themselves into a fatal defensive cocoon.

Ganguly's miserable form continued into the ODIs and when he was handed a six-match ban (later reduced to four) once again for a slow over rate in the fourth game, his forced absence from the last two matches was a mercy at least for him as India were thoroughly outclassed, losing the last four on the trot.

The biggest success story of the season was on the domestic front. The unheralded Railways teams with no glamour boys in their ranks lifted the Ranji Trophy for the second time in four years.

TSUNAMI IN INDIA

Anil Kumble was holidaying with his family in Chennai when the tsunami struck the southern coast of India on 26 December. Kumble had been replaced after the two-Test series in Bangladesh and missed the three ODI games which followed.

Disaster struck even as his team-mates were starting their second match at Dhaka, having won the first at Chittagong three days earlier by the narrow margin of 11 runs.

'I consider myself very lucky,' said the veteran leg spinner, and the highest Test wicket-taker for his country. 'I was about 60 metres from the beach. I was with my family and about ten minutes before the tsunami hit I checked out of the resort where we had been staying. We knew something was wrong but we thought it was just a high tide. We did not know what a tsunami was.'

Kumble played in both tsunami benefit matches, in Melbourne early in 2005 and then at Lord's in June. Sachin Tendulkar also made an appearance despite not being fit to play in either match.

The Indian cricket board, too, was planning such a match but amidst the controversy and chaos that plagued the BCCI throughout the season, the event didn't happen. Word was just beginning to trickle through to the Indian team when the match began in Dhaka.

All-rounder Sridharan Sriram of Tamil Nadu was the only player from the south. But if he was distracted by the events back home, it didn't show. He top scored with 57 and picked up one wicket. But India still suffered their most humiliating defeat since losing to Sri Lanka in the 1979 Prudential World Cup before the future world champions had gained Test status.

Ironically, even as seemingly the whole of Bangladesh was out on the streets celebrating their first ODI win at home, the country remained unscathed by the devastating disaster. Surrounded by turbulent rivers, over the last 35 years Bangladesh has suffered perhaps the highest casualty rate per capita of any country in the world through natural disasters like floods and cyclones.

It's a daily routine for Chennai's citizens to make an early morning pilgrimage to their beloved Marina, the second-longest continuous beach in the world. Sunday morning sees the Marina packed with hundreds of people taking walks, kids playing games of cricket and fishermen getting their boats ready for the morning catch; 26 December was just another day on the beach.

The kids playing cricket and volleyball, mainly from families who make their living from the sea, were quick to scurry to the safety of the broad streets adjacent to the beach.

Those who died on the Marina were mainly city folk taking a Sunday stroll with their families. The major casualties among the fishing community occurred in other parts of the city that lay by the sea.

The survivors are presently being housed in temporary camps and are being given monthly rations plus financial help by the government and charities. Many have resumed fishing in boats given by the government and aid agencies. According to Tamil Nadu state government figures, a total of 8,005 people were killed.

Just two weeks after the disaster struck, children were back to their beach games. For those who live from the sea and by the sea, life goes on.

Gulu Ezekiel

FIRST TEST – INDIA v. AUSTRALIA
6–10 October 2004 at Bangalore

AUSTRALIA

	First Innings		Second Innings	
JL Langer	b Pathan	52	lbw b Pathan	0
ML Hayden	c Yuvraj Singh b Harbhajan Singh	26	run out	30
SM Katich	b Kumble	81	c Dravid b Kumble	39
DR Martyn	c Chopra b Kumble	3	c sub b Harbhajan Singh	45
DS Lehmann	c Dravid b Kumble	17	c Chopra b Harbhajan Singh	14
MJ Clarke	c Patel b Khan	151	c Chopra b Harbhajan Singh	17
*AC Gilchrist (capt)	c & b Harbhajan Singh	104	c Chopra b Kumble	26
SK Warne	c Dravid b Harbhajan Singh	1	c Yuvraj Singh b Harbhajan Singh	31
JN Gillespie	not out	7	c Yuvraj Singh b Harbhajan Singh	8
MS Kasprowicz	c Yuvraj Singh b Harbhajan Singh	3	c Dravid b Harbhajan Singh	8
GD McGrath	lbw b Harbhajan Singh	0	not out	3
Extras	b 5, lb 15, w 1, nb 8	29	b 2, lb 1, w 1, nb 3	7
	(130 overs)	**474**	(78.1 overs)	**228**

	First Innings				Second Innings			
	O	M	R	W	O	M	R	W
Pathan	21	6	62	1	12	2	38	1
Khan	22	2	60	1	13	1	45	0
Harbhajan Singh	41	7	146	5	30.1	5	78	6
Kumble	39	4	157	3	23	4	64	2
Sehwag	5	0	26	0	-	-	-	-
Yuvraj Singh	2	0	3	0	-	-	-	-

Fall of Wickets
1-50, 2-124, 3-129, 4-149, 5-256, 6-423, 7-427, 8-471, 9-474
1-0, 2-65, 3-86, 4-104, 5-146, 6-167, 7-204, 8-216, 9-217

INDIA

	First Innings		Second Innings	
A Chopra	lbw b McGrath	0	lbw b Gillespie	5
V Sehwag	c Langer b Kasprowicz	39	lbw b McGrath	0
R Dravid	b McGrath	0	lbw b Kasprowicz	60
SC Ganguly (capt)	c Gilchrist b Kasprowicz	45	run out	5
VVS Laxman	b Warne	31	lbw b Warne	3
Yuvraj Singh	c Gilchrist b McGrath	5	c Gilchrist b McGrath	27
*PA Patel	b Gillespie	46	lbw b Warne	4
IK Pathan	c Gilchrist b Warne	31	c Gilchrist b Gillespie	55
A Kumble	b Gillespie	26	b Kasprowicz	2
Harbhajan Singh	c Lehmann b McGrath	8	c McGrath b Gillespie	42
Z Khan	not out	0	not out	22
Extras	b 5, lb 2, w 5, nb 3	15	b 6, lb 5, nb 3	14
	(89.2 overs)	**246**	(87.4 overs)	**239**

	First Innings				Second Innings			
	O	M	R	W	O	M	R	W
McGrath	25	8	55	4	20	10	39	2
Gillespie	16.2	3	63	2	14.4	4	33	3
Warne	28	4	78	2	32	8	115	2
Kasprowicz	20	4	43	2	14	7	23	2
Lehmann	-	-	-	-	6	3	14	0
Clarke	-	-	-	-	1	0	4	0

Fall of Wickets
1-0, 2-4, 3-87, 4-98, 5-124, 6-136, 7-196, 8-227, 9-244
1-1, 2-7, 3-12, 4-19, 5-81, 6-86, 7-118, 8-125, 9-214

Umpires: BF Bowden & SA Bucknor
Toss: Australia
Test debut: MJ Clarke
Man of the Match: MJ Clarke

Australia won by 217 runs

SECOND TEST – INDIA v. AUSTRALIA
14–18 October 2004 at Chennai

AUSTRALIA

	First Innings		Second Innings	
JL Langer	c Dravid b Harbhajan Singh	71	c Dravid b Kumble	19
ML Hayden	c Laxman b Harbhajan Singh	58	c Laxman b Kumble	39
SM Katich	not out	36	(4) lbw b Khan	9
DR Martyn	c Yuvraj Singh b Kumble	26	(5) c Dravid b Harbhajan Singh	104
DS Lehmann	c Patel b Kumble	0	(8) c Patel b Kumble	31
MJ Clarke	lbw b Kumble	5	(7) not out	39
*AC Gilchrist (capt)	c Yuvraj Singh b Kumble	3	(3) b Kumble	49
SK Warne	c and b Kumble	4	(9) c Laxman b Kumble	0
JN Gillespie	c Kaif b Kumble	5	(6) c Dravid b Harbhajan Singh	26
MS Kasprowicz	c Laxman b Kumble	4	lbw b Kumble	5
GD McGrath	run out	2	b Harbhajan Singh	2
Extras	b 7, lb 4, w 1, nb 4, p 5	21	b 19, lb 15, w 3, nb 4, p 5	46
	(71.3 overs)	**235**	(133.5 overs)	**369**

	First Innings				Second Innings			
	O	M	R	W	O	M	R	W
Pathan	12	3	29	0	12	3	39	0
Khan	11	2	44	0	22	6	36	1
Harbhajan Singh	29	2	90	2	46.5	12	108	3
Kumble	17.3	4	48	7	47	8	133	6
Sehwag	2	1	8	0	1	0	5	0
Yuvraj Singh	-	-	-	-	2	0	7	0
Ganguly	-	-	-	-	3	1	2	0

Fall of Wickets
1-136, 2-136, 3-189, 4-191, 5-204, 6-210, 7-216, 8-224, 9-228
1-53, 2-76, 3-121, 4-145, 5-284, 6-285, 7-347, 8-347, 9-364

INDIA

	First Innings		Second Innings	
Yuvraj Singh	c Gilchrist b Warne	8	not out	7
V Sehwag	c Clarke b Warne	155	not out	12
IK Pathan	c Hayden b Warne	14		
R Dravid	b Kasprowicz	26		
SC Ganguly (capt)	c Gilchrist b Gillespie	9		
VVS Laxman	b Gillespie	4		
M Kaif	run out	64		
*PA Patel	c Gilchrist b Warne	54		
A Kumble	b Warne	20		
Harbhajan Singh	c & b Warne	5		
Z Khan	not out	0		
Extras	b 6, lb 3, w 2, nb 6	17		0
	(134.3 overs)	**376**	(0 wkts 3 overs)	**19**

	First Innings				Second Innings			
	O	M	R	W	O	M	R	W
McGrath	25	4	74	0	2	0	18	0
Gillespie	35	8	70	2	1	0	1	0
Warne	42.3	5	125	6	-	-	-	-
Kasprowicz	25	5	65	1	-	-	-	-
Lehmann	5	0	26	0	-	-	-	-
Katich	2	0	7	0	-	-	-	-

Fall of Wickets
1-28, 2-83, 3-178, 4-203, 5-213, 6-233, 7-335, 8-369, 9-372

Umpires: RE Koertzen & DR Shepherd
Toss: Australia
Man of the Match: A Kumble

Match drawn

THIRD TEST – INDIA v. AUSTRALIA
26–29 October 2004 at Nagpur

AUSTRALIA

	First Innings		Second Innings	
JL Langer	c Dravid b Khan	44	c Laxman b Kartik	30
ML Hayden	c Patel b Khan	23	b Khan	9
SM Katich	c Chopra b Kumble	4	lbw b Kartik	99
DR Martyn	c Agarkar b Kumble	114	c Patel b Khan	97
DS Lehmann	c Dravid b Kartik	70		
MJ Clarke	c Patel b Khan	91	(5) c Kaif b Kumble	73
*AC Gilchrist (capt)	c & b Kartik	2	(6) not out	3
SK Warne	st Patel b Kartik	2		
JN Gillespie	lbw b Khan	9		
MS Kasprowicz	c Patel b Agarkar	0		
GD McGrath	not out	11		
Extras	b 6, lb 13, w 1, nb 8	28	b 1, lb 15, w 2	18
	(100.2 overs)	**398**	(5 wkts dec 98.1 overs)	**329**

	First Innings				Second Innings			
	O	M	R	W	O	M	R	W
Agarkar	23	2	99	1	21	7	68	0
Khan	26.2	6	95	4	21.1	5	64	2
Kumble	25	6	99	2	21	1	89	1
Kartik	20	1	57	3	26	5	74	2
Tendulkar	6	1	29	0	8	1	12	0
Sehwag	-	-	-	-	1	0	6	0

Fall of Wickets
1-67, 2-79, 3-86, 4-234, 5-314, 6-323, 7-337, 8-376, 9-377
1-19, 2-99, 3-171, 4-319, 5-329

INDIA

	First Innings		Second Innings	
A Chopra	c Warne b Gillespie	9	b Gillespie	1
V Sehwag	c Gilchrist b McGrath	22	c Clarke b Warne	58
R Dravid (capt)	c Warne b McGrath	21	b Gillespie	2
SR Tendulkar	lbw b Gillespie	8	c Martyn b McGrath	2
VVS Laxman	c Clarke b Warne	13	c McGrath b Kasprowicz	2
M Kaif	c Warne b McGrath	55	c Gilchrist b Kasprowicz	7
*PA Patel	c Hayden b Warne	20	c Gilchrist b Gillespie	32
AB Agarkar	c Clarke b Gillespie	15	not out	44
A Kumble	not out	7	b Gillespie	2
M Kartik	c Clarke b Gillespie	3	c Gilchrist b McGrath	22
Z Khan	b Gillespie	0	c Martyn b Warne	25
Extras	lb 10, w 1, nb 1	12	lb 2, nb 1	3
	(91.5 overs)	**185**	(53.3 overs)	**200**

	First Innings				Second Innings			
	O	M	R	W	O	M	R	W
McGrath	25	13	27	3	16	1	79	2
Gillespie	22.5	8	56	5	16	7	24	4
Kasprowicz	21	4	45	0	7	1	39	2
Warne	23	8	47	2	14.3	2	56	2

Fall of Wickets
1-31, 2-34, 3-49, 4-75, 5-103, 6-150, 7-173, 8-178, 9-181
1-1, 2-9, 3-20, 4-29, 5-37, 6-102, 7-114, 8-122, 9-148

Umpires: Aleem Dar & DR Shepherd
Toss: Australia
Man of the Match: DR Martyn

Australia won by 342 runs

FOURTH TEST – INDIA v. AUSTRALIA
3–5 November 2004 at Mumbai

INDIA

	First Innings		Second Innings	
G Gambhir	lbw b Gillespie	3	c Clarke b McGrath	1
V Sehwag	b McGrath	8	lbw b McGrath	5
R Dravid (capt)	not out	31	(5) c Gilchrist b Clarke	27
SR Tendulkar	c Gilchrist b Gillespie	5	c Clarke b Hauritz	55
VVS Laxman	c Gilchrist b Gillespie	1	(3) c & b Hauritz	69
M Kaif	lbw b Gillespie	2	b Clarke	25
*KKD Karthik	b Kasprowicz	10	c Ponting b Clarke	4
A Kumble	c Ponting b Hauritz	16	not out	13
Harbhajan Singh	c Katich b Hauritz	14	c Hayden b Clarke	0
M Kartik	c Gilchrist b Hauritz	0	b Clarke	2
Z Khan	b Kasprowicz	0	lbw b Clarke	0
Extras	b 6, lb 7, nb 1	14	b 4	4
	(41.3 overs)	**104**	(68.2 overs)	**205**

	First Innings				Second Innings			
	O	M	R	W	O	M	R	W
McGrath	16	9	35	1	12	6	29	2
Gillespie	12	2	29	4	15	1	47	0
Kasprowicz	8.3	3	11	2	13	5	29	0
Hauritz	5	0	16	3	22	4	87	2
Clarke	-	-	-	-	6.2	0	9	6

Fall of Wickets
1-11, 2-11, 3-29, 4-31, 5-33, 6-46, 7-68, 8-100, 9-102
1-5, 2-14, 3-105, 4-153, 5-182, 6-188, 7-195, 8-195, 9-199

AUSTRALIA

	First Innings		Second Innings	
JL Langer	c Dravid b Khan	12	c Karthik b Khan	0
ML Hayden	c Kaif b Kartik	35	b Harbhajan Singh	24
RT Ponting (capt)	lbw b Kumble	11	c Laxman b Kartik	12
DR Martyn	b Kartik	55	lbw b Kartik	0
SM Katich	c Kaif b Kumble	7	c Dravid b Harbhajan Singh	1
MJ Clarke	st Karthik b Kumble	17	b Kartik	7
*AC Gilchrist	c Kaif b Kartik	26	c Tendulkar b Harbhajan Singh	5
JN Gillespie	c Kaif b Kumble	2	not out	9
NM Hauritz	c Harbhajan Singh b Kumble	0	lbw b Kumble	15
MS Kasprowicz	c Kumble b Kartik	19	c Dravid b Harbhajan Singh	7
GD McGrath	not out	9	c Laxman b Harbhajan Singh	0
Extras	b 2, lb 4, nb 4	10	b 8, lb 5	13
	(61.3 overs)	**203**	(30.5 overs)	**93**

	First Innings				Second Innings			
	O	M	R	W	O	M	R	W
Khan	6	0	10	1	2	0	14	1
Harbhajan Singh	21	4	53	0	10.5	2	29	5
Kumble	19	0	90	5	6	3	5	1
Kartik	15.3	1	44	4	12	3	32	3

Fall of Wickets
1-17, 2-37, 3-81, 4-101, 5-121, 6-157, 7-167, 8-171, 9-184
1-0, 2-24, 3-24, 4-33, 5-48, 6-48, 7-58, 8-78, 9-93

Umpires: Aleem Dar & RE Koertzen
Toss: India
Man of the Match: M Kartik
Man of the Series: DR Martyn

India won by 13 runs

SERIES AVERAGES
India v. Australia

INDIA

Batting	M	Inns	NO	Runs	HS	Av	100	50	c/st
AB Agarkar	1	2	1	59	44*	59.00	-	-	1/-
V Sehwag	4	8	1	299	155	42.71	1	1	-/-
IK Pathan	2	3	0	100	55	33.33	-	1	-/-
PA Patel	3	5	0	156	54	31.20	-	1	7/1
M Kaif	3	5	0	153	64	30.60	-	2	6/-
R Dravid	4	7	1	167	60	27.83	-	1	13/-
SC Ganguly	2	3	0	59	45	19.66	-	-	-/-
VVS Laxman	4	7	0	123	69	17.57	-	1	7/-
SR Tendulkar	2	4	0	70	55	17.50	-	1	1/-
A Kumble	4	7	2	86	26	17.20	-	-	2/-
Yuvraj Singh	2	4	1	47	27	15.66	-	-	6/-
Harbhajan Singh	3	5	0	69	42	13.80	-	-	2/-
Z Khan	4	7	3	47	25	11.75	-	-	-/-
KKD Karthik	1	2	0	14	10	7.00	-	-	1/1
M Kartik	2	4	0	27	22	6.75	-	-	1/-
A Chopra	2	4	0	15	9	3.75	-	-	5/-
G Gambhir	1	2	0	4	3	2.00	-	-	-/-

Bowling	Overs	Mds	Runs	Wkts	Av	Best	5/inn	10m
M Kartik	73.3	10	207	12	17.25	4-44	-	-
Harbhajan Singh	178.5	32	504	21	24.00	6-78	3	1
A Kumble	197.3	30	685	27	25.37	7-48	3	1
Z Khan	123.3	22	368	10	36.80	4-95	-	-
IK Pathan	57	14	168	2	84.00	1-38	-	-
AB Agarkar	44	9	167	1	167.00	1-99	-	-

Also bowled: SC Ganguly 3-1-2-0, Yuvraj Singh 4-0-10-0, SR Tendulkar 14-2-41-0, V Sehwag 9-1-45-0.

AUSTRALIA

Batting	M	Inns	NO	Runs	HS	Av	100	50	c/st
MJ Clarke	4	8	1	400	151	57.14	1	2	7/-
DR Martyn	4	8	0	444	114	55.50	2	2	2/-
SM Katich	4	8	1	276	99	39.42	-	2	1/-
AC Gilchrist	4	8	1	218	104	31.14	1	-	16/-
ML Hayden	4	8	0	244	58	30.50	-	1	3/-
JL Langer	4	8	0	228	71	28.50	-	2	1/-
DS Lehmann	3	5	0	132	70	26.40	-	1	1/-
JN Gillespie	4	7	2	66	26	13.20	-	-	-/-
RT Ponting	1	2	0	23	12	11.50	-	-	2/-
SK Warne	3	5	0	38	31	7.60	-	-	4/-
NM Hauritz	1	2	0	15	15	7.50	-	-	1/-
GD McGrath	4	7	3	27	11*	6.75	-	-	2/-
MS Kasprowicz	4	7	0	46	19	6.57	-	-	-/-

Bowling	Overs	Mds	Runs	Wkts	Av	Best	5/inn	10m
MJ Clarke	7.2	0	13	6	2.16	6-9	1	-
JN Gillespie	132.5	33	323	20	16.15	5-56	1	-
NM Hauritz	27	4	103	5	20.60	3-16	-	-
GD McGrath	141	51	356	14	25.42	4-55	-	-
MS Kasprowicz	108.3	29	255	9	28.33	2-11	-	-
SK Warne	140	27	421	14	30.07	6-125	1	-

Also bowled: SM Katich 2-0-7-0, DS Lehmann 11-3-40-0.

FIRST TEST – INDIA v. SOUTH AFRICA
20–24 November 2004 at Kanpur

SOUTH AFRICA

	First Innings		Second Innings	
GC Smith (capt)	b Kumble	37	c Gambhir b Kartik	47
AJ Hall	b Kumble	163	c Karthik b Harbhajan Singh	26
M van Jaarsveld	lbw b Kumble	2	lbw b Kartik	13
JH Kallis	lbw b Kumble	37	not out	28
JA Rudolph	b Kumble	0	c Karthik b Harbhajan Singh	2
HH Dippenaar	c Karthik b Ganguly	48	not out	31
Z de Bruyn	c Dravid b Harbhajan Singh	83		
SM Pollock	not out	44		
*TL Tsolekile	lbw b Kumble	9		
RJ Peterson	b Harbhajan Singh	34		
M Ntini				
Extras	b 9, lb 22, w 1, nb 16, p 5	53	b 12, lb 5, nb 5	22
	(9 wkts dec 190.4 overs)	510	(4 wkts 64 overs)	169

	First Innings				Second Innings			
	O	M	R	W	O	M	R	W
Khan	29	7	59	0	8	2	26	0
Ganguly	12	2	45	1	-	-	-	-
Kumble	54	13	131	6	21	8	52	0
Harbhajan Singh	44.4	9	127	2	16	5	39	2
Kartik	42	12	76	0	14	6	17	2
Tendulkar	9	0	36	0	5	0	18	0

Fall of Wickets
1-61, 2-69, 3-154, 4-154, 5-241, 6-385, 7-445, 8-467, 9-510
1-67, 2-100, 3-110, 4-115

INDIA

	First Innings	
V Sehwag	lbw b Hall	164
G Gambhir	c Tsolekile b Pollock	96
R Dravid	c Tsolekile b Ntini	54
SR Tendulkar	b Hall	3
SC Ganguly (capt)	c Peterson b de Bruyn	57
VVS Laxman	b Ntini	9
*KKD Karthik	lbw b Pollock	1
A Kumble	c Tsolekile b Ntini	9
Harbhajan Singh	c Dippenaar b Peterson	17
Z Khan	b Hall	30
M Kartik	not out	0
Extras	b 10, lb 9, nb 7	26
	(134.4 overs)	466

	First Innings			
	O	M	R	W
Pollock	38	11	100	2
Ntini	39	0	135	3
Peterson	21	2	90	1
Hall	25.4	7	93	3
de Bruyn	11	3	29	1

Fall of Wickets
1-218, 2-294, 3-298, 4-394, 5-407, 6-408, 7-419, 8-420, 9-456

Umpires: DJ Harper & SJA Taufel
Toss: South Africa
Test debut: Z de Bruyn, TL Tsolekile
Man of the Match: AJ Hall

<u>Match drawn</u>

SECOND TEST – INDIA v. SOUTH AFRICA
28 November–2 December 2004 at Kolkata

SOUTH AFRICA

	First Innings			Second Innings	
GC Smith (capt)	c Karthik b Pathan	0		c Laxman b Harbhajan Singh	71
AJ Hall	c Karthik b Khan	7		c Karthik b Harbhajan Singh	21
JA Rudolph	b Khan	61		lbw b Harbhajan Singh	3
JH Kallis	b Ganguly	121		c & b Harbhajan Singh	55
HM Amla	b Pathan	24		c Laxman b Harbhajan Singh	2
HH Dippenaar	c Karthik b Pathan	1		c Sehwag b Kumble	2
Z de Bruyn	c Karthik b Khan	15		not out	32
SM Pollock	c Dravid b Kumble	18		c Gambhir b Harbhajan Singh	6
JL Ontong	not out	16		c Karthik b Harbhajan Singh	0
*TL Tsolekile	c & b Harbhajan Singh	15		b Kumble	1
M Ntini	c Pathan b Harbhajan Singh	0		c Dravid b Kumble	12
Extras	lb 17, nb 10	27		b 12, lb 2, nb 3	17
	(121.3 overs)	305		(74.4 overs)	222

	First Innings				Second Innings			
	O	M	R	W	O	M	R	W
Pathan	31	7	72	3	5	1	17	0
Khan	27	7	64	3	5	0	22	0
Kumble	30	6	76	1	34.4	7	82	3
Ganguly	9	3	14	1	-	-	-	-
Harbhajan Singh	21.3	6	54	2	30	3	87	7
Tendulkar	3	0	8	0	-	-	-	-

Fall of Wickets
1-0, 2-21, 3-130, 4-176, 5-182, 6-230, 7-261, 8-273, 9-305
1-77, 2-81, 3-126, 4-138, 5-147, 6-183, 7-193, 8-193, 9-194

INDIA

	First Innings			Second Innings	
V Sehwag	c Smith b Ntini	88		c Smith b Ntini	10
G Gambhir	lbw b Pollock	7		lbw b Rudolph	26
R Dravid	b Hall	80		not out	47
SR Tendulkar	b de Bruyn	20		not out	32
SC Ganguly (capt)	lbw b de Bruyn	40			
VVS Laxman	c Ontong b Ntini	38			
*KKD Karthik	lbw b Pollock	46			
IK Pathan	c Smith b Ntini	24			
A Kumble	c Kallis b Ntini	8			
Harbhajan Singh	c Dippenaar b Ontong	14			
Z Khan	not out	11			
Extras	lb 19, w 6, nb 10	35		lb 1, nb 4	5
	(150.1 overs)	411		(2 wkts 39.4 overs)	120

	First Innings				Second Innings			
	O	M	R	W	O	M	R	W
Pollock	45	13	101	2	7	1	22	0
Ntini	44	9	112	4	4	0	11	1
Ontong	18.1	1	79	1	10.4	1	44	0
Hall	27	5	68	1	3	2	2	0
de Bruyn	16	4	32	2	-	-	-	-
Rudolph	-	-	-	-	8	1	24	1
Smith	-	-	-	-	7	1	16	0

Fall of Wickets
1-17, 2-144, 3-189, 4-238, 5-267, 6-308, 7-366, 8-382, 9-387
1-15, 2-60

Umpires: DJ Harper & SJA Taufel
Toss: South Africa
Test debut: HM Amla
Man of the Match: Harbhajan Singh
Man of the Series: V Sehwag

India won by 8 wickets

SERIES AVERAGES
India v. South Africa

INDIA

Batting	M	Inns	NO	Runs	HS	Av	100	50	c/st
R Dravid	2	3	1	181	80	90.50	-	2	3/-
V Sehwag	2	3	0	262	164	87.33	1	1	1/-
SC Ganguly	2	2	0	97	57	48.50	-	1	-/-
G Gambhir	2	3	0	129	96	43.00	-	1	2/-
Z Khan	2	2	1	41	30	41.00	-	-	-/-
SR Tendulkar	2	3	1	55	32*	27.50	-	-	-/-
IK Pathan	1	1	0	24	24	24.00	-	-	1/-
VVS Laxman	2	2	0	47	38	23.50	-	-	2/-
KKD Karthik	2	2	0	47	46	23.50	-	-	9/-
Harbhajan Singh	2	2	0	31	17	15.50	-	-	2/-
A Kumble	2	2	0	17	9	8.50	-	-	-/-
M Kartik	1	1	1	0	0*	-	-	-	-/-

Bowling	Overs	Mds	Runs	Wkts	Av	Best	5/inn	10m
Harbhajan Singh	112.1	23	307	13	23.61	7-87	1	-
SC Ganguly	21	5	59	2	29.50	1-14	-	-
IK Pathan	36	8	89	3	29.66	3-72	-	-
A Kumble	139.4	34	341	10	34.10	6-131	1	-
M Kartik	56	18	93	2	46.50	2-17	-	-
Z Khan	69	16	171	3	57.00	3-64	-	-

Also bowled: SR Tendulkar 17-0-62-0.

SOUTH AFRICA

Batting	M	Inns	NO	Runs	HS	Av	100	50	c/st
JH Kallis	2	4	1	241	121	80.33	1	1	1/-
Z de Bruyn	2	3	1	130	83	65.00	-	1	-/-
AJ Hall	2	4	0	217	163	54.25	1	-	-/-
GC Smith	2	4	0	155	71	38.75	-	1	3/-
SM Pollock	2	3	1	68	44*	34.00	-	-	-/-
RJ Peterson	1	1	0	34	34	34.00	-	-	1/-
HH Dippenaar	2	4	1	82	48	27.33	-	-	2/-
JA Rudolph	2	4	0	66	61	16.50	-	1	-/-
JL Ontong	1	2	1	16	16*	16.00	-	-	1/-
HM Amla	1	2	0	26	24	13.00	-	-	-/-
TL Tsolekile	2	3	0	25	15	8.33	-	-	3/-
M van Jaarsveld	1	2	0	15	13	7.50	-	-	-/-
M Ntini	2	2	0	12	12	6.00	-	-	-/-

Bowling	Overs	Mds	Runs	Wkts	Av	Best	5/inn	10m
Z de Bruyn	27	7	61	3	20.33	2-32	-	-
JA Rudolph	8	1	24	1	24.00	1-24	-	-
M Ntini	87	9	258	8	32.25	4-112	-	-
AJ Hall	55.4	14	163	4	40.75	3-93	-	-
SM Pollock	90	25	223	4	55.75	2-100	-	-
RJ Peterson	21	2	90	1	90.00	1-90	-	-
JL Ontong	28.5	2	123	1	123.00	1-79	-	-

Also bowled: GC Smith 7-1-16-0.

FIRST TEST – INDIA v. PAKISTAN
8–12 March 2005 at Mohali

PAKISTAN

	First Innings		Second Innings	
Salman Butt	b Pathan	5	c Karthik b Pathan	5
Taufeeq Umar	b Balaji	44	c & b Balaji	4
Younis Khan	lbw b Khan	9	b Balaji	1
Inzamam-ul-Haq (capt)	lbw b Kumble	57	(5) lbw b Kumble	86
Yousuf Youhana	c Karthik b Pathan	6	(4) b Kumble	68
Asim Kamal	b Balaji	91	lbw b Balaji	48
Abdul Razzaq	c Karthik b Balaji	26	c Dravid b Kumble	71
*Kamran Akmal	c Dravid b Kumble	15	c sub b Balaji	109
Mohammad Sami	b Balaji	20	c & b Kumble	10
Naved-ul-Hasan	lbw b Balaji	11	not out	38
Danish Kaneria	not out	8	not out	4
Extras	b 11, lb 5, w 1, nb 3	20	b 17, lb 20, w 13, nb 2	52
	(86.4 overs)	312	(9 wkts dec 144 overs)	496

	First Innings				Second Innings			
	O	M	R	W	O	M	R	W
Pathan	23	5	68	2	27	7	70	1
Khan	17	2	70	1	22	0	93	0
Balaji	20.4	5	76	5	30	5	95	4
Kumble	22	6	76	2	54	16	160	4
Ganguly	2	0	3	0	-	-	-	-
Sehwag	2	1	3	0	3	1	11	0
Tendulkar	-	-	-	-	8	0	30	0

Fall of Wickets
1-11, 2-30, 3-89, 4-104, 5-156, 6-191, 7-239, 8-282, 9-303
1-6, 2-10, 3-10, 4-149, 5-193, 6-243, 7-427, 8-436, 9-467

INDIA

	First Innings		Second Innings	
G Gambhir	c Naved-ul-Hasan b D Kaneria	41	not out	32
V Sehwag	c Yousuf Youhana b A Razzaq	173	st Kamran Akmal b Younis Khan	36
R Dravid	c Asim Kamal b M Sami	50		
SR Tendulkar	c Asim Kamal b Naved-ul-Hasan	94		
SC Ganguly (capt)	c Salman Butt b Danish Kaneria	21		
VVS Laxman	b Danish Kaneria	58		
*KKD Karthik	c Naved-ul-Hasan b M Sami	6		
IK Pathan	st Kamran Akmal b D Kaneria	13		
L Balaji	c Kamran Akmal b D Kaneria	31		
A Kumble	not out	1		
Z Khan	c & b Danish Kaneria	0		
Extras	b 1, lb 5, w 1, nb 21	28	b 5, lb 8, nb 4	17
	(147.4 overs)	516	(1 wkt 17 overs)	85

	First Innings				Second Innings			
	O	M	R	W	O	M	R	W
Mohammad Sami	36	6	120	2	7	0	25	0
Naved-ul-Hasan	32	1	133	1	2	0	6	0
Abdul Razzaq	26	1	107	1	-	-	-	-
Danish Kaneria	53.4	12	150	6	6	2	17	0
Younis Khan	-	-	-	-	2	0	24	1

Fall of Wickets
1-113, 2-216, 3-334, 4-381, 5-417, 6-444, 7-465, 8-507, 9-516
1-85

Umpires: DB Hair & RE Koertzen
Toss: India
Man of the Match: Kamran Akmal

Match drawn

SECOND TEST – INDIA v. PAKISTAN
16–20 March 2005 at Kolkata

INDIA

	First Innings		Second Innings	
V Sehwag	c Inzamam-ul-Haq b S Afridi	81	b Mohammad Sami	15
G Gambhir	lbw b Danish Kaneria	29	b Mohammad Sami	1
R Dravid	c Kamran Akmal b D Kaneria	110	c Asim Kamal b Danish Kaneria	135
SR Tendulkar	c Kamran Akmal b Shahid Afridi	52	c Kamran Akmal b Abdul Razzaq	52
SC Ganguly (capt)	c Kamran Akmal b Abdul Razzaq	12	c & b Mohammad Sami	12
VVS Laxman	lbw b Abdul Razzaq	0	st Kamran Akmal b Danish Kaneria	24
*KKD Karthik	run out	28	b Danish Kaneria	93
IK Pathan	c Younis Khan b Danish Kaneria	8	not out	38
L Balaji	b Shahid Afridi	3	(10) c Kamran Akmal b A Razzaq	0
Harbhajan Singh	lbw b Abdul Razzaq	27	(9) b Abdul Razzaq	0
A Kumble	not out	21	not out	14
Extras	b 2, lb 12, w 6, nb 16	36	b 5, lb 5, w 1, nb 12	23
	(111.1 overs)	407	(9 wkts dec 104 overs)	407

	First Innings				Second Innings			
	O	M	R	W	O	M	R	W
Mohammad Sami	22	3	76	0	23	5	82	3
Mohammad Khalil	11	3	39	0	12	0	64	0
Danish Kaneria	35	1	136	3	34	7	123	3
Abdul Razzaq	22.1	4	62	3	19	3	80	3
Shahid Afridi	21	0	80	3	15	2	47	0
Younis Khan	-	-	-	-	1	0	1	0

Fall of Wickets
1-80, 2-156, 3-278, 4-298, 5-298, 6-344, 7-345, 8-357, 9-363
1-14, 2-23, 3-121, 4-154, 5-321, 6-331, 7-377, 8-378, 9-378

PAKISTAN

	First Innings		Second Innings	
Taufeeq Umar	c Harbhajan Singh b Balaji	18	c Sehwag b Balaji	35
Shahid Afridi	c Tendulkar b Pathan	29	c Ganguly b Kumble	59
Younis Khan	c Laxman b Kumble	147	st Karthik b Kumble	0
Yousuf Youhana	lbw b Balaji	104	(5) c Gambhir b Kumble	22
Inzamam-ul-Haq (capt)	c Karthik b Pathan	30	(4) b Kumble	13
Asim Kamal	run out	6	c sub b Kumble	50
Abdul Razzaq	c Dravid b Kumble	17	b Kumble	6
*Kamran Akmal	c Tendulkar b Harbhajan Singh	0	b Harbhajan Singh	7
Mohammad Sami	c Ganguly b Harbhajan Singh	7	lbw b Kumble	9
Mohammad Khalil	c Sehwag b Kumble	4	not out	0
Danish Kaneria	not out	3	b Harbhajan Singh	3
Extras	b 5, lb 13, w 2, nb 8	28	b 17, lb 3, w 1, nb 1	22
	(113.1 overs)	393	(91.3 overs)	226

	First Innings				Second Innings			
	O	M	R	W	O	M	R	W
Pathan	23	6	90	2	7	1	32	0
Balaji	21	1	81	2	16	4	60	1
Kumble	37.1	11	98	3	38	16	63	7
Ganguly	2	0	12	0	-	-	-	-
Harbhajan Singh	30	6	94	2	30.3	16	51	2

Fall of Wickets
1-35, 2-70, 3-281, 4-331, 5-347, 6-361, 7-362, 8-378, 9-378
1-93, 2-95, 3-115, 4-115, 5-178, 6-188, 7-203, 8-214, 9-223

Umpires: SA Bucknor & DB Hair
Toss: India
Man of the Match: R Dravid

India won by 195 runs

THIRD TEST – INDIA v. PAKISTAN
24–28 March 2005 at Bangalore

PAKISTAN

	First Innings		Second Innings	
Yasir Hameed	c Karthik b Pathan	6	lbw b Kumble	76
Shahid Afridi	c Dravid b Balaji	0	st Karthik b Tendulkar	58
Younis Khan	c Pathan b Harbhajan Singh	267	not out	84
Inzamam-ul-Haq (capt)	lbw b Balaji	184	not out	31
Yousuf Youhana	c Karthik b Harbhajan Singh	37		
Asim Kamal	c Ganguly b Harbhajan Singh	4		
Abdul Razzaq	c & b Harbhajan Singh	5		
*Kamran Akmal	b Harbhajan Singh	28		
Mohammad Sami	run out	17		
Arshad Khan	not out	1		
Danish Kaneria	c Laxman b Harbhajan Singh	0		
Extras	b 8, lb 5, w 4, nb 4	21	b 4, lb 1, w 5, nb 2	12
	(167.5 overs)	570	(2 wkts dec 50 overs)	261

	First Innings				Second Innings			
	O	M	R	W	O	M	R	W
Pathan	34	4	105	1	5	0	45	0
Balaji	29	4	114	2	3	0	26	0
Kumble	46	8	159	0	21	1	88	1
Harbhajan Singh	51.5	9	152	6	6	0	35	0
Tendulkar	3	0	14	0	15	1	62	1
Ganguly	4	0	13	0	-	-	-	-

Fall of Wickets
1-4, 2-7, 3-331, 4-415, 5-428, 6-446, 7-504, 8-565, 9-569
1-91, 2-183

INDIA

	First Innings		Second Innings	
G Gambhir	c Younis Khan b M Sami	24	lbw b Mohammad Sami	52
V Sehwag	c & b Danish Kaneria	201	run out	38
R Dravid	lbw b Danish Kaneria	22	c Younis Khan b Arshad Khan	16
SR Tendulkar	c Younis Khan b Shahid Afridi	41	c Asim Kamal b Shahid Afridi	16
VVS Laxman	not out	79	lbw b Shahid Afridi	5
SC Ganguly (capt)	st Kamran Akmal b D Kaneria	1	b Shahid Afridi	2
*KKD Karthik	c Asim Kamal b M Sami	10	b Mohammad Sami	9
IK Pathan	c Yousuf Youhana b M Sami	5	(9) c Yousuf Youhana b A Khan	0
Harbhajan Singh	c Abdul Razzaq b Danish Kaneria	1	(10) c Younis Khan b D Kaneria	8
L Balaji	c Kamran Akmal b Danish Kaneria	2	(11) lbw b Danish Kaneria	0
A Kumble	b Shahid Afridi	22	(8) not out	37
Extras	b 9, lb 13, w 1, nb 18	41	b 8, lb 8, w 10, nb 5	31
	(128.4 overs)	449	(90 overs)	214

	First Innings				Second Innings			
	O	M	R	W	O	M	R	W
Mohammad Sami	34	5	106	3	21	5	84	2
Abdul Razzaq	17	0	77	0	13	3	34	0
Danish Kaneria	39	7	127	5	25	11	46	2
Arshad Khan	28	3	87	0	14	8	21	2
Shahid Afridi	10.4	3	30	2	17	7	13	3

Fall of Wickets
1-98, 2-172, 3-257, 4-337, 5-343, 6-374, 7-386, 8-388, 9-396
1-87, 2-108, 3-118, 4-127, 5-135, 6-164, 7-164, 8-189, 9-210

Umpires: BF Bowden & SJA Taufel
Toss: Pakistan
Man of the Match: Younis Khan
Man of the Series: V Sehwag

Pakistan won by 168 runs

SERIES AVERAGES
India v. Pakistan

INDIA

Batting	M	Inns	NO	Runs	HS	Av	100	50	c/st
A Kumble	3	5	4	95	37*	95.00	-	-	1/-
V Sehwag	3	6	0	544	201	90.66	2	1	2/-
R Dravid	3	5	0	333	135	66.60	2	1	4/-
SR Tendulkar	3	5	0	255	94	51.00	-	3	2/-
VVS Laxman	3	5	1	166	79*	41.50	-	2	2/-
G Gambhir	3	6	1	179	52	35.80	-	1	1/-
KKD Karthik	3	5	0	146	93	29.20	-	1	6/2
IK Pathan	3	5	1	64	38*	16.00	-	-	1/-
SC Ganguly	3	5	0	48	21	9.60	-	-	3/-
Harbhajan Singh	2	4	0	36	27	9.00	-	-	2/-
L Balaji	3	5	0	36	31	7.20	-	-	1/-
Z Khan	1	1	0	0	0	0.00	-	-	-/-

Bowling	Overs	Mds	Runs	Wkts	Av	Best	5/inn	10m
L Balaji	119.4	19	452	14	32.28	5-76	1	-
Harbhajan Singh	118.2	31	332	10	33.20	6-152	1	-
A Kumble	218.1	58	644	17	37.88	7-63	1	1
IK Pathan	119	23	410	6	68.33	2-68	-	-
SR Tendulkar	26	1	106	1	106.00	1-62	-	-
Z Khan	39	2	163	1	163.00	1-70	-	-

Also bowled: V Sehwag 5-2-14-0, SC Ganguly 8-0-28-0.

PAKISTAN

Batting	M	Inns	NO	Runs	HS	Av	100	50	c/st
Younis Khan	3	6	1	508	267	101.60	2	1	5/-
Inzamam-ul-Haq	3	6	1	401	184	80.20	1	2	1/-
Naved-ul-Hasan	1	2	1	49	38*	49.00	-	-	2/-
Yousuf Youhana	3	5	0	237	104	47.40	1	1	3/-
Yasir Hameed	1	2	0	82	76	41.00	-	1	-/-
Asim Kamal	3	5	0	199	91	39.80	-	2	5/-
Shahid Afridi	2	4	0	146	59	36.50	-	2	-/-
Kamran Akmal	3	5	0	159	109	31.80	1	-	7/4
Taufeeq Umar	2	4	0	101	44	25.25	-	-	-/-
Abdul Razzaq	3	5	0	125	71	25.00	-	1	1/-
Mohammad Sami	3	5	0	63	20	12.60	-	-	1/-
Danish Kaneria	3	5	3	18	8*	9.00	-	-	2/-
Salman Butt	1	2	0	10	5	5.00	-	-	1/-
Mohammad Khalil	1	2	1	4	4	4.00	-	-	-/-
Arshad Khan	1	1	1	1	1*	-	-	-	-/-

Bowling	Overs	Mds	Runs	Wkts	Av	Best	5/inn	10m
Shahid Afridi	63.4	12	170	8	21.25	3-13	-	-
Younis Khan	3	0	25	1	25.00	1-24	-	-
Danish Kaneria	192.4	40	599	19	31.52	6-150	2	-
Mohammad Sami	143	24	493	10	49.30	3-82	-	-
Abdul Razzaq	97.1	11	360	7	51.42	3-62	-	-
Arshad Khan	42	11	108	2	54.00	2-21	-	-
Naved-ul-Hasan	34	1	139	1	139.00	1-133	-	-

Also bowled: Mohammad Khalil 23-3-103-0.

ONE-DAY INTERNATIONALS
v. Pakistan

Match One
2 April 2005 at Kochi
India 281 for 8 (50 overs) (V Sehwag 108,
R Dravid 104, Arshad Khan 4 for 33)
Pakistan 194 (45.2 overs)
(SR Tendulkar 5 for 50)
India won by 87 runs

Match Two
5 April 2005 at Visakhapatnam
India 356 for 9 (50 overs) (MS Dhoni 148,
V Sehwag 74, R Dravid 52)
Pakistan 298 (44.1 overs) (Abdul Razzaq 88,
Yousuf Youhana 71, A Nehra 4 for 72)
India won by 58 runs

Match Three
9 April 2005 at Jamshedpur
Pakistan 319 for 9 (50 overs) (Salman Butt 101,
Shoaib Malik 75)
India 213 (41.4 overs) (IK Pathan 64,
Naved-ul-Hasan 6 for 27)
Pakistan won by 106 runs

Match Four
12 April 2005 at Ahmedabad
India 315 for 6 (48 overs) (SR Tendulkar 123)
Pakistan 319 for 7
(48 overs)
(Shoaib Malik 65,
Inzamam-ul-Haq 60*)
Pakistan won by 3 wickets

Match Five
15 April 2005 at Kanpur
India 249 for 6 (50 overs)
(R Dravid 86, M Kaif 78)
Pakistan 252 for 5
(42.1 overs)
(Shahid Afridi 102)
Pakistan won by 5 wickets

A touch of fate: Virender Sehwag enjoyed a prolific Test series against Pakistan, with 544 runs in the three matches at an average of 90. Here, though, at Calcutta, he was unlucky to play on to Mohammad Sami and was gone for 15.

NEW ZEALAND

NEW ZEALAND REPORT
By Bryan Waddle

One of the fascinating, never-ending rituals of the current game is the comparisons made between great cricket teams of various eras: the 1948 Australians, Clive Lloyd's West Indies team of the late 1970s and early 1980s, and the Australian sides led by Steve Waugh and Ricky Ponting.

They are subjective arguments, of course, and hardly likely to be resolved successfully, but the fact that Ponting's Australians were mentioned in such august company was enough to represent the scale of the challenge facing New Zealand over the past 12 months.

By any yardstick the Black Caps didn't measure up to it. Despite the bookends of successful series against extremely modest opposition in Bangladesh and Zimbabwe, New Zealand lost ground against the Australians. Five Tests played and four lost might not have fairly reflected New Zealand's overall performance, but in reality the Australian dominance was as emphatic as the series result suggested.

Two Test wins and three ODI victories in Bangladesh was hardly the preparation New Zealand needed for the series against Australia. Those wins were so comprehensive that, individually and collectively, it was hard to gauge the Black Caps' performance. They did what they had to, ruthlessly disposing of opposition that hasn't yet reached any consistency at international level.

Individuals were able to shine in the harsh environment of Dhaka and Chittagong with Daniel Vettori clearly the main star. Vettori prospered in conditions that encouraged spin bowling. So often in the past Vettori hasn't had an adequate workload heading into busy international programmes but in two Tests the left-arm spinner gained valuable time at the bowling crease completing 111 overs and taking 20 wickets at 11.2 – including three bags of five in an innings and 12 scalps overall in the second Test in Chittagong.

There were cameo performances of quality, also, from James Franklin and Stephen Fleming. A genuine swing bowler, Franklin's left-armers have troubled many Test batsmen in a relatively brief

career. His play though has been a little like his Test appearances – erratic – but when he gains greater consistency he is likely to become a more potent force. In Dhaka, Franklin became only the second New Zealander to take a Test match hat-trick, after Peter Petherick's astonishing debut feat against Pakistan in Lahore in 1976–77, ending with 5 for 28 from seventeen overs in Bangladesh's first innings. Fleming was the individual batting star of the second Test, his 202 helping New Zealand to 545 for 6 declared before Vettori exercised his by-now familiar control over the Bangladesh batsmen.

New Zealand's international summer programme, however, was severely curtailed by the Asian Tsunami. No sooner had the series against Sri Lanka started – and the first ODI completed – than the Sri Lankans quite rightly returned home to face the horror of the devastation in the south of their country.

A hastily arranged series of matches between New Zealand and a World XI captained by Shane Warne plugged the gap in the summer programme. The goodwill and generosity of players and public alike made the results irrelevant but the matches ensured that New Zealand Cricket was able to donate more than $1million to the Tsunami Relief effort.

After the comprehensive defeats in Australia pre-Christmas, New Zealand needed a strong home performance to regain some credibility. The omens for the Test series were not great, though, as Australia handed out a one-day lesson with a resounding clean sweep of the five-match ODI series.

On the first day of the Test series there were at least some positive signs that New Zealand might match the world champions. Sent in on a hard, well-grassed Jade Stadium pitch, New Zealand compiled 433 with Hamish Marshall in his first home Test producing a mature innings of 146. As dominant as the home team were on the first day, however, reaching 265 for 3, they could not sustain any pressure to make life tough for the Australians.

With Australia at 201 for 6 in reply, New Zealand still appeared to have the grip they wanted but they hadn't counted on the power of Adam Gilchrist's game. The Aussie keeper, with sound support from Simon Katich, took Australia to within a run of New Zealand's total and from there it was one-way traffic.

Just out of reach: James Franklin attempts something spectacular off his own bowling during New Zealand's Napier Test match against Sri Lanka.

In between time Adam Gilchrist gave another display of his brilliance. His second successive hundred of the series ended at 162, made off just 146 balls, and with Damien Martyn he added a record 256 for the sixth wicket against New Zealand.

The old firm of Warne and McGrath kept the foot on the New Zealand throat in the third Test, snaring 14 of the 20 Black Cap wickets to fall. In fact, that pair collected 17 and 18 wickets respectively in the three-Test series which, with the commanding batting of Gilchrist, who scored 343 runs at 171.5, highlighted the difference between the sides.

By contrast New Zealand's top performers with the ball were Franklin and Vettori – Franklin taking a creditable 12 wickets while Vettori shouldered another big workload for a return of just eight. But Vettori's control of flight and spin, and clever changes of pace, kept a hold on the Australian batsmen who were content to survive the left-armer and attack what was a relatively

The irresistible power of the Australian bowling had New Zealand out in just 50 overs in the second innings for 131, and a nine-wicket victory.

In Wellington it was much of the same although the weather had the first and final say – washing out the entire first day and ending play early on the last.

innocuous bowling line-up at the other end.

With the rugby season in full swing and late afternoon light hardly conducive to good cricket, New Zealand had to play two Tests in April to fulfil its series with Sri Lanka. April, though, is not a good month for cricket in New Zealand – yet the weather conditions held long enough for the Black Caps to complete a 1-0 series win over an underdone Sri Lankan unit.

McLean Park in Napier was a bowlers' graveyard during the first Test, with New Zealand reaching 561 and then matched by Sri Lanka's 498. Both sides had two centurions, Hamish Marshall and Astle for the Kiwis and Atapattu and Jayawardene for the tourists, while Brendon McCullum fell in the 90s for the second time in his brief Test career.

While the Napier pitch proved difficult for bowlers, Sri Lanka unleashed a bowler of unusual style on the New Zealanders – and he almost stole the Test. Lasith Malinga has an awkward low slinging action and delivers at lively pace. Coupled with good control of swing he ended with nine wickets in the match, taking 5 for 80 in the second innings as New Zealand slumped to 238 all out.

Lou Vincent and pace bowler Chris Martin gave New Zealand the telling advantage in the second

Test. Martin took the first six wickets to leave Sri Lanka teetering at 86 for 7 soon after lunch on the first day, and although they recovered to reach 211 it was only a minor revival. Vincent gave a command performance over the next two days in reaching his highest Test score, 224, ensuring that New Zealand took a first innings lead of 311. The match was then wrapped up with a day to spare, Franklin the chief destroyer in the second innings with 4 for 71.

Forgetting the opposition, New Zealand's overall record during the year was satisfactory: five Test wins from 11 played and ten ODI wins from 18. Yet, by true international standards, they wouldn't have gained a pass mark. Perhaps the long-awaited, and initially successful, return from injury of fast bowler Shane Bond to international cricket late in New Zealand's year will herald an upturn in fortunes during the coming 12 months. Bond's cutting edge had been badly missed.

Auckland won the domestic first-class title by beating Wellington in the final by seven wickets. Auckland were the top qualifiers after winning five of eight preliminary games. Their one-day performances, however, were not as successful with just one win from ten games. Northern Districts took the limited-overs title, beating top qualifiers Central Districts in the final.

Left-arm spinner Daniel Vettori gained the respect of Australia's batsmen during the Test series won 2-0 by the world champions.

ONE-DAY INTERNATIONALS
v. Sri Lanka

Match One
26 December 2004 at Auckland
Sri Lanka 141 (42 overs)
(CL Cairns 4 for 33)
New Zealand 144 for 3 (33 overs)
(SP Fleming 77*)
New Zealand won by 7 wickets

ONE-DAY INTERNATIONALS
v. Australia

Match One
19 February 2005 at Wellington
Australia 236 for 7 (50 overs) (ML Hayden 71,
RT Ponting 61, A Symonds 53, SB Styris 4 for 40)
New Zealand 226 (48.4 overs) (HJH Marshall 76,
NJ Astle 65, GD McGrath 4 for 16)
Australia won by 10 runs

Match Two
22 February 2005 at Christchurch
Australia 314 for 6 (50 overs)
(ML Hayden 114, DR Martyn 58, RT Ponting 53)
New Zealand 208 (40.4 overs)
(DL Vettori 83)
Australia won by 106 runs

Match Three
26 February 2005 at Auckland
Australia 264 for 5 (50 overs)
(MJ Clarke 71*, MEK Hussey 65*, SM Katich 58)
New Zealand 178 for 9 (41.5 overs)
(HJH Marshall 55)
Australia won by 86 runs

Match Four
1 March 2005 at Wellington
New Zealand 233 (49.5 overs)
Australia 236 for 3 (34.2 overs)
(DR Martyn 65*, AC Gilchrist 54)
Australia won by 7 wickets

Match Five
5 March 2005 at Napier
Australia 347 for 5 (50 overs)
(RT Ponting 141*, AC Gilchrist 91)
New Zealand 225 for 8 (50 overs)
(CD McMillan 63)
Australia won by 122 runs

FIRST TEST – NEW ZEALAND v. AUSTRALIA
10–13 March 2005 at Christchurch

NEW ZEALAND

	First Innings		Second Innings	
CD Cumming	c Gillespie b Kasprowicz	74	lbw b Gillespie	7
SP Fleming (capt)	lbw b Warne	18	lbw b McGrath	17
HJH Marshall	b Warne	146	b Warne	22
L Vincent	lbw b Clarke	27	lbw b Gillespie	4
NJ Astle	lbw b McGrath	74	b Kasprowicz	21
CD McMillan	c Gilchrist b McGrath	13	c Katich b Warne	5
*BB McCullum	c Langer b McGrath	29	lbw b Gillespie	24
DL Vettori	not out	24	lbw b Warne	23
JEC Franklin	lbw b McGrath	0	not out	5
IEO'Brien	c Gilchrist b McGrath	5	lbw b Warne	0
CS Martin	c Gilchrist b McGrath	1	lbw b Warne	0
Extras	b 4, lb 14, w 2, nb 2	22	b 1, lb 1, nb 1	3
	(141 overs)	433	(50 overs)	131

	First Innings				Second Innings			
	O	M	R	W	O	M	R	W
McGrath	42	9	115	6	14	7	19	1
Gillespie	29	5	87	0	12	2	38	3
Kasprowicz	25	6	85	1	10	3	33	1
Warne	40	6	112	2	14	3	39	5
Clarke	5	0	16	1	-	-	-	-

Fall of Wickets
1-56, 2-153, 3-199, 4-330, 5-355, 6-388, 7-403, 8-403, 9-415
1-20, 2-30, 3-34, 4-71, 5-78, 6-87, 7-121, 8-127, 9-131

AUSTRALIA

	First Innings		Second Innings	
JL Langer	b Franklin	23	not out	72
ML Hayden	c Astle b O'Brien	35	c Cumming b Vettori	15
RT Ponting (capt)	c McCullum b Martin	46	not out	47
DR Martyn	lbw b Vettori	32		
JN Gillespie	c Cumming b Vettori	12		
MJ Clarke	c McCullum b Franklin	8		
SM Katich	c Vincent b Astle	118		
*AC Gilchrist	c O'Brien b Vettori	121		
SK Warne	c Astle b Vettori	2		
MS Kasprowicz	not out	13		
GD McGrath	lbw b Vettori	0		
Extras	b 2, lb 13, w 3, nb 4	22	nb 1	1
	(123.2 overs)	432	(1 wkt 31.3 overs)	135

	First Innings				Second Innings			
	O	M	R	W	O	M	R	W
Martin	29	6	104	1	8	0	27	0
Franklin	26	5	102	2	5	1	26	0
O'Brien	14	3	73	1	5	0	27	0
Vettori	40.2	13	106	5	13.3	0	55	1
Astle	14	6	32	1	-	-	-	-

Fall of Wickets
1-48, 2-75, 3-140, 4-147, 5-160, 6-201, 7-413, 8-418, 9-426
1-25

Umpires: Aleem Dar & DR Shepherd
Toss: Australia
Test debuts: CD Cumming, IE O'Brien
Man of the Match: AC Gilchrist

<u>**Australia won by 9 wickets**</u>

SECOND TEST – NEW ZEALAND v. AUSTRALIA
18–22 March 2005 at Wellington

AUSTRALIA

	First Innings		
JL Langer	c McCullum b Vettori	46	
ML Hayden	c Vincent b Franklin	61	
RT Ponting (capt)	lbw b Vettori	9	
DR Martyn	c McCullum b O'Brien	165	
MJ Clarke	c Fleming b Astle	8	
SM Katich	c McCullum b Franklin	35	
*AC Gilchrist	c & b Franklin	162	
SK Warne	not out	50	
JN Gillespie	b Franklin	2	
MS Kasprowicz	not out	2	
GD McGrath			
Extras	b 4, lb 8, w 2, nb 16	30	
	(8 wkts dec 140 overs)	**570**	

	First Innings			
	O	M	R	W
Martin	28	6	123	0
Franklin	28	4	128	4
O'Brien	24	4	97	1
Vettori	47	5	170	2
Astle	13	2	40	1

Fall of Wickets
1-82, 2-100, 3-146, 4-163, 5-247, 6-503, 7-557, 8-559

NEW ZEALAND

	First Innings		Second Innings	
CD Cumming	b Kasprowicz	37	not out	10
SP Fleming (capt)	lbw b McGrath	0	lbw b McGrath	1
HJH Marshall	c Gillespie b McGrath	18	lbw b McGrath	0
L Vincent	c Gilchrist b Kasprowicz	63	b Kasprowicz	24
NJ Astle	c Warne b Clarke	9	not out	4
JEC Franklin	c Gilchrist b Kasprowicz	26		
CD McMillan	b Warne	20		
*BB McCullum	c Clarke b Warne	3		
DL Vettori	c Martyn b Warne	45		
IEO'Brien	b Gillespie	5		
CS Martin	not out	0		
Extras	b 4, lb 8, w 1, nb 5	18	b 3, lb 5, nb 1	9
	(81.1 overs)	244	(3 wkts 17.2 overs)	48

	First Innings				Second Innings			
	O	M	R	W	O	M	R	W
McGrath	14	3	50	2	6	3	10	2
Gillespie	20	4	63	1	5	2	5	0
Kasprowicz	16	2	42	3	3	0	11	1
Warne	28.1	7	69	3	3.2	0	14	0
Clarke	3	1	8	1	-	-	-	-

Fall of Wickets
1-9, 2-55, 3-78, 4-108, 5-166, 6-180, 7-184, 8-201, 9-212
1-3, 2-3, 3-37

Umpires: RE Koertzen & DR Shepherd
Toss: New Zealand
Man of the Match: AC Gilchrist

Match drawn

THIRD TEST – NEW ZEALAND v. AUSTRALIA
26–29 March 2005 at Auckland

NEW ZEALAND

	First Innings		Second Innings	
CD Cumming	lbw b Gillespie	5	lbw b McGrath	0
JAH Marshall	c Hayden b McGrath	29	c Langer b McGrath	3
HJH Marshall	c Ponting b Warne	76	c Gilchrist b McGrath	7
SP Fleming (capt)	b Kasprowicz	65	c & b Gillespie	3
NJ Astle	c Langer b McGrath	19	c Katich b Warne	69
L Vincent	b Gillespie	2	run out	40
*BB McCullum	c Gilchrist b McGrath	25	lbw b Warne	0
DL Vettori	not out	41	c McGrath b Warne	65
JEC Franklin	c Katich b Warne	3	c Ponting b Warne	23
PJ Wiseman	c Gillespie b Warne	8	b McGrath	23
CS Martin	c Clarke b Kasprowicz	0	not out	4
Extras	b 4, lb 13, nb 2	19	b 1, lb 14, nb 2	17
	(116.2 overs)	292	(69.2 overs)	254

	First Innings				Second Innings			
	O	M	R	W	O	M	R	W
McGrath	34	20	49	3	16.2	5	40	4
Gillespie	25	8	64	2	16	4	63	1
Kasprowicz	30.2	7	89	2	14	2	59	0
Warne	23	4	63	3	23	5	77	4
Ponting	4	1	10	0	-	-	-	-

Fall of Wickets
1-15, 2-53, 3-179, 4-183, 5-194, 6-228, 7-247, 8-262, 9-288
1-0, 2-9, 3-15, 4-23, 5-93, 6-93, 7-174, 8-220, 9-227

AUSTRALIA

	First Innings		Second Innings	
JL Langer	b Franklin	6	not out	59
ML Hayden	lbw b Franklin	38	run out	9
RT Ponting (capt)	c McCullum b Astle	105	not out	86
DR Martyn	b Wiseman	38		
MJ Clarke	run out	22		
JN Gillespie	c McCullum b Martin	35		
SM Katich	c Wiseman b Franklin	35		
*AC Gilchrist	not out	60		
SK Warne	c Fleming b Franklin	1		
MS Kasprowicz	b Franklin	23		
GD McGrath	c McCullum b Franklin	0		
Extras	b 4, lb 7, nb 9	20	lb 10, nb 2	12
	(118.1 overs)	383	(1 wkt 29.3 overs)	166

	First Innings				Second Innings			
	O	M	R	W	O	M	R	W
Martin	21	4	92	1	8	1	51	0
Franklin	26.1	3	119	6	7	0	40	0
Astle	21	7	50	1	7	0	33	0
Vettori	19	4	47	0	4	0	19	0
Wiseman	31	7	64	1	3.3	0	13	0

Fall of Wickets
1-8, 2-84, 3-187, 4-215, 5-226, 6-297, 7-297, 8-303, 9-377
1-18

Umpires: JW Lloyds & RE Koertzen
Toss: New Zealand
Test debut: JAH Marshall
Man of the Match: RT Ponting
Man of the Series: AC Gilchrist

Australia won by 9 wickets

SERIES AVERAGES
New Zealand v. Australia

NEW ZEALAND

Batting	M	Inns	NO	Runs	HS	Av	100	50	c/st
DL Vettori	3	5	2	198	65	66.00	-	1	-/-
HJH Marshall	3	6	0	269	146	44.83	1	1	-/-
NJ Astle	3	6	1	196	74	39.20	-	2	2/-
L Vincent	3	6	0	160	63	26.66	-	1	2/-
CD Cumming	3	6	1	133	74	26.60	-	1	2/-
SP Fleming	3	6	0	104	65	17.33	-	1	2/-
BB McCullum	3	5	0	81	29	16.20	-	-	8/-
JAH Marshall	1	2	0	32	29	16.00	-	-	-/-
PJ Wiseman	1	2	0	31	23	15.50	-	-	1/-
JEC Franklin	3	5	1	57	26	14.25	-	-	1/-
CD McMillan	2	3	0	38	20	12.66	-	-	-/-
IE O'Brien	2	3	0	10	5	3.33	-	-	1/-
CS Martin	3	5	2	5	4*	1.66	-	-	-/-

Bowling	Overs	Mds	Runs	Wkts	Av	Best	5/inn	10m
JEC Franklin	92.1	13	415	12	34.58	6-119	1	-
DL Vettori	123.5	22	397	8	49.62	5-106	1	-
NJ Astle	55	15	155	3	51.66	1-32	-	-
PJ Wiseman	34.3	7	77	1	77.00	1-64	-	-
IE O'Brien	43	7	197	2	98.50	1-73	-	-
CS Martin	94	17	397	2	198.50	1-92	-	-

AUSTRALIA

Batting	M	Inns	NO	Runs	HS	Av	100	50	c/st
AC Gilchrist	3	3	1	343	162	171.50	2	1	7/-
RT Ponting	3	5	2	293	105	97.66	1	1	2/-
DR Martyn	3	3	0	235	165	78.33	1	-	1/-
JL Langer	3	5	2	206	72*	68.66	-	2	3/-
SM Katich	3	3	0	188	118	62.66	1	-	3/-
MS Kasprowicz	3	3	2	38	23	38.00	-	-	-/-
ML Hayden	3	5	0	158	61	31.60	-	1	1/-
SK Warne	3	3	1	53	50*	26.50	-	1	1/-
JN Gillespie	3	3	0	49	35	16.33	-	-	4/-
MJ Clarke	3	3	0	38	22	12.66	-	-	2/-
GD McGrath	3	2	0	0	0	0.00	-	-	1/-

Bowling	Overs	Mds	Runs	Wkts	Av	Best	5/inn	10m
MJ Clarke	8	1	24	2	12.00	1-8	-	-
GD McGrath	126.2	47	283	18	15.72	6-115	1	-
SK Warne	131.3	25	374	17	22.00	5-39	1	-
MS Kasprowicz	98.2	20	319	8	39.87	3-42	-	-
JN Gillespie	107	25	320	7	45.71	3-38	-	-

Also bowled: RT Ponting 4-1-10-0.

FIRST TEST – NEW ZEALAND v. SRI LANKA
4–8 April 2005 at Napier

NEW ZEALAND

	First Innings		Second Innings	
CD Cumming	lbw b Vaas	12	lbw b Malinga	16
JAH Marshall	c Samaraweera b Chandana	52	lbw b Jayasuriya	39
HJH Marshall	c Vaas b Malinga	160	lbw b Malinga	6
SP Fleming (capt)	b Malinga	16	(5) c Kulasekara b Malinga	41
NJ Astle	c Jayasuriya b Vaas	114	(6) run out	19
L Vincent	c Dilshan b Kulasekara	0	(7) b Chandana	52
*BB McCullum	lbw b Malinga	99	(8) c Samaraweera b Jayasuriya	7
JEC Franklin	c Malinga b Herath	55	(9) b Malinga	7
KD Mills	b Malinga	4	(10) c Jayasuriya b Herath	22
PJ Wiseman	c Atapattu b Herath	27	(4) lbw b Malinga	0
CS Martin	not out	1	not out	4
Extras	b 5, lb 4, w 2, nb 10	21	b 6, lb 7, w 2, nb 10	25
	(159.1 overs)	561	(92.4 overs)	238

	First Innings			Second Innings		
	O	M	R	W	O	M	R	W
Vaas	33	5	125	2	17	4	38	0
Malinga	34	5	130	4	24.4	4	80	5
Kulasekara	25	7	70	1	11	2	19	0
Herath	30.1	5	91	2	11	4	29	1
Chandana	33	4	123	1	7	2	12	1
Jayasuriya	3	1	8	0	21	8	41	2
Dilshan	1	0	5	0	-	-	-	-
Samaraweera	-	-	-	-	1	0	6	0

Fall of Wickets
1-35, 2-142, 3-187, 4-312, 5-317, 6-446, 7-487, 8-497, 9-540
1-51, 2-64, 3-69, 4-85, 5-115, 6-128, 7-148, 8-181, 9-222

SRI LANKA

	First Innings		Second Innings	
MS Atapattu (capt)	c Fleming b Astle	127	not out	2
ST Jayasuriya	lbw b Martin	48	not out	5
*KC Sangakkara	b Martin	5		
DPMD Jayawardene	c McCullum b Franklin	141		
TT Samaraweera	c Fleming b Martin	88		
TM Dilshan	c Vincent b Martin	28		
WPUJC Vaas	c Astle b Wiseman	17		
UDU Chandana	c Martin b Franklin	19		
HMRKB Herath	b Franklin	0		
KMDN Kulasekara	c Fleming b Franklin	0		
SL Malinga	not out	0		
Extras	b 1, lb 6, w 6, nb 12	25		0
	(148.1 overs)	498	(0 wkts 1.3 overs)	7

	First Innings			Second Innings		
	O	M	R	W	O	M	R	W
Martin	37	9	132	4	1	0	1	0
Franklin	32.1	8	126	4	0.3	0	6	0
Wiseman	38	7	128	1	-	-	-	-
Mills	23	6	59	0	-	-	-	-
Astle	18	6	46	1	-	-	-	-

Fall of Wickets
1-95, 2-101, 3-285, 4-407, 5-452, 6-463, 7-488, 8-491, 9-497

Umpires: SA Bucknor & DB Hair
Toss: New Zealand
Test debut: KMDN Kulasekara
Man of the Match: SL Malinga

Match drawn

SECOND TEST – NEW ZEALAND v. SRI LANKA
11–14 April 2005 at Wellington

SRI LANKA

	First Innings		Second Innings	
MS Atapattu (capt)	c Vincent b Martin	0	(2) c Fleming b Franklin	16
ST Jayasuriya	c Astle b Martin	22	(1) c Vincent b Martin	2
*KC Sangakkara	c Marshall JAH b Martin	16	(4) b Franklin	45
DPMD Jayawardene	lbw b Martin	1	(5) c McCullum b Franklin	13
TT Samaraweera	lbw b Astle	73	(6) c Fleming b Astle	17
TM Dilshan	c McCullum b Martin	9	(7) b Astle	73
S Kalavitigoda	c Vincent b Martin	7	(8) c McCullum b Mills	1
WPUJC Vaas	b Franklin	5	(9) b Franklin	38
UDU Chandana	lbw b Astle	41	(10) b Astle	8
MF Maharoof	c sub b Astle	12	(3) c Astle b Mills	36
SL Malinga	not out	4	not out	0
Extras	b 4, lb 5, w 1, nb 11	21	b 4, lb 10, w 2, nb 8	24
	(65.1 overs)	211	(92.5 overs)	273

	First Innings				Second Innings			
	O	M	R	W	O	M	R	W
Martin	20	7	54	6	18	4	50	1
Franklin	11	1	51	1	23.5	4	71	4
Mills	20	6	50	0	11	4	34	2
Astle	12.1	2	35	3	13	4	27	3
Wiseman	2	0	12	0	26	7	75	0
Vincent	–	–	–	–	1	0	2	0

Fall of Wickets
1-0, 2-34, 3-36, 4-41, 5-60, 6-80, 7-86, 8-175, 9-200
1-6, 2-47, 3-95, 4-117, 5-137, 6-164, 7-177, 8-255, 9-267

NEW ZEALAND

	First Innings	
CD Cumming	lbw b Vaas	47
JAH Marshall	lbw b Vaas	28
HJH Marshall	c Jayawardene b Vaas	6
L Vincent	run out	224
NJ Astle	c Dilshan b Vaas	0
SP Fleming (capt)	c Kalavitigoda b Vaas	88
*BB McCullum	c & b Vaas	0
JEC Franklin	lbw b Malinga	15
KD Mills	c Jayawardene b Malinga	31
PJ Wiseman	not out	32
CS Martin	not out	4
Extras	b 11, lb 23, w 1, nb 12	47
	(9 wkts dec 146 overs)	522

	First Innings			
	O	M	R	W
Vaas	40	12	108	6
Malinga	34	2	124	2
Maharoof	28	11	96	0
Jayawardene	6	2	14	0
Chandana	28	4	97	0
Jayasuriya	9	2	34	0
Dilshan	1	0	15	0

Fall of Wickets
1-61, 2-70, 3-153, 4-153, 5-294, 6-294, 7-342, 8-440, 9-499

Umpires: SA Bucknor & DB Hair
Toss: New Zealand
Test debut: S Kalavitigoda
Man of the Match: L Vincent

New Zealand won by an innings and 38 runs

SERIES AVERAGES
New Zealand v. Sri Lanka

NEW ZEALAND

Batting	M	Inns	NO	Runs	HS	Av	100	50	c/st
L Vincent	2	3	0	276	224	92.00	1	1	4/-
HJH Marshall	2	3	0	172	160	57.33	1	–	-/-
SP Fleming	2	3	0	145	88	48.33	–	1	5/-
NJ Astle	2	3	0	133	114	44.33	1	–	3/-
JAH Marshall	2	3	0	119	52	39.66	–	1	1/-
BB McCullum	2	3	0	106	99	35.33	–	1	4/-
PJ Wiseman	2	3	1	59	32*	29.50	–	–	-/-
JEC Franklin	2	3	0	77	55	25.66	–	1	-/-
CD Cumming	2	3	0	75	47	25.00	–	–	-/-
KD Mills	2	3	0	57	31	19.00	–	–	-/-
CS Martin	2	3	3	9	4*	–	–	–	1/-

Bowling	Overs	Mds	Runs	Wkts	Av	Best	5/inn	10m
NJ Astle	43.1	12	108	7	15.42	3-27	–	–
CS Martin	76	20	237	11	21.54	6-54	1	–
JEC Franklin	67.3	13	254	9	28.22	4-71	–	–
KD Mills	54	16	143	2	71.50	2-34	–	–
PJ Wiseman	66	14	215	1	215.00	1-128	–	–

Also bowled: L Vincent 1-0-2-0.

SRI LANKA

Batting	M	Inns	NO	Runs	HS	Av	100	50	c/st
TT Samaraweera	2	3	0	178	88	59.33	–	2	2/-
DPMD Jayawardene	2	3	0	155	141	51.66	1	–	2/-
MS Atapattu	2	4	1	145	127	48.33	1	–	1/-
TM Dilshan	2	3	0	110	73	36.66	–	1	2/-
ST Jayasuriya	2	4	1	77	48	25.66	–	–	2/-
MF Maharoof	1	2	0	48	36	24.00	–	–	-/-
UDU Chandana	2	3	0	68	41	22.66	–	–	-/-
KC Sangakkara	2	3	0	66	45	22.00	–	–	-/-
WPUJC Vaas	2	3	0	60	38	20.00	–	–	2/-
S Kalavitigoda	1	2	0	8	7	4.00	–	–	1/-
HMRKB Herath	1	1	0	0	0	0.00	–	–	-/-
KMDN Kulasekara	1	1	0	0	0	0.00	–	–	1/-
SL Malinga	2	3	3	4	4*	–	–	–	1/-

Bowling	Overs	Mds	Runs	Wkts	Av	Best	5/inn	10m
SL Malinga	92.4	11	334	11	30.36	5-80	1	–
WPUJC Vaas	90	21	271	8	33.87	6-108	1	–
HMRKB Herath	41.1	9	120	3	40.00	2-91	–	–
ST Jayasuriya	33	11	83	2	41.50	2-41	–	–
KMDN Kulasekara	36	9	89	1	89.00	1-70	–	–
UDU Chandana	68	10	232	2	116.00	1-12	–	–

Also bowled: TT Samaraweera 1-0-6-0, DPMD Jayawardene 6-2-14-0, TM Dilshan 2-0-20-0, MF Maharoof 28-11-96-0.

PAKISTAN

PAKISTAN REPORT
By Qamar Ahmed

Pakistan have bounced back under the captaincy of Inzamam-ul-Haq during the past 12 months following the massive dent to their pride handed out by the previous year's home defeat to India. Initially, however, a drawn home series against Sri Lanka and a 3-0 whitewash against Australia drew heaps of criticism. Even their former captain Imran Khan joined in to slate Pakistan's capitulation Down Under as 'spineless'. 'There was no leadership, and no plans,' said Imran as Pakistan suffered in Australia. He was soon to be proved wrong, though, as Inzamam emerged not only as an inspirational leader but also as a consistent performer with the bat.

Inzamam's 184 in his hundredth Test against India in the decisive final match at Bangalore, and then another century (117) in the second Test against West Indies in Jamaica, helped Pakistan to level both series. A 4-2 margin of victory in the one-day series against India, after being 2-0 down, and a 3-0 whitewash against the West Indies in the Caribbean also owed much to the leadership of 'Inzy' and his performances with the bat.

All this, in fact, led the great Imran to change his mind and say, 'Inzamam has now matured as a captain and to me he is probably the greatest batting match-winner in the game – much more so than any of his contemporary batsmen.' Pakistan's success on overseas tours in India and West Indies also owed a lot to batsmen Younis Khan, Yousuf Youhana, Asim Kamal, Kamran Akmal, all-rounders Shahid Afridi, Abdul Razzaq and Naved-ul-Hasan and leg-spinner Danish Kaneria – all of whom performed to their full potential.

Of the three overseas tours, though, their trip to India surely must have been the most satisfying. Beating India on their own patch to level the Test series and an emphatic 4-2 victory in the one-day games were their crowning moments.

Trailing by 204 runs on the first innings in the first Test at Mohali, Pakistan did

Younis Khan has emerged as one of Pakistan's leading batsmen during the past few years.

A master of deception: Danish Kaneria is now one of the world's best as a leg spinner who can perform both the roles of strike bowler and stock bowler.

themselves proud as they hung on to a draw with the help of a maiden Test century (109) by their keeper Kamran Akmal. He and Razzaq (71) put on a record 184-run seventh-wicket stand after Pakistan had lost three wickets for 10 runs earlier on. Inzamam with 87 and Youhana with 68 had, meanwhile, laid the foundation for Kamran and Razzaq's match-saving stand.

At 256 for 6 on the fourth day, Pakistan led only by 53 runs but they later managed to declare at 496 for 9 – leaving India an impossible 293 to make in 25 overs.

India, in reply to Pakistan's first innings 312, had made 516 with the help of 173 by opener Virender Sehwag and 94 by Sachin Tendulkar, plus half-centuries from VVS Laxman and Rahul Dravid. Kaneria had bowled impressively for his 6 for 150; so did Laxmipathy Balaji who had match figures of 9 for 171.

At Kolkata, Pakistan lost the second Test by 195 runs. Set to make 422 for victory, they were 95 for one on the fourth evening but collapsed to 226 as Anil Kumble picked up 7 for 63 to finish with 10 for 161 in the match, his seventh ten wicket haul in his 94th match.

In the first innings Dravid scored 110, his 19th century, Sehwag 81 and Tendulkar 52 to become the fifth in Test history to reach the landmark of 10,000 runs. For Steve

Bucknor this was his hundredth Test – the first umpire to achieve this feat.

When Pakistan replied, both Younis Khan (147) and Youhana (104) made a century each. In the second innings Dravid scored another ton (135) in India's 407 for 9 to emulate his feat against New Zealand at Hamilton in 1998–99.

In the decisive Test, at Bangalore, Pakistan bounced back to win by 168 runs and level the series. Having accumulated 570 with the help of a magnificent 267 by Younis Khan and 184 by Inzamam, who shared a record 324-run partnership for the third wicket, Pakistan led by 121 on the first innings despite Sehwag's 201 in India's reply.

Set 383 to win, India were 25 for one on the fourth evening and 102 for 1 at lunch on the final day but slumped to 135 for 5 at tea to be all out for 214. Tendulkar was at the crease for 140 minutes for his 16 as the Pakistan bowlers tightened the screw. Afridi had started the slide by taking the wickets of Laxman, Ganguly and Tendulkar.

In the one-day series that followed, Pakistan's defeats in the first two matches were disappointing but they bounced back to win the remaining four games to add to their six-wicket win earlier in the season in the Platinum Jubilee match of BCCI at Kolkata.

On their tour of the Caribbean, aiming to win a series for the first time in the West Indies, Pakistan suffered defeat by 276 runs in the first Test at Bridgetown, Barbados, but later avenged their humiliation with an impressive 136-run victory in Jamaica to level the two-match series.

Handicapped by bans slapped on Inzamam and Shoaib Malik for showing dissent and excessive appealing in the final Test against India, and in the case of Malik for admitting to purposely throwing away a domestic Twenty20 match, Pakistan conceded defeat after tea on the fourth day of the first Test.

Brian Lara's 130 and Shivnarine Chanderpaul's 92, in a 169-run fourth-wicket partnership, enabled West Indies to take a first innings lead of 201. In the second innings Chanderpaul's 153, his 14th Test hundred, later set Pakistan 373 to win but Chris Gayle, bowling a tantalising length, took 5 for 91 as Pakistan were dismissed despite Afridi scoring 122, his third hundred, and Asim Kamal 55.

In the second Test, at Kingston, the Pakistanis turned the tables to win on the final day by 136 runs. Lara hammered 153, his 30th Test hundred, in West Indies' 404, and it won the home side a 30-run first innings lead. In Pakistan's 374 Younis Khan had made 106, Inzamam and Asim Kamal 51 each.

Inzamam's second innings 117, his 22nd century in Tests, and Younis Khan's 64 then left West Indies with 280 to win but they found themselves all out for 143 as medium-pacer Shabbir Ahmed, with 4 for 55, and spinner Kaneria, with 5 for 46, made life difficult for the home batsmen. Kaneria finished with 12 wickets in the series.

Pakistan ended the tour on a high note with three victories in the one-day series.

Earlier, however, Pakistan had endured that disappointing tour of Australia, losing three Tests in a row at Perth, the MCG and at Sydney. They lost the first by 491 runs and the last two by nine wickets each.

In the first Test Australia led by 202 runs on the first innings with the help of 191 by Justin Langer, and despite Shoaib Akhtar's 5 for 99. Choosing not to enforce the follow on, Australia totalled 361 for 5 in their second innings – Damien Martyn making 100, Langer 97 and Ricky Ponting 98 – and thus set Pakistan 564 for victory. It was merely a fantasy target, with Glenn McGrath taking an astonishing 8 for 24 and Pakistan being tumbled out for just 72.

At the MCG Youhana, leading Pakistan in the absence of back injury victim Inzamam, hit a responsible 111, while Salman Butt made 79 and Younis Khan 87 as Pakistan reached 341. But Martyn scored yet another hundred (142), and in their second innings Pakistan were out cheaply for 163 – leaving Australia only 126 to win. This they reached for the loss of only one wicket.

In the Sydney Test Salman Butt scored 108 and Yasir Hameed 58, but again the Pakistanis were outgunned by Australia. Ponting's 207 contained 30 fours and Adam Gilchrist made a hundred with 14 fours and five sixes.

Australia, who led by 264 runs on the first innings, in the end needed only 62 runs for a clean sweep of the series.

Pakistan had wins against West Indies and Australia in the one-day VB Series, to reach the best-of-three final, but then they lost the first two matches to the Australians.

In the only home Test series of the past year, against Sri Lanka at the start of the season, Pakistan were humiliated in the first Test at Faisalabad as Sri Lanka won by 201 runs. But then fought back to level the series at Karachi with a six-wicket victory.

Thilan Samarweera made his fourth Test century and Sanath Jayasuriya 253 during Sri Lanka's triumph in the first Test, but at Karachi the

Shoaib Malik was in prime form during the PakTel Cup, which Pakistan lost to Sri Lanka in the final after being unbeaten in the group stage.

Pakistanis came out strongly with centuries each from Younis Khan (124) and Inzamam (117) earning them a first innings lead of 270. Jayasuriya then scored 107 and Kumara Sangakkara 128, but Kaneria kept his side in the game by taking 7 for 118 and, in the end, Pakistan needed just 137 to win and reached their target for the loss of only four wickets.

In the Triangular one-day series Pakistan made short work of Zimbabwe to reach the Paktel Cup final but lost to Sri Lanka by 119 runs.

The Quaid-e-Azam Trophy, Pakistan's premier first-class tournament, was won by Peshawar who regained the title with their first innings lead against Faisalabad. The Patron's Trophy first-class competition was shared by PIA and Habib Bank. Lahore Lions won the national one-day tournament against Sialkot Stallions by 95 runs.

Pakistan's first Twenty20 competition, the ABN-AMRO Cup, was won by Faisalabad Wolves who defeated Karachi Dolphins by two wickets, while Karachi won the first national women's tournament by beating Lahore by six wickets.

Hasan Raza of Karachi and Habib Bank made 1,288 runs in six first-class matches at an average of 77.55 – also hitting four centuries. Riaz Afridi, a medium-pacer from Peshawar, had a bag of 80 wickets at an average of 19.53.

PAKTEL CUP

Match One
30 September 2004 at Multan
Pakistan 292 for 7 (50 overs)
(Abdul Razzaq 107*,
Inzamam-ul-Haq 73, Shahid Afridi 58)

Zimbabwe 148 (38.3 overs) (V Sibanda 57)
Pakistan won by 144 runs

Match Two
3 October 2004 at Peshawar
Zimbabwe 252 for 4 (50 overs)
(BRM Taylor 73, DD Ebrahim 71*)
Pakistan 258 for 7 (48.1 overs)
(Shoaib Malik 80, Younis Khan 77)
Pakistan won by 3 wickets

Match Three
6 October 2004 at Karachi
Sri Lanka 232 for 9 (50 overs)
(ST Jayasuriya 53)
Pakistan 233 for 2 (48.4 overs)
(Yousuf Youhana 107*, Shoaib Malik 86*)
Pakistan won by 8 wickets

Match Four
9 October 2004 at Rawalpindi
Zimbabwe 104 (33 overs)
Sri Lanka 108 for 3 (18.1 overs)
Sri Lanka won by 7 wickets

Match Five
11 October 2004 at Rawalpindi
Sri Lanka v. **Zimbabwe**
Match abandoned – no result

Match Six
14 October 2004 at Lahore
Sri Lanka 293 for 6 (50 overs)
(MS Atapattu 111, KC Sangakkara 69)
Pakistan 297 for 4 (48.5 overs)
(Inzamam-ul-Haq 76*, Salman Butt 57,
Shoaib Malik 56)
Pakistan won by 6 wickets

	P	W	L	T	NR	RR	Pts
Pakistan	4	4	0	0	0	0.89	21
Sri Lanka	4	1	2	0	1	1.05	11
Zimbabwe	4	0	3	0	1	-2.29	4

Final
16 October 2004 at Lahore
Sri Lanka 287 for 7 (50 overs)
(KC Sangakkara 68, MS Atapattu 66)
Pakistan 168 (38 overs)
(ST Jayasuriya 5 for 17)
Sri Lanka won by 119 runs

FIRST TEST – PAKISTAN v. SRI LANKA
20–24 October 2004 at Faisalabad

SRI LANKA

	First Innings		Second Innings	
MS Atapattu (capt)	lbw b Shoaib Akhtar	0	lbw b Shoaib Akhtar	0
ST Jayasuriya	c Asim Kamal b Mohammad Sami	38	lbw b Danish Kaneria	253
KC Sangakkara	c Imran Farhat b Shoaib Akhtar	2	c Moin Khan b Shoaib Akhtar	59
DPMD Jayawardene	c Moin Khan b Mohammad Sami	0	c Moin Khan b Danish Kaneria	57
TT Samaraweera	c M Sami b Shoaib Akhtar	100	run out	21
J Mubarak	c Inzamam-ul-Haq b M Sami	34	c Moin Khan b Shoaib Akhtar	0
*RS Kaluwitharana	c & b Danish Kaneria	4	c sub b Danish Kaneria	1
WPUJC Vaas	c Yousuf Youhana b Shoaib Akhtar	22	b Shoaib Malik	4
HMRKB Herath	not out	33	lbw b Danish Kaneria	5
CRD Fernando	b Shoaib Akhtar	0	run out	1
SL Malinga	b Mohammad Sami	1	not out	0
Extras	lb 3, nb 6	9	b 12, lb 5, w 3, nb 12, p 5	37
	(81.4 overs)	243	(109.2 overs)	438

	First Innings				Second Innings			
	O	M	R	W	O	M	R	W
Shoaib Akhtar	19	3	60	5	25	1	115	3
Mohammad Sami	21.4	5	71	4	12	1	48	0
Abdul Razzaq	15	5	33	0	22	7	78	0
Danish Kaneria	18	3	53	1	38.2	4	117	4
Shoaib Malik	8	1	23	0	12	1	58	1

Fall of Wickets
1-0, 2-6, 3-9, 4-77, 5-142, 6-147, 7-180, 8-237, 9-242
1-0, 2-98, 3-216, 4-309, 5-314, 6-319, 7-330, 8-337, 9-438

PAKISTAN

	First Innings		Second Innings	
Yasir Hameed	c Mubarak b Fernando	58	lbw b Fernando	17
Imran Farhat	c Mubarak b Malinga	11	lbw b Fernando	53
Asim Kamal	c Jayawardene b Fernando	17	b Fernando	1
Inzamam-ul-Haq (capt)	c Malinga b Herath	32	b Fernando	3
Yousuf Youhana	c Kaluwitharana b Herath	17	lbw b Herath	44
Shoaib Malik	run out	48	c & b Herath	59
Abdul Razzaq	c Jayawardene b Vaas	39	lbw b Herath	0
*Moin Khan	b Jayasuriya	5	c Kaluwitharana b Vaas	1
Mohammad Sami	not out	5	run out	6
Shoaib Akhtar	lbw b Herath	9	st Kaluwitharana b Herath	12
Danish Kaneria	run out	1	not out	0
Extras	b 6, lb 4, nb 12	22	b 4, lb 1, w 6, nb 9	20
	(84.1 overs)	264	(79.2 overs)	216

	First Innings				Second Innings			
	O	M	R	W	O	M	R	W
Vaas	26	5	62	1	16	4	54	1
Malinga	10	1	50	1	6	2	13	0
Fernando	16	0	65	2	20	4	77	4
Herath	27.1	6	68	3	32.2	10	64	4
Samaraweera	1	0	5	0	-	-	-	-
Jayasuriya	4	1	4	1	4	2	2	0
Mubarak	-	-	-	-	1	0	1	0

Fall of Wickets
1-28, 2-94, 3-109, 4-134, 5-188, 6-227, 7-246, 8-248, 9-262
1-59, 2-65, 3-86, 4-91, 5-154, 6-158, 7-159, 8-187, 9-215

Umpires: BF Bowden & SA Bucknor
Toss: Sri Lanka
Man of the Match: ST Jayasuriya

Sri Lanka won by 201 runs

SECOND TEST – PAKISTAN v. SRI LANKA
28 October–1 November 2004 at Karachi

SRI LANKA

	First Innings		Second Innings	
ST Jayasuriya	lbw b Danish Kaneria	26	c Shoaib Malik b Danish Kaneria	107
MS Atapattu (capt)	c Younis Khan b Danish Kaneria	44	c Yasir Hameed b Danish Kaneria	25
*KC Sangakkara	c Danish Kaneria b Riaz Afridi	13	c Kamran Akmal b N-ul-Hasan	138
DPMD Jayawardene	c Inzamam-ul-Haq b Riaz Afridi	16	c Yasir Hameed b Danish Kaneria	32
TT Samaraweera	c Imran Farhat b Abdul Razzaq	13	c Younis Khan b Danish Kaneria	22
J Mubarak	c Yasir Hameed b Abdul Razzaq	13	c Imran Farhat b Danish Kaneria	2
RS Kaluwitharana	c Kamran Akmal b Danish Kaneria	54	b Danish Kaneria	7
WPUJC Vaas	c Imran Farhat b Abdul Razzaq	7	not out	32
MF Maharoof	c Kamran Akmal b Abdul Razzaq	2	b Danish Kaneria	3
HMRKB Herath	c Kamran Akmal b Abdul Razzaq	12	c & b Naved-ul-Hasan	6
CRD Fernando	not out	0	c Kamran Akmal b N-ul-Hasan	4
Extras	b 4, lb 3, w 1	8	b 6, lb 10, nb 12	28
	(82.1 overs)	208	(141.5 overs)	406

	First Innings				Second Innings			
	O	M	R	W	O	M	R	W
Naved-ul-Hasan	17	2	52	0	24.5	4	83	3
Riaz Afridi	19	7	42	2	12	3	45	0
Abdul Razzaq	23.1	9	35	5	29	8	99	0
Danish Kaneria	23	3	72	3	60	20	118	7
Shoaib Malik	-	-	-	-	16	5	45	0

Fall of Wickets
1-66, 2-79, 3-97, 4-106, 5-126, 6-140, 7-158, 8-164, 9-208
1-117, 2-170, 3-253, 4-333, 5-351, 6-359, 7-360, 8-364, 9-387

PAKISTAN

	First Innings		Second Innings	
Yasir Hameed	c Sangakkara b Maharoof	3	c Atapattu b Herath	15
Imran Farhat	lbw b Vaas	72	c Jayawardene b Vaas	19
Younis Khan	c Samaraweera b Herath	124	c Atapattu b Vaas	14
Inzamam-ul-Haq (capt)	c Jayawardene b Vaas	117		
Riaz Afridi	b Vaas	9		
Yousuf Youhana	c Sangakkara b Fernando	46	(4) lbw b Herath	1
Shoaib Malik	lbw b Fernando	44	(5) not out	53
Abdul Razzaq	c Fernando b Jayasuriya	16	(6) not out	35
*Kamran Akmal	c Jayawardene b Herath	15		
Naved-ul-Hasan	b Fernando	11		
Danish Kaneria	not out	5		
Extras	lb 9, nb 7	16	lb 1, nb 1	2
	(137.1 overs)	478	(4 wkts 37 overs)	139

	First Innings				Second Innings			
	O	M	R	W	O	M	R	W
Vaas	33	5	106	3	14	0	45	2
Maharoof	23	4	62	1	2	0	13	0
Fernando	22.1	1	96	3	3	0	11	0
Herath	33	3	125	2	15	2	63	2
Mubarak	9	2	33	0	-	-	-	-
Jayasuriya	11	3	35	1	3	1	6	0
Samaraweera	6	0	12	0	-	-	-	-

Fall of Wickets
1-13, 2-135, 3-284, 4-298, 5-372, 6-387, 7-437, 8-462, 9-464
1-31, 2-43, 3-47, 4-57

Umpires: BF Bowden & SA Bucknor
Toss: Pakistan
Test debuts: Naved-ul-Hasan, Riaz Afridi
Man of the Match: Danish Kaneria
Man of the Series: ST Jayasuriya

Pakistan won by 6 wickets

SERIES AVERAGES
Pakistan v. Sri Lanka

PAKISTAN

Batting	M	Inns	NO	Runs	HS	Av	100	50	c/st
Younis Khan	1	2	0	138	124	69.00	1	-	2/-
Shoaib Malik	2	4	1	204	59	68.00	-	2	1/-
Inzamam-ul-Haq	2	3	0	152	117	50.66	1	-	2/-
Imran Farhat	2	4	0	155	72	38.75	-	2	4/-
Abdul Razzaq	2	4	1	90	39	30.00	-	-	-/-
Yousuf Youhana	2	4	0	108	46	27.00	-	-	1/-
Yasir Hameed	2	4	0	93	58	23.25	-	1	3/-
Kamran Akmal	1	1	0	15	15	15.00	-	-	5/-
Mohammad Sami	1	2	1	11	6	11.00	-	-	1/-
Naved-ul-Hasan	1	1	0	11	11	11.00	-	-	1/-
Shoaib Akhtar	1	2	0	21	12	10.50	-	-	-/-
Asim Kamal	1	2	0	18	17	9.00	-	-	1/-
Riaz Afridi	1	1	0	9	9	9.00	-	-	-/-
Danish Kaneria	2	3	2	6	5*	6.00	-	-	2/-
Moin Khan	1	2	0	6	5	3.00	-	-	4/-

Bowling	Overs	Mds	Runs	Wkts	Av	Best	5/inn	10m
Shoaib Akhtar	44	4	175	8	21.87	5-60	1	-
Danish Kaneria	139.2	30	360	15	24.00	7-118	1	1
Mohammad Sami	33.4	6	119	4	29.75	4-71	-	-
Riaz Afridi	31	10	87	2	43.50	2-42	-	-
Naved-ul-Hasan	41.5	6	135	3	45.00	3-83	-	-
Abdul Razzaq	89.1	29	245	5	49.00	5-35	1	-
Shoaib Malik	36	7	126	1	126.00	1-58	-	-

SRI LANKA

Batting	M	Inns	NO	Runs	HS	Av	100	50	c/st
ST Jayasuriya	2	4	0	424	253	106.00	2	-	-/-
KC Sangakkara	2	4	0	212	138	53.00	1	1	2/-
TT Samaraweera	2	4	0	156	100	39.00	1	-	1/-
DPMD Jayawardene	2	4	0	105	57	26.25	-	1	5/-
WPUJC Vaas	2	4	1	65	32*	21.66	-	-	-/-
HMRKB Herath	2	4	1	56	33*	18.66	-	-	1/-
MS Atapattu	2	4	0	69	44	17.25	-	-	2/-
RS Kaluwitharana	2	4	0	66	54	16.50	-	1	2/1
J Mubarak	2	4	0	49	34	12.25	-	-	2/-
MF Maharoof	1	2	0	5	3	2.50	-	-	-/-
CRD Fernando	2	4	1	5	4	1.66	-	-	1/-
SL Malinga	1	2	1	1	1	1.00	-	-	-/-

Bowling	Overs	Mds	Runs	Wkts	Av	Best	5/inn	10m
ST Jayasuriya	22	7	47	2	23.50	1-4	-	-
CRD Fernando	61.1	5	249	9	27.66	4-77	-	-
HMRKB Herath	107.3	21	320	11	29.09	4-64	-	-
WPUJC Vaas	89	14	267	7	38.14	3-106	-	-
SL Malinga	16	3	63	1	63.00	1-50	-	-
MF Maharoof	25	4	75	1	75.00	1-62	-	-

Also bowled: TT Samaraweera 7-0-17-0, J Mubarak 10-2-34-0.

SRI LANKA

SRI LANKA REPORT
By Charlie Austin

Sri Lanka will never forget 2005, an emotional year filled with heartache and pain for many thousands. The tsunami waves that ripped apart the island's coastline on Boxing Day, killing over 30,000 and robbing thousands more of their homes and livelihoods, pushed cricket onto the backburner. For much of the year, as tours to New Zealand and India were postponed, the cricketers concentrated their minds on the rebuilding of a nation.

On the field, it was therefore a low-key year with unusually little cricket. The Sri Lanka team prospered most in the one-day game, winning all the series they played after the Champions Trophy and rising up to second place in the ICC's ODI rankings. In Test cricket, without their talisman, Muttiah Muralitharan, who struggled through two shoulder operations, their fortunes were mixed with a 1-1 draw against Pakistan, a 1-0 away defeat to New Zealand and 2-0 wins against West Indies and Bangladesh.

Off the field, though, the year was action-packed, filled not only with the tsunami but selection rows and the cricket board controversy. Indeed, once again, the crisis-ridden administration displayed a disgraceful inability to professionally manage and develop the game. Consequently, while Sri Lanka remains an island with abundant talent and potential, the prospect of sustained success in both forms of the game at home and away appears a distant dream.

However, those prospects did improve towards the end of the year as a government-appointed interim management committee, headed by Jayantha Dharmadasa, a local businessman, appointed Tom Moody, the former Australian all-rounder and Director of Cricket at Worcestershire, as the new head coach. Moody replaced fellow Australian John Dyson who, despite presiding over the team during a relative upturn in fortunes, had failed to win the full confidence of the players.

Unlike Dyson and Dav Whatmore before him, Moody was given wider powers for the appointment of his own backroom coaching and support staff, including an assistant coach in the former Warwickshire batsman and star fielder Trevor Penney, and a new Australian physio, Tom Simsek. In addition, Moody was handed overall responsibility for the development of the coaching structures feeding into the national team, including the Under-15, Under-17 and Under-19 teams as well as the A squad and the Academy.

Moody soon settled into the new role, impressing senior players and, crucially, winning their trust. His recent international experience helped him to relate well to individuals and a firm, uncluttered and coherent approach to coaching brought immediate improvements. When cricket did finally resume after the tsunami, he started with a honeymoon run as Sri Lanka swept West Indies and Bangladesh aside 2-0 in two-Test series and also clinched the Indian Oil Cup against India and West Indies in August.

The cricket year kicked off with a tour of Pakistan in October, when Sri Lanka were still smarting from defeat against England in the Champions Trophy. They started the Paktel Cup tri-series unconvincingly with two early defeats. But a woefully weak Zimbabwe team, struggling with their own off-field troubles, provided little competition and Sri Lanka still qualified for the final, which they won with ease despite the eruption of a furious selection row.

Midway through the tournament Sri Lanka's selection chairman, former fast bowler Ashantha de Mel, had launched a stinging public attack on the team management, accusing them of blocking the blooding of new players. De Mel's selection committee followed up with the shock axing of Tillekeratne Dilshan for the two-Test series in Pakistan, a move designed to force Marvan Atapattu to play a young player in the middle order. Atapattu and the senior players were astonished by de Mel's out-of-the-blue comments to the media back home and furious with his committee's sudden sacking of Dilshan, a centurion against England and Australia during the previous year, without prior consultation.

Pakistan bore the brunt of Sri Lankan frustration as the tourists closed ranks and produced their most cohesive performance in the tournament final at Lahore, piling up 287 and cruising to a 118-run win.

Tom Moody, the new head coach of Sri Lanka, takes over the role from fellow Australian John Dyson.

The row simmered on for several weeks and eventually Thilanga Sumathipala, the former board president, acted as a mediator in a face-to-face meeting to let off tension. But before that Sri Lanka faced the tricky prospect of Pakistan without Muralitharan.

In the first Test at Faisalabad, powered by a magnificent second innings 253 from Sanath Jayasuriya and 7 for 132 from Rangana Herath, their left-arm spinner, they completed an emphatic 201-run victory. But in the second Test at Karachi, despite fine hundreds from Jayasuriya and Kumar Sangakkara, Pakistan were finally able to exploit the weakened middle order. Sri Lanka slipped from 333 for 3 to 406 all out and although Pakistan wobbled early, losing four quick wickets, the series finished 1-1.

Sri Lanka's next assignment proved short-lived as a five-match ODI series and two-match Test series in New Zealand was postponed on humanitarian

grounds. Sri Lanka produced a miserable display in the opening ODI at Auckland as they were bundled out for 141 on a lively pitch. But their woeful batting was immediately forgotten when they returned to the team hotel and switched on their televisions to witness the Asian tsunami disaster unfolding in their country.

Obviously, with family and friends struggling back home, Sri Lanka's players immediately asked for the tour to be cancelled. But the cricket board had failed to grasp the enormity of the natural disaster and the farce of playing cricket in its aftermath. Initially, they refused to call the tour off completely, arguing they would face crippling financial penalties for doing so. The players fumed silently in their hotel rooms before common sense prevailed and Sri Lanka Cricket finally realised that neither the ICC nor New Zealand cricket objected to a postponement.

The players returned and joined the relief effort, supporting various organisations and also helping the board's own Cricket Aid programme. The domestic season was effectively cancelled – although the new four-day Provincial Tournament was staged later in the year – and no international cricket was played for four months when the two postponed Tests against New Zealand were slotted into the end of the southern hemisphere summer (or rather the start of the winter).

But before the cricket started, the administrators hogged the limelight as cricket politics erupted on a grand scale. As the cricket board prepared for its annual elections at the end of March, the government announced that it was stepping in to take over the board's management on the grounds of financial mismanagement. However, the real unspoken reason for the sudden decision was Sumathipala's decision to contest the board elections to seek a new term in office.

Sumathipala had given up the board presidency in March 2004 after his entanglement in a passport fraud police investigation involving an accused contract murderer. But he remained an unofficial power, controlling the board's affairs through loyal supporters. However, he wanted the limelight back again by 2005 and was on the point of contesting when the Sports Minister, apparently on the instructions of Sri Lanka's president, Chandika Kumaratunga, intervened.

Sumathipala, though, refused to step aside and instead denied the new government-appointed board members access to the board headquarters and simultaneously launched a legal fight. The row rumbled on for weeks, paralysing the administration. On one occasion, as they tried to prepare for their New Zealand tour, Sri Lanka were forced to abandon a team practice because no one was able to authorise the release of cricket balls from the storeroom.

Finally, the government, following the drafting of amendments to the Sports Law and with the public support of the International Cricket Council (ICC), who were also concerned about Sumathipala's family links with the gambling industry in Sri Lanka, was able to take control and some sense of normality returned in time for home series against West Indies and India.

The national players tried hard to stay away from the political infighting and the lucky ones were able to sign early-season county cricket contracts. Chaminda Vaas (Worcestershire), Sanath Jayasuriya (Somerset), Muttiah Muralitharan (Lancashire) and Upul Chandana (Gloucestershire) formed the largest-ever Sri Lankan contingent to play in England, a development that was widely welcomed as part of Sri Lanka's long-term effort to improve their performances overseas.

Before starting in England though, Sri Lanka's players resumed their series against New Zealand. The end-of-season weather, coupled with the distraction of politics at home and the resultant insecurity of the team management, contributed to a disappointing short tour. The first Test was drawn on a featherbed in Napier, with Atapattu (127) and Mahela Jayawardene (141) scoring heavily, but Sri Lanka then crumbled at a bitterly cold Basin Reserve in Wellington, losing by an innings and 38 runs.

The players returned in July for the start of Moody's tenure, which kicked off with a hopelessly one-sided Test series against a West Indies squad missing ten key players – including Brian Lara, Ramnaresh Sarwan and Chris Gayle – because of the long-running contracts dispute created by the signing of an exclusive team sponsorship deal with Digicel. At one stage the tour came

Mahela Jayawardene was a century-maker against New Zealand at McLean Park.

close to cancellation before Tony Howard, the West Indies team manager, was able to persuade several A team players, by coincidence also touring Sri Lanka, into signing tour contracts.

The first Test marked the return to international cricket for Muralitharan after an 11-month absence – a return he celebrated with a match-winning second innings performance, claiming 6 for 36 as West Indies were skittled for 113. But, although Sri Lanka won comfortably in the end by six wickets, their top order produced a nervy display against hostile pace bowling from the young West Indian trio of quicks, led by Jermaine Lawson.

During the second Test, too, Sri Lanka's batsmen struggled to shrug off their early season rustiness on a difficult pitch in Kandy. However, Sangakkara held the innings together with a brilliant seven-hour 157 not out to set West Indies an improbable 378-run target. Muralitharan – supported in the first innings by Vaas who snapped up 6 for 22, swinging the ball prodigiously – cleaned up with 8 for 46 as West Indies' chronically weak batting crumpled again.

Although expected to win, the West Indies victory boosted confidence, which was then carried into the Indian Oil Cup, a triangular series in August that was billed as the start of Sri Lanka's 2007 World Cup campaign. It could not have started better, either, as Sri Lanka dominated the series, beating India on three separate occasions in emphatic style. Jayawardene, the Man of the Series, was the star performer with a remarkable 94 not out to steal victory in one of the group games and then a fine 83 in the final.

Sri Lanka finished up the year with a ruthless demolition of Bangladesh in September, whitewashing them in both the ODI and Test series. Moody's first three months at the helm could not have progressed better. But Moody and the team faced far tougher assignments on the horizon in 2006, including a long tour to India and an early summer visit to England.

ENGLAND A IN SRI LANKA
By Kate Laven

The news that Kevin Pietersen would not join England A for their tour of Sri Lanka, following his roof-raising performances in South Africa, served to highlight the scale of opportunity presented by the ECB National Academy's winter excursions to hostile environments.

But while Pietersen's absence was a constant reminder of reachable goals, many of Ian Bell's touring squad struggled to see off the searing tropical heat which sucked energy from their ill-prepared bodies and vitality from their ambitions.

Bell emerged with credit in all departments. His brief, as outlined by Duncan Fletcher during his frustrating tour of South Africa as part of England's one-day squad, was simply to get a barrel-load of runs. So, when he made a match-winning 144 in the opening four-day game against Sri Lanka A at Colombo Colts CC, under the influential gaze of chairman of selectors David Graveney and England A coach Rod Marsh, his future as an international batsman was set fair.

His willingness to bowl was also a bonus. It allowed him to keep lather levels to a minimum among his pace bowling attack, which was spearheaded by Gloucestershire's Jon Lewis and Sajid Mahmood of Lancashire, and also earned his side a few handy wickets.

Jon Lewis was often the pick of England A's quicker bowlers on their tour of Sri Lanka.

As captain, Bell commanded respect and instilled a fighting spirit that brought England A to the brink of an unlikely victory in the second four-day game, having at one stage been floundering hopelessly on 21 for 5. An ebullient century from Sussex wicketkeeper Matt Prior closed the gap to just 39 runs and the portents looked encouraging.

But after posting an emphatic win in the opening match of the triangular one-day tournament, immaturity and inexperience led Bell to bat first in the second against Pakistan A on a dire Colombo CC track. England were skittled out for 79 and, although Mahmood and Lewis fought back with two wickets apiece in the first 12 overs, the tourists were back in their five-star hotel in time for afternoon tea, having suffered a heavy five-wicket defeat.

Bell made light of his disastrous decision but it marked the turning point in what had, thus far, been a successful tour. As expected, England A had won all their warm-up games in United Arab Emirates with Vikram Solanki and Prior showing especially good form with the bat.

For Solanki, landing in Colombo, where the team were confined due to the devastation created by the Boxing Day tsunami, coincided with the onset of flu. Forced to sit out the first game, his rhythm was disturbed and one attractive half-century apart, his lacklustre contributions in the top order left the rest with an uphill struggle, though his fielding in the slips remained magical as ever.

The quicker pace of the one-day game presented a stern test of their fitness and stamina and physio Stuart Osborne stayed busy dishing out tips on how to prevent dehydration.

For Owais Shah, warnings over eating curry and drinking tea went unheeded and he was despatched to hospital, his limbs shaking uncontrollably, to be put on a saline drip after England A's one tournament win against Sri Lanka, in which he had made 63.

When Alex Gidman and David Harrison were violently sick in the outfield, after strenuous bowling spells later in the series, and when Prior virtually collapsed behind the stumps complaining of dizziness, the quick-fix remedies were duly administered to keep them on the park. These problems, however, pointed to a general lack of preparedness and explained why England A's performances fell away so dramatically, leaving them way off the pace when Sri Lanka and Pakistan qualified for the final.

Lewis stayed cool throughout, his economical action matching his stingy returns and he proved the pick of the bowlers to earn Marsh's repeated commendations. Off spinner Graeme Swann shed his soft downy feathers to emerge a real prospect for the future while Prior made enough progress with bat and gloves to retain his place as next in line to the top job.

Essex's young opener Alastair Cook, who was brought in at the last minute to replace Pietersen, made an indelible mark on the lower rungs of the England ladder with a promising display of composure and sound technique.

'Some of the players found the going tough but in the end they weren't fit enough for such hard cricket,' said Marsh as he bowed out of England A cricket after four years in charge. 'I'll take the rap for that, but it is disappointing. However, there have been a couple of fine performers on this tour who will go on and play cricket this year for England and do it with distinction.'

Kate Laven writes on cricket for the Daily Telegraph.

Matt Prior showcased his strokemaking talents with a century against Sri Lanka A in Colombo.

TSUNAMI IN SRI LANKA

arrow School's First XI were sweating their way through fielding drills on a sweltering Boxing Day morning when a concerned mother called out the first warning. Within minutes Galle International Stadium, one of the world's most picturesque venues, was ruined – drowned by the tsunami waves that were carving a trail of destruction throughout the Indian Ocean.

Fortunately, the match had not started and Harrow's cricketers had a lucky escape, rushing to the safety of the main pavilion before the swirling waters, ringing their way around the 16th-century Galle Fort, engulfed the island's south coast town. Tragically, though, one of the boys' stepfather who was travelling from the team hotel was swept to his death on a day in which an estimated 32,000 died in Sri Lanka.

The tsunami disaster, a tragedy that impacted heavily upon the cricket world, affecting fans and players, officially started at 00.58 GMT when a violent underwater earthquake, the largest to hit the planet for 40 years, ruptured the seabeds to the north and west off Indonesia. The sudden movement of the tectonic plates created a series of giant waves travelling up to 500 miles per hour.

Approximately two hours later, at 03.36 GMT (09.36am local time), those waves pounded into Sri Lanka's east coast, surging up to a mile inland in some low-lying areas. There was no warning. Entire coastal villages, especially those of the many hard-up fishing communities who live in flimsy housing, were flattened. Vehicles were swept away. Most human survivors either ran to high ground or clung on to coconut palms.

The waves circled around the southern tip of the island and then moved more slowly up the west coast to Colombo. Galle was hit several minutes after the east coast impact. Fortunately, by the time the waves reached Kalutara a further 40 miles to the north, they had lost some of their speed and power. Muttiah Muralitharan,

driving south to a charity function with his fiancée and family, was alerted just in time to turn his car around and speed back home.

Muralitharan's team-mates were losing to New Zealand in Auckland when the waves arrived. By the time they reached their hotel rooms the first news alerts had started. Text messages from loved ones back home started to flow. Several waited throughout the night, fretting for the safety of family and friends who lived along the coast. With so much chaos and confusion, it was a long wait for some.

Sanath Jayasuriya's 60-year-old mother, Breeda, had been shopping for vegetables in Matara, a small fishing town on the southern tip of the island. She was caught up in the first wave but then plucked to safety by a bystander. Upul Chandana's mother was also saved but then watched in horror as her brave rescuer was carried away. Nuwan Zoysa's aunt, and three relatives of Dilhara Fernando's wife, died.

The worst cricket-related tragedy though – aside from the hundreds of cricket-playing children swept to their deaths along India's Coromandel Coast – was in Hambantota, a south coast fishing town that was so severely hit that the entire seaside city centre was reduced to rubble. Seven players of the promotion-seeking Division Two team were killed.

Most of Sri Lanka's cricketers, like most Sri Lankans, know people who died and it was no surprise that they became so heavily involved in relief work. Muralitharan spearheaded their involvement during the early days, working with the United Nations World Food Programme to organise three aid convoys to Jaffna, Trincomalee and Hambantota, delivering over 30 tonnes of essential provisions and medical supplies into refugee camps.

Muralitharan was joined by his team-mates as soon as they were able to persuade Sri Lanka Cricket (SLC), who had initially refused to cancel the New Zealand tour on financial grounds, to allow them to return home. Several other international cricketers, including Shane Warne and Brian Lara, also pledged their support to Muralitharan's efforts.

The cricket world also reacted with remarkable and heart-warming speed to the disaster, playing a full part in both emergency relief and long-term rehabilitation. Indeed, within just 15 days, thanks to the efforts of the International Cricket Council (ICC) and the Federation of International Cricketers (FICA), an official one-day international was played between a World XI and Asian XI in front of 70,000 spectators – the event raised an incredible £6 million.

There were many more smaller scale fund-raising events in the months that followed, including a FICA XI series against New Zealand, a sell-out MCC XI v. World XI game at Lord's during the English summer and a successful Twenty20 World XI v. Asia XI at The Oval organised by Surrey County Cricket Club. Cricket clubs throughout the world played equally valuable roles, organising dinners, auctions, raffles and walks to raise much-needed funds.

Unfortunately, Sri Lanka's own cricket officials did not respond with the same genuine selflessness. A charity called Cricket Aid was hastily set up to run refugee camps, rebuild housing and help orphans, but it soon lost credibility as it descended into a public relations exercise. Potential donors reneged on promised pledges and gave their funds instead to more trusted organisations.

But, Cricket Aid aside, the efforts of so many within the cricketing world did play an important role in the regeneration of the island. The feared epidemics were avoided, temporary houses for many thousands were built, fishing boats were repaired and, during the course of 2005, tsunami-hit communities, with little help from their own sadly corrupt and incompetent government, climbed back on their feet with remarkable speed.

Fittingly, too, the Galle International Stadium will soon be rebuilt. In the immediate aftermath there had been serious doubts about its future with SLC officials claiming it would be irresponsible of them to rebuild in the same location. But, gradually, the case for moving the stadium away from its historic home waned, and reconstruction is expected to start by the end of this year.

The return of cricket to the stadium will be a symbolic moment for the town, and Sri Lanka as a whole, marking as it will the resumption of some kind of normality. For some, however, there will be years of hard work ahead to completely rebuild their shattered livelihoods. And when play does resume, world cricket will be able to look on knowing that it played its part.

Charlie Austin

The Tsunami tragedy initiated a heroic response from the world of cricket. A number of high-profile matches were organised to raise funds for the grieving and the dispossessed, including a fixture at Lord's on 14 June when MCC took on an International XI. Here, Brian Lara sweeps.

FIRST TEST – SRI LANKA v. WEST INDIES
13–16 July 2005 at Colombo

WEST INDIES

	First Innings		Second Innings	
SC Joseph	lbw b Wijekoon	28	c Jayawardene b Muralitharan	2
XM Marshall	lbw b Vaas	10	lbw b Vaas	2
RS Morton	b Muralitharan	43	lbw b Vaas	0
N Deonarine	c Sangakkara b Malinga	12	lbw b Vaas	7
S Chanderpaul (capt)	lbw b Vaas	69	not out	48
DR Smith	lbw b Malinga	4	lbw b Vaas	0
*D Ramdin	b Wijekoon	56	lbw b Muralitharan	11
OAC Banks	b Malinga	32	c Dilshan b Muralitharan	7
DB Powell	c Jayawardene b Malinga	3	c Jayawardene b Muralitharan	0
TL Best	b Vaas	4	st Sangakkara b Muralitharan	27
JJC Lawson	not out	4	c sub b Muralitharan	0
Extras	lb 7, nb 13	20	b 8, nb 1	9
	(88.4 overs)	285	(60 overs)	113

	First Innings				Second Innings			
	O	M	R	W	O	M	R	W
Vaas	16.4	4	35	3	18	9	15	4
Malinga	14	1	71	4	12	5	22	0
Wijekoon	10	1	49	2	-	-	-	-
Muralitharan	29	8	56	1	21	8	36	6
Herath	14	1	52	0	3	0	12	0
Jayasuriya	5	1	15	0	6	1	20	0

Fall of Wickets
1-14, 2-72, 3-95, 4-109, 5-113, 6-192, 7-273, 8-276, 9-281
1-3, 2-3, 3-15, 4-21, 5-21, 6-48, 7-69, 8-69, 9-113

SRI LANKA

	First Innings		Second Innings	
MS Atapattu (capt)	b Powell	1	(2) c Ramdin b Lawson	28
ST Jayasuriya	c Smith b Lawson	3	(1) c Marshall b Lawson	15
*KC Sangakkara	c Ramdin b Banks	34	c Joseph b Lawson	0
DPMD Jayawardene	c Morton b Powell	3	not out	41
TT Samaraweera	c & b Lawson	11	lbw b Lawson	51
TM Dilshan	c Smith b Banks	32	not out	27
WPUJC Vaas	b Smith	49		
G Wijekoon	c Joseph b Best	12		
HMRKB Herath	c Ramdin b Lawson	24		
M Muralitharan	b Lawson	36		
SL Malinga	not out	5		
Extras	lb 6, nb 11	17	lb 6, w 2, nb 2	10
	(57.3 overs)	227	(4 wkts 38.3 overs)	172

	First Innings				Second Innings			
	O	M	R	W	O	M	R	W
Powell	13	4	31	2	8	0	44	0
Lawson	14.3	3	59	4	12	1	43	4
Best	11	1	47	1	8.3	1	37	0
Banks	16	3	70	2	7	0	31	0
Deonarine	1	0	9	0	-	-	-	-
Smith	2	0	5	1	3	1	11	0

Fall of Wickets
1-4, 2-7, 3-32, 4-47, 5-91, 6-93, 7-113, 8-149, 9-215
1-34, 2-34, 3-49, 4-135

Umpires: Nadeem Ghauri & SJA Taufel
Toss: West Indies
Test debuts: G Wijekoon, XM Marshall, RS Morton, D Ramdin
Man of the Match: WPUJC Vaas

Sri Lanka won by 6 wickets

SECOND TEST – SRI LANKA v. WEST INDIES
22–25 July 2005 at Kandy

SRI LANKA

	First Innings		Second Innings	
MS Atapattu (capt)	b Best	17	(2) c Banks b Powell	19
ST Jayasuriya	c Ramdin b Powell	2	(1) c Morton b Lawson	36
*KC Sangakkara	c Morton b Powell	6	not out	157
DPMD Jayawardene	c Morton b Best	6	b Lawson	43
TT Samaraweera	c Deonarine b Banks	37	c Ramdin b Lawson	0
TM Dilshan	run out	36	c Morton b Banks	49
WPUJC Vaas	c Ramdass b Best	6	(8) b Banks	19
G Wijekoon	c Ramdass b Powell	14	(7) b Powell	12
HMRKB Herath	c Ramdin b Powell	1	not out	15
M Muralitharan	not out	18		
SL Malinga	c Ramdin b Powell	0		
Extras	lb 6, nb 1	7	b 4, lb 6, w 6, nb 9	25
	(46.1 overs)	150	(7 wkts dec 107 overs)	375

	First Innings				Second Innings			
	O	M	R	W	O	M	R	W
Powell	13.1	4	25	5	28	3	89	2
Lawson	10	0	29	0	29	1	104	3
Best	10	1	50	3	20	3	84	0
Banks	13	1	40	1	19	5	47	2
Deonarine	-	-	-	-	3	0	13	0
Morton	-	-	-	-	5	0	15	0
Chanderpaul	-	-	-	-	3	1	13	0

Fall of Wickets
1-3, 2-17, 3-35, 4-42, 5-98, 6-107, 7-127, 8-130, 9-143
1-55, 2-57, 3-155, 4-155, 5-264, 6-278, 7-321

WEST INDIES

	First Innings		Second Innings	
XM Marshall	c Atapattu b Vaas	4	lbw b Malinga	1
R Ramdass	run out	3	c Jayawardene b Muralitharan	23
RS Morton	b Vaas	1	lbw b Muralitharan	9
S Chanderpaul (capt)	lbw b Vaas	13	c Jayawardene b Herath	24
SC Joseph	c Dilshan b Vaas	18	c Jayawardene b Muralitharan	0
N Deonarine	c & b Jayasuriya	40	b Muralitharan	29
*D Ramdin	lbw b Vaas	13	b Muralitharan	28
OAC Banks	c Dilshan b Muralitharan	17	c Sangakkara b Muralitharan	1
DB Powell	b Vaas	0	c Jayawardene b Muralitharan	0
TL Best	not out	26	b Muralitharan	8
JJC Lawson	b Muralitharan	3	not out	1
Extras	b 4, lb 2, nb 4	10	b 4, lb 2, w 2, nb 5	13
	(58.1 overs)	148	(41.2 overs)	137

	First Innings				Second Innings			
	O	M	R	W	O	M	R	W
Vaas	15	6	22	6	-	-	-	-
Malinga	9	3	22	0	12	2	48	1
Wijekoon	5	2	9	0	4	1	8	0
Muralitharan	9.1	0	37	2	16.2	4	46	8
Herath	9	0	26	0	9	2	29	1
Jayasuriya	11	3	26	1	-	-	-	-

Fall of Wickets
1-9, 2-9, 3-12, 4-27, 5-75, 6-97, 7-101, 8-101, 9-122
1-2, 2-38, 3-49, 4-49, 5-77, 6-105, 7-111, 8-119, 9-131

Umpires: AL Hill & SJA Taufel
Toss: West Indies
Test debut: RR Ramdass
Man of the Match: KC Sangakkara
Man of the Series: WPUJC Vaas

Sri Lanka won by 240 runs

SERIES AVERAGES
Sri Lanka v. West Indies

SRI LANKA

Batting	M	Inns	NO	Runs	HS	Av	100	50	c/st
KC Sangakkara	2	4	1	197	157*	65.66	1	–	2/1
M Muralitharan	2	2	1	54	36	54.00	–	–	-/-
TM Dilshan	2	4	1	144	49	48.00	–	–	3/-
DPMD Jayawardene	2	4	1	93	43	31.00	–	–	7/-
TT Samaraweera	2	4	0	99	51	24.75	–	1	-/-
WPUJC Vaas	2	3	0	74	49	24.66	–	–	-/-
HMRKB Herath	2	3	1	40	24	20.00	–	–	-/-
MS Atapattu	2	4	0	65	28	16.25	–	–	1/-
ST Jayasuriya	2	4	0	56	36	14.00	–	–	1/-
G Wijekoon	2	3	0	38	14	12.66	–	–	-/-
SL Malinga	2	2	1	5	5*	5.00	–	–	-/-

Bowling	Overs	Mds	Runs	Wkts	Av	Best	5/inn	10m
WPUJC Vaas	49.4	19	72	13	5.53	6-22	1	–
M Muralitharan	75.3	20	175	17	10.29	8-46	2	1
SL Malinga	47	11	163	5	32.60	4-71	–	–
G Wijekoon	19	4	66	2	33.00	2-49	–	–
ST Jayasuriya	22	5	61	1	61.00	1-26	–	–
HMRKB Herath	35	3	119	1	119.00	1-29	–	–

WEST INDIES

Batting	M	Inns	NO	Runs	HS	Av	100	50	c/st
S Chanderpaul	2	4	1	154	69	51.33	–	1	-/-
D Ramdin	2	4	0	108	56	27.00	–	1	7/-
N Deonarine	2	4	0	88	40	22.00	–	–	1/-
TL Best	2	4	1	65	27	21.66	–	–	-/-
OAC Banks	2	4	0	57	32	14.25	–	–	1/-
RS Morton	2	4	0	53	43	13.25	–	–	5/-
R Ramdass	1	2	0	26	23	13.00	–	–	2/-
SC Joseph	2	4	0	48	28	12.00	–	–	2/-
XM Marshall	2	4	0	17	10	4.25	–	–	1/-
JJC Lawson	2	4	2	8	4*	4.00	–	–	1/-
DR Smith	1	2	0	4	4	2.00	–	–	2/-
DB Powell	2	4	0	3	3	0.75	–	–	-/-

Bowling	Overs	Mds	Runs	Wkts	Av	Best	5/inn	10m
DR Smith	5	1	16	1	16.00	1-5	–	–
DB Powell	62.1	11	189	9	21.00	5-25	1	–
JJC Lawson	65.3	5	235	11	21.36	4-43	–	–
OAC Banks	55	9	188	5	37.60	2-47	–	–
TL Best	49.3	6	218	4	54.50	3-50	–	–

Also bowled: S Chanderpaul 3-1-13-0, RS Morton 5-0-15-0, N Deonarine 4-0-22-0.

ONE-DAY INTERNATIONALS
v. Bangladesh

Match One
31 August 2005 at Colombo (SSC)
Sri Lanka 269 for 9 (50 overs) (WU Tharanga 60, MS Atapattu 55, DPMD Jayawardene 50)
Bangladesh 181 for 9 (50 overs)
Sri Lanka won by 88 runs

Match Two
2 September 2005 at Colombo (RPS)
Sri Lanka 295 for 5 (50 overs) (WU Tharanga 105, MS Atapattu 53*)
Bangladesh 220 for 6 (50 overs) (Shahriar Nafees 51)
Sri Lanka won by 75 runs

FIRST TEST – SRI LANKA v. BANGLADESH
12–14 September 2005 at Colombo (RPS)

BANGLADESH

	First Innings		Second Innings	
Javed Omar	c Sangakkara b Fernando	30	c Sangakkara b Malinga	9
Shahriar Nafees	b Malinga	3	b Muralitharan	13
Habibul Bashar (capt)	run out	84	c Sangakkara b Vaas	15
Mohammad Ashraful	c Fernando b Herath	17	lbw b Muralitharan	0
Tushar Imran	b Herath	0	b Muralitharan	3
Aftab Ahmed	c Samaraweera b Herath	0	c Samaraweera b Muralitharan	8
*Khaled Mashud	c Samaraweera b Muralitharan	2	b Malinga	15
Mohammad Rafique	lbw b Muralitharan	9	c Samaraweera b Muralitharan	4
Syed Rasel	st Sangakkara b Herath	19	b Malinga	1
Shahadat Hossain	lbw b Muralitharan	2	not out	5
Enamul Haque jnr	not out	0	st Sangakkara b Muralitharan	2
Extras	b 8, lb 2, w 1, nb 11	22	b 4, w 5, nb 2	11
	(44 overs)	188	(27.4 overs)	86

	First Innings				Second Innings			
	O	M	R	W	O	M	R	W
Vaas	6	1	25	0	10	4	31	1
Malinga	8	1	44	1	6	1	32	3
Fernando	4	1	29	1	–	–	–	–
Muralitharan	14	1	42	3	10.4	4	18	6
Herath	12	4	38	4	1	0	1	0

Fall of Wickets
1-4, 2-63, 3-155, 4-156, 5-156, 6-158, 7-158, 8-170, 9-176
1-9, 2-35, 3-35, 4-39, 5-47, 6-50, 7-59, 8-73, 9-83

SRI LANKA

	First Innings	
ST Jayasuriya	c A Ahmed b Shahadat Hossain	46
MS Atapattu (capt)	lbw b Rasel	18
*KC Sangakkara	c M Ashraful b M Rafique	30
TT Samaraweera	c K Mashud b Shahadat Hossain	78
DPMD Jayawardene	c K Mashud b M Rafique	63
TM Dilshan	b Rasel	86
WPUJC Vaas	lbw b Mohammad Rafique	5
HMRKB Herath	c K Mashud b M Rafique	13
M Muralitharan	c K Mashud b M Rafique	3
CRD Fernando	not out	1
SL Malinga		
Extras	lb 6, w 1, nb 20	27
	(9 wkts dec 110.2 overs)	370

	First Innings			
	O	M	R	W
Rasel	19.2	2	67	2
Shahadat Hossain	20	0	75	2
Mohammad Rafique	37	9	114	5
Enamul Haque jnr	33	8	106	0
Mohammad Ashraful	1	0	2	0

Fall of Wickets
1-41, 2-97, 3-130, 4-231, 5-295, 6-306, 7-337, 8-345, 9-370

Umpires: Asda Rauf & SA Bucknor
Toss: Sri Lanka
Test debuts: Shahriar Nafees, Syed Rasel
Man of the Match: M Muralitharan

Sri Lanka won by an innings and 96 runs

Match Three
4 September 2005 at Colombo (RPS)
Bangladesh 108 (38.2 overs)
Sri Lanka 106 for 4 (21.2 overs) (DA Gunawardene 52)
Sri Lanka won by 6 wickets – DL Method: target 106 from 46 overs

SECOND TEST – SRI LANKA v. BANGLADESH
20–22 September 2005 at Colombo (PSS)

SRI LANKA

	First Innings	
ST Jayasuriya	lbw b Rasel	13
MS Atapattu (capt)	c K Mashud b Shahadat Hossain	11
*KC Sangakkara	b Rasel	5
DPMD Jayawardene	b Shahadat Hossain	2
TT Samaraweera	c Nafees b Rasel	138
TM Dilshan	c K Mashud b Aftab Ahmed	168
WPUJC Vaas	b Rasel	65
HMRKB Herath	lbw b Shahadat Hossain	1
M Muralitharan	b Shahadat Hossain	24
CRD Fernando	not out	4
SL Malinga		
Extras	b 4, lb 10, w 1, nb 11	26
	(9 wkts dec 92.3)	**457**

	First Innings			
	O	M	R	W
Rasel	21.3	2	129	4
Shahadat Hossain	20	3	108	4
Aftab Ahmed	8	2	33	1
Mohammad Rafique	23	1	92	0
Enamul Haque jnr	18	2	70	0
Mohammad Ashraful	2	0	11	0

Fall of Wickets
1-28, 2-28, 3-33, 4-48, 5-328, 6-397, 7-400, 8-453, 9-457

BANGLADESH

	First Innings		Second Innings	
Javed Omar	b Fernando	18	(2) c Atapattu b Vaas	9
Shahriar Nafees	c Sangakkara b Malinga	5	(4) c Samaraweera b Muralitharan	51
Habibul Bashar (capt)	c Vaas b Fernando	18	c Muralitharan b Fernando	10
Nafees Iqbal	c Sangakkara b Fernando	5	(1) c Sangakkara b Fernando	30
Mohammad Ashraful	c Atapattu b Fernando	42	c Samaraweera b Vaas	26
Aftab Ahmed	c Sangakkara b Fernando	23	(7) c Samaraweera b Herath	25
*Khaled Mashud	st Sangakkara b Muralitharan	26	(8) lbw b Muralitharan	18
Mohammad Rafique	c Dilshan b Muralitharan	6	(9) b Herath	9
Syed Rasel	c Vaas b Muralitharan	5	(10) c Jayasuriya b Herath	1
Shahadat Hossain	c Sangakkara b Malinga	7	(6) b Vaas	1
Enamul Haque jnr	not out	2	not out	1
Extras	b 8, lb 9, w 1, nb 16	34	b 7, lb 3, nb 6	16
	(45.4 overs)	**191**	(60.4 overs)	**197**

	First Innings				Second Innings			
	O	M	R	W	O	M	R	W
Vaas	10	0	31	0	13	1	36	3
Malinga	9	1	32	2	7	0	31	0
Fernando	11	2	60	5	10	0	35	2
Muralitharan	14.4	2	47	3	14	6	28	2
Herath	1	0	4	0	15.4	3	52	3
Dilshan	-	-	-	-	1	0	5	0

Fall of Wickets
1-16, 2-46, 3-52, 4-72, 5-115, 6-135, 7-143, 8-157, 9-166
1-22, 2-44, 3-56, 4-131, 5-136, 6-139, 7-172, 8-194, 9-196

Umpires: BF Bowden & SA Bucknor
Toss: Sri Lanka
Man of the Match: TT Samaraweera
Man of the Series: TM Dilshan

<u>Sri Lanka won by an innings and 69 runs</u>

SERIES AVERAGES
Sri Lanka v. Bangladesh

SRI LANKA

Batting	M	Inns	NO	Runs	HS	Av	100	50	c/st
TM Dilshan	2	2	0	254	168	127.00	1	1	1/-
TT Samaraweera	2	2	0	216	138	108.00	1	1	7/-
WPUJC Vaas	2	2	0	70	65	35.00	-	1	2/-
DPMD Jayawardene	2	2	0	65	63	32.50	-	1	-/-
ST Jayasuriya	2	2	0	59	46	29.50	-	-	1/-
KC Sangakkara	2	2	0	35	30	17.50	-	-	8/3
MS Atapattu	2	2	0	29	18	14.50	-	-	2/-
M Muralitharan	2	2	0	27	24	13.50	-	-	1/-
HMRKB Herath	2	2	0	14	13	7.00	-	-	-/-
CRD Fernando	2	2	2	5	4*	-	-	-	1/-
SL Malinga	2	0	0	0	0	-	-	-	-/-

Bowling	Overs	Mds	Runs	Wkts	Av	Best	5/inn	10m
M Muralitharan	53.2	13	135	14	9.64	6-18	1	-
HMRKB Herath	29.4	7	95	7	13.57	4-38	-	-
CRD Fernando	25	3	124	8	15.50	5-60	1	-
SL Malinga	30	3	139	6	23.16	3-32	-	-
WPUJC Vaas	39	6	123	4	30.75	3-36	-	-
TM Dilshan	1	0	5	0	-	-	-	-

BANGLADESH

Batting	M	Inns	NO	Runs	HS	Av	100	50	c/st
Habibul Bashar	2	4	0	127	84	31.75	-	1	-/-
Mohammad Ashraful	2	4	0	85	42	21.25	-	-	1/-
Shahriar Nafees	2	4	0	72	51	18.00	-	1	1/-
Nafees Iqbal	1	2	0	35	30	17.50	-	-	-/-
Javed Omar	2	4	0	66	30	16.50	-	-	-/-
Khaled Mashud	2	4	0	61	26	15.25	-	-	6/-
Aftab Ahmed	2	4	0	56	25	14.00	-	-	1/-
Mohammad Rafique	2	4	0	28	9	7.00	-	-	-/-
Syed Rasel	2	4	0	26	19	6.50	-	-	-/-
Enamul Haque jnr	2	4	3	5	2*	5.00	-	-	-/-
Shahadat Hossain	2	4	1	15	7	5.00	-	-	-/-
Tushar Imran	1	2	0	3	3	1.50	-	-	-/-

Bowling	Overs	Mds	Runs	Wkts	Av	Best	5/inn	10m
Shahadat Hossain	40	3	183	6	30.50	4-108	-	-
Syed Rasel	40.5	4	196	6	32.66	4-129	-	-
Aftab Ahmed	8	2	33	1	33.00	1-33	-	-
Mohammad Rafique	60	10	206	5	41.20	5-114	1	-
Mohammad Ashraful	3	0	13	0	-	-	-	-
Enamul Haque jnr	51	10	176	0	-	-	-	-

WEST INDIES

WEST INDIES REPORT
By Tony Cozier

As restricted as the tournament was, the West Indies' triumph in the ICC Champions Trophy in England in September 2004 seemed a timely catalyst to put an end to the depressing decline of the previous decade during which they had tumbled from top to virtual bottom in both forms of the game. It proved a cruel illusion. They quickly lurched, yet again, from one crisis to another, each eating away at the already vulnerable state of a team once the envy of the rest of the cricket world.

A year after their uplifting victory over England in the final at The Oval, the West Indies remained firmly entrenched at No. 8 in both ICC ranking lists, above only Zimbabwe and Bangladesh. Most of the

Shivnarine Chanderpaul was given the West Indies captaincy as Caribbean cricket lurched from one new crisis to another.

The fast bowling of Tino Best provided some rays of sunshine for West Indies cricket, amid the shadows of off-the-field wrangles and on-field disappointments.

turmoil involved the decision of the West Indies Cricket Board (WICB) to replace Cable & Wireless, the giant British telecommunications company that had been its main sponsor for 18 years, with Digicel, the Irish mobile phone group and Cable & Wireless' direct competitor.

Within six weeks of their Champions Trophy success, an acrimonious row blew up between the WICB and the West Indies Players Association (WIPA) over what the WIPA claimed to be restrictive stipulations on players' endorsement rights in the new Digicel contract. Nearly a year later, it was still simmering. Only the intervention of the sub-committee on cricket of the relevant Caribbean Community (Caricom) governments, and a temporary ruling by a High Court judge on the disputed clauses, cleared the way for the

best team to be chosen for the triangular one-day VB Series in January and February in Australia, the first engagement after the Champions Trophy.

The euphoria of The Oval well and truly evaporated as the West Indies won only one of their six matches and were eliminated after the first round.

Still not settled on the team's return home, the dispute led to the end of Brian Lara's second term as captain when he withdrew from the first Test of the season, against South Africa, in protest against the exclusion of six players because of their agreements with Cable & Wireless that clashed with the overall Digicel sponsorship.

Although Lara and the others were brought back for the remainder of the series against South Africa and Pakistan, when Cable & Wireless freed them of their obligations, trouble was never far away. As the WICB and the WIPA failed to resolve their differences, ten of the 13 players chosen for the subsequent tour of Sri Lanka in July and August, Lara among them, pulled out at the last moment. Stating that it was committed to fulfilling its obligations to the ICC – a US$2 million fine was a persuasive factor – the WICB hurriedly cobbled together replacements, mostly from the A team that was, coincidentally, just ending a separate tour of Sri Lanka.

Of the 14 eventually assembled, only Shivnarine Chanderpaul, who had distanced himself from the WIPA's position from the start and had replaced Lara as captain, boasted more than ten Tests on his CV.

The situation became even more complex when seven of the A players reneged on a signed, collective statement rejecting the WICB's invitation and joined the senior team. The rift caused such internal resentment that the teams had to be shifted into different hotels for the last week of the A tour.

While all this was taking place, a committee of three, headed by Trinidad and Tobago High Court judge Anthony Lucky, was appointed by WICB president Teddy Griffith to 'review all aspects of the negotiations' that led to the change of sponsors. The issue had created widespread public debate, with Cable & Wireless claiming it had been unfairly dealt with, and Griffith's move was welcomed as a rare example of transparency and accountability by the board.

When the Lucky Report was released it proved to be anything but for Griffith and the WICB. Both were heavily criticised in the 50,000-word document that concluded that Cable & Wireless had, indeed, been unfairly treated and claimed that the Digicel contract was 'legally flawed'.

The report was adamantly rejected by Griffith and the WICB in public responses which further inflamed the controversy, rather than putting it to rest. By then, Griffith, 69, had resigned as WICB president citing 'personal and family considerations', his position taken at the annual general meeting in July by Ken Gordon, 75. A media executive and former minister of the Trinidad and Tobago government with no previous cricketing background, either as player or administrator, Gordon was the fourth president in six years. He right away found himself confronted by yet another resignation and another crisis. Less than two years in the post, Rawle Brancker, 67, a company director from Barbados and left-handed all-rounder who toured England with the West Indies in 1966, quit as board chairman of the company set up by the WICB to preside over preparations for the 2007 World Cup in the Caribbean.

He gave as the essential reason for his departure his differences with his chief executive, Chris Dehring, and the lack of support from Griffith and other board members. Brancker said he made way to ensure the success of the tournament, the first in the West Indies and a massive undertaking for the eight small territories that will host the event from 11 March to 28 April. Yet his exit increased the doubts of those who remained sceptical that the region would be ready in time, in spite of the confidence of International Cricket Council (ICC) officials.

Given such a chaotic environment, the West Indies' struggles on the field were only to be expected. In the year following the Champions Trophy, they lost five of their eight Tests against a solitary win. Their limited-overs record was even more unflattering: 15 defeats against two victories. In that time, they used 29 players, a turnover that

rendered the job of new head coach, the Australian Bennett King, all but impossible.

King assumed his post as the first foreign coach within a month of the Champions Trophy, replacing Gus Logie, the West Indies middle-order batsman of the 1980s. He brought with him an all-Australian support staff of assistant coach, physiotherapist and fitness trainer but at no time could he be sure what players he would have under him or, indeed, whether he would have any at all.

It was an instructive paradox that, as a team, the West Indies showed strongest when without their leading players because of the sponsorship disagreement. With Lara, Chris Gayle, Ramnaresh Sarwan and Dwayne Bravo excluded, they forced South Africa to follow on after amassing 543 for 5 declared in the first Test of the home series. There were double-centuries from Wavell Hinds and Chanderpaul, in his first Test as captain, and they might even have won but for three missed catches in South Africa's second innings.

Back to full strength, they were beaten in the next two Tests to lose the series that ended in a pointless draw as Antigua's infamous Recreation Ground pitch yielded a Test record eight individual hundreds.

An unprecedented sequence of defeats in all eight home one-day internationals – five to South Africa, three to Pakistan – followed. A comprehensive victory by 275 runs in Bridgetown over a typically divided Pakistan team, minus captain Inzamam-ul-Haq (suspended) and Yousaf Youhana (who returned home following his father's illness), came as a welcome respite but it was brief. Defeat in Kingston in the second Test denied them the series.

There were outstanding individual performances, not least from Lara, but the lack of cohesion and consistency remained an insoluble problem. In his five Tests for the season, Lara reeled off four hundreds and 724 runs at an average of 80.44, even though he did not play even a club match in the three months following the VB Series. Chanderpaul was just as prolific, with three hundreds, 723 runs and an average of 90.37. The season's most imposing innings was Chris Gayle's 317 in the run-glut in Antigua but his form was typical of the overall fickleness. His highest score in eight other innings was 50.

As usual, it was the batting, supposedly their strongest department, that let West Indies down. Their two Test losses to South Africa and one to Pakistan followed second innings totals of 194, 166 and 143.

Daren Powell, one of the new fast bowlers in West Indies colours, celebrates a wicket with team-mates.

In the circumstances, the results in the Tests in Sri Lanka – defeat by six wickets and by 240 runs – were not unexpected. Yet the spirit of Chanderpaul's novices earned the respect of their opponents who had their backs to the wall more than once.

Nothing was more encouraging than the fast bowling combination of Jermaine Lawson, Daren Powell and Tino Best and the support provided by new wicketkeeper Dinesh Ramdin, 20, and in the field. The gradual improvement was evident in their last two matches in the limited-overs Indian Oil Cup that brought them a deserving win over Sri Lanka and a narrow loss, by seven runs, to India.

At domestic level, there was an unmistakable shift in the balance of power. Barbados, champions of the first-class Carib Beer Series for the previous two seasons and unbeaten for 21 matches, lost six of their ten in 2005, slipped from top to last but one in the table and were replaced as the dominant force by Jamaica. The Jamaicans, well balanced and well led, comfortably headed the standings after the home-and-away round-robin round with seven victories against one defeat.

The Leeward Islands, an often-disjointed team, enjoyed its best season since the heady days of Viv Richards, Richie Richardson, Eldine Baptiste, Curtly Ambrose and the Benjamins. Their second position in the league sent them into the five-day final against Jamaica but they were outplayed in spite of a spirited second innings fight. Their inspiration was provided by their 37-year-old wicketkeeper Ridley Jacobs who signed off on a distinguished career with 816 runs, the highest aggregate of the season, at an average of 62.72. His last innings was a typically dogged 140 in the final but it was not enough to prevent defeat. Gayle trumped it for Jamaica with hundreds in each innings, 131 and 150 not out.

Jacobs was one of the several familiar names that were, once more, dominant. The newcomers who came most noticeably to the fore were Nikita Miller, a left-arm spinner from Jamaica, whose season's high 39 wickets earned him selection on the A team, and Ryan Ramdass, a heavy-set opener from Jamaica, whose three hundreds were enough to propel him into the decimated Test team in Sri Lanka.

The surprise performance of the year was Trinidad and Tobago's triumph in the limited-overs President's Cup. They made light of the absence, for one reason or another, of Brian Lara and four other Test players to defeat Barbados in the semi-final and defending champions Guyana in the final.

Dinesh Ramdin, the 20-year-old West Indies wicketkeeper, looks on as Sri Lanka's Rangana Herath attempts to sweep during the first Test in Colombo.

FIRST TEST – WEST INDIES v. SOUTH AFRICA
31 March–4 April 2005 at Georgetown

WEST INDIES

	First Innings	
WW Hinds	c Boucher b Langeveldt	213
DS Smith	c Boucher b Nel	11
D Ganga	c Boucher b Nel	0
DJ Pagon	c Kallis b Nel	35
S Chanderpaul (capt)	not out	203
RO Hinds	c Kallis b Boje	48
N Deonarine	not out	15
*CO Browne		
DB Powell		
PT Collins		
RD King		
Extras	lb 8, w 2, nb 8	18
	(5 wkts dec 152.1 overs)	**543**

	First Innings			
	O	M	R	W
Ntini	23	5	98	0
Nel	33	8	93	3
Langeveldt	27	5	65	1
Hall	16	4	53	0
Kallis	14	3	70	0
Boje	29.1	2	106	1
Smith	10	0	50	0

Fall of Wickets
1-24, 2-24, 3-106, 4-390, 5-506

SOUTH AFRICA

	First Innings		Second Innings	
GC Smith (capt)	c Browne b Collins	2	(2) b Collins	34
AB de Villiers	c Browne b King	41	(1) b King	20
JA Rudolph	c Hinds RO b Powell	0	lbw b Deonarine	24
JH Kallis	b Powell	0	not out	109
HH Gibbs	lbw b Collins	5	b Hinds RO	49
*MV Boucher	c Chanderpaul b Collins	41		
AJ Hall	c Collins b King	2		
N Boje	b King	34		
M Ntini	lbw b Powell	8		
CK Langeveldt	c Hinds RO b Deonarine	10		
A Nel	not out	6		
Extras	lb 6, w 2, nb 31	39	b 16, lb 2, w 2, nb 9	29
	(66.5 overs)	**188**	(4 wkts 161 overs)	**269**

	First Innings				Second Innings			
	O	M	R	W	O	M	R	W
Collins	18	5	39	3	24	10	44	1
Powell	18	2	61	3	28	15	46	0
King	16	2	48	3	24	5	54	1
Hinds R.O.	13	5	29	0	27	13	27	1
Deonarine	1.5	0	5	1	30	15	35	1
Hinds W.W.	-	-	-	-	14	5	16	0
Chanderpaul	-	-	-	-	13	6	25	0
Ganga	-	-	-	-	1	0	4	0

Fall of Wickets
1-15, 2-16, 3-16, 4-30, 5-71, 6-95, 7-158, 8-169, 9-172
1-46, 2-68, 3-119, 4-258

Umpires: Aleem Dar & DR Shepherd
Toss: West Indies
Test debuts: N Deonarine & DJ Pagon
Man of the Match: S Chanderpaul

Match drawn

SECOND TEST – WEST INDIES v. SOUTH AFRICA
8–12 April 2005 at Port of Spain

WEST INDIES

	First Innings		Second Innings	
WW Hinds	c Smith b Ntini	32	lbw b Boje	22
CH Gayle	c Boucher b Ntini	6	c de Villiers b Ntini	1
RR Sarwan	c Nel b Ntini	5	not out	107
BC Lara	b Nel	196	b Boje	4
S Chanderpaul (capt)	c & b Boje	35	lbw b Ntini	1
DJ Pagon	b Ntini	0	b Ntini	2
DJJ Bravo	b Nel	5	c Boucher b Ntini	33
*CO Browne	c Rudolph b Ntini	26	lbw b Ntini	2
DB Powell	b Ntini	15	c Kallis b Nel	1
PT Collins	lbw b Nel	2	b Ntini	0
RD King	not out	1	b Ntini	0
Extras	b 4, lb 8, w 2, nb 5, p 5	24	b 6, lb 10, w 1, nb 4	21
	(104.4 overs)	**347**	(89.5 overs)	**194**

	First Innings				Second Innings			
	O	M	R	W	O	M	R	W
Nel	28.4	7	71	3	21	6	42	1
Ntini	28	3	95	6	19.5	7	37	7
Kallis	13	4	41	0	11	3	29	0
Zondeki	15	0	71	0	11	4	24	0
Boje	20	2	52	1	20	6	37	2
Smith	-	-	-	-	7	1	9	0

Fall of Wickets
1-7, 2-13, 3-108, 4-203, 5-204, 6-225, 7-299, 8-318, 9-325
1-14, 2-79, 3-85, 4-86, 5-92, 6-180, 7-188, 8-189, 9-190

SOUTH AFRICA

	First Innings		Second Innings	
GC Smith (capt)	lbw b Hinds	148	(2) c Gayle b Bravo	41
AB de Villiers	c Chanderpaul b King	33	(1) b Powell	62
JA Rudolph	c Browne b Bravo	8	not out	7
JH Kallis	lbw b Bravo	39	not out	19
M Zondeki	b Collins	14		
HH Gibbs	b Collins	34		
AG Prince	c Chanderpaul b Gayle	45		
*MV Boucher	c & b Gayle	28		
N Boje	not out	13		
M Ntini	b Gayle	4		
A Nel	b Gayle	6		
Extras	b 2, lb 2, w 2, nb 20	26	b 5, lb 2, w 3, nb 7	17
	(166.5 overs)	**398**	(2 wkts 44.5 overs)	**146**

	First Innings				Second Innings			
	O	M	R	W	O	M	R	W
Collins	29	5	78	2	4	0	27	0
Powell	22	3	86	0	10	2	27	1
King	26	7	50	1	11.5	1	28	0
Bravo	37	8	98	2	6	2	27	1
Gayle	37.5	18	50	4	11	3	16	0
Chanderpaul	2	0	6	0	-	-	-	-
Hinds	8	5	9	1	2	0	14	0
Sarwan	5	0	17	0	-	-	-	-

Fall of Wickets
1-70, 2-86, 3-181, 4-222, 5-274, 6-303, 7-374, 8-375, 9-384
1-117, 2-119

Umpires: Aleem Dar & DR Shepherd
Toss: West Indies
Man of the Match: M Ntini

South Africa won by 8 wickets

THIRD TEST – WEST INDIES v. SOUTH AFRICA
21–24 April 2005 at Bridgetown

WEST INDIES

	First Innings		Second Innings	
WW Hinds	c Smith b Ntini	1	(2) c Gibbs b Nel	11
CH Gayle	c Boucher b Nel	0	(1) c Smith b Ntini	5
RR Sarwan	c Prince b Nel	10	c Gibbs b Ntini	0
BC Lara	b Nel	176	lbw b Nel	13
S Chanderpaul (capt)	c Boucher b Zondeki	53	lbw b Nel	31
RO Hinds	c Boucher b Kallis	10	(7) c Kallis b Boje	15
DJJ Bravo	c Smith b Zondeki	26	(6) c Boucher b Kallis	6
*CO Browne	c Zondeki b Nel	5	c Dippenaar b Nel	68
DB Powell	c Boucher b Zondeki	3	lbw b Nel	5
FH Edwards	c Dippenaar b Zondeki	2	c Ntini b Nel	2
RD King	not out	0	not out	3
Extras	b 1, lb 3, w 1, nb 5	10	b 1, lb 2, nb 4	7
	(92.2 overs)	296	(54.2 overs)	166

	First Innings				Second Innings			
	O	M	R	W	O	M	R	W
Nel	21.2	3	56	4	16.2	3	32	6
Ntini	17	2	61	1	11	2	40	2
Kallis	14	6	37	1	6	3	7	1
Zondeki	16	1	50	4	8	3	43	0
Smith	8	1	23	0	2	0	8	0
Boje	16	2	65	0	11	1	33	1

Fall of Wickets
1-2, 2-12, 3-12, 4-150, 5-171, 6-286, 7-288, 8-292, 9-296
1-17, 2-17, 3-17, 4-54, 5-63, 6-71, 7-107, 8-130, 9-143

SOUTH AFRICA

	First Innings	
GC Smith (capt)	c Hinds WW b Gayle	104
AB de Villiers	c Browne b King	178
HH Dippenaar	run out	71
JH Kallis	c sub (DR Smith) b Hinds WW	78
HH Gibbs	c Bravo b Gayle	8
AG Prince	c Bravo b Gayle	23
*MV Boucher	b Powell	28
N Boje	not out	20
M Zondeki	c Chanderpaul b Powell	2
M Ntini	c Bravo b Powell	16
A Nel	not out	4
Extras	b 1, lb 2, nb 13	16
	(9 wkts dec 177.5 overs)	548

	First Innings			
	O	M	R	W
Edwards	32.5	3	112	0
King	30	5	80	1
Powell	31	2	103	3
Bravo	29	3	73	0
Hinds RO	18	1	67	0
Gayle	27	3	85	3
Hinds WW	9	2	18	1
Sarwan	1	0	7	0

Fall of Wickets
1-191, 2-334, 3-392, 4-410, 5-450, 6-496, 7-502, 8-504, 9-542

Umpires: BF Bowden & SJA Taufel
Toss: West Indies
Man of the Match: A Nel

South Africa won by an innings and 86 runs

FOURTH TEST – WEST INDIES v. SOUTH AFRICA
29 April–3 May 2005 at St John's

SOUTH AFRICA

	First Innings		Second Innings	
AB de Villiers	c Browne b Best	114	(2) c Washington b Best	12
GC Smith (capt)	c Washington b Powell	126	(1) not out	50
HH Dippenaar	run out	5	not out	56
JH Kallis	c Washington b Powell	147		
HH Gibbs	c Deonarine b Gayle	23		
AG Prince	c Browne b Bravo	131		
*MV Boucher	not out	11		
SM Pollock	not out	13		
N Boje				
M Ntini				
M Zondeki				
Extras	b 4, lb 1, w 5, nb 8	18	b 1, w 1, nb 7	9
	(6 wkts dec 163 overs)	588	(1 wkt 31 overs)	127

	First Innings				Second Innings			
	O	M	R	W	O	M	R	W
Powell	32	3	137	2	8	2	27	0
Best	26	4	116	1	5	0	31	1
Washington	22	3	73	0	7	1	20	0
Bravo	27	4	97	1	3	0	12	0
Gayle	31	11	65	1	1	0	3	0
Hinds	6	0	24	0	3	1	10	0
Deonarine	18	1	69	0	3	1	20	0
Sarwan	1	0	2	0	1	0	3	0

Fall of Wickets
1-245, 2-245, 3-251, 4-295, 5-562, 6-563
1-14

WEST INDIES

	First Innings	
CH Gayle	c Smith b Zondeki	317
WW Hinds	c & b Ntini	0
RR Sarwan	c Prince b Zondeki	127
BC Lara	c Boucher b Zondeki	4
S Chanderpaul (capt)	run out	127
N Deonarine	c Boucher b Smith	4
DJJ Bravo	c Prince b Boucher	107
*CO Browne	lbw b Smith	0
DB Powell	b de Villiers	12
TL Best	c Gibbs b de Villiers	5
DM Washington	not out	7
Extras	b 2, lb 9, w 3, nb 23	37
	(235.2 overs)	747

	First Innings			
	O	M	R	W
Pollock	34	5	111	0
Ntini	33	3	106	1
Zondeki	25	4	120	3
Kallis	36	6	96	0
Boje	30	6	76	0
Smith	43	3	145	2
de Villiers	21	6	49	2
Prince	9	1	22	0
Dippenaar	2	1	1	0
Boucher	1.2	0	6	1
Gibbs	1	0	4	0

Fall of Wickets
1-14, 2-345, 3-363, 4-512, 5-535, 6-665, 7-665, 8-700, 9-712

Umpires: BF Bowden & SJA Taufel
Toss: South Africa
Test debut: DM Washington
Man of the Match: CH Gayle
Man of the Series: GC Smith

Match drawn

SERIES AVERAGES
West Indies v. South Africa

WEST INDIES

Batting	M	Inns	NO	Runs	HS	Av	100	50	c/st
S Chanderpaul	4	6	1	450	203*	90.00	2	1	4/-
BC Lara	3	5	0	393	196	78.60	2	-	-/-
CH Gayle	3	5	0	329	317	65.80	1	-	2/-
RR Sarwan	3	5	1	249	127	62.25	2	-	-/-
WW Hinds	4	6	0	279	213	46.50	1	-	1/-
DJJ Bravo	3	5	0	177	107	35.40	1	-	3/-
RO Hinds	2	3	0	73	48	24.33	-	-	2/-
CO Browne	4	5	0	101	68	20.20	-	1	6/-
N Deonarine	2	2	1	19	15*	19.00	-	-	1/-
DJ Pagon	2	3	0	37	35	12.33	-	-	-/-
DS Smith	1	1	0	11	11	11.00	-	-	-/-
DB Powell	4	5	0	36	15	7.20	-	-	-/-
TL Best	1	1	0	5	5	5.00	-	-	-/-
RD King	3	4	3	4	3*	4.00	-	-	-/-
FH Edwards	1	2	0	4	2	2.00	-	-	-/-
PT Collins	2	2	0	2	2	1.00	-	-	1/-
D Ganga	1	1	0	0	0	0.00	-	-	-/-
DM Washington	1	1	1	7	7*	-	-	-	3/-

Bowling	Overs	Mds	Runs	Wkts	Av	Best	5/inn	10m
CH Gayle	107.5	35	219	8	27.37	4-50	-	-
PT Collins	75	20	188	6	31.33	3-39	-	-
RD King	107.5	20	260	6	43.33	3-48	-	-
WW Hinds	42	13	91	2	45.50	1-9	-	-
DB Powell	149	29	487	9	54.11	3-61	-	-
N Deonarine	52.5	17	129	2	64.50	1-5	-	-
TL Best	31	4	147	2	73.50	1-31	-	-
DJJ Bravo	102	17	307	4	76.75	2-98	-	-
RO Hinds	58	19	123	1	123.00	1-27	-	-

Also bowled: D Ganga 1-0-4-0, RR Sarwan 8-0-29-0, S Chanderpaul 15-6-31-0, DM Washington 29-4-93-0, FH Edwards 32.5-3-112-0.

SOUTH AFRICA

Batting	M	Inns	NO	Runs	HS	Av	100	50	c/st
JH Kallis	4	6	2	392	147	98.00	2	1	4/-
GC Smith	4	7	1	505	148	84.16	3	1	5/-
N Boje	4	3	2	67	34	67.00	-	-	1/-
AG Prince	3	3	0	199	131	66.33	1	-	3/-
HH Dippenaar	2	3	1	132	71	66.00	-	2	2/-
AB de Villiers	4	7	0	460	178	65.71	2	1	1/-
MV Boucher	4	5	2	112	41	37.33	-	-	12/-
HH Gibbs	4	5	0	119	49	23.80	-	-	3/-
A Nel	3	3	2	16	6*	16.00	-	-	1/-
JA Rudolph	2	4	1	39	24	13.00	-	-	1/-
CK Langeveldt	1	1	0	10	10	10.00	-	-	-/-
M Ntini	4	3	0	28	16	9.33	-	-	2/-
M Zondeki	3	2	0	16	14	8.00	-	-	1/-
AJ Hall	1	1	0	2	2	2.00	-	-	-/-
SM Pollock	1	1	1	13	13*	-	-	-	-/-

Bowling	Overs	Mds	Runs	Wkts	Av	Best	5/inn	10m
MV Boucher	1.2	0	6	1	6.00	1-6	-	-
A Nel	120.2	27	294	17	17.29	6-32	1	1
AB de Villiers	21	6	49	2	24.50	2-49	-	-
M Ntini	131.5	22	437	17	25.70	7-37	2	1
M Zondeki	75	12	308	7	44.00	4-50	-	-
CK Langeveldt	27	5	65	1	65.00	1-65	-	-
N Boje	126.1	19	369	5	73.80	2-37	-	-
GC Smith	70	5	235	2	117.50	2-145	-	-
JH Kallis	94	25	280	2	140.00	1-7	-	-

Also bowled: HH Dippenaar 2-1-1-0, HH Gibbs 1-0-4-0, AG Prince 9-1-22-0, AJ Hall 16-4-53-0, SM Pollock 34-5-111-0.

ONE-DAY INTERNATIONALS
v. South Africa

Match One
7 May 2005 at Kingston
West Indies 253 (48.5 overs) (RR Sarwan 72, M Ntini 4 for 46)
South Africa 255 for 2 (45 overs) (GC Smith 103, HH Dippenaar 56, JH Kallis 51*)
South Africa won by 8 wickets

Match Two
8 May 2005 at Kingston
West Indies 152 for 7 (50 overs)
South Africa 124 for 2 (26.4 overs) (HH Dippenaar 60*)
South Africa won by 8 wickets – DL Method: target 124 from 33 overs

Match Three
11 May 2005 at Bridgetown
South Africa 284 for 6 (50 overs) (HH Dippenaar 123, JH Kallis 87)
West Indies 283 (49.5 overs) (CH Gayle 132, CK Langeveldt 5 for 62)
South Africa won by 1 run

Match Four
14 May 2005 at Port of Spain
West Indies 231 for 8 (50 overs) (S Chanderpaul 85*)
South Africa 232 for 4 (46.5 overs) (AG Prince 89*, JM Kemp 65)
South Africa won by 6 wickets

Match Five
15 May 2005 at Port of Spain
West Indies 138 for 7 (20 overs)
South Africa 141 for 3 (19.1 overs) (HH Dippenaar 61*)
South Africa won by 7 wickets

FIRST TEST – WEST INDIES v. PAKISTAN
26–29 May 2005 at Bridgetown

WEST INDIES

	First Innings		Second Innings	
CH Gayle	c Abdul Razzaq b Shabbir Ahmed	4	c Asim Kamal b Danish Kaneria	50
DS Smith	c Yasir Hameed b Abdul Razzaq	19	c Kamran Akmal b Abdul Razzaq	10
RR Sarwan	c Bazid Khan b Shabbir Ahmed	6	c Kamran Akmal b Shahid Afridi	1
BC Lara	b Danish Kaneria	130	st Kamran Akmal b Shahid Afridi	48
S Chanderpaul (capt)	c Bazid Khan b Danish Kaneria	92	not out	153
WW Hinds	run out	28	b Danish Kaneria	52
*CO Browne	c Kamran Akmal b Shabbir Ahmed	12	c Kamran Akmal b Shahid Afridi	1
DB Powell	b Abdul Razzaq	10	b Naved-ul-Hasan	5
FH Edwards	c Yasir Hameed b Danish Kaneria	3	c Kamran Akmal b Shabbir Ahmed	20
RD King	c Kamran Akmal b Abdul Razzaq	3	b Shabbir Ahmed	5
CD Collymore	not out	0	lbw b Abdul Razzaq	0
Extras	b 3, lb 6, w 2, nb 27	38	b 4, lb 9, w 2, nb 11	26
	(83.3 overs)	**345**	(102 overs)	**371**

	First Innings				Second Innings			
	O	M	R	W	O	M	R	W
Naved-ul-Hasan	18	2	66	0	24	7	88	1
Shabbir Ahmed	18	4	66	3	20	2	70	2
Abdul Razzaq	17	3	58	3	15	4	36	2
Danish Kaneria	24.3	1	114	3	26	4	115	2
Shahid Afridi	6	0	32	0	17	3	49	3

Fall of Wickets
1-12, 2-25, 3-45, 4-214, 5-263, 6-287, 7-336, 8-336, 9-343
1-59, 2-64, 3-65, 4-137, 5-271, 6-274, 7-307, 8-353, 9-367

PAKISTAN

	First Innings		Second Innings	
Salman Butt	c Browne b Collymore	27	c Gayle b Edwards	0
Shahid Afridi	c Smith b Edwards	16	(6) c Chanderpaul b Powell	122
Yasir Hameed	b Edwards	12	(2) c Browne b Powell	11
Younis Khan (capt)	c Collymore b Edwards	31	(3) run out	0
Bazid Khan	c Browne b Collymore	9	(4) lbw b Collymore	23
Asim Kamal	c Sarwan b King	0	(5) c Smith b Gayle	55
Abdul Razzaq	lbw b Edwards	10	st Browne b Gayle	41
*Kamran Akmal	c Hinds b King	4	b Gayle	21
Naved-ul-Hasan	c Sarwan b Collymore	17	c Lara b Gayle	6
Shabbir Ahmed	b Edwards	6	not out	0
Danish Kaneria	not out	4	c Browne b Gayle	0
Extras	b 4, nb 4	8	lb 7, nb 10	17
	(43.4 overs)	**144**	(62.3 overs)	**296**

	First Innings				Second Innings			
	O	M	R	W	O	M	R	W
Edwards	14	1	38	5	1.2	1	0	1
Powell	10	4	36	0	11	1	47	2
King	11	1	46	2	11.4	0	70	0
Collymore	8.4	3	20	3	19	2	80	1
Gayle	-	-	-	-	18.3	3	91	5
Hinds	-	-	-	-	1	0	1	0

Fall of Wickets
1-26, 2-54, 3-76, 4-96, 5-96, 6-100, 7-113, 8-120, 9-132
1-0, 2-1, 3-16, 4-47, 5-162, 6-257, 7-277, 8-295, 9-296

Umpires: DB Hair & DR Shepherd
Toss: West Indies
Test debut: Bazid Khan
Man of the Match: S Chanderpaul

West Indies won by 276 runs

SECOND TEST – WEST INDIES v. PAKISTAN
3–7 June 2005 at Kingston

PAKISTAN

	First Innings		Second Innings	
Shoaib Malik	c Browne b Collymore	13	c Browne b Collymore	64
Yasir Hameed	c Gayle b Powell	14	c Smith b Collymore	26
Younis Khan	c Hinds b Collymore	106	c & b Gayle	43
Inzamam-ul-Haq (capt)	c Smith b Gayle	50	(5) not out	117
Asim Kamal	b Collymore	51	(4) lbw b Collymore	0
Shahid Afridi	c Browne b Collymore	33	c Smith b Best	43
Abdul Razzaq	lbw b Collymore	19	b Best	2
*Kamran Akmal	lbw b Powell	49	c Browne b Best	1
Naved-ul-Hasan	not out	7	b King	0
Shabbir Ahmed	c Browne b Collymore	0	c Browne b Best	0
Danish Kaneria	b Collymore	6	c & b Collymore	0
Extras	b 4, lb 3, w 2, nb 17	26	lb 2, w 3, nb 8	13
	(100.3 overs)	**374**	(77.5 overs)	**309**

	First Innings				Second Innings			
	O	M	R	W	O	M	R	W
Powell	21	4	69	2	22	0	100	0
Best	12	1	59	0	13	1	46	4
Collymore	27.3	5	78	7	16.5	2	56	4
King	13	1	65	0	16	1	70	1
Gayle	25	1	85	1	10	2	35	1
Sarwan	2	0	11	0	-	-	-	-

Fall of Wickets
1-16, 2-43, 3-130, 4-247, 5-260, 6-298, 7-336, 8-360, 9-374
1-66, 2-119, 3-119, 4-194, 5-267, 6-273, 7-279, 8-280, 9-295

WEST INDIES

	First Innings		Second Innings	
CH Gayle	c Kamran Akmal b Abdul Razzaq	33	c Yasir Hameed b Shabbir Ahmed	15
DS Smith	b Abdul Razzaq	25	c Kamran Akmal b Danish Kaneria	49
RR Sarwan	c Danish Kaneria b Shabbir Ahmed	55	hit wkt b Danish Kaneria	8
BC Lara	c Kamran Akmal b Shabbir Ahmed	153	c Kamran Akmal b Danish Kaneria	0
S Chanderpaul (capt)	c Kamran Akmal b Danish Kaneria	28	lbw b Danish Kaneria	0
WW Hinds	c Yasir Hameed b Shahid Afridi	63	c Younis Khan b Abdul Razzaq	19
*CO Browne	c Kamran Akmal b Shabbir Ahmed	0	c Kamran Akmal b Shabbir Ahmed	10
DB Powell	c Kamran Akmal b Shabbir Ahmed	14	c Yasir Hameed b Danish Kaneria	12
TL Best	b Shahid Afridi	18	c Shahid Afridi b Shabbir Ahmed	4
RD King	lbw b Shahid Afridi	0	c Kamran Akmal b Shabbir Ahmed	4
CD Collymore	not out	2	not out	7
Extras	b 3, lb 7, w 1, nb 2	13	lb 5, nb 10	15
	(112 overs)	**404**	(52.5 overs)	**143**

	First Innings				Second Innings			
	O	M	R	W	O	M	R	W
Naved-ul-Hasan	6	0	50	0	-	-	-	-
Shabbir Ahmed	22	4	64	4	18.5	4	55	4
Abdul Razzaq	23	4	83	2	14	5	37	1
Danish Kaneria	28.5	7	94	1	20	8	46	5
Shahid Afridi	13.1	3	51	3	-	-	-	-
Shoaib Malik	19	2	52	0	-	-	-	-

Fall of Wickets
1-48, 2-59, 3-205, 4-275, 5-326, 6-326, 7-356, 8-385, 9-393
1-27, 2-48, 3-48, 4-56, 5-94, 6-100, 7-126, 8-126, 9-130

Umpires: DB Hair & DR Shepherd
Toss: Pakistan
Man of the Match: Danish Kaneria
Man of the Series: BC Lara

Pakistan won by 136 runs

SERIES AVERAGES
West Indies v. Pakistan

WEST INDIES

Batting	M	Inns	NO	Runs	HS	Av	100	50	c/st
S Chanderpaul	2	4	1	273	153*	91.00	1	1	1/-
BC Lara	2	4	0	331	153	82.75	2	-	1/-
WW Hinds	2	4	0	162	63	40.50	-	2	2/-
DS Smith	2	4	0	103	49	25.75	-	-	5/-
CH Gayle	2	4	0	102	50	25.50	-	1	3/-
RR Sarwan	2	4	0	70	55	17.50	-	1	2/-
FH Edwards	1	2	0	23	20	11.50	-	-	-/-
TL Best	1	2	0	22	18	11.00	-	-	-/-
DB Powell	2	4	0	41	14	10.25	-	-	-/-
CD Collymore	2	4	3	9	7*	9.00	-	-	2/-
CO Browne	2	4	0	23	12	5.75	-	-	10/1
RD King	2	4	0	12	5	3.00	-	-	-/-

Bowling	Overs	Mds	Runs	Wkts	Av	Best	5/inn	10m
FH Edwards	15.2	2	38	6	6.33	5-38	1	-
CD Collymore	72	12	234	15	15.60	7-78	1	1
TL Best	25	2	105	4	26.25	4-46	-	-
CH Gayle	53.3	6	211	7	30.14	5-91	1	-
DB Powell	64	9	252	4	63.00	2-47	-	-
RD King	51.4	3	251	3	83.66	2-46	-	-

Also bowled: WW Hinds 1-0-1-0, RR Sarwan 2-0-11-0.

PAKISTAN

Batting	M	Inns	NO	Runs	HS	Av	100	50	c/st
Inzamam-ul-Haq	1	2	1	167	117*	167.00	1	1	-/-
Shahid Afridi	2	4	0	214	122	53.50	1	-	1/-
Younis Khan	2	4	0	180	106	45.00	1	-	1/-
Shoaib Malik	1	2	0	77	64	38.50	-	1	-/-
Asim Kamal	2	4	0	106	55	26.50	-	2	1/-
Kamran Akmal	2	4	0	75	49	18.75	-	-	15/1
Abdul Razzaq	2	4	0	72	41	18.00	-	-	1/-
Bazid Khan	1	2	0	32	23	16.00	-	-	2/-
Yasir Hameed	2	4	0	63	26	15.75	-	-	5/-
Salman Butt	1	2	0	27	27	13.50	-	-	-/-
Naved-ul-Hasan	2	4	1	30	17	10.00	-	-	-/-
Danish Kaneria	2	4	1	10	6	3.33	-	-	1/-
Shabbir Ahmed	2	4	1	6	6	2.00	-	-	-/-

Bowling	Overs	Mds	Runs	Wkts	Av	Best	5/inn	10m
Shabbir Ahmed	78.5	14	255	13	19.61	4-55	-	-
Shahid Afridi	36.1	6	132	6	22.00	3-49	-	-
Abdul Razzaq	69	16	214	8	26.75	3-58	-	-
Danish Kaneria	99.2	20	369	11	33.54	5-46	1	-
Naved-ul-Hasan	48	9	204	1	204.00	1-88	-	-

Also bowled: Shoaib Malik 19-2-52-0.

ONE–DAY INTERNATIONALS
v. Pakistan

Match One
18 May 2005 at Arnos Vale
Pakistan 192 (44.3 overs)
West Indies 133 (45.2 overs) (Abdul Razzaq 4 for 29)
Pakistan won by 59 runs

Match Two
21 May 2005 at Boursejour
Pakistan 258 for 8 (50 overs) (Shoaib Malik 51, Inzamam-ul-Haq 51)
West Indies 218 (48.2 overs) (RS Morton 55, Shahid Afridi 4 for 38)
Pakistan won by 40 runs

Match Three
22 May 2005 at Boursejour
Pakistan 303 for 6 (50 overs) (Bazid Khan 66, Shahid Afridi 56, Yousuf Youhana 50)
West Indies 281 (49.3 overs) (CH Gayle 124, Abdul Razzaq 4 for 45)
Pakistan won by 22 runs

OTHER ONE-DAY INTERNATIONAL TOURNAMENTS

BCCI Platinum Jubilee Match

13 November 2004 at Kolkata
India 292 for 6 (50 overs) (Yuvraj Singh 78,
V Sehwag 53)
Pakistan 293 for 4 (49 overs) (Salman Butt 108*,
Inzamam-ul-Haq 75, Shoaib Malik 61)
Pakistan won by 6 wickets

World Cricket Tsunami Appeal Match

10 January 2005 at Melbourne
ICC World XI 344 for 8 (50 overs) (RT Ponting 115,
CL Cairns 69, BC Lara 52)
Asian Cricket Council XI 232 (39.5 overs) (R Dravid 75*)
ICC World XI won by 112 runs

Indian Oil Cup
(India, Sri Lanka and West Indies)

Match One
30 July 2005 at Dambulla
India 205 for 9 (50 overs) (R Dravid 54)
Sri Lanka 209 for 7 (48.2 overs)
Sri Lanka (5pts) won by 3 wickets – India (1pt)

Match Two
31 July 2005 at Dambulla
West Indies 178 (47.4 overs)
India 180 for 4 (36 overs) (R Dravid 52*)
India (6pts) won by 6 wickets

Match Three
2 August 2005 at Dambulla
Sri Lanka 241 for 6 (50 overs) (KC Sangakkara 79,
MS Atapattu 70)
West Indies 191 (45.1 overs) (DR Smith 68)
Sri Lanka (6pts) won by 50 runs

Match Four
3 August 2005 at Dambulla
India 220 for 8 (50 overs) (SC Ganguly 51,
TM Dilshan 4 for 29)
Sri Lanka 221 for 6 (48 overs)
(DPMD Jayawardene 94*)
Sri Lanka (5pts) won by 4 wickets – India (1pt)

Match Five
6 August 2005 at Colombo (RPS)
West Indies 226 for 7 (50 overs) (SC Joseph 58,
S Chanderpaul 57)
Sri Lanka 193 (47 overs) (RP Arnold 59)
West Indies (5pts) won by 33 runs – Sri Lanka (1pt)

Match Six
7 August 2005 at Colombo (RPS)
India 262 for 4 (50 overs)
(Yuvraj Singh 110, M Kaif 83*)
West Indies 255 for 9 (50 overs) (RS Morton 84,
D Ramdin 74*)
India (5pts) won by 7 runs – West Indies (1pt)

FINAL TABLE

	P	W	L	T	NR	RR	Pts
Sri Lanka	4	3	1	0	0	0.19	17
India	4	2	2	0	0	0.26	13
West Indies	4	1	3	0	0	-0.46	6

Final
9 August 2005 at Colombo (RPS)
Sri Lanka 281 for 9 (50 overs)
(DPMD Jayawardene 83, ST Jayasuriya 67,
RP Arnold 64, A Nehra 6 for 59)
India 263 for 9 (50 overs) (R Dravid 69)
Sri Lanka won by 18 runs

Afro-Asian Cup

Match One
17 August 2005 at Centurion
Africa XI 198 (44.3 overs)
(AG Prince 78*)
Asia XI 196 (48.1 overs)
Africa XI won by 2 runs

Match Two
20 August 2005 at Durban
Asia XI 267 for 7 (50 overs)
(KC Sangakkara 61, DPMD Jayawardene 52)
Africa XI 250 (49.2 overs)
Asia XI won by 17 runs

Match Three
21 August 2005 at Durban
Africa XI 106 (32.5 overs)
Asia XI 8 for 2 (3 overs)
Match abandoned – no result

Videocon Series
(India, New Zealand and Zimbabwe)

Match One
24 August 2005 at Bulawayo
New Zealand 397 for 5 (44 overs)
(L Vincent 172, SP Fleming 93, BB McCullum 51*)
Zimbabwe 205 (43 overs)
New Zealand (6pts) won by 192 runs

Match Two
26 August 2005 at Bulawayo
New Zealand 215 (43.1 overs)
(CD McMillan 54)
India 164 (37.2 overs)
(JP Yadav 69, IK Pathan 50, SE Bond 6 for 19)
New Zealand (6pts) won by 51 runs

Match Three
29 August 2005 at Harare
India 226 for 6 (50 overs)
(M Kaif 65, MS Dhoni 56, Yuvraj Singh 53*);
Zimbabwe 65 (24.3 overs)
(IK Pathan 5 for 27, AB Agarkar 4 for 18)
India (6pts) won by 161 runs

Match Four
31 August 2005 at Harare
New Zealand 238 (49.1 overs)
(SB Styris 63, NJ Astle 61, AM Blignaut 4 for 46)

Zimbabwe 211 (49 overs)
(AM Blignaut 50, SE Bond 4 for 17)
New Zealand (5pts) won by 27 runs – Zimbabwe (1pt)

Match Five
2 September 2005 at Harare
New Zealand 278 for 9 (50 overs) (SB Styris 56)
India 279 for 4 (47.3 overs) (M Kaif 102*)
India (5pts) won by 6 wickets – New Zealand (1pt)

Match Six
4 September 2005 at Harare
Zimbabwe 250 (50 overs)
(CK Coventry 74, T Taibu 71)
India 255 for 6 (48.1 overs)
(Yuvraj Singh 120, MS Dhoni 67*)
India (5pts) won by 4 wickets – Zimbabwe (1pt)

FINAL TABLE

	P	W	L	T	NR	RR	Pts
New Zealand	4	3	1	0	0	1.33	18
India	4	3	1	0	0	0.68	16
Zimbabwe	4	0	4	0	0	-2.04	2

Final
6 September 2005 at Harare
India 276 (49.3 overs) (M Kaif 93*,
V Sehwag 75, JDP Oram 4 for 58)
New Zealand 278 for 4 (48.1 overs)
(NJ Astle 115*, SP Fleming 61)
New Zealand won by 6 wickets

ENGLAND: FIRST-CLASS COUNTIES FORM CHARTS

DERBYSHIRE

DURHAM

ESSEX

GLAMORGAN

GLOUCESTERSHIRE

HAMPSHIRE

KENT

LANCASHIRE

LEICESTERSHIRE

MIDDLESEX

NORTHAMPTONSHIRE

NOTTINGHAMSHIRE

SOMERSET

SURREY

SUSSEX

WARWICKSHIRE

WORCESTERSHIRE

YORKSHIRE

DERBYSHIRE CCC

FIRST–CLASS MATCHES
BATTING

	AG Botha	J Moss	LD Sutton	G Welch	SD Stubbings	Hassan Adnan	MJ Di Venuto	ID Hunter	NGE Walker	CWG Bassano	AKD Gray	BJ France	MA Sheikh	JDC Bryant	KJ Dean	TJ Friend	T Lungley	PMR Havell	PM Borrington	WA White	J Needham	Extras	Total	Wickets	Result	Points
v. Worcestershire	16	9	21	9	5	15	0	2	12*	30					12							4	135	10		
(Derby) 13-16 April	6	7	47	29	58	0	111	9	0	6					6*							6	285	10	L	3
v. Oxford UCCE	0	35	17	26	46	9	17	23*	2	48					7							16	246	10		
(The Parks) 20-22 April		109*			8	60*	43															6	226	2	D	
v. Northamptonshire	36	33	3	8	3	44	25	0	0*	76					4							9	241	10		
(Derby) 27-30 April					58*		55*															6	119	0	D	7
v. Lancashire	31	9	95	1	6	17	28	20*	0		0			4								4	215	10		
(Old Trafford) 6-9 May	8*	12	4	0	65	1	40	2	8		28			1								13	182	10	L	3
v. Worcestershire	43	25	19	29	12	35	0	22		32					11			2*				33	263	10		
(Worcester) 11-14 May	29*	75	45	63	7	6	51	4		0					12			0				22	314	10	L	5
v. Leicestershire	26	4	23	42	1	2	76	9			28*			21				2*				17	251	9		
(Derby) 26-29 May	30	5	8	13	32	16	73	8			14			61				0*				25	285	10	L	5
v. Essex	40	38	11	112	92		23		11		0*	42	45	0								48	462	10		
(Chelmsford) 1-4 June		29					110*		21			56		9*								11	236	3	D	11
v. Lancashire	1	11	38	19		30	31	3*			7	30	0	4								17	191	10		
(Derby) 15-17 June	0	51	17	27		1	18	0*			14	7	0	32								18	185	10	L	3
v. Durham	13	7	29	40	14	1	32	1*	0			6				3						15	161	10		
(Derby) 21-24 July	25*	0	5	67*	28	106	203					0				82						23	539	7	D	7
v. Yorkshire	30	52	31	42	2	0	79	40	8*		43					0						23	350	10		
(Headingley) 26-29 July		50	43*	6*	34	0	16									14						10	173	5	D	11
v. Somerset	91	24	1	72	31	74		2*			77*	1				20						45	438	8		
(Derby) 4-7 August	4	106	19	1	55	48		0			0	7				1		6*				15	262	10	L	7
v. Northamptonshire	11	0	32	14	44	24	43	20			7*	0	14									10	219	10		
(Northampton) 10-13 August	24	6	2	47	14	0	47	0			8*	11	8									38	205	10	L	4
v. Essex	39	21	88	4	64	52	27		4	30			55								1*	41	426	10		
(Derby) 16-19 August	22	74	46*	0	5	13	4		7	1			9								6	29	216	10	L	6
v. Durham	1	92	55*	0	11	7	5	12		87	11		6									39	326	10		
(The Riverside) 30 August-2 September	7*	2	36*	22	101	17	36			22												34	277	6	D	10
v. Leicestershire	34*	14	18	6	25	0		35		29		0					5		4			20	190	10		
(Leicester) 8-11 September																									D	5
v. Yorkshire	28*	19	17	19	63	6			4	16		17					0			2		25	216	10		
(Derby) 16-19 September	156*	49	10	1	91	42			79	5		12					36			6		36	523	10	D	7
v. Somerset	57	53	53	99*	151	191				47									28			28	707	7		
(Taunton) 21-24 September																									W	22

	AG Botha	J Moss	LD Sutton	G Welch	SD Stubbings	Hassan Adnan	MJ Di Venuto	ID Hunter	NGE Walker	CWG Bassano	AKD Gray	BJ France	MA Sheikh	JDC Bryant	KJ Dean	TJ Friend	T Lungley	PMR Havell	PM Borrington	WA White	J Needham
Matches	17	17	17	17	16	16	13	13	10	9	8	7	5	4	4	3	3	3	2	2	1
Innings	28	31	29	29	29	29	26	20	14	14	13	13	8	8	6	6	3	5	2	2	2
Not Out	7	1	4	3	1	1	2	6	3	0	5	0	0	1	1	0	0	4	0	0	1
Highest Score	156*	109*	95	112	151	191	203	40	79	87	77*	56	55	61	12	82	36	6*	28	6	6
Runs	808	1021	833	818	1126	817	1193	212	156	429	237	189	137	132	52	120	41	10	32	8	7
Average	38.47	34.03	33.32	31.46	40.21	29.17	49.70	15.14	14.18	30.64	29.62	14.53	17.12	18.85	10.40	20.00	13.66	10.00	16.00	4.00	7.00
100s	1	2	0	1	2	2	3	0	0	0	0	0	0	0	0	0	0	0	0	0	0
50s	2	7	4	4	8	3	5	0	1	2	1	1	1	1	0	1	0	0	0	0	0
Catches/Stumpings	7/0	11/0	52/0	9/0	9/0	9/0	12/0	3/0	4/0	4/0	9/0	3/0	0/0	2/0	0/0	2/0	1/0	0/0	0/0	0/0	0/0

Home Ground: Derby
Address: County Ground, Nottingham Road, Derby, DE21 6DA
Tel: 01332 383211
Fax: 01332 290251
Email: derby@ecb.co.uk
Directions: *By road:* From the South & East, exit M1 junction 25, follow the A52 into Derby, take the fourth exit off the Pentagon Island. From the North, exit M1 junction 28, join the A38 into Derby, follow directional signs, the cricket ground is seen on the left approaching the city. From the West, on A50 follow signs for A52 Nottingham and on leaving the city centre inner ring road take the second exit off the Pentagon Island into the ground.

Capacity: 9,500
Other grounds used: Chesterfield
Year Formed: 1870

Chief Executive: Tom Sears
General Manager: Keith Stevenson
Director of Cricket: Dave Houghton
Academy Director & 2nd XI Coach: Karl Krikken
Captain: Luke Sutton
County Colours: Blue, brown and gold

Honours
County Championship
1936
Sunday League/NCL
1990
Benson & Hedges Cup
1993
Gillette Cup/NatWest/C&G Trophy
1981

Website:
www.dccc.org.uk

DERBYSHIRE CCC

FIRST-CLASS MATCHES

BOWLING

	G Welch	ID Hunter	AG Botha	J Moss	NGE Walker	MA Sheikh	AKD Gray	KJ Dean	PMR Havell	WA White	T Lungley	J Needham	BJ France	Hassan Adnan	Overs	Total	Byes/Leg-byes	Wickets	Run outs
v. Worcestershire (Derby) 13-16 April	23-8-51-2	30-4-92-2	7-2-15-0	16-7-38-2	17.3-0-63-2			22-5-80-0							115.3	350	11	9	1
	3-0-7-0	4-0-28-0			4-1-13-0			2.5-0-20-0							13.5	71	3	0	
v. Oxford UCCE (The Parks) 20-22nd April	22-6-53-2	26-6-64-1	22-1-105-0	10.3-4-38-2	18-4-55-1			21-9-36-3					2-0-3-0		121.3	372	18	10	1
															-	-	-	-	
v. Northamptonshire (Derby) 27-30 April	22-3-91-4	24-4-90-1	8-1-41-0	22-7-63-1	17-2-78-1			27-5-74-0					2-0-7-0		122	451	7	7	
															-	-	-	-	
v. Lancashire (Old Trafford) 6-9 May	25-3-61-1	21-0-98-1	32.3-7-104-6	20-4-81-1	17-3-54-1		22-2-62-0								137.3	469	9	10	
															-	-	-	-	
v. Worcestershire (Worcester) 11-14 May	28-8-77-1	26-1-108-3	11-1-42-0	7-0-36-0				29-3-93-3	24.5-4-106-3						125.5	478	16	10	
	3-0-18-0	4-0-30-1	1-0-10-0	1.2-0-2-0				3-0-16-0	4-0-18-0						16.2	100	6	1	
v. Leicestershire (Derby) 26-29 May	18.2-4-48-4	14-5-47-0	13-3-41-2	18-7-42-1			17-2-57-2		9-2-41-0						89.2	279	3	10	1
	24-7-52-1	8-1-34-0	9.1-0-54-1	14-7-22-1			18-5-41-2		12-0-45-1						85.1	258	10	6	
v. Essex (Chelmsford) 1-4 June	20-5-63-5		7-3-20-0	15-5-51-0	10-0-51-0	26.5-10-67-4	21-3-53-1								99.5	320	15	10	
	6-3-13-2		14-1-66-0	5-1-20-1	14-0-76-2	6-1-22-0	11-2-38-0								56	245	10	5	
v. Lancashire (Derby) 15-17 June	17.1-5-65-4	22-2-102-3		12-5-30-1		25-7-39-2	2-1-1-0								78.1	241	4	10	
	7-0-35-1	9-3-29-3		13.5-3-40-4		8-2-28-1									37.5	136	4	9	
v. Durham (Derby) 21-24 July	23-8-51-3	19.5-3-79-2	18-4-74-1	18-5-47-0	20-4-69-4								8-2-33-0	1-0-5-0	107.5	371	13	10	
	10-5-27-0	13.3-3-36-0	6-3-10-2	7-1-19-0											36	93	1	2	
v. Yorkshire (Headingley) 26-29 July	26-6-68-2	23-1-127-2	35-2-143-3	17-3-74-0	17-1-92-0		10.5-1-56-3								128.5	570	10	10	
															-	-	-	-	
v. Somerset (Derby) 4-7 August	25-5-82-4	28-3-113-2	28-7-70-2	11-3-32-0			19.5-4-53-2				17-1-105-0				128.5	460	5	10	
	11-7-14-0	12-5-46-2	31-12-68-1				13-3-43-0				15-2-70-2				82	245	4	5	
v. Northamptonshire (Northampton) 10-13 August	10-4-21-3	15.5-3-50-4	1-0-11-0	5-1-21-1		15-7-24-2									46.5	140	13	10	
	18-6-63-2	13-0-91-0	21.3-1-87-1	5-1-23-0		17-2-63-1	30-4-130-2								104.3	466	9	6	
v. Essex (Derby) 16-19 August	26-8-68-5		16-7-26-0	2-0-13-0	18.2-4-74-1	24-9-74-1						11-3-42-2			97.2	306	9	10	1
	21.4-5-77-2		27-3-97-1	9-2-23-1	10-2-55-0	13-2-45-0						4-1-26-0			84.4	337	14	5	1
v. Durham (The Riverside) 30 August-2 September	23-7-43-2	24.5-4-63-5	13-4-32-1	20-6-61-3		14-3-40-0	3-0-15-0								84.5	230	8	10	
	22-4-83-0	23-6-86-0		24-7-56-4		27-7-96-2	7-1-16-0								116	375	6	8	1
v. Leicestershire (Leicester) 8-11 September	27-9-65-0	22-2-93-2	51-11-155-2	23-4-56-0							25-5-95-1		8-1-37-1	10-0-37-0	166	552	14	6	
															-	-	-	-	
v. Yorkshire (Derby) 16-19 September	31-3-87-1		29.3-5-90-4	18-9-37-1	18-2-84-2					23-3-107-0	23-4-91-2				142.3	520	24	10	
	11-3-29-1		23-12-20-2	12.3-6-19-1	6-1-18-1					6-1-16-1					58.3	114	12	6	
v. Somerset (Taunton) 21-24 September	15-3-42-3	10-2-32-0		13-2-46-1						12.5-1-77-4	14-2-54-2				64.5	259	8	10	
	31.2-4-105-5	39-17-93-4		10-1-64-1						17-3-80-0	17-1-80-0				114.2	430	8	10	

	G Welch	ID Hunter	AG Botha	J Moss	NGE Walker	MA Sheikh	AKD Gray	KJ Dean	PMR Havell	WA White	T Lungley	J Needham	BJ France	Hassan Adnan
Overs	549.3	382.3	473.4	326.1	209.5	175.5	174.4	104.5	81.5	58.5	79	15	16	15
Maidens	139	56	109	98	27	44	28	22	9	8	12	4	3	0
Runs	1559	1506	1506	944	892	498	565	319	385	280	320	68	70	52
Wickets	60	34	33	25	17	13	12	6	6	5	5	2	1	0
Average	25.98	44.29	45.63	37.76	52.47	38.30	47.08	53.16	64.16	56.00	64.00	34.00	70.00	-

FIELDING

52	LD Sutton (52 ct, 0 st)
12	MJ Di Venuto
11	J Moss
9	G Welch
9	SD Stubbings
9	AKD Gray
9	Hassan Adnan
7	AG Botha
4	CWG Bassano
4	NGE Walker
3	ID Hunter
3	BJ France
2	JDC Bryant
2	TJ Friend
1	T Lungley
0	KJ Dean
0	MA Sheikh
0	PMR Havell
0	PM Borrington
0	J Needham
0	WA White

DURHAM CCC

FIRST–CLASS MATCHES

BATTING

Match	DM Benkenstein	GR Breese	GJ Muchall	P Mustard	LE Plunkett	PD Collingwood	M Davies	MEK Hussey	JJB Lewis	N Peng	GM Scott	AA Noffke	NJ Astle	N Killeen	ML Lewis	CD Thorp	G Onions	SJ Harmison	BA Williams	GD Bridge	ML Turner	JP Maher	JA Lowe	Extras	Total	Wickets	Result	Points
v. Leicestershire	16	10	82	28	11*	18		253	50	39														16	523	8		
(Leicester) 13-15 April																											W	22
v. Worcestershire	38	10	38	3	0	129	1	2	37	24								0*						4	286	10		
(The Riverside) 20-21 April	1*		1			4		15	9*															2	32	3	W	19
v. Somerset	6	2	12	0	74*	6	62	47	36									0		6				47	298	10		
(Stockton-on-Tees) 6-9 May	51	79*	23	16	3*	8		51	7															6	244	6	W	19
v. Lancashire	5	0	34	77	11	20		144*	36	0					1			1						9	338	10		
(Old Trafford) 11-13 May						2*		26*	5															2	35	1	W	20
v. Yorkshire	21	64	48	78	16	7	8*	26	23	13					2									10	316	10		
(The Riverside) 20-23 May	28*	13	47	8	5	0	7*	61	19	11														27	226	8	D	10
v. Durham UCCE	0	35	10	44		1		20		87		13	11			5				31*				20	277	10		
(Durham) 25-27 May	53	19	27*					68		18		0	65							0*				8	258	7	D	
v. Worcestershire	15	32	32	39	37	26	0*		18	19		18	11											9	256	10		
(Worcester) 1-4 June			9*			103*			49	5														14	180	2	D	9
v. Essex	110	63	123	17		6		24		26		25*	15	23							18			55	505	10		
(The Riverside) 9-11 June																											W	22
v. Northamptonshire	80	55	4	80		1				3		65	32	0							1*			7	334	10		
(Northampton) 15-18 June	83*	69*	10						52	16			58											5	293	4	D	
v. Lancashire	1	0	0	15	0*	1			36	4	29	4	58											19	167	10		
(The Riverside) 8-10 July	8	1	20	32	0	0*				17	19	3	23											12	135	10	L	1
v. Derbyshire	98	11	8	0	0	190	4	10			18	10*					4							18	371	10		
(Derby) 21-24 July			0*		12			42*			28													11	93	2	D	11
v. Somerset	43	51	57	20	11	181	7*	63			4				4									35	476	9		
(Taunton) 26-29 July						105*		27			61*													15	208	1	W	22
v. Essex	36	24	37	17	7	5		8		0	19				20		0*							23	196	10		
(Southend) 3-6 August	124	42	34	20	20	46	17	0			1				10		9*							24	347	10	L	3
v. Leicestershire	41	0	7	17	5	39		146							7*	10	0						26	17	315	10		
(The Riverside) 12-15 August			22*		5			61*															14	1	103	2	D	10
v. Yorkshire	126	13	64	21	0	33		92			14			3*		10			6					32	414	10		
(Scarborough) 24-27 August																											D	11
v. Derbyshire	49	13	26	12	10	13					45			13		23			8*			9		9	230	10		
(The Riverside) 30 August-2 September	162*	31	14	5	0	112					21					0			15*			7		8	375	8	D	8
v. Northamptonshire	41	78	2	2	46	22					36			0		1			22*			0		20	270	10		
(The Riverside) 14-17 September		0*				22					12*											2		2	38	2	D	8
Matches	17	17	17	17	14	13	12	10	10	10	7	6	5	5	5	5	4	4	3	2	2	2	1					
Innings	25	24	29	23	19	23	14	18	17	15	13	8	8	5	6	6	4	3	4	3	2	4	2					
Not Out	4	2	4	1	4	3	5	4	1	0	2	2	0	1	1	0	2	1	3	2	1	0	0					
Highest Score	162*	79*	123	80	74*	190	62	253	68	87	61*	65	65	23	20	23	9*	1	22*	31*	18	9	26					
Runs	1236	715	764	578	256	1103	120	1074	495	282	307	138	273	39	44	49	13	1	51	37	19	18	40					
Average	58.85	32.50	30.56	26.27	17.06	55.15	13.33	76.71	30.93	18.80	27.90	23.00	34.12	9.75	8.80	8.16	6.50	0.50	51.00	37.00	19.00	4.50	20.00					
100s	4	0	1	0	0	6	0	3	0	0	0	0	0	0	0	0	0	0	0	0	0	0	0					
50s	5	7	3	3	1	0	1	5	3	1	1	1	3	0	0	0	0	0	0	0	0	0	0					
Catches/Stumpings	12/0	16/0	6/0	45/3	6/0	15/0	2/0	19/0	8/0	0/0	2/0	1/0	3/0	3/0	2/0	3/0	1/0	1/0	1/0	2/0	0/0	3/0	0/0					

Home Ground: Chester-le-Street
Address: County Ground, The Riverside, Chester-le-Street, County Durham, DH3 3QR
Tel: 0191 3871717
Fax: 0191 3871616
Email: reception.durham@ecb.co.uk
Directions: *By rail:* Chester-le-Street (approx 5 minutes by taxi or a 10-minute walk). *By road:* Easily accessible from junction 63 of the A1(M).

Capacity: 10,000
Other grounds used: Darlington CC, Hartlepool CC, Stockton CC
Year formed: 1882

Chief Executive: David Harker
Director of Cricket: Geoff Cook
First XI Coach: Martyn Moxon
Captain: Mike Hussey/Dale Benkenstein/Paul Collingwood
County colours: Yellow, blue and burgundy

Honours
None yet

Website:
www.durhamccc.co.uk

DURHAM CCC

FIRST–CLASS MATCHES
BOWLING

	LE Plunkett	M Davies	GR Breese	SJ Harmison	ML Lewis	PD Collingwood	AA Noffke	DM Benkenstein	N Killeen	BA Williams	GD Bridge	CD Thorp	G Onions	NJ Astle	ML Turner	MEK Hussey	GM Scott	GJ Muchall	Overs	Total	Byes/Leg-byes	Wickets	Run outs
v. Leicestershire	14-1-43-5	8-4-19-2		11-0-36-0		6-1-15-1													39	123	10	10	2
(Leicester) 13-15 April	18.3-4-55-3	13-5-34-2	7-2-18-0	19-7-30-4		8-3-15-0		10-4-26-1											75.3	184	6	10	
v. Worcestershire	13-2-55-0	15-7-32-6		11.1-1-25-3		9-0-45-1		4-2-11-0											52.1	171	3	10	
(The Riverside) 20-21 April	11-3-25-3	6-0-33-1		13.4-2-61-5		3-0-22-1													33.4	146	5	10	
v. Somerset	19-3-53-1	12-3-49-2		18-2-72-2		11.3-1-52-5					3-1-12-0								63.3	252	14	10	
(Stockton-on-Tees) 6-9 May	17-3-78-1	12-3-40-2	6-0-26-0	26-6-84-4		10.1-2-46-3													71.1	288	14	10	
v. Lancashire	18.3-6-47-3		8-3-16-0	16-6-32-3	14-2-53-3	11-2-37-0		5-1-10-0											72.3	199	4	10	1
(Old Trafford) 11-13 May	12-4-38-1			16.2-2-52-6	11-1-53-2	5-1-28-1													44.2	173	2	10	
v. Yorkshire	21-6-67-2	14-3-32-2	7-1-26-1		21.4-7-77-4	11-2-39-1													74.4	254	13	10	
(The Riverside) 20-23 May	19-2-93-3	13-2-48-2	2-0-24-0		21.2-3-80-5	11-1-43-0		2-0-9-0											68.2	306	9	10	
v. Durham UCCE		23-8-39-2	12-4-27-1				19-4-51-1	9-2-24-1			17-2-42-0	2-0-9-1		11.4-6-20-3					93.4	228	16	9	
(Durham) 25-27 May		10-1-40-0	24-4-86-3				9-3-33-0	7-3-20-1			18-4-54-4			6-3-17-0					74	261	11	9	1
v. Worcestershire	19-1-83-1	17-6-43-3	10-1-22-0			12.5-5-29-2	25-8-75-4												83.5	267	15	10	
(Worcester) 1-4 June																			-	-	-	-	
v. Essex		12-6-15-4	3-1-4-0				15-9-19-4		10-5-24-2					2-1-4-0	13-2-36-0				55	106	4	10	
(The Riverside) 9-11 June		24-6-86-5	10-1-48-0				24-7-79-2	8-0-47-1	14.1-2-46-1					11-3-20-0	13-1-47-1				104.1	380	7	10	
v. Northamptonshire		13-5-38-2	3-0-15-1				13-4-31-1	7.4-1-29-4	13-6-31-1					4-1-12-0	13-0-51-1				66.4	214	7	10	
(Northampton) 15-18 June		7-4-5-1	17-2-45-2				15-4-51-0	5-1-19-1	11-4-37-0					4-1-4-0	10-2-32-0				69	205	12	4	
v. Lancashire	28-4-116-2	30.1-6-109-4	21-3-80-2				34-6-89-2	13-3-47-0						14-2-40-0			7-1-28-0		147.1	530	21	10	
(The Riverside) 8-10 July																			-	-	-	-	
v. Derbyshire	13-2-61-3	6.1-5-4-3					14-0-61-2						8-0-28-1						41.1	161	7	10	1
(Derby) 21-24 Juy	33-7-109-2	21.5-5-64-0	31-4-86-1			20-3-64-0		18-2-84-2					20-4-83-2			5-0-23-0	1-0-7-0		149.5	539	19	7	
v. Somerset	12-1-69-2	16.3-8-29-3	19-3-83-5		14-1-65-0								5-0-33-0				2-0-13-0		68.3	303	11	10	
(Taunton) 26-29 July	6-2-23-1	7-1-25-1	27-9-55-4		12-2-49-3	4-1-5-0							4-1-8-1						60	174	9	10	
v. Essex	11-2-45-0	11-4-17-1	7.2-1-22-3		20-4-69-4	6-1-27-0		3-1-7-1					11-2-54-0						69.2	245	4	10	1
(Southend) 3-6 August	16-4-74-2	5-2-9-1	32.1-6-73-2		33-3-85-2	7-2-16-1							7-0-30-0						100.1	299	12	8	
v. Leicestershire	22-4-100-2		19.4-8-91-5		22-4-83-3	7-0-24-0						20-6-58-0	12-1-73-0						102.4	443	14	10	
(The Riverside) 12-15 August																			-	-	-	-	
v. Yorkshire	25-4-100-2		22-2-82-0			14-1-56-3			18-2-61-0	26-8-80-0		12-2-37-0				7-0-36-1		5-0-11-0	129	475	12	6	
(Scarborough) 24-27 August																			-	-	-	-	
v. Derbyshire	30-9-70-3		6-1-12-0			13-2-40-1			21.4-9-40-3	23-3-73-3		17-3-54-0						2-0-7-0	112.4	326	30	10	
(The Riverside) 30 August-2 September	13-2-44-2		20-4-60-1			3-0-22-0			12-3-40-1	13-0-69-1		5-0-16-0							66	277	26	6	1
v. Northamptonshire	24-4-86-5		18-1-79-0			9-0-45-1			20-6-57-0	15.2-1-88-1		11-1-43-0							97.2	414	16	7	
(The Riverside) 14-17 September	8-0-39-2								3-0-21-0	6-0-25-2		4-1-10-3							21	101	6	7	

	LE Plunkett	M Davies	GR Breese	SJ Harmison	ML Lewis	PD Collingwood	AA Noffke	DM Benkenstein	N Killeen	BA Williams	GD Bridge	CD Thorp	G Onions	NJ Astle	ML Turner	MEK Hussey	GM Scott	GJ Muchall
Overs	423	296.4	332.1	131.1	169	181.3	168	91.4	122.5	83.2	38	71	67	52.4	49	12	10	7
Maidens	80	94	61	26	27	28	45	20	37	12	7	13	8	17	5	0	1	0
Runs	1573	810	1080	392	614	670	489	333	357	335	108	227	309	117	166	59	48	18
Wickets	51	49	31	27	26	21	16	12	8	7	4	4	4	3	2	1	0	0
Average	30.84	16.53	34.83	14.51	23.61	31.90	30.56	27.75	44.62	47.85	27.00	56.75	77.25	39.00	83.00	59.00	-	-

FIELDING

48	P Mustard (45 ct, 3 st)
19	MEK Hussey
16	GR Breese
15	PD Collingwood
12	DM Benkenstein
8	JJB Lewis
6	GJ Muchall
6	LE Plunkett
3	N Killeen
3	NJ Astle
3	JP Maher
3	CD Thorp
2	M Davies
2	GD Bridge
2	GM Scott
2	ML Lewis
1	BA Williams
1	SJ Harmison
1	AA Noffke
1	G Onions
0	N Peng
0	JA Lowe
0	ML Turner

ESSEX CCC

FIRST–CLASS MATCHES — BATTING

	JS Foster	RS Bopara	RC Irani	AN Cook	JD Middlebrook	A Flower	WI Jefferson	AR Adams	GW Flower	D Gough	GR Napier	Danish Kaneria	DW Steyn	AP Palladino	TJ Phillips	AJ Tudor	RN ten Doeschate	AP Cowan	ND Thornicroft	JE Bishop	A Nel	MA Chambers	MS Westfield	JS Ahmed	Extras	Total	Wickets	Result	Points
v. Cambridge UCCE	58	69*	11		40*		61		11																57	307	4		
(Fenner's) 9-11 April	17	19	58		21*		35		4	36*					25*	29									29	273	6	W	
v. Yorkshire		46	56*	11		62*	149		65																12	401	4		
(Chelmsford) 13-16 April																												D	12
v. Somerset	78*	71	32	111	26	2	11				0					57									39	427	8		
(Taunton) 27-30 April		22*		25			23*																		8	78	1	W	22
v. Leicestershire	13	25	46	28	40	10	93	27		15*	34		0												31	362	10		
(Chelmsford) 6-9 May	0*	0	34	59		74*	13																		11	191	4	W	21
v. Northamptonshire	26	12	36	16	0	32	38	0			3			1*											14	178	10		
(Northampton) 11-14 May	34	79	1	195	0	142*	11							2*											31	495	6	D	6
v. Worcestershire	22	5	85	39	37	4	16		4				0	0*				0							8	220	10		
(Chelmsford) 20-23 May	39	4	21	46	0	85	42		29				11	2*				27							23	329	10	L	4
v. Yorkshire	92	18	103	42	44*	188	4		0	93															38	622	8	D	12
(Headingley) 25-28 May																													
v. Derbyshire	67	0	67	6	71	29	19		7	36												2*			16	320	10		
(Chelmsford) 1-4 June	15	105*		59	2*	41	12		0																11	245	5	D	9
v. Durham	2	9		39	8	20	0	12	11				0*						0						5	106	10		
(The Riverside) 9-11 June	78	21		8	37	24	2	103	6				82	0					4*						15	380	10	L	3
v. Northamptonshire	11	87	47	66	42	72	48	29*	55			22													24	506	10		
(Chelmsford) 10-12 July				0*			4*																		0	4	0	W	22
v. Lancashire	24	17	59	32	64	138	1	48	115				0*												38	536	9	D	9
(Old Trafford) 21-24 July																													
v. Leicestershire	32	17	97	62	12	3		36	4	2				17											15	297	10		
(Leicester) 26-29 July		48*		4		0*			24																4	80	2	D	8
v. Durham	8	11	4	107	0	14		6	15		51			17											12	245	10		
(Southend) 3-6 August	2	9	48	44	8	132*		17	1		10		1*												27	299	8	W	18
v. Derbyshire	0	1	99	1	42	22	8		61	51	0														21	306	10		
(Derby) 16-19 August	22*	10	88*	14		104	83		0																16	337	5	W	19
v. Somerset	107*	42	86	0	42*	14	93		5																11	400	6	L	
(Colchester) 24-27 August																													
v. Lancashire	0	20	15	64	50	22	1	38	0	15		19*													23	267	10		
(Chelmsford) 9-11 September	24	42	10	19	19	5	35	19	13	15		6*													20	227	10	L	5
v. Worcestershire	0	13	99	35	4		116	38			55				89		98							14*	13	574	10		
(Worcester) 21-24 September		58*		117*			20																		6	201	1	D	10
Matches	17	17	16	16	16	15	15	12	12	10	8	7	6	5	3	3	2	1	1	1	1	1	1	1					
Innings	25	29	23	28	23	24	26	12	19	10	7	6	7	7	4	2	1	2	2	0	0	1	2	1					
Not Out	4	5	2	2	5	5	2	1	0	2	0	5	2	4	2	0	0	0	1	0	0	1	0	1					
Highest Score	107*	105*	103	195	71	188	149	103	115	93	55	22	82	17	89	57	98	27	4*	0	0	2*	0	14*					
Runs	771	880	1202	1249	609	1239	938	373	397	296	153	47	94	40	116	86	98	27	4	0	0	2	0	14					
Average	36.71	36.66	57.23	48.03	33.83	65.21	39.08	33.90	20.89	37.00	21.85	47.00	18.80	13.33	58.00	43.00	98.00	13.50	4.00	–	–	–	0.00	–					
100s	1	1	1	4	0	5	2	1	1	0	0	0	0	0	0	0	0	0	0	0	0	0	0	0					
50s	5	5	10	5	3	4	4	0	3	2	2	0	1	0	1	1	1	0	0	0	0	0	0	0					
Catches/Stumpings	35/6	7/0	5/0	12/0	9/0	11/0	11/0	14/0	5/0	1/0	2/0	2/0	2/0	1/0	0/0	2/0	1/0	1/0	0/0	2/0	1/0	0/0	0/0	0/0					

Home Ground: Chelmsford
Address: County Ground, New Writtle Street, Chelmsford, Essex, CM2 0PG
Tel: 01245 252420
Fax: 01245 254030
Email: administration.essex@ecb.co.uk
Directions: *By rail:* Chelmsford Station (8 minutes' walk away). *By road:* M25 then A12 to Chelmsford. Exit Chelmsford and follow AA signs to Essex Cricket Club.
Capacity: 6,000

Other grounds used: Colchester, Southend-on-Sea
Year formed: 1876

Chief Executive: David East
Cricket Operations Manager: Alan Lilley
Club Coach: Graham Gooch
Captain: Ronnie Irani/James Foster
County colours: Blue, gold and red

Honours
County Championship
1979, 1983, 1984, 1986, 1991, 1992
Sunday League/NCL
1981, 1984, 1985, 2005
Refuge Assurance Cup
1989
Benson & Hedges Cup
1979, 1998
Gillette Cup/NatWest/C&G Trophy
1985, 1997

Website:
www.essexcricket.org.uk

ESSEX CCC

FIRST-CLASS MATCHES

BOWLING

Each cell gives the bowling analysis (overs–maidens–runs–wickets); where two innings were bowled the first innings is given above the second.

Bowlers (part 1)

Match	AR Adams	Danish Kaneria	JD Middlebrook	D Gough	RS Bopara	GR Napier	DW Steyn	GW Flower
v. Cambridge UCCE (Fenner's) 9-11 April			18.5-8-54-5 9-4-15-1	15-2-51-1 5-3-7-1	10-0-67-0 2-0-21-0			3-2-4-0 18-5-50-0
v. Yorkshire (Chelmsford) 13-16 April	15-4-52-3 2-1-9-0			16-6-44-1 3-1-7-0	3.2-0-13-2 2-0-9-1	12-3-59-2 5-0-31-0	 4-1-18-0	
v. Somerset (Taunton) 27-30 April	15-4-52-2 20-6-67-4		 22.5-5-60-4	18.3-5-62-3 17-1-61-1	 3-0-14-0	9-2-25-3 16-2-82-1		
v. Leicestershire (Chelmsford) 6-9 May	23-11-49-2 21-9-48-2		 10-2-37-0	19-7-46-3 21.1-5-60-4	8-1-19-1 5-0-31-0	14-3-34-1 16-5-49-2	17-3-69-3 21-3-102-2	
v. Northamptonshire (Northampton) 11-14 May	33-7-95-1		17.1-1-64-1		11-3-33-0	12-3-36-1	30-2-153-1	
v. Worcestershire (Chelmsford) 20-23 May			27-2-89-4 11-2-33-1	19-1-72-2 2-0-18-0	6-0-37-1			14-1-81-1 8-1-53-1
v. Yorkshire (Headingley) 25-28 May 2005	39-11-96-2 9-0-38-1		28-7-78-0 29-8-75-2	29-6-85-5 5-2-13-0	7-0-43-1 3-1-9-0		26.2-9-70-2 13-3-67-0	6-0-21-0 5-2-8-1
v. Derbyshire (Chelmsford) 1-4 June			36-7-95-1 18-1-64-0	30.4-6-90-1 8-4-8-0	29-7-93-4 6-0-25-0		28-8-78-0 11-2-60-1	2-1-4-2 19-0-64-2
v. Durham (The Riverside) 9-11 June	36-7-121-4		11-1-42-0		8-1-34-1		31-6-105-3	8-2-18-0
v. Northamptonshire (Chelmsford) 10-12 July	10.2-1-41-0 16-4-56-1	31-9-83-2 32.4-10-74-6	28-12-72-4 16-3-48-0		 5-1-7-0			5-1-14-0 3-0-19-0
v. Lancashire (Old Trafford) 21-24 July	19-6-65-1	70.2-10-208-0	41.4-11-119-1		18-3-64-1			47.3-17-112-3
v. Leicestershire (Leicester) 26-29 July	27-7-83-3	18-3-72-1	9-2-34-0	31-11-81-2	5-0-21-0			
v. Durham (Southend) 3-6 August	25.1-11-60-5 29-9-83-2	19-9-30-3 40.3-7-103-2	7-1-25-1 34-7-92-4		 3-1-6-0	9-1-47-1 9-2-28-1		
v. Derbyshire (Derby) 16-19 August		60.1-16-111-6 26-6-65-5	27.3-6-67-1 6-1-13-1	22.3-4-54-1	17-2-73-1 11-2-65-2	24-6-78-0 9.2-0-25-2		2-1-6-0 7-0-29-0
v. Somerset (Colchester) 24-27 August		14-2-46-0 24-4-80-1	5-0-20-0 7.1-0-39-0		4-0-20-0 10-0-40-1	6-3-13-0 6-1-21-0		 2-0-26-1
v. Lancashire (Chelmsford) 9-11 September	20-8-37-2 6-2-32-0	36-6-136-4 23-4-61-2	8.3-0-52-2 13.5-3-30-0	14-5-41-1 7-1-24-0	9-2-46-1 2-0-6-0			
v. Worcestershire (Worcester) 21-24 September	8-2-41-1 18-1-93-0		31-5-91-0 6-0-42-0		10-0-50-1 15-2-95-2	13-1-73-0 6-0-33-0		

Bowlers (part 2)

Match	AJ Tudor	AP Palladino	TJ Phillips	A Nel	AN Cook	JE Bishop	WI Jefferson	ND Thornicroft	MA Chambers	MS Westfield	AP Cowan	JS Ahmed	RN ten Doeschate
v. Cambridge UCCE (Fenner's) 9-11 April	11-3-30-2 5-1-17-1	5-1-28-0 15-5-52-0				12-3-32-1 4.5-0-19-1							10-1-51-0 9-1-67-0
v. Yorkshire (Chelmsford) 13-16 April	9-1-30-2 4-0-16-1				 4-0-15-0								
v. Somerset (Taunton) 27-30 April	18-6-48-2 9-2-24-0												
v. Leicestershire (Chelmsford) 6-9 May													
v. Northamptonshire (Northampton) 11-14 May		43-5-149-3											
v. Worcestershire (Chelmsford) 20-23 May		7.1-1-38-1 2.1-0-17-0									16-3-59-1 9-3-40-0		
v. Yorkshire (Headingley) 25-28 May 2005					 4-0-16-1								
v. Derbyshire (Chelmsford) 1-4 June					6-2-19-0		15-1-73-1 1-0-11-0						
v. Durham (The Riverside) 9-11 June					6-3-10-0			22-6-70-1		18-0-90-1			
v. Northamptonshire (Chelmsford) 10-12 July	8-2-24-3 8-2-13-0	 3-1-13-3											
v. Lancashire (Old Trafford) 21-24 July	16-4-45-0				4-0-11-0		4-1-15-0						
v. Leicestershire (Leicester) 26-29 July		25-6-80-2											
v. Durham (Southend) 3-6 August		6-0-23-0 3-1-31-0											
v. Derbyshire (Derby) 16-19 August								2-0-15-0					
v. Somerset (Colchester) 24-27 August				6-2-12-2 17-1-76-2									
v. Lancashire (Chelmsford) 9-11 September													
v. Worcestershire (Worcester) 21-24 September			14-2-69-0 4-0-24-3									16-4-90-1 11-0-51-0	

Match totals

Match	Overs	Total	Byes/Leg-byes	Wickets	Run outs
v. Cambridge UCCE (Fenner's) 9-11 April	84.5 67.5	321 255	4 7	10 4	1
v. Yorkshire (Chelmsford) 13-16 April	55.2 24	205 105	7 0	10 2	
v. Somerset (Taunton) 27-30 April	60.3 87.5	190 313	3 5	10 10	
v. Leicestershire (Chelmsford) 6-9 May	81 94.1	220 332	3 5	10 10	
v. Northamptonshire (Northampton) 11-14 May	146.1 -	552 -	17 -	7 -	
v. Worcestershire (Chelmsford) 20-23 May	89.1 32.1	383 167	7 6	10 2	
v. Yorkshire (Headingley) 25-28 May 2005	135.2 68	408 238	15 12	10 5	
v. Derbyshire (Chelmsford) 1-4 June	146.4 63	462 236	10 4	10 3	1
v. Durham (The Riverside) 9-11 June	140 -	505 -	15 -	10 -	
v. Northamptonshire (Chelmsford) 10-12 July	82.2 83.4	247 261	13 31	10 10	1
v. Lancashire (Old Trafford) 21-24 July	220.3 -	655 -	16 -	6 -	
v. Leicestershire (Leicester) 26-29 July	115 -	382 -	11 -	8 -	
v. Durham (Southend) 3-6 August	69.1 115.3	196 347	5 10	10 10	 1
v. Derbyshire (Derby) 16-19 August	155.1 59.2	426 216	22 14	10 10	1
v. Somerset (Colchester) 24-27 August	35 66.1	112 292	1 10	2 5	
v. Lancashire (Chelmsford) 9-11 September	87.3 51.5	340 155	28 2	10 2	
v. Worcestershire (Worcester) 21-24 September	92 60	424 348	10 10	3 5	

Season bowling averages

Bowler	Overs	Maidens	Runs	Wickets	Average
AR Adams	391.3	111	1218	36	33.83
Danish Kaneria	394.4	86	1069	32	33.40
JD Middlebrook	467.3	97	1417	32	44.28
D Gough	291.5	72	839	27	31.07
RS Bopara	214.2	26	959	20	47.95
GR Napier	166.2	32	634	14	45.28
DW Steyn	199.2	38	838	14	59.85
GW Flower	131.3	32	393	9	43.66
AJ Tudor	56	13	165	8	20.62
AP Palladino	75.2	16	271	6	45.16
TJ Phillips	81	13	322	6	53.66
A Nel	23	3	88	4	22.00
AN Cook	13	1	54	3	18.00
JE Bishop	16.5	3	51	2	25.50
WI Jefferson	20	6	60	1	60.00
ND Thornicroft	22	6	70	1	70.00
MA Chambers	16	1	84	1	84.00
MS Westfield	18	0	90	1	90.00
AP Cowan	25	6	99	1	99.00
JS Ahmed	27	4	141	1	141.00
RN ten Doeschate	19	2	118	0	-

FIELDING

41	JS Foster (35 ct, 6 st)
14	AR Adams
12	AN Cook
11	A Flower
11	WI Jefferson
9	JD Middlebrook
7	RS Bopara
5	GW Flower
5	RC Irani
2	AJ Tudor
2	GR Napier
2	JE Bishop
2	Danish Kaneria
2	DW Steyn
1	D Gough
1	AP Cowan
1	AP Palladino
1	A Nel
1	RN ten Doeschate
0	TJ Phillips
0	ND Thornicroft
0	MA Chambers
0	MS Westfield
0	JS Ahmed

GLAMORGAN CCC

FIRST-CLASS MATCHES
BATTING

Match	MA Wallace	RDB Croft	DL Hemp	MJ Powell	DS Harrison	DD Cherry	J Hughes	DA Cosker	AG Wharf	MTG Elliott	AP Davies	SD Thomas	HT Waters	SC Ganguly	RE Watkins	RN Grant	IJ Thomas	MP O'Shea	SP Jones	MP Maynard	AJ Harrison	Extras	Total	Wickets	Result	Points
v. Warwickshire (Edgbaston) 13-16 April	3	7	8	31	2				1	84		9					24		0*	20		9	198	10		
	11	33	96	31	23				0	69		46					1		0*	0		13	323	10	L	1
v. Surrey (Cardiff) 27-30 April	96	2	60	11	3		0		1	0		15					29		7*			26	250	10		
	55	2	24	22	1*		0		34	4		10					1		0			20	173	10	L	5
v. Gloucestershire (Cardiff) 6-9 May	52	31	0	0	12		0	15*	35	38		17					18					21	239	10		
	32	8	57	39	4		1	0*	0	123		21					40					20	345	10	L	4
v. Surrey (The Oval) 11-14 May	5	27	24	43	75*	47	30	17			37	12					4					24	345	10		
	0	7	95	93	0	0	6	12			0*	2					12					21	248	10	L	6
v. Hampshire (The Rose Bowl) 20-23 May	9	29	38	4	0	2	0			51	4	63							12*			17	229	10		
	5	30	21	68	0	40	17			15	16*	13							0			25	250	10	L	3
v. Sussex (Swansea) 1-4 June	24	9	128	16	1	0		19*		85	0	23		0								19	301	10		
			56	24*		87				162				15*								10	354	3	D	8
v. Kent (Cardiff) 8-10 June	25	45	69	6	14	7		17*		28	24	26		69								28	358	10		
	3	33	4	0	0	0		1		8	35*	17		142								17	260	10	L	6
v. Middlesex (Southgate) 15-18 June			103			226	134*			59				22*								40	584	3		
			29			16	100*			20				84*								7	256	3	L	6
v. Nottinghamshire (Trent Bridge) 8-10 July	45	4	44	30	26	8	5				41*		3	47		8						6	267	10		
	12	20	12	27	21	27	20				0		0*	22		33						20	214	10	L	5
v. Middlesex (Cardiff) 21-23 July	23	84	22	18	5	14	7		21				1*	4	1							32	232	10		
	64	25	5	58	8	4	41		1				2*	55	6							10	279	10	L	4
v. Bangladesh A (Abergavenny) 26-28 July	51	40		111		4	13	11*	77		15		1		13			10				34	380	10		
																									D	
v. Kent (Canterbury) 3-5 August	0	2	171*	23	4	0	1	18	21				34					0				32	306	10		
	10	12	13	6	19	21	27	7*	5				0					24				13	157	10	L	5
v. Warwickshire (Colwyn Bay) 10-12 August	3	66*	31	26	19	21	7	22	0						16			4				24	239	10		
	68	33	19	72*	25	24	10	23	1						7			14				12	308	10	L	3
v. Gloucestershire (Bristol) 25-28 August	49	23	23	8	8	166	21	23	40				0*			1						20	382	10		
	0	21*	45	26	15	40	21	52	28				0			27						15	290	10	W	21
v. Nottinghamshire (Cardiff) 30 August-2 September	7	5	21	62	0	10	3	12*	22				0		1							8	151	10		
	14	0	14	96	13	4	10	10	113				0*		12							21	307	10	L	3
v. Sussex (Hove) 7-8 September	4	35	71	34	1	8	32	6	11				0*			30						23	255	10		
	12	0	1	22	0	39	5	0	0				0*			4						13	96	10	L	5
v. Hampshire (Cardiff) 15-18 September	31*	20	51	7	11	0		39	0		0				41	25						24	249	10		
	33*	90	14	24	8	23		0	19		0				2	8						23	244	10	L	4
Matches	17	17	16	16	16	14	13	12	12	7	7	7	7	5	5	4	4	3	3	1	1					
Innings	30	30	32	31	29	27	25	20	21	14	12	14	13	9	9	7	8	5	6	2	1					
Not Out	2	2	1	2	2	0	2	7	0	0	4	0	7	2	0	1	0	0	4	0	0					
Highest Score	96	90	171*	111	75*	226	134*	52	113	162	41*	63	34	142	41	33	40	24	12*	20	0					
Runs	746	743	1369	1038	318	838	511	304	430	746	172	274	41	438	131	103	129	52	19	20	0					
Average	26.64	26.53	44.16	35.79	11.77	31.03	22.21	23.38	20.47	53.28	21.50	19.57	6.83	62.57	14.55	17.16	16.12	10.40	9.50	10.00	0.00					
100s	0	0	3	1	0	2	2	0	1	2	0	0	0	1	0	0	0	0	0	0	0					
50s	6	3	8	6	1	1	0	1	1	6	0	0	1	3	0	0	0	0	0	0	0					
Catches/Stumpings	31/4	5/0	9/0	9/0	8/0	1/0	10/0	5/0	10/0	6/0	3/0	0/0	0/0	2/0	0/0	1/0	2/0	1/0	2/0	1/0	0/0					

Home Ground: Cardiff
Address: Sophia Gardens, Cardiff, CF11 9XR
Tel: 0871 2823401
Fax: 0871 2823405
Email: info@glamorgancricket.co.uk
Directions: *By rail:* Cardiff central train station. *By road:* From North, A470 and follow signs to Cardiff until junction with Cardiff bypass then A48 Port Talbot and City Centre. Cathedral Road is situated off A48 for Sophia Gardens.

Capacity: 4,000
Other grounds used: Swansea, Colwyn Bay, Abergavenny
Year formed: 1888

Chief Executive: Mike Fatkin
Chairman: Paul Russell
First XI Coach: John Derrick
Captain: Robert Croft
County colours: Navy blue and yellow/gold

Honours
County Championship
1948, 1969, 1997
Sunday League/NCL
1993, 2002, 2004

Website:
www.glamorgancricket.com

GLAMORGAN CCC

FIRST-CLASS MATCHES

BOWLING

First-class matches	RDB Croft	AG Wharf	DA Cosker	DS Harrison	AP Davies	HT Waters	SP Jones	SD Thomas	RE Watkins	SC Ganguly	AJ Harrison	MTG Elliott	DD Cherry	RN Grant	Overs	Total	Byes/Leg-byes	Wickets	Run outs
v. Warwickshire (Edgbaston) 13-16 April	46-13-121-2	31-3-120-1		29-4-107-0			29-2-121-3	16.4-0-83-2							151.4	564	12	8	
															-	-	-	-	
v. Surrey (Cardiff) 27-30 April	6-3-6-0	19-4-52-3		17-5-52-1			18.4-3-62-3	14-2-63-3							74.4	248	13	10	
	11-3-41-2	8-0-52-2		7-0-31-0			9-2-42-1	1-0-6-0							36	178	6	5	
v. Gloucestershire (Cardiff) 6-9 May	27-3-107-1	30.1-4-127-3	29-6-79-2	16-4-77-1				21-3-66-1							123.1	466	10	10	2
	15.3-6-38-1		17-3-43-2	4-0-14-0				8-1-24-0							44.3	119	0	3	
v. Surrey (The Oval) 11-14 May	29.4-3-116-2		34.3-3-120-2	20-6-72-3	24-4-121-3			0.3-0-8-0							108.4	444	7	10	
	29-5-125-1		20-1-87-0	14-4-45-0	15-1-76-2			13.3-1-84-1							91.3	425	8	4	
v. Hampshire (The Rose Bowl) 20-23 May	25-2-107-2			20-5-63-1	26-8-76-2		34-12-73-3	11-0-71-0							116	401	11	8	
	6-0-28-1			3.4-0-20-0	2-0-8-0		3-0-24-0								14.4	80	0	1	
v. Sussex (Swansea) 1-4 June	25-1-100-2		28-2-116-1	25-6-94-0	27-4-120-1					4-1-7-0	15-2-54-1				124	497	6	5	
															-	-	-	-	
v. Kent (Cardiff) 8-10 June	46-6-161-3		44.3-6-149-2	23-4-72-2	23-5-73-1			19-2-99-2		3-0-8-0					158.3	568	6	10	
				4-0-20-0				3.5-0-31-0							7.5	51	0	0	
v. Middlesex (Southgate) 15-18 June	25-2-95-0	18.3-1-103-1	34-4-133-2	15-1-85-1									3-0-12-0		95.3	435	7	4	
	25-0-141-2	9-0-39-0	25.5-1-123-1	9-1-59-0					7-1-30-0				2-0-8-0		77.5	408	8	4	1
v. Nottinghamshire (Trent Bridge) 8-10 July	23-3-82-0			22-1-83-1	26-2-107-1	23-2-75-4				16-0-68-3					110	425	10	10	1
	6.4-4-15-0			4-1-17-0	2-0-10-0					3-2-5-0			2-1-5-0		17.4	57	5	0	
v. Middlesex (Cardiff) 21-23 July	38-1-146-2	28-4-143-0		23.3-1-117-5		26-4-75-3				5-0-30-0				3-0-18-0	123.3	534	5	10	
															-	-	-	-	
v. Bangladesh A (Abergavenny) 26-28 July		5-0-36-0			5.1-2-17-2										10.1	54	1	2	
															-	-	-	-	
v. Kent (Canterbury) 3-5 August	39-5-160-1	24-5-93-2	30-5-123-3	24.5-4-125-3		18-1-83-1									135.5	587	3	10	
															-	-	-	-	
v. Warwickshire (Colwyn Bay) 10-12 August	37-3-126-3	22-3-129-2	27-5-106-1	26-4-101-1				14-0-76-0							126	545	7	7	
		1-0-1-0		1.2-1-1-0											2.2	3	1	0	
v. Gloucestershire (Bristol) 25-28 August		17-4-59-6		16-2-59-4		13-3-45-2				1-0-12-0					34	133	3	10	
	42-2-11-1	16-2-62-5	18-10-24-1	10.1-2-24-1						7-0-38-0					68.3	217	13	10	
v. Nottinghamshire (Cardiff) 30 August-2 September	27-5-57-3	18-4-39-0	22.5-5-57-4	14-2-51-1		13-3-36-0				12-2-30-1					106.5	283	8	10	1
	22.1-3-77-1	5-0-23-0	22-5-48-1	3-0-19-0									1-0-4-0		53.1	179	8	2	
v. Sussex (Hove) 7-8 September	26.4-2-97-3	21-3-75-3	17-0-61-1	16-2-47-0		7-2-18-1				9-3-14-2					96.4	317	0	10	
	2-0-17-0	3.4-0-8-0	1-0-7-1												6.4	35	3	1	
v. Hampshire (Cardiff) 15-18 September	25.4-2-103-5	15-3-39-0	18-4-78-3	15-4-49-1	14-4-38-1					8-0-31-0					95.4	350	12	10	
	10-0-57-5	6-0-45-0	7-0-51-1	5-0-43-1	4-0-18-0										32	218	4	7	

	RDB Croft	AG Wharf	DA Cosker	DS Harrison	AP Davies	HT Waters	SP Jones	SD Thomas	RE Watkins	SC Ganguly	AJ Harrison	MTG Elliott	DD Cherry	RN Grant
Overs	577.4	297.2	395.4	387.3	168.1	100	93.4	122.3	37	38	15	5	3	3
Maidens	77	40	60	64	30	15	19	9	5	4	2	0	1	0
Runs	2134	1245	1405	1547	664	332	322	611	125	148	54	20	9	18
Wickets	43	28	28	27	13	11	10	9	3	3	1	0	0	0
Average	49.62	44.46	50.17	57.29	51.07	30.18	32.20	67.88	41.66	49.33	54.00	-	-	-

FIELDING

35	MA Wallace (31 ct, 4 st)
10	AG Wharf
10	J Hughes
9	DL Hemp
9	MJ Powell
8	DS Harrison
6	MTG Elliott
5	RDB Croft
5	DA Cosker
3	AP Davies
2	SC Ganguly
2	SP Jones
2	IJ Thomas
1	MP Maynard
1	DD Cherry
1	RN Grant
1	MP O'Shea
0	SD Thomas
0	RE Watkins
0	AJ Harrison
0	HT Waters

GLOUCESTERSHIRE CCC

FIRST-CLASS MATCHES
BATTING

	SJ Adshead	APR Gidman	CM Spearman	WPC Weston	Kadeer Ali	MA Hardinges	SP Kirby	J Lewis	MGN Windows	JMM Averis	CG Taylor	ID Fisher	CM Bandara	RR Sarwan	UDU Chandana	JA Pearson	THC Hancock	WD Rudge	CG Greenidge	MCJ Ball	SD Snell	MW Alleyne	GP Hodnett	RJ Sillence	Extras	Total	Wickets	Result	Points
v. Oxford UCCE	54	0	18	103	6	41*				13	21						22		11						16	305	9		
(The Parks) 9-11 April		42*	216*	66	38						85*						23								20	490	4	D	
v. Hampshire	0	5	34	66	33	2	0*	40		4	3						2								32	221	10		
(The Rose Bowl) 13-16 April	18	24	66	57	10	2	0	3*		0	7						0								16	203	10	L	4
v. Kent	7	43	35	19	3		0*	18		22	66				0		23								12	248	10		
(Bristol) 27-30 April																												D	8
v. Glamorgan	59	16	73	29	55		6*	5			176	16			14		0								17	466	10		
(Cardiff) 6-9 May			18	23	20*						15						41*								2	119	3	W	22
v. Middlesex	27	19	69	24	0		15*	0		21	17				12		9								19	232	10		
(Lord's) 11-13 May	0	5	20	9	12		4*	19		0	46				17		21								7	160	10	L	4
v. Nottinghamshire	45	37		45	16	27	8			4	0				17	15			20*						16	250	10		
(Bristol) 25-27 May	2	9		1	12	5	5			5	12				49*	68			7						12	192	10	L	5
v. Kent	2	2		5		27	4*		39		0	39			7	13			25						20	183	10		
(Maidstone) 1-3 June	3	13	0			19	4*		15		18	22			1	0			0						3	98	10	L	3
v. Warwickshire	43		35	1		21			37		13	8			0*	52			5			16			23	254	10		
(Gloucester) 10-12 June	23		7	2		0			3		45	43			19	0			4*			51			20	217	10	L	4
v. Surrey	2	93	29	10	33		0*		30	6	21	36				0									28	288	10		
(Bristol) 8-11 July	93	142	47	52	24	2			6	29*	18	22				34									25	494	10	D	8
v. Bangladesh A	8	13		13	0					33		0	4		17			0			83*				14	232	10		
(Bristol) 20-22 July	41	100*		63	1							36			7*						42				40	330	5	W	
v. Sussex	28*	18	48	7		9	2	8	0	0		0		9											13	142	10		
(Hove) 26-29 July	5	1	22	21		23		5*	28	15		14*		30											28	192	8	D	7
v. Hampshire	73	115	9	22	33	8	24*	33	33			19	0	18				7		7					9	363	10		
(Cheltenham) 3-6 August	13*	17	34	26	5	4	0	50	50			12	1	48				0*		0					22	232	10	L	7
v. Sussex	39	7		46	3		0*	33	33			15	20	26				15							21	224	10		
(Cheltenham) 10-12 August	6	7			6			0	0			13	16	117											8	179	10	L	4
v. Surrey	148*	84	1	0	7				21	29		13	8	0				0							24	350	10		
(The Oval) 16-19 August	0	40*	7		66	14			38			2*		99				13							28	294	6	D	11
v. Glamorgan	36	2	9	11	0	36*			8				14	0				0		1				12	5	133	10		
(Bristol) 25-28 August	14	56	39	2	4	9*			6				6	54				0		1				0	14	217	10	L	4
v. Middlesex	59	57	0	46	6	30*		28	28				70	4											32	333	10		
(Bristol) 30 August-2 September	36	25	10	61		58*	2	28	28				29	26											11	287	10	D	10
v. Nottinghamshire	0	0	2	55*	5	7	10	2	2	0			4	11											7	103	10		
(Trent Bridge) 5-6 September	3	20	38	1	10	13*		55	8	13			6	0											2	169	10	L	3
v. Warwickshire	14	2	1	7	2*		13	1	1				0							1	13		49		15	118	10		
(Edgbaston) 21-24 September	19		42	38	15	15	0	65*					16							0	3		10		6	229	10	L	3
Matches	18	16	14	13	13	13	13	11	11	10	9	9	8	7	6	5	5	5	4	3	2	1	1	1					
Innings	33	30	27	24	25	25	21	19	22	16	17	17	14	14	10	10	9	8	7	6	4	2	2	2					
Not Out	3	3	0	0	2	2	11	6	1	1	1	2	0	0	2	1	1	1	2	0	1	0	0	0					
Highest Score	148*	142	216	103	66	58*	15*	55	65*	33	176	43	70	117	49*	68	41*	15	25	7	83*	51	49	12					
Runs	920	1012	930	710	494	404	105	324	479	194	563	310	194	442	136	206	141	35	72	10	141	67	59	12					
Average	30.66	37.48	34.44	29.58	21.47	17.56	10.50	24.92	22.80	12.93	35.18	20.66	13.85	31.57	17.00	22.88	17.62	5.00	14.40	1.66	47.00	33.50	29.50	6.00					
100s	1	3	1	1	0	0	0	0	0	0	1	0	0	1	0	0	0	0	0	0	0	0	0	0					
50s	5	4	3	5	4	1	0	1	2	0	2	0	1	2	0	2	0	0	0	0	1	1	0	0					
Catches/Stumpings	40/6	14/0	13/0	4/0	8/0	10/0	0/0	5/0	2/0	2/0	5/0	8/0	6/0	9/0	2/0	2/0	11/0	2/0	0/0	5/0	4/0	0/0	1/0	0/0					

Home Ground: Bristol
Address: County Ground, Nevil Road, Bristol, BS7 9EJ
Tel: 01179 108000
Fax: 01179 241193
Directions: *By road:* M5, M4, M32 into Bristol, exit at second exit (Fishponds/Horfield), then third exit – Muller Road. Almost at end of Muller Road (bus station on right), turn left at Ralph Road. Go to the top, turn left and then right almost immediately into Kennington Avenue. Follow the signs for County Cricket.

Capacity: 8,000
Other grounds used: Gloucester, Cheltenham College
Year formed: 1870

Chief Executive: Tom Richardson
Chairman: Alan Haines
Director of Cricket: Andy Stovold
Head Coach: Mark Alleyne
Captain: Chris Taylor/Craig Spearman/Alex Gidman/Jon Lewis
County colours: Blue, brown, gold, green and red

Honours
Sunday League/NCL
2000
Benson & Hedges Cup
1977, 1999, 2000
Gillette Cup/NatWest/C&G Trophy
1973, 1999, 2000, 2003, 2004

Website:
www.gloscricket.co.uk

GLOUCESTERSHIRE CCC

FIRST-CLASS MATCHES
BOWLING

FIRST-CLASS MATCHES	CM Bandara	SP Kirby	J Lewis	MA Hardinges	JMM Averis	ID Fisher	UDU Chandana	WD Rudge	APR Gidman	CG Greenidge	MCJ Ball	Kadeer Ali	RR Sarwan	RJ Sillence	THC Hancock	CG Taylor	MW Alleyne	Overs	Total	Byes/Leg-byes	Wickets	Run outs
v. Oxford UCCE		13-7-20-4		10.4-4-24-3	8-5-6-1				6-1-11-1	12-3-39-1								49.4	116	16	10	
(The Parks) 9-11 April		10-5-26-1		6-2-13-1	8-5-11-3				6-1-22-0	6-1-21-0					2-0-17-0			38	114	4	6	1
v. Hampshire		16-2-64-2	16.5-5-51-3	12-4-40-3	10-4-20-1				6-2-21-1									60.5	197	1	10	
(The Rose Bowl) 13-16 April		22-6-71-2	25-8-59-3	10.3-1-43-2	11-1-58-2				11-2-42-1									79.3	275	2	10	
v. Kent		26-6-73-2	34-9-57-5		24-10-66-0		38-4-105-2		11-1-45-0									133	359	13	10	1
(Bristol) 27-30 April		10-1-38-2	10-2-27-0		7-1-24-1		17-5-44-0		6-0-29-0			5-0-15-0			5-2-14-1	8-1-26-1		68	229	12	5	
v. Glamorgan		14-1-50-2	16-6-48-1			5-2-12-0	21-2-73-3		10-1-47-4									66	239	9	10	
(Cardiff) 6-9 May		15-2-55-0	12-3-34-1			34-10-89-4	36.1-9-117-5		8-0-31-0							2-0-7-0		107.1	345	12	10	
v. Middlesex		19-3-84-3	24.2-6-82-4		13-2-49-0		24-6-74-1		20-1-89-2									100.2	390	12	10	
(Lord's) 11-13 May		17.5-4-58-1	23-6-48-1		17-2-66-2		32-5-104-1		11.1-0-55-1									101	342	11	6	
v. Nottinghamshire		20-5-70-1		25-4-115-4	23-3-65-1	25-2-89-1			3-0-19-1	21-4-104-2								117	469	7	10	
(Bristol) 25-27 May																		–	–	–	–	
v. Kent		14-3-42-1		18-2-51-5		5-1-15-1	7-0-19-0		9-2-28-2	14-4-36-1								67	204	13	10	
(Maidstone) 1-3 June		8.4-2-38-3		5-0-23-0						3-1-6-0								16.4	78	11	3	
v. Warwickshire				22-3-82-0		39-12-99-3	39-5-115-3			23.5-4-78-2							24-3-84-1	147.5	473	15	10	1
(Gloucester) 10-12 June																		–	–	–	–	
v. Surrey		30.1-3-130-3		29-6-100-3	27-4-138-2		32-4-149-1		17-0-69-0							3-0-10-0		138.1	603	7	10	1
(Bristol) 8-11 July		6-0-30-3		2-0-13-0	3-0-32-0													11	84	9	3	
v. Bangladesh A	21-5-61-1		17-3-75-3		12-2-32-2	10-1-25-1		12-3-46-3										72	251	12	10	
(Bristol) 20-22 July	17.3-7-45-5		12-1-51-0		10-2-28-0	11-4-33-3		5-1-23-2										55.3	181	1	10	
v. Sussex		13-2-55-2	17-7-62-4	6-2-12-1		10-3-54-3												46	191	8	10	
(Hove) 26-29 July		15-6-29-2	27-2-88-5	8-2-24-0		11-0-45-0	25.1-4-75-2						1-0-1-0					87.1	267	5	10	1
v. Hampshire	30-4-110-4	20.4-4-53-4	20-5-112-2	8-1-41-0		15-3-57-0												93.4	385	12	10	
(Cheltenham) 3-6 August	31.5-2-108-3	10-3-24-2	15-3-69-1	13-1-52-0		34-2-108-1							4-0-17-0					107.5	388	10	7	
v. Sussex	23-4-64-4	4.3-1-15-0				24.3-5-93-3		15.1-4-75-2			25-1-108-0							92.1	365	10	10	1
(Cheltenham) 10-12 August	26-3-112-4					4-0-16-0		7-1-53-0			21-6-70-0	5-2-12-1						63	264	1	5	
v. Surrey	27.1-4-88-3			23-5-66-2	27-6-96-2	17-1-78-0		25-4-97-3				2-0-11-0	3-0-18-0					124.1	463	9	10	
(The Oval) 16-19 August																		–	–	–	–	
v. Glamorgan	27-9-56-3		30.2-7-77-1	22-6-67-3				13-1-68-0				4-1-8-0	1-0-5-0	17-2-90-2				114.2	382	11	10	1
(Bristol) 25-28 August	37-9-85-4		16-3-39-1	3-0-19-0				6-0-36-1				2-0-4-1	18-5-38-2	13-1-54-0				95	290	15	10	1
v. Middlesex	26.1-8-71-5			22-6-61-0	8-3-31-0			18-6-75-3			19-7-31-1	6-1-19-0						99.1	297	9	10	1
(Bristol) 30 August-2 September	22-3-65-1			10-5-20-1				9-1-32-0			26-6-56-2		5-0-20-0					72	203	10	4	
v. Nottinghamshire	15-3-65-0		20-2-71-2	19-2-80-4	13.4-3-38-3	15-0-75-0												82.4	336	7	10	1
(Trent Bridge) 5-6 September																		–	–	–	–	
v. Warwickshire	25-6-67-4		15-10-23-3	14-6-33-1	12-3-48-2						24-11-36-0							90	208	1	10	
(Edgbaston) 21-24 September	24-2-90-4		10-1-51-0	17-3-64-2	3-1-13-0						34-7-99-3							88	320	3	9	

	CM Bandara	SP Kirby	J Lewis	MA Hardinges	JMM Averis	ID Fisher	UDU Chandana	WD Rudge	APR Gidman	CG Greenidge	MCJ Ball	Kadeer Ali	RR Sarwan	RJ Sillence	THC Hancock	CG Taylor	MW Alleyne
Overs	352.4	349.5	397.3	259.5	236	255.4	239.1	110.1	124.1	79.5	149	24	32	30	7	13	24
Maidens	69	79	98	53	50	49	38	21	11	17	38	4	5	3	2	1	3
Runs	1087	1170	1237	915	865	849	740	505	508	284	400	69	99	144	31	43	84
Wickets	45	45	43	32	20	19	16	14	13	6	6	2	2	2	1	1	1
Average	24.15	26.00	28.76	28.59	43.25	44.68	46.25	36.07	39.07	47.33	66.66	34.50	49.50	72.00	31.00	43.00	84.00

FIELDING

46	SJ Adshead (40 ct, 6 st)
14	APR Gidman
13	CM Spearman
11	THC Hancock
10	MA Hardinges
9	RR Sarwan
8	ID Fisher
8	Kadeer Ali
6	CM Bandara
5	MCJ Ball
5	J Lewis
5	CG Taylor
4	WPC Weston
4	SD Snell
2	MGN Windows
2	JMM Averis
2	UDU Chandana
2	JA Pearson
2	WD Rudge
1	GP Hodnett
0	MW Alleyne
0	CG Greenidge
0	RJ Sillence
0	SP Kirby

HAMPSHIRE CCC

FIRST-CLASS MATCHES
BATTING

	JP Crawley	SM Ervine	N Pothas	MJ Brown	AD Mascarenhas	SK Warne	CT Tremlett	SD Udal	GA Lamb	JHK Adams	BV Taylor	SM Katich	KP Pietersen	JJ McLean	RJ Logan	SR Watson	CC Benham	AJ Bichel	CD McMillan	JTA Bruce	TG Burrows	DA Kenway	Extras	Total	Wickets	Result	Points
v. Gloucestershire	4	11	4	35		22	3			22	2	72*			5							0	17	197	10		
(The Rose Bowl) 13-16 Apr 2005	0	25	0	32		62	64			16	4*	20			28							20	4	275	10	W	17
v. Sussex	28	23	84	6		34	0	20*		32	4	39	0										10	280	10		
(Hove) 20-23 April	22	57	6*	7		6		4*		35	24	27	61										18	267	8	D	9
v. Middlesex	84	26	18	51	34	0	13*			5	0	27	0										17	275	10		
(The Rose Bowl) 6-9 May	40	30	65	15	44*	12	1			11	9	28	28										21	304	10	W	19
v. Kent	0	18		32	9	107*	35			0		56	1		4						42		24	328	10		
(Canterbury) 11-14 May	25	57		54	8	26*	4			1		128	125		0*						13		20	461	9	D	10
v. Glamorgan	106	34	21	16	5*	13*	4		42		1*	20	126										13	401	8		
(The Rose Bowl) 20-23 May	24*		28*									28											0	80	1	W	22
v. Warwickshire	34	16	1	15		0		34	0		0*		42	5		21							16	184	10		
(Stratford) 25-26 May	3	32	0	49	4		0	2					12	0	13*	4							5	124	10	L	3
v. Nottinghamshire	39	15	27	26		46	24*	16	15			0			4				52				13	277	10		
(Trent Bridge) 1-4 June	6	16*		54				75					41						26*				2	220	4	W	17
v. Surrey	1	0	9	34		3	11*		5	1	4					41			17				20	146	10		
(The Rose Bowl) 15-17 June	67	11	0	20		14	12*		11	1	0					0			4				20	160	10	L	3
v. Middlesex	62	33	26	15	39	101		24	7		2*					20			7				19	355	10		
(Southgate) 8-11 July	14	8	19	1	35	4		1	51		3*					15			15				26	192	10	L	7
v. Sussex	16	69	135	15	8			0	0		1*					43	2		14				6	309	10		
(The Rose Bowl) 20-23 July	5	3	74	16	1		44*	5	0							82	6		34				7	277	10	W	20
v. Gloucestershire	11	6	139	1	0		47*					0				26	0	138	0				17	385	10		
(Cheltenham) 3-6 August	120	22	54*	8	16*		4					68				52	8						36	388	7	W	21
v. Kent	24	74	74*	19	4		0		2	8		0				16		87					17	325	10		
(The Rose Bowl) 12-15 August	46	69	15*	11	6			6*	12			19				30		2					25	241	8	D	10
v. Surrey	42	2	100*	0	49*			20				32				88							28	361	6		
(The Oval) 24-27 August																										D	11
v. Warwickshire	60	60	30		102*			2	65			4				203*							50	576	6		
(The Rose Bowl) 30 August-1 September																										W	22
v. Glamorgan	17	20	26	67	24		9		71			50				52	2			0*			12	350	10		
(Cardiff) 15-18 September	35	75		10*	15		28					49				0*	0			2			4	218	7	W	22
v. Nottinghamshire	311*	9	46	103*			50			53		67											75	714	5		
(The Rose Bowl) 21-23 September																										W	22

	JP Crawley	SM Ervine	N Pothas	MJ Brown	AD Mascarenhas	SK Warne	CT Tremlett	SD Udal	GA Lamb	JHK Adams	BV Taylor	SM Katich	KP Pietersen	JJ McLean	RJ Logan	SR Watson	CC Benham	AJ Bichel	CD McMillan	JTA Bruce	TG Burrows	DA Kenway
Matches	16	16	15	13	11	11	11	11	9	8	8	7	6	6	6	5	5	4	4	4	1	1
Innings	29	28	24	25	18	18	14	14	15	13	14	13	11	9	9	8	10	3	8	3	2	2
Not Out	2	1	5	1	7	3	5	4	0	0	6	1	0	1	2	1	0	0	1	1	0	0
Highest Score	311*	75	139	54	103*	107*	64	47*	75	71	24	128	126	68	28	203*	41	138	52	2	42	20
Runs	1246	821	973	560	540	493	219	196	250	310	66	597	424	242	61	540	117	227	169	2	55	20
Average	46.14	30.40	51.21	23.33	49.09	32.86	24.33	19.60	16.66	23.84	8.25	49.75	38.54	30.25	8.71	77.14	11.70	75.66	24.14	1.00	27.50	10.00
100s	3	0	3	0	2	2	0	0	0	0	0	1	2	0	0	1	0	1	0	0	0	0
50s	4	7	5	3	1	1	1	0	2	3	0	4	1	3	0	3	0	1	1	0	0	0
Catches/Stumpings	14/1	8/0	48/3	13/0	5/0	13/0	3/0	7/0	13/0	8/0	0/0	7/0	4/0	4/0	0/0	10/0	5/0	1/0	0/0	3/0	5/0	3/0

Home Ground: Southampton
Address: The Rose Bowl, Botley Road, West End, Southampton, SO30 3XH
Tel: 02380 472002
Fax: 02380 472122
Email: enquiries@rosebowlplc.com
Directions: From the North: M3 Southbound to junction 14, follow signs for M27 Eastbound (Fareham and Portsmouth). At junction 7 of M27, filter left onto Charles Watts Way (A334) and from there follow the brown road signs to The Rose Bowl. From the South: M27 to junction 7 and follow the brown road signs to The Rose Bowl.

Capacity: 9,950
Year formed: 1863

Chief Executive: Roger Bransgrove
Director of Cricket: Tim Tremlett
Captain: Shane Warne/Shaun Udal
County colours: Navy blue, old gold

Honours
County Championship
1961, 1973
Sunday League/NCL
1975, 1978, 1986
Benson & Hedges Cup
1988, 1992
Gillette Cup/NatWest/C&G Trophy
1991, 2005

Website:
www.hampshirecricket.com

HAMPSHIRE CCC

FIRST-CLASS MATCHES

BOWLING

Figures are given as overs-maidens-runs-wickets, top line first innings, lower line second innings.

Match	SK Warne	CT Tremlett	SD Udal	SM Ervine	AD Mascarenhas	BV Taylor	JTA Bruce	AJ Bichel
v. Gloucestershire (The Rose Bowl) 13-16 April	23-3-50-3 22-2-56-3	17-2-51-1 13-3-43-1		11-3-38-2 5-2-20-0		12-2-38-3 14.4-3-45-6		
v. Sussex (Hove) 20-23 April	23-5-72-2 21-2-81-4	17.5-4-44-6 25-6-69-1	7-0-29-0 3-0-8-0	18-8-55-1 23-11-37-2		10-0-36-1 30-6-86-2		
v. Middlesex (The Rose Bowl) 6-9 May	27-2-73-3 30-7-58-4	22.2-8-41-3 19-6-59-4		9-2-34-1 5-0-28-0	20-3-66-3 16-2-49-2	15-4-51-0 13-2-33-0		
v. Kent (Canterbury) 11-14 May	19-3-50-3 37-13-65-3	14-2-61-2 31-7-88-4		12-2-66-2 30-4-104-2	20-5-53-0 23-7-65-0			
v. Glamorgan (The Rose Bowl) 20-23 May	21-3-63-1 12-1-34-1	13-4-42-4 17-3-54-3		10.2-1-30-0 23.4-7-60-5		15-4-50-2 19-2-48-0		
v. Warwickshire (Stratford) 25-26 May	24.2-2-88-6		7-1-16-1	19-2-59-1		14-4-54-2 2-0-10-0		
v. Nottinghamshire (Trent Bridge) 1-4 June	7-0-26-0 12.2-1-37-2	11.5-1-42-1 16-1-80-5	2-0-9-0 5-0-19-1	15-5-36-2 11-1-54-0				
v. Surrey (The Rose Bowl) 15-17 June	21-0-89-2	20-2-106-4		17.4-3-84-2		11-3-39-2		
v. Middlesex (Southgate) 8-11 July	23-4-57-2 29.4-4-108-2		9.3-4-18-3 21-5-60-3	14-3-53-1 5-2-17-0	15-5-38-3 6-1-18-0	21-2-71-1 7-2-10-0		
v. Sussex (The Rose Bowl) 20-23 July		15-0-70-1 11-0-56-1	10-0-68-2 2-0-10-0	19.5-4-73-5 17-4-54-4	15-5-25-1 20.4-4-64-5	4-0-16-0		
v. Gloucestershire (Cheltenham) 3-6 August		11-3-60-1 12-3-37-0	22-5-70-1 22.5-5-61-6	12-2-41-1 8-2-28-0	12-2-46-0 5-1-16-1		12-1-42-3	17.1-6-57-2 17-4-46-1
v. Kent (The Rose Bowl) 12-15 August		22-1-78-1 1-0-9-0	18-4-51-2 7-0-19-1	11-0-56-0 5-0-29-1	25-8-77-3 14-4-33-3			27-3-122-4 15.3-1-56-3
v. Surrey (The Oval) 24-27 August			19-4-65-3 30-9-65-5	17-3-63-1 12-2-52-1	14-1-55-1 6-1-22-0		14-1-82-3 14-3-50-1	13-2-49-1
v. Warwickshire (The Rose Bowl) 30 August-1 September		18-1-93-2 7-0-49-1	8-1-23-1 22-8-44-6	7.2-3-17-1 6-0-24-1	16-5-52-3 8-3-12-0			14-6-39-2 17-3-72-1
v. Glamorgan (Cardiff) 15-18 September	22-5-50-4 9-0-31-1			19-3-42-0 12-1-46-1	10-1-38-1 12.4-1-60-5	5-2-8-1 6-1-9-1	14-3-38-2 13-0-51-2	
v. Nottinghamshire (The Rose Bowl) 21-23 September	1.2-0-6-0 13-4-67-1			16.2-4-39-4 11.5-0-70-4	7.4-1-50-0	14-2-55-5 13-3-38-2	7-1-19-1 17-4-42-2	
Overs	397.4	334	274.3	374.1	273.4	187.4	91	120.4
Maidens	61	57	54	79	65	34	13	25
Runs	1161	1232	832	1360	801	587	324	441
Wickets	47	46	44	42	34	19	14	14
Average	24.70	26.78	18.90	32.38	23.55	30.89	23.14	31.50

Match	SR Watson	RJ Logan	SM Katich	GA Lamb	CD McMillan	JP Crawley	JHK Adams	KP Pietersen	Overs	Total	Byes/Leg-byes	Wickets	Run outs
v. Gloucestershire (The Rose Bowl) 13-16 April		10.1-1-34-1 9-1-27-0					2-0-9-0		73.1 65.4	221 203	10 3	10 10	
v. Sussex (Hove) 20-23 April			6-1-16-1				1-0-9-0	1-0-7-0	77.5 108	252 312	0 15	10 10	
v. Middlesex (The Rose Bowl) 6-9 May			1-0-3-0						93.2 84	279 236	14 6	10 10	
v. Kent (Canterbury) 11-14 May		15.3-3-59-3 18-0-98-0					2-1-7-0		80.3 141	305 447	16 20	10 9	
v. Glamorgan (The Rose Bowl) 20-23 May			5-0-25-2 13-3-42-1	4-0-16-0					68.2 84.4	229 250	3 7	10 10	1
v. Warwickshire (Stratford) 25-26 May		16-4-36-0 2-0-22-0		0.4-0-12-0				1-1-0-0	81.2 4.4	265 44	12 0	10 0	
v. Nottinghamshire (Trent Bridge) 1-4 June		8-0-50-0 8-2-22-1			13-3-49-2 11-1-36-1				56.5 63.2	222 261	10 13	5 10	
v. Surrey (The Rose Bowl) 15-17 June				4-1-11-0	8-2-22-0				81.4 –	361 –	10 –	10 –	
v. Middlesex (Southgate) 8-11 July				8-0-30-2	4-1-12-0 3-0-19-0				86.3 79.4	272 278	18 16	10 8	1
v. Sussex (The Rose Bowl) 20-23 July	11-2-49-1 10-1-40-0				2-0-12-0				76.5 60.4	316 235	3 11	10 10	
v. Gloucestershire (Cheltenham) 3-6 August	12-5-42-2 17-4-35-2								98.1 81.5	363 232	5 9	10 10	
v. Kent (The Rose Bowl) 12-15 August	14-0-43-0 8-2-33-2			1-0-9-0					118 50.3	446 185	10 6	10 10	
v. Surrey (The Oval) 24-27 August	15-2-52-0 10-3-29-0			19-4-67-1		25-0-7-1			92 93.5	378 302	12 10	10 10	1 1
v. Warwickshire (The Rose Bowl) 30 August-1 September	9-2-27-1 6-1-22-1								72.2 66	258 232	7 9	10 10	
v. Glamorgan (Cardiff) 15-18 September		11-1-67-1 10-1-36-0							81 62.4	249 244	6 11	10 10	1
v. Nottinghamshire (The Rose Bowl) 21-23 September		9-2-35-0 12-0-86-1					1-0-1-0		55.2 67.5	213 313	9 9	10 10	
Overs	112	128.4	25	36.4	41	2.5	6	2					
Maidens	22	15	4	5	7	0	1	1					
Runs	372	572	86	145	150	7	26	7					
Wickets	9	7	4	3	3	1	0	0					
Average	41.33	81.71	21.50	48.33	50.00	7.00	–	–					

FIELDING

51	N Pothas (48 ct, 3 st)
15	JP Crawley (14 ct, 1 st)
13	SK Warne
13	MJ Brown
13	GA Lamb
10	SR Watson
8	JHK Adams
8	SM Ervine
7	SD Udal
7	SM Katich
5	AD Mascarenhas
5	CC Benham
5	TG Burrows
4	KP Pietersen
4	JJ McLean
3	DA Kenway
3	CT Tremlett
3	JTA Bruce
1	AJ Bichel
0	CD McMillan
0	RJ Logan
0	BV Taylor

KENT CCC

FIRST–CLASS MATCHES

BATTING

	DI Stevens	M van Jaarsveld	MJ Walker	DP Fulton	MM Patel	RWT Key	NJ O'Brien	A Khan	SJ Cook	AJ Hall	MJ Saggers	JM Kemp	MJ Dennington	NJ Dexter	GO Jones	JC Tredwell	RH Joseph	PG Dixey	MA Carberry	RS Ferley	JL Denly	KJF Jones	DA Stiff	SMJ Cusden	Extras	Total	Wickets	Result	Points
v. Warwickshire	88	118	3	53	10	4		4	1				2		32									6*	26	347	10		
(Canterbury) 20-23 April	0	111	54*	75		21		14*					12		3										18	308	6	D	10
v. Gloucestershire	5	2	109	2	2	164		4	22*		6		13		2										28	359	10		
(Bristol) 27-30 April	54	32	56	8		18							4*		36*										21	229	5	D	11
v. Hampshire	68	1	12	74	0	20		5*	4		17		50		6										48	305	10		
(Canterbury) 11-14 May	58	77	37	37	41*	54		0*	37		23		55		22										31	447	9	D	10
v. Nottinghamshire	33	0	51	57	22	32	64	19	0	0	12*														11	301	10		
(Trent Bridge) 20-23 May	47	0	48	51	37*	32	8	5*	38	0															32	298	8	W	20
v. Surrey	1	0	0	45	3	112	1		5	61	5*	3													26	262	10		
(Tunbridge Wells) 25-28 May		168	32*	18		189					19	28*													13	467	4	D	9
v. Gloucestershire	35	10	13	21	29		13	11*	23	25		0									4				20	204	10		
(Maidstone) 1-3 June	23*	15	19*	0																	10				11	78	3	W	18
v. Glamorgan	80	262*	20	0	87	6	16	0		15	45					27									10	568	10		
(Cardiff) 8-10 June			25*		24*																				2	51	0	W	22
v. Warwickshire	163	62	140	6	0	75	21*	0	1	49		25													27	569	10		
(Edgbaston) 15-18 June																												W	22
v. Sussex	50	32	56	1	8	74	34	0*	9	68	6														10	348	10		
(Canterbury) 10-13 July	0	4	32	4	2	31	10	8	7	12	2*														7	119	10	L	6
v. Surrey	0	36	173	39	27	65	46	1*	13	24		124													24	572	10		
(Guildford) 20-23 July	4	25	18	31		47	23*			17		47*													20	232	6	W	21
v. Glamorgan	208	41	11	15	64	35	0	0*	13	133		39													28	587	10		
(Canterbury) 3-5 August																												W	22
v. Hampshire	101	1	9	45	54*	88	9	33	4	23		69													10	446	10		
(The Rose Bowl) 12-15 August	22	24	21	25	1	36	7	7*	0	31		3													8	185	10	D	12
v. Bangladesh A							12				44		6	1		0	12	24	0	23		0	15*		16	153	10		
(Canterbury) 16-17 August							1						19	54		13		16*	47	10		14	12*		2	188	7	W	
v. Middlesex	106	50	12	110		142	1*			27*		57													44	549	6		
(Canterbury) 24-27 August																												D	11
v. Middlesex	43	0	11	16	0	94	13	58*	0	16		102													31	384	10		
(Lord's) 7-10 September	15	26	0	9	0*	52	9			37*		30													14	192	7	D	9
v. Nottinghamshire	0	9	11	35		43	56*							79*											4	237	5		
(Canterbury) 14-17 September	11	64	3	12	37	6	28	15	2		18*			4											5	205	10	L	3
v. Sussex	26	11	34	6	51	8	61				16*			34		0	0								10	257	10		
(Hove) 21-23 September	36	17	33	13	12	84	9				3			4		15	0*								12	238	10	L	5
Matches	16	16	16	16	16	15	14	14	14	11	9	8	4	3	3	3	2	1	1	1	1	1	1	1					
Innings	27	28	28	29	21	27	22	17	18	16	13	12	8	6	6	5	3	2	2	2	2	2	2	1					
Not Out	1	1	3	1	4	1	4	9	2	2	5	2	1	1	1	0	1	1	0	0	0	0	2	1					
Highest Score	208	262*	173	110	87	189	64	58*	38	133	45	124	55	79*	36*	27	12	24	47	23	10	14	15*	6*					
Runs	1277	1198	993	833	487	1556	442	170	193	538	216	527	161	176	101	55	12	40	47	33	14	14	27	6					
Average	49.11	44.37	39.72	29.75	28.64	59.84	24.55	21.25	12.06	38.42	27.00	52.70	23.00	35.20	20.20	11.00	6.00	40.00	23.50	16.50	7.00	7.00	–	–					
100s	4	4	3	1	0	4	0	0	0	1	0	2	0	0	0	0	0	0	0	0	0	0	0	0					
50s	6	4	4	5	4	8	3	1	0	2	0	2	2	2	0	0	0	0	0	0	0	0	0	0					
Catches/Stumpings	13/0	18/0	8/0	16/0	3/0	8/0	46/5	2/0	3/0	9/0	5/0	8/0	3/0	4/0	13/1	1/0	1/0	3/0	1/0	0/0	0/0	1/0	0/0	0/0					

Home Ground: Canterbury
Address: St Lawrence Ground, Old Dover Road, Canterbury, CT1 3NZ
Tel: 01227 456886
Fax: 01227 762168
Email: jon.fordham.kent@ecb.co.uk
Directions: From the North, From M20 junction 7 turn left onto A249. At M2 junction 5 (Sittingbourne) bear right onto M2. At junction 7 (Boughton Street) turn right on to A2. Follow this to junction with A2050, turn left. Follow yellow signs to cricket ground. From the South, From M20 junction 13 bear right onto A20. Follow this road to junction with A260. Bear left and continue to junction with A2 (north). Continue to junction with A2050 and then proceed as north.
Capacity: 10,000
Other grounds used: Beckenham, Maidstone, Tunbridge Wells
Year formed: 1870

Chief Executive: Paul Millman
Director of Cricket: Graham Ford
Coaching Co-Ordinator: Simon Willis
Captain: David Fulton
County Colours: Red, yellow and black

Honours
County Championship
1906, 1909, 1910, 1913, 1970, 1978
Joint Champions 1977
Sunday League/NCL
1972, 1973, 1976, 1995, 2001
Benson & Hedges Cup
1973, 1978
Gillette Cup/NatWest/C&G Trophy
1967, 1974

Website:
www.kentccc.com

KENT CCC

FIRST-CLASS MATCHES

BOWLING

	MM Patel	A Khan	SJ Cook	AJ Hall	MJ Saggers	DI Stevens	JM Kemp	RH Joseph	MJ Dennington	MJ Walker	M van Jaarsveld	SMJ Cusden	JC Tredwell	DA Stiff	NJ Dexter	RS Ferley	DP Fulton	RWT Key	Overs	Total	Byes/Leg-byes	Wickets	Run outs
v. Warwickshire (Canterbury) 20-23 April	35-8-90-3	22.5-7-73-6	24-7-62-0						7-3-9-0	1-0-2-0		16-1-57-1							105.5	309	16	10	
	32-20-32-4	19-6-42-1	22-11-51-2			3-1-8-0			7-1-23-0		6-2-18-0	12-0-50-2							101	233	9	9	
v. Gloucestershire (Bristol) 27-30 April	27-3-57-2	20-7-55-2	25.1-9-57-5		19-7-32-0	2-2-0-0			15-4-40-1										108.1	248	7	10	
																			-	-	-	-	
v. Hampshire (Canterbury) 11-14 May	3.5-1-28-1	15-2-82-1	16-4-62-2		19-4-64-2	3-1-13-0			17-5-63-3										73.5	328	16	10	1
	33.2-5-108-2	20-0-106-4	18-1-104-0		26-4-82-2	6-1-20-0			6-0-25-0										109.2	461	16	9	1
v. Nottinghamshire (Trent Bridge) 20-23 May	1-0-2-0	12-1-38-2	18-5-44-5	16-3-33-1	17-3-66-1														64	184	1	10	1
	20.2-6-61-3	11-3-36-2	9-2-30-1	18-5-42-4	15-7-38-0														73.2	219	12	10	
v. Surrey (Tunbridge Wells) 25-28 May	38-5-124-6		9-0-48-0	10-0-40-0	18-3-53-1	13-4-22-3	3-0-24-0												91	324	13	10	
	42.3-9-120-1		7-2-16-0	17-1-64-2	8-0-54-1	10-1-34-0					14-4-28-0								98.3	333	17	4	
v. Gloucestershire (Maidstone) 1-3 June	1-0-4-0	11.3-2-31-3	19-6-54-3	16-4-47-2		8-4-16-1	5-2-25-1												60.3	183	6	10	
		13-3-25-2	6-0-18-2	12.1-4-36-3		11-2-19-3	1-1-0-0												43.1	98	0	10	
v. Glamorgan (Cardiff) 8-10 June	21-3-90-1	18-6-65-2		19-4-65-1	21.4-4-71-2	5-0-18-1							14-4-37-2						98.4	358	12	10	1
	4-0-11-0	9-0-44-3		10-1-38-4	10-2-42-1	10.4-1-83-2							2-0-26-0						45.4	260	16	10	
v. Warwickshire (Edgbaston) 15-18 June	3-1-4-0	18-4-64-3	23-5-79-4	24-12-39-1		11-3-33-1	5-1-24-1												84	252	9	10	
	25-10-53-6	15.3-4-52-2	6-0-23-0	11-3-14-2							1-0-4-0								58.3	153	7	10	
v. Sussex (Canterbury) 10-13 July	10-1-51-1	15-1-65-1	24.1-11-57-3	24-1-73-2	20-1-65-1	19-2-43-1													112.1	378	24	10	1
	17-5-27-3	10.3-2-39-4	7-3-19-0	13-2-44-2	8-4-16-1														55.3	155	10	10	
v. Surrey (Guildford) 20-23 July	30-6-96-3	21-4-92-1	17-3-78-2	21.4-4-73-1		11-0-40-1	17-0-60-0											1-0-5-0	118.4	452	8	8	
	47.2-8-110-4	20-2-86-1	15.3-3-77-1	15-5-22-2		13-0-25-0	3-0-16-0			4-1-6-1	2-0-12-1								119.2	350	36	10	
v. Glamorgan (Canterbury) 3-5 August	21-3-53-1	20-0-96-3	13.5-5-35-3	15-4-36-1		7-0-32-1	13-1-38-1			3-0-3-0							2-0-5-0		95.5	306	8	10	
	8-1-26-1	7-1-34-1	12-5-26-2	13-4-32-4		3-0-12-0	9-2-23-2				1-1-0-0								52	157	4	10	
v. Hampshire (The Rose Bowl) 12-15 August	11.4-4-28-3	20-3-89-2	21-2-74-1	19-3-62-3		4-0-29-0	8-1-30-1												83.4	325	13	10	
	17-1-54-0	16-2-43-1	17-6-32-3	19-4-57-2			12.5-3-34-2				1-0-4-0								82.5	241	17	8	
v. Bangladesh A (Canterbury) 16-17 August					14-4-48-5			9.2-1-58-1	5.1-1-23-3				1.5-1-4-0	10-1-41-1	1-0-7-0				41.2	185	4	10	
					12-4-24-2			7.3-2-19-5	5-1-23-0					7-0-44-1	2-1-4-0	8-1-26-1			41.3	155	15	10	1
v. Middlesex (Canterbury) 24-27 August	27-6-90-3	20-6-83-4	18-4-60-0		22-3-98-1	10-0-27-0	12-1-32-0												109	400	10	8	
	22.4-8-34-4	6-0-27-1	6-1-13-0		8-2-21-1	3-2-1-0					6-3-7-1								51.4	114	11	7	
v. Middlesex (Lord's) 7-10 September	47-10-110-1	24-3-106-1	19-2-59-0	25-2-92-1		19-3-62-2	21-2-53-3			13-0-42-1	1-0-1-0								169	550	25	9	
																			-	-	-	-	
v. Nottinghamshire (Canterbury) 14-17 September	18-1-48-0	31-11-82-2	25-6-109-2		25.5-4-100-1	18-1-70-1				4-0-12-1					10-1-55-0				131.5	486	10	8	1
					2-1-1-0	3-0-19-0				9-0-95-1	4-1-12-1				6-0-42-1				24	170	1	3	
v. Sussex (Hove) 21-23 September	25-4-81-5					18-3-71-0	7-0-29-0	18.5-4-69-2					11-3-38-1		11-1-44-1				90.5	348	11	10	1
	10-3-34-1					5-0-27-0		6-0-33-1					8-0-41-0		2-0-9-0				31	151	7	2	

	MM Patel	A Khan	SJ Cook	AJ Hall	MJ Saggers	DI Stevens	JM Kemp	RH Joseph	MJ Dennington	MJ Walker	M van Jaarsveld	SMJ Cusden	JC Tredwell	DA Stiff	NJ Dexter	RS Ferley	DP Fulton	RWT Key
Overs	598.4	415.2	397.1	347.5	258.3	199.4	109.5	41.4	62.1	35	35	28	36.5	17	32	8	2	1
Maidens	132	80	103	71	55	28	14	7	15	1	11	1	8	1	3	1	0	0
Runs	1626	1555	1247	1028	854	655	359	179	206	164	82	107	146	85	161	26	5	5
Wickets	59	55	41	40	20	17	11	9	7	4	3	3	3	2	2	1	0	0
Average	27.55	28.27	30.41	25.70	42.70	38.52	32.63	19.88	29.42	41.00	27.33	35.66	48.66	42.50	80.50	26.00	-	-

FIELDING

51	NJ O'Brien (46 ct, 5 st)
18	M van Jaarsveld
16	DP Fulton
14	GO Jones (13 ct, 1 st)
13	DI Stevens
9	AJ Hall
8	MJ Walker
8	RWT Key
8	JM Kemp
5	MJ Saggers
4	NJ Dexter
3	MM Patel
3	SJ Cook
3	MJ Dennington
3	PG Dixey
2	A Khan
1	MA Carberry
1	JC Tredwell
1	RH Joseph
1	KJF Jones
0	RS Ferley
0	DA Stiff
0	SMJ Cusden
0	JL Denly

LANCASHIRE CCC

FIRST-CLASS MATCHES
BATTING

	MJ Chilton	MB Loye	JM Anderson	IJ Sutcliffe	SG Law	WK Hegg	DG Cork	G Chapple
v. Somerset	39	53	0	34	37	4	65	
(Old Trafford) 13-16 April	31*	92		0	10	4*		
v. Worcestershire	26	19	18	14	28	69*	11	
(Worcester) 27-30 April	2	40	10*	21	83	29	57	
v. Derbyshire	50	101	14		112	39	4	41
(Old Trafford) 6-9 May								
v. Durham	32	10	37*		22	6	0	7
(Old Trafford) 11-13 May	13	12	4		17	12	7	7
v. Somerset	36	11		150				
(Taunton) 20-23 May								
v. Oxford UCCE	33			25				
(The Parks) 25-27 May	15*			14*				
v. Northamptonshire	0	0	24	2	14	48	25	0
(Old Trafford) 1-4 June	113*	6	0	0	7	14	12	5
v. Yorkshire	0	67	0	153	46	11	31	2
(Headingley) 8-11 June	112	43		52	53*	32*		13
v. Derbyshire	3	8	4	32	23	25	64	8
(Derby) 15-17 June	2	28	0	62*	6	9	2	12
v. Durham	52	200	4	48	27	11	102*	6
(The Riverside) 8-10 July								
v. Essex	4	194		66		57*	19*	
(Old Trafford) 21-24 July								
v. Leicestershire	19	22	0	93	32	9	8	22
(Leicester) 3-6 August	0	19		3	47	77*	4	60
v. Yorkshire	130	11	12	93	0	68	52	0
(Old Trafford) 16-19 August								
v. Worcestershire	0	187		12	143	8*	14	82
(Blackpool) 25-28 August								
v. Northamptonshire	0	38	1*	19	111	15	11	15
(Northampton) 30 August-2 September	38	8	4*	4	3	12	14	0
v. Essex	37	10	0	50	18	0*	70	
(Chelmsford) 9-11 September	42	16		80*	13*			
v. Leicestershire	30		5*	3	6		33	27
(Old Trafford) 21-23 September	36	3*	8	16	0		20	10
Matches	17	16	16	15	15	15	14	14
Innings	28	25	19	25	24	21	19	20
Not Out	3	1	5	3	2	6	2	1
Highest Score	130	200	37*	153	143	77*	102*	82
Runs	895	1198	145	1046	858	502	540	422
Average	35.80	49.91	10.35	47.54	39.00	33.46	31.76	22.21
100s	3	4	0	2	3	0	1	0
50s	2	3	0	7	2	3	5	3
Catches/Stumpings	10/0	11/0	8/0	15/0	18/0	41/5	12/0	5/0

	G Keedy	A Symonds	BJ Hodge	SI Mahmood	PJ Horton	M Muralitharan	A Flintoff	SJ Marshall
v. Somerset	2*			57	19			
(Old Trafford) 13-16 April					41			
v. Worcestershire				1		0	0	
(Worcester) 27-30 April				29		0	83	
v. Derbyshire	1*		65			24	5	
(Old Trafford) 6-9 May								
v. Durham	34		8			12	12	
(Old Trafford) 11-13 May	0*		16			4	55	
v. Somerset			110*				29*	
(Taunton) 20-23 May								
v. Oxford UCCE	3			38	84			35*
(The Parks) 25-27 May								
v. Northamptonshire	0*		7			10		
(Old Trafford) 1-4 June	1*		25					
v. Yorkshire	1*		15	24				
(Headingley) 8-11 June			8					
v. Derbyshire			37	5		24*		
(Derby) 15-17 June			1	0		4*		
v. Durham	5		39					
(The Riverside) 8-10 July								
v. Essex		134			99			
(Old Trafford) 21-24 July								
v. Leicestershire		45		13				17*
(Leicester) 3-6 August		121		11				9
v. Yorkshire	0*	146						
(Old Trafford) 16-19 August								
v. Worcestershire		1						26*
(Blackpool) 25-28 August								
v. Northamptonshire		37						17
(Northampton) 30 August-2 September		4						0
v. Essex		98		0	19			
(Chelmsford) 9-11 September								
v. Leicestershire		14		43				
(Old Trafford) 21-23 September		9		21				
Matches	9	7	7	7	6	6	4	4
Innings	10	10	11	10	9	8	6	6
Not Out	7	0	1	0	0	2	1	3
Highest Score	34	146	110*	57	99	24*	83	35*
Runs	47	623	331	177	350	78	184	104
Average	15.66	62.30	33.10	17.70	38.88	13.00	36.80	34.66
100s	0	3	1	0	0	0	0	0
50s	0	1	1	1	2	0	2	0
Catches/Stumpings	1/0	4/0	6/0	0/0	2/1	3/0	4/0	1/0

	MJ North	AR Crook	SP Crook	GD Cross	KW Hogg	M Kartik	SJ Croft	TCP Smith	Extras	Total	Wickets	Result	Points
v. Somerset					3				10	323	10		
(Old Trafford) 13-16 April					6				11	195	5	D	10
v. Worcestershire					9				1	196	10		
(Worcester) 27-30 April					0				23	377	10	W	17
v. Derbyshire									13	469	10		
(Old Trafford) 6-9 May												W	22
v. Durham									19	199	10		
(Old Trafford) 11-13 May									26	173	10	L	3
v. Somerset									15	351	3		
(Taunton) 20-23 May												D	11
v. Oxford UCCE		88	66	2			6	0	40	420	10		
(The Parks) 25-27 May									3	32	0	W	
v. Northamptonshire									19	149	10		
(Old Trafford) 1-4 June									7	190	8	D	7
v. Yorkshire									29	379	10		
(Headingley) 8-11 June									24	337	5	D	11
v. Derbyshire									8	241	10		
(Derby) 15-17 June									10	136	9	W	18
v. Durham			5						31	530	10		
(The Riverside) 8-10 July												W	22
v. Essex		43							39	655	6		
(Old Trafford) 21-24 July												D	10
v. Leicestershire									11	291	10		
(Leicester) 3-6 August									17	368	9	W	19
v. Yorkshire	2								23	537	10		
(Old Trafford) 16-19 August												D	11
v. Worcestershire	60								29	562	8		
(Blackpool) 25-28 August												W	22
v. Northamptonshire	30								7	301	10		
(Northampton) 30 August-2 September	9								7	103	10	L	6
v. Essex						0			38	340	10		
(Chelmsford) 9-11 September									4	155	2	W	20
v. Leicestershire				14		7			9	191	10		
(Old Trafford) 21-23 September				22		4			21	170	10	L	3
Matches	3	2	2	2	2	2	1	1					
Innings	4	2	2	3	4	3	1	1					
Not Out	0	0	0	0	0	0	0	0					
Highest Score	60	88	66	22	9	7	6	0					
Runs	101	131	71	38	18	11	6	0					
Average	25.25	65.50	35.50	12.66	4.50	3.66	6.00	0.00					
100s	0	0	0	0	0	0	0	0					
50s	1	1	1	0	0	0	0	0					
Catches/Stumpings	2/0	4/0	0/0	9/2	2/0	1/0	0/0	1/0					

Home Ground: Old Trafford
Address: Old Trafford, Manchester, M16 0PX
Tel: 0870 0625000
Fax: 0870 0624614
Email: enquiries@lccc.co.uk
Directions: By rail, Manchester Piccadilly or Victoria then Metro link to Old Trafford. By road: M63, Stretford slip-road (junction 7) on to A56; follow signs.
Capacity: 21,500
Other grounds used: Blackpool, Liverpool
Year formed: 1864

Chairman: Jack Simmons
Chief Executive: Jim Cumbes
First XI Coach: Mike Watkinson
Captain: Mark Chilton
County colours: Red and white

Website:
www.lccc.co.uk

Honours
County Championship
1881, 1897, 1904, 1926, 1927, 1928, 1930, 1934. Joint champions 1879, 1882, 1889, 1950
Sunday League/NCL
1970, 1989, 1998, 1999
Benson & Hedges Cup
1984, 1990, 1995, 1996
Gillette Cup/NatWest/C>rophy
1970, 1971, 1972, 1975, 1990, 1996, 1998

LANCASHIRE CCC

FIRST-CLASS MATCHES
BOWLING

Match	JM Anderson	G Chapple	DG Cork	M Muralitharan	G Keedy	M Kartik	A Symonds	SI Mahmood	SJ Marshall	AR Crook	KW Hogg	MJ North	MJ Chilton	BJ Hodge	TCP Smith	A Flintoff	SJ Croft	SP Crook	Overs	Total	Byes/Leg-byes	Wickets	Run outs
v. Somerset (Old Trafford) 13-16 April	23-8-58-1 8-2-28-1		22-5-52-2 7-3-21-0		16-3-68-2 4-3-2-2			16.1-6-41-3 3.3-0-6-0			12-4-40-2								89.1 22.3	272 69	13 12	10 3	
v. Worcestershire (Worcester) 27-30 April	18-3-102-1 12-3-52-2		20-3-64-3 16-4-51-4		26-5-69-5 18.3-5-33-3			4-0-35-0			8.2-1-28-1 14-4-45-0								76.2 60.3	306 191	8 10	10 10	 1
v. Derbyshire (Old Trafford) 6-9 May	21-4-62-4 16-4-60-1	18-3-53-1 5-1-10-1	20-7-31-1 5-4-10-0	18.4-3-45-2 26.1-17-31-2	4-1-22-0 26-6-60-0														81.4 78.1	215 182	2 6	10 10	2
v. Durham (Old Trafford) 11-13 May	11-1-49-0 4-0-26-1	12-3-43-1	10-3-28-0 3.1-1-7-0	39-11-107-5	25.5-6-82-2									4-0-14-1		5-3-11-1			106.5 7.1	338 35	4 2	10 1	
v. Somerset (Taunton) 20-23 May	23-7-57-2	19.1-7-50-2	14-2-66-1	26-6-56-5												15-3-48-0			97.1 –	294 –	17 –	10 –	
v. Oxford UCCE (The Parks) 25-27 May				17-3-46-4 26.3-11-33-6				19.5-5-68-2 14-4-31-1	12-2-28-1 14-4-23-2	13-1-40-1 12-4-21-0					10-5-24-1 10-3-22-0		11-1-49-0	16-4-39-0 4-0-13-0	98.5 80.3	300 151	6 8	9 10	 1
v. Northamptonshire (Old Trafford) 1-4 June	19.5-6-51-4 12-3-40-2	8-2-16-0 13-2-27-1	13-3-26-2 19-5-43-2	23-6-57-3 16-3-68-4	3-1-12-0 15.1-5-29-1														66.5 75.1	175 225	13 18	10 10	1
v. Yorkshire (Headingley) 8-11 June	25.2-3-97-4 21-7-69-3	30-10-70-3 18-5-45-3	22.2-7-44-0 13-2-35-1		22-2-65-2 15-6-33-1			5.4-0-42-0 20-4-56-1						8-3-7-0 5-0-14-0					113.2 92	335 273	10 21	10 9	1
v. Derbyshire (Derby) 15-17 June	13-2-52-0 6-1-21-1	19-10-29-3 13-1-44-1	14.3-2-40-4 11-1-44-0	13-3-24-1 27-10-50-6				8-0-31-2 7.1-1-15-1											67.3 64.1	191 185	15 11	10 10	 1
v. Durham (The Riverside) 8-10 July	16-4-65-2 15-5-47-2	13.3-4-24-3 12-4-18-4	16-5-35-2 9.1-1-30-3		13-6-17-3 3-1-9-0													4-1-9-0 5-1-19-0	62.3 44.1	167 135	17 12	10 10	 1
v. Essex (Old Trafford) 21-24 July	36-4-140-0	30-13-55-2	29-8-91-3		15-0-86-1		20-4-62-0			10-2-71-3									140 –	536 –	31 –	9 –	
v. Leicestershire (Leicester) 3-6 August	17-3-61-2 19-4-79-5	19-2-60-3 9-4-28-2	20.5-5-44-2 13-4-41-2				19-4-43-2	18-2-46-1 3.3-1-8-1											93.5 44.3	261 164	7 8	10 10	
v. Yorkshire (Old Trafford) 16-19 August	23-2-100-3 14-3-48-1	23-2-78-3 14-2-34-0	27-7-58-0 14-1-61-1		25-4-101-2 35-9-88-1			20-5-53-1 10-3-18-1				7-2-16-1 17-4-41-1	 5-1-9-1						125 109	417 323	11 24	10 6	
v. Worcestershire (Blackpool) 25-28 August	19-3-61-4 13-3-33-2	15-3-56-0 13.4-4-32-5	22.3-4-103-4 7-2-20-2					13-0-32-2 7-2-16-1	18-2-63-0			11-2-39-0							98.3 40.4	376 113	22 12	10 10	
v. Northamptonshire (Northampton) 30 August-2 September	20-4-56-1 28-2-108-2	19-5-45-2 15-2-58-0	17-9-27-4 10-0-46-0					24-6-64-2 23-4-80-3	12-2-39-1 17-2-59-1			15-2-46-0 6-0-34-0							107 99	289 400	12 15	10 6	
v. Essex (Chelmsford) 9-11 September	14-0-56-3 15-0-53-2	8-3-19-1 7-2-42-0				23.4-2-93-5 25.2-9-75-5	19-4-63-1 10-1-28-0	5-0-33-0 6-0-21-3											69.4 63.2	267 227	3 8	10 10	
v. Leicestershire (Old Trafford) 21-23 September	14-5-37-0 16.3-3-45-4	14.5-4-22-5 15-0-52-1				22-7-43-4 19-3-49-2	6-1-17-1 6-3-8-2	12-1-43-0 7-1-28-1											68.5 63.3	165 200	3 13	10 10	

	JM Anderson	G Chapple	DG Cork	M Muralitharan	G Keedy	M Kartik	A Symonds	SI Mahmood	SJ Marshall	AR Crook	KW Hogg	MJ North	MJ Chilton	BJ Hodge	TCP Smith	A Flintoff	SJ Croft	SP Crook
Overs	512.4	383.1	395.3	233.2	265.3	90	177	128.2	94.3	35	34.2	56	5	17	20	20	11	29
Maidens	99	98	98	69	67	21	37	22	15	7	9	10	1	3	8	6	1	6
Runs	1813	1010	1118	540	753	260	484	450	266	132	113	176	9	35	46	59	49	80
Wickets	60	47	43	36	33	16	16	14	7	4	3	2	1	1	1	1	0	0
Average	30.21	21.48	26.00	15.00	22.81	16.25	30.25	32.14	38.00	33.00	37.66	88.00	9.00	35.00	46.00	59.00	–	–

FIELDING

46	WK Hegg (41 ct, 5 st)
18	SG Law
15	IJ Sutcliffe
12	DG Cork
11	MB Loye
11	GD Cross (9 ct, 2 st)
10	MJ Chilton
8	JM Anderson
6	BJ Hodge
5	G Chapple
4	A Symonds
4	A Flintoff
4	AR Crook
3	M Muralitharan
3	PJ Horton (2 ct, 1 st)
2	MJ North
2	KW Hogg
1	G Keedy
1	SJ Marshall
1	M Kartik
1	TCP Smith
0	SI Mahmood
0	SJ Croft
0	SP Crook

LEICESTERSHIRE CCC

FIRST-CLASS MATCHES
BATTING

	HD Ackerman	DDJ Robinson	PA Nixon	JK Maunders	DL Maddy	CW Henderson	OD Gibson	CM Willoughby	A Habib	DD Masters	D Mongia	SCL Broad	TJ New	JL Sadler	PAJ DeFreitas	CJL Rogers	JN Snape	RAG Cummins	JJ Krejza	DS Brignull	CJ Liddle	Extras	Total	Wickets	Result	Points
v. Durham (Leicester) 13-15 April	7	14	17*	4	10	22	0		15	1					0		19					14	123	10		
	19	19	32	50	2	0*	0		8	19					0		23					12	184	10	L	1
v. Northamptonshire (Northampton) 20-23 April	16	100	16	5	45	30*	18	9	38						19		28					15	339	10		
	50*	6*	1*	14	11				2								31					0	115	4	D	9
v. Durham UCCE (Leicester) 27-29 April				55	124				82		57			36*								30	384	4		
				47		17*				8		11	4	82*								18	187	4	D	
v. Essex (Chelmsford) 6-9 May	25	73	0		34	6	4	2*	2	27	6				20							21	220	10		
	93	57	2		6	55	22	4	30	2*	39				0							22	332	10	L	4
v. Yorkshire (Leicester) 11-14 May	85*	42	0		53	5	6	2	41	8	0				6							30	278	10		
	30	6	68		27	10	9		16	9*	70				17							14	276	9	L	5
v. Derbyshire (Derby) 26-29 May	9	110	0	5	44	6	5	6		25*	51			13								5	279	10		
	57	14	33	23	8		4*				47			56*								16	258	6	W	19
v. Somerset (Oakham School) 1-4 June	117	47	17	1	42	50	0	9*			26	17		0								12	338	10		
																									D	10
v. Worcestershire (Leicester) 15-18 June	14	31	11	19	49	1	6	1			66	2*		22								3	225	10		
	2	16	85	3	21	5		16*			36	14		19								16	238	10	W	18
v. Somerset (Taunton) 8-10 July	35	33	62*	30	8	25	0	3			0			52		48						34	330	10		
	51	19	36*	67	7	8	13	0			7			18		0						27	253	10	L	6
v. Australia (Leicester) 15-17 July	12	0		17		30	0*			15	0	18		4*		56			38			27	217	10		
	1	81		33								1*				209			19			19	363	5	D	
v. Yorkshire (Scarborough) 20-23 July	20	26	10	3	40	49	91	0	0		10*					93						24	366	10		
	10	0	22	48	0	21	33*	4	26		2					35						16	217	10	L	7
v. Essex (Leicester) 26-29 July	9	5	85	46	3	36			153*	2	4							4*				35	382	8		
																									D	11
v. Lancashire (Leicester) 3-6 August	41		2	1	20	0	9		84	36	0		50					1*				17	261	10		
	2		0	17	4	0	23		22	29*	31		20					1				15	164	10	L	5
v. Durham (The Riverside) 12-15 August	61	73	26	22	12	30*	0	10	7	0	164											38	443	10		
																									D	12
v. Northamptonshire (Leicester) 24-27 August	6	139	36*	19	34		74*		32		41											24	405	6		
																									D	12
v. Worcestershire (Worcester) 30 August-2 September	12	16	58	148	34	37		1*	9	0		31	31									28	405	10		
	16	11	28*	8	22				90*				49									31	255	5	D	12
v. Derbyshire (Leicester) 8-11 September	125	123	50*	0		19*			42		71		89									33	552	6		
																									D	12
v. Lancashire (Old Trafford) 21-23 September	48	14	11	40			2	0	6	9*	2	6	18									9	165	10		
	67	33	0	34			6	0	0	5*	14	7	8									25	200	10	W	17
Matches	17	16	16	16	15	15	15	14	13	13	11	10	7	6	4	3	2	2	1	1	1					
Innings	29	27	27	27	25	21	24	17	21	16	17	12	11	10	7	6	4	3	2	0	0					
Not Out	2	1	7	0	0	4	4	5	2	6	0	2	1	4	0	0	0	2	0	0	0					
Highest Score	125	139	85	148	124	55	91	16*	153*	36	164	31	89	82*	20	209	31	4*	38	0	0					
Runs	1040	1108	708	759	660	413	379	68	705	195	684	107	329	302	62	441	101	6	57	0	0					
Average	38.51	42.61	35.40	28.11	26.40	24.29	18.95	5.66	37.10	19.50	40.23	10.70	32.90	50.33	8.85	73.50	25.25	6.00	28.50	-	-					
100s	2	4	0	1	1	0	0	0	1	0	1	0	1	0	0	1	0	0	0	0	0					
50s	7	4	6	3	1	2	2	0	3	0	5	0	2	3	0	2	0	0	0	0	0					
Catches/Stumpings	9/0	13/0	40/4	7/0	17/0	6/0	2/0	2/0	8/0	4/0	5/0	1/0	7/1	4/0	0/0	4/0	0/0	1/0	0/0	0/0	0/0					

Home Ground: Grace Road, Leicester
Address: County Ground, Grace Road, Leicester, LE2 8AD
Tel: 0871 2821879
Fax: 0871 2821873
Email: enquiries@leicestershireccc.co.uk
Directions: *By road:* Follow signs from city centre, or from southern ring road from M1 or A6.
Capacity: 5,500
Other grounds used: Oakham School
Year formed: 1879

Operations Manager: Gus Mackay
Director of Cricket: James Whitaker
Head Coach: Phil Whitticase
Club Captain: Hylton Ackerman
County Colours: Dark green and scarlet

Website:
www.leicestershireccc.com

Honours
County Championship
1975, 1996, 1998
Sunday League/NCL
1974, 1977
Benson & Hedges Cup
1972, 1975, 1985
Twenty20 Cup
2004

LEICESTERSHIRE CCC

FIRST-CLASS MATCHES
BOWLING

FIRST-CLASS MATCHES	OD Gibson	DD Masters	CM Willoughby	CW Henderson	SCL Broad	JK Maunders	DL Maddy	PAJ DeFreitas
v. Durham (Leicester) 13-15 April	44-10-121-3	33-9-117-2		34-5-104-0		1-0-7-0	16-4-59-1	25-8-84-0
	–							
v. Northamptonshire (Northampton) 20-23 April	31-4-123-1		30-9-79-1	19-4-86-0		1-0-6-0	4-0-30-0	23-4-76-4
	13-2-48-1		10-1-49-0	10-0-69-0				16-2-67-2
v. Durham UCCE (Leicester) 27-29 April		21-5-66-2		43-14-60-4	15-5-40-1			
		–						
v. Essex (Chelmsford) 6-9 May	30-3-118-3	16-3-60-1	24.4-4-90-1	12-5-17-0				21-4-68-3
	12.2-1-38-2	7-2-26-1	8-1-48-0	6-0-32-0				11-2-43-1
v. Yorkshire (Leicester) 11-14 May	17-3-56-6	8-1-28-2	8-1-18-0	6.4-0-19-1			2-0-6-1	4-0-18-0
	24.1-1-124-0	11-2-36-0	13-0-69-0	16-5-41-1			18-2-70-1	11-1-50-2
v. Derbyshire (Derby) 26-29 May	22-7-48-2	15-2-28-2	19-2-59-1	22.3-5-48-1		9-2-23-1	12-3-26-2	
	23-4-66-3	11-3-22-1	25-7-66-2	38-9-76-3		2-0-7-0	18-8-25-1	
v. Somerset (Oakham School) 1-4 June	15-2-34-3		15-6-27-2	7.3-1-13-3	7-2-21-1		6-3-9-1	
	17-3-42-0		16-4-39-1	28-8-47-1	18-6-40-1	5-2-9-0	9-3-21-0	
v. Worcestershire (Leicester) 15-18 June	25-1-101-3		29-10-56-1	28-9-62-1	17.1-2-64-4		11-2-22-1	
	11-1-41-3		8-1-24-1	9-1-15-0	8-0-31-3		4-1-5-0	
v. Somerset (Taunton) 8-10 July	18-0-104-0		23-2-130-2	23-1-109-1	20.3-0-119-3	3-0-26-0	14-1-65-4	
				3-0-9-0			3-0-9-0	
v. Australia (Leicester) 15-17 July	18-1-77-1	20-0-98-1	17-1-77-0		22-1-77-2	21-1-89-3		
	–							
v. Yorkshire (Scarborough) 20-23 July	18-4-36-3		17-2-55-3	3-1-22-0	8.3-1-35-3		10-2-33-1	
	28-7-82-1		25-6-88-1	40-11-91-2	14-0-60-0	3-0-19-0	13-1-44-0	
v. Essex (Leicester) 26-29 July		25-11-65-4	28.1-8-73-2	13-3-32-1		5-0-17-0	7-1-27-0	
		5-2-9-1	6-1-15-0	9-1-33-0			5-2-16-0	
v. Lancashire (Leicester) 3-6 August	17.3-0-80-3	21-9-38-2		33-6-69-2		7-2-33-0	5-1-22-0	
	22.3-1-101-3	9-5-28-1		20-2-72-1		11-1-37-3	14-0-47-0	
v. Durham (The Riverside) 12-15 August	22-7-48-0	26.2-6-74-6	31-9-92-4	20-4-61-0		4-1-21-0	3-1-5-0	
	8-3-27-1	5-0-16-0	4-0-16-0	14-9-24-1				
v. Northamptonshire (Leicester) 24-27 August	18-7-41-1	15-3-59-1		19.4-4-63-5	16-4-58-1		10-5-22-2	2-0-11-0
	–							
v. Worcestershire (Worcester) 30 August-2 September		17-7-49-3	20-4-80-2	34-8-72-4	16-5-69-1		3-0-5-0	2-0-11-0
		14-3-47-1	16-5-49-2	26-5-70-1	12-2-65-1		3-0-13-0	3-1-5-0
v. Derbyshire (Leicester) 8-11 September	14-5-39-1	18-7-30-2	16-9-27-3		16-5-46-3		6-1-13-0	
	–							
v. Lancashire (Old Trafford) 21-23 September	16-3-52-0	8-5-7-1	11-3-27-1		14-1-57-3		8-0-28-4	
	14-4-35-1		10-1-32-3		10-3-49-3		3-1-9-1	
Overs	498.3	305.2	429.5	537.2	214.1	105	181	111
Maidens	84	85	97	121	37	16	36	21
Runs	1682	903	1385	1416	831	384	568	406
Wickets	45	34	33	33	30	14	13	12
Average	37.37	26.55	41.96	42.90	27.70	27.42	43.69	33.83

FIRST-CLASS MATCHES	RAG Cummins	D Mongia	DS Brignull	JN Snape	DDJ Robinson	CJL Rogers	CJ Liddle	JJ Krejza	Overs	Total	Byes/Leg-byes	Wickets	Run outs
v. Durham (Leicester) 13-15 April				8-1-23-1					161	523	8	8	1
									–	–	–	–	
v. Northamptonshire (Northampton) 20-23 April				3-0-16-0					111	433	17	6	
									49	238	5	3	
v. Durham UCCE (Leicester) 27-29 April			13.2-4-36-3				14-2-45-0		106.2	255	8	10	
									–	–	–	–	
v. Essex (Chelmsford) 6-9 May		1-1-0-0							104.4	362	9	10	2
									44.2	191	4	4	
v. Yorkshire (Leicester) 11-14 May									45.4	151	6	10	
		3-0-7-0							96.1	406	9	4	
v. Derbyshire (Derby) 26-29 May		4-0-11-0							103.3	251	8	9	
		6-1-12-0							123	285	11	10	
v. Somerset (Oakham School) 1-4 June									50.3	105	1	10	
		7-1-18-0							100	225	9	3	
v. Worcestershire (Leicester) 15-18 June		7-2-13-0							117.1	323	5	10	
		5.1-1-8-2							45.1	128	4	10	1
v. Somerset (Taunton) 8-10 July									101.3	566	13	10	
									6	18	0	0	
v. Australia (Leicester) 15-17 July						2-0-5-0		25-0-136-0	125	582	23	7	
									–	–	–	–	
v. Yorkshire (Scarborough) 20-23 July									56.3	187	6	10	
						3-0-9-0			126	400	7	4	
v. Essex (Leicester) 26-29 July	12-2-49-3	4-0-22-0							94.1	297	12	10	
	4-2-3-1								29	80	4	2	
v. Lancashire (Leicester) 3-6 August	10-2-32-3	5-1-10-0							98.3	291	7	10	
	16-3-52-1	8-2-17-0							100.3	368	14	9	
v. Durham (The Riverside) 12-15 August									106.2	315	9	10	
		5-1-18-0				1-0-1-0			37	103	1	2	
v. Northamptonshire (Leicester) 24-27 August									80.4	261	7	10	
									–	–	–	–	
v. Worcestershire (Worcester) 30 August-2 September									92	290	4	10	
						1-0-2-0			75	258	7	5	
v. Derbyshire (Leicester) 8-11 September		3.4-0-18-1							73.4	190	17	10	
									–	–	–	–	
v. Lancashire (Old Trafford) 21-23 September		3-1-13-0							60	191	7	10	1
		14.3-3-42-2							51.3	170	3	10	
Overs	42	76.2	13.2	11	2	5	14	25					
Maidens	9	14	4	1	0	0	2	0					
Runs	136	209	36	39	3	14	45	136					
Wickets	8	5	3	1	0	0	0	0					
Average	17.00	41.80	12.00	39.00	–	–	–	–					

FIELDING

44	PA Nixon (40 ct, 4 st)
17	DL Maddy
13	DDJ Robinson
9	HD Ackerman
8	A Habib
8	TJ New (7 ct, 1 st)
7	JK Maunders
6	CW Henderson
5	D Mongia
4	JL Sadler
4	DD Masters
4	CJL Rogers
2	OD Gibson
2	CM Willoughby
1	RAG Cummins
1	SCL Broad
0	PAJ DeFreitas
0	JN Snape
0	DS Brignull
0	CJ Liddle
0	JJ Krejza

MIDDLESEX CCC

FIRST-CLASS MATCHES

BATTING

	ET Smith	BL Hutton	OA Shah	EC Joyce	PN Weekes	BJM Scott	JWM Dalrymple	A Richardson	SB Styris	MM Betts	PD Trego	CT Peploe	AJ Strauss	SR Clark	M Hayward	IK Pathan	CB Keegan	PM Hutchison	CD Whelan	CJC Wright	YA Golwalker	DC Nash	AD Poynter	NRD Compton	CMP Jones	BA Godleman	ST Finn	Extras	Total	Wickets	Result	Points
v. Nottinghamshire	39	2	5	192	24	1		15					4	12*			28	0										23	345	10		
(Lord's) 20-23 April	49	76*	19*										2															12	158	2	D	9
v. Warwickshire	0	7	19	92	11	37		10	53				13	6				26*										24	298	10		
(Edgbaston) 27-30 April	30	12	54	63	14	5		10*	6				37	1				2										12	246	10	L	5
v. Hampshire	11	6	83	70	13	11		1*	33				6				17		1									27	279	10		
(The Rose Bowl) 6-9 May	52	24	24	20	49	22		0	0				19				3		9*									14	236	10	L	5
v. Gloucestershire	13	14	63	75	69	58		4	16	12*		8	27															31	390	10		
(Lord's) 11-13 May	35	19	111*	93	1	13*			36				10															24	342	6	W	21
v. Sussex	41	4	58	82	55	19	0	10	34	36*						41												21	401	10		
(Hove) 25-28 May	29	7	20	6	71	4	65	0	2	6						13*												21	244	10	D	12
v. Cambridge UCCE	35	111			43*	20																		39*				25	273	3		
(Fenner's) 1-3 June	11											4											1	56*		69*		13	154	3	L	
v. Surrey	60	44	0	24	39	64*	77	19	8							68				13								21	437	10		
(Lord's) 8-11 June	88	10	21	60	28*	61*	15		55																			15	353	6	D	12
v. Glamorgan	92	19	49	155*		14*			85																			21	435	4		
(Southgate) 15-18 June	145	7*	155	70*		4			6							4*												17	408	4	W	20
v. Hampshire	22	42	16	54	6	2	62	4*	15	0		12																37	272	10		
(Southgate) 8-11 July	60	5	60	35	39*	14	24	16	3			0*																22	278	8	W	19
v. Glamorgan	29	73	101	32	42	25	108		30	0	72	11*																11	534	10		
(Cardiff) 21-23 July																															W	22
v. Warwickshire	0	49	63	13	92*	0	9		30	26	23	4																14	323	10		
(Lord's) 3-6 August	21	92	156*	11	1	1	17		1	1	7	6																16	330	10	L	6
v. Nottinghamshire	128	31	27	5	38	20*	60	25	13	1										0								8	325	10		
(Trent Bridge) 10-13 August	25	31	173*	101		45																						10	385	4	D	10
v. Sussex	13	6	4	36	6	13	10			16		16		2	0*													6	128	10		
(Lord's) 16-17 August	69	21	0	0	0	0	0			0		42		14	1*													15	162	10	L	3
v. Kent	40	10	105	12	128*	4	5				51	4*										12						29	400	8		
(Canterbury) 24-27 August	2	5	13	27	51		0				3*	0*										0						13	114	7	D	11
v. Gloucestershire	70		26	73	5	2	14	0	34			24		17*														21	297	10		
(Bristol) 30 August-2 September	8	43	25	90	3*		22*																					12	203	4	D	9
v. Kent	14	152	128	68	26*	4	76	8*	4	28											3							39	550	9		
(Lord's) 7-10 September																															D	12
v. Surrey	36	79	58	90	17*		0		100*																			24	404	5		
(The Oval) 21-24 September	7	29	14	19	14	23	75	10*	2	36											2							12	243	10	L	6

	ET Smith	BL Hutton	OA Shah	EC Joyce	PN Weekes	BJM Scott	JWM Dalrymple	A Richardson	SB Styris	MM Betts	PD Trego	CT Peploe	AJ Strauss	SR Clark	M Hayward	IK Pathan	CB Keegan	PM Hutchison	CD Whelan	CJC Wright	YA Golwalker	DC Nash	AD Poynter	NRD Compton	CMP Jones	BA Godleman	ST Finn
Matches	17	17	16	16	16	16	13	13	9	9	7	7	4	4	4	3	2	2	2	2	2	1	1	1	1	1	1
Innings	32	31	30	29	26	23	23	16	17	10	10	10	8	7	5	4	3	3	2	2	2	2	1	2	0	1	0
Not Out	0	2	4	2	7	5	2	5	1	2	1	2	0	3	3	2	0	1	1	0	0	0	0	2	0	1	0
Highest Score	145	152	173*	192	128*	64*	108	25	100*	36*	72	42	37	17*	12*	68	28	26*	9*	13	3	12	1	56*	0	69*	0
Runs	1274	1010	1650	1668	842	442	721	137	484	136	234	147	118	47	20	126	48	28	10	13	5	12	1	95	0	69	0
Average	39.81	34.82	63.46	61.77	44.31	24.55	34.33	12.45	30.25	17.00	26.00	18.37	14.75	11.75	10.00	63.00	16.00	14.00	10.00	6.50	2.50	6.00	1.00	-	-	-	-
100s	2	2	7	3	1	0	1	0	1	0	0	0	0	0	0	0	0	0	0	0	0	0	0	0	0	0	0
50s	7	4	7	13	5	3	6	0	3	0	2	0	0	0	0	1	0	0	0	0	0	0	0	1	0	1	0
Catches/Stumpings	12/0	24/0	22/0	15/0	7/0	44/6	3/0	2/0	4/0	0/0	2/0	2/0	3/0	1/0	1/0	1/0	0/0	2/0	0/0	1/0	0/0	0/0	2/0	0/0	0/0	0/0	0/0

Home Ground: Lord's
Address: Lord's Cricket Ground, London, NW8 8QN
Tel: 0207 289 1300
Fax: 0207 289 5831
Email: enquiries@middlesexccc.com
Directions: *By underground:* St John's Wood on Jubilee Line. *By bus:* 13, 82, 113 stop along east side of ground; 139 at south-west corner; 274 at top of Regent's Park.
Capacity: 28,000

Other grounds used: Southgate, Uxbridge, Richmond
Year formed: 1864

Chief Executive: Vinny Codrington
Head Coach: John Emburey
Captain: Ben Hutton
County Colours: Navy

Website:
www.middlesexccc.co.uk

Honours
County Championship
1903, 1920, 1921, 1947, 1976, 1980, 1982, 1985, 1990, 1993. Joint champions 1949, 1977
Sunday League/NCL
1992
Benson & Hedges Cup
1983, 1986
Gillette Cup/NatWest/C&G Trophy
1977, 1980, 1984, 1988, 1989

MIDDLESEX CCC

FIRST-CLASS MATCHES
BOWLING

	A Richardson	SB Styris	JWM Dalrymple	MM Betts	CT Peploe	PD Trego	SR Clark	PN Weekes	M Hayward	CD Whelan	YA Golwalker	PM Hutchison	IK Pathan	CMP Jones	EC Joyce	ST Finn	OA Shah	CB Keegan	BL Hutton	CJC Wright	Overs	Total	Byes/Leg-byes	Wickets	Run outs
v. Nottinghamshire	38-10-113-7							37.2-8-83-3	25-3-91-0			18-2-70-0					1-0-4-0	26-7-103-0	10-0-54-0		155.2	546	28	10	
(Lord's) 20-23 April	9-1-36-1							7-0-41-0	9-1-23-2			11-0-59-2						14-1-45-0			50	212	8	5	
v. Warwickshire	27-2-87-4	17-2-62-0						28-2-74-2	21-3-73-2			17.4-0-83-1							8-1-38-0		118.4	430	13	10	1
(Edgbaston) 27-30 April	7-4-11-0							11-2-40-0	4-1-11-1			7-1-43-2					12-0-3-0		1-0-4-0		31.2	115	3	3	
v. Hampshire	26.5-8-53-4	22-8-45-4						3-0-10-0		14-4-58-1							1-0-4-0	25-7-78-1	4-1-13-0		95.5	275	14	10	
(The Rose Bowl) 6-9 May	31-9-90-1	29.5-8-73-6						17-7-37-1		8-0-54-2								5-3-7-0	10-0-34-0		100.5	304	9	10	
v. Gloucestershire	19.5-8-32-5	13-2-51-1		15-0-86-4	17-5-49-0			1-0-8-0													65.5	232	6	10	
(Lord's) 11-13 May	14.4-2-42-3	7-1-18-1		11-0-58-4	10-4-35-2																42.4	160	7	10	
v. Sussex	31-6-124-3	18-4-42-2	4-2-4-0	13-2-61-0				3-1-7-1				25-5-81-4									94	332	13	10	
(Hove) 25-28 May	23-8-40-4	29-4-83-4	3-1-9-0	8-1-40-0				10-1-34-0				17-0-68-1									90	286	7	9	
v. Cambridge UCCE		18-4-54-3			13-6-18-2					7.4-1-36-2			11-3-26-2		6-1-16-1						55.4	151	1	10	
(Fenner's) 1-3 June		15-2-66-2			20-6-34-1					12-3-34-2			19.2-3-64-1		14-5-37-1					7-0-31-1	87.2	277	11	8	
v. Surrey	32-7-106-6	24-5-80-1	2-0-7-0					15-3-36-1				23-3-73-0			2-0-16-1		5-2-20-0	23-2-103-0			126	460	19	10	1
(Lord's) 8-11 June																					–	–	–	–	
v. Glamorgan	19-6-86-0	19-0-100-0	12-0-52-0	20-5-80-1				22-1-103-1		19-4-66-0	4-1-13-0	11-1-44-0			7-0-25-0						133	584	15	3	1
(Southgate) 15-18 June	8-2-24-3		12-2-43-0	4-1-15-0				10-0-57-0		5-1-36-0	6-0-36-0	3-1-16-0			4-0-27-0						52	256	2	3	
v. Hampshire	22-2-97-1	17-1-61-3		18.2-5-62-3	14-2-85-3			3-0-16-0							2-0-13-0				4-1-14-0		80.2	355	7	10	
(Southgate) 8-11 July	11-3-30-1		18.4-2-53-4	9-0-22-1	27-6-77-3																65.4	192	10	10	1
v. Glamorgan		11-3-42-3	3-0-31-1	15-5-37-1	10-4-43-0	13-1-52-3									0.3-0-4-1				4-3-4-0		56.3	232	19	10	1
(Cardiff) 21-23 July		17-4-57-5	13-1-46-1	16-2-44-2	28-5-82-2	9-2-37-0	5-1-9-0														88	279	4	10	
v. Warwickshire				27-8-77-2	23-6-54-2	7-1-40-0	24-7-61-5	43-0-25-1							1-0-4-0				2-1-2-0		88.3	272	9	10	
(Lord's) 3-6 August			20-0-77-1	18-5-71-1	21-2-119-1	4-0-33-2	21-3-68-2											0.1-0-2-0			84.1	383	13	7	
v. Nottinghamshire	16-3-54-3			11-6-23-1		17-3-59-6													1-0-5-0	10-1-31-0	55	181	9	10	
(Trent Bridge) 10-13 August	10-4-24-1			10-2-24-0		6-2-18-0		9-1-25-0											2-1-10-0	5-0-25-0	42	128	2	1	
v. Sussex			6-0-43-2			17-2-71-1	21-5-87-2	22.4-3-109-1	15-2-75-1	15-1-65-2							7-0-50-1		1-0-10-0		104.4	522	12	10	
(Lord's) 16-17 August																					–	–	–	–	
v. Kent	27-4-95-1		22-0-115-0					15-1-82-0	26-5-79-3	5-1-15-0	20-0-117-1						2-0-16-0				117	549	25	6	1
(Canterbury) 24-27 August																					–	–	–	–	
v. Gloucestershire	18.2-2-77-4		19-2-84-4	8-1-39-0	24-4-61-0				13-3-38-1	10-0-20-1											92.2	333	14	10	
(Bristol) 30 August-2 September	15-4-29-0		20-4-58-2	10.5-1-33-2	25-5-73-1				14-1-57-3	14-3-29-2							1-0-3-0				99.5	287	5	10	
v. Kent	27-4-90-3		5-0-15-1	20-2-74-0	20-1-88-3					31-7-112-3											103	384	5	10	
(Lord's) 7-10 September	16-6-38-2		16-1-50-2	5-1-16-0	6-1-27-0					25.4-12-41-3									4-0-13-0		72.4	192	7	7	
v. Surrey	23-4-60-0	7-2-16-1	30-2-109-0				13-4-53-0			8-0-21-0		48-6-176-1						10-0-68-0	21.3-1-95-2	17-0-74-0	177.3	686	14	5	1
(The Oval) 21-24 September																					–	–	–	–	

	A Richardson	SB Styris	JWM Dalrymple	MM Betts	CT Peploe	PD Trego	SR Clark	PN Weekes	M Hayward	CD Whelan	YA Golwalker	PM Hutchison	IK Pathan	CMP Jones	EC Joyce	ST Finn	OA Shah	CB Keegan	BL Hutton	CJC Wright
Overs	471.4	230.5	248.4	229.1	249	131	120.4	237.5	94	41.4	104.4	53.4	89	30.2	32.3	20	40	70	93	38
Maidens	109	44	25	45	57	21	22	33	9	8	25	3	13	6	1	6	3	18	10	3
Runs	1438	730	940	838	801	576	412	765	380	182	329	255	324	90	204	53	171	233	394	159
Wickets	57	31	23	22	18	16	15	14	8	7	7	5	5	3	3	2	2	1	1	0
Average	25.22	23.54	40.86	38.09	44.50	36.00	27.46	54.64	47.50	26.00	47.00	51.00	64.80	30.00	68.00	26.50	85.50	233.00	394.00	-

FIELDING

50	BJM Scott (44 ct, 6 st)
24	BL Hutton
22	OA Shah
15	EC Joyce
12	ET Smith
7	PN Weekes
4	SB Styris
3	AJ Strauss
3	JWM Dalrymple
2	A Richardson
2	PM Hutchison
2	PD Trego
2	CT Peploe
2	AD Poynter
1	M Hayward
1	SR Clark
1	IK Pathan
1	CJC Wright
0	MM Betts
0	DC Nash
0	CB Keegan
0	NRD Compton
0	CMP Jones
0	CD Whelan
0	BA Godleman
0	ST Finn
0	YA Golwalker

NORTHAMPTONSHIRE CCC

FIRST–CLASS MATCHES
BATTING

	U Afzaal	BM Shafayat	DJG Sales	DG Wright	ML Love	RA White	J Louw	JF Brown	MH Wessels	BJ Phillips	MS Panesar	PS Jones	C Pietersen	SP Crook	GL Brophy	TW Roberts	AR White	TB Huggins	MJ Friedlander	JP Wolstenholme	TM Baker	RE King	Extras	Total	Wickets	Result	Points
v. Leicestershire (Northampton) 20-23 April	11	59	113	8	50	95			22*						52*								23	433	6		
	5	14	79		112*	22*																	6	238	3	D	12
v. Derbyshire (Derby) 27-30 April	2	161	39	8	168	35*	4*		21						0								13	451	7	D	12
v. Yorkshire (Headingley) 6-9 May	0	4	33	36	42	15	58	0	55*			13			0								25	281	10		
	19	25	16	15	4	5	10	7*	3			51											20	175	10	L	5
v. Essex (Northampton) 11-14 May	168*	153	20	55	20	21	15		26	33*													41	552	7	D	12
v. Bangladesh (Northampton) 20-22 May	47*	76				14			20							16	30*	8	7				12	230	6	D	
v. Somerset (Northampton) 25-27 May	0	8	0	9	166	49	37	4*	102	5		14											14	408	10		
	3	4	15	14*	33	8	5		8	3		0											7	100	10	L	8
v. Lancashire (Old Trafford) 1-4 June	42	43	9	11	0	34	0	1*	15	6			1										13	175	10		
	48	0	43	30	8	23	0	1	23	31*			0										18	225	10	D	7
v. Durham (Northampton) 15-18 June	16	22	50*	26	49	13	0	0	3	24			0										11	214	10		
	0	38	23*		62	11			57*														14	205	4	D	8
v. Essex (Chelmsford) 10-12 July	43	9		53*	21			0	3	58						44							16	247	10		
	47	84	12	11	32			0	0	35	0*		0			0							40	261	10	L	3
v. Worcestershire (Northampton) 20-23 July	0	12	53	4	74		1	22	0	0	39*					53							41	299	10		
	21	84	19	47	27		5	0*	102	17	0					1							41	364	10	W	19
v. Worcestershire (Worcester) 4-6 August	41	1	31	0	53	30	0	0*	13	5	5												10	189	10		
	6	7	190	85	14	12	27	5*	17	5													18	386	10	W	17
v. Derbyshire (Northampton) 10-13 August	9	1	1	22	2	25	0	0*	17	48													15	140	10		
	59	22	93	43	177	0			50*														22	466	6	W	17
v. Leicestershire (Leicester) 24-27 August	6	56	20	18	67	26	18		17	24	1*										0		8	261	10	D	8
v. Lancashire (Northampton) 30 August-2 September	38	33	66	5	44	41	3	5	18	18*	0												18	289	10		
	147	80	77	5	11	9			30*	22*													19	400	6	W	19
v. Somerset (Taunton) 7-10 September	112	23	154	71	14	24	64	2	0		0			91*									19	574	10	D	12
v. Durham (The Riverside) 14-17 September	119	13	11	21		84	5*		107					19*			0						35	414	7		
	21*	22	0	1		22	9*		0					10			6						10	101	7	D	12
v. Yorkshire (Northampton) 21-24 September	157	4	4	11	95	26	16		2	25*				97									39	476	9	W	22
Matches	17	17	16	16	15	15	15	15	14	13	8	6	4	3	3	3	2	1	1	1	1	1					
Innings	28	28	27	25	25	24	20	16	23	20	11	6	3	4	3	5	3	1	1	0	1	0					
Not Out	3	0	2	2	1	2	3	7	3	6	4	0	0	2	1	0	1	0	0	0	0	0					
Highest Score	168*	161	190	85	177	95	64	22	107	58	39*	51	1	97	52*	53	30*	8	7	0	0	0					
Runs	1187	1058	1171	609	1345	644	277	47	613	447	75	78	1	217	52	114	36	8	7	0	0	0					
Average	47.48	37.78	46.84	26.47	56.04	29.27	16.29	5.22	30.65	31.92	10.71	13.00	0.33	108.50	26.00	22.80	18.00	8.00	7.00	-	0.00	-					
100s	5	2	3	0	4	0	0	0	3	0	0	0	0	0	0	0	0	0	0	0	0	0					
50s	1	6	6	4	6	2	2	0	2	2	0	1	0	2	1	1	0	0	0	0	0	0					
Catches/Stumpings	9/0	21/0	20/0	6/0	36/0	10/0	2/0	1/0	23/4	2/0	2/0	0/0	2/0	0/0	6/0	0/0	1/0	1/0	1/0	2/0	1/0	0/0					

Home Ground: Northampton
Address: Wantage Road, Northampton, NN1 4TJ
Tel: 01604 514455
Fax: 01604 514488
Email: commercial@nccc.co.uk
Directions: Junction 15 from M1 onto A508 (A45) towards Northampton. Follow the dual carriageway for approx 3 miles. Keeping in left-hand lane, take next exit from dual carriageway marked A428 Bedford and Town Centre. Move into middle lane approaching the roundabout at bottom of slip road. Take second exit following signs for Abington/Kingsthorpe onto Rushmere Road. Follow Rushmere Road (A5095) across the junction with Billing Road and continue straight on through Abington Park to traffic lights at main junction with Wellingborough Road.
Capacity: 4,250
Other grounds used: Campbell Park, Milton Keynes, Stowe School
Year formed: 1878

Chief Executive: Mark Tagg
Chairman: Lynn Wilson
First XI Manager: Kepler Wessels
Captain: David Sales
County Colours: Claret and gold

Honours
Benson & Hedges Cup
1980
Gillette Cup/NatWest/C&G Trophy
1976, 1992

Website:
www.nccc.co.uk

NORTHAMPTONSHIRE CCC

FIRST-CLASS MATCHES

BOWLING

Match	JF Brown	DG Wright	MS Panesar	J Louw	BJ Phillips	PS Jones	C Pietersen	SP Crook	MJ Friedlander	RE King	TM Baker	U Afzaal	RA White	BM Shafayat	JP Wolstenholme	AR White	Overs	Total	Byes/Leg-byes	Wickets	Run outs
v. Leicestershire	16-3-58-1	27-9-68-1		27-9-85-2	15.2-6-33-1	20-3-74-4						2-0-10-1					107.2	339	11	10	
(Northampton) 20-23 April	11-3-34-1	8-2-17-0		12-3-31-0	5-1-12-1	8-3-16-2								3-0-5-0			47	115	0	4	
v. Derbyshire	17-8-20-0	29-10-57-1		30.5-10-71-6	20-7-45-2	13-3-39-1											109.5	241	9	10	
(Derby) 27-30 April	11-2-33-0	8-5-16-0		9-0-30-0	5-3-2-0	12-3-30-0						5-2-4-0					50	119	4	0	
v. Yorkshire	25.1-3-81-0	24.4-8-60-8		21-3-72-1	12-1-52-0	14-6-33-1								1.5-0-7-0			98.4	328	23	10	
(Headingley) 6-9 May		4-0-16-0		6-0-43-0	4-0-30-0	6-2-39-0											20	132	4	0	
v. Essex	14.5-4-24-2	14-4-36-1		14-4-51-6	10-5-23-1	14-4-30-0						10-2-38-0	10-3-19-0	2-1-1-0			66.5	178	14	10	
(Northampton) 11-14 May	56-15-110-2	20-2-73-0		31-7-95-1	19-6-44-3	28-7-90-0											176	495	25	6	
v. Bangladesh							16-0-74-3		14-1-67-3	7-2-32-1			9-0-39-0		9-3-14-0	15-1-82-0	70	309	1	7	
(Northampton) 20-22 May																	-	-	-	-	
v. Somerset	34.5-7-112-6	20-2-78-1		13-3-59-0	18-4-52-1	8-1-46-1											93.5	356	9	10	1
(Northampton) 25-27 May	13.1-3-51-1	12-1-26-1		13-4-43-2	3-0-15-0							5-1-17-0					46.1	155	3	4	
v. Lancashire	4.3-1-15-1	13-5-34-3		10-2-34-3	4-0-22-2		10-0-31-1										41.3	149	13	10	
(Old Trafford) 1-4 June	17-5-73-4	11-3-21-1		12.5-0-66-3			2-0-17-0						1-0-8-0				43.5	190	5	8	
v. Durham	28.5-6-92-3	28-8-71-4		24-5-92-2	19-5-46-1		6-1-30-0										105.5	334	3	10	
(Northampton) 15-18 June	33-12-82-1	22-4-83-2		19-1-65-1	10-2-31-0		7-0-29-0										91	293	3	4	
v. Essex	47-13-136-2	23-8-52-1	56.3-15-181-7		13-2-39-0	21-2-77-0											160.3	506	21	10	
(Chelmsford) 10-12 July			0.2-0-4-0														0.2	4	0	0	
v. Worcestershire	29-7-65-0	18-1-80-3	29-5-91-3	16-1-77-3	15-3-43-0									3-0-13-0			110	381	12	10	1
(Northampton) 20-23 July	20-3-55-2	3-0-21-0	26.5-3-77-6	9-2-27-2													58.5	200	20	10	
v. Worcestershire		23-8-87-3	4-0-8-0	22.1-7-66-4	14-5-42-3									3-1-7-0			66.1	216	6	10	
(Worcester) 4-6 August		14-5-39-1	12.2-3-40-4	14-1-60-2	14-3-56-3									3-0-19-0			57.2	222	8	10	
v. Derbyshire	9-2-20-1	22-7-54-2	24.3-7-56-4	15-3-42-2	13-3-39-1												83.3	219	8	10	
(Northampton) 10-13 August	45-22-61-5	9.2-7-10-1	43-15-82-4	2-1-20-0													99.2	205	32	10	
v. Leicestershire		32-10-87-4	26-3-80-0	21-4-81-0	25.4-9-76-1						13-2-55-1			5-0-9-0			122.4	405	17	6	
(Leicester) 24-27 August																	-	-	-	-	
v. Lancashire	36.3-9-113-5	19-6-55-4	33-6-88-1	2-1-12-0	13-6-26-0												103.3	301	7	10	
(Northampton) 30 August-2 September	16-8-22-5	6-2-21-0	16-3-32-3	7-3-21-1	2-2-0-1												47	103	7	10	
v. Somerset	24-8-65-1	19-5-83-2	26.5-7-66-4	19-2-70-1				20-2-86-1									108.5	396	26	10	1
(Taunton) 7-10 September	16-7-33-1	12-7-30-3	17-3-58-0	4-1-17-0				5-0-21-0									54	163	4	4	
v. Durham	19-9-33-1	24-5-79-5		25-7-67-1			7-0-23-0	14.3-4-54-3									89.3	270	14	10	
(The Riverside) 14-17 September	1-0-3-0	5-2-13-1		7-5-13-1				2-0-7-0									15	38	2	2	
v. Yorkshire	34-10-65-5	5-1-23-0	27.5-11-32-5	7-3-9-0				9-2-23-0									82.5	177	25	10	
(Northampton) 21-24 September	50.5-14-95-5	5-2-8-0	46-14-96-5	3-2-5-0				4-0-15-0					1-0-25-0				109.5	278	34	10	

	JF Brown	DG Wright	MS Panesar	J Louw	BJ Phillips	PS Jones	C Pietersen	SP Crook	MJ Friedlander	RE King	TM Baker	U Afzaal	RA White	BM Shafayat	JP Wolstenholme	AR White
Overs	629.4	480	389.1	415.5	254	144	48	54.3	14	7	13	23	20	20.5	9	15
Maidens	184	139	95	94	73	34	1	8	1	2	2	5	3	2	3	1
Runs	1551	1398	991	1424	728	474	204	206	67	32	55	94	66	61	14	82
Wickets	55	53	46	44	21	9	4	4	3	1	1	1	0	0	0	0
Average	28.20	26.37	21.54	32.36	34.66	52.66	51.00	51.50	22.33	32.00	55.00	94.00	-	-	-	-

FIELDING

36	ML Love
27	MH Wessels (23 ct, 4 st)
21	BM Shafayat
20	DJG Sales
10	RA White
9	U Afzaal
6	GL Brophy
6	DG Wright
2	BJ Phillips
2	MS Panesar
2	JP Wolstenholme
2	J Louw
2	C Pietersen
1	JF Brown
1	TM Baker
1	TB Huggins
1	AR White
1	MJ Friedlander
0	PS Jones
0	TW Roberts
0	RE King
0	SP Crook

NOTTINGHAMSHIRE CCC

FIRST–CLASS MATCHES

BATTING

	JER Gallian	DJ Bicknell	DJ Hussey	CMW Read	MA Ealham	GP Swann	RJ Sidebottom	GJ Smith	AJ Harris	SP Fleming	RJ Warren	A Singh	PJ Franks	Younis Khan	WR Smith	SR Patel	OJ Newby	MHA Footitt	D Alleyne	GD Clough	Extras	Total	Wickets	Result	Points
v. Loughborough UCCE (Trent Bridge) 13–15 April	57	91	62	41		63	22*	2	0		21	131	6								36	532	10	D	
v. Middlesex (Lord's) 20–23 April	46	56	118	63	47	9	31	9		0		25	104*								38	546	10	D	12
	8	111	57	9*	4*					1		14									8	212	5		
v. Sussex (Trent Bridge) 27–30 April	199	7	89	51	5	7*				111		7	8								25	509	8	W	22
	13*	17*																			0	30	0		
v. Surrey (The Oval) 6–9 May	141	91	74	13	57*					238		0	26*			2					50	692	7	W	22
v. Kent (Trent Bridge) 20–23 May	18	63	23	0	0		0			24		11				12	11			14*	8	184	10	L	3
	36	17	26	0	21		31			20		11				3	38*			0	16	219	10		
v. Gloucestershire (Bristol) 25–27 May	46	48	98*	23	27		4	26		92		57				10	0				38	469	10	W	22
v. Hampshire (Trent Bridge) 1–4 June	17	4	42	59*	41*					7		27									25	222	5	L	4
	20	13	64	8	2	0	0	0	0*	105		18									31	261	10		
v. Sussex (Arundel Castle) 15–18 June	5	88	13	17*	13	11	2	0	35	129	25										22	360	10	D	11
v. Glamorgan (Trent Bridge) 8–10 July	21	61	81	103*	6	0		4		78	34							16			11	425	10	W	22
	31*	20*																			6	57	0		
v. Warwickshire (Edgbaston) 20–22 July	62	84	77	26	11	19	0	5	1*	41	5										10	341	10	W	20
		4*				8*															0	12	0		
v. Surrey (Trent Bridge) 26–29 July	37	0	29		55	29	4	18	1*		21			10					6		16	226	10	D	8
	2	17	30		46	0	2*	0*			13			0					40		19	169	8		
v. Middlesex (Trent Bridge) 10–13 August	11	33	9	10	26	53	0	6*	0					7	6						20	181	10	D	7
	56*	62													5*						5	128	1		
v. Warwickshire (Trent Bridge) 14–16 August	20	11	232*	89	36	39	12	2	21					29	0						23	514	10	W	22
v. Glamorgan (Cardiff) 30 August–2 September	0	123	1	9	1	0	12	17	1*		51			53							15	283	10	W	19
	70	16									60*			20*							13	179	2		
v. Gloucestershire (Trent Bridge) 5–6 September	0	13	157	0	14	38	8*	9	0		60			12							25	336	10	W	20
v. Kent (Canterbury) 14–17 September	199	64	11	75	72	23	1*	9*		1	8										23	486	8	W	20
	74*		0	63						6*	16										11	170	3		
v. Hampshire (The Rose Bowl) 21–23 September	26	11		34		9		7	5	42	8		27*		13			0			31	213	10	L	2
	5	97		63		14		23	1	13	29		24		10			19*			15	313	10		
Matches	17	17	16	16	15	15	15	15	12	11	9	7	5	5	3	3	2	2	1	1					
Innings	27	27	21	21	19	17	15	16	12	16	13	10	6	7	5	4	3	3	2	2					
Not Out	4	3	2	4	3	2	4	3	4	1	1	0	3	1	1	0	1	1	0	1					
Highest Score	199	123	232*	103*	72	63	31	26	35	238	60*	131	104*	53	13	12	38*	19*	40	14*					
Runs	1220	1222	1293	756	484	322	129	137	75	908	351	301	195	131	34	27	49	35	46	14					
Average	53.04	50.91	68.05	44.47	30.25	21.46	11.72	10.53	9.37	60.53	29.25	30.10	65.00	21.83	8.50	6.75	24.50	17.50	23.00	14.00					
100s	3	2	3	1	0	0	0	0	0	4	0	1	1	0	0	0	0	0	0	0					
50s	5	10	8	7	3	2	0	0	0	2	3	1	1	0	1	0	0	0	0	0					
Catches/Stumpings	14/0	3/0	30/0	62/2	5/0	5/0	6/0	4/0	4/0	14/0	6/0	2/0	0/0	4/0	1/0	0/0	0/0	1/0	5/0	0/0					

Home Ground: Trent Bridge
Address: Trent Bridge, Nottingham, NG2 6AG
Tel: 01159 823000
Fax: 01159 455730
Email: administration.notts@ecb.co.uk
Directions: *By road:* Follow signs from ring road towards city centre.
Capacity: 14,500 (16,000 during international matches)
Other grounds used: Cleethorpes
Year formed: 1841

Chief Executive: Derek Brewer
Director of Cricket: Mike Newell
Captain: Stephen Fleming/Jason Gallian
County colours: Green and gold

Website:
www.nottsccc.co.uk

Honours
County Championship
1883, 1884, 1885, 1886, 1907, 1929, 1981, 1987, 2005
Sunday League/NCL
1991
Benson & Hedges Cup
1976, 1989
Gillette Cup/NatWest/C&G Trophy
1987

NOTTINGHAMSHIRE CCC

FIRST–CLASS MATCHES
BOWLING

FIRST–CLASS MATCHES	MA Ealham	GJ Smith	RJ Sidebottom	AJ Harris	GP Swann	PJ Franks	DJ Hussey	SR Patel	MHA Footitt	OJ Newby	Younis Khan	GD Clough	DJ Bicknell	JER Gallian	A Singh	WR Smith	Overs	Total	Byes/Leg-byes	Wickets	Run outs
v. Loughborough UCCE (Trent Bridge) 13-15 April		13-5-19-5 6-6-0-0	11.1-4-28-1 7-4-8-1	14-6-43-1 7.3-0-36-1	3-2-1-0	12-3-43-1 8-1-50-0	7-2-19-2 8-1-31-1						9.3-2-41-0		1-0-13-0		60.1 47	164 185	11 6	10 4	 1
v. Middlesex (Lord's) 20-23 April	17-2-68-2	22-6-67-3 2-1-2-0	17.5-2-85-2 2-1-6-0		21-6-59-2 20-7-43-0	16-3-59-1	24-6-61-1							9-1-37-0			93.5 57	345 158	7 9	10 2	 1
v. Sussex (Trent Bridge) 27-30 April	24-5-69-3 4-0-12-0	27.3-11-83-2 14-4-56-2	30-12-73-2 8.4-4-15-4		23-5-51-1 22-5-51-3	19-4-84-2 5-1-19-1											123.3 53.4	379 159	19 6	10 10	
v. Surrey (The Oval) 6-9 May	14-4-53-4 34-9-81-3		19-3-78-2 37-12-82-2		7.1-1-40-1 33.1-8-94-4	9-1-37-2 18-3-72-1	1-0-7-0	17-2-43-0					1-0-2-0				49.1 141.1	217 404	9 18	10 10	1
v. Kent (Trent Bridge) 20-23 May	24-5-69-2 15-2-47-1		27.2-9-61-5 14-4-35-1					14-2-37-1 21-6-73-3		20-6-79-2 15-1-78-2		17-2-45-0 7-0-39-1					102.2 72	301 298	10 26	10 8	
v. Gloucestershire (Bristol) 25-27 May	16-10-26-3 19-4-64-3	15-2-55-1 18-5-41-2	25-6-65-4 18-6-35-4				1-0-4-0	13.4-6-24-1 11.3-1-41-1		12-3-66-1							81.4 67.3	250 192	14 7	10 10	
v. Hampshire (Trent Bridge) 1-4 June	11-4-33-1	17-6-45-0	25-5-89-2	23.4-6-83-6	5-1-16-1		14-1-105-4						4.3-0-44-0	10-1-71-0			81.4 28.3	277 220	11 0	10 4	
v. Sussex (Arundel Castle) 15-18 June	14-5-39-0 5-1-18-0	27.2-3-116-3 11-3-31-0	4.4-3-6-0	28.2-3-131-5 8-0-33-1	13-2-55-1 11-1-41-1		10-0-59-0							11-2-72-0			87.2 56	355 256	8 2	10 3	1 1
v. Glamorgan (Trent Bridge) 8-10 July	15-1-58-2 7-1-15-2	17-4-64-4 16-7-39-1		14-2-62-3 15-2-50-2	3-0-16-0 25-7-48-1		1-0-5-0		12-2-62-1 14.3-4-45-4								61 78.3	267 214	5 12	10 10	
v. Warwickshire (Edgbaston) 20-22 July	13-3-41-2 8-1-20-1	12-1-58-3 9.1-2-23-2	14-4-41-2 13-8-13-1	15-3-48-3 6-0-15-0	9-2-21-0 23-7-57-6												63 59.1	219 133	10 5	10 10	
v. Surrey (Trent Bridge) 26-29 Jul	9.5-5-12-2 16-6-40-1	8-2-33-3 19-4-57-3	15-7-27-2 20-2-73-1	16-3-55-3 16-2-82-1	7-2-21-0						4-0-16-0						48.5 82	136 292	9 3	10 6	
v. Middlesex (Trent Bridge) 10-13 August	17-3-66-2 17-3-61-2	18-3-68-3 15-2-60-0	15-4-41-0 15-7-28-0	21.3-4-86-4 16-0-107-0	12-1-40-1 10-0-43-0		5-1-13-0				6-0-20-0 16.5-1-67-2						89.3 94.5	325 385	4 6	10 4	
v. Warwickshire (Trent Bridge) 14-16 August	13-3-39-2 6-1-11-0	5-0-29-0 15-3-64-3	17-4-41-4 16-6-34-1	9.4-0-41-4 9-1-33-1	10-2-41-2						4.2-0-21-2						44.4 60.2	156 207	6 3	10 10	 1
v. Glamorgan (Cardiff) 30 August-2 September	11-3-29-2 17-3-50-4	17-10-28-4 6-1-32-1	10-1-31-3 16-4-36-2	10-3-57-1 19.4-2-70-3	26-4-75-0						6-0-27-0						48 90.4	151 307	6 17	10 10	
v. Gloucestershire (Trent Bridge) 5-6 September	11-2-31-5 10-2-44-4	9-1-33-3 4.1-0-20-1	7-3-18-1 7-1-19-2	8-4-15-1 5-1-22-1	10-3-62-2												35 36.1	103 169	6 2	10 10	
v. Kent (Canterbury) 14-17 September	14-2-44-2 9-0-25-1	15-2-43-0 4.4-0-18-2	14-3-36-0 8-1-28-1	16-4-44-0 17-0-76-6	21-5-66-3 14-3-55-0												80 52.4	237 205	4 3	5 10	
v. Hampshire (The Rose Bowl) 21-23 September		31-3-130-0		30-8-104-2	39-5-145-1	20-1-89-1			17-0-153-1							9.3-0-70-0	146.3 –	714 –	23	5	
Overs	390.5	393.5	433.4	325.2	367.2	107	71	77.1	43.3	47	37.1	24	15	30	1	9.3					
Maidens	90	97	130	54	79	17	11	17	6	10	1	2	2	4	0	0					
Runs	1165	1314	1132	1293	1141	453	304	218	260	223	151	84	87	180	13	70					
Wickets	56	51	50	49	30	9	8	6	6	5	4	1	0	0	0	0					
Average	20.80	25.76	22.64	26.38	38.03	50.33	38.00	36.33	43.33	44.60	37.75	84.00	-	-	-	-					

FIELDING

64	CMW Read (62 ct, 2 st)
30	DJ Hussey
14	JER Gallian
14	SP Fleming
6	RJ Warren
6	RJ Sidebottom
5	MA Ealham
5	GP Swann
5	D Alleyne
4	AJ Harris
4	GJ Smith
4	Younis Khan
3	DJ Bicknell
2	A Singh
1	WR Smith
1	MHA Footitt
0	PJ Franks
0	GD Clough
0	SR Patel
0	OJ Newby

SOMERSET CCC

FIRST-CLASS MATCHES

BATTING

	ID Blackwell	JD Francis	JC Hildreth	MJ Wood	AR Caddick	RL Johnson	M Burns	RJ Turner	AW Laraman	KA Parsons	CM Gazzard	WJ Durston	AV Suppiah	ST Jayasuriya	SRG Francis	CK Langeveldt	NAM McLean	GM Andrew	GC Smith	ME Trescothick	RJ Woodman	M Parsons	NJ Edwards	MK Munday	Extras	Total	Wickets	Result	Points
v. Durham UCCE	191	123	0	95			19	22*	50*														42		38	580	6		
(Taunton) 9-11 April		3*	112	72*			9																		15	211	2	D	
v. Lancashire	122	1	14	10	0*	27	40	21	6											11					20	272	10		
(Old Trafford) 13-16 April	1*		0	27			5*													22					14	69	3	D	9
v. Yorkshire	33	11	18	23*	15	23	0	21						0			18								20	182	10		
(Headingley) 20-23 April	21	125*	0	13	11	0	24	53						7			0								21	275	10	L	3
v. Essex	0	35	22		4	18	8	20	43					31			0*			4					5	190	10		
(Taunton) 27-30 April	38	64	0		30	24	3	68*	8					0			40			18					20	313	10	L	2
v. Durham	48	35	70	19	8	11	11	6						2	5*					21					16	252	10		
(Stockton-on-Tees) 6-9 May	87	4	21	54	4	34	5	2						17	20*					20					20	288	10	L	5
v. Lancashire	3	17	4	4		0	87	45	2					73				32				6*			21	294	10		
(Taunton) 20-23 May																												D	7
v. Northamptonshire	59	43	20	53		32	34	27*	16					55			0	0							17	356	10		
(Northampton) 25-27 May	2*	55	7*	5			48							22											16	155	4	W	21
v. Leicestershire	0	4	6				37	7	2					24	2*	1		8	10						4	105	10		
(Oakham School) 1-4 June		104*	25*				59							9					9						19	225	3	D	7
v. Worcestershire	54	1		127	19	21	18	8	11					66	5*				55						23	408	10		
(Bath) 8-11 June	8	0		10	11	0	49	19	16					21	1*				6						11	152	10	L	8
v. Leicestershire	59	0	18	74	23					6	24	0			13	18*			311						20	566	10		
(Taunton) 8-10 July		4*																	14*						0	18	0	W	22
v. Durham	59	1	86	59	0*	0				26	2		20			0			28						22	303	10		
(Taunton) 26-29 July	8	16	3	2	10	23				45	3		2			9*			39						14	174	10	L	5
v. Derbyshire	18	19	73	4	0	35				14	7	146*	123												21	460	10		
(Derby) 4-7 August	88*	34	30	10						15*		44	14												10	245	5	W	21
v. Yorkshire	62	30	31	297	5					94	0	16	6		9	5*									26	581	10		
(Taunton) 10-13 August																												D	12
v. Worcestershire	9	2	4	21	6					34	74	3	72		3						46*				44	318	10		
(Worcester) 16-19 August	5	15	12	72	39					11	44*	26	34		29						0				35	322	10	L	4
v. Essex		31*	76*	0								0	0												5	112	2		
(Colchester) 24-27 August	59	51	125*	0						12*		0	29												16	292	5	W	16
v. Northamptonshire	98	8	25	58		0				31	3	27	91			6		10*							39	396	10		
(Taunton) 7-10 September	1*	64	50	4								36*	0												8	163	4	D	10
v. Derbyshire	16	54	84	25						20	12*	25	0					3			2	1			17	259	10		
(Taunton) 21-24 September	107	108	1	29						93*	21	0	28					15			6	4			18	430	10	L	3
Matches	17	17	16	13	11	11	9	9	9	8	8	7	7	7	6	6	6	5	4	4	3	2	1	1					
Innings	28	31	29	23	16	15	17	13	13	12	10	11	13	13	9	6	7	6	8	6	4	3	1	0					
Not Out	4	5	4	1	3	0	1	3	1	3	2	2	0	0	5	3	1	1	1	0	1	1	0	0					
Highest Score	191	125*	125*	297	54	35	87	68*	53	94	74	146*	123	73	29	18*	40	32	311	22	46*	6*	42	0					
Runs	1256	1062	937	1058	256	218	484	277	236	401	190	323	419	327	87	38	59	68	472	96	54	11	42	0					
Average	52.33	40.84	37.48	48.09	19.69	14.53	30.25	27.70	19.66	44.55	23.75	35.88	32.23	25.15	21.75	12.66	9.83	13.60	67.42	16.00	18.00	5.50	42.00	-					
100s	3	4	2	2	0	0	0	0	0	0	0	1	1	0	0	0	0	0	1	0	0	0	0	0					
50s	9	5	6	7	1	0	2	1	2	2	1	0	2	3	0	0	0	0	1	0	0	0	0	0					
Catches/Stumpings	5/0	8/0	15/0	4/0	3/0	5/0	4/0	22/1	2/0	5/0	15/0	5/0	1/0	2/0	6/0	0/0	1/0	1/0	7/0	6/0	0/0	0/0	0/0	0/0					

Home Ground: Taunton
Address: County Ground, St James Street, Taunton, Somerset, TA1 1JT
Tel: 01823 272946
Fax: 01823 332395
Email: somerset@ecb.co.uk
Directions: *By road:* M5 junction 25, follow A358 to town centre. Signposted from there.

Other grounds used: Bath
Year formed: 1875

Chief Executive: Peter Anderson
Head Coach: Mark Garaway
Captain: Graeme Smith/Marcus Trescothick/Rob Turner/Ian Blackwell
County colours: Black, white and maroon

Honours
Sunday League/NCL
1979
Benson & Hedges Cup
1981, 1982
Gillette Cup/NatWest/C&G Trophy
1979, 1983, 2001
Twenty20 Cup
2005

Website:
www.somersetcountycc.com

SOMERSET CCC

FIRST-CLASS MATCHES
BOWLING

FIRST-CLASS MATCHES	AR Caddick	ID Blackwell	RL Johnson	CK Langeveldt	AW Laraman	NAM McLean	GM Andrew	KA Parsons	WJ Durston	ST Jayasuriya	SRG Francis	M Burns	AV Suppiah	RJ Woodman	GC Smith	MK Munday	M Parsons	JC Hildreth	Overs	Total	Byes/Leg-byes	Wickets	Run outs
v. Durham UCCE (Taunton) 9-11 April	27-8-60-2	36-9-95-0	25-6-61-0		21-1-55-0	20-4-72-1						14.4-3-51-1						4-0-24-0	147.4 –	433 –	15 –	4 –	
v. Lancashire (Old Trafford) 13-16 April	26-6-78-4 19-4-50-1	18-5-44-2 19-1-63-2	20.3-3-84-2 5-0-26-0		15-2-39-1 11-1-28-1	17-4-69-1 7-2-21-1													96.3 61	323 195	9 7	10 5	
v. Yorkshire (Headingley) 20-23 April	22-3-95-2	20-4-70-0	25-5-92-1		30-3-100-3	18-3-107-3				7-0-27-0									122 –	501 –	10 –	9 –	
v. Essex (Taunton) 27-30 April	33.5-4-110-3	22-6-51-0 6-2-12-0	30-6-98-3 4-1-17-0		17-3-54-0	13-3-50-1 7-0-39-1				5-0-18-0 1.1-0-10-0			6-0-31-0						126.5 18.1	427 78	15 0	8 1	1
v. Durham (Stockton-on-Tees) 6-9 May	28-7-106-6 25-7-98-6	7-2-27-0 12-1-56-0	17-3-66-1 16-2-52-0		13-2-45-1 5-1-25-0					3-1-2-2 3-1-13-0	12-2-40-0								80 61	298 244	12 0	10 6	
v. Lancashire (Taunton) 20-23 May		9-1-43-0			8-0-54-0		14.1-0-106-1			16-0-99-2							9-1-47-0		56.1 –	351 –	2 –	3 –	
v. Northamptonshire (Northampton) 25-27 May		24-6-85-2 1-1-0-2	17-3-54-3		13-2-56-2 7-2-21-2	20-5-91-1 9-3-29-1	10.2-1-66-1 12-4-31-3			10-3-33-1 1-1-0-0		8-1-19-0 6.5-1-12-2							102.2 36.5	408 100	4 7	10 10	
v. Leicestershire (Oakham School) 1-4 June		25.4-8-66-3			23-3-68-3	12-3-29-2	16-2-58-0			5-1-12-0	25-2-81-2	1-0-10-0			4-1-12-0				111.4 –	338 –	2 –	10 –	
v. Worcestershire (Bath) 8-11 June	31-4-132-5 6-0-49-2	19.5-2-58-2 5-0-27-0	31-9-93-3 7-0-36-0		13-1-43-0 1-0-14-0					5-0-16-0	12-1-50-0 2.4-0-12-0	4-0-19-0							115.5 21.4	423 138	12 0	10 2	
v. Leicestershire (Taunton) 8-10 July	30-9-83-3 19-8-46-3	16-4-42-1 20.2-2-59-3	23.1-9-67-3 20-3-67-3					14-5-18-2 4-0-19-0	5-0-21-0 4-1-21-0		14-2-69-0 7-1-34-1				7-3-17-0			1-0-5-0	109.1 75.2	330 253	13 2	10 10	1
v. Durham (Taunton) 26-29 July	36-6-130-3 7-0-30-0	28-7-90-1 4-1-15-0	21-4-76-2 8-2-34-0	27-8-80-1 5-0-25-0				10-2-41-1 5-0-24-0					12.2-4-28-1 3-0-39-0		2-0-8-0 7-0-34-1				136.2 39	476 208	23 7	9 1	
v. Derbyshire (Derby) 4-7 August	40-10-102-4 13-0-66-2	41-5-105-2 15.4-1-86-4	22-5-63-0 5-0-35-1	32-7-78-2 6-1-35-0				3-0-14-0	8-2-39-0 4-0-33-1			3-1-9-0							149 43.4	438 262	28 7	8 10	2
v. Yorkshire (Taunton) 10-13 August	29.3-7-96-6 19.5-7-51-2	21-3-47-0 12-4-32-0		30-10-98-2 18-5-42-2				7-1-27-0	7-1-37-1 3-2-1-0		13-1-79-1 9-4-43-0	3-1-10-0							110.3 61.5	406 179	12 10	10 4	
v. Worcestershire (Worcester) 16-19 August	31-4-119-0	38.2-9-146-2						18-3-81-3	16-1-93-1		20-3-112-1		6-1-38-0	14-0-79-1				5-0-15-0	148.2 –	696 –	13 –	8 –	
v. Essex (Colchester) 24-27 August		38-10-105-2		33-12-71-1				16.1-4-56-0						24-8-78-1		14-0-77-1		1-0-10-0	126.1 –	400 –	3 –	6 –	
v. Northamptonshire (Taunton) 7-10 September		37-5-118-0	25-2-118-4		21-4-74-1		21.2-2-105-2	19-2-74-1	17-0-82-2										140.2 –	574 –	3 –	10 –	
v. Derbyshire (Taunton) 21-24 September		31-9-70-0					31-5-134-4	16-2-74-0	28-1-122-1				15.5-1-67-1	28-3-111-0			18-2-88-0	4-0-19-0	171.5 –	707 –	22 –	7 –	1

	AR Caddick	ID Blackwell	RL Johnson	CK Langeveldt	AW Laraman	NAM McLean	GM Andrew	KA Parsons	WJ Durston	ST Jayasuriya	SRG Francis	M Burns	AV Suppiah	RJ Woodman	GC Smith	MK Munday	M Parsons	JC Hildreth
Overs	443.1	517.5	287.3	215.1	177	123	104.5	112.1	92	56.1	114.4	40.3	43.1	66	20	14	27	15
Maidens	94	107	52	59	21	27	14	19	8	7	16	5	8	11	4	0	3	0
Runs	1501	1569	1048	637	602	507	500	428	449	230	520	142	191	268	71	77	135	73
Wickets	54	28	20	15	13	12	11	7	6	5	5	3	2	2	1	1	0	0
Average	27.79	56.03	52.40	42.46	46.30	42.25	45.45	61.14	74.83	46.00	104.00	47.33	95.50	134.00	71.00	77.00	–	–

FIELDING

23	RJ Turner (22 ct, 1 st)
15	CM Gazzard
15	JC Hildreth
8	JD Francis
7	GC Smith
6	ME Trescothick
6	SRG Francis
5	KA Parsons
5	RL Johnson
5	ID Blackwell
5	WJ Durston
4	M Burns
4	MJ Wood
3	AR Caddick
2	ST Jayasuriya
2	AW Laraman
1	NAM McLean
1	GM Andrew
1	AV Suppiah
0	MK Munday
0	NJ Edwards
0	M Parsons
0	CK Langeveldt
0	RJ Woodman

SURREY CCC

FIRST-CLASS MATCHES
BATTING

FIRST-CLASS MATCHES	SA Newman	AD Brown	JN Batty	MR Ramprakash	M Akram	R Clarke	RS Clinton	ND Doshi	Azhar Mahmood	TJ Murtagh	J Ormond	MP Bicknell	GP Thorpe	IDK Salisbury	MA Butcher	Saqlain Mushtaq	JGE Benning	Harbhajan Singh	JW Dernbach	DJ Thornely	RJ Hamilton-Brown	AJ Hodd	NC Saker	Extras	Total	Wickets	Result	Points
v. Sussex	5	74*	70	152		10*	10						59											22	402	5		
(The Oval) 13-16 April																											D	12
v. Glamorgan	44	8	18	107	0	35	7	0		5*	0		5											19	248	10		
(Cardiff) 27-30 April	48	34	9	68*		5*	1						5											8	178	5	W	18
v. Nottinghamshire	44	9	16	0	4*	14		0			15	28	9				56							22	217	10		
(The Oval) 6-9 May	17	21	27	107	27*	14		33			35	59	0				20							44	404	10	L	3
v. Glamorgan	117	122	25	2	0	84	1	0			2	17*					57							17	444	10		
(The Oval) 11-14 May	219	42*		97		34	24																	9	425	4	W	22
v. Kent	21	56	34	4	1*	124	33	16				2			3	14								16	324	10		
(Tunbridge Wells) 25-28 May	167	29	4*		3*	105										3								22	333	4	D	10
v. Warwickshire	4	40	84*	39	4	12	84			23	9	11						0						30	340	10		
(Whitgift School) 1-4 June	37	14	31	18		29				74*	20	58						15*						14	310	7	D	10
v. Middlesex	8	152*	45	28*		73				8	4	33	4					0		81				24	460	10		
(Lord's) 8-11 June																											D	12
v. Hampshire	111	28	10	2*	16	30					7	26	10					25		73				23	361	10		
(The Rose Bowl) 15-17 June																											W	21
v. Gloucestershire	82	7	55			17	66	0*	89		33	76	73					84						21	603	10		
(Bristol) 8-11 July	6	18*				17	26		26				3*											14	84	3	D	12
v. Kent		107	50	97		18	0	0*	41		2*		95	15										27	452	8		
(Guildford) 20-23 July		34	55	62	0	7	45	4	25		2*		47	20										49	350	10	L	8
v. Nottinghamshire	15	28	0	42	0	0	8	4*	19	7		0												13	136	10		
(Trent Bridge) 26-29 July	40	18	32	7		127*	15		7			37*												9	292	6	D	7
v. Sussex	1	0	16	97	16	34	0	0	57*	6									1					20	248	10		
(Hove) 3-5 August	74	1	15	12	9	75	12	0	41	9									1*					5	254	10	L	8
v. Bangladesh A	8					56								59*	5		124				5	57*		22	336	5		
(The Oval) 10-12 August	48					22								44*	90		51				9	55*	0	13	332	6	D	
v. Gloucestershire	14	35	56	192	4*		10	0	0	66			36	6	8									36	463	10		
(The Oval) 16-19 August																											D	12
v. Hampshire	71	8	124	6	0		0	0	49	24					75	4*								17	378	10		
(The Oval) 24-27 August	7	42	33	37	0	51	26	0	0	44*					45	2								15	302	10	D	10
v. Warwickshire	12	1	3	16	12	63			24	30					30	31			0*					3	225	10		
(Edgbaston) 10-13 September	15		76*	126	45										27	10								14	313	5	D	8
v. Middlesex	51	30*	73	252	22				204*						5									49	686	5		
(The Oval) 21-24 September																											W	20

	SA Newman	AD Brown	JN Batty	MR Ramprakash	M Akram	R Clarke	RS Clinton	ND Doshi	Azhar Mahmood	TJ Murtagh	J Ormond	MP Bicknell	GP Thorpe	IDK Salisbury	MA Butcher	Saqlain Mushtaq	JGE Benning	Harbhajan Singh	JW Dernbach	DJ Thornely	RJ Hamilton-Brown	AJ Hodd	NC Saker
Matches	16	16	16	14	14	13	13	11	9	9	9	8	8	5	5	5	4	4	3	2	1	1	1
Innings	27	26	25	23	15	22	22	14	13	11	11	11	12	5	8	5	7	5	3	2	2	2	1
Not Out	0	5	3	2	5	4	0	3	2	3	2	2	1	2	0	1	0	1	2	0	0	2	0
Highest Score	219	152*	124	252	27*	127*	105	33	204*	74*	35	76	95	59*	90	31	124	84	1*	81	9	57*	0
Runs	1286	958	961	1568	79	776	672	93	582	296	129	347	346	141	283	55	325	124	2	154	14	112	0
Average	47.62	45.61	43.68	74.66	7.90	43.11	30.54	8.45	52.90	37.00	14.33	38.55	31.45	47.00	35.37	13.75	46.42	31.00	2.00	77.00	7.00	-	0.00
100s	4	3	1	6	0	2	1	0	1	0	0	0	0	0	0	0	1	0	0	0	0	0	0
50s	4	2	8	5	0	3	5	0	2	2	0	3	3	1	2	0	3	1	0	2	0	2	0
Catches/Stumpings	14/0	19/0	50/4	8/0	1/0	16/0	8/0	1/0	10/0	4/0	2/0	4/0	1/0	4/0	3/0	3/0	1/0	2/0	1/0	1/0	1/0	1/0	0/0

Home Ground: The Brit Oval
Address: The Brit Oval, Kennington, London, SE11 5SS
Tel: 0207 582 6660
Fax: 0207 735 7769
Email: enquiries@surreycricket.com
Directions: *By road:* The Brit Oval is located south of the Thames in Kennington on the A202, near the junction with the A3 and A24, just south of Vauxhall Bridge and 10 minutes from Victoria and Waterloo (Eurostar). *By rail:* Take South West Trains to Vauxhall which is a short walk from the ground. The station is well served by trains from throughout Surrey and Hampshire as well as from the Greater London area. Connections include Clapham Junction and Waterloo.

Capacity: 16,500
Other grounds used: Guildford, Whitgift School
Year formed: 1845

Chief Executive: Paul Sheldon
Cricket Manager: Steve Rixon
Captain: Mark Butcher/Mark Ramprakash/Graham Thorpe
County colours: Blue, white and yellow

Website:
www.surreycricket.com

Honours
County Championship
1890, 1891, 1892, 1894, 1895, 1899, 1914, 1952, 1953, 1954, 1955, 1956, 1957, 1958, 1971, 1999, 2000, 2002
Joint Champions 1950
Sunday League/NCL
1996, 2003
Benson & Hedges Cup
1974, 1997, 2001
Gillette Cup/NatWest/C&G Trophy
1982, 1992
Twenty20 Cup
2003

SURREY CCC

FIRST-CLASS MATCHES
BOWLING

FIRST-CLASS MATCHES	M Akram	J Ormond	MP Bicknell	Azhar Mahmood	ND Doshi	Harbhajan Singh	R Clarke	Saqlain Mushtaq	TJ Murtagh	IDK Salisbury	JGE Benning	JW Dernbach	DJ Thornely	NC Saker	MR Ramprakash	AD Brown	MA Butcher	RS Clinton	SA Newman	Overs	Total	Byes/Leg-byes	Wickets	Run outs
v. Sussex (The Oval) 13–16 April	25-2-104-2	26-9-67-3		18-5-59-1			22.1-2-91-4		12-1-28-0											103.1	370	21	10	
																				–	–	–	–	
v. Glamorgan (Cardiff) 27–30 April	16.3-3-67-4	19.1-4-62-2			7-2-21-1		13-2-64-1	8.3-3-32-2												64.1	250	4	10	
	7.5-0-62-2	18.4-4-63-7			12-4-17-1		4-1-14-0											4.1-0-6-0		46.4	173	11	10	
v. Nottinghamshire (The Oval) 6–9 May	34-1-155-1	21-1-88-2	28-1-156-2		24-2-126-0		14-1-64-1				11-0-73-1				2-0-6-0					134	692	19	7	
																				–	–	–	–	
v. Glamorgan (The Oval) 11–14 May	17-3-98-1	18-7-45-1		19.5-3-74-6	9-2-32-0		9-0-61-2				2-0-29-0									74.5	345	6	10	
	12.1-1-63-4	12-3-47-1		17-5-55-2	6-0-27-0		8-1-46-3													55.1	248	10	10	
v. Kent (Tunbridge Wells) 25–28 May	20-6-51-0		24-10-31-4		13.4-1-58-3		12-2-45-0			7-2-16-0	16-1-57-3									92.4	262	4	10	
	17.2-3-55-1		17.4-3-74-1		31-1-124-1					19-1-85-0	23-2-94-1							5-1-23-0		113	467	12	4	
v. Warwickshire (Whitgift School) 1–4 June	12-4-51-5	14-5-37-2	7-1-40-0			20-4-57-2			4-0-21-0											57	209	3	10	1
	12-5-25-0	23-4-68-2	16-6-39-0			26-9-60-1			5-2-6-0									1-0-10-0		83	222	14	3	
v. Middlesex (Lord's) 8–11 June		30-6-98-3	31.4-5-116-4			35-10-87-2			26-5-86-1				12-3-36-0					7-1-32-0	3-0-17-0	134.4	437	14	10	
		15-2-67-2	20-4-73-1			10-2-37-1			17-1-77-0				10-0-40-2							82	353	10	6	
v. Hampshire (The Rose Bowl) 15–17 June	7-3-27-1			7-1-20-1	16-2-36-6								3-1-11-0							49.5	146	10	10	
	9.3-2-41-5			6-1-26-0	8-1-47-2								3-0-21-0							33.3	160	5	10	
v. Gloucestershire (Bristol) 8–11 July		12-5-31-1	15-5-51-1	12-2-46-1	9-2-20-0	23.1-6-51-4	17-4-74-3													88.1	288	15	10	
		31.2-9-89-4	17-4-57-0	18-4-81-1	24-11-48-1	49-8-142-2	18-2-55-2													157.2	494	22	10	
v. Kent (Guildford) 20–23 July	24-2-114-1	28-1-109-1		24-2-104-3	30-3-111-3		9-0-53-0	14.5-0-71-2												129.5	572	10	10	
	6-0-30-2	9-0-68-0		8.1-0-40-1	7-0-58-2			4-0-25-1												34.1	232	11	6	
v. Nottinghamshire (Trent Bridge) 26–29 July	12-2-42-1		22-6-56-6	22-2-90-1		7-5-6-1	2-0-22-0		10-1-32-2											66	226	6	10	
	10.2-1-37-2		3.4-0-13-1	12-2-65-3					5-1-25-0											40	169	1	8	1
v. Sussex (Hove) 3–5 August	28-5-104-1			27-6-72-5	18-5-45-1			23.5-6-71-3				17-2-69-0						1-0-9-0		114.5	378	8	10	
	8.1-0-21-2			6-1-16-2	7-1-46-0			6-1-22-1				1-0-18-0								28.1	125	2	5	
v. Bangladesh A (The Oval) 10–12 August				20-6-75-2				29-5-82-3			7-0-40-1	12.2-2-68-2		16-3-62-1			1-0-6-0			85.2	336	3	10	1
				4-0-25-0				6-4-5-1				6-0-40-0		6-0-31-0			2-0-5-0			24	113	7	1	
v. Gloucestershire (The Oval) 16–19 August	17-3-63-2			18-7-63-3	20-5-75-2	28-3-110-1	13-2-37-2													96	350	2	10	
	9.5-0-67-0			16.1-5-52-2	21-5-68-3	25-3-82-1	5-1-19-0													77	294	6	6	
v. Hampshire (The Oval) 24–27 August	22-5-80-3			17-3-69-0	24.3-3-105-2	28-7-59-1	16-4-44-0													107.3	361	4	6	
																				–	–	–	–	
v. Warwickshire (Edgbaston) 10–13 September	11-2-42-0			18-4-70-3		5-0-32-0		28.5-4-80-4	12-1-38-1			12-1-66-2				5-0-14-0				86.5	338	10	10	
						6-0-10-0														11	26	2	0	
v. Middlesex (The Oval) 21–24 September	19-0-99-2		11-1-57-0			3-0-30-0	25-1-98-2	12-2-53-0	14.1-0-61-1											84.1	404	6	5	
	9-1-44-1					10-1-47-2	20-1-77-3	20-1-77-3	11.3-0-73-3											50.3	243	2	10	1

	M Akram	J Ormond	MP Bicknell	Azhar Mahmood	ND Doshi	Harbhajan Singh	R Clarke	Saqlain Mushtaq	TJ Murtagh	IDK Salisbury	JGE Benning	JW Dernbach	DJ Thornely	NC Saker	MR Ramprakash	AD Brown	MA Butcher	RS Clinton	SA Newman
Overs	366.4	301	251.5	227.2	294.1	187.1	152.1	189.5	163.2	82.3	59	48.2	28	22	2	5	3	18.1	3
Maidens	54	65	55	44	58	42	16	28	30	4	3	5	4	3	0	0	0	2	0
Runs	1542	1001	881	884	1087	517	708	593	563	359	293	261	108	93	6	14	11	80	17
Wickets	43	36	29	26	23	20	18	16	12	7	6	4	2	1	0	0	0	0	0
Average	35.86	27.80	30.37	34.00	47.26	25.85	39.33	37.06	46.91	51.28	48.83	65.25	54.00	93.00	–	–	–	–	–

FIELDING

54	JN Batty (50 ct, 4 st)
19	AD Brown
16	R Clarke
14	SA Newman
10	Azhar Mahmood
8	MR Ramprakash
8	RS Clinton
4	MP Bicknell
4	IDK Salisbury
4	TJ Murtagh
3	MA Butcher
3	Saqlain Mushtaq
2	J Ormond
2	Harbhajan Singh
1	GP Thorpe
1	M Akram
1	ND Doshi
1	JGE Benning
1	AJ Hodd
1	JW Dernbach
1	DJ Thornely
1	RJ Hamilton-Brown
0	NC Saker

SUSSEX CCC

FIRST-CLASS MATCHES
BATTING

	MH Yardy	RR Montgomerie	CJ Adams	RJ Kirtley	MJ Prior	Mushtaq Ahmed	MW Goodwin	RSC Martin-Jenkins	JD Lewry	IJ Ward	Naved-ul-Hasan	CD Hopkinson	TR Ambrose	LJ Wright	MJG Davis	JJ van der Wath	SA Heather	CD Nash	Extras	Total	Wickets	Result	Points
v. Loughborough UCCE	46	140	1	2*			45	0		150		31	38		2				35	490	9		
(Hove) 9-11 April																						D	
v. Surrey	111	22	5	23*	59	14	31	40	5	22			15						23	370	10		
(The Oval) 13-16 April																						D	9
v. Hampshire	104	5	29	1*	4	0	87	2	2	3					5				10	252	10		
(Hove) 20-23 April	13	7	79*	17	12	36	28	0	0	86					1				33	312	10	D	9
v. Nottinghamshire	54	4	46	7	65	12	33	66*	17	21						20			34	379	10		
(Trent Bridge) 27-30 April	0	1	3	0*	0	16	41	49	0	22						19			8	159	10	L	6
v. Warwickshire	88	3	67	30	4	30*	108	21	0	3						34			24	412	10		
(Hove) 10-12 May																						W	21
v. Bangladesh	257	49			51							64	78	1		16*	7		26	549	7		
(Hove) 15-17 May																						W	
v. Middlesex	9	6	72	14	41	57	67	25	12*	6						0			23	332	10		
(Hove) 25-28 May	5	52	9	4*	42	0	88	32	0*	24						6			24	286	9	D	10
v. Glamorgan	38	184*	32		30		158			35						9*			11	497	5		
(Swansea) 1-4 June																						D	12
v. Nottinghamshire	31	0	58	9*	103	11	39	37	14				0	27					26	355	10		
(Arundel Castle) 15-18 June	7	16	120*		8		102*												3	256	3	D	11
v. Kent	6	21	83	21*		7	63	2	4	100	23		13						35	378	10		
(Canterbury) 10-13 July	34	17	31	0		4	26	6	1*	3	6		12						15	155	10	W	21
v. Hampshire	0	64	41	0	24	21*	49		5	27	39	25							21	316	10		
(The Rose Bowl) 20-23 July	34	1	21	3*	1	3	71		1	60	25	0							15	235	10	L	6
v. Gloucestershire	20	32	5	8*	6	4	16		23		13		31	0					33	191	10		
(Hove) 26-29 July	106	0	61	1*	3	0	43		6		2		10	15					20	267	10	D	7
v. Surrey	65	68	2	0	18	14	25	88			26*	24		26					22	378	10		
(Hove) 3-5 August	35	4	5		66*	4	5*					2							4	125	5	W	21
v. Gloucestershire	13	25	66	0*	52	22	51	35			6	59			24				12	365	10		
(Cheltenham) 10-12 August	59*	37	8		109		5				8*	35							3	264	5	W	21
v. Middlesex	179	27	17	9*	38	7	20	8			139	10			50				18	522	10		
(Lord's) 16-17 August																						W	22
v. Warwickshire	75	0	66	10*	13	5	150	43			34	4		8					20	428	10		
(Edgbaston) 25-28 August	9	11	8	6	7	0	16	27*			2	23		12					5	126	10	L	8
v. Glamorgan	22	4	84	12	15	7	59	35*		48	19				2				10	317	10		
(Hove) 7-8 September	2*	18*								10									5	35	1	W	20
v. Kent	43	7	41	17	4	90*		20			4	7	44	37					34	348	10		
(Hove) 21-23 September	55*	26										57	3*						10	151	2	W	20
Matches	18	18	17	17	16	16	15	15	12	10	9	8	7	7	6	5	1	1					
Innings	30	30	27	23	25	22	25	20	16	16	14	13	10	8	6	7	1	0					
Not Out	3	2	2	13	1	3	1	4	3	0	2	0	1	0	0	2	0	0					
Highest Score	257	184*	120*	30	109	90*	158	88	23	150	139	64	78	37	50	34	7	0					
Runs	1520	851	1060	194	775	360	1380	586	90	620	346	341	244	126	84	104	7	0					
Average	56.29	30.39	42.40	19.40	32.29	18.94	57.50	36.62	6.92	38.75	28.83	26.23	27.11	15.75	14.00	20.80	7.00	-					
100s	5	2	1	0	2	0	4	0	0	1	0	0	0	0	0	0	0	0					
50s	6	3	9	0	5	2	7	2	0	2	0	3	1	0	1	0	0	0					
Catches/Stumpings	16/0	11/0	23/0	8/0	43/1	4/0	8/0	4/0	3/0	3/0	5/0	3/0	14/2	5/0	0/0	1/0	0/0	1/0					

Home Ground: Hove
Address: County Ground, Eaton Road, Hove, BN3 3AN
Tel: 0871 2822000
Fax: 01273 771549
Email: simon.dyke@sussexcricket.co.uk
Directions: *By rail:* Hove station is a 10-minute walk. *By road:* Follow AA signs. Street parking at no cost.
Capacity: 5,500

Other grounds used: Horsham, Arundel Castle
Year formed: 1839

Chief Executive: Hugh Griffiths
Director of Cricket: Peter Moores
Captain: Chris Adams
County colours: Red, black and white

Honours
County Championship
2003
Sunday League/NCL
1982
Gillette Cup/NatWest/C&G Trophy
1963, 1964, 1978, 1986

Website:
www.sussexcricket.co.uk

SUSSEX CCC

FIRST-CLASS MATCHES

BOWLING

	Mushtaq Ahmed	RJ Kirtley	Naved-ul-Hasan	JD Lewry	RSC Martin-Jenkins	LJ Wright	JJ van der Wath	MH Yardy	MJG Davis	CJ Adams	RR Montgomerie	IJ Ward	CD Hopkinson	Overs	Total	Byes/Leg-byes	Wickets	Run outs
v. Loughborough UCCE		19-5-56-3		20-6-42-3	20-8-40-2	11-2-32-0			27.2-7-52-2					97.2	237	15	10	
(Hove) 9-11 April		8-2-25-1		8-5-12-2	5-2-11-1			8-2-21-0	6-3-5-0	2-0-4-0	1-1-0-0		5-0-11-0	43	103	14	5	1
v. Surrey	28.2-3-126-1	31-14-65-1		26-8-96-2	20-5-72-0			4-0-24-1						109.2	402	19	5	
(The Oval) 13-16 April														-	-	-	-	
v. Hampshire	25-5-84-2	24-5-54-4		19-1-62-1	18-8-51-3				4-0-19-0					90	280	5	10	
(Hove) 20-23 April	24-3-89-3	27-3-88-4		13-2-40-1	10-3-32-0									74	267	18	8	
v. Nottinghamshire	29-1-131-1	24.4-2-96-2		28-2-99-1	21-4-53-0		22-5-113-2							124.4	509	17	8	2
(Trent Bridge) 27-30 April		3-0-15-0		2.5-0-15-0										5.5	30	0	0	
v. Warwickshire	24-4-73-4	6-0-16-0		21.2-9-46-5	8-5-8-1		3-0-22-0							62.2	179	14	10	
(Hove) 10-12 May	17.1-2-65-4	11-5-17-3		7-2-18-2	8-1-17-0		8-1-22-1							51.1	146	7	10	
v. Bangladesh				10-1-42-3		9-4-18-2	13-5-21-3	2-0-4-0	10-2-26-1				3-0-6-0	47	127	10	10	
(Hove) 15-17 May				11-4-14-0		18-3-56-1	12-3-31-3	22.2-6-83-5						63.2	196	12	10	
v. Middlesex	30.5-3-117-1	32-8-80-6		27-3-92-1	18-1-45-2			18-6-54-0	1-0-1-0					126.5	401	12	10	
(Hove) 25-28 May	24.3-2-77-3	12-2-37-1		16-5-65-6	4-0-29-0			7-2-25-0						63.3	244	11	10	
v. Glamorgan	13-1-77-3	11-1-49-1		21-4-77-6	6-0-46-0			9-2-38-0	1-0-5-0					61	301	9	10	
(Swansea) 1-4 June	15-0-92-0	10-3-23-0		11-1-42-0	6-0-28-0			12-0-73-1	16-1-62-2	4-0-17-0	5-0-13-0	1-1-0-0		80	354	4	3	
v. Nottinghamshire	22-4-71-0	28-7-87-2		24.1-3-74-6	24-4-74-1	8-2-39-1								106.1	360	10	10	
(Arundel Castle) 15-18 June														-	-	-	-	
v. Kent	34-2-134-3	19-6-73-1	19.1-1-46-3	19-5-63-2	11-2-24-1									102.1	348	8	10	
(Canterbury) 10-13 July	15-3-58-4	10-3-20-2	12.2-3-28-4	7-3-10-0										44.2	119	3	10	
v. Hampshire	22-5-66-2	21-8-68-2	26-7-82-3	26.2-8-50-3				3-0-15-0					4-1-25-0	102.2	309	3	10	
(The Rose Bowl) 20-23 July	23.2-9-91-2	24-10-67-5	17.4-3-73-2	12-2-39-1										76.4	277	7	10	
v. Gloucestershire		17-5-39-2	13-5-26-4	14-4-30-2		12-4-36-2								56	142	11	10	
(Hove) 26-29 July	19-10-25-3	20-8-41-1	19.4-8-53-2	6.2-2-16-1		9-0-33-1								74	192	24	8	
v. Surrey	11-1-33-3	16-5-52-2		16-2-62-0	15-5-52-2	11-3-33-3								69	248	16	10	
(Hove) 3-5 August	21-1-96-3	20-10-39-2		21-5-70-4	14-3-45-1									76	254	4	10	
v. Gloucestershire	23-2-65-6	9-1-25-0		15.1-3-53-4	9-5-8-0				16-2-53-0					72.1	224	20	10	
(Cheltenham) 10-12 August	15.3-1-46-3	8-2-32-1		15-1-81-5	7-2-12-0									45.3	179	8	10	1
v. Middlesex	14-5-24-3	7-0-27-0		9-1-42-3	11.4-2-31-4									41.4	128	4	10	
(Lord's) 16-17 August	16.2-5-44-6	13-1-54-0		17-4-54-4										46.2	162	10	10	
v. Warwickshire	34-5-127-3	31-2-99-3		33.1-5-135-1	22-7-51-1	16-3-39-2								136.1	475	24	10	
(Edgbaston) 25-28 August	12-1-37-2	12.1-2-27-3		17-2-55-4	9-1-30-0	9-2-24-1								59.1	180	7	10	
v. Glamorgan	25.3-3-89-5	15-4-42-4		19-5-51-0	3-0-18-0			4-0-15-1	11-2-22-0					77.3	255	18	10	
(Hove) 7-8 September	9-0-29-5	8-0-22-0		11-1-41-5										28	96	4	10	
v. Kent	27.4-5-81-2	19-5-53-4		20-0-83-4	7-1-25-0	5-0-11-0								78.4	257	4	10	
(Hove) 21-23 September	26-3-92-3	9.2-1-46-3		12-2-41-2	7-2-22-1	3-0-8-0		6-1-22-0						63.2	238	8	10	1

	Mushtaq Ahmed	RJ Kirtley	Naved-ul-Hasan	JD Lewry	RSC Martin-Jenkins	LJ Wright	JJ van der Wath	MH Yardy	MJG Davis	CJ Adams	RR Montgomerie	IJ Ward	CD Hopkinson
Overs	600.5	525.1	313.1	350	283.4	111	104	67.2	74.2	6	6	1	12
Maidens	82	130	58	80	71	23	24	10	16	0	1	1	1
Runs	2139	1533	1076	1044	824	329	399	252	177	21	13	0	42
Wickets	80	63	54	48	20	13	10	9	3	0	0	0	0
Average	26.73	24.33	19.92	21.75	41.20	25.30	39.90	28.00	59.00	-	-	-	-

FIELDING

44	MJ Prior (43 ct, 1 st)
23	CJ Adams
16	MH Yardy
16	TR Ambrose (14 ct, 2 st)
11	RR Montgomerie
8	RJ Kirtley
8	MW Goodwin
5	LJ Wright
5	Naved-ul-Hasan
4	Mushtaq Ahmed
4	RSC Martin-Jenkins
3	IJ Ward
3	JD Lewry
3	CD Hopkinson
1	CD Nash
1	JJ van der Wath
0	MJG Davis
0	SA Heather

WARWICKSHIRE CCC

FIRST–CLASS MATCHES
BATTING

Match	UJ Trott	NV Knight	AGR Loudon	DR Brown	T Frost	NM Carter	MJ Powell	JO Troughton	IJ Westwood	HH Streak	IR Bell	D Pretorius	M Ntini	JE Anyon	NA Warren	LC Parker	N Tahir	AF Giles	MA Wagh	MM Ali	KJ Piper	T Mees	PW Harrison	SM Eustace	Extras	Total	Wickets	Result	Points
v. MCC	75	115	7*	27*			28				14								66						13	345	5		
(Lord's) 8-11 April	72*		5		91		32				20														5	225	4	L	
v. Glamorgan	10	44		122		39	146			41*	96							20	28						18	564	8		
(Edgbaston) 13-16 April																												W	22
v. Kent	19	100	40	22	5	6*	4			12	63				0			18							20	309	10		
(Canterbury) 20-23 April	20	0	64	13	82*	9	21			0	9				0*			0							15	233	9	D	10
v. Middlesex	21	3	39	12	8	7	7			17	231	0*						62							23	430	10		
(Edgbaston) 27-30 April	11	29	8*				5				47*														15	115	3	W	22
v. Sussex	29	45	6	9	7	1	45			0	1	1						19*							16	179	10		
(Hove) 10-12 May	7	17	13	18	23	1	13			0*	35	12						0							7	146	10	L	2
v. Cambridge UCCE	150*		5				32	0	9								32			57			0*		11	296	6		
(Fenner's) 21-23 May			46				8*		73*																0	127	1	W	
v. Hampshire	28	51	18	12	2	6	5	22	68	22							5*								26	265	10		
(Stratford) 25-26 May		39*							3*																2	44	0	W	19
v. Surrey	41	37	58	0	3	0	18	12	18	19							0*								3	209	10		
(Whitgift School) 1-4 June	37	35	61*				65*		2																22	222	3	D	8
v. Gloucestershire	128	19	47	20	35	20	1	60		28	79				5*										31	473	10		
(Gloucester) 10-12 June																												W	22
v. Kent	0	8	14	10	23	82	49	1		51	1				2*										11	252	10		
(Edgbaston) 15-18 June	12	26	37	12	7*	15	16	11		4	0				4										9	153	10	L	3
v. Nottinghamshire	17	57	2	0	4	11		24	36			22		0		34*									12	219	10		
(Edgbaston) 20-22 July	1	11	4	17	24	4		6	33			0		8*		18									7	133	10	L	4
v. Middlesex	6	13	27	92	27	4		7	0			21*	12			43									20	272	10		
(Lord's) 3-6 August	0	75	95*	19	5	17		119	5							27*									21	383	7	W	19
v. Glamorgan	152	36	42	64	3	36*		68	106							19*									19	545	7		
(Colwyn Bay) 10-12 August		2*							0*																1	3	0	W	22
v. Nottinghamshire	31	5	8	34*	2	0		0	49				4	0		17									6	156	10		
(Trent Bridge) 14-16 August	19		46	6	10	45*		16	17				0	2		37									9	207	10	L	3
v. Sussex	210	69	32	21	22	39	3		29				18	0*		4									28	475	10		
(Edgbaston) 25-28 August	16	15	1	34	40	2	36		8				9	0*		1									18	180	10	W	22
v. Hampshire	1	116	10	24	19		13	11	0				27*	10			4								23	258	10		
(The Rose Bowl) 30 August-1 September	27	24	16	2	0		1	76	48				4	0*			14								20	232	10	L	4
v. Surrey	9	117	60	0	13	6	60	9	45				0	1*											18	338	10		
(Edgbaston) 10-13 September		14*							10*																2	26	0	D	10
v. Gloucestershire	9	6	19	10	27	18		84	10		2			2*			18								3	208	10		
(Edgbaston) 21-24 September	3	94	4	16	0	21		57	55		37			6*			22*								5	320	9	W	18
Matches	18	17	17	17	16	15	13	12	11	9	8	6	6	6	6	5	5	4	2	1	1	1	1	1					
Innings	30	30	30	26	25	23	22	18	22	11	14	6	8	11	5	9	7	6	2	1	0	0	1	0					
Not Out	2	3	4	2	2	3	2	0	4	2	1	2	1	7	3	3	3	1	0	0	0	0	1	0					
Highest Score	210	117	95*	122	91	82	146	119	106	51	231	22	27*	10	5*	43	32	62	66	57	0	0	0*	0					
Runs	1161	1222	834	616	482	389	608	583	624	194	635	56	74	29	11	200	95	119	94	57	0	0	0	0					
Average	41.46	45.25	32.07	25.66	20.95	19.45	30.40	32.38	34.66	21.55	48.84	14.00	10.57	7.25	5.50	33.33	23.75	23.80	47.00	57.00	-	-	-	-					
100s	4	4	0	1	0	0	1	1	1	0	1	0	0	0	0	0	0	0	0	0	0	0	0	0					
50s	2	5	5	2	2	1	2	5	3	1	3	0	0	0	0	0	0	1	1	1	0	0	0	0					
Catches/Stumpings	32/0	9/0	12/0	14/0	42/1	7/0	8/0	6/0	6/0	8/0	6/0	3/0	1/0	3/0	0/0	1/0	0/0	0/0	0/0	2/0	2/2	0/0	1/0	1/0					

Home Ground: Edgbaston
Address: County Ground, Edgbaston, Birmingham, B5 7QU
Tel: 0870 0621902
Fax: 0121 4467516
Email: info@thebears.co.uk
Directions: *By rail:* New Street station, Birmingham.
By road: M6 to A38(M) to city centre, then follow signs to county ground.
Capacity: 20,000

Other grounds used: Stratford upon Avon
Year formed: 1882

Chief Executive: Dennis Amiss MBE
Diector of Coaching: John Inverarity
Captain: Nick Knight
County colours: Blue and white

Honours
County Championship
1911, 1951, 1972, 1994, 1995, 2004
Sunday League/NCL
1980, 1994, 1997
Benson & Hedges Cup
1994, 2002
Gillette Cup/NatWest/C&G Trophy
1989, 1993, 1995

Website:
www.thebears.co.uk

WARWICKSHIRE CCC

FIRST-CLASS MATCHES

BOWLING

	DR Brown	NM Carter	AGR Loudon	HH Streak	AF Giles	M Ntini	JE Anyon	D Pretorius	N Tahir	IJL Trott	NA Warren	IR Bell	JO Troughton	MJ Powell	IJ Westwood	T Mees	MM Ali	Overs	Total	Byes/Leg-byes	Wickets	Run outs
v. MCC (Lord's) 8–11 April	11-3-40-0 12-1-50-1		19-3-80-0 11-0-74-0	14-3-39-0 9-0-45-1			6-1-18-0			7-1-27-0 4-0-13-1	10.5-2-40-1 10-1-58-0	5-1-13-1 8-1-49-0		4-0-14-0				76.5 54	275 296	4 7	2 3	
v. Glamorgan (Edgbaston) 13–16 April	9-4-23-1 7-1-46-1	4-0-24-0 12-1-48-1		14-3-45-0 17-4-46-2	17.3-1-44-6 27-4-85-3						11-1-40-3 4-0-26-0	8-3-18-0 15-2-64-3						63.3 82	198 323	4 8	10 10	
v. Kent (Canterbury) 20–23 April	15-2-63-1 19-5-39-0	17-1-59-1 18-4-69-2	8-0-25-0 1-0-4-0	19.2-5-53-2 14-0-49-0	29-6-86-5 25-2-71-3					1-0-8-0	10-2-32-0 15-3-48-1	6-0-16-0 4-0-17-0						105.2 96	347 308	5 11	10 6	1
v. Middlesex (Edgbaston) 27–30 April	15-5-40-1 13-2-27-1	13.1-6-37-3	13-3-40-1 24-2-67-3	18-6-64-2 11-3-18-0	12-3-31-1 42.2-9-91-6			15-1-60-2 12-1-35-0				1-0-6-0						87.1 102.2	298 246	20 8	10 10	
v. Sussex (Hove) 10–12 May	34-10-71-1	31-10-60-2	11-2-27-1	28-8-50-2	11-1-37-0			25.5-4-88-3		12-0-39-0		4-0-18-0						156.5 –	412 –	22 –	10 –	1
v. Cambridge UCCE (Fenner's) 21–23 May			2-2-0-0 15-1-48-3							5-0-18-1 8-0-31-0	6-2-21-0 15-1-42-2	8-1-43-0 9.1-1-34-2	9-1-63-2	7-4-16-1		5-2-26-0 5-0-23-0	2-0-15-0	26 70.1	109 296	1 24	1 10	
v. Hampshire (Stratford) 25–26 May	14-3-59-4 13-0-51-3	15-5-18-1 4-1-9-0		17-6-39-2 13-5-31-6				13-2-45-2 7-2-30-1	2.5-1-16-1									61.5 37	184 124	7 3	10 10	
v. Surrey (Whitgift School) 1–4 June	26-10-63-3 11-1-38-0	19-3-77-3 14-4-43-1	16-2-39-1 25-1-89-1	26-4-98-2 12-4-37-0				9-1-42-1 8-0-28-3	8-2-35-1						3-0-30-1			96 81	340 310	21 10	10 7	
v. Gloucestershire (Gloucester) 10–12 June	24.5-7-51-4 15-6-29-2	21-6-57-4 10-2-40-1	7-0-27-1 15-1-33-1	22-7-42-1 15.5-6-44-6						9-1-23-0	10-5-16-0 7-2-37-0	5-2-18-0	4-3-3-0 4-0-22-0					102.5 66.5	254 217	17 12	10 10	
v. Kent (Edgbaston) 15–18 June	28-4-71-1	31.5-1-127-1	43.1-7-130-3	4.1-3-8-0						15-2-37-0	24-2-104-2	14-5-45-2	7-0-37-0					167.1 –	569 –	10 –	10 –	1
v. Nottinghamshire (Edgbaston) 20–22 July	18-0-78-2	20-7-59-1 1-0-8-0	26.4-2-92-6				6-1-34-0	15-2-54-1 0.4-0-4-0					3-0-16-0					88.4 1.4	341 12	8 0	10 0	
v. Middlesex (Lord's) 3–6 August	6.1-0-27-1 9-2-31-1	19-1-58-0 14-0-67-0	16-0-66-2 21-2-71-2			17-3-79-4 22-1-69-5		20-0-85-2 16-2-56-2		6-0-18-0			2-0-10-0					78.1 90	323 330	8 8	10 10	1
v. Glamorgan (Colwyn Bay) 10–12 August	17-2-58-4 17-3-54-1	16-4-69-3 22-4-73-3	1-0-4-0 21-5-57-1			13.1-2-49-1 13-2-59-2		11-2-46-2 5-0-18-0			4-0-19-2		6.1-1-24-1					58.1 88.1	239 308	13 4	10 10	
v. Nottinghamshire (Trent Bridge) 14–16 August	30.3-3-128-5	25-3-96-3	22-2-91-0			22-4-96-1	16-0-86-1			3-0-14-0								118.3 –	514 –	3 –	10 –	
v. Sussex (Edgbaston) 25–28 August	22-2-89-3 9-4-19-0	26.4-4-95-2 7-2-13-2	4-0-19-0 4-0-11-2			24-2-115-3 12-3-45-2			14-3-45-2 14-2-33-4	11-0-57-0								101.4 46	428 126	8 5	10 10	
v. Hampshire (The Rose Bowl) 3 August–1 September	30-7-111-2		28-3-93-0			35-9-98-2	20-4-103-0	17-1-71-0		17-2-65-2			4-1-11-0					151 –	576 –	24 –	6 –	
v. Surrey (Edgbaston) 10–13 September	22-6-58-3 16-3-41-2	10-4-54-2 10-0-40-0	20-3-81-1			13-0-46-1 21-3-65-1			15-1-64-4 13-2-44-0	9-3-15-0			3.1-0-19-1					60 92.1	225 313	3 8	10 5	
v. Gloucestershire (Edgbaston) 21–24 September	16-10-27-2 16-4-58-0	16-6-30-4 14-4-48-1	11.3-2-22-2 31-5-66-6				7-2-16-1	5-2-10-1 11-3-38-2					2-0-15-1					55.3 74	118 229	13 4	10 10	

	DR Brown	NM Carter	AGR Loudon	HH Streak	AF Giles	M Ntini	JE Anyon	D Pretorius	N Tahir	IJL Trott	NA Warren	IR Bell	JO Troughton	MJ Powell	IJ Westwood	T Mees	MM Ali
Overs	495.3	410.4	416.2	254.2	163.5	192.1	105	126.3	83	129.5	119	70	44.2	11	3	10	2
Maidens	110	83	48	67	26	29	15	13	11	15	20	14	6	4	0	2	0
Runs	1540	1378	1356	708	445	721	425	464	313	449	478	264	220	30	30	49	15
Wickets	50	41	37	26	24	22	12	12	11	9	9	6	5	1	1	0	0
Average	**30.80**	**33.60**	**36.64**	**27.23**	**18.54**	**32.77**	**35.41**	**38.66**	**28.45**	**49.88**	**53.11**	**44.00**	**44.00**	**30.00**	**30.00**	**–**	**–**

FIELDING

43	T Frost (42 ct, 1 st)
32	IJL Trott
14	DR Brown
12	AGR Loudon
9	NV Knight
8	HH Streak
8	MJ Powell
7	NM Carter
6	IR Bell
6	JO Troughton
6	IJ Westwood
4	KJ Piper (2 ct, 2 st)
3	D Pretorius
3	JE Anyon
2	MM Ali
1	M Ntini
1	LC Parker
1	PW Harrison
1	SM Eustace
0	AF Giles
0	MA Wagh
0	T Mees
0	NA Warren
0	N Tahir

WORCESTERSHIRE CCC

FIRST–CLASS MATCHES
BATTING

	BF Smith	SC Moore	GA Hick	MS Mason	VS Solanki	GJ Batty	Kabir Ali	DJ Pipe	SM Davies	Z de Bruyn	RW Price	SD Peters	MN Malik	WPUJC Vaas	DKH Mitchell	Shoaib Akhtar	DH Wigley	CH Gayle	A Sheriyar	SA Wedge	DA Leatherdale	SA Khalid	Extras	Total	Wickets	Result	Points
v. Derbyshire	48	19	80	18	0	47		33				55					7*		3*		14		26	350	9		
(Derby) 13-16 April		26*										39*											6	71	0	W	21
v. Durham	5	46	26	13	1	4		6				30		26			2*		5				7	171	10		
(The Riverside) 20-21 April	3	28	6	0	8	15		23				9		42*			0		5				7	146	10	L	3
v. Lancashire	0	0	176	18	4	13	21	9				27		22			2*						14	306	10		
(Worcester) 27-30 April	37	1	57	0*	52	14	2	7				0	3										18	191	10	L	6
v. Loughborough UCCE	0	0						23	6	81	8	0	1		5					0*		0	9	133	10		
(Kidderminster) 8-10 May	68	27						4	37	3	20	8	1		12					0*		20	9	209	10	L	
v. Derbyshire	0	246	12	4	27	1	20	80*		25		2		45									16	478	10		
(Worcester) 11-14 May		28*	62*									2											8	100	1	W	22
v. Essex	100	39	19	31*	31	54	53	3		0		10	10										33	383	10		
(Chelmsford) 20-23 May		63*	76*					11				0											17	167	2	W	21
v. Durham	123	16	13	0*	0		7	12	4	2	20			45									25	267	10		
(Worcester) 1-4 June																										D	9
v. Somerset	140	86	55	2		16*		0	1	30	6	3*		45	4								35	423	10		
(Bath) 8-11 June	39*	66*	17						1														15	138	2	W	22
v. Leicestershire	45	41	13	4			47	0	67	5		3	20		63*								15	323	10		
(Leicester) 15-18 June	14	3	8	11*			0	49	13	0		3	13		10								4	128	10	L	6
v. Yorkshire	38	74	8	4		57	57	10	59	2		1*			20								15	345	10		
(Worcester) 8-11 July	1	26	22	24		29	20*	32	5	41			0		0								22	222	10	L	6
v. Northamptonshire	27	20	10	26	80	48	24		95	10	7					20*							14	381	10		
(Northampton) 20-23 July	57	17	0	5	22	24*	7		37	10	0					1							20	200	10	L	7
v. Australia	1	69	21	3	36		4	22*		4	0	0	16										11	187	10		
(Worcester) 30 July-1 August																										D	
v. Northamptonshire	38	62	0	30*	17	0	7	4		6		3				35							14	216	10		
(Worcester) 4-6 August	92	8	0	5	29	2	5	0		43		6*				19							13	222	10	L	4
v. Somerset	172	28				3	25		148	161	16	88			23*								32	696	8		
(Worcester) 16-19 August																										W	22
v. Lancashire	133	40	0	4	65			11	35		1*	6	2					43					36	376	10		
(Blackpool) 25-28 August	8	0	24	11	7			14	0		14	6	1*					8					20	113	10	L	6
v. Leicestershire	13	23	38	0	44	46	37*		25	4					0			51					9	290	10		
(Worcester) 30 August-2 September	87*	4	19		1	52*			29									57					9	258	5	D	9
v. Yorkshire	27	27	19	38	48	14	14		44				21*		1			29					26	308	10		
(Headingley) 7-10 September	0	30	27	16	74*	7	0		26				0		8			4					19	211	10	D	10
v. Essex	154*	191	17		24*										6								32	424	3		
(Worcester) 21-24 September	76	45	107		15	10*			26*						53								16	348	5	D	11
Matches	18	18	16	16	13	13	13	12	11	11	10	9	9	7	6	4	4	3	2	2	1	1					
Innings	30	33	29	23	21	20	18	19	19	16	13	16	14	10	10	7	4	6	3	2	1	2					
Not Out	3	4	2	5	2	4	2	2	1	0	1	1	5	1	2	1	3	0	1	2	0	0					
Highest Score	172	246	176	38	80	57	57	80*	148	161	20	88	21*	45	63*	35	7*	57	5	0*	14	20					
Runs	1546	1399	932	267	585	456	328	326	627	498	101	282	61	271	196	84	11	192	13	0	14	20					
Average	57.25	48.24	34.51	14.83	30.78	28.50	20.50	19.17	34.83	31.12	8.41	18.80	6.77	30.11	24.50	14.00	11.00	32.00	6.50	-	14.00	10.00					
100s	6	2	2	0	0	0	0	0	1	1	0	0	0	0	0	0	0	0	0	0	0	0					
50s	5	6	5	0	4	3	2	1	2	2	0	2	0	0	2	0	0	2	0	0	0	0					
Catches/Stumpings	20/0	11/0	36/0	2/0	9/0	10/0	9/0	43/2	11/3	10/0	6/0	6/0	0/0	3/0	6/0	1/0	2/0	6/0	0/0	0/0	0/0	0/0					

Home Ground: New Road, Worcester
Address: County Ground, New Road, Worcester, WR2 4QQ
Tel: 01905 748474
Fax: 01905 748005
Email: info@wccc.co.uk
Directions: From the M5 Junction 7, follow the brown 'broken stumps' logos to WCCC.
Capacity: 4,500

Other grounds used: None
Year formed: 1865

Chief Executive: Mark Newton
First XI Coach: Tom Moody
Captain: Vikram Solanki/Gareth Batty/Graeme Hick
County colours: Green, black and white

Honours
County Championship
1964, 1965, 1974, 1988, 1989
Sunday League/NCL
1971, 1987, 1988
Benson & Hedges Cup
1991
Gillette Cup/NatWest/C&G Trophy
1994

Website:
www.wccc.co.uk

WORCESTERSHIRE CCC

FIRST-CLASS MATCHES

BOWLING

Match	MS Mason	Kabir Ali	MN Malik	GJ Batty	RW Price	WPUJC Vaas	Shoaib Akhtar	DH Wigley	Z de Bruyn	A Sheriyar	SA Wedge	CH Gayle	SC Moore	DA Leatherdale	DKH Mitchell	BF Smith	VS Solanki	SA Khalid	Overs	Total	Byes/Leg-byes	Wickets	Run outs
v. Derbyshire (Derby) 13-16 April	10-6-6-2			5-1-7-1				15-2-53-3		20.5-6-48-3				9-3-18-1					59.5	135	3	10	
	24-11-30-1			38-9-87-5				20-6-68-4		16-2-68-0				8-1-29-0					106	285	3	10	
v. Durham (The Riverside) 20-21 April	29-12-65-1			20-6-51-1		26-6-65-3		10.5-1-39-3		20-5-62-2									105.5	286	4	10	
	5-1-12-2							6-0-15-1		2-0-3-0									13	32	2	3	
v. Lancashire (Worcester) 27-30 April	14-6-22-3	17-3-70-3		17-2-84-0		22-8-49-3		12-3-54-1					9-0-36-1						65	196	1	10	
	31.3-6-107-4	6-1-23-1				32-7-110-3													95.3	377	17	10	1
v. Loughborough UCCE (Kidderminster) 8-10 May			26-10-65-3		15-3-49-2				17-2-80-1		17.2-2-68-0							16-3-39-0	91.2	304	3	6	
			5.5-2-14-2						5-0-26-0										10.5	41	1	2	
v. Derbyshire (Worcester) 11-14 May	16-3-43-2	20.3-3-77-4		15-4-21-1				23-7-79-3	9-2-30-0										83.3	263	13	10	
	18-6-34-3	16-2-69-2		25-8-61-2				23.4-2-85-3	14-2-56-0										96.4	314	9	10	
v. Essex (Chelmsford) 20-23 May	14-1-48-4	14-2-55-2		10.5-2-26-3		12-4-33-0			14-2-54-1										64.5	220	4	10	
	23-6-66-3	18-4-49-2		14-2-51-3		27-10-73-2			18-2-71-0										100	329	10	10	
v. Durham (Worcester) 1-4 June	13-5-49-2	20.5-3-72-3			21-6-60-1	22-10-36-3			5-0-37-0										81.5	256	2	10	1
	11-5-25-0	8-0-43-1			9-1-36-0	6-1-8-0			16-4-61-1										50	180	7	2	
v. Somerset (Bath) 8-11 June	27-7-82-4		26-3-87-2	15-0-55-1	6-1-31-0	30-5-88-3			14-2-50-0										118	408	15	10	
	17-7-34-5		12-5-25-1		24-9-26-1	18-4-53-2			5-1-13-1										76	152	1	10	
v. Leicestershire (Leicester) 15-18 June	10-1-43-0		24.1-8-71-5		16-5-29-3	18-6-37-1			14-3-44-0										82.1	225	1	10	1
	4-0-21-0		16-4-74-3		27.2-10-64-4	26-10-63-2													73.2	238	16	10	1
v. Yorkshire (Worcester) 8-11 July	23.2-5-60-2	22-4-59-3	22-5-79-3	17-4-45-1					7-0-41-1										91.2	300	16	10	
	22.5-6-61-2	22-6-70-4	12-2-53-0	13-2-34-1					5-0-28-0										74.5	269	23	7	
v. Northamptonshire (Northampton) 20-23 July	18-5-61-2	17.4-2-87-2		15-3-51-0	2-0-2-0		14-3-47-6		9-2-36-0										75.4	299	15	10	
	10-4-30-0	12-1-56-3		24.1-5-99-3	32-6-92-3		13-3-67-1												91.1	364	20	10	
v. Australia (Worcester) 30 July-1 August	22-5-65-2	20-2-124-1	22-6-78-3					19-2-68-2			15-3-58-1								98	406	13	9	
	7-2-34-0	6-2-34-0	7-1-30-0					12-2-26-0			6-1-26-1								38	161	11	2	1
v. Northamptonshire (Worcester) 4-6 August	12-4-26-1	9-0-56-0	17-5-44-3	2-1-5-1			9.2-1-55-5				11-1-45-1								49.2	189	3	10	
	13-2-59-2	9-0-56-2	15-2-57-2	13-0-88-1			13.1-2-72-2												74.1	386	9	10	
v. Somerset (Worcester) 16-19 August	18-6-56-2	20-9-51-2	16.3-3-63-3	19-2-65-1	16-3-34-2						8-0-24-0								97.3	318	25	10	
	10-2-39-1	8.5-0-50-1	3-0-23-0	43-8-121-4	44-21-67-4														108.5	322	22	10	
v. Lancashire (Blackpool) 25-28 August	24-3-101-2	24-3-107-1	24-0-136-2		47-4-167-3							14-2-30-0	1-0-8-0				1-0-4-0		135	562	9	8	
	-	-	-		-														-	-	-	-	
v. Leicestershire (Worcester) 30 August-2 September	22-7-88-1	24-5-95-4		29-3-91-0	25.1-6-61-3		15-4-43-0					7-2-18-2							122.1	405	9	10	
	8-2-22-0	12-2-64-3		14-2-43-0	22-4-44-1		7-0-34-0					9-0-29-1							72	255	19	5	
v. Yorkshire (Headingley) 7-10 September	13-1-73-0	16-1-79-4	16-1-71-3	8-1-20-2			12-2-69-0					3-2-1-0							68	317	4	10	1
	7-0-24-0	9-0-40-1	6-1-32-1				3-0-18-0												25	125	11	2	
v. Essex (Worcester) 21-24 September		25-4-92-2		28-7-91-1	35-7-108-1	28.2-4-126-1			31-5-112-5				1-1-0-0		7-1-40-0	7-1-41-0	10-0-45-0		155.2	574	5	10	
						5-1-25-0			6-1-31-0						8-0-59-1				36	201	0	1	

	MS Mason	Kabir Ali	MN Malik	GJ Batty	RW Price	WPUJC Vaas	Shoaib Akhtar	DH Wigley	Z de Bruyn	A Sheriyar	SA Wedge	CH Gayle	SC Moore	DA Leatherdale	DKH Mitchell	BF Smith	VS Solanki	SA Khalid
Overs	496.4	376.5	270.3	385	372.3	285.4	86.3	97.1	192	58.5	54.2	33	11	17	15	7	11	16
Maidens	137	59	58	72	90	80	15	17	27	13	8	6	1	4	1	1	0	3
Runs	1486	1578	1002	1196	964	779	405	380	780	181	211	78	44	47	99	41	49	39
Wickets	53	51	36	32	30	28	14	13	8	5	5	3	1	1	1	0	0	0
Average	28.03	30.94	27.83	37.37	32.13	27.82	28.92	29.23	97.50	36.20	42.20	26.00	44.00	47.00	99.00	-	-	-

FIELDING

45	DJ Pipe (43 ct, 2 st)
36	GA Hick
20	BF Smith
14	SM Davies (11 ct, 3 st)
11	SC Moore
10	GJ Batty
10	Z de Bruyn
9	VS Solanki
9	Kabir Ali
6	SD Peters
6	CH Gayle
6	RW Price
6	DKH Mitchell
3	WPUJC Vaas
2	MS Mason
2	DH Wigley
1	Shoaib Akhtar
0	DA Leatherdale
0	A Sheriyar
0	MN Malik
0	SA Khalid
0	SA Wedge

YORKSHIRE CCC

FIRST–CLASS MATCHES

BATTING

	MJ Wood	A McGrath	C White	GJ Kruis	TT Bresnan	RKJ Dawson	PA Jaques	IJ Harvey	I Dawood	MJ Lumb	JJ Sayers	CEW Silverwood	MJ Hoggard	SM Guy	MAK Lawson	DJ Wainwright	RM Pyrah	MP Vaughan	MF Cleary	JAR Blain	CR Taylor	DS Lucas	SA Patterson	ME Claydon	Extras	Total	Wickets	Result	Points
v. Essex (Chelmsford) 13-16 April	29	4	59*	3		13	2	0	6	18		57	7												7	205	10		
	0	27					67*			11*															0	105	2	D	6
v. Somerset (Headingley) 20-23 April	95	2	0	16*	74	21	27	209*	5	21		4													27	501	9		
																												W	22
v. Northamptonshire (Headingley) 6-9 May	12	26	12	5*	5	0	176	0	51				0					12							29	328	10		
	56*						70*																		6	132	0	W	20
v. Leicestershire (Leicester) 11-14 May	17	0	0	4	2	29	14	1	62*				2					9							11	151	10		
	48	165*	34*				37	47										53							22	406	4	W	17
v. Durham (The Riverside) 20-23 May	0	18	11	37*	7	86	12	1	25	28		2													27	254	10		
	8	133*	12	5	5	0	1	0	12	27		80													23	306	10	D	9
v. Essex (Headingley) 25-28 May	17	35	60	26*	70	1	2	76	21	33		40													27	408	10		
	31	50	17*				89	15	5*	3															28	238	5	D	9
v. Lancashire (Headingley) 8-11 June	8	4	71	10*	17	9	97	14	7	68			19												11	335	10		
	3	3	33	13*	1	28	44	48	4	1			64*												31	273	9	D	10
v. Worcestershire (Worcester) 8-11 July	14	29	56	0*	19	0	38		14		14	20					78								18	300	10		
	9	41	27		9*	51*	67		5		24						0								36	269	7	W	20
v. Leicestershire (Scarborough) 20-23 July	21	4	33	0	3	20	22	4	45		5				20*										10	187	10		
	70	89	18*				55	54*			104														10	400	4	W	17
v. Derbyshire (Headingley) 26-29 July	13	134	67*	4	7	18	219	83	0	8	1														16	570	10		
																												D	12
v. Bangladesh A (Headingley) 3-5 August	202*									14	115										14*				12	357	2		
											103*			35		62	0			19*	0				21	240	4	W	
v. Somerset (Taunton) 10-13 August	34	22	50	0	4*	15	106		8	130	0	0													37	406	10		
	0	68	9*				14			19*	51														18	179	4	D	11
v. Lancashire (Old Trafford) 16-19 August	86	35	110*	35	11	27	14		28	34	14	6													17	417	10		
	54	57	66*			0*	14		28	1	48														55	323	6	D	11
v. Durham (Scarborough) 24-27 August	47	30	29		58*	63*	172	24			31														21	475	6		
																												D	12
v. Worcestershire (Headingley) 7-10 September	4	173*	5	4	6	49*		11		3	22			7					11						22	317	10		
	8	65*								16*	22														14	125	2		10
v. Derbyshire (Derby) 16-19 September	76	158	7	8*	4			103		9	46			42	5				12						50	520	10		
	0	13	1		0			7		9	50*			12*											22	114	6	D	12
v. Northamptonshire (Northampton) 21-24 September	30	10	51	0*	14			1		0	32			9	3	0									27	177	10		
	13	30	35	4	23			74		36	6			12	3	4*									38	278	10	L	3

	MJ Wood	A McGrath	C White	GJ Kruis	TT Bresnan	RKJ Dawson	PA Jaques	IJ Harvey	I Dawood	MJ Lumb	JJ Sayers	CEW Silverwood	MJ Hoggard	SM Guy	MAK Lawson	DJ Wainwright	RM Pyrah	MP Vaughan	MF Cleary	JAR Blain	CR Taylor	DS Lucas	SA Patterson	ME Claydon
Matches	17	16	16	16	15	14	13	13	12	11	10	6	6	5	3	2	2	2	2	2	1	1	1	1
Innings	30	28	26	18	20	18	23	20	17	21	17	7	7	6	4	3	3	3	2	1	2	0	0	0
Not Out	2	4	8	9	3	4	2	2	2	4	1	0	1	1	1	1	0	0	0	1	1	0	0	0
Highest Score	202*	173*	110*	37*	74	86	219	209*	62*	130	115	80	64*	42	20*	62	78	53	12	19*	14*	0	0	0
Runs	1005	1425	873	174	339	430	1359	772	326	584	592	186	116	117	31	66	78	74	23	19	14	0	0	0
Average	35.89	59.37	48.50	19.33	19.94	30.71	64.71	42.88	21.73	34.35	37.00	26.57	19.33	23.40	10.33	33.00	26.00	24.66	11.50	-	14.00	-	-	-
100s	1	5	1	0	0	0	4	2	0	2	2	0	0	0	0	0	0	0	0	0	0	0	0	0
50s	6	5	8	0	3	3	6	4	2	1	2	2	1	0	0	1	1	1	0	0	0	0	0	0
Catches/Stumpings	20/0	20/0	10/0	5/0	4/0	8/0	14/0	8/0	34/1	10/0	11/0	3/0	2/0	13/1	0/0	2/0	1/0	0/0	0/0	1/0	1/0	0/0	1/0	0/0

Home Ground: Headingley
Address: Headingley Cricket Ground, Leeds, LS6 3BU
Tel: 01132 787394
Fax: 01132 784099
Email: rachel@yorkshireccc.org.uk
Directions: From M1 South leave at junction 43 to M621 as far as junction 2. From M62 West leave at junction 27 to take M621 as far as junction 2. From M62 East leave at junction 29 to join M1 northbound to junction 2 of M621. At junction 2 of the M621 follow the signs for Headingley stadium along A643. Follow Leeds Inner Ring Road (A58(M)) to A660 which is signposted to Headingley stadium. Signs along this route will indicate when you have reached the Headingley area and on Test match days additional temporary signing will direct you to the free Park & Ride car park to the north of Headingley at Beckett Park.
Other grounds used: Scarborough
Year formed: 1863

Chief Executive: Colin Graves
Operations Director: Geoff Cope
Director of Cricket: David Byas
Captain: Craig White
County colours: Blue and gold

Website:
www.yorkshireccc.org.uk

Honours
County Championship
1867, 1869, 1870, 1893, 1896, 1898, 1901, 1902, 1905, 1908, 1912, 1919, 1922, 1923, 1924, 1925, 1931, 1932, 1933, 1935, 1937, 1938, 1939, 1946, 1949, 1959, 1960, 1962, 1963, 1966, 1967, 1968, 2001
Sunday League/NCL
1983
Benson & Hedges Cup
1987
Gillette Cup/NatWest/C&G Trophy
1965, 1969, 2002

YORKSHIRE CCC

FIRST-CLASS MATCHES

BOWLING

	GJ Kruis	TT Bresnan	IJ Harvey	RKJ Dawson	MJ Hoggard	A McGrath	CEW Silverwood	DS Lucas	MF Cleary	DJ Wainwright	MAK Lawson	RM Pyrah	JAR Blain	MJ Lumb	C White	ME Claydon	JJ Sayers	SA Patterson	PA Jaques	Overs	Total	Byes/Leg-byes	Wickets	Run outs
v. Essex	30-6-108-0		24-10-47-1	10-1-35-0	30-8-86-2	9.5-1-35-0	21-0-72-0							2-0-7-1						126.5	401	11	4	
(Chelmsford) 13-16 April																				–	–	–	–	
v. Somerset	12-3-39-3	13-2-50-3	4.5-1-14-2		14-4-49-1	5-1-12-0														48.5	182	18	10	1
(Headingley) 20-23 April	14-4-41-3	16-4-46-0	13-5-29-1	27-6-68-2	23-9-50-2									3-1-11-0	5-1-21-1					101	275	9	10	1
v. Northamptonshire	19-7-59-5	16-2-51-0	9-2-24-0	8-1-37-0	19-6-50-2	9.1-0-35-3									3-0-16-0					83.1	281	9	10	
(Headingley) 6-9 May	14-5-30-3	16-2-48-3	7.3-1-16-2		18-4-72-1															55.3	175	9	10	1
v. Leicestershire	20-8-40-3	17-6-38-2	13-2-61-1	6-1-18-1	20.5-1-57-1	26-7-52-2														102.5	278	12	10	
(Leicester) 11-14 May	13.5-3-45-1	12-4-32-1	22-5-54-2	12-1-42-2	16-4-53-2	15-1-42-1														90.5	276	8	9	
v. Durham	24-7-97-1	20-2-69-4	19-5-48-1	4-0-13-1		1-0-5-0	14-2-63-2							5-0-17-1						87	316	4	10	
(The Riverside) 20-23 May	30-4-96-4	16-5-62-1	15-6-32-2				8-2-23-0													69	226	13	8	1
v. Essex	32-8-93-2	32-6-101-2	23-8-80-0	33.3-2-147-1		20-4-58-2	29-13-80-1							8-1-26-0	7-1-25-0					184.3	622	12	8	
(Headingley) 25-28 May																				–	–	–	–	
v. Lancashire	21-6-92-2	19-2-76-3	19-3-51-4	18-2-52-0	20-6-80-1	6-2-17-0														103	379	11	10	
(Headingley) 8-11 June	19-4-64-1	9-2-44-0	6-0-31-0	17-3-53-1	25-2-91-3	16-1-46-0														92	337	8	5	
v. Worcestershire	22-4-94-2	17.1-3-78-2		16-3-63-2	22-6-68-3	12-3-26-0						3-1-9-1								92.1	345	7	10	
(Worcester) 8-11 July	16-2-59-2	16-1-42-5			21-3-76-2	5-0-29-1														58	222	16	10	
v. Leicestershire	24.5-5-90-4	25-4-88-1	12-4-35-1	28-4-70-2		10-2-30-1					11-2-44-1									110.5	366	9	10	
(Scarborough) 20-23 July	22.5-7-39-1	16-4-44-3	6-1-21-0	13-0-54-4		10-1-28-2					3-0-23-0									70.5	217	8	10	
v. Derbyshire	26-7-95-1	21-4-60-2	13-6-18-0	23-3-66-3		7-1-25-1	18.2-3-73-3													108.2	350	13	10	
(Headingley) 26-29 July	18-5-51-3	6-0-24-0	5-1-12-0	15-5-34-1		6-1-14-0	10-2-32-1													60	173	6	5	
v. Bangladesh A								15.4-2-49-5		21-6-56-3		5-0-21-1	16-3-64-1			13-2-65-0	2-0-9-0	15-0-46-0		87.4	325	15	10	
(Headingley) 3-5 August								14-2-35-3		12-4-22-3		2-1-4-1	9-2-40-2			11-3-27-1		3-0-7-0		51	146	11	10	
v. Somerset	30-2-134-0	27-4-110-2		33-3-132-4		22-2-93-2	29-5-94-2							1-0-2-0						142	581	16	10	
(Taunton) 10-13 August																				–	–	–	–	
v. Lancashire	34-9-102-5	41-11-111-4		41.1-5-151-1		19-3-63-0	13-1-47-0							4-0-29-0	2-0-9-0				3-0-19-0	157.1	537	11	10	
(Old Trafford) 16-19 August																				–	–	–	–	
v. Durham	36-9-106-5	30.5-6-101-4	17-5-54-1	3-1-18-0		10-5-28-0							19-0-97-0							115.5	414	10	10	
(Scarborough) 24-27 August																				–	–	–	–	
v. Worcestershire	22-7-88-2	13-3-45-3	11-3-25-1	18-5-45-2		4-0-25-1			17-2-70-1											85	308	10	10	
(Headingley) 7-10 September	17-2-65-4	9-0-47-0	4.4-1-21-2			1-0-4-0			12-1-65-3											43.4	211	9	10	1
v. Derbyshire	14-3-52-1	15-5-44-1	17.4-9-40-5			3-0-12-0			14-3-46-3											63.4	216	22	10	
(Derby) 16-19 September	30-4-107-1	22-3-93-1	20-5-51-2			8-1-24-0			24-4-69-1		38-6-155-5									142	523	24	10	
v. Northamptonshire	23-4-75-5	14-2-67-0	6.5-0-24-2			6-0-24-0				29-5-86-1	30-1-150-1						5-0-26-0			113.5	476	24	9	
(Northampton) 21-24 September																				–	–	–	–	

	GJ Kruis	TT Bresnan	IJ Harvey	RKJ Dawson	MJ Hoggard	A McGrath	CEW Silverwood	DS Lucas	MF Cleary	DJ Wainwright	MAK Lawson	RM Pyrah	JAR Blain	MJ Lumb	C White	ME Claydon	JJ Sayers	SA Patterson	PA Jaques
Overs	584.3	459	288.3	325.4	228.5	231	142.2	29.4	67	62	82	10	44	23	17	24	7	18	3
Maidens	135	87	83	46	53	36	28	4	10	15	9	2	5	2	2	5	0	0	0
Runs	1961	1571	788	1098	732	727	479	84	250	164	372	34	201	92	71	92	35	53	19
Wickets	64	47	30	27	20	16	9	8	8	7	7	3	3	2	1	1	0	0	0
Average	30.64	33.42	26.26	40.66	36.60	45.43	53.22	10.50	31.25	23.42	53.14	11.33	67.00	46.00	71.00	92.00	–	–	–

FIELDING

35	I Dawood (34 ct, 1 st)
20	A McGrath
20	MJ Wood
14	SM Guy (13 ct, 1 st)
14	PA Jaques
11	JJ Sayers
10	C White
10	MJ Lumb
8	IJ Harvey
8	RKJ Dawson
5	GJ Kruis
4	TT Bresnan
3	CEW Silverwood
2	MJ Hoggard
2	DJ Wainwright
1	JAR Blain
1	CR Taylor
1	RM Pyrah
1	SA Patterson
0	MP Vaughan
0	DS Lucas
0	MAK Lawson
0	MF Cleary
0	ME Claydon